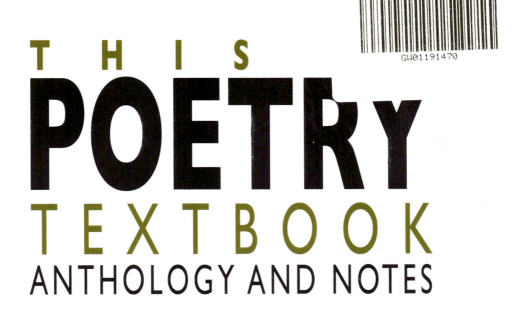

HIGHER LEVEL LEAVING CERT
2013

Brian Forristal & Billy Ramsell

FORUM PUBLICATIONS

Published by
Forum Publications
23 Washington St., Cork.
Tel: (021) 4270525 · (021) 4270500
Fax: (01) 6335347

Copyright © Brian Forristal MA and Billy Ramsell MA 2011
The moral right of the authors has been asserted

Additional writing and research by Siobhán Collins

Design and layout: Dominic Carroll
Printed in Ireland by ColourBooks

ISBN: 978-1-906565-13-8

© All rights reserved.
No part of this publication may be reproduced, copied or transmitted in any form or by any means without written permission of the publishers or else under the terms of any licence permitting limited copying issued by the Irish Copyright Licensing Agency, The Writers' Centre, Parnell Square, Dublin 1.

Acknowledgements

'The Armadillo', 'At the Fishhouses', 'The Bight', 'Filling Station', 'First Death in Nova Scotia', 'The Fish', 'In the Waiting Room', 'The Prodigal', 'Questions of Travel' and 'Sestina' from *The Complete Poems 1927-1979* by Elizabeth Bishop. Copyright © 1979, 1983 by Alice Helen Methfessel. Reprinted by permission of Farrar, Straus and Giroux, LLC.; Poems by Thomas Kinsella are reproduced by kind permission of Carcanet Press Ltd.; 'The Uncle Speaks in the Drawing Room', 'Our Whole Life' from *Collected Early Poems 1950–1970* by Adrienne Rich. Copyright © 1993 by Adrienne Rich. Copyright © 1967, 1963, 1962, 1961, 1960, 1959, 1958, 1957, 1956, 1955, 1954, 1953, 1952, 1951 by Adrienne Rich. Copyright © 1984, 1975, 1971, 1969, 1966 by W.W. Norton & Company, Inc. Used by permission of the author and W.W. Norton & Company, Inc. 'Aunt Jennifer's Tigers', 'Storm Warnings', 'Living in Sin', 'The Roofwalker', 'Trying to Talk with a Man', 'Diving into the Wreck', 'From a Survivor' and 'Power' from *The Fact of Doorframe: Selected Poems 1950–2001* by Adrienne Rich. Copyright © 2002 by Adrienne Rich. Copyright © 2001, 1999, 1995, 1991, 1989, 1986, 1984, 1981, 1967, 1963, 1962, 1961, 1960, 1959, 1958, 1957, 1956, 1955, 1954, 1953, 1952, 1951 by Adrienne Rich. Copyright © 1978, 1975, 1973, 1971, 1969, 1966 by W.W. Norton & Company, Inc. Used by permission of the author and W.W. Norton & Company, Inc; 'Hotel Room 12th Floor' by Norman MacCaig, by kind permission of Gardner Books. Poems by Sylvia Plath are reproduced by kind permission of Faber and Faber Ltd. Poems by Derek Mahon are reproduced by kind permission of the author and The Gallery Press. 'I Want to Write' by Margaret Walker from *This is My Century: New and Collected Poems*, University of Georgia Press, 1989.

Despite their very best efforts, in the case of some copyright material the publishers have not been able to contact the copyright holders but will be glad to make the appropriate arrangements with them as soon as they make contact.

CONTENTS

WHAT IS POETRY?	5
TIMELINE	6
GLOSSARY OF POETRY TERMS & IDEAS	7

POEMS

WILLIAM SHAKESPEARE — 11
- Sonnet 12 ('When I do count') — 13
- Sonnet 18 ('Shall I compare thee') — 14
- Sonnet 23 ('As an unperfect actor') — 15
- Sonnet 29 ('When in disgrace') — 16
- Sonnet 30 ('When to the sessions') — 17
- Sonnet 60 ('Like as the waves') — 18
- Sonnet 65 ('Since brass, nor stone') — 19
- Sonnet 66 ('Tired with all these') — 20
- Sonnet 73 ('That time of year') — 21
- Sonnet 94 ('They that have power') — 22
- Sonnet 116 ('Let me not') — 23
- Fear No More the Heat o' the Sun — 24

WILLIAM WORDSWORTH — 26
- Lines Composed a Few Miles Above Tintern Abbey, on Revisiting the Banks of the Wye During a Tour. July 13, 1798 — 28
- She Dwelt Amongthe Untrodden Ways — 33
- A Slumber DidMy Spirit Seal — 34
- To My Sister — 35
- The Stolen Boat — 37
- Skating — 39
- The Solitary Reaper — 41
- Lines Composed Upon Westminster Bridge, Sept. 3, 1802 — 43
- It is a Beauteous Evening — 44

GERARD MANLEY HOPKINS — 45
- As Kingfishers Catch Fire, Dragonflies Draw Flame — 47
- God's Grandeur — 48
- The Windhover — 49
- Pied Beauty — 50
- Spring — 51
- Felix Randal — 52
- Inversnaid — 53
- No Worst, There is None — 54
- I Wake and Feel the Fell of Dark — 55
- Thou Art Indeed Just, Lord … — 56

ELIZABETH BISHOP — 57
- The Fish — 59
- The Bight — 61
- At the Fishhouses — 63
- The Prodigal — 66
- Questions of Travel — 68
- The Armadillo — 71
- Sestina — 73
- First Death in Nova Scotia — 75
- Filling Station — 77
- In the Waiting Room — 79

THOMAS KINSELLA — 82
- Thinking of Mr D. — 84
- Dick King — 85
- Chrysalides — 87
- Mirror in February — 88
- Tear — 89
- Hen Woman — 93
- His Father's Hands — 96
- Model School, Inchicore — 99
- VII — 101
- VI – Littlebody — 103
- Echo — 106

ADRIENNE RICH — 107
- Aunt Jennifer's Tigers — 107
- The Uncle Speaks in the Drawing Room — 108
- Storm Warnings — 109
- Living in Sin — 110
- The Roofwalker — 111
- Our Whole Life — 112
- Trying to Talk with a Man — 113
- Diving into the Wreck — 114
- From a Survivor — 116
- Power — 117

SYLVIA PLATH — 118
- The Times Are Tidy — 120
- Black Rook in Rainy Weather — 121
- Morning Song — 123
- Mirror — 124
- Finisterre — 125
- Pheasant — 127
- Elm — 128
- The Arrival of the Bee Box — 130
- Poppies in July — 132
- Child — 133

DEREK MAHON — 134
- Grandfather — 136
- Day Trip to Donegal — 137
- After the *Titanic* — **139**
- Ecclesiastes — 140
- As it Should Be — 142
- A Disused Shed in Co. Wexford — 143
- The Chinese Restaurant in Portrush — 146
- Rathlin — 147
- Antarctica — 149
- Kinsale — 150

NOTES

WILLIAM SHAKESPEARE 152
Themes 152
Sonnet 12 ('When I do count') 157
Sonnet 18 ('Shall I compare thee') 158
Sonnet 23 ('As an unperfect actor') 161
Sonnet 29 ('When in disgrace') 163
Sonnet 30 ('When to the sessions') 166
Sonnet 60 ('Like as the waves') 168
Sonnet 65 ('Since brass, nor stone') 172
Sonnet 66 ('Tired with all these') 174
Sonnet 73 ('That time of year') 177
Sonnet 94 ('They that have power') 179
Sonnet 116 ('Let me not') 183
Fear No More the Heat o' the Sun 185

WILLIAM WORDSWORTH 188
Themes 188
Lines Composed a Few Miles Above Tintern Abbey, on Revisiting the Banks of the Wye During a Tour. July 13, 1798 191
She Dwelt Among the Untrodden Ways 196
A Slumber Did My Spirit Seal 198
To My Sister 199
The Stolen Boat 200
Skating 204
The Solitary Reaper 207
Lines Composed Upon Westminster Bridge, Sept. 3, 1802 209
It is a Beauteous Evening, Calm and Free 210

GERARD MANLEY HOPKINS 212
Themes 212
As Kingfishers Catch Fire, Dragonflies Draw Flame 217
God's Grandeur 220
The Windhover 222
Pied Beauty 225
Spring 227
Felix Randal 230
Inversnaid 232
No Worst, There is None 235
I Wake and Feel the Fell of Dark 239
Thou Art Indeed Just, Lord … 241

ELIZABETH BISHOP 244
Themes 244
The Fish 248
The Bight 250
At the Fishhouses 252
The Prodigal 256
Questions of Travel 260
The Armadillo 265
Sestina 269
First Death in Nova Scotia 273
Filling Station 276
In the Waiting Room 278

THOMAS KINSELLA 281
Themes 281
Thinking of Mr D. 287
Dick King 289
Chrysalides 292
Mirror in February 295
Tear 298
Hen Woman 303
His Father's Hands 307
from Settings: Model School, Inchicore 313
VII 316
VI – Littlebody 317
Echo 319

SYLVIA PLATH 320
Themes 320
The Times Are Tidy 324
Black Rook in Rainy Weather 325
Morning Song 329
Mirror 331
Finisterre 335
Pheasant 340
Elm 341
The Arrival of the Bee Box 345
Poppies in July 349
Child 351

DEREK MAHON 353
Themes 353
Grandfather 356
Day Trip to Donegal 358
After the *Titanic* 361
Ecclesiastes 365
As it Should Be 369
A Disused Shed in Co. Wexford 370
The Chinese Restaurant in Portrush 376
Rathlin 379
Antarctica 383
Kinsale 386

QUICK REFERENCE 388
EXAM PREPARATION 395
THE UNSEEN POEM 410

WHAT IS POETRY?

Poetry is finer and more philosophical than history; for poetry expresses the universal, and history only the particular.
Aristotle

poetry = the best words in their best order.
Samuel Taylor Coleridge

It is a test that genuine poetry can communicate before it is understood.
T. S. Eliot

A poem ... begins as a lump in the throat, a sense of wrong, a homesickness, a lovesickness. It is a reaching-out toward expression; an effort to find fulfillment. A complete poem is one where an emotion finds the thought and the thought finds the words.
Robert Frost

Poetry is the language in which man explores his own amazement.
Christopher Fry

Poetry is not an expression of the party line. It's that time of night, lying in bed, thinking what you really think, making the private world public, that's what the poet does.
Allen Ginsberg

Poetry is the art of uniting pleasure with truth, by calling imagination to the help of reason.
Samuel Johnson

Poetry should begin with emotion in the poet, and end with the same emotion in the reader. The poem is simply the instrument of transferance
Philip Larkin

You can tear a poem apart to see what makes it technically tick ... You're back with the mystery of having been moved by words. The best craftsmanship always leaves holes and gaps in the works of the poem so that something that is not in the poem can creep, crawl, flash or thunder in.
Dylan Thomas

A good poem helps to change the shape and significance of the universe, helps to extend everyone's knowledge of himself and the world around him.
Dylan Thomas

It is difficult
to get the news from poems
yet men die miserably every day
for lack
of what is found there.
William Carlos Williams

I have said that poetry is the spontaneous overflow of powerful feelings: it takes its origin from emotion recollected in tranquility.
William Wordsworth

We make out of the quarrel with others, rhetoric, but of the quarrel with ourselves, poetry.
W.B. Yeats

For a man to become a poet he must be in love, or miserable.
Lord Byron

TIMELINE

Year	Poets featured on the course	Historical events
1492		Columbus sails to America
1539		Copernicus publishes theory that the earth is not the centre of the universe
1564	William Shakespeare born	Galileo born
1607		The Flight of the Earls
1616	William Shakespeare dies	
1641		The Irish rebellion
1770	William Wordsworth born	
1789		The French Revolution
1844	Gerard Manley Hopkins born	
1845		The Irish Famine begins
1850	William Wordsworth dies	
1859		Darwin publishes *On the Origin of the Species*
1889	Gerard Manley Hopkins dies	
1911	Elizabeth Bishop born	
1912		The *Titanic* sinks
1914		World War I begins
1922		Irish Free State proclaimed
1928	Thomas Kinsella born	
1929	Adrienne Rich born	
1932	Sylvia Plath born	
1939		World War II begins
1941	Derek Mahon born	
1957		European Economic Community (EEC) established
1963	Sylvia Plath dies	
1969		Neil Armstrong walks on the moon
1979	Elizabeth Bishop dies	
1981		Personal computers (PCs) introduced by IBM

GLOSSARY OF POETRY IDEAS & TERMS

RHYME

Rhyme schemes

Since time immemorial, rhyme has been deeply associated with poetry. The poem's rhyme scheme describes how rhymes are arranged in each stanza. When we describe a rhyme scheme, we refer to lines that rhyme with one another by the same letter.

- In 'A Summer Morning', for example, the first line of each stanza rhymes with the third line, while the second line rhymes with the fourth. We say, therefore, that the poem has an ABAB rhyme scheme:

> Her young employers, having got in late   A
> From seeing friends in town   B
> And scraped the right front fender on the gate,   A
> Will not, the cook expects, be coming down.   B

- In 'The Uncle Speaks in the Drawing Room', meanwhile, each stanza rhymes ABBACC:

> I have seen the mob of late   A
> Standing sullen in the square,   B
> Gazing with a sullen stare   B
> At window, balcony, and gate.   A
> Some have talked in bitter tones,   C
> Some have held and fingered stones.   C

Half-rhyme

An important technique to watch out for is half-rhyme. This is where two lines end in words that almost rhyme.

- Larkin makes use of half-rhyme in 'Ambulances'. In the first stanza, the poet rhymes 'absorb' and 'kerb', while in the final stanza he rhymes 'room' and 'come'.
- We can also see this in the 'Harvest Bow' by Seamus Heaney. In this poem, 'braille' ryhmes with 'palpable', 'midges' with 'hedges', and 'rust' with 'twist'.

METAPHOR & SIMILE

Metaphors and similes are incredibly common in poetry, and many poems owe their most vivid and memorable moments to these techniques. The ability to correctly identify similes and metaphors is very important when it comes to dealing with the unseen poem.

- A metaphor is when one thing is compared to something else.
- A simile is very similar to a metaphor in that it also compares one thing to something else. The big difference is that it uses the words 'like' or 'as'.

Each of the following phrases compares the hurler D.J. Carey to a lion:

- 'D.J. was like a lion in attack.'
- 'D.J. played as if he was a lion in attack.'
- 'D.J. was a lion in attack.'

The first two comparisons are similes because they use the words 'like' or 'as'. The third comparison is a metaphor because it does not feature the words 'like' or 'as'. Very often a metaphor is referred to as a 'strong' or 'direct' comparison, while a simile is referred to as a 'weak' or 'indirect' comparison. As a general rule, similes tend to occur more often than metaphors, especially in modern poetry.

Consider the following phrases, and in the case of each say whether it is a metaphor or a simile:

- 'The words are shadows' (*Eavan Boland*)
- 'One tree is yellow as butter' (*Eavan Boland*)
- 'Suspicion climbed all over her face, like a kitten, but not so playfully' (*Raymond Chandler*)
- 'A leaping tongue of bloom' (*Robert Frost*)
- 'Love set you going like a fat gold watch' (*Sylvia Plath*)
- 'a dump of rocks/ Leftover soldiers from old, messy wars' (*Sylvia Plath*)
- 'The mists are … Souls' (*Sylvia Plath*)
- 'He stumbles on like a rumour of war' (*Eavan Boland*)
- 'My red filaments burn and stand, a hand of wires' (*Sylvia Plath*)
- 'I thought of London spread out in the sun/ Its postal districts packed like squares of wheat' (*Philip Larkin*)
- 'The sky is a torn sail' (*Adrienne Rich*)

PERSONIFICATION

This is a technique whereby an inanimate object is described as if it had the qualities of a living thing.

- In 'Out, Out –', for example, Robert Frost suggests that a buzz-saw was 'snarling', making it seem like a hungry and dangerous animal.

Glossary of Poetry Terms & Ideas

- In 'The Sun' by Mary Oliver, the poet describes the setting sun being 'relaxed and easy'. She also says that the sun 'reaches out' to us with its warmth, suggesting that the sun is acting in a conscious, deliberate manner.
- Personification also occurs in 'The Explosion', where Philip Larkin describes the 'slagheap' as sleeping in the sun. This suggests that the vast slagheap is a living thing, a menacing giant that could awake at any moment.

HYPERBOLE

This is where we deliberately exaggerate to make a point. For example:
- These books weigh a ton. (These books are heavy.)
- I could sleep for a year. (I could sleep for a long time.)
- The path went on forever. (The path was very long.)
- I'm doing a million things right now. (I'm busy.)
- I could eat a horse. (I'm hungry.)

METONYMY

This is a technique whereby we describe something without mentioning the thing itself; instead, we mention something closely associated with it:
- For example, we use the phrase 'White House' to refer to the president of the US and his advisors, or 'Hollywood' to refer to the film industry.
- An example of metonymy occurs in line 8 of 'A Constable Calls' where Seamus Heaney refers to the constable as 'the law'.

SYNECDOCHE

In this technique we identify something by referring to a part of the thing instead of naming the thing itself:
- A good example is the phrase 'All hands on deck'. In this instance, the sailors are identified by a part of their bodies, i.e. their hands. Similarly, we might use the word 'wheels' to refer to a car, or 'head' to refer to cattle.

SOUND EFFECTS

One of the features that most distinguishes poetry from ordinary language is its 'musical' quality. Much of this 'word music' is generated by alliteration, assonance and onomatopoeia.

ALLITERATION

Alliteration occurs when a number of words in close proximity start with the same sound.
- We see this in the repeated 's' sounds in the fourth line of 'The Explosion': 'In the sun the slagheap slept'.
- It also occurs in line 5 of 'Aunt Jennifer's Tigers' with the repeated 'f' sound in 'fingers fluttering'.

ASSONANCE

Assonance occurs when a number of words in close proximity have similar vowel sounds.

- We see this in 'A Call' with the repeated 'u' sounds in 'sunstruck pendulums'. Heaney again uses assonance in 'The Underground' with the repeated 'o' sounds in 'moonlit stones'.
- We also see it in 'Mirror in February' with the repeated 'a' sounds in 'fading lamp'.

ONOMATOPOEIA

Onomatopoeia occurs when a word or a group of words sounds like the noise it describes. Examples of onomatopoeic words include buzz, murmur and clang.

- It also occurs in line 12 of Seamus Heaney's 'A Call': we can hear the tick-tock of the clock in the phrase 'The amplified grave ticking of the hall clocks'.
- We also see it in 'Out, Out –' by Robert Frost where we are told 'The buzz-saw snarled and rattled in the yard'. In this phrase we can almost hear the growling of the saw as it cuts the wood.

EUPHONY & CACOPHONY

Euphony and cacophony are also important concepts. Euphony can be defined as any pleasing or agreeable combination of sounds. Cacophony, meanwhile, is a harsh, jarring or discordant combination of sounds.

- Euphony features in 'This Moment' by Eavan Boland in the lines 'Stars and moths,/ And rinds slanting around fruit' where the soft 's' and 'r' sounds create a pleasant and soothing musical effect.
- Cacophony can be seen in 'Mirror in February' where the repeated 'b', 't' and 'k' sounds create a harsh musical effect: 'the awakening trees,/ Hacked clean for better bearing'.

OTHER USEFUL POETIC TERMS

Allegory ▸ A poem in which the characters or descriptions convey a hidden symbolic or moral message.

Allusion ▸ Where a poem makes reference to another poem or text.

Anaphora ▸ The repetition of words or phrases at the beginning of lines.

Antithesis ▸ Figure of speech where contrasting words or ideas are placed in close proximity.

Ballad ▸ Term originating from the Portuguese word balada, meaning 'dancing song'. However, it normally refers to either a simple song or to a narrative poem (often with a tragic ending).

Beat ▸ The rhythmic or musical quality of a poem. In metrical verse, this is determined by the regular pattern of stressed and unstressed syllables.

Couplet ▸ A unit comprised of two lines.

Elegy ▸ Poem written to lament the dead.

Ellipsis ▸ Omission from a sentence of words needed to complete its construction, but without a loss of sense.

Enjambment ▸ The continuation of a sentence or phrase across a line break – as opposed to an end-stopped line.

Form ▸ The structural components of a poem – e.g. stanza pattern, metre, syllable count, etc. – as opposed to the content. T.S. Eliot said: 'In the perfect poem they (form and content) fit and are the same thing'.

Free verse ▸ Verse without formal metre or rhyme patterns.

Imagery ▸ When detail and description causes an image to appear before our mind's eye.

Internal rhyme ▸ Where a word in the middle of a line of poetry rhymes with the word at the end of the line.

Irony ▸ Very similar to sarcasm – the sentence means the opposite of what it seems to mean. We might say 'Oh, that's brilliant' in response to a very bad event.

Neologism ▸ The coining or use of new words.

Oxymoron ▸ Figure of speech containing two seemingly contradictory expressions: e.g. a happy funeral.

Paradox ▸ Seemingly absurd statement which, on closer examination, reveals an important truth: e.g. Wordsworth's ' The child is father of the man'.

Pathetic fallacy ▸ Term coined by Ruskin to describe a tendency of poets (particularly Wordsworth) and painters to attribute human feelings to nature.

Pun ▸ Playful device where similar-sounding words with different meanings, or single words with multiple meanings, are employed.

Quatrain ▸ A stanza comprised of four lines

Refrain ▸ A line or phrase that recurs throughout a poem – especially at the end of stanzas.

Sonnet ▸ A fourteen-line poem usually in iambic pentameters consisting of an octave and a sestet. The octave presents and develops the theme, while the sestet reflects and brings the poem to a conclusion.

Italian or Petrarchan sonnet

The sonnet was originated by the Italian poet Guittone of Arezzo and then popularised by Petrarch (1304–74). The term 'sonnet' derives from the Italian for 'little song'. The Italian sonnet has the following rhyme scheme: A-B-B-A, A-B-B-A, C-D-E, C-D-E.

Shakespearean or English sonnet

The Shakespearean or English sonnet employs an A-B-A-B, C-D-C-D, E-F-E-F, G-G rhyme scheme. Essentially, it consists of three quatrains and a final couplet, and usually features a break between the octave and the sestet.

WILLIAM SHAKESPEARE
BIOGRAPHY

For all his fame and celebration, we know almost nothing about William Shakespeare. His father John was a glover and leather merchant. He married Mary Arden, the daughter of the wealthy Robert Arden of Wilmecote, who owned a sixty-acre farm.

The precise date of Shakespeare's birth is not known, but 23 April – St George's Day – has been accepted as his birthday.

Shakespeare probably began his education at the age of six or seven at the Stratford grammar school. As was the case in all Elizabethan grammar schools, the focus would have been very much on Latin history, poetry and drama.

There are other fragmented and dubious details about Shakespeare's life when growing up in Stratford. Many believe that after leaving school he worked as a butcher and in his father's glove business.

When Shakespeare was eighteen, he married Anne Hathaway, who was twenty-six and already several months' pregnant. William's first child, Susanna, was baptised in Stratford some time in May 1583. Baptism records reveal that twins – Hamnet and Judith – were born in February 1592. Hamnet, William's only son, died in 1596 when just eleven years old.

No one knows for certain how Shakespeare first started his career in the theatre, but by 1592 he had become an established actor. By late 1594, Shakespeare was an actor, writer and part-owner of a playing company known as the Lord Chamberlain's Men. He wrote many great plays, achieving great fame, fortune and the praise of the king and queen. He died on 23 April 1616 at the age of fifty-two.

Shakespeare & the sonnet

The sonnet is a type of poem invented in Italy in the 1200s. The sonnet's defining feature is that it has fourteen lines. Many great Italian poets, such as Dante and Michelangelo, made extensive use of the sonnet. However, the form is particularly associated with a poet called Petrarch, who wrote a highly influential book of sonnets about his futile love for a woman called Laura.

In the sixteenth century, English poets began writing sonnets of their own, creating a new English version of the form in the process. It became the fashion among English poets to a create long, carefully structured sequences of sonnets. Shakespeare was no exception to this trend. The eleven sonnets on this course come from his sequence of 154 sonnets written over many years but eventually published in 1609.

The English version of the sonnet – often referred to as the Shakespearean sonnet – is divided into three quatrains and a couplet. This was the form used by Shakespeare. It has the following rhyme scheme:

Shall I compare thee to a summer's day?	A
Thou art more lovely and more temperate:	B
Rough winds do shake the darling buds of May,	A
And summer's lease hath all too short a date:	B
Sometime too hot the eye of heaven shines,	C
And often is his gold complexion dimm'd;	D
And every fair from fair sometime declines,	C
By chance or nature's changing course untrimm'd;	D
But thy eternal summer shall not fade	E
Nor lose possession of that fair thou owest;	F
Nor shall Death brag thou wander'st in his shade,	E
When in eternal lines to time thou growest:	F
So long as men can breathe or eyes can see,	G
So long lives this and this gives life to thee.	G

Sometimes, the first eight lines outline a problem or issue, while the remaining six provide some resolution to this issue or cause us to see it in a new way. In these instances, the transition between line 8 and line 9 is known as the volta, or turn.

Sometimes, however, the first twelve lines outline the problem while only the final two provide some resolution or cause us to see the problem in a new way. In such instances, the volta is said to occur between line 12 and line 13.

Sonnet sequences – whether they were written by Italian masters like Petrarch or by Shakespeare's contemporaries in England – dealt with themes such as death, immortality, time and the nature of poetry itself. In this regard, Shakespeare's book of sonnets is no exception. As we shall see, his sonnets deal with each of these themes at considerable length.

However, from Petrarch's time, sonnet sequences were especially associated with the theme of love. Sonneteers typically wrote an entire sequence of sonnets about their frustrated love for a particular unattainable woman. In such sequences, the beloved often belonged to a higher social class than the poet himself. The sequences tended to be written in what might be described as highly romantic or exaggerated language, the poet providing lavish, unrealistic descriptions of the beloved's beauty and over-the-top almost hysterical descriptions of his despair at being unable to win her affections.

Shakespeare's sequence is different in that the first 127 sonnets are addressed to another man, generally referred to as the Fair Youth. The Fair Youth seems to be younger, richer, better-looking and of higher social status than the poet. The exact nature of the relationship between the poet and the Fair Youth is hard to pin down. Sometimes it seems to be an intensely close bond of friendship. Sometimes the poet comes across as a father figure to the Fair Youth, giving advice and urging him to procreate. Sometimes the Fair Youth seems to be the poet's wealthy patron, supporting his writing financially and emotionally. Sometimes their relationship even seems to have an erotic element. What cannot be doubted is that the poet's love for the Fair Youth is overwhelmingly powerful.

Over the centuries, scholars have speculated over who the Fair Youth actually was. Some say it was William Herbert, the Earl of Pembroke. Others say that it was Henry Wriothesley, the Earl of Southampton. Some scholars think that the Fair Youth is based on several people that Shakespeare knew. Yet others insist that the Fair Youth should be regarded as a fictional character rather than one based on any real-life historical person.

Sonnet 12

When I do count the clock that tells the time,
And see the brave day sunk in hideous night;
When I behold the violet past prime,
And sable curls all silver'd o'er with white;
When lofty trees I see barren of leaves,   5
Which erst from heat did canopy the herd,
And summer's green all girded up in sheaves,
Borne on the bier with white and bristly beard;
Then of thy beauty do I question make,
That thou among the wastes of time must go,   10
Since sweets and beauties do themselves forsake,
And die as fast as they see others grow,
    And nothing 'gainst Time's scythe can make defence
    Save breed to brave him when he takes thee hence.

[1] **count:** *count the strokes of*
[2] **brave:** *fine, splendid, beautiful*
[4] **sable:** *black*
[6] **erst:** *formerly, erstwhile*
[7] **summer's green:** *This refers to the wheat or barley growing in the fields*
[7] **girded up:** *To surround with a belt; to tie firmly*
[8] **bier:** *A framework for carrying; a handbarrow; the movable stand on which a corpse is placed before burial*
[11] **sweets and beauties:** *abstract for concrete sweet things and beautiful things*
[11] **do themselves forsake:** *change, leave their beauty and sweetness behind*
[14] **breed:** *offspring*
[14] **brave:** *challenge, defy*

COMPREHENSION

1. Read the first eight lines and list the things that make the poet aware of the passage of time.
2. The poet imagines 'Time' to be someone with a 'scythe'. What does the image suggest about time? What does it mean to say that 'nothing 'gainst Time's scythe can make defence'?
3. Beautiful things 'die as fast as they see others grow'. What do you think the poet means by this? To what do you think he is referring when he says 'sweets and beauties'?
4. The poet says that his beloved must eventually go 'among the wastes of time'. What do you think the 'wastes of time' are?
5. The various things that the poet sees lead him to ask a question. What question does he find himself asking when he witnesses the things mentioned in lines 1–8?
6. In the final line, the poet suggests a way for his beloved to somehow defy time. What does he suggest?

PERSONAL RESPONSE

1. What do you think is the central theme of the poem?
2. What does the poem suggest to you about the poet's feelings for his beloved?
3. Do you agree with the poet's belief that 'nothing 'gainst Time's scythe can make defence'?
4. Do you think this is a hopeful poem? Give reasons for your answer.

IN CONTEXT

1. Compare this sonnet with Sonnet 60 ('Like as the waves make towards the pebbled shore'). How do each describe the passage of time? Does the poet use similar imagery and comparisons in both sonnets?
2. Compare and contrast the ways in which sonnets 12, 60 and 65 suggest time might be defeated.

William Shakespeare

Sonnet 18

Shall I compare thee to a summer's day?
Thou art more lovely and more temperate:
Rough winds do shake the darling buds of May,
And summer's lease hath all too short a date;
Sometime too hot the eye of heaven shines,   5
And often is his gold complexion dimmed,
And every fair from fair sometime declines,
By chance or nature's changing course untrimm'd:
But thy eternal summer shall not fade,
Nor lose possession of that fair thou owest;   10
Nor shall Death brag thou wand'rest in his shade,
When in eternal lines to time thou growest.
    So long as men can breathe or eyes can see,
    So long lives this, and this gives life to thee.

[4] **lease:** *a legal agreement allowing use of property or land for a certain amount of time*
[7] **every fair:** *every fair thing*
[8] **untrimm'd:** *stripped, undressed*
[10] **that fair thou owest:** *the fairness you own or possess*

COMPREHENSION

1. What comparison does the poet consider making in the first line?
2. Why does he reject this comparison?
3. In lines 3–6 the poet identifies several 'problems' that can detract from the beauty of a summer's day. What are these?
4. *Class Discussion:* 'and every fair from fair sometime declines'. What does the poet mean by this?
5. What does the poet mean by the expression 'thy eternal summer' in line 9?
6. In line 14 the poet writes 'so long lives this'. What does the word 'this' refer to in this line?
7. In line 11 the poet claims that the Fair Youth will never die. How does he justify this extraordinary claim?

PERSONAL RESPONSE

1. *Group Discussion:* Summarise the poet's argument in three or four sentences. Do you find it convincing?
2. How would you describe the poet's tone in this sonnet? Is he happy or sad, confused or confident? Give reasons for your answer.
3. What does this poem say about beauty? Give reasons for your answer.

Sonnet 23

As an unperfect actor on the stage,
Who with his fear is put besides his part,
Or some fierce thing replete with too much rage,
Whose strength's abundance weakens his own heart;
So I, for fear of trust, forget to say					5
The perfect ceremony of love's rite,
And in mine own love's strength seem to decay,
O'er-charged with burden of mine own love's might:
O let my books be then the eloquence
And dumb presagers of my speaking breast,					10
Who plead for love, and look for recompense,
More than that tongue that more hath more expressed.
    O learn to read what silent love hath writ:
    To hear with eyes belongs to love's fine wit.

[1] **unperfect actor:** *an actor who does not know his lines*
[2] **put beside his part:** *is made to forget his part*
[3] **replete with:** *full of*
[8] **O'er-charged:** *overburdened*
[10] **dumb presagers:** *silent witnesses that go before*
[14] **fine wit:** *sharp intelligence*

COMPREHENSION

1. What do you understand an 'unperfect' actor to be? Why do you think such an actor would be unable to perform his part?
2. In the third line the poet describes 'some fierce thing' that is full of 'rage'. What do you think this 'fierce thing' might be?
3. The rage that the 'fierce thing' experiences is so intense that it 'weakens his own heart'. What do understand this to mean?
4. The first two lines of the poem are linked with lines 5 and 6. How does the 'unperfect actor' correspond with the poet's forgetting 'to say/ The perfect ceremony of love's rite'?
5. Lines 3 and 4 are linked with lines 7 and 8. How does the 'fierce thing replete with too much rage' correspond with the poet and the strength of his love?
6. The poet is having difficulty expressing his feelings when he is with his beloved. What does he suggest as a remedy for the problem in lines 9 and 10?
7. What does the poet hope his books will achieve? In what way might the poet's books be better than the 'tongue'?
8. What does the poet call on his beloved to do in the last two lines of the poem?

PERSONAL RESPONSE

1. What does the poem suggest to you about love?
2. What do you think the poet means by 'for fear of trust'? Do you think he is afraid to trust himself or his beloved?
3. Do you think that poems better express feelings than the tongue?

IN CONTEXT

1. Write an essay about Shakespeare's use of metaphor and simile in sonnets 23, 65 and 73. Which comparisons do you find most effective?
2. Read sonnets 23 and 94. What do they tell us about the poet's relationship with the Fair Youth? Do you get a sense that the relationship is one of equality, or do you think the poet is in a weaker and more vulnerable position?

Sonnet 29

When in disgrace with Fortune and men's eyes
I all alone beweep my outcast state,
And trouble deaf heaven with my bootless cries,
And look upon myself and curse my fate,
Wishing me like to one more rich in hope, 5
Featured like him, like him with friends possessed,
Desiring this man's art, and that man's scope,
With what I most enjoy contented least;
Yet in these thoughts myself almost despising,
Haply I think on thee, and then my state 10
(Like to the lark at break of day arising)
From sullen earth sings hymns at heaven's gate.
    For thy sweet love remembered such wealth brings
    That then I scorn to change my state with kings.

[2] **beweep:** *mourn, lament, bewail*
[3] **bootless:** *useless, futile*
[5] **like to:** *similar to*
[6] **featured like him:** *having his features or looks*
[7] **scope:** *range of abilities*
[8] **contented:** *happy, content*
[10] **haply:** *luckily, by a stroke of good fortune*
[12] **sullen:** *dark, dull, gloomy*

COMPREHENSION

1. Read line 1 carefully. What is troubling the poet?
2. How according to lines 2–4 does he respond to this predicament?
3. What response does the poet receive to his prayers?
4. In lines 5–7 the poet describes how he envies his fellow men. What qualities does he envy?
5. *Group Discussion:* What does the poet mean when he describes himself as being 'With what I most enjoy contented least'?
6. What causes a sudden change in the poet's state of mind?
7. What simile does he use to describe this change? Do you think it is a good comparison? Give a reason for your answer.

PERSONAL RESPONSE

1. Identify one line or phrase in this poem that you found memorable. Give a reason for your choice.
2. 'This poem skilfully conjures and contrasts two very different moods'. Would you agree with this statement? Write a short paragraph giving reasons for your answer.
3. *Class Discussion:* 'The poem's last two lines suggest an exaggerated and implausible view of love'. Would you agree?
4. Did you like or dislike this poem? Write a paragraph giving three or four reasons for your answer.

Sonnet 30

When to the sessions of sweet silent thought
I summon up remembrance of things past,
I sigh the lack of many a thing I sought,
And with old woes new wail my dear time's waste;
Then can I drown an eye (unused to flow)   5
For precious friends hid in death's dateless night,
And weep afresh love's long-since-cancelled woe,
And moan the expense of many a vanished sight;
Then can I grieve at grievances fore-gone,
And heavily from woe to woe tell o'er   10
The sad account of fore-bemoaned moan,
Which I new pay as if not paid before.
    But if the while I think on thee (dear friend)
    All losses are restored, and sorrows end.

[6] **dateless:** *having no determined time of expiry*
[9] **foregone:** *in the past*
[10] **heavily:** *sadly*
[10] **tell o'er:** *(a) relate again (b) sum up*
[11] **fore-bemoaned:** *already lamented*

COMPREHENSION

1. In certain moments of silent contemplation the poet begins to think about the past. What does he think about on such occasions?
2. How does the poem convey the sense that past hurts are never quite forgotten?
3. What do you think the poet means by 'death's dateless night'?
4. Compile a list of the different verbs in the poem that express sorrow.
5. What do you the poet means when he says he new pays his moans 'as if not paid before'?
6. Can you identify words and phrases in the sonnet that have legal or accounting associations? Why do you think the poet uses such terminology to describe his experience? In what way does the poet's woe resemble a debt?

PERSONAL RESPONSE

1. Did you sympathise with the poet in this poem or did you feel that he was wallowing in his misery?
2. What does the poem suggest to you about the poet's love for his 'dear friend'?

IN CONTEXT

1. Compare this sonnet with sonnet 29. Is the poet being made miserable by the same things in both sonnets, or does the cause of his misery differ in each?
2. In sonnets 29, 30 and 66 the poet states that thoughts of the Fair Youth enable him to overcome all misery, fear and doubt. Compare the endings of these sonnets and say whether or not you think that they are convincing.

Sonnet 60

Like as the waves make towards the pebbled shore,
So do our minutes hasten to their end,
Each changing place with that which goes before,
In sequent toil all forwards do contend.
Nativity, once in the main of light,   5
Crawls to maturity, wherewith being crowned
Crookèd eclipses 'gainst his glory fight,
And Time that gave doth now his gift confound.
Time doth transfix the flourish set on youth,
And delves the parallels in beauty's brow,   10
Feeds on the rarities of nature's truth,
And nothing stands but for his scythe to mow.
    And yet to times in hope my verse shall stand,
    Praising thy worth, despite his cruel hand.

[1] **Like as:** *just as*
[1] **make towards:** *move towards*
[2] **hasten:** *rush, hurry*
[4] **sequent:** *following in continuous succession*
[5] **Nativity:** *the time of birth*
[5] **Main:** *great expanse, open sea*
[6] **wherewith being crowned:** *with which being crowned*
[7] **Crookèd eclipses:** *malign or evil eclipses; misfortune; in Shakespeare's time eclipses were associated with bad luck and reversals of fortune*
[8] **confound:** *destroy, overturn, reverse*
[9] **transfix:** *to pierce or run through with a sword or weapon*
[10] **delves:** *digs deeply*
[10] **parallels:** *trenches*
[13] **to times:** *in time to come, for all time*

COMPREHENSION

1. In lines 1–4 the poet makes a comparison between waves and minutes. What similarities does he claim they share?
2. What do you understand by the expression 'sequent toil'?
3. *Class Discussion:* What do we understand by the phrase 'main of light'?
4. What does the poet mean when he says that 'nativity' was once in this main of light? Where does 'nativity' go when it leaves the 'main of light' behind?
5. What is 'maturity' crowned with?
6. *Class Discussion:* The phrase 'crooked eclipses' is unusual. What do we think Shakespeare meant by this?
7. List the different words and phrases used by Shakespeare to describe the damage done by time to the human body.
8. In the concluding couplet a new concept is introduced. What is this?

PERSONAL RESPONSE

1. Would you agree that Shakespeare creates a sense of speed and haste in the opening four lines? Give a reason for your answer.
2. Describe in your own words the central argument of this poem. Do you find the argument convincing?
3. How would you describe the poet's tone in this piece? Does he come across as happy or despairing, uncertain or confident?
4. Pick one phrase or image from this poem that you found interesting or memorable. Say why.

IN CONTEXT

Compare this poem with Sonnet 18 ('Shall I compare thee'). Write a paragraph describing one significant similarity and one significant difference between these poems.

Sonnet 65

Since brass, nor stone, nor earth, nor boundless sea,
But sad mortality o'er sways their power,
How with this rage shall beauty hold a plea,
Whose action is no stronger than a flower?
O how shall summer's honey breath hold out   5
Against the wreckful siege of batt'ring days,
When rocks impregnable are not so stout,
Nor gates of steel so strong, but time decays?
O fearful meditation; where, alack,
Shall Time's best jewel from Time's chest lie hid?   10
Or what strong hand can hold his swift foot back,
Or who his spoil of beauty can forbid?
    O none, unless this miracle have might,
    That in black ink my love may still shine bright.

[2] **sad mortality:** *mortality that causes sadness; solemn, ugly, hideous mortality*
[2] **o'er sways their power:** *has greater power than they do*
[6] **wreckful:** *destructive*
[7] **impregnable:** *invincible, unassailable*

COMPREHENSION
1. What do brass, stone, earth and sea have in common? How might 'sad mortality' be said to possess greater power than these?
2. Why does the poet compare 'beauty' to a flower and 'summer's honey breath'? What do the comparisons suggest about beauty's ability to stand up to the passage of time?
3. How is 'Time' characterised in the poem? To what does the poet compare the effects of time?
4. What do you think 'Time's best jewel' and 'Time's chest' represent?
5. What does the poet hope his writing might achieve?
6. Read the first four lines of the sonnet. Can you identify the legal metaphor that the poet uses? What is the dominant metaphor in lines 5–8?

PERSONAL RESPONSE
1. How would you describe the tone of this poem? Does the tone change throughout?
2. Do you agree with the poet's description of time as a cruel and destructive force against which nothing can survive?
3. Do you think that the written word still holds the kind of power that the poet ascribes to it?

IN CONTEXT
1. How does Shakespeare characterise the passage of time in his sonnets? Consider the poet's use of personification in his depiction of time in sonnets 60, 65 and 116.
2. 'O fearful meditation'. What is it exactly that the poet fears about the passage of time? Refer to three of the sonnets in your answer.

William Shakespeare

Sonnet 66

Tired with all these, for restful death I cry:
As to behold desert a beggar born,
And needy nothing trimmed in jollity,
And purest faith unhappily forsworn,
And guilded honour shamefully misplaced,   5
And maiden virtue rudely strumpeted,
And right perfection wrongfully disgraced,
And strength by limping sway disablèd,
And art made tongue-tied by authority,
And folly (doctor-like) controlling skill,   10
And simple truth miscalled simplicity,
And captive good attending captain ill.
    Tired with all these, from these would I be gone,
    Save that to die I leave my love alone.

[2] **as to:** *as in the following*
[2] **desert:** *the quality of deservingness*
[3] **trimmed:** *dressed*
[4] **forsworn:** *1) prejured, falsely sworn 2) renounce*
[5] **gilded:** *covered with gold*
[6] **strumpeted:** *turned into a prostitute, declared to be a prostitute*
[8] **sway:** *power, authority*
[9] **art:** *skill, knowledge; in Shakespeare this rarely refers to the creative arts*
[9] **tongue-tied:** *silenced*
[10] **folly:** *foolishness, stupidity*
[11] **simple truth:** *plain truth*
[11] **miscalled:** *wrongly called*
[11] **simplicity:** *simple-mindedness*
[12] **attending:** *serving*
[14] **save that:** *except that*

COMPREHENSION

1. *Class discussion:* In this poem Shakespeare makes extensive use of a technique called 'personification'. What is personification?
2. *Group Discussion:* In lines 2–12 Shakespeare uses eleven different personifications. Working in small groups, outline as best you can what each personification is meant to describe.
3. Write a few lines describing in your own words the poet's state of mind.
4. What has brought him to this particular mental state?
5. What solution does he have in mind for this predicament?
6. What prevents him following this course of action?
7. *Class Discussion:* 'Shakespeare's sonnets always have a turn, or volta, that marks a change in argument, mood or feeling'. Where does the turn occur in this poem? Is it effective?

PERSONAL RESPONSE

1. What, in your opinion, is the main theme of this poem? Is it love, death, despair or something else? Write a paragraph justifying your answer.
2. Write a short paragraph describing in your own words the view of life put forward in this poem. Do you find this view convincing or exaggerated?
3. Would you agree that this view of life is as applicable to our own times as it is to Shakespeare's?
4. Write a paragraph describing Shakespeare's argument in this poem.
5. Several notable critics have found the sonnet's ending a little forced or unconvincing. Would you agree? Give a reason for your answer.

IN CONTEXT

Write a paragraph comparing the attitude towards death in this poem with that portrayed in 'Fear No More the Heat o' the Sun'. Which of these two poems do you find more optimistic in outlook? Give reasons for your answer.

William Shakespeare

◁▶ Sonnet 73

That time of year thou mayst in me behold
When yellow leaves, or none, or few, do hang
Upon those boughs which shake against the cold,
Bare ruined choirs, where late the sweet birds sang.
In me thou seest the twilight of such day 5
As after sunset fadeth in the west,
Which by and by black night doth take away,
Death's second self, that seals up all in rest.
In me thou seest the glowing of such fire
That on the ashes of his youth doth lie, 10
As the death-bed whereon it must expire,
Consumed with that which it was nourished by.
    This thou perceiv'st, which makes thy love more strong,
    To love that well, which thou must leave ere long.

[4] **choirs:** *the part of a church where singers perform*
[12] **Consumed with:** *choked with*

COMPREHENSION

1. What time of year do the first four lines of the poem describe? How might this time of year be evident in the poem?
2. What time of day is being described in lines 5–8? How does this time of day correspond with the poem?
3. What does 'Death's second self' represent?
4. In lines 9–12 the poet describes a fire. What condition is the poet in? How might such a fire represent the poet's condition?
5. How might a fire be 'Consumed with that which it was nourished by'?
6. The poet says that his beloved can see or behold such things as the day's twilight and the dying fire in him. How does he think his beloved ought to react to this?

PERSONAL RESPONSE

1. In this poem the poet uses three metaphors to describe his ageing self. What stage of life do you think the poet is at?
2. Which of the three metaphors do you think is most effective? Give reasons for your choice.
3. The poet wants his beloved's love to be 'more strong'. Do you think that the poet's description of his ageing self will result in his being loved 'well'?

IN CONTEXT

1. Compare the mood and tone of sonnets 73, 66 and 29. Which sonnet did you find most moving?
2. Discuss Shakespeare's depiction of death in sonnets 73, 30 and 66.

William Shakespeare

Sonnet 94

They that have power to hurt and will do none,
That do not do the thing they most do show,
Who, moving others, are themselves as stone,
Unmovèd, cold, and to temptation slow:
They rightly do inherit heaven's graces, 5
And husband nature's riches from expense.
They are the lords and owners of their faces,
Others but stewards of their excellence.
The summer's flower is to the summer sweet,
Though to itself it only live and die, 10
But if that flower with base infection meet,
The basest weed outbraves his dignity:
    For sweetest things turn sourest by their deeds;
    Lilies that fester smell far worse than weeds.

[1] **will do none:** *will do no hurt*
[4] **unmoved:** *experiencing or displaying little emotion*
[5] **inherit:** *possess, receive as a possession*
[6] **husband:** *use sparingly or economically, carefully manage*
[6] **expense:** *waste*
[8] **stewards:** *one who administers a house or property on behalf of a great lord*
[10] **to itself:** *for itself*
[11] **base:** *worthless, of little or no value*
[12] **outbraves:** *outshines, surpasses*

COMPREHENSION

Lines 1–4

1. *Class Discussion:* What does the word 'none' in the opening line refer to?
2. Lines 1–4 describe a certain type of person. What characteristics does such a person possess?
3. *Group Discussion:* Examine line 2 carefully. Write out in your own words what it means.
4. According to line 2 there is something that these people being described by the poet 'don't do'. In your opinion, what is this action they omit to perform?

Lines 5–8

5. Would you describe lines 5–8 as praise or criticism of these people? Give a reason for your answer.
6. *Group Discussion:* Readers of Shakespeare are often puzzled by line 6. What in your opinion are the 'nature's riches' mentioned here? How could such riches be husbanded?
7. What might it mean to be 'the lord and owner' of one's face? In your opinion, does this suggest positive or negative personal traits?

8. *Class Discussion:* In line 8 what does the word 'their' refer to? Could it refer to more than one thing?

Lines 9–14

9. What happens to the sweet summer flowers if they become infected with a disease or parasite?
10. What happens to lilies when they fester?

PERSONAL RESPONSE

1. *Group Discussion:* Read the last six lines of this poem very carefully. What do they say about human nature?
2. This poem seems to divide naturally into two parts: lines 1–8 and line 9–14. Write a paragraph describing your understanding of the relationship between these parts.
3. Try to summarise the argument put forward by the poet in a single paragraph.
4. Do you consider the poem's final lines effective as a conclusion? Write a few lines justifying your answer.

William Shakespeare

Sonnet 116

Let me not to the marriage of true minds
Admit impediments: love is not love
Which alters when it alteration finds,
Or bends with the remover to remove.
O no, it is an evèr-fixed mark,   5
That looks on tempests and is never shaken;
It is the star to every wandering bark,
Whose worth's unknown, although his height be taken.
Love's not Time's fool, though rosy lips and cheeks
Within his bending sickle's compass come.   10
Love alters not with his brief hours and weeks,
But bears it out even to the edge of doom.
    If this be error and upon me proved,
    I never writ, nor no man ever loved.

[5] **mark:** *landmark*
[7] **wandering bark:** *ship lost at sea*
[10] **compass:** *range*
[12] **bears it out:** *endures*

COMPREHENSION

1. The poet does not wish to 'Admit impediments' 'to the marriage of true minds'. What do you think he means by the 'marriage of true minds'?
2. In lines 2–4 the poet says that if love 'alters when it alteration finds,/ Or bends with the remover to remove' then it is not love. What do you think he means by this?
3. In lines 5–8 the poet gives a definition of what he thinks true or pure love is. What does he say such love resembles?
4. How does the poet characterise the passage of time?
5. 'Love's not Time's fool'. Is true love subject to time? Do 'rosy lips and cheeks' have the same relationship with time?
6. In the last two lines the poet says that if his view of love is wrong then he 'never writ, nor no man ever loved'. What do you think he means by this?

PERSONAL RESPONSE

1. Do you think that the poet's description of love is idealistic and unreal, or do you think that we should expect such things of love?
2. Imagine that someone you know is getting married and wants you to recommend a poem that will be read at the wedding. Write a short essay in which you attempt to persuade your friend that this sonnet by Shakespeare is the ideal poem.

IN CONTEXT

Many of Shakespeare's sonnets are concerned with the destructive passage of time. With reference to sonnets 12, 65 and 116, write a short essay in which you discuss the poet's ardent desire to find something that will counter time and last forever.

Fear No More the Heat o' the Sun

GUIDERIUS
Fear no more the heat o' the sun,
Nor the furious winter's rages;
Thou thy worldly task hast done,
Home art gone, and ta'en thy wages:
Golden lads and girls all must,   5
As chimney-sweepers, come to dust.

ARVIRAGUS
Fear no more the frown o' the great;
Thou art past the tyrant's stroke;
Care no more to clothe and eat;
To thee the reed is as the oak: 10
The sceptre, learning, physic, must
All follow this, and come to dust.

GUIDERIUS
Fear no more the lightning flash,

ARVIRAGUS
Nor the all-dreaded thunder-stone;

GUIDERIUS
Fear not slander, censure rash;   15

ARVIRAGUS
Thou hast finish'd joy and moan:

GUIDERIUS ARVIRAGUS
All lovers young, all lovers must
Consign to thee, and come to dust.

GUIDERIUS
No exorciser harm thee!

ARVIRAGUS
Nor no witchcraft charm thee!   20

GUIDERIUS
Ghost unlaid forbear thee!

ARVIRAGUS
Nothing ill come near thee!

GUIDERIUS ARVIRAGUS
Quiet consummation have;
And renowned be thy grave

This poem features in *Cymbeline*, act 4, scene 2

[11] **sceptre:** *a rod carried by a king as a symbol of his authority*
[11] **physic:** *the science of medicine*
[14] **thunder-stone:** *meteorite*
[15] **slander:** *a malicious and false attack on somebody's good name*
[15] **censure rash:** *over-hasty criticism or reproach*
[18] **consign to thee:** *join with you*
[21] **ghost unlaid:** *a ghost that walks the earth, that has not been subjected to rituals that will grant it rest*
[22] **ill:** *evil*
[24] **renowned:** *celebrated, famous*

PRE-READING

What work by Shakespeare do these lines come from? What situation or context are they spoken in?

COMPREHENSION

1. *Group Discussion:* Lines 1–18 mention a number of things Imogen no longer has to fear. List them.
2. In line 4 we are told Imogen has gone 'home' and has received her 'wages'. What is meant by each of these phrases?
3. What must happen to the 'Golden lads and girls'?
4. What does the phrase 'frown o' the great' refer to?
5. *Class Discussion:* 'To thee the reed is as the oak'. What do you understand by this expression?
6. *Group Discussion:* What is meant by the words 'sceptre', 'learning' and 'physic'?
7. What must happen to these three things or concepts?
8. Why can Imogen be said to have finished 'joy and moan'?
9. What do you think the phrase 'consign to thee' in line 18 means?
10. What do lines 19–22 suggest about the poem's two speakers?
11. *Class Discussion:* What might it mean for a ghost to be 'unlaid'?
12. Look up the word 'consummation' online or in a dictionary. What kind of consummation do you think the speakers are wishing for Imogen?
13. What final thing do the speakers wish Imogen?

PERSONAL RESPONSE

1. Read the poem again carefully. Would you describe it as mournful or as an optimistic piece?
2. What view of life is put forward in this poem? Write a short paragraph justifying your answer.
3. What view of death is put forward in this poem? Write a short paragraph justifying your answer.
4. Identify two phrases or images you found memorable in this poem, and say why in each case.
5. Write a short paragraph describing how this made you feel.

IN CONTEXT

'The view of life and death put forward in this poem is very similar to that portrayed in Sonnet 66 ('Tired with all these')'. Write a paragraph either agreeing or disagreeing with this statement and giving reasons for your opinion.

WILLIAM WORDSWORTH

BIOGRAPHY

William Wordsworth was born on 7 April 1770 in Cumberland, England. His father was law agent and rent collector for Lord Lonsdale, and the family was fairly well off. His sister – the poet and diarist Dorothy Wordsworth, to whom he was close all his life – was born in 1771. After the death of their mother in 1778, John Wordsworth sent William to Hawkshead Grammar School and Dorothy to live with relatives in Yorkshire; she and William would not meet again for another nine years.

Wordsworth's enthusiasm for the French Revolution took him to France in 1791, where he had an affair with Annette Vallon, who bore him an illegitimate daughter, Caroline, in 1792. Having run out of money, Wordsworth returned to England the following year. The Anglo-French war, following the Reign of Terror, prevented his return to France for nine years. In 1794 he was reunited with his sister Dorothy, who became his companion, close friend, moral support and housekeeper until her physical and mental decline in the 1830s.

The year 1797 marked the beginning of Wordsworth's long friendship with Samuel Taylor Coleridge. Together they began to formulate their ideas for a book of poems that would eventually be published as *Lyrical Ballads*. Wordsworth's most memorable contribution to this volume was 'Lines Composed a Few Miles Above Tintern Abbey', which he wrote just in time to include it.

Lyrical Ballads, published in 1798, is generally considered to have marked the beginning of the English Romantic movement in literature. This movement can be seen as a reaction against the increase in efforts to scientifically describe the natural world in a rational manner, as well as the growth of industrialisation. Romantic poets wanted to create a new kind of poetry that emphasised strong emotion, intuition and spontaneity. In his preface to *Lyrical Ballads* Wordsworth wrote that 'all good poetry is the spontaneous overflow of powerful feelings'.

Romantic poetry often focused on the natural world, and dealt with powerful feelings of sadness and loss. Wordsworth wished to deal with such themes in simple settings, and to write in a language close to that of everyday speech. He described his intentions in the preface to *Lyrical Ballads*:

> The principal object … which I proposed to myself in these Poems was to choose incidents and situations from common life, and to relate or describe them, throughout, as far as was possible, in a selection of language really used by men … Low and rustic life was generally chosen, because in that condition, the essential passions of the heart find a better soil in which they can attain their maturity, are less under restraint, and speak a plainer and more emphatic language; because in that condition of life our elementary feelings co-exist in a state of greater simplicity, and, consequently, may be more accurately contemplated, and more forcibly communicated … and lastly, because in that condition the passions of men are incorporated with the beautiful and permanent forms of nature.

William, Dorothy and Coleridge travelled to Germany in the autumn of 1797. Wordsworth wrote all but one of what became known as his 'Lucy' poems while living in Germany – a period during which he struggled with loneliness and anxiety. The 'Lucy' poems' are a series of poems comprising five verses (two of which appear on the Leaving Cert course: 'She Dwelt Among the Untrodden Ways' and 'A Slumber Did My Spirit Steal'), and were first published in the second edition of

Lyrical Ballads. The poems – dealing with the death of a young girl who lived close to nature – explore the 'still, sad music of humanity' that Wordsworth perceived in the natural world. Although they share stylistic and thematic similarities, it was not Wordsworth but literary critics who first described the five poems as a unified set called the 'Lucy' poems.

After their return from Germany, William and Dorothy settled in his beloved Lake District, near Grasmere. In the summer of 1802 Wordsworth spent a few weeks in France, where he was reunited with his daughter. Travelling through London on the way to France, he was inspired by the silent beauty of the city to write 'Lines Composed On Westminster Bridge'. He later wrote a poem based on a walk taken with his daughter along a beach in Calais: 'It is a Beauteous Evening, Calm and Free'.

When he returned to England, Wordsworth married his childhood friend, Mary Hutchinson. Dorothy continued to live with the couple and grew close to Mary. The following year, Mary gave birth to the first of five children. The yea 1807 saw the publication of Wordsworth's *Poems in Two Volumes*.

Two of Wordsworth's children, Thomas and Catherine, died in 1812. The following year, he received an appointment as 'distributor of stamps' for Westmorland, and the £400-per-year income from the post made him financially secure.

Wordsworth had for years been making plans to write a long philosophical poem in three parts, which he intended to call 'The Recluse'. He had in 1798 started an autobiographical poem, which he never named but simply called the 'poem to Coleridge'. In 1804 he began expanding this autobiographical work. By 1805 he had completed it, but refused to publish such a personal work until he had completed the whole of 'The Recluse'.

Wordsworth's relationship with Coleridge had deteriorated after their return from Germany, mainly due to the latter's addiction to opium. However, by 1828 they had mended relations, and they toured the Rhineland together that year. Dorothy suffered from a severe illness in 1829 that rendered her an invalid for the remainder of her life.

Wordsworth received an honorary doctor of civil law degree in 1838 from Durham University, and the same honour from Oxford University the next year. In 1842 the government awarded him a Civil List pension amounting to £300 a year. With the death in 1843 of Robert Southey, Wordsworth became the poet laureate. When his daughter Dora died in 1847, his production of poetry came to a standstill.

William Wordsworth died on 23 April 1850, and was buried at St Oswald's church in Grasmere. His widow Mary published his lengthy autobiographical 'poem to Coleridge' as *The Prelude* several months after his death. Though this failed to arouse great interest in 1850, it has since come to be recognised as his masterpiece.

Lines Composed a Few Miles Above Tintern Abbey, on Revisiting the Banks of the Wye During a Tour. July 13, 1798

FIVE years have past; five summers, with the length
Of five long winters! and again I hear
These waters, rolling from their mountain-springs
With a soft inland murmur. – Once again
Do I behold these steep and lofty cliffs, 5
That on a wild secluded scene impress
Thoughts of more deep seclusion; and connect
The landscape with the quiet of the sky.
The day is come when I again repose
Here, under this dark sycamore, and view 10
These plots of cottage-ground, these orchard-tufts,
Which at this season, with their unripe fruits,
Are clad in one green hue, and lose themselves
'Mid groves and copses. Once again I see
These hedge-rows, hardly hedge-rows, little lines 15
Of sportive wood run wild: these pastoral farms,
Green to the very door; and wreaths of smoke
Sent up, in silence, from among the trees!
With some uncertain notice, as might seem
Of vagrant dwellers in the houseless woods, 20
Or of some Hermit's cave, where by his fire
The Hermit sits alone.

                      These beauteous forms,
Through a long absence, have not been to me
As is a landscape to a blind man's eye: 25
But oft, in lonely rooms, and 'mid the din
Of towns and cities, I have owed to them
In hours of weariness, sensations sweet,
Felt in the blood, and felt along the heart;
And passing even into my purer mind, 30
With tranquil restoration: – feelings too
Of unremembered pleasure: such, perhaps,
As have no slight or trivial influence
On that best portion of a good man's life,
His little, nameless, unremembered, acts 35
Of kindness and of love. Nor less, I trust,
To them I may have owed another gift,
Of aspect more sublime; that blessed mood,
In which the burthen of the mystery,
In which the heavy and the weary weight 40
Of all this unintelligible world,
Is lightened: – that serene and blessed mood,

In which the affections gently lead us on, –
Until, the breath of this corporeal frame
And even the motion of our human blood   45
Almost suspended, we are laid asleep
In body, and become a living soul:
While with an eye made quiet by the power
Of harmony, and the deep power of joy,
We see into the life of things.   50
                     If this
Be but a vain belief, yet, oh! how oft –
In darkness and amid the many shapes
Of joyless daylight; when the fretful stir
Unprofitable, and the fever of the world,   55
Have hung upon the beatings of my heart –
How oft, in spirit, have I turned to thee,
O sylvan Wye! thou wanderer thro' the woods,
How often has my spirit turned to thee!
And now, with gleams of half-extinguished thought,   60
With many recognitions dim and faint,
And somewhat of a sad perplexity,
The picture of the mind revives again:
While here I stand, not only with the sense
Of present pleasure, but with pleasing thoughts   65
That in this moment there is life and food
For future years. And so I dare to hope,
Though changed, no doubt, from what I was when first
I came among these hills; when like a roe
I bounded o'er the mountains, by the sides   70
Of the deep rivers, and the lonely streams,
Wherever nature led: more like a man
Flying from something that he dreads, than one
Who sought the thing he loved. For nature then
(The coarser pleasures of my boyish days,   75
And their glad animal movements all gone by)
To me was all in all. – I cannot paint
What then I was. The sounding cataract
Haunted me like a passion: the tall rock,
The mountain, and the deep and gloomy wood,   80
Their colours and their forms, were then to me
An appetite; a feeling and a love,
That had no need of a remoter charm,
By thought supplied, nor any interest
Unborrowed from the eye. – That time is past,   85
And all its aching joys are now no more,
And all its dizzy raptures. Not for this
Faint I, nor mourn nor murmur, other gifts
Have followed; for such loss, I would believe,
Abundant recompence. For I have learned   90
To look on nature, not as in the hour
Of thoughtless youth; but hearing oftentimes

continued over

The still, sad music of humanity,
Nor harsh nor grating, though of ample power
To chasten and subdue. And I have felt					95
A presence that disturbs me with the joy
Of elevated thoughts; a sense sublime
Of something far more deeply interfused,
Whose dwelling is the light of setting suns,
And the round ocean and the living air,					100
And the blue sky, and in the mind of man;
A motion and a spirit, that impels
All thinking things, all objects of all thought,
And rolls through all things. Therefore am I still
A lover of the meadows and the woods,					105
And mountains; and of all that we behold
From this green earth; of all the mighty world
Of eye, and ear, – both what they half create,
And what perceive; well pleased to recognise
In nature and the language of the sense,					110
The anchor of my purest thoughts, the nurse,
The guide, the guardian of my heart, and soul
Of all my moral being.

                Nor perchance,
If I were not thus taught, should I the more			115
Suffer my genial spirits to decay:
For thou art with me here upon the banks
Of this fair river; thou my dearest Friend,
My dear, dear Friend; and in thy voice I catch
The language of my former heart, and read				120
My former pleasures in the shooting lights
Of thy wild eyes. Oh! yet a little while
May I behold in thee what I was once,
My dear, dear Sister! and this prayer I make,
Knowing that Nature never did betray					125
The heart that loved her; 'tis her privilege,
Through all the years of this our life, to lead
From joy to joy: for she can so inform
The mind that is within us, so impress
With quietness and beauty, and so feed					130
With lofty thoughts, that neither evil tongues,
Rash judgments, nor the sneers of selfish men,
Nor greetings where no kindness is, nor all
The dreary intercourse of daily life,
Shall e'er prevail against us, or disturb					135
Our cheerful faith, that all which we behold
Is full of blessings. Therefore let the moon
Shine on thee in thy solitary walk;
And let the misty mountain-winds be free
To blow against thee: and, in after years,					140
When these wild ecstasies shall be matured

Into a sober pleasure; when thy mind
Shall be a mansion for all lovely forms,
Thy memory be as a dwelling-place
For all sweet sounds and harmonies; oh! then,   145
If solitude, or fear, or pain, or grief,
Should be thy portion, with what healing thoughts
Of tender joy wilt thou remember me,
And these my exhortations! Nor, perchance –
If I should be where I no more can hear   150
Thy voice, nor catch from thy wild eyes these gleams
Of past existence – wilt thou then forget
That on the banks of this delightful stream
We stood together; and that I, so long
A worshipper of Nature, hither came   155
Unwearied in that service: rather say
With warmer love – oh! with far deeper zeal
Of holier love. Nor wilt thou then forget,
That after many wanderings, many years
Of absence, these steep woods and lofty cliffs,   160
And this green pastoral landscape, were to me
More dear, both for themselves and for thy sake!

Tintern Abbey: *Ruins of a medieval abbey situated in the valley of the River Wye, in Monmouthshire, noted for its beautiful scenery*
[14] **copses:** *small bushes*
[58] **sylvan:** *spirit of the woods*
[75] **coarser:** *unrefined; primarily physical*
[88] **Faint I:** *become discouraged*
[116] **genial spirits:** *vital energies*
[118] **my dearest Friend:** *Wordsworth's sister Dorothy, who went with him on the walking trip here commemorated*

COMPREHENSION

1. How long does the speaker say it is since he last visited Tintern Abbey?
2. Read the first twenty-two lines carefully. How do you think the speaker feels on having returned to this location?
3. How often is the word 'again' repeated in the first twenty lines? What is the effect of this repetition?
4. Focussing on lines 22–57, write a few paragraphs on how the poet's memory of these 'beauteous forms' has worked upon and influenced him in his absence from them.
5. What is the speaker's attitude towards the city?
6. Discuss the relationship between past memories, present feeling and future memories as suggested in lines 58–65.
7. What is the speaker's mood in these lines?
8. Read lines 65–111 closely. In what way does the speaker think that he is different now from how he was when, as a boy, he 'bounded o'er the mountains' and through the streams?
9. Does the speaker mourn for his younger self, and his past close relationship with nature? Support your answer with reference to the text.
10. How is the speaker's 'moral being' (line 113) linked to his love of nature?
11. What is the poet's feeling towards his sister? Does she remind him of his former self? If so, in what way?
12. The final section of the poem (lines 120–59) is a form of prayer. How does the poet link nature with religious and moral feeling?
13. 'Tintern Abbey' is composed in unrhymed lines in iambic pentameter. What effect does this style of blank verse have on the meaning of the poem?
14. List the places in the poem where mid-line breaks – between the end of one sentence and the beginning of the next – are used by the poet to indicate an important break of subject or shift in focus.
15. What do you think is the main theme of 'Tintern Abbey'?
16. The language of the poem is strikingly simple and forthright. Why do you think that Wordsworth writes in such a plain and straightforward manner?
17. Compare the poet's representation of nature, the past and the imagination in this poem.

PERSONAL RESPONSE

1. How does Wordsworth imply the connections between God, nature and the human mind in this poem?
2. Do you think that Wordsworth's poem is relevant to today's society?
3. Why do you think that the speaker places so much emphasis on memory?
4. Where in the poem does the speaker suggest that images in the memory may serve as a source of healing? What do you think of this suggestion?
5. Think about your own memories. How important are they to your sense of identity?

IN CONTEXT

1. Discuss the theme of memory as it runs through 'Tintern Abbey' and 'The Solitary Reaper.' How does Wordsworth believe memory works on the human character? How is memory important in sustaining the connection between the individual and nature?

William Wordsworth

She Dwelt Among the Untrodden Ways

She dwelt among the untrodden ways
    Beside the springs of Dove,
A Maid whom there were none to praise
    And very few to love:

A violet by a mossy stone   5
    Half hidden from the eye!
– Fair as a star, when only one
    Is shining in the sky.

She lived unknown, and few could know
    When Lucy ceased to be;   10
But she is in her grave, and, oh,
    The difference to me!

[1] **untrodden:** *not travelled over or through;*
[2] **Dove:** *Several rivers in England are named Dove*
[3] **mossy:** *covered in moss*

COMPREHENSION

1. What do we learn about Lucy's life from the poem's first stanza?
2. What two comparisons does the poet use to describe Lucy in stanza 2? What do these suggest about Lucy's appearance and personality? Would you agree that they are effective?
3. What has happened to Lucy?
4. 'Oh! The difference to me'. What event has caused the poet's life to be different? Is this a positive or a negative change?
5. The poet declares that only a 'few' people realised that Lucy 'ceased to be'. What was the reason for this?
6. Describe the poem's rhyme scheme.
7. *Group Discussion:* In stanza 3, the poet says that there were people who knew Lucy but that there was no one to 'praise' her. Why do you think this is?

PERSONAL RESPONSE

1. How does the poet feel about Lucy's life and death? Write down the three words that best describe his emotional state. Would you agree that this is a poem of mixed emotions?
2. What kind of relationship do you think the poet had with Lucy?
3. *Writing Task:* Imagine you are Lucy. Write three paragraphs describing your life beside the streams of Dove.
4. *Class Discussion:* This poem is both celebratory of Lucy's life and full of grief for her passing.
5. What is the speaker's attitude towards nature in this poem?
6. Identify and comment on the poet's uses of metaphor and simile in this poem.
7. In your opinion, how well does the speaker portray Lucy's uniqueness? Support your answer with examples from the poem.

IN CONTEXT

Compare and contrast Wordsworth's representation of nature, love and death in 'She Dwelt Among the Untrodden Ways' and 'A Slumber Did My Spirit Seal'.

William Wordsworth

A Slumber Did My Spirit Seal

A slumber did my spirit seal;
I had no human fears:
She seemed a thing that could not feel
The touch of earthly years.

No motion has she now, no force;   5
She neither hears nor sees;
Rolled round in earth's diurnal course
With rocks, and stones, and trees.

[7] **earth's diurnal course:** *the daily rotation of the earth*

COMPREHENSION

1. 'A slumber did my spirit seal'. What does the speaker mean by this line? What has happened to him?
2. *Class Discussion:* Consider the phrase 'human fears'? What does the speaker mean by this? What might be an example of a 'human fear'?
3. This poem is about a girl named Lucy. In line 3, the speaker refers to Lucy as a 'thing'. Why do you think he does this? What effect does this choice of word have?
4. How does Lucy appear to the speaker in lines 3–4?
5. *Class Discussion:* There is a shift in tense between the first and second stanzas. What is this shift and what effect does it create?
6. In line 5 we're told that Lucy has no 'motion' and no 'force'. What does this suggest about her?
7. Lucy, we're told, is now rolled around with the earth's daily rotation. What does this mean? What has happened to her?

PERSONAL RESPONSE

1. Find an example of recurrent *sibilants* ('s' sounds) in this poem. Where else does the poet use alliteration in this poem?
2. What other literary devices, if any, does the poet use in this poem?
3. 'This short lyric poem communicates a strong sense of personal emotion'. What emotion or emotions is the poet expressing in this poem? Would you agree that there is a mix of emotions here?
4. *Class Discussion:* 'In this poem the speaker searches for consolation in a time of great personal loss'. Discuss this statement with reference to the poem.
5. *Group Discussion:* Which of the following best describes the speaker's reaction to Lucy's death: acceptance or denial? Compose a paragraph giving the reasons for your answer and share it with the rest of the class.
6. What view of life-after-death is put forward in this poem? Is it a religious view?
7. Would you agree that this is a simple poem? Give reasons for your answer.

IN CONTEXT

Many of Wordsworth's poems illustrate the speaker's growth in spiritual awareness through the experience of some personal event. Discuss this statement with reference to 'A Slumber Did My Spirit Seal' and 'She Dwelt Among the Untrodden Ways'.

To My Sister

It is the first mild day of March:
Each minute sweeter than before,
The redbreast sings from the tall larch
That stands beside our door.

There is a blessing in the air,   5
Which seems a sense of joy to yield
To the bare trees, and mountains bare,
And grass in the green field.

My sister! ('tis a wish of mine)
Now that our morning meal is done,   10
Make haste, your morning task resign;
Come forth and feel the sun.

Edward will come with you; – and, pray,
Put on with speed your woodland dress;
And bring no book: for this one day   15
We'll give to idleness.

No joyless forms shall regulate
Our living calendar:
We from today, my Friend, will date
The opening of the year.   20

Love, now a universal birth,
From heart to heart is stealing,
From earth to man, from man to earth:
– It is the hour of feeling.

One moment now may give us more   25
Than years of toiling reason:
Our minds shall drink at every pore
The spirit of the season.

Some silent laws our hearts will make,
Which they shall long obey: 30
We for the year to come may take
Our temper from today.

And from the blessed power that rolls
About, below, above,
We'll frame the measure of our souls: 35
They shall be tuned to love.

Then come, my Sister! come, I pray,
With speed put on your woodland dress;
And bring no book: for this one day
We'll give to idleness.   40

[3] **larch:** *deciduous tree*
[13] **Edward:** *identified by Wordsworth as the five-year-old son of his friend, Basil Montagu*
[17] **forms:** *rituals; set observances*
[19–20] *Until 1751 New Year's Day fell on 25 March*
[29] **silent laws:** *New Year resolutions*
[35] **Measure:** *musical connotation – with the sense of a melody*

COMPREHENSION

1. Describe what the poet sees and hears in the opening stanzas. Why does the poet urge his sister to dress with 'speed'? What is the urgency of the situation?
2. What is the poet's mood on this day? How does he wish to spend his time?
3. What natural elements does the poet associate with his sister?
4. How does the speaker link love and nature in this poem? Consider, in particular, stanza 6 in your answer to this question.
5. 'One moment now may give us more/ Than years of toiling reason' (lines 25–6). According to the poem, how does the natural world benefit us?
6. What does the speaker hope to gain from his experience of 'the first mild day of March'?
7. What is the 'spirit of the season' the speaker refers to?
8. What do you think the poet means by the phrase 'joyless forms'?
9. How effective is the poet's use of alliteration in this poem? In what way does it contribute to the poem's meaning?

PERSONAL RESPONSE

1. What emotions did you experience when you first read this poem?
2. Write a paragraph describing what you imagine Wordsworth's sister is like. Base your description loosely on this poem.
3. 'Wordsworth often has a spiritual response to nature in his poems.' Discuss this statement with reference to 'To My Sister'.
4. Have you ever made resolutions or 'silent laws'? What motivated your resolutions? Why do you think Wordsworth refers to such resolutions as 'silent'

IN CONTEXT

Although many of Wordsworth's poems reveal an air of melancholy, 'To My Sister' and 'It is a Beauteous Evening' succeed in conveying a completely positive and spiritual mood. Discuss.

from *The Prelude* [Book I, lines 357–400]
The Stolen Boat

One summer evening (led by her) I found
A little boat tied to a willow tree
Within a rocky cave, its usual home.
Straight I unloosed her chain, and stepping in   360
Pushed from the shore. It was an act of stealth
And troubled pleasure, nor without the voice
Of mountain-echoes did my boat move on;
Leaving behind her still, on either side,
Small circles glittering idly in the moon,   365
Until they melted all into one track
Of sparkling light. But now, like one who rows,
Proud of his skill, to reach a chosen point
With an unswerving line, I fixed my view
Upon the summit of a craggy ridge,   370
The horizon's utmost boundary; for above
Was nothing but the stars and the grey sky.
She was an elfin pinnace; lustily
I dipped my oars into the silent lake,
And, as I rose upon the stroke, my boat   375
Went heaving through the water like a swan;
When, from behind that craggy steep till then
The horizon's bound, a huge peak, black and huge,
As if with voluntary power instinct,
Upreared its head. I struck and struck again,   380
And growing still in stature the grim shape
Towered up between me and the stars, and still,
For so it seemed, with purpose of its own
And measured motion like a living thing,
Strode after me. With trembling oars I turned,   385
And through the silent water stole my way
Back to the covert of the willow tree;
There in her mooring-place I left my bark, –
And through the meadows homeward went, in grave
And serious mood; but after I had seen   390
That spectacle, for many days, my brain
Worked with a dim and undetermined sense
Of unknown modes of being; o'er my thoughts
There hung a darkness, call it solitude
Or blank desertion. No familiar shapes   395
Remained, no pleasant images of trees,
Of sea or sky, no colours of green fields;
But huge and mighty forms, that do not live
Like living men, moved slowly through the mind
By day, and were a trouble to my dreams.   400

[361] **stealth:** *shifty; furtive; covert*
[373] **elfin pinnace:** *small vessel; light boat propelled by oars*

COMPREHENSION

1. List all of the verbs in the first four and a half lines of this poem, and use them to give a brief account of the poet's boyhood activities in this poem.
2. Who does the pronoun 'her' in the opening line refer to?
3. What do you understand by the phrase 'troubled pleasure'?
4. Why do you think that the poet's pleasure is mixed with anxiety in this poem?
5. What literary device does the poet employ in this phrase: 'nor without the voice/ Of mountain-echoes did my boat move on'?
6. Do you think that the speaker was skilled at rowing? Give a reason for your answer.
7. Where in this poem does the poet give a fairy-like quality to his boat and his surroundings?
8. Where did the speaker fix his gaze in order to row in an unswerving line?
9. Where in the poem does the magical, fairy-tale experience transform into a threatening one?
10. Write a few paragraphs on the importance of alliteration, word choice and grammatical form to the meaning and impact of the following lines:

    > I struck and struck again,
    > And growing still in stature the grim shape
    > Towered up between me and the stars, and still,
    > For so it seemed, with purpose of its own
    > And measured motion like a living thing,
    > Strode after me.

11. Does the speaker's mood change during the course of the poem? If so, explain where and why this happens.
12. What does the speaker learn through his experience?
13. What new understanding of nature haunts the speaker's mind days after the event?
14. Does the poet represent solitude in a positive or negative light in this poem, or does he allow it more ambiguous associations?
15. What troubles the poet in his dreams at night?
16. This poem reveals how nature affects the inner life of the speaker-poet. Discuss.

PERSONAL RESPONSE

1. Is there any particular landscape or place which provides you with a sense of comfort and security when you visit or think of it? Describe such a place – real or imagined – and explain why you think it has the power to provide emotional comfort.
2. Have you ever experienced mixed feelings of both pleasure and fear in the contemplation of something that you did not quite understand? Do you think this feeling of awe is confined to childhood experiences?
3. *Group Discussion:* Do you think that 'The Stolen Boat' has a moral message?

IN CONTEXT

Wordsworth's boyhood experience informs his profound awareness of the wisdom and spirit of the universe. Discuss this statement with reference to 'The Stolen Boat' and one other poem by Wordsworth on your course.

William Wordsworth

from *The Prelude* [Book I, lines 425–63]
Skating

And in the frosty season, when the sun 425
Was set, and visible for many a mile
The cottage windows blazed through twilight gloom,
I heeded not their summons: happy time
It was indeed for all of us – for me
It was a time of rapture! Clear and loud 430
The village clock tolled six, – I wheeled about,
Proud and exulting like an untired horse
That cares not for his home. All shod with steel,
We hissed along the polished ice in games
Confederate, imitative of the chase 435
And woodland pleasures, – the resounding horn,
The pack loud chiming, and the hunted hare.
So through the darkness and the cold we flew,
And not a voice was idle; with the din
Smitten, the precipices rang aloud; 440
The leafless trees and every icy crag
Tinkled like iron; while far distant hills
Into the tumult sent an alien sound
Of melancholy not unnoticed, while the stars
Eastward were sparkling clear, and in the west 445
The orange sky of evening died away.
Not seldom from the uproar I retired
Into a silent bay, or sportively
Glanced sideway, leaving the tumultuous throng,
To cut across the reflex of a star 450
That fled, and, flying still before me, gleamed
Upon the glassy plain; and oftentimes,
When we had given our bodies to the wind,
And all the shadowy banks on either side
Came sweeping through the darkness, spinning still 455
The rapid line of motion, then at once
Have I, reclining back upon my heels,
Stopped short; yet still the solitary cliffs
Wheeled by me – even as if the earth had rolled
With visible motion her diurnal round! 460
Behind me did they stretch in solemn train,
Feebler and feebler, and I stood and watched
Till all was tranquil as a dreamless sleep.

[432] **exulting:** *rejoicing greatly; triumphant*
[435] **Confederate:** *joining together; part of a confederacy*
[440] **precipices:** *steep cliff; overhanging rock*
[449] **tumultuous:** *excited; noisy; passionate; disorderly*

COMPREHENSION

1. Describe in your own words the scene presented in the first five lines. What time of day is it?
2. What 'summons' does the young Wordsworth receive? Why does he ignore this summons?
3. What does Wordsworth compare himself to?
4. Wordsworth uses an interesting comparison to describe the children's games. What is this?
5. *Group Discussion*: Read lines 434–41 carefully. Compose a paragraph describing, in your own words, the echoes produced by the children's games.
6. What indications are there that the young Wordsworth is perhaps more solitary and thoughtful than his childhood companions?
7. What do you understand by the phrase 'when we had given our bodies to the wind'?
8. 'the shadowy banks on either side/ Came sweeping through the darkness'. What optical effect is Wordsworth describing here?
9. When the young Wordsworth breaks suddenly he experiences another optical illusion. What is this?

PERSONAL RESPONSE

1. Identify one line or image in this poem that appealed to you, and say why.
2. What mood or atmosphere is created by this poem? Would you agree that the atmosphere changes throughout the piece? In each case give reasons for your answer.
3. Would you describe this as a sad or a happy poem? Is it possible that it contains elements of both happiness and sorrow?
4. 'For Wordsworth, solitude and poetry are inextricably linked'. Discuss this statement with reference to 'Skating'.
5. *Class Discussion*: Wordsworth often claimed that *The Prelude* showed how he had been taught, or 'mentored', by nature. Is there any sense of that 'mentoring' in this poem?

IN CONTEXT

1. 'In both "Skating" and "The Stolen Boat" nature is presented not only as something beautiful and peaceful but also as something strange, sad and threatening'. Write two paragraphs explaining whether you agree or disagree with this statement.
2. Write a brief note comparing Wordsworth's descriptions of sound and music in this poem with that in 'The Solitary Reaper'.

The Solitary Reaper

Behold her, single in the field,
Yon solitary Highland Lass!
Reaping and singing by herself;
Stop here, or gently pass!
Alone she cuts and binds the grain,   5
And sings a melancholy strain;
O listen! for the Vale profound
Is overflowing with the sound.

No Nightingale did ever chaunt
More welcome notes to weary bands   10
Of travellers in some shady haunt,
Among Arabian sands:
A voice so thrilling ne'er was heard
In springtime from the Cuckoo-bird,
Breaking the silence of the seas   15
Among the farthest Hebrides.

Will no one tell me what she sings? –
Perhaps the plaintive numbers flow
For old, unhappy, far-off things,
And battles long ago: 20
Or is it some more humble lay,
Familiar matter of today?
Some natural sorrow, loss, or pain,
That has been, and may be again?

Whate'er the theme, the Maiden sang   25
As if her song could have no ending;
I saw her singing at her work,
And o'er the sickle bending; –
I listened, motionless and still;
And, as I mounted up the hill,   30
The music in my heart I bore,
Long after it was heard no more.

---

[3] **Reaping:** *harvest; cut with a sickle*
[6] **melancholy:** *sad; depression of spirits*
[9] **chaunt:** *archaic version of chant*
[16] **Hebrides:** *islands off the west coast of Scotland*
[18] **plaintive:** *expressive of grief or suffering*
[21] **lay:** *a simple narrative poem; ballad*
[28] **sickle:** *implement with curved metal blade*

COMPREHENSION

Stanza 1
1. Where is this poem taking place? Write a couple of lines describing its setting in your own words.
2. What work is the 'highland lass' doing?
3. What effect does her singing have on the speaker? Give reasons for your answer.
4. What emotions does he associate with her song?
5. What do you understand by the expression 'Vale profound'?

Stanza 2
6. What comparisons does the speaker use to describe the beauty of the lass' singing?
7. *Group Discussion:* What similarities are there between these images? What are the main differences between them?
8. Would you agree that both of these comparisons are atmospheric and effective? Give reasons for your answer.

Stanza 3
9. The speaker doesn't know what the girl is singing about. Why is this?
10. Do you think it is a little strange that the poet is so drawn to a song even though he does not understand what it is about?
11. What does he imagine she might be singing about?
12. The speaker says that the girl's songs 'flow'. What does this suggest about the quality of her singing?

Stanza 4
13. *Group Discussion:* To the speaker it seemed that the lass' song 'could have no ending'. What do you think he means by this?
14. This final stanza features a shift in grammatical tense. What is this? What effect does this have?
15. The effect of the girl's singing remained with the poet for some time after he left the valley behind. How does he convey this?

PERSONAL RESPONSE

1. Write a few lines describing the poem's structure and its rhyming scheme.
2. In this poem the speaker addresses the reader directly. Identify the instances where he uses this technique. What is its effect?
3. 'The tone of this poem mingles sorrow and happiness, showing how we can take joy in the saddest of songs'. Would you agree with this statement? Give reasons for your answer.
4. What line or image did you find most effective in this poem? Write a brief paragraph giving the reason for your answer.
5. Read the third stanza carefully. How important is it that the speaker understands the words and meaning of the maiden's song? Do you think that it is important to fully understand a work of art in order to have an emotional response to it?
6. Do you think that there is a connection between music and poetry? If so, explain what it is you think they have in common.

IN CONTEXT

1. Discuss the close relationship between music and nature for Wordsworth with reference to three or more of his poems.
2. The poet places much emphasis on the fact that the young girl is alone (he mentions it four times in the first five lines of the poem). Write a paragraph comparing and contrasting the treatment of solitude in this poem with that in two other Wordsworth poems on the syllabus.

Lines Composed Upon Westminster Bridge, Sept. 3, 1802

Written on the roof of a coach, on my way to France

Earth has not anything to show more fair:
Dull would he be of soul who could pass by
A sight so touching in its majesty:
This City now doth, like a garment, wear
The beauty of the morning; silent, bare,   5
Ships, towers, domes, theatres, and temples lie
Open unto the fields, and to the sky;
All bright and glittering in the smokeless air.
Never did sun more beautifully steep
In his first splendour, valley, rock, or hill;   10
Ne'er saw I, never felt, a calm so deep!
The river glideth at his own sweet will:
Dear God! the very houses seem asleep;
And all that mighty heart is lying still!

COMPREHENSION

1. Examine the poet's word choice in the opening lines of the sonnet. Which words have religious connotations?
2. Do you think that the time of day is relevant to the speaker's praise of the city? Explain with reference to the poem.
3. What does Wordsworth compare to a garment in this poem? Do you think that this is an effective simile?
4. What great monuments of civilisation does Wordsworth mention in this poem?
5. Why do you think the poet compares the city to natural wonders in this poem?
6. Do you think that the city is in conflict with nature in this poem? Refer to the poem in your answer.
7. Why do you think the speaker describes the air as 'smokeless'?
8. Discuss in detail the effect of the speaker's personification of the scene, with reference to the sun, the river, the houses and to the city's heart.
9. Why do you think it is important to the overall scene and atmosphere of the poem that the river 'glideth at his own sweet will'?
10. How important is it to the speaker's appreciation of the scene that the city's 'mighty' heart is 'lying still'?
11. Note the rhyming scheme in this sonnet. Is it a Petrarchan or Shakespearean sonnet? Do you think the sonnet form is an unusual choice for a poem that celebrates the beauty of the city? Give reasons for your answer.

PERSONAL RESPONSE

1. Trace how the spiritual atmosphere is developed throughout the poem by means of word choice and tone.
2. Examine how Wordsworth appeals to his reader's senses of sight, touch, taste, smell and hearing in this poem. Do you think that Wordsworth deserves to be described as a sensual poet?
3. From reading this poem, can you sense the 'splendour' of the city? Have you ever experienced a sight that you found 'touching in its majesty'? Try to describe such a scene, real or imagined.
4. Do you think that there is a relationship between the experience of beauty and spiritual feeling?

IN CONTEXT

Wordsworth's poetry usually idealises natural landscapes and expresses distaste for urban life. Compare and contrast this poem with 'Tintern Abbey' and 'It is a Beauteous Evening'.

William Wordsworth

It is a Beauteous Evening

It is a beauteous evening, calm and free,
The holy time is quiet as a Nun
Breathless with adoration; the broad sun
Is sinking down in its tranquillity;
The gentleness of heaven broods o'er the Sea: 5
Listen! the mighty Being is awake,
And doth with his eternal motion make
A sound like thunder – everlastingly.
Dear Child! dear Girl! that walkest with me here,
If thou appear untouched by solemn thought,   10
Thy nature is not therefore less divine:
Thou liest in Abraham's bosom all the year,
And worship'st at the Temple's inner shrine,
God being with thee when we know it not.

[12] **Abraham's bosom:** *The phrase 'Bosom of Abraham' refers to the place where the Jews said the righteous dead awaited Judgement Day. It is believed to be a place of comfort. The phrase 'Bosom of Abraham' is found in Luke 16:22–3.*

COMPREHENSION

1. What do you think of the poet's description of the evening as 'holy'? What does this description suggest about his attitude to nature?
2. Explain the simile in lines 2–3. Do you think that this simile is effective?
3. Discuss the personification in line 5 of the poem.
4. What do you think 'the mighty Being' is a reference to?
5. Who is the speaker addressing in the sestet of this poem?
6. What line in the poem suggests that the speaker's response to nature is different to the child's?
7. Explain the meaning and significance of the allusion (reference) to 'Abraham's bosom.'
8. What does the speaker mean about the child's worshiping at the 'Temple's inner shrine'?
9. What traditional religious imagery does the poet employ in this poem?
10. Do you see a change in tone or argument between the octet and the sestet?
11. How does Wordsworth combine religious and natural imagery in this poem?
12. What does the speaker say about the state of childhood in this poem?
13. Why do you think the poet choose the sonnet form for a poem about nature?

PERSONAL RESPONSE

1. This poem is thought to have originated from a real moment in Wordsworth's life, when he walked on the beach with his ten-year-old illegitimate daughter, whom he had not previously known. What do you think this poem says about the poet's feelings towards his daughter?
2. Read the first eight lines aloud. Do you think that the poet's use of broad vowels adds to the spiritual quality of the poem?
3. Do you think that Wordsworth's daughter would be pleased if she were to read this poem? Give reasons for your answer.

IN CONTEXT

Wordsworth's poetry reveals his spiritual and emotional self. Discuss this statement with reference to 'It is a Beauteous Evening' and 'Tintern Abbey'.

GERARD MANLEY HOPKINS
BIOGRAPHY

Hopkins was born in Stratford, in the county of Essex, on 28 July 1844. His parents were prosperous and cultured. Hopkins' father dabbled in literature, writing books and articles on a variety of subjects, including several books of poetry. Hopkins seems to have had a relatively happy childhood; his education began at home and was influenced by his father's literary interests. In later years, however, relations with his family became strained following his conversion to Roman Catholicism. He attended the prestigious Highgate School, where he endured a classical Victorian education, focusing on subjects such as history, Greek and Latin.

Though Hopkins was small and physically unimposing, he was as sporty as any boy his age, and got on quite well with his fellow schoolmates. However, there were hints that he was not quite the average schoolboy: the austere, self-punishing streak that eventually led him to the strict life of a Jesuit priest was even then evident. Once, for a bet, he decided to drink no water or other liquids for three days. Though his tongue became discoloured due to dehydration, he won the bet. Hopkins' stubborn nature often caused him to run afoul of the school authorities, and he was once whipped and threatened with expulsion. At Highgate, too, Hopkins' poetic instincts began to stir, and he won a prize for writing a long poem.

After school, Hopkins went to Oxford University, where he continued to write poetry. Though he could be stubborn, touchy and arrogant, he was popular with his fellow students and enjoyed the university's social life, especially boating with friends on the River Cherwell. At the time, Oxford was buzzing with theological debate. Many young students of an artistic bent, including Hopkins, were unhappy with their own Protestant religion. They were also unwilling to contemplate the possibility of atheism.

These thoughtful, sensitive young men were attracted to the Catholic religion – beguiled by what they regarded as the drama and mystery of rituals such as Mass and confession. They regarded Catholic rituals as a kind of theatre, and its rich symbolism appealed to their artistic nature. The interest in Catholicism of these young Protestant men was a form of rebellion, since at the time the Roman Church was held in deep suspicion by the majority of English people. Protestants who adopted the ceremonies and rituals of the Catholic Church while retaining their Protestant beliefs were known as 'Anglo-Catholics'. Throughout his time at Oxford, then, Hopkins – like many young students – was an Anglo-Catholic. More and more, however, he drifted toward Roman Catholicism proper. He adopted Catholic customs, such as going to confession and not eating meat on Fridays. He would even chastise himself with a whip during Lent. Hopkins, it seems, was attracted to Catholicism not only by its symbolism and mystery but by the opportunity it offered for him to indulge his masochistic self-punishing streak. Hopkins eventually took the leap and converted to the Roman faith in 1866, aged twenty-two.

Much has been made of Hopkins' sexuality. At Oxford he decided to remain celibate for life. Many critics, however, suspect that Hopkins had homosexual tendencies with which he was deeply uncomfortable. There is evidence to suggest he was deeply attracted to a young poet called Digby Dolben, who drowned in 1865, shortly before Hopkins' conversion. Several critics maintain that it was Hopkins' discomfort with his own sexuality that led to his personal vow of celibacy at Oxford and his decision to join the priesthood. It also, perhaps, gave rise to the feelings of self-loathing expressed in poems such as 'No Worst, There is None' and his notorious tendency toward self-punishment. Throughout his life Hopkins was to dwell on his own faults with an almost painful attention to detail. He would be overcome with remorse for even the tiniest failing or transgression.

Having graduated from Oxford, Hopkins taught for nine months at the Oratory school founded by John Henry Newman, one of England's leading Catholics. While there he decided to become a priest. His decision to join the Jesuit order – known as the 'spiritual army' of the Church – shows his desire for rigorous order and soldierly discipline. Once again, Hopkins' self-punishing streak is in evidence. Life as a Jesuit was incredibly demanding and austere – an endless succession of fasting, praying and penance. Throughout this time Hopkins studied at Manresa House, which is the Jesuit school in London, and also at Stonyhurst, near Blackburn in Lancashire.

Hopkins' health was consistently poor, however, and the order sent him to St Bueno's in Wales to recuperate. The period in Wales was one of the happiest in Hopkins' life. He fell in love with the Welsh countryside, and – prompted by the rector at St Bueno's – began writing poetry again. Many of Hopkins' best-known poems date from this period, including 'Spring', 'The Windhover' and 'God's Grandeur'. From 1877 onwards Hopkins spent much of his time in the bleak slums of industrialised northern Britain. He spent several periods at Stonyhurst, a few months in Glasgow, and a particularly dismal time in Liverpool. The bleakness of urban industrialised life did not agree with Hopkins, and he struggled to find inspiration for his poetry ('Felix Randal', however – written during his Liverpool period – was inspired by the death of one of his parishioners).

In 1884 the Jesuits moved Hopkins to Dublin so as to teach at the newly formed Catholic university. This was a particularly unhappy period in Hopkins' life. He felt out of place in Ireland, and despised the slums of dirty Dublin. He was overworked at the university, and his health, always fragile, became very poor. Hopkins' 'terrible sonnets' – including 'No Worst, There is None' and 'I Wake and Feel the Fell of Dark' – stem from this bleak period. Hopkins spent five years in Dublin, until his poor health, exacerbated by the filth and squalor of the city, finally got the better of him. He died, harassed and exhausted, from typhoid fever in 1889. As one critic put it, he was a 'sensitive, over-scrupulous and unusual man who had been formed with too little capacity for human happiness'.

As Kingfishers Catch Fire, Dragonflies Draw Flame

As kingfishers catch fire, dragonflies draw flame;
   As tumbled over rim in roundy wells
     Stones ring; like each tucked string tells, each hung bell's
Bow swung finds tongue to fling out broad its name;
Each mortal thing does one thing and the same:
   Deals out that being indoors each one dwells;
     Selves — goes itself; *myself* it speaks and spells,
Crying *What I do is me: for that I came.*

I say more: the just man justices;
   Keeps grace: that keeps all his goings graces;
Acts in God's eye what in God's eye he is —
   Christ. For Christ plays in ten thousand places,
Lovely in limbs, and lovely in eyes not his
   To the Father through the features of men's faces.

[2] **roundy:** *round shaped*

COMPREHENSION

1. In lines 1–4 Hopkins refers to four different creatures and objects. What are they? What does he describe each one doing?
2. What are the physical characteristics of kingfishers and dragonflies? Is it obvious why Hopkins might describe them as 'catching fire' and 'drawing flame'? Would you agree that this is a successful metaphor?
3. In line 4 we are told that a bell 'finds tongue'. What does Hopkins mean by this? How might a bell be said to 'find tongue'? When does this happen?
4. *Class Discussion:* 'Each mortal thing does one thing and the same'. Read lines 5–8 carefully. What is it that each mortal thing does?
5. Explain what you understand by the phrase 'selves – goes itself'.
6. *Group Discussion:* Consider the phrase: 'Christ plays in ten thousand places,/ Lovely in limbs, and lovely in eyes not his'. What does Hopkins mean by this? How can Christ be present in all these different places, limbs and eyes?

PERSONAL RESPONSE

1. Would you agree with Hopkins that individual natures reveal their own true selves?
2. 'Hopkins celebrates the phenomenon that by expressing itself, every creature gives us a glimpse of God'. Discuss this statement.
3. Hopkins' poetry has been described as 'a sequence of alliteration, internal rhymes and crisp consonants wrapped around closely packed contrasting vowel sounds'. Discuss this statement with detailed reference to the poem.
4. Read this poem aloud a number of times. Identify two or more internal rhymes in this poem. Do you find this intense sound patterning pleasant or disconcerting?

God's Grandeur

The world is charged with the grandeur of God.
    It will flame out, like shining from shook foil;
    It gathers to a greatness, like the ooze of oil
Crushed. Why do men then now not reck his rod?
Generations have trod, have trod, have trod;   5
    And all is seared with trade; bleared, smeared with toil;
    And wears man's smudge and shares man's smell: the soil
Is bare now, nor can foot feel, being shod.

And, for all this, nature is never spent;
    There lives the dearest freshness deep down things;   10
And though the last lights off the black West went
    Oh, morning, at the brown brink eastwards, springs –
Because the Holy Ghost over the bent
    World broods with warm breast and with ah! bright wings.

[4] **reck:** *heed*
[6] **seared:** *parched, dry*
[6] **bleared:** *blurred, reddened*
[6] **smeared:** *soiled, tarnished*

COMPREHENSION

1. Think about the word 'charged'. What generally happens when something is charged? What does the verb suggest about the 'grandeur of God'?
2. Do you see a link between the verb 'charged' in the opening line and 'flame' in line 2? If so, explain this link.
3. To what does the pronoun 'it' refer to in the second line?
4. Explain what you understand by the phrase 'reck his rod'.
5. Why do you think the poet feels that humans fail to heed God's divine authority?
6. *Class Discussion:* Identify the repetition, alliteration and internal rhymes in lines 5 and 6, and discuss how these literary devices contribute to the meaning and mood of these lines.
7. What is the poet's attitude towards 'toil' and 'trade', and the increasing industrialisation and urbanisation of his time?
8. What does line 8 suggest about the relationship between people and nature?
9. What do the shoes people wear symbolise for the poet?
10. Comment on the change of tone in the sestet. Do you see a turn or shift in the argument? If you do, explain.
11. What do you think the poet means when he uses the word 'spent'?
12. What does 'morning' represent for the speaker in this poem?
13. What is the connection between the 'Holy Ghost' and the 'warm breast' and 'bright wings'?

PERSONAL RESPONSE

1. Do you think that this can be read as an environmental poem before its time?
2. How is contemporary human life described in the second quatrain? Is this an appealing way of life in your opinion?
3. Do you think that Hopkins rejects the increasing urbanisation and scientific advances (including interest in the area of electricity) of his time as being counter to spirituality? Discuss with reference to the poem.

IN CONTEXT

'The belief in the beauty and glory of God being evident in nature is a theme Hopkins returns to again and again in his poetry.' Discuss this theme with reference to 'God's Grandeur' and two other Hopkins poems on your course.

The Windhover

to Christ Our Lord

I caught this morning morning's minion, king-
    dom of daylight's dauphin, dapple-dáwn-drawn Falcon, in his riding
    Of the rólling level úndernéath him steady áir, and stríding
High there, how he rung upon the rein of a wimpling wing
In his ecstasy! then off, off forth on swing,   5
    As a skate's heel sweeps smooth on a bow-bend: the hurl and gliding
    Rebuffed the big wind. My heart in hiding
Stirred for a bird, – the achieve of, the mastery of the thing!

Brute beauty and valour and act, oh, air, pride, plume, here
    Buckle! AND the fire that breaks from thee then, a billion   10
Times told lovelier, more dangerous, o my chevalier!

    No wónder of it: shéer plód makes plóugh down sillion
Shine, and blue-bleak embers, ah my dear,
    Fall, gáll themsélves, and gásh góld-vermilion.

Windhover: *a falcon*
[1] **minion:** *favourite*
[2] **dauphin:** *crown prince*
[4] **wimpling:** *rippling; undulating*
[11] **chevalier:** *horseman; knight; image of Christ as*
[12] **sillion:** *coined by Hopkins*
[14] **vermilion:** *red, the colour of nobility and royalty*

COMPREHENSION

1. The poem is dedicated to Christ. Does this dedication add to or alter your expectations about the poem?
2. What comparison does the poet use to describe the bird's pattern of flight? What do the words 'High there' refer to in line 4? Do they have more than one meaning?
3. What do the following words have in common (explain your answers): kingdom, dauphin, plume, buckle, chevalier, blue, gold, vermilion?
4. In line 5 we are told that the bird is off again, in flight. What does the speaker compare his movement to in line 6? Is this an apt simile in your opinion?
5. Why do you think the speaker says that the bird now 'rebuffed the big wind'?
6. What is it about the bird that so moves the speaker's heart?
7. Why do you think the speaker describes his own heart as having been in hiding?
8. Comment on the alliteration in 'brute beauty'.
9. What does the verb 'buckle' denote in line 9?
10. Who and what do you think the speaker is referring to when he says 'the fire that breaks from thee'?
11. Who is the 'chevalier'? Why does the poet address him as 'O my chevalier!'?
12. What contrast exists between the octave and the sestet?

PERSONAL RESPONSE

1. Is this a religious poem in your opinion?
2. Comment on the poet's use of alliteration in this poem. Why do you think that Hopkins was so concerned with the lyrical quality of his verse?
3. 'However the poem is read, it's quite a trick of metaphor-magic to turn a hungry bird looking for breakfast into, among much else, a prince, a horseman, a knight, a plough, a fire's embers, and maybe Christ himself.' Discuss this statement with detailed reference to the poem.

Gerard Manley Hopkins

Pied Beauty

Glory be to God for dappled things –
    For skies of couple-colour as a brinded cow;
      For rose-moles all in stipple upon trout that swim;
Fresh-firecoal chestnut-falls; finches' wings;
    Landscape plotted and pieced – fold, fallow, and plough;   5
      And áll trades, their gear and tackle and trim.

All things counter, original, spáre, strange;
    Whatever is fickle, frecklèd, (who knows how?)
      With swíft, slów; sweet, sour; adázzle, dím;
He fathers-forth whose beauty is pást change: 10
           Praise Him.

[1] **dappled:** *mottled*
[2] **brinded:** *streaked; brindled*
[3] **stipple:** *fleck; speckle*
[4] **firecoal:** *coal that is turned the colour of fire*
[5] **fallow:** *ploughed but left unseeded*

COMPREHENSION

1. What is the simile in line 2? Have you ever come across this comparison before? Is it an effective simile?
2. Hopkins coins the compound word 'couple-colour'. How effective is this term as a description of the sky?
3. What does Hopkins compare the inside of the fallen chestnuts to?
4. Why do you think that the poet mentions the wings of finches?
5. List the several examples of 'dappled things' Hopkins mentions. How many of these are natural and how many are man-made?
6. What is the poet's attitude towards trades in this poem?
7. What do you think attracts the poet to diversity and variety?
8. Comment on the form of this poem. Why do you think Hopkins has shortened the sonnet?
9. Does Hopkins attach moral qualities to the 'dappled things' he mentions? Discuss with detailed reference to the poem.
10. Why do you think Hopkins chooses to commend 'dappled things' in particular?
11. Whose 'beauty is past change' in this poem?
12. Do you think there's irony in the notion that the great variety in the natural world is a testimony to the perfect unity of God?
13. What is the poem's rhyme scheme? Is it regular or irregular? Why do you think the poet chose this particular rhyming scheme?
14. Comment on the praise of God as He who 'fathers-forth'. Do you think the poet's role can be compared to God's in terms of creation?

PERSONAL RESPONSE

1. Do you think the 'dappled things' Hopkins praises God for are traditionally considered to be praiseworthy? Or is Hopkins being unconventional in what he considers to be beautiful?
2. Read this poem aloud a couple of times. Do you think that Hopkins successfully approximates the rhythms and style of normal speech, as was his aim?
3. Would you agree that diversity and contrasts increase the richness of our surroundings?

IN CONTEXT

'For Hopkins, the role of the poet is to show how God is reflected in nature.' Do you agree with this statement? Detail your answer with reference to at least three poems on your course.

Spring

Nothing is so beautiful as spring –
    When weeds in wheels, shoot long and lovely and lush;
    Thrush's eggs look little low heavens, and thrush
Through the echoing timber does so rinse and wring
The ear, it strikes like lightnings to hear him sing;   5
    The glassy peartree leaves and blooms, they brush
    The descending blue; that blue is all in a rush
With richness; the racing lambs too have fair their fling.

What is all this juice and all this joy?   10
    A strain of the earth's sweet being in the beginning
In Eden garden. Have, get, before it cloy,
    Before it cloud, Christ, lord, and sour with sinning,
Innocent mind and Mayday in girl and boy,
    Most, O maid's child, thy choice and worthy the winning.

[4] **wring:** *squeeze out, twist*
[11] **cloy:** *to sicken*
[13] **Mayday:** *The first day of May, traditionally associated with the Virgin Mary*

COMPREHENSION

1. What, according to the poet, compares to the beauty of spring?
2. *Group Discussion:* The poet refers to 'weeds'. What has he got in mind here? In what sense could 'weeds' be said to resemble 'wheels'?
3. *Group Discussion:* Can you imagine how 'thrush's eggs' might resemble 'little low heavens'?
4. What effect does the thrush's singing have on the poet?
5. List each of the different sights and sounds mentioned in the first eight lines.
6. Why do you think spring reminds the poet of the Garden of Eden?
7. What view of children is put forward in line 14?
8. *Class Discussion:* What does the poet fear will happen to children? What does he call on God to do about this? How might this task be accomplished?
9. Who does the poet refer to when he mentions maid's child?

PERSONAL RESPONSE

1. Do you think that this poem suggests a relationship between time and innocence?
2. What is your favourite line or image in this poem? Give reasons for your answer.
3. Do you think this poem is concerned with birth and renewal or with decay and death? Could it be concerned with both? Support your answer with references to the text.
4. The sonnet's sestet begins with the question 'What is all this juice and joy?' Do you think that it provides an answer to this question? If so, what is it?

IN CONTEXT

How does Hopkins combine the subjects of nature and religion in his poetry? Discuss with reference to 'Spring' and two other poems on the course.

Felix Randal

Felix Randal the farrier, O is he dead then? my duty all ended,
    Who have watched his mould of man, big-boned and hardy-handsome
    Pining, pining, till time when reason rambled in it, and some
Fatal four disorders, fleshed there, all contended?
Sickness broke him. Impatient, he cursed at first, but mended   5
    Being anointed and all; though a heavenlier heart began some
    Months earlier, since I had our sweet reprieve and ransom
Tendered to him. Ah well, God rest him all road ever he offended!

This seeing the sick endears them to us, us too it endears.
My tongue had taught thee comfort, touch had quenched thy tears,   10
    Thy tears that touched my heart, child, Felix, poor Felix Randal;
How far from then forethought of, all thy more boisterous years,
When thou at the random grim forge, powerful amidst peers
    Didst fettle for the great grey drayhorse his bright and battering sandal!

[1] **farrier:** *blacksmith*
[6] **heavenlier:** *more heavenly*
[7] **sweet reprieve and ransom:** *Holy Communion. Christ as ransom reprieved the human race through his own death on the cross.*
[14] **fettle:** *fix*

COMPREHENSION

1. The poet says his duty toward Felix Randal is 'all ended'. Why is this?
2. What physical characteristics did Felix have?
3. *Group Discussion:* Hopkins refers to Felix's 'mould of man'. What does he mean by this?
4. The phrase 'till time when' in line 3 is an example of Hopkins' compression of language. Rewrite this phrase in your own words.
5. What happened to Felix's sanity, to his powers of reason?
6. *Class Discussion:* Consider the phrase: 'some/ Fatal four disorders, fleshed there, all contended'. What is happening to Felix in these lines?
7. How did Felix initially react to his illness?
8. Read again lines 5–8. What two duties did the poet perform for Felix? What change of attitude did this help to bring about?
1. One of a priest's duties is tending to the sick. What effect does this duty have on the sick person? What effect does it have on the priest?
2. *Group Discussion:* Line 12 is an example of Hopkins' experimentation with and compression of language. Rewrite the meaning of this line, as you understand it, in your own words.
3. What scene is presented in lines 13–14? Describe it in your own words.
4. Write a paragraph contrasting this portrayal of Felix when he was at the height of his powers and Felix in his illness as described by the poet in lines 2–5.
5. What do you understand by the expression 'powerful amidst peers' and 'random grim forge'. Could these phrases have more than one interpretation?

PERSONAL RESPONSE

1. Would you agree that there are several different portrayals of Felix in this poem? Describe them. How do you think Felix would like to be remembered?
2. Alliteration plays a very important part throughout this poem. Choose the two lines from the poem that you feel give the best example of the poet's use of alliteration. How does the use of alliteration contribute to the meaning and atmosphere in these lines?
3. What colloquial expressions does Hopkins use in this poem? What effect do they have on the poem's tone?
4. Write a paragraph describing your personal response to this poem.

Gerard Manley Hopkins

Inversnaid

Sept. 28 1881

This darksome burn, horseback brown,
His rollrock highroad roaring down,
In coop and in comb the fleece of his foam
Flutes and low to the lake falls home.

A windpuff-bonnet of fawn-froth   5
Turns and twindles over the broth
Of a pool so pitchblack, fell-frowning,
It rounds and rounds Despair to drowning.

Degged with dew, dappled with dew
Are the groins of the braes that the brook treads through,   10
Wiry heathpacks, flitches of fern,
And the beadbonny ash that sits over the burn.

What would the world be, once bereft
Of wet and of wildness? Let them be left,
O let them be left, wildness and wet;   15
Long live the weeds and the wilderness yet.

Inversnaid: *place in the Scottish Highlands*
[1] **darksome:** *mixture of 'dark' and 'handsome'*
[1] **burn:** *small stream*
[3] **coop:** *'enclosed hollow' (definition from Hopkins' notebook)*
[3] **comb:** *rippling stretch of water*
[4] **Flutes:** *ornamental vertical groove; long-stemmed glass*
[5] **bonnet:** *hat*
[6] **twindles:** *a mixture of 'twists', 'twitches' and 'dwindles'*
[9] **Degged:** *sprinkled (Scots dialect)*
[10] **braes:** *steep bank or hillside (Scots dialect)*
[11] **heathpacks:** *heather clumps*
[11] **flitches:** *side of meat*
[12] **bonny:** *beautiful*

COMPREHENSION

1. How does Hopkins describe the colour of the water in the first stanza?
2. What do you think the poet means by the term 'rollrock'?
3. Detail how the poet uses a horse metaphor to describe the movement and look of the river in stanza 1.
4. What does he mean when he says 'to the lake falls home'?
5. How does the image of the flute contribute to your visualisation of the waterfall?
6. In stanza 2, what does the white froth of the river remind the poet of?
7. In this poem, the poet has coined the words 'fawn-froth' and 'fell-frowning' – what do you think they mean?
8. Why do you think Hopkins worries about the destruction of the wild areas of nature?
9. Can you identify where the tone is happy and full of celebration, and where it is dark and anxious?
10. Give a couple of examples of where Hopkins uses compound words. Do you think that they effectively add to the descriptive quality of the poem?
11. What does the final line of the poem pray for?
12. Can you identify two rhyming couplets and two internal rhymes (i.e. rhyming that occurs within a single line) in this poem?
13. Is there a change in mood between the first three stanzas and the final verse?

PERSONAL RESPONSE

1. What do you think of Hopkins' coinage of the word 'beadbonny'. Working within a group, try to make up three new words to describe some object of your choice.
2. In your opinion, does Hopkins despair for the future of nature in this poem?
3. In your own words, and with as much detail as possible, describe the landscape that Hopkins depicts in this poem.
4. What do you think the world would be like if there were only towns, and no countryside left?

Gerard Manley Hopkins

No Worst, There is None

No worst, there is none. Pitched past pitch of grief,
More pangs will, schooled at forepangs, wilder wring.
Comforter, where, where is your comforting?
Mary, mother of us, where is your relief?
My cries heave, herds-long; huddle in a main, a chief   5
Woe, world-sorrow; on an age-old anvil wince and sing –
Then lull, then leave off. Fury had shrieked 'No ling-
ering! Let me be fell: force I must be brief'.

O the mind, mind has mountains; cliffs of fall
Frightful, sheer, no-man-fathomed. Hold them cheap   10
May who ne'er hung there. Nor does long our small
Durance deal with that steep or deep. Here! creep,
Wretch, under a comfort serves in a whirlwind: all
Life death does end and each day dies with sleep.

[2] **forepangs:** *earlier pangs*
[2] **wring:** *squeeze out*
[8] **fell:** *fall*
[12] **Durance:** *endurance*

COMPREHENSION

1. *Class Discussion:* What different meanings does the word 'pitch' have? What do you think it means to be 'Pitched past pitch of grief'? Could this phrase have a number of different meanings?
2. *Group Discussion:* Consider the phrase: 'More pangs will, schooled at forepangs, wilder wring.' Together, try to work out what Hopkins means by this.
3. Who do you think is the 'comforter' referred to in line 3?
4. *Group Discussion:* What does the speaker compare his cries to in line 5? Is this a surprising metaphor? Do you think it is effective?
5. In line 6, the poet refers to an 'anvil'. Who or what is being beaten on this anvil? Why do you think the anvil is described as being 'age-old'? In each case, give reasons for your answer.
6. What effect does the splitting of the word 'ling-/ering' have?
7. What personification takes place in lines 7–8? Would you agree that this is effective?
8. *Class Discussion:* What metaphor for the mind does the poet introduce in the sestet? How is this metaphor developed over the next few lines?
9. In line 10, the poet states that the mind's mountains are 'no-man-fathomed'. What do you understand by this phrase?
10. What does the image of the 'whirlwind' suggest to you?
11. The final line suggests a relationship between sleep and death. What does it suggest they have in common?
12. Do you think that the last line is offered as a form of consolation?

PERSONAL RESPONSE

1. Write a paragraph describing the poet's state of mind in your own words.
2. Comment on the poet's use of punctuation. What effect does this unusual punctuation have?
3. How does the poet's use of alliteration and repetition contribute to the meaning and the atmosphere of the poem?
4. Would you agree that this is a difficult poem to like? Write a couple of paragraphs giving the reason for your answer.

I Wake and Feel the Fell of Dark

I wake and feel the fell of dark, not day.
What hours, O what black hours we have spent
This night! what sights you, heart, saw, ways you went!
And more must, in yet longer light's delay.
With witness I speak this. But where I say   5
Hours I mean years, mean life. And my lament
Is cries countless, cries like dead letters sent
To dearest him that lives alas! away.
I am gall, I am heartburn. God's most deep decree
Bitter would have me taste: my taste was me;   10
Bones built in me, flesh filled, blood brimmed the curse.
Selfyeast of spirit a dull dough sours. I see
The lost are like this, and their scourge to be
As I am mine, their sweating selves; but worse.

[12] **Selfyeast:** *coined by Hopkins from the words 'self' and 'yeast'*
[13] **scourge:** *to inflict pain*

COMPREHENSION

1. Who is the 'we' mentioned in line 2?
2. Who does the speaker compare his sufferings to? Look particularly at lines 7, 8 and 13 when answering this question.
3. Has the speaker been suffering for hours, days or years?
4. What is the speaker's 'lament'?
5. Why does he compare his 'cries' to dead letters?
6. Who do you think 'dearest him' refers to?
7. Is his beloved present or absent?
8. What is the difference in tone and content between the octave and the sestet?
9. Is his suffering at an end, or does he expect it to continue into the future?
10. Why do you think the speaker describes the suffering of the 'lost' as worse than his?
11. Do you think the opening of the sestet suggests that the speaker blames God for his problems? Give reasons for your answer.
12. What do you think is 'the curse' the speaker refers to in line 11?
13. Analyse the phrase: 'Selfyeast of spirit a dull dough sours'. Do you think that this suggests that the speaker takes on responsibility for his own pain and suffering?
14. Describe the speaker's emotional state as it develops throughout the poem?
15. In the final lines, what, according to the speaker, is the 'scourge' of the 'lost'?
16. Do you think the poet's portrayal of the terrifying nature of isolation is effective?

PERSONAL RESPONSE

1. In your opinion, does the speaker see suffering as God's will? Support your answer with reference to the text.
2. Do you think that the speaker is overly harsh in his self-judgement? Write a few lines about a time (real or imagined) when you were overly critical of yourself.
3. 'sights/ saw' and 'ways/ went' are two of the sound pairs in this poem. Make a list of any others that you can find.
4. What do you think the phrase 'my taste was me' means?

IN CONTEXT

'Hopkins' sonnets typically shift from a personal, often sensual experience rooted in the physical world to moral, philosophical, and theological reflections'. Discuss this statement with reference to 'I Wake and Feel the Fell of Dark' and two other sonnets on your course.

Gerard Manley Hopkins

Thou Art Indeed Just, Lord …

*Justus quidem tu es, Domine, si disputem tecum: verumtamen
justa loquar ad te: Quare via impiorum prosperatur? &c.* (Jerem xii 1)

Thou art indeed just, Lord, if I contend
With thee; but, sir, so what I plead is just.
Why do sinners' ways prosper? and why must
Disappointment all I endeavour end?
Wert thou my enemy, O thou my friend, 5
How wouldst thou worse, I wonder, than thou dost
Defeat, thwart me? Oh, the sots and thralls of lust
Do in spare hours more thrive than I that spend,
Sir, life upon thy cause. See, banks and brakes
Now, leavèd how thick! lacèd they are again 10
With fretty chervil, look, and fresh wind shakes
Them; birds build – but not I build; no, but strain,
Time's eunuch, and not breed one work that wakes.
Mine, O thou lord of life, send my roots rain.

[1] **contend:** *argue*
[2] **plead:** *address the court on behalf of someone; make an appeal*
[4] **endeavour:** *strive to do something*
[7] **thwart:** *frustrate, prevent something from happening*
[7] **sots:** *drunkards*
[7] **thrall:** *bondage, something that ties one up*
[8] **spend:** *exhaust, wear out, to become consumed*
[11] **fretty:** *adorned with interlaced design*
[11] **chervil:** *fragile herb*
[13] **eunuch:** *impotent man, lacking virility or power; castrated*

COMPREHENSION

1. In what setting might you expect to hear terms such as 'contend', 'plead' and 'sir'? How do these terms contribute to the tone and atmosphere of the poem's first eight lines?
2. Who does the poet contrast himself with in lines 3 and 4?
3. According to the poet, how do sinners get on in life? How does he get on in comparison?
4. Read lines 5–7 carefully. How does the poet feel he's being treated by God? Does he feel that God could actually treat him any worse?
5. What do you understand by the phrase 'sots' and 'thralls' of lust?
6. What has the poet 'spent' his life doing?
7. In lines 9–14 what comparison does the poet make between nature and himself?
8. *Group Discussion:* What does the poet means when he says that he 'strains' but is unable to 'breed one work that wakes'? What 'works' might he be referring to here?
9. There are several instances in these lines where the normal order of words in a sentence is reversed. Identify these instances. What effect do these reversals have on our reading of the poem?
10. What does the poet ask God to do in the final line? What might he mean by this?

PERSONAL RESPONSE

1. Do you think that the speaker actually considers God to be just and his 'friend'? Pay close attention to the text when developing your answer to this question.
2. *Group Discussion:* Identify the many images of fertility in this poem. How you think they contribute to its meaning ?
3. Have you ever known or heard of a time when the wicked prosper and the good seem to be punished? Write an account (real or imagined) of such a situation taking place.

ELIZABETH BISHOP
BIOGRAPHY

Like many of the poets on the Leaving Cert course, Bishop had what in many ways could be regarded as a difficult life. She was born in Massachusetts in 1913. Her troubles began early, with her father dying when she was only eight months old. This terrible loss seemed to drive Bishop's mother insane, and she received various treatments for mental illness, finally being institutionalised when Bishop was only five. Bishop, unfortunately, would never see her mother again. This early trauma would haunt Bishop's writing (it is evident in 'Sestina' in particular). The notion of motherhood occurs again and again in Bishop's poetry, though Bishop's mother herself only appears once, in 'First Death in Nova Scotia'. (The mother also appears in the terrifying short story *In the Village*, which recounts the five-year-old Bishop's memories of her mother's breakdown and provides an immense psychological insight into her life and work.)

After her mother was hospitalised, Bishop was raised by various relatives in different locations. The result of this was that Bishop was in later life a somewhat unsettled person, and suffered from 'itchy feet'. Her happiest childhood days were spent in Great Village, Nova Scotia, where she was looked after mainly by her maternal grandmother. Nova Scotia, then, was the closest thing to a 'home' she ever had.

During her college years, it became apparent that Bishop's troubled childhood had had a profoundly negative effect on her. She suffered from low self-esteem and depression, and began to drink heavily. Bishop's health was poor, and she suffered from chronic asthma – a disease that then was far less treatable than it is today. At college, she also discovered that she was a lesbian, which, in those far more conservative times, was sure to make life difficult for her. However, it was not all doom and gloom. Bishop was lucky enough to have a substantial inheritance, which meant she never really had to work. She received a cheque each month that was enough for her, just about, to get by on (Bishop's luck in this regard ran out in the 1970s when inflation rendered her inheritance worthless). It was during this Vassar College period that Bishop's poetic talent began to blossom. The great American poet Marianne Moore became her friend and mentor, guiding Bishop through the years of her poetic apprenticeship, and helping her to have her first poems and stories published.

After leaving college, Bishop's itchy feet began to kick in. She spent a great many years shuttling between New York, Key West in Florida and other locations. (When in Florida, Bishop enjoyed the sport of fishing, a pastime that 'The Fish' reflects.) It was also at this time that she developed into a full-blown alcoholic. To a large extent, Bishop's drinking stemmed from feelings of inadequacy. Surprisingly, given her obvious talent, Bishop had little confidence in her own artistic ability, and felt overwhelmed by the gifted and clever people who populated New York's literary and artistic world. Bishop dealt with these feelings of inadequacy in the worst possible way: by getting completely and utterly drunk. Her alcoholism caused her great guilt and embarrassment, which, of course, led to more drinking. Bishop's life gradually became more of a mess during this period (1945–51) even as her literary career was taking off with the publication in 1946 of her first (award-winning) book *North and South*. 'The Prodigal' and 'The Bight' were written during this unhappy period in Bishop's life.

Bishop's alcohol addiction seemed to contribute to her restlessness. Like many addicts, she was given to blaming her surroundings for her problems rather than fully facing up to the fact that the difficulty lay within. However, Bishop finally settled in Brazil in 1951, where she began a relationship with

Lota Soares, a Brazilian woman she had known for many years. She became fascinated with Brazilian culture, and translated many poems and stories from Portuguese into English. Her attraction to Brazil is evident in 'Questions of Travel' and 'The Armadillo'. In 1956 Bishop won the prestigious Pulitzer Prize for her second collection: *A Cold Spring*. Despite this success, Bishop still seemed to have little confidence in her writing. She suffered from excruciating bouts of writer's block, and often spent months or even years attempting to finish a poem. She would hang the poem in big writing on cardboard sheets above her desk, leaving gaps for the perfect words she could never come up with.

Bishop's final years were difficult. She was greatly saddened by the death of her partner Lota in 1967, and left Brazil for the United States. At this point, as we have seen, inflation wiped out her inheritance, which meant she had to earn a living for the first time. She found a part-time teaching job at the prestigious Harvard University, and supplemented her income by giving public readings of her work. Bishop's last years coincided with the beginning of her rise to literary fame. Yet they were a difficult, lonely time, as she dealt with alcoholism, depression, asthma and general physical illness. She died suddenly in 1979. Bishop, then, was a writer who neither seldom nor for long knew personal happiness. But she rarely if ever used her writing to complain. Her work, instead, was devoted to celebrating and exploring the physical world around us, with its terror and beauty, and our inner psyches, with all their mysteries and dissatisfactions.

The Fish

I caught a tremendous fish
and held him beside the boat
half out of water, with my hook
fast in a corner of his mouth.
He didn't fight.
He hadn't fought at all.
He hung a grunting weight,
battered and venerable
and homely. Here and there
his brown skin hung in strips
like ancient wallpaper,
and its pattern of darker brown
was like wallpaper:
shapes like full-blown roses
stained and lost through age.
He was speckled with barnacles,
fine rosettes of lime,
and infested
with tiny white sea-lice,
and underneath two or three
rags of green weed hung down.
While his gills were breathing in
the terrible oxygen
– the frightening gills,
fresh and crisp with blood,
that can cut so badly –
I thought of the coarse white flesh
packed in like feathers,
the big bones and the little bones,
the dramatic reds and blacks
of his shiny entrails,
and the pink swim-bladder
like a big peony.
I looked into his eyes
which were far larger than mine
but shallower, and yellowed,
the irises backed and packed
with tarnished tinfoil
seen through the lenses
of old scratched isinglass.
They shifted a little, but not
to return my stare.
– It was more like the tipping
of an object toward the light.
I admired his sullen face,
the mechanism of his jaw,
and then I saw
that from his lower lip
– if you could call it a lip –
grim, wet, and weaponlike,
hung five old pieces of fish-line,
or four and a wire leader
with the swivel still attached,
with all their five big hooks
grown firmly in his mouth.
A green line, frayed at the end
where he broke it, two heavier lines,
and a fine black thread
still crimped from the strain and snap
when it broke and he got away.
Like medals with their ribbons
frayed and wavering,
a five-haired beard of wisdom
trailing from his aching jaw.
I stared and stared
and victory filled up
the little rented boat,
from the pool of bilge
where oil had spread a rainbow
around the rusted engine
to the bailer rusted orange,
the sun-cracked thwarts,
the oarlocks on their strings,
the gunnels – until everything
was rainbow, rainbow, rainbow!
And I let the fish go.

[40] *isinglass: a gelatin-like substance obtained from the bladders of certain fish*

COMPREHENSION

1. *Class Discussion*: Having read the poem twice, and discuss your reaction to it with the rest of the class. What did you find most striking about this poem?
2. How did the poet feel about her catch in the opening lines?
3. In lines 8–9 the poet uses three words to describe the fish: she says that he is 'battered and venerable/ and homely'. What does each word suggest to you about the fish? With what would you ordinarily associate the word 'venerable'?
4. Throughout the poem Bishop uses a number of similes to describe the fish. Lines 9–15, for example, compare the fish's skin to 'wallpaper'. Write a short paragraph about this particular simile and say whether or not you found the comparison effective.
5. Why is the oxygen considered to be 'terrible' in line 24?
6. The poet performs an imaginary dissection of the fish in lines 26–32. Consider the language that she uses to achieve this, focusing in particular on her use of simile and colour.
7. 'In describing the fish, the poet seeks to be as accurate and as thorough as possible.' Discuss her account of the fish's eyes in light of this statement.
8. 'It was more like the tipping/ of an object toward the light'. Though the poet seeks to capture the fish in language, to make him familiar, on a number of occasions she is forced to acknowledge his very otherness and his indifference to her curiosity. Where is this apparent in the poem?
9. 'I admired his sullen face'. In order to make the fish familiar, Bishop sometimes uses descriptions and expressions that would ordinarily be applied to people. Identify where these occur, and discuss how the fish is thus personified.
10. When the poet comes to focus on the fish's jaw, she realises that she is not the first person to have attempted to catch this fish. What brings about this realisation?
11. The poet greatly admires the fish's strength and experience. Where is this apparent in the poem?
12. By the close of the poem, the poet has become transfixed by the fish. Suddenly, it reveals something to her that causes the world around her to become 'rainbow, rainbow, rainbow'. What gives rise to this wonderful moment?

PERSONAL RESPONSE

1. Did you find the poem unusual? Were you surprised by the extent of the detail given in the poem?
2. Do you think that the poet was always sympathetic to the fish or do you think her attitude changed during the course of the poem?
3. 'He was speckled with barnacles … and infested/ with tiny white sea-lice'. Did you find the poet's need to be as thorough and as accurate as possible in her description too much, or did you admire her willingness to capture every aspect of the fish in the poem?
4. Do you think this poem has anything to say about the way people relate to the natural world?

IN CONTEXT

1. The poetry of Elizabeth Bishop reveals a fascination with places and things that would not ordinarily be considered beautiful or poetic. In 'The Bight', for example, the bay she describes is 'frowsy' and far from picturesque. Similarly, 'Filling Station' is preoccupied with an environment that is three times referred to as 'dirty'. The world of 'The Prodigal' is particularly unpleasant, the stench 'sickening'. Here, in 'The Fish', the poet's world is the boat she fishes from with its 'pool of bilge' and 'rusted engine'. Making reference to three of her poems, discuss Bishop's fascination with unattractive environments.
2. When Bishop's first volume of poetry was published, the poet Randall Jarrell wrote that 'all her poems testify to having been somewhere'. Referring to 'The Fish' and two other poems, discuss the poetry of Elizabeth Bishop with regards to Jarrell's statement.

The Bight

(On my birthday)

At low tide like this how sheer the water is.
White, crumbling ribs of marl protrude and glare
and the boats are dry, the pilings dry as matches.
Absorbing, rather than being absorbed,
the water in the bight doesn't wet anything, 5
the color of the gas flame turned as low as possible.
One can smell it turning to gas; if one were Baudelaire
one could probably hear it turning to marimba music.
The little ocher dredge at work off the end of the dock
already plays the dry perfectly off-beat claves. 10
The birds are outsize. Pelicans crash
into this peculiar gas unnecessarily hard,
it seems to me, like pickaxes,
rarely coming up with anything to show for it,
and going off with humorous elbowings. 15
Black-and-white man-of-war birds soar
on impalpable drafts
and open their tails like scissors on the curves
or tense them like wishbones, till they tremble.
The frowsy sponge boats keep coming in 20
with the obliging air of retrievers,
bristling with jackstraw gaffs and hooks
and decorated with bobbles of sponges.
There is a fence of chicken wire along the dock
where, glinting like little plowshares, 25
the blue-gray shark tails are hung up to dry
for the Chinese-restaurant trade.
Some of the little white boats are still piled up
against each other, or lie on their sides, stove in,
and not yet salvaged, if they ever will be, from the last bad storm, 30
like torn-open, unanswered letters.
The bight is littered with old correspondences.
Click. Click. Goes the dredge,
and brings up a dripping jawful of marl.
All the untidy activity continues, 35
awful but cheerful.

Bight: *a large curved and shallow bay*
[2] **marl:** *a muddy, earthy deposit that is rich in either lime or calcium*
[3] **pilings:** *a structure made from heavy beams called piles*
[7] **Baudelaire:** *Charles Baudelaire (1821–67) was a French poet*
[8] **marimba:** *a xylophone-like musical instrument*
[9] **ocher [ochre]:** *a shade of colour; golden yellow or yellowish brown*
[10] **claves:** *a jazzy rhythmic pattern used in much Cuban music*
[17] **impalpable:** *intangible, incapable of being touched*
[20] **frowsy:** *not neat, unkempt, slovenly or dishevelled*

Elizabeth Bishop

PRE-READING

Think of a bay or a coastal area that you are familiar with. Write a paragraph about this area describing its features and landmarks.

COMPREHENSION

1. The first six lines of the poem describe the water in the bight. What is particularly strange about the water that the poet observes?
2. The bight is an inhospitable place. How is this conveyed in the opening lines?
3. 'The birds are outsize'. What does the poet mean by this?
4. Consider the similes that the poet uses to describe the birds. The pelicans are said to crash 'like pickaxes', whilst the man-of-war birds 'open their tails like scissors'. Discuss the poet's choice of comparison, and say how they impact on your impression of the bight.
5. The 'pilings' in the bight are said to be 'absorbing, rather than being absorbed'. Discuss how the objects in the poem fail to function properly or do what they are supposed to do.
6. Whereas bay areas are generally supposed to be pleasant and picturesque, this bay seems dangerous and inhospitable. How might the bight be considered threatening and uninviting?
7. Although the bight seems an unpleasant place, the poet remains somewhat upbeat and quirky. Where is this apparent in the poem?
8. Whereas the birds and 'shark-tails' are compared to mechanical devices, the machines and boats are likened to animals. Identify the similes that the poet uses when describing the 'sponge boats' and the 'dredge' in the poem, and discuss the comparisons she makes.
9. The damaged boats that 'lie on their sides' are compared to 'torn-open, unanswered letters'. Why do you think the poet draws this comparison? Do you think that the bay in any way reflects how she views her own affairs?
10. How does the structure of the poem correspond with its subject matter?
11. In the last line of the poem, Bishop describes the activity of the bight as 'awful but cheerful'. Discuss the poem in light of this description, commenting upon what you consider to be the 'awful' and the 'cheerful' aspects of the bight.

PERSONAL RESPONSE

1. How does reading this poem make you feel? Can you sympathise with the way the poet views her environment?
2. The poet says in parenthesis under the title that she experienced this bight on 'her birthday'. Does this fact have any bearing upon how you read and understand the poem? Do you think that the poet's perception of the bight is influenced by it being her birthday?
3. What images from the poem did you find most effective and memorable. Write a short essay discussing the images of the poem.

IN CONTEXT

1. Write an essay about the poetry of Elizabeth Bishop – referring to 'The Bight' and two other poems – in which you discuss how the poet deals with place.
2. Bishop's attention to detail is remarkable and her similes often vivid. Referring to three of her poems, write an essay in which you discuss the poet's use of simile.

At the Fishhouses

Although it is a cold evening,
down by one of the fishhouses
an old man sits netting,
his net, in the gloaming almost invisible,
a dark purple-brown, 5
and his shuttle worn and polished.
The air smells so strong of codfish
it makes one's nose run and one's eyes water.
The five fishhouses have steeply peaked roofs
and narrow, cleated gangplanks slant up 10
to storerooms in the gables
for the wheelbarrows to be pushed up and down on.
All is silver: the heavy surface of the sea,
swelling slowly as if considering spilling over,
is opaque, but the silver of the benches, 15
the lobster pots, and masts, scattered
among the wild jagged rocks,
is of an apparent translucence
like the small old buildings with an emerald moss
growing on their shoreward walls. 20
The big fish tubs are completely lined
with layers of beautiful herring scales
and the wheelbarrows are similarly plastered
with creamy iridescent coats of mail,
with small iridescent flies crawling on them. 25
Up on the little slope behind the houses,
set in the sparse bright sprinkle of grass,
is an ancient wooden capstan,
cracked, with two long bleached handles
and some melancholy stains, like dried blood, 30
where the ironwork has rusted.
The old man accepts a Lucky Strike.
He was a friend of my grandfather.
We talk of the decline in the population
and of codfish and herring 35
while he waits for a herring boat to come in.
There are sequins on his vest and on his thumb.
He has scraped the scales, the principal beauty,
from unnumbered fish with that black old knife,
the blade of which is almost worn away. 40

Down at the water's edge, at the place
where they haul up the boats, up the long ramp
descending into the water, thin silver
tree trunks are laid horizontally
across the gray stones, down and down 45
at intervals of four or five feet.

continued over

Cold dark deep and absolutely clear,
element bearable to no mortal,
to fish and to seals … One seal particularly
I have seen here evening after evening.
He was curious about me. He was interested in music;
like me a believer in total immersion,
so I used to sing him Baptist hymns.
I also sang 'A Mighty Fortress is Our God.'
He stood up in the water and regarded me
steadily, moving his head a little.
Then he would disappear, then suddenly emerge
almost in the same spot, with a sort of shrug
as if it were against his better judgement.
Cold dark deep and absolutely clear,
the clear gray icy water … Back, behind us,
the dignified tall firs begin.
Bluish, associating with their shadows,
a million Christmas trees stand
waiting for Christmas. The water seems suspended
above the rounded gray and blue-gray stones.
I have seen it over and over, the same sea, the same,
slightly, indifferently swinging above the stones,
icily free above the stones,
above the stones and then the world.
If you could dip your hand in,
your wrist would ache immediately,
your bones would begin to ache and your hand would burn
as if the water were a transmutation of fire
that feeds on stones and burns with a dark gray flame.
If you tasted it, it would first taste bitter,
then briny, then surely burn your tongue.
It is like what we imagine knowledge to be:
dark, salt, clear, moving, utterly free,
drawn from the cold hard mouth
of the world, derived from the rocky breasts
forever, flowing and drawn, and since
our knowledge is historical, flowing, and flown.

[4] **gloaming:** *dusk, twilight*
[10] **gangplanks:** *boards used as a removable foot-bridge between a ship and a pier*
[23] **iridescent:** *an iridescent surface appears to change colour when we view it from a different angle or when the light hits it from a different angle*
[53] **Baptist:** *a Protestant Christian denomination, popular in the United States and usually Calvinist in doctrine. New members are baptised by being completely immersed in water*
[54] **A Mighty Fortress Is Our Lord:** *a popular Protestant hymn composed by Martin Luther. It is associated with the Lutheran and Anglican traditions rather than with the Baptist denomination mentioned in line 53*

COMPREHENSION

Lines 1–40

1. How would you describe the general atmosphere of the first section of the poem?
2. The fisherman's net is said to be 'in the gloaming almost invisible'. Consider how the first section of the poem conveys a sense of transience and impermanence.
3. The sea is said to be 'opaque, but the silver of the benches,/ the lobster pots, and masts … is of an apparent translucence'. Discuss how the coastal scene, despite her best efforts, eludes the poet's desire to capture it completely in language.
4. *Group Discussion:* Some of the descriptions given are matter-of-fact and objective (i.e. they are not influenced by the poet's personal feelings or interpretations; for example, when the poet says that the fishhouses 'have steeply peaked roofs' we would consider this an objective description as this is how they might appear to anyone), whilst others are subjective (i.e. they are described in a way that is particular or peculiar to the poet; for example, that the sea is said to be 'considering spilling over' is not an objective fact but, rather, the poet's interpretation of the sea's appearance or intention). Discuss the many descriptions in the opening section of the poem, and say which ones are objective and which are subjective. Do some descriptions combine objective and subjective elements?

Lines 41–83

5. Line 41 brings us down to the water's edge. However, when the poet comes to describe the sea in line 49 she stops short and moves quickly on to a light-hearted description of a seal. Why do you think she hesitates in her description of the sea?
6. Consider the poet's brief description of the sea in lines 47–9. Would you consider that the terms she uses to describe the sea are in any way contradictory? What do you think she means when she says that it is 'bearable to no mortal'?
7. In line 60 the poet returns to the sea and tries once again to describe it. Yet again she stops and focuses on something else. Why is the sea so difficult for her to comprehend?
8. Although she is briefly distracted by the fir trees behind her, the poet quickly gets back to contemplating the sea. Consider the language she uses in lines 65–70. How is a sense of urgency conveyed in these lines? Why do you think the poet writes in this manner here?
9. Why does the sea appear so different to the rest of the area? In what sense can the sea be considered 'free'?
10. Lines 71–7 describe how the poet imagines the water would feel and taste. Why do you think she likens the cold water to fire?
11. *Class Discussion:* Having described the sea, the poet tells us that 'we imagine knowledge to be' similar. In what way, if any, can knowledge be thought of as 'dark, salt, clear moving' and 'utterly free'?
12. Bishop tells us that 'knowledge' is 'drawn from the cold hard mouth/ of the world, derived from the rocky breasts'. What sort of knowledge is she referring to? Why do you think she describes the place of origin as having feminine features that are cold and hard?

PERSONAL RESPONSE

Were you surprised by the poem's movement from relatively straightforward description in the opening section to complex, abstract philosophical considerations of knowledge in the final lines? Did you find the poem frustrating or did you find it stimulating and thought-provoking? Can you draw a link between the early part of the poem and the final meditations upon the sea?

IN CONTEXT

1. 'The need to comprehend and understand her environment as thoroughly as possible through language is at the heart of many Elizabeth Bishop poems'. How does 'At the Fishhouses' compare to other poems on the course in this regard?
2. In 'The Bight' Bishop summarises the scene before her as 'awful but cheerful'. These words might deftly summarise how the world often appears in the poems of Elizabeth Bishop. Compare and contrast 'At the Fishhouses' and 'The Bight' based upon this opinion.

The Prodigal

The brown enormous odor he lived by
was too close, with its breathing and thick hair,
for him to judge. The floor was rotten; the sty
was plastered halfway up with glass-smooth dung.
Light-lashed, self-righteous, above moving snouts,   5
the pigs' eyes followed him, a cheerful stare –
even to the sow that always ate her young –
till, sickening, he leaned to scratch her head.
But sometimes mornings after drinking bouts
(he hid the pints behind a two-by-four),   10
the sunrise glazed the barnyard mud with red;
the burning puddles seemed to reassure.
And then he thought he almost might endure
his exile yet another year or more.

But evenings the first star came to warn.   15
The farmer whom he worked for came at dark
to shut the cows and horses in the barn
beneath their overhanging clouds of hay,
with pitchforks, faint forked lightnings, catching light,
safe and companionable as in the Ark.   20
The pigs stuck out their little feet and snored.
The lantern – like the sun, going away –
laid on the mud a pacing aureole.
Carrying a bucket along a slimy board,
he felt the bats' uncertain staggering flight,   25
his shuddering insights, beyond his control,
touching him. But it took him a long time
finally to make up his mind to go home.

Prodigal: *a spendthrift, someone who has wasted his or her money in an extravagant fashion.*
[23] **Aureole:** *a halo of light*

PRE-READING

What do you understand by the word 'prodigal'? Are you familiar with the story of the prodigal son from the Bible? Write a brief paragraph retelling that story in your own words.

COMPREHENSION

1. Describe, in your own words, the prodigal's dwelling place.
2. What is the prodigal's occupation?
3. It has been suggested that the poem's opening stanza contains lines that 'appeal to all five senses'. Identify at least one phrase from this stanza that appeals to each sense.
4. Bishop describes the pigs' odour as being 'brown and enormous'. What do you think she means by this?
5. According to Bishop, the smell of the pigsty was 'too close' for the prodigal to judge. What do you think she means by this?'
6. What indications are there in lines 1–10 that the prodigal is unhappy with his current way of life?
7. What indication is there that he is ashamed of his 'drinking bouts'?
8. On certain mornings the farmyard has a peculiar beauty. Describe, in your own words, how the farmyard looks on these particular mornings.
9. How does the prodigal feel on these particular mornings?
10. How does the opening stanza indicate that the prodigal is far from home?
11. 'But evenings the first star came to warn'. What warning do you think the 'first star' gives the prodigal?
12. What does the farmer do each evening?
13. 'The lantern – like the sun, going away'. Who does this lantern belong to?
14. How do the animals spend the night? How does this compare with the way the prodigal spends his nights?
15. According to Bishop, the prodigal felt the 'bats' uncertain staggering flight'. What do you think is meant by this expression? How could the prodigal 'feel' the flight of the bats overhead?
16. 'But it took him a long time/ finally to make up his mind to go home'. Why do you think the prodigal was reluctant or hesitant to change his life, leave the pigsty behind and return to his home place?
17. *Class Discussion:* What is the form of this poem?

PERSONAL RESPONSE

1. Bishop's poems are famous for their well-crafted images. Identify two images in this poem that you found particularly memorable or effective. Give reasons for your choice.
2. *Class Discussion:* What are the main themes of 'The Prodigal'? Is it a poem with a clear and well-defined message or moral?
3. '"The Prodigal" is a masterful study of addiction. It provides a wonderfully grim depiction of the squalor and misery endured by those who suffer from the various forms of this terrible disease.' Would you agree with this interpretation of the poem? Give reasons for your answer.

IN CONTEXT

'The Prodigal' presents us with a character who has a sudden moment of understanding or realisation – what Bishop refers to as moments of 'shuddering insights'. Identify two other poems by Bishop that also contain moments of realisation, and compare or contrast them with 'The Prodigal'.

Questions of Travel

There are too many waterfalls here; the crowded streams
hurry too rapidly down to the sea,
and the pressure of so many clouds on the mountaintops
makes them spill over the sides in soft slow-motion,
turning to waterfalls under our very eyes.
— For if those streaks, those mile-long, shiny, tearstains,
aren't waterfalls yet,
in a quick age or so, as ages go here,
they probably will be.
But if the streams and clouds keep traveling, traveling,
the mountains look like the hulls of capsized ships,
slime-hung and barnacled.

Think of the long trip home.
Should we have stayed at home and thought of here?
Where should we be today?
Is it right to be watching strangers in a play
in this strangest of theaters?
What childishness is it that while there's a breath of life
in our bodies, we are determined to rush
to see the sun the other way around?
The tiniest green hummingbird in the world?
To stare at some inexplicable old stonework,
inexplicable and impenetrable,
at any view,
instantly seen and always, always delightful?
Oh, must we dream our dreams
and have them, too?
And have we room
for one more folded sunset, still quite warm?

But surely it would have been a pity
not to have seen the trees along this road,
really exaggerated in their beauty,
not to have seen them gesturing
like noble pantomimists, robed in pink.
— Not to have had to stop for gas and heard
the sad, two-noted, wooden tune
of disparate wooden clogs
carelessly clacking over
a grease-stained filling-station floor.
(In another country the clogs would all be tested.
Each pair there would have identical pitch.)
— A pity not to have heard
the other, less primitive music of the fat brown bird
who sings above the broken gasoline pump
in a bamboo church of Jesuit baroque:
three towers, five silver crosses.

– Yes, a pity not to have pondered,
blurr'dly and inconclusively,
on what connection can exist for centuries   50
between the crudest wooden footwear
and, careful and finicky,
the whittled fantasies of wooden footwear
and, careful and finicky,
the whittled fantasies of wooden cages.   55
– Never to have studied history in
the weak calligraphy of songbirds' cages.
– And never to have had to listen to rain
so much like politicians' speeches:
two hours of unrelenting oratory   60
and then a sudden golden silence
in which the traveler takes a notebook, writes:

'Is it lack of imagination that makes us come
to imagined places, not just stay at home?
Or could Pascal have been not entirely right   65
about just sitting quietly in one's room?

Continent, city, country, society:
the choice is never wide and never free.
And here, or there ... No. Should we have stayed at home,
wherever that may be?'

[45] **Jesuit baroque:** *a dramatic and complex style of architecture that was developed in seventeen-century Europe and brought to South America by Jesuit priests*
[62] **Pacscal:** *Blaise Pascal (1623–62) was a French mathematician, philosopher and inventor*

Elizabeth Bishop

PRE-READING
Think about a trip you made to a foreign country. What aspects of the trip did you enjoy most? Were there any aspects of the trip you didn't like?

COMPREHENSION
Lines 1–12
1. Describe, in your own words, the scene depicted in the poem's first ten lines.
2. Do you think the speaker finds this scene attractive? Give reasons for your answer.
3. Identify two metaphors or similes in this section of the poem, and say whether or not you find them effective.
4. 'in a quick age or so, as ages go here'. What do you understand by this expression?

Lines 13–29
5. What negative aspects of travel does the speaker identify in this section?
6. How would you describe the tone of this section?
7. According to the speaker what kind of behaviour is down to 'childishness'?
8. Comment on the use of the word 'delightful'.
9. What do you think the speaker means when she asks 'Oh, must we dream our dreams/ and have them, too?'?
10. What do you understand by the expression 'folded sunset, still quite warm'? What does it mean for a sunset to be 'folded'?

Lines 30–59
11. In this section the speaker mentions a number of experiences it would have been 'a pity' to miss out on. List them. Which of these experiences seems most appealing to you? Which seems least appealing? Give reasons for your answers.
12. What simile does Bishop use to describe the trees?
13. Describe, in your own words, the songbird's cage.
14. How would you describe the atmosphere of the gas station?
15. The speaker claims that she is 'studying history' when she looks at the songbird's cage. What might she mean by this?
16. What simile does Bishop use to describe the sound of the tropical rain?

Lines 60–6
17. What do you understand by the speaker's suggestion that Pascal may not have been 'entirely right'?
18. *Class Discussion:* 'The choice is never wide and never free'. What does Bishop mean by this rather enigmatic pronouncement?

PERSONAL RESPONSE
1. Consider the poem's title. What do you feel are the questions of travel Bishop wants to address?
2. 'This poem is an extremely balanced meditation on travel. Every experience Bishop describes is shown to have both a negative and positive aspect. The poem, therefore, simply does not make up its mind on the question of whether travel is a good thing or a bad thing.' Write a paragraph in response to this statement.
3. Did you like this poem? Write a paragraph explaining your answer.

IN CONTEXT
Compare and contrast the depiction of the filling station in this poem with that in 'Filling Station'. Which poem, in your opinion, provides the more positive depiction of a filling station?

The Armadillo

for Robert Lowell

This is the time of year
when almost every night
the frail, illegal fire balloons appear.
Climbing the mountain height,

rising toward a saint
still honored in these parts,
the paper chambers flush and fill with light
that comes and goes, like hearts.

Once up against the sky it's hard
to tell them from the stars —
planets, that is — the tinted ones:
Venus going down, or Mars,

or the pale green one. With a wind,
they flare and falter, wobble and toss;
but if it's still they steer between
the kite sticks of the Southern Cross,

receding, dwindling, solemnly
and steadily forsaking us,
or, in the downdraft from a peak,
suddenly turning dangerous.

Last night another big one fell.
It splattered like an egg of fire
against the cliff behind the house.
The flame ran down. We saw the pair

of owls who nest there flying up
and up, their whirling black-and-white
stained bright pink underneath, until
they shrieked up out of sight.

The ancient owls' nest must have burned.
Hastily, all alone,
a glistening armadillo left the scene,
rose-flecked, head down, tail down,

and then a baby rabbit jumped out,
short-eared, to our surprise.
So soft! — a handful of intangible ash
with fixed, ignited eyes.

Too pretty, dreamlike mimicry!
O falling fire and piercing cry
and panic, and a weak mailed fist
clenched ignorant against the sky!

[16] **Southern Cross:** *a distinctive constellation visible in the Southern hemisphere*

COMPREHENSION

1. Where is this poem set?
2. Why do the local people launch the fire balloons?
3. Describe, in your own words, the appearance of the fire balloons. What are they constructed from?
4. According to the speaker, what do the fire balloons resemble when they are 'up against the sky'?
5. In lines 12–20 the speaker describes three different ways in which the fire balloons move, depending on the weather conditions. Describe these in your own words.
6. What is the 'pale green one'?
7. Based on your reading of lines 1–20, how would you describe the speaker's reaction to the fire balloons?
8. 'Last night another big one fell'. What damage is caused by this falling fire balloon?
9. Why are the owls described as being stained 'bright pink underneath'?
10. Why is the rabbit 'short-eared'?
11. *Class Discussion*: Why did Bishop choose to print the poem's final stanza in italics?
12. *Class Discussion*: What do you understand by the expression 'Too pretty, dreamlike mimicry!'? What do you think is being referred to here?
13. What do you understand by the 'weak mailed fist' in line 39? Who or what does this fist belong to?
14. Identify three similes in this poem. In the case of each say whether or not you find it effective. Give reasons for your answer.

PERSONAL RESPONSE

1. What emotions did you experience when you first read 'The Armadillo'?
2. How would you describe the tone or atmosphere of this poem? Would you agree that the tone changes throughout the piece?
3. *Class Discussion*: Many critics have suggested that the fire balloons in this poem serve a 'symbolic function'. What do you think the fire balloons might symbolise?
4. 'The reference to Venus, god of love, and Mars, god of war, are vitally important.' Do you agree with this statement? What significance do you think these references might have in the context of the poem as a whole?
5. The conclusion of this poem is often considered to be one of Bishop's most directly emotional pieces of writing. What emotions, in your opinion, are expressed in the poem's last four lines?
6. 'This poem is about the stupidity of men'. Write a paragraph agreeing or disagreeing with this statement.
7. Would you agree that this is a pessimistic poem? Give reasons for your answer.
8. 'This poem is about things that are dangerous but that we can't stay away from. Things like war, love and art exert a glamorous attraction on us despite – or perhaps because of – their danger.' Write a paragraph in response to this statement.

Sestina

September rain falls on the house.
In the failing light, the old grandmother
sits in the kitchen with the child
beside the Little Marvel Stove,
reading the jokes from the almanac,
laughing and talking to hide her tears.

She thinks that her equinoctial tears
and the rain that beats on the roof of the house
were both foretold by the almanac,
but only known to a grandmother.
The iron kettle sings on the stove.
She cuts some bread and says to the child,

It's time for tea now; but the child
is watching the teakettle's small hard tears
dance like mad on the hot black stove,
the way the rain must dance on the house.
Tidying up, the old grandmother
hangs up the clever almanac

on its string. Birdlike, the almanac
hovers half open above the child,
hovers above the old grandmother
and her teacup full of dark brown tears.
She shivers and says she thinks the house
feels chilly, and puts more wood in the stove.

It was to be, says the Marvel Stove.
I know what I know, says the almanac.
With crayons the child draws a rigid house
and a winding pathway. Then the child
puts in a man with buttons like tears
and shows it proudly to the grandmother.

But secretly, while the grandmother
busies herself about the stove,
the little moons fall down like tears
from between the pages of the almanac
into the flower bed the child
has carefully placed in the front of the house.

Time to plant tears, says the almanac.
The grandmother sings to the marvelous stove
and the child draws another inscrutable house.

COMPREHENSION

1. Consider the poem's title. What is a 'sestina'? In what sense is this poem a sestina?
2. Describe, in your own words, the poem's setting.
3. What do you understand by the expression 'equinoctial tears'?
4. What, according to the grandmother, did the almanac predict?
5. Why is the almanac described as 'clever'?
6. Why is the almanac described as 'birdlike'?
7. *Class Discussion:* 'Then the child/ puts in a man with buttons like tears'. What is the significance of this statement?
8. What is your understanding of the expression 'teacup full of dark brown tears'?
9. What is your reaction to the depiction of the almanac in stanza 4?
10. It was to be, says the Marvel Stone. What, based on your reading of the poem, do you think was 'to be'?
11. What is happening in stanza 6?
12. Why are the houses drawn by the child described as 'inscrutable'?
13. Comment on the role played by the weather in the poem.
14. Comment on the form of the poem.

PERSONAL RESPONSE

1. Write a paragraph describing the emotions you experienced when you first read 'Sestina'.
2. *Class Discussion:* What, based on the clues given in the poem, is the background to the scene depicted in 'Sestina'?
3. 'Sestina' has often been described as a poem where 'almost everything is left unsaid'. Do you think this accurately describes the poem?
4. How would you describe the poem's atmosphere? Would you agree that the atmosphere changes throughout the poem? Give reasons for your answers.
5. Would you agree that this poem contains some strange and startling images? Identify the two images you found most effective. Say why.
6. Write three paragraphs saying why you liked or did not like 'Sestina'. Each paragraph should focus on a different aspect of the poem.
7. 'In 'Sestina' Bishop wonderfully recreates the world of childhood'. Would you agree with this statement? Give reasons for your answer.
8. Do you think this is a realistic poem? Would you agree that certain aspects of it are unrealistic? Give reasons for your answer.
9. Imagine you are the child's grandmother. Write a diary entry describing the events that led up to the little scene depicted in this poem.

IN CONTEXT

'Sestina', like 'First Death in Nova Scotia' and 'In the Waiting Room', is a poem of childhood. Write a paragraph comparing and contrasting the depiction of childhood in these three poems.

First Death in Nova Scotia

In the cold, cold parlor
my mother laid out Arthur
beneath the chromographs:
Edward, Prince of Wales,
with Princess Alexandra,   5
and King George with Queen Mary.
Below them on the table
stood a stuffed loon
shot and stuffed by Uncle
Arthur, Arthur's father.   10

Since Uncle Arthur fired
a bullet into him,
he hadn't said a word.
He kept his own counsel
on his white, frozen lake,   15
the marble-topped table.
His breast was deep and white,
cold and caressable;
his eyes were red glass,
much to be desired.   20

'Come,' said my mother,
'Come and say good-bye
to your little cousin Arthur.'
I was lifted up and given
one lily of the valley   25
to put in Arthur's hand.
Arthur's coffin was
a little frosted cake,
and the red-eyed loon eyed it
from his white, frozen lake.   30

Arthur was very small.
He was all white, like a doll
that hadn't been painted yet.
Jack Frost had started to paint him
the way he always painted   35
the Maple Leaf (Forever).
He had just begun on his hair,
a few red strokes, and then
Jack Frost had dropped the brush
and left him white, forever.   40

The gracious royal couples
were warm in red and ermine;
their feet were well wrapped up
in the ladies' ermine trains.
They invited Arthur to be   45
the smallest page at court.
But how could Arthur go,
clutching his tiny lily,
with his eyes shut up so tight
and the roads deep in snow?   50

[3] **chromograph:** *an early form of colour photograph*
[8] **loon:** *short-tailed birds with a distinctive cry that dive to catch fish.*
[36] **Maple Leaf:** *the national emblem of Canada; 'The Maple Leaf Forever' was a popular patriotic song*
[42] **ermine:** *an expensive type of fur which comes from the rodent of the same name*

COMPREHENSION

1. Describe, in your own words, the setting of this poem.
2. How old do you think the speaker is? Give reasons for your answer.
3. 'Since Uncle Arthur had fired a bullet into him'. Who had Uncle Arthur shot?
4. What relationship does the speaker have with little Arthur?
5. Why is Arthur described as being 'all white'?
6. What simile is used to describe the marble-topped table?
7. What simile is used to describe the cousin's body?
8. What do you understand by the expression 'Maple Leaf (Forever)'?
9. Comment on the repetition of the word 'forever' in the poem's fourth stanza.
10. Who are the 'gracious royal couples' referred to in stanza 5?
11. Where does the child's mother tell her that Arthur is going?
12. Why do you think she tells her daughter this?
13. Comment on the use of colours in this poem.

PERSONAL RESPONSE

1. Write a short paragraph describing the emotions you experienced when you first read this poem.
2. Do you think this poem manages to depict events as they would be experienced by a child? Give reasons for your answer.
3. 'This poem movingly recounts a child's first confrontation with death. It shows her attempts to come to grips with this strange new concept and also her attempts to avoid thinking about her cousin's alien, altered state.' Write a short paragraph in response to this statement.

IN CONTEXT

'In the Waiting Room' is another poem that addresses Bishop's childhood. Write a short paragraph discussing the similarities and differences between these two poems. Would you agree that both poems deal with important moments of realisation?

Filling Station

Oh, but it is dirty!
– this little filling station,
oil-soaked, oil-permeated
to a disturbing, over-all
black translucency.
Be careful with that match!

Father wears a dirty,
oil-soaked monkey suit
that cuts him under the arms,
and several quick and saucy
and greasy sons assist him
(it's a family filling station),
all quite thoroughly dirty.

Do they live in the station?
It has a cement porch
behind the pumps, and on it
a set of crushed and grease –
impregnated wickerwork;
on the wicker sofa
a dirty dog, quite comfy.

Some comic books provide
the only note of color –
of certain color. They lie
upon a big dim doily
draping a taboret
(part of the set), beside
a big hirsute begonia.

Why the extraneous plant?
Why the taboret?
Why, oh why, the doily?
(Embroidered in daisy stitch
with marguerites, I think,
and heavy with gray crochet.)

Somebody embroidered the doily.
Somebody waters the plant,
or oils it, maybe. Somebody
arranges the rows of cans
so that they softly say:
ESSO–SO–SO–SO

to high-strung automobiles.
Somebody loves us all.

[24] **doily:** *an ornamental mat, often made from cotton or linen*
[25] **taboret:** *a short stool without a back or arms*
[32] **marguerites:** *daisy-like flowers*

COMPREHENSION

1. How would you characterise the 'voice' of the poem? Is there any reason to presume it is a woman who speaks?
2. The second stanza introduces, or at least recognises, the filling-station family. What sort of people run the filling station?
3. Where do you think the speaker of the poem is located?
4. Why does the speaker think that the people working at the station might live there? Why does the thought of living there cause her concern?
5. In the fourth stanza the speaker says that the comic books 'provide/ the only note of … certain color'. Why are the other colours of the filling station 'uncertain'?
6. The plant of the taboret is 'a big hirsute begonia.' Why does the description of the plant seem so appropriate given its location?
7. Why does the presence of the 'doily' so surprise the speaker?
8. Does the detailed description of the doily make it any easier for us to know what sort of person the speaker of the poem might be?
9. The fifth stanza asks many questions. Do you think the speaker of the poem knows the answer to these questions and is just using them for dramatic effect, or do you think she is genuinely curious?
10. The final stanza refers to the 'somebody' who must have been responsible for the presence of the surprising objects mentioned in the fourth stanza. Who do you think this 'somebody' might be? Does the poem lead us to an obvious answer?
11. Is the last line of the poem an honest remark, intended to mean just what it says? Or do you think the speaker is being sarcastic or ironic?

PERSONAL RESPONSE

1. 'At first the speaker's attitude seems harshly judgemental, but the following stanzas highlight the determinedness with which this speaker looks into the translucency in order to see the humanity existing at the filling station.' Would you agree with this point of view?
2. This is a poem about taking things for granted. Would you agree?
3. 'There is an understood presence at the end of "Filling Station", a nurturing and artistic overseer to this otherwise casual business. It is on the care and the arrangement of objects that survival depends. The soft utterances of the oil cans gently mock and soothe the high-strung automobiles that so cruelly embody the idea of cultural and social progress.' Discuss the poem in light of these comments.

IN CONTEXT

1. 'The descriptively self-contained stanzas of "Filling Station" cause it to resemble "Sestina" more than any other Bishop poem. The theatrical positioning of props and people echoes the dominant image patterns of that poem'. Write a short essay based upon this observation.
2. 'Bishop's work is preoccupied with motherhood, sometimes in the most unlikely places'. Discuss the poetry of Elizabeth Bishop in light of this remark.
3. '"Filling Station", like many Bishop poems, is a poem of place. And though it may be a more whimsical poem than "At the Fishhouses" and "The Bight", it nevertheless shares many characteristics with these poems.' Write a short essay based on this observation.

In the Waiting Room

In Worcester, Massachusetts,
I went with Aunt Consuelo
to keep her dentist's appointment
and sat and waited for her
in the dentist's waiting room.　　　　　5
It was winter. It got dark
early. The waiting room
was full of grown-up people,
arctics and overcoats,
lamps and magazines.　　　　　　　　10
My aunt was inside
what seemed like a long time
and while I waited and read
the *National Geographic*
(I could read) and carefully　　　　　15
studied the photographs:
the inside of a volcano,
black, and full of ashes;
then it was spilling over
in rivulets of fire.　　　　　　　　　20
Osa and Martin Johnson
dressed in riding breeches,
laced boots, and pith helmets.
A dead man slung on a pole
– 'Long Pig,' the caption said.　　　25
Babies with pointed heads
wound round and round with string;
black, naked women with necks
wound round and round with wire
like the necks of light bulbs.　　　　30
Their breasts were horrifying.
I read it right straight through.
I was too shy to stop.
And then I looked at the cover:
the yellow margins, the date.　　　　35

Suddenly, from inside,
came an *oh!* of pain
– Aunt Consuelo's voice –
not very loud or long.
I wasn't at all surprised;　　　　　　40
even then I knew she was
a foolish, timid woman.
I might have been embarrassed,
but wasn't. What took me
completely by surprise　　　　　　　45
was that it was *me*:
my voice, in my mouth.
Without thinking at all
I was my foolish aunt,

continued over

I – we – were falling, falling,
our eyes glued to the cover
of the *National Geographic*,
February, 1918.

I said to myself: three days
and you'll be seven years old.
I was saying it to stop
the sensation of falling off
the round, turning world
into cold, blue-black space.
But I felt: you are an *I*,
you are an *Elizabeth*,
you are one of *them*.
Why should you be one, too?
I scarcely dared to look
to see what it was I was.
I gave a sidelong glance
– I couldn't look any higher –
at shadowy gray knees,
trousers and skirts and boots
and different pairs of hands
lying under the lamps.
I knew that nothing stranger
had ever happened, that nothing
stranger could ever happen.
Why should I be my aunt,
or me, or anyone?
What similarities –
boots, hands, the family voice
I felt in my throat, or even
the *National Geographic*
and those awful hanging breasts –
held us all together
or made us all just one?
How I didn't know any
word for it how 'unlikely' …
How had I come to be here,
like them, and overhear
a cry of pain that could have
got loud and worse but hadn't?

The waiting room was bright
and too hot. It was sliding
beneath a big black wave,
another, and another.

Then I was back in it.
The War was on. Outside,
in Worcester, Massachusetts,
were night and slush and cold,
and it was still the fifth
of February, 1918.

[21] **Osa and Martin Johnson:** *an American couple who became famous in the early twentieth century for their travels in Africa and other exotic locations*
[25] **Long Pig:** *this refers to cannibalism: in certain Polynesian islands, human flesh was known as 'long-pig'*
[95] **The War:** *First World War*

PRE-READING

Do you recall a time in your childhood when something that you took for granted was shown to be unsound or untrue? How did you feel at the time?

COMPREHENSION

Lines 1–35

1. How did the language used in the poem suggest that it is a small child who speaks?
2. What details concern the child in the opening lines of the poem?
3. How is the child's sense of importance and uniqueness made evident by what she says in the first twenty lines of the poem?
4. What is her opinion of the aunt whom she accompanies to the dentist?
5. Describe the articles that the young girl looks at in the *National Geographic*. What is her reaction to the images she sees?
6. Why did she continue to read the articles although they obviously disturbed her?

Lines 36–53

7. What does the child hear?
8. Where does she think this noise originates from?
9. What is her impression of her aunt having heard this noise?
10. 'What took me/ completely by surprise/ was that it was me'. What is happening here? How is the voice she heard now considered to be her own? Was she mistaken to think that it was the aunt who made the noise in the first place?
11. What might have caused the young girl to make the noise herself?

Lines 54–74

12. What does she do to steady herself and regain her grip on the world?
13. In line 60 she tells herself that she is an 'I', and in line 62 she must also acknowledge that she is 'one of them'. What does it mean that she is now 'one of them'?
14. What does she do in order to get a better understanding of what being 'one of them' entails?
15. What does she see when she looks around her? Why can't she raise her eyes?
16. 'I knew that nothing stranger/ had ever happened'. Is there a sense that the young girl is now coming to terms with the strange event?

Lines 75–99

17. The girl reveals an awareness that she is not quite as unique as she once thought she was. How is this apparent in what she says in lines 75–85?
18. What additional acknowledgement must she now make about the disturbing articles that she read in the magazine?
19. Why do you think the 'hanging breasts' are particularly disturbing for the young girl?
20. Why do you think that she describes the cry as something that could have 'got loud and worse' but hadn't?
21. She says that the waiting room 'was sliding/ beneath a big black wave,/ another, and another'. What is happening here?
22. How do the last six lines restore a sense of order and stability to the child's world?

PERSONAL RESPONSE

1. How does this poem explore the painful transition from childhood to adulthood?
2. Do you think that Bishop captures the world of the child well in the lines of this poem? Which lines do you think especially illustrate what it's like to think as a young child about the world?
3. Did you find the event that the child described initially confusing? How did this confusion arise?

IN CONTEXT

'Very few poets deal with childhood as sympathetically and as realistically as Elizabeth Bishop. In her poems, the child does not symbolise or represent some innocence that the older poet now desires to recapture. Instead, childhood is revealed as a troubled time of uncertainty when notions of innocence are constantly under threat.' Write an essay discussing three poems dealing with childhood by Elizabeth Bishop in light of this statement.

THOMAS KINSELLA

BIOGRAPHY

Kinsella was born in Inchicore, Dublin, in 1928. Both his father and his grandfather worked for Guinness' brewery in Dublin. In his later years his grandfather retired from the brewery and worked as a cobbler, a fact referenced in the poem 'His Father's Hands'. Kinsella's father was a highly political individual. A committed socialist, he was among those responsible for establishing the trade union movement in the Guinness company. The father's argumentative, somewhat abrasive personality is also referenced in 'His Father's Hands'. However, there can be little doubt that the father's political zeal influenced Kinsella's determination to speak out against injustice in his poetry.

Kinsella grew up in the area of Dublin around James's Street and Inchicore. Both his grandmothers kept shops in this area. This part of Dublin forms the backdrop to much of Kinsella's poetry; for instance, the grandmother's shop is mentioned in 'Tear', while this inner-city world of yards and lanes is featured in poems such as 'Hen Woman' and 'Dick King'.

Kinsella was educated at the Model School in Inchicore – an experience powerfully described in the poem of the same name. His later education took place in the Christian Brothers' O'Connell School and in UCD, where he studied science. His university education was cut short when he was offered and accepted a position in the civil service. However, he continued to attend night classes.

This was an exciting period in Kinsella's life. He began to seriously explore the possibility of poetry. He formed important friendships with influential figures such as Liam Miller, founder of the Dolmen Press, and with the great composer Seán Ó Riada. With these and other young artists and intellectuals, Kinsella enjoyed many late-night conversations about life, art, music and politics. It was also at this time that he met his future wife, Eleanor, whose companionship was destined to have a great impact on his life and poetry. His first book of poetry, simply entitled *Poems*, was published as a wedding present to her on the occasion of their marriage in 1956.

Kinsella's early poetry was very successful and won him a measure of fame both in Ireland and in Britain. His urban, sophisticate verse set him apart from the mainstream of Irish poetry, which was dominated by the more rural example of Patrick Kavanagh and the by-now-tired influence of W.B. Yeats. His civil service career was also successful, with Kinsella rising high in the Department of Finance and eventually serving as secretary to its director, T.K. Whitaker. Kinsella's translations from the Irish language also met with good reviews. At Liam Miller's suggestion, he translated the ancient Irish epic called *The Táin*, and with Seán O'Tuama translated *An Duanaire: The Poems of the Dispossessed*.

In the late Sixties and the Seventies Kinsella's work started to become looser and more experimental in form. The earlier carefully rhymed poems like 'Mirror in February' were replaced by free verse influenced by American poets such as Ezra Pound and William Carlos Williams. Instead of focusing on individual poems, he began to see his entire output as part of one long, almost endless poetic sequence.

His poetry also grew thematically denser, coming under the influence of Irish myth and the psychology of Carl Gustav Jung. Jung's influence is evident in the poetry's focus on origins, beginnings and inheritance. Another influence on Kinsella at this point was the concept of numerology. He began to structure his work around a complex and very personal idea of numbers and their significances. We see this in 'Hen

Woman', with its focus on zero, and in 'His Father's Hands', with its focus on the digit 1.

At around this time Kinsella's reputation suffered something of a setback. Critics and readers found his new, more experimental style confusing and off-putting. His poem 'Butcher's Dozen' alienated the British reading public as it bitterly criticised the official British response to the Bloody Sunday massacre in Derry in 1972. He founded Pepper Cannister Press and began publishing his work in small, limited-edition booklets rather than in conventional book form. This development also diminished his presence in the eyes of the reading public. Furthermore, in a world where literature became increasingly media-driven, Kinsella refused to play the celebrity game, and seldom gave interviews.

In 1965 Kinsella left the civil service and took up a position in the US, initially as a writer-in-residence in Illinois and then as a professor in Temple University, Philadelphia. For many years afterwards, he would divide his time between Ireland and the US. Over this time, he continued his Pepper Cannister series of publications, creating a vast and complicated body of work that deals with both the personal and the political, with both the mythic and the historic.

In recent years Kinsella's work has found the reputation it deserves. His writing has been championed by a new generation of readers, and many younger poets have claimed him as an influence. In the past decade, his work has been the subject of many books as well as several radio and television documentaries. In 2007 he was given the Freedom of the City of Dublin.

Thinking of Mr D.

A man still light of foot, but ageing, took
An hour to drink his glass, his quiet tongue
Danced to such cheerful slander.

He sipped and swallowed with a scathing smile,
Tapping a polished toe.   5
His sober nod withheld assent.

When he died I saw him twice.
Once as he used retire
On one last murmured stabbing little tale
From the right company, tucking in his scarf.   10

And once down by the river, under wharf-
Lamps that plunged him in and out of light,
A priestlike figure turning, wolfish-slim,
Quickly aside from pain, in a bodily plight,
To note the oiled reflections chime and swim.   15

[3] **slander:** *a malicious statement, damaging to a person's reputation*
[11] **wharf:** *a level quayside area*

COMPREHENSION

Lines 1–6

1. Read the first six lines of the poem. Think of three words that best describe the character of Mr D.
2. Although Mr D. is an ageing man, he seems full of vitality. How is this evident?
3. How do you think Mr D. would have appeared to the other people in the pub? Do you think he was a pleasant character?

Lines 7–15

4. Where does the poet say he saw Mr D. after he had died?
5. Describe Mr D.'s appearance in lines 11–15. How does the description given here differ to that given in the first six lines?
6. How does the poet convey Mr D.'s suffering in the last six lines of the poem?
7. What is Mr D. looking at in the final line of the poem?

PERSONAL RESPONSE

1. 'A priestlike figure turning, wolfish-slim,/ Quickly aside from pain, in a bodily plight,/ To note the oiled reflections chime and swim.' What do you think Mr D. is thinking about as he looks out on the river?
2. The poet says that he 'saw him twice' after Mr D. died. What does the poet mean by this?
3. Mr D. was a man who seemed to manage his appearance very carefully. How is this evident in the poem?
4. Did you feel any sympathy for Mr D.?
5. Why do you think the poet chose to write a poem about Mr D.?

IN CONTEXT

1. 'Kinsella's poems often deal with the negative effects of ageing.' Discuss this statement in relation to 'Thinking of Mr D.', 'Dick King' and 'Tear'.
2. 'There is a sense in the poetry of Thomas Kinsella that death is not final, that the dead continue to somehow live on in the lives of those who knew them.' Discuss this statement in relation to 'Thinking of Mr D.' and 'His Father's Hands'.

Dick King

In your ghost, Dick King, in your phantom vowels I read
That death roves our memories igniting
Love. Kind plague, low voice in a stubbled throat,
You haunt with the taint of age and of vanished good,
Fouling my thought with losses.   5

Clearly now I remember rain on the cobbles,
Ripples in the iron trough, and the horses' dipped
Faces under the Fountain in James's Street,
When I sheltered my nine years against your buttons
And your own dread years were to come: 10

And your voice, in a pause of softness, named the dead,
Hushed as though the city had died by fire,
Bemused, discovering … discovering
A gate to enter temperate ghosthood by;
And I squeezed your fingers till you found again   15
My hand hidden in yours.

                I squeeze your fingers:

Dick King was an upright man.
Sixty years he trod
The dull stations underfoot.   20
Fifteen he lies with God.

By the salt seaboard he grew up
But left its rock and rain
To bring a dying language east
And dwell in Basin Lane.   25

By the Southern Railway he increased:
His second soul was born
In the clangour of the iron sheds,
The hush of the late horn.

An invalid he took to wife.   30
She prayed her life away;
Her whisper filled the whitewashed yard
Until her dying day.

And season in, season out,
He made his wintry bed.   35
He took the path to the turnstile
Morning and night till he was dead.

He clasped his hands in a Union ward
To hear St James's bell.
I searched his eyes though I was young,   40
The last to wish him well.

[2] **roves:** *wanders*
[14] **temperate:** *can mean showing moderation or self-restraint. Can also mean mild or warm.*
[37] **Union ward:** *a workhouse, or an institution for the poor*

COMPREHENSION

Lines 1–5

1. What effect do the opening lines suggest death has on our memories?
2. Although Dick King is dead, he continues to be present in the life of the poet. How does the old man's presence make the poet feel? Do the opening lines convey conflicting emotions?
3. What do the opening lines of the poem tell us about the type of man Dick King was?

Lines 6–17

4. The poet recalls a memory from his childhood when he stood next to Dick King on James's Street. What details does he remember from this occasion?
5. How do these lines suggest the child's vulnerability?
6. What sort of atmosphere do these lines convey? Think about the sounds of the words that the poet has chosen to use, how assonance and alliteration contribute to the overall atmosphere.
7. What do you think Dick King is thinking about on this occasion?
8. There is a shift in tense in line 17. Why do you think the poet does this?

Lines 18–41

9. Where did Dick King grow up?
10. Where did he move to? What 'dying language' did he bring with him when he moved?
11. What does the poet mean when he says Dick King 'increased' by the Southern Railway?
12. How does the poet convey the sense of Dick King starting a new life in line 27?
13. What did he work as?
14. What sort of woman did he marry?
15. What sort of life did Dick King live after his wife's death?
16. Do you think Dick King was happy or unhappy in his later years?
17. How does the structure of lines 18–41 differ from lines 1–17? What effect does this have on the tone and mood of the poem?

PERSONAL RESPONSE

1. Make a list of the main images in the poem. Which of these did you find most effective, and why?
2. The second half of the poem is considerably different to the first half. Did you find that the poem worked as a whole?
3. This poem is an elegy. How does the poet use language to convey melancholy and sadness?
4. How would you describe Dick King? Do you think he lived a very happy life?

IN CONTEXT

1. Kinsella's poetry often deals with childhood innocence and vulnerability. Discuss this statement in relation to 'Dick King', 'Model School, Inchicore' and 'Tear'.
2. This poem seems to present a somewhat positive view of death, linking it with love. Compare Kinsella's treatment of death in this poem with Thinking of Mr D.' and 'Tear'.
3. Kinsella's poems are often remarkable for the detailed and vivid memories they describe. Discuss this in relation to 'Hen Woman', 'Dick King' and 'Chrysalides'.

Chrysalides

Our last free summer we mooned about at odd hours
Pedalling slowly through country towns, stopping to eat
Chocolate and fruit, tracing our vagaries on the map.

At night we watched in the barn, to the lurch of melodeon music,
The crunching boots of countrymen – huge and weightless
As their shadows – twirling and leaping over the yellow concrete.

Sleeping too little or too much, we awoke at noon
And were received with womanly mockery into the kitchen,
Like calves poking our faces in with enormous hunger.

Daily we strapped our saddlebags and went to experience
A tolerance we shall never know again, confusing
For the last time, for example, the licit and the familiar.

Our instincts blurred with change; a strange wakefulness
Sapped our energies and dulled our slow-beating hearts
To the extremes of feeling – insensitive alike

To the unique succession of our youthful midnights,
When by a window ablaze softly with the virgin moon
Dry scones and jugs of milk awaited us in the dark,

Or to lasting horror, a wedding flight of ants
Spawning to its death, a mute perspiration
Glistening like drops of copper, agonised, in our path.

Chrysalides: *plural form of chrysalid (also known as chrysalis): the dormant stage of an insect, especially of a butterfly or moth, before it gets its wings*

COMPREHENSION

1. In what sense do you think this is the poet's 'last free summer'?
2. How do the poet and his companion spend their days during this summer? How do they spend their nights?
3. *Group Discussion:* 'A tolerance we shall never know again'. In what sense are the poet and his companion tolerated by those around them?
4. *Class Discussion:* 'Our instincts blurred with change'. What change do you think the poet and his companion are experiencing? What effect does this change have on them?
5. What unsettling or disturbing sight do the poet and his companion witness? Describe this sight in your own words.

PERSONAL RESPONSE

1. *Group Discussion:* There are several references to sex and sexuality in this poem. Identify them.
2. *Class Discussion:* Some readers feel this poem describes sexual awakening. Others disagree. What is your opinion?
3. Did you like this poem? Give reasons for your answer.
4. Identify a line or image in this poem that you found powerful or memorable, and say why.

IN CONTEXT

'Many of Kinsella's poems deal with a growing awareness of mortality and a loss of innocence.' Write a couple of paragraphs comparing 'Chrysalides' to 'Tear' and 'Mirror in February' in light of this statement.

Mirror in February

The day dawns with scent of must and rain
Of opened soil, dark trees, dry bedroom air.
Under the fading lamp, half dressed – my brain
Idling on some compulsive fantasy –
I towel my shaven jaw and stop, and stare,   5
Riveted by a dark exhausted eye,
A dry downturning mouth.

It seems again that it is time to learn,
In this untiring, crumbling place of growth
To which, for the time being, I return.   10
Now plainly in the mirror of my soul
I read that I have looked my last on youth
And little more; for they are not made whole
That reach the age of Christ.

Below my window the awakening trees,   15
Hacked clean for better bearing, stand defaced
Suffering their brute necessities,
And how should the flesh not quail that span for span
Is mutilated more? In slow distaste
I fold my towel with what grace I can,   20
Not young and not renewable, but man.

[18] **quail:** *to feel or show fear*

FIRST ENCOUNTER

1. Where is the speaker? What is he doing?
2. What time of day do you think it is? Why do you think this?
3. *Class Discussion:* What do you think the speaker is fantasising about?
4. The speaker says he is 'riveted'. What does he mean by this? What has riveted him?
5. *Class Discussion:* The speaker describes the world as an 'untiring, crumbling place of growth'. What does he mean by this?
6. The speaker says he looks in the 'mirror of his soul'. What dies he mean by this? What does he see in this mirror?
7. What is the 'age of Christ'? According to the speaker, what does or does not happen to those who reach this age?
8. What has happened to the trees outside the speaker's window? Why has this happened?
9. *Group Discussion:* What similarities does the speaker find between himself and the defaced trees? What important differences does he find?
10. 'that span for span/ Is mutilated more'. What is the speaker referring to in these lines? What does he mean by the expression 'span for span'? What has been 'mutilated'?

PERSONAL RESPONSE

1. *Group Discussion:* How would you describes the atmosphere conjured by the poem's opening lines? Pick the three words that in your opinion best describe it, and give reasons for your answer.
2. The speaker says that it is time for him to 'learn'. What, if anything, do you think he learns in this poem?
3. How would you describe the speaker's tone and attitude in the poem's concluding lines? Is he depressed, defiant, anxious, hopeful?
4. Would you agree that this poem presents a sad or bleak view of human life? Is there any hope or positivity in its outlook on human existence?

Tear

I was sent in to see her.
A fringe of jet drops
chattered at my ear
as I went in through the hangings.

I was swallowed in chambery dusk.
My heart shrank
at the smell of disused
organs and sour kidney.

The black aprons I used to
bury my face in
were folded at the foot of the bed
in the last watery light from the window

(Go in and say goodbye to her)
and I was carried off
to unfathomable depths.
I turned to look at her.

She stared at the ceiling
and puffed her cheek, distracted,
propped high in the bed
resting for the next attack.

The covers were gathered close
up to her mouth,
that the lines of ill-temper still
marked. Her grey hair

was loosened out like a young woman's
all over the pillow,
mixed with the shadows
criss-crossing her forehead

and at her mouth and eyes,
like a web of strands tying down her head
and tangling down toward the shadow
eating away the floor at my feet.

I couldn't stir at first, nor wished to,
for fear she might turn and tempt me
(my own father's mother)
with open mouth

continued over

– with some fierce wheedling whisper –
to hide myself one last time
against her, and bury my
self in her drying mud. 40

Was I to kiss her? As soon
kiss the damp that crept
in the flowered walls
of this pit.

Yet I had to kiss. 45
I knelt by the bulk of the death bed
and sank my face in the chill
and smell of her black aprons.

Snuff and musk, the folds against my eyelids,
carried me into a derelict place 50
smelling of ash: unseen walls and roofs
rustled like breathing.

I found myself disturbing
dead ashes for any trace
of warmth, when far off 55
in the vaults a single drop

splashed. And I found
what I was looking for
– not heat nor fire,
not any comfort, 60

but her voice, soft, talking to someone
about my father: 'God help him, he cried
big tears over there by the machine
for the poor little thing.' Bright

drops on the wooden lid 65
for my infant sister.
My own wail of child-animal grief
was soon done, with any early guess

at sad dullness and tedious pain
and lives bitter with hard bondage. 70
How I tasted it now –
her heart beating in my mouth!

She drew an uncertain breath
and pushed at the clothes
and shuddered tiredly.   75
I broke free

and left the room
promising myself
when she was really dead
I would really kiss.   80

My grandfather half looked up
from the fireplace as I came out,
and shrugged and turned back
with a deaf stare to the heat.

I fidgeted beside him for a minute   85
and went out to the shop.
It was still bright there
and I felt better able to breathe.

Old age can digest
anything: the commotion   90
at Heaven's gate – the struggle
in store for you all your life.

How long and hard it is
before you get to Heaven,
unless like little Agnes   95
you vanish with early tears.

[50] **derelict:** *in very poor condition; disused and neglected*
[95] **Agnes:** *the poet's baby sister*

LINE BY LINE

Stanzas 1–4

1. How does the speaker feel about having to enter the room of his dying grandmother?
2. Describe the room that he enters. What sights, sounds and smells does the poet mention?
3. What do you think he means when he says that he 'was carried off/ to unfathomable depths'?

Stanzas 5–11

4. Describe the grandmother's appearance. How does the poet respond to what he sees?
5. How is the poet's sense of horror and disgust conveyed in these stanzas?
6. What do these stanzas suggest about the grandmother's personality? Do you think she was a kind and caring woman?

Stanzas 12–18

7. *Class Discussion:* Why do you think the speaker buries his head in the grandmother's aprons?
8. With his eyes closed the speaker is carried off to a strange and eerie 'derelict' place. Describe what he experiences? How would you interpret what is happening in this part of the poem?
9. The poet says that he was not searching for 'heat nor fire,/ not any comfort'. What do you think he was searching for?
10. The speaker suddenly recalls a moment from his childhood. Describe what he remembers.
11. How did the poet respond to the death of his infant sister?
12. What does stanza 18 (lines 69–72) tell us about the kind of lives his grandparents and father lived?

Stanzas 19–24

13. What snaps the poet out of his remembrance of the past?
14. How does his grandfather respond to the poet's emergence from the grandmother's room? What does his response suggest about him and his relationship with his grandson?
15. Read the last two stanzas of the poem. What do they say about life and old age?

PERSONAL RESPONSE

1. The poem describes a very significant moment in the life of the young poet. What knowledge and understanding do you think the young boy gained from encountering his dying grandmother? Do you think that this encounter marks the end of childhood innocence and the beginning of adulthood?
2. How did you feel about Kinsella's depiction of his grandmother and the honest description of his reaction to the dying woman? Do you think that the poem benefits from the poet's brutal honesty, or did you find the descriptions shocking?

IN CONTEXT

1. A number of Kinsella poems describe childhood encounters with older people. Compare 'Dick King', 'His Father's Hands' and 'Tear' in terms of their depiction of old age. What did the poet learn from his encounters with the older people described in these poems?
2. Memory is a key theme in the poetry of Thomas Kinsella. Compare 'Tear' with 'Hen Woman' in terms of memory. What do each of these poems have to say about the way memory works?

Hen Woman

The noon heat in the yard
smelled of stillness and coming thunder.
A hen scratched and picked at the shore.
It stopped, its body crouched and puffed out.
The brooding silence seemed to say 'Hush …'

The cottage door opened,
a black hole
in a whitewashed wall so bright
the eyes narrowed.
Inside, a clock murmured 'Gong …'

(I had felt all this before.)

She hurried out in her slippers
muttering, her face dark with anger,
and gathered the hen up jerking
languidly. Her hand fumbled.
Too late. Too late.

It fixed me with its pebble eyes
(seeing what mad blur).
A white egg showed in the sphincter;
mouth and beak opened together;
and time stood still.

Nothing moved: bird or woman,
fumbled or fumbling – locked there
(as I must have been) gaping.

*

There was a tiny movement at my feet,
tiny and mechanical; I looked down.
A beetle like a bronze leaf
was inching across the cement,
clasping with small tarsi
a ball of dung bigger than its body.

The serrated brow pressed the ground humbly,
lifted in a short stare, bowed again;
the dung-ball advanced minutely,
losing a few fragments,
specks of staleness and freshness.

*

continued over

A mutter of thunder far off
– time not quite stopped.
I saw the egg had moved a fraction:
a tender blank brain
under torsion, a clean new world.   40

As I watched, the mystery completed.
The black zero of the orifice
closed to a point
and the white zero of the egg hung free,
flecked with greenish brown oils.   45

It fell and turned over slowly.
Dreamlike, fussed by her splayed fingers,
it floated outward, moon-white,
leaving no trace in the air,
and began its drop to the shore.   50

              *

I feed upon it still, as you see;
there is no end to that which, not understood,
may yet be hoarded in the imagination,
in the yolk of one's being, so to speak,
there to undergo its (quite animal) growth, 55

dividing blindly, twitching, packed with will,
searching in its own tissue
for the structure in which it may wake.
Something that had – clenched in its cave –
not been now as was: an egg of being.   60

Through what seemed a whole year it fell
– as it still falls, for me, solid and light,
the red gold beating in its silvery womb,
alive as the yolk and white of my eye.
As it will continue to fall, probably, until I die, 65
through the vast indifferent spaces
with which I am empty.

              *

It smashed against the grating
and slipped down quickly out of sight.
It was over in a comical flash.   70
The soft mucous shell clung a little longer,
then drained down.

She stood staring, in blank anger.
Then her eyes came to life, and she laughed
and let the bird flap away.   75

              'It's all the one.
There's plenty more where that came from!'

[3] **shore:** *a grating that allows water flow into a drain*

[19] **sphincter:** *a muscle that surrounds an opening. Its function is to guard or close it.*

[29] **tarsi:** *the feet of an insect, usually ending in a claw*

[40] **torsion:** *the action of twisting*

COMPREHENSION

Lines 1–35

1. Pick the three words that in your opinion best describe the atmosphere created by these lines. In each case give reasons for your choice.
2. *Group Discussion:* 'The brooding silence seemed to say "Hush …"'. What are we to make of this rather enigmatic line?
3. Why do the young poet's eyes narrow?
4. The hen's body 'crouched and puffed out'. What is happening here?
5. The woman runs out of her house, her face 'dark with anger'. What is she angry about?
6. What does the woman attempt to do? Is she successful?
7. What is the young poet's reaction to these events?
8. The young poet notices something moving at his feet. Describe what he sees there in your own words.
9. *Class Discussion:* 'I had felt all this before'. What does Kinsella mean by this?

Lines 36–77

10. It has been suggested that lines 36–50 produce a kind of 'slow-motion effect'. What do you think is meant by this? Would you agree?
11. *Class Discussion:* The poet hoards something in his imagination and continues 'to feed upon it'. What is he hoarding and in what sense is he feeding upon it?
12. *Class Discussion:* Kinsella describes something that twitches and divides blindly, that searches for a 'structure' to wake itself. What is he talking about?
13. *Group Discussion:* The poet says that for him the egg will continue to fall until he dies. What does he mean by this?
14. What eventually happens to the egg?
15. What is the woman's response to this event?
16. Does her response surprise you?

PERSONAL RESPONSE

1. *Group Discussion:* What message, if any, is Kinsella trying to convey to the reader in this poem? Discuss this question in small groups and write a brief paragraph outlining your opinions.
2. What is your personal response to this poem? Identity one aspect of the poem you liked and one aspect you didn't like. In each case give reasons for your answer.
3. 'This poem very effectively captures the wonder and mystery we experience as children, even in the face of very ordinary events'. Would you agree that the poem accomplishes this feat?
4. 'The most startling feature of "Hen Woman" is the intense detail with which Kinsella describes the physical word'. Identify two examples of such detailed description in the poem, and in each case say whether or not you found it effective.
5. Did you like or dislike this poem? Write a paragraph saying why.

IN CONTEXT

Like many of Kinsella's poems, "Hen Woman" describes the process of memory, powerfully illustrating how seemingly unimportant things can stick in our memories forever'. Discuss this statement in relation to 'Hen Woman' and two other poems by Kinsella on the course.

His Father's Hands

I drank firmly
and set the glass down between us firmly.
You were saying.

My father
Was saying.

His fingers prodded and prodded,
marring his point. Emphas-
emphasemphasis.

I have watched
his father's hands before him

      cupped, and tightening the black Plug
between knife and thumb,
carving off little curlicues
to rub them in the dark of his palms,

or cutting into new leather at his bench,
levering a groove open with his thumb,
insinuating wet sprigs for the hammer.

He kept the sprigs in mouthfuls
and brought them out in silvery
units between his lips.

I took a pinch out of their hole
and knocked them one by one into the wood,
bright points among hundreds gone black,
other children's – cousins and others, grown up.

      Or his bow hand scarcely moving,
scraping in the dark corner near the fire,
his plump fingers shifting on the strings.

To his deaf, inclined head
he hugged the fiddle's body
whispering with the tune

with breaking heart
whene'er I hear
in privacy, across a blocked void,

the wind that shakes the barley.
The wind …
round her grave …

on my breast in blood she died …
But blood for blood without remorse
I've ta'en …

Beyond that.

      *

Your family, Thomas, met with and helped
many of the Croppies in hiding from the Yeos
or on their way home after the defeat
in south Wexford. They sheltered the Laceys
who were later hanged on the Bridge in Ballinglen   45
between Tinahely and Anacorra,

From hearsay, as far as I can tell
the Men Folk were either Stone Cutters
or masons or probably both.
                              In the 18   50
and late 1700s even the farmers
had some other trade to make a living.

They lived in Farnese among a Colony
of North of Ireland or Scotch settlers left there
in some of the dispersals or migrations   55
which occurred in this Area of Wicklow and Wexford
and Carlow. And some years before that time
the Family came from somewhere around Tullow.

Beyond that.

                      *

Littered uplands. Dense grass. Rocks everywhere,   60
wet underneath, retaining memory of the long cold.

First, a prow of land
chosen, and wedged with tracks;
then boulders chosen
and sloped together, stabilised in menace.   65

I do not like this place.
I do not think the people who lived here
were ever happy. It feels evil.
Terrible things happened.
I feel afraid here when I am on my own.   70

                      *

Dispersals or migrations.
Through what evolutions or accidents
toward that peace and patience
by the fireside, that blocked gentleness …

That serene pause, with the slashing knife,   75
in kindly mockery,
as I busy myself with my little nails
at the rude block, his bench.

The blood advancing
– gorging vessel after vessel –   80
and altering in them
one by one.

continued over

Behold, that gentleness already
modulated twice, in others:
to earnestness and iteration;
to an offhandedness, repressing various impulses. 85

*

Extraordinary … The big block – I found it
years afterward in a corner of the yard
in sunlight after rain
and stood it up, wet and black: 90
it turned under my hands, an axis
of light flashing down its length,
and the wood's soft flesh broke open,
countless little nails
squirming and dropping out of it. 95

[11] **plug:** *a piece of tobacco cut for chewing*
[17] **sprigs:** *headless nails*
[42] **Croppies:** *name given to the Irish who fought in the 1798 Rebellion*
[42] **Yeos:** *short for Yeomen. A section of the British army that fought against the Irish in 1798.*

COMPREHENSION

Lines 1–40

1. The poem begins with the poet drinking with his father. In what manner does the father seem to be speaking? How does the poet feel about this?
2. The poet then thinks of his grandfather. What does he remember his grandfather doing?
3. The young poet then takes some nails and drives them into his grandfather's workbench. What does he notice about this bench as he does this?
4. How would you describe the mood of this section?
5. What do you think the poet means when he writes 'Beyond that'? Might it have something to do with going back in time?

Lines 41–70

6. In lines 41–58, we receive a version of the Kinsella family history. What do we learn about the Kinsella family here?
7. Then, in lines 59–69, the poet imagines the beginnings of Irish civilization. What type of landscape does he imagine himself in?
8. What do you think are the 'Terrible things' that happened?

Lines 71–95

9. Kinsella ponders on how the Irish race has evolved since those first settlers up to the point of his grandfather. In what way does he think the Irish race has evolved?
10. How does the poet think of his grandfather in lines 73–8?
11. In lines 87–95, the poet remembers finding the block that had been his grandfather's workbench. How do you think the poet feels when he finds his grandfather's block again, years later? What happens when he touches it?

PERSONAL RESPONSE

1. What sort of impression of the world are you left with after reading this poem?
2. What do you think this poem has to say about hardship?
3. Make a list of the imagery in this poem. Which image do you find most effective. Give reasons for your answer.
4. Some consider this poem to be an elegy for the poet's grandfather. Do you agree with this assessment of the poem?

IN CONTEXT

1. Kinsella has a tendency to depict the dead in a brutally honest fashion. Compare Kinsella's portrait of his grandfather in this poem to his depiction of other dead figures in 'Dick King', 'Thinking of Mr D.' and 'Tear'.
2. Discuss the theme of the isolation of the individual as it runs through this poem. How does Kinsella's depiction of this in 'His Father's Hands' compare with its depiction in 'Tear'?

from *Settings*
Model School, Inchicore

Miss Carney handed us out blank paper and marla,
old plasticine with the colours
all rolled together into brown.

You started with a ball of it
and rolled it into a snake curling
around your hand, and kept rolling it
in one place until it wore down into two
with a stain on the paper.

We always tittered at each other
when we said the adding-up table in Irish
and came to her name.

    *

In the second school we had Mr Browne.
He had white teeth in his brown man's face.

He stood in front of the blackboard
and chalked a white dot.

    'We are going to start
        decimals.'

    I am going to know
        everything.

    *

One day he said:
'Out into the sun!'
We settled his chair under a tree
and sat ourselves down delighted
in two rows in the greeny gold shade.

A fat bee floated around
shining amongst us
and the flickering sun
warmed our folded coats
and he said: 'History …!'

    *

When the Autumn came
and the big chestnut leaves
fell all over the playground
we piled them in heaps
between the wall and the tree trunks
and the boys ran races
jumping over the heaps
and tumbled into them shouting.

continued over

    *

I sat by myself in the shed
and watched the draught
blowing the papers
around the wheels of the bicycles.

Will God judge
      our most secret thoughts and actions?
God will judge
      our most secret thoughts and actions
and every idle word that man shall speak
he shall render an account of it
on the Day of Judgement.

*

The taste
of ink off
the nib shrank your
mouth.

COMPREHENSION

1. What is 'marla'? What do the young poet and his classmates do with it?
2. *Class Discussion*: What makes the young poet and his schoolmates 'titter'? Why do they laugh at this point?
3. Why does Mr Browne take the class outside for a history lesson?
4. What is the poet's reaction to the taste of his pen's ink?
5. What do you understand by his description of how his mouth 'shrank' from this taste?
6. Describe in your own words the game played by the poet and his schoolmates in the autumn.
7. Based on the information given in the poem, what kind of person do you the young poet was? Write a short paragraph describing your impressions of what he might have been like.

PERSONAL RESPONSE

1. This poem has several shifts in atmosphere. Describe them.
2. Write a paragraph describing the thoughts you imagine passing through the young poet's mind as he sits alone in the shed.
3. Lines 41–8 come from the catechism. What is the catechism? If necessary, look this up online. How does this information affect your response to these lines and, indeed, to the poem as a whole?
4. 'This poem vividly describes how seemingly inconsequential details can stick in our minds to be remembered forever more'. Would you agree with this statement? Give reasons for your answer.
5. *Group Discussion*: 'The young speaker in this poem is hungry for knowledge. But just like Adam in the Garden of Eden, knowledge does not bring him happiness'. Discuss this statement and write a paragraph in response to it.
6. Would you describe this as a broadly happy or a broadly sad poem? Give reasons for your answer.

IN CONTEXT

'Kinsella's poetry is haunted by an awareness of mortality and death'. Compare 'Model School, Inchicore' to two other Kinsella poems from the course in light of this statement.

from *The Familiar*

VII

I was downstairs at first light,
looking out through the frost on the window
at the hill opposite and the sheets of frost
scattered down among the rocks.

The cat back in the kitchen. 5
Folded on herself. Torn and watchful.

                    *

A chilled grapefruit
– thin-skinned, with that little gloss.
I took a mouthful, looking up along the edge of the wood

at the two hooded crows high in the cold 10
talking to each other,
flying up toward the tundra, beyond the waterfall.

                    *

I sliced the tomatoes in thin discs
in damp sequence into their dish;
scalded the kettle; made the tea, 15

and rang the little brazen bell.
And saved the toast.   Arranged the pieces

in slight disorder around the basket.
Fixed our places, one with the fruit 20
and one with the plate of sharp cheese.

                    *

And stood in my dressing gown
with arms extended
over the sweetness of the sacrifice.

Her shade showed in the door. 25
Her voice responded:
'You are very good. You always made it nice.'

---

[12] **tundra:** *an area of land that is permanently frozen and upon which very little grows*

COMPREHENSION
1. Where is the poet? What is he doing?
2. Describe the landscape that the poet sees.
3. What animals are described in the poem? Is there anything unusual about their behaviour?
4. What items of food does he prepare? How would you describe his preparation?
5. Who is the poet preparing the breakfast for? How does he describe her appearance?
6. How does the poet behave when she appears?

PERSONAL RESPONSE
1. Did any descriptions or features of the poem strike you as odd or unusual? What were they? Why did you find them strange?
2. Some readers have identified the figure who appears at the door as the muse – the personification of poetic inspiration. What does the poem suggest about the nature of the relationship between the poet and his muse?
3. Would you describe this as a love poem?
4. How would you describe the atmosphere of this poem? What words and images work to create this atmosphere?

IN CONTEXT
1. How might the setting of this poem be compared to that of 'Mirror in February'?
2. What do 'The Familiar: VII' and 'Hen Woman' tell us about artistic inspiration and creativity?

from *Glenmacnass*
VI – Littlebody

Up on the high road, as far as the sheepfold
into the wind, and back. The sides of the black bog channels
dug down in the water. The white cottonheads
on the old cuttings nodding everywhere.
Around one more bend, towards the car shining in the distance.   5

From a stony slope half way, behind a rock prow
with the stones on top for an old mark,
the music of pipes, distant and clear.

*

I was climbing up, making no noise
and getting close, when the music stopped,   10
leaving a pagan shape in the air.

There was a hard inhale,
a base growl,
and it started again, in a guttural dance.

I looked around the edge   15
– and it was Littlebody. Hugging his bag
under his left arm, with his eyes closed.

I slipped. Our eyes met.
He started scuttling up the slope with his gear
and his hump, elbows out and neck back.   20

But I shouted:
            'Stop, Littlebody!
I found you fair and I want my due.'

He stopped and dropped his pipes,
and spread his arms out, waiting for the next move.   25
I heard myself reciting:

'Demon dwarf
with the German jaw,
surrender your purse
with the ghostly gold.'   30

He took out a fat purse,
put it down on a stone
and recited in reply, in a voice too big for his body:

continued over

'You found me fair,
and I grant your wishes.
But we'll meet again,
when I dance in your ashes.'

He settled himself down once more
and bent over the bag,
                looking off to one side.

'I thought I was safe up here.
You have to give the music a while to itself sometimes,
up out of the huckstering

– jumping around in your green top hat
and showing your skills
with your eye on your income.'

He ran his fingers up and down the stops,
then gave the bag a last squeeze.
His face went solemn,

his fingertips fondled all the right places,
and he started a slow air
                out across the valley.

*

I left him to himself.
And left the purse where it was.
I have all I need for the while I have left

without taking unnecessary risks.
And made my way down to the main road
with my mind on our next meeting.

        Littlebody: *A leprechaun known from Irish folklore*
[43] **huckstering:** *selling small items; bargaining and haggling*

LINE BY LINE

Lines 1–20
1. Where is the poet?
2. What is he doing?
3. What does he hear?
4. Describe who he encounters?

Lines 21–40
5. What does the poet expect to get from Littlebody? Why do you think it is his 'due' to receive this?
6. How does Littlebody respond to the poet's demand?

Lines 41–58
7. In lines 41–6 Littlebody talks about playing music. What different types of performance does he describe? Does he favour one kind over the other, or do you think he believes in the necessity of both?
8. The poet decides to leave Littlebody 'to himself' and does not take his money. Why do you think he decides to leave the gold behind?
9. When do you think that the poet's 'next meeting' with Littlebody will be?

PERSONAL RESPONSE

1. What was your initial response to reading this poem?
2. Why do you think Kinsella chose to write a poem about an encounter with a leprechaun?
3. What do you think this poem has to say about art and the commercialisation of art?

IN CONTEXT

1. Both 'The Familiar: VII' and 'Littlebody' deal with the conditions needed for the artist to produce his work. What do each of these poems have to say about this?
2. Compare Kinsella's descriptions of the natural world in 'Mirror in February', 'The Familiar: VII' and 'Littlebody'.

Thomas Kinsella

from *Belief and Unbelief*
Echo

He cleared the thorns
from the broken gate,
and held her hand
through the heart of the wood
to the holy well.   5

They revealed their names
and told their tales
as they said that they would
on that distant day
when their love began.   10

And hand in hand
they turned to leave.
When she stopped and whispered
a final secret
down to the water.   15

Echo: *most commonly refers to a reflection of a sound. In Greek mythology, however, Echo was the name of a nymph who loved her own voice. Echo would often distract Hera while her husband Zeus was off having affairs with other nymphs. As punishment, Hera took away Echo's voice, except in foolish repetition of another's shouted words. She fell in love with Narcissus, a handsome but vain young man who did not return her affections. Heartbroken, she fled to isolated glens, left alone with her voice.*

LINE BY LINE

1. What sort of condition is the entrance to the wood in? Do you think that the path the couple take to the well is much used?
2. What do the couple do when they reach the well?
3. What 'tales' do you think they tell?
4. When did the couple decide that they would make this trip to the well?
5. What does the girl do just before they leave the well? Do you think the man hears what she says?

PERSONAL RESPONSE

1. Why do you think did the couple make this trip to the well? What is the significance of them speaking their names and telling their tales to the well? Is their something almost religious about their act?
2. Would you consider this a love poem? What does the poem suggest to you about relationships?
3. Why do you think Kinsella called this poem 'Echo'?

IN CONTEXT

How might 'Echo', 'His Father's Hands' and 'Littlebody' be compared in terms of pagan rituals and beliefs?

ADRIENNE RICH

For reasons of copyright, questions and notes on Adrienne Rich do not appear in this book. Please visit our webpage for further information: www.forum-publications.com

Aunt Jennifer's Tigers

Aunt Jennifer's tigers prance across a screen,
Bright topaz denizens of a world of green.
They do not fear the men beneath the tree;
They pace in sleek chivalric certainty.

Aunt Jennifer's fingers fluttering through her wool   5
Find even the ivory needle hard to pull.
The massive weight of Uncle's wedding band
Sits heavily upon Aunt Jennifer's hand.

When Aunt is dead, her terrified hands will lie
Still ringed with ordeals she was mastered by.   10
The tigers in the panel that she made
Will go on prancing, proud and unafraid.

The Uncle Speaks in the Drawing Room

I have seen the mob of late
Standing sullen in the square,
Gazing with a sullen stare
At window, balcony, and gate.
Some have talked in bitter tones, 5
Some have held and fingered stones.

These are follies that subside.
Let us consider, none the less,
Certain frailties of glass
Which, it cannot be denied, 10
Lead in times like these to fear
For crystal vase and chandelier.

Not that missiles will be cast;
None as yet dare lift an arm.
But the scene recalls a storm 15
When our grandsire stood aghast
To see his antique ruby bowl
Shivered in a thunder-roll.

Let us only bear in mind
How these treasures handed down 20
From a calmer age passed on
Are in the keeping of our kind.
We stand between the dead glass-blowers
And murmurings of missile-throwers.

Adrienne Rich

Storm Warnings

The glass has been falling all the afternoon,
And knowing better than the instrument
What winds are walking overhead, what zone
Of gray unrest is moving across the land,
I leave the book upon a pillowed chair   5
And walk from window to closed window, watching
Boughs strain against the sky

And think again, as often when the air
Moves inward toward a silent core of waiting,
How with a single purpose time has traveled   10
By secret currents of the undiscerned
Into this polar realm. Weather abroad
And weather in the heart alike come on
Regardless of prediction.

Between foreseeing and averting change   15
Lies all the mastery of elements
Which clocks and weatherglasses cannot alter.
Time in the hand is not control of time,
Nor shattered fragments of an instrument
A proof against the wind; the wind will rise, 20
We can only close the shutters.

I draw the curtains as the sky goes black
And set a match to candles sheathed in glass
Against the keyhole draught, the insistent whine
Of weather through the unsealed aperture.   25
This is our sole defense against the season;
These are the things that we have learned to do
Who live in troubled regions.

Living in Sin

She had thought the studio would keep itself;
no dust upon the furniture of love.
Half heresy, to wish the taps less vocal,
the panes relieved of grime. A plate of pears,
a piano with a Persian shawl, a cat   5
stalking the picturesque amusing mouse
had risen at his urging.
Not that at five each separate stair would writhe
under the milkman's tramp; that morning light
so coldly would delineate the scraps   10
of last night's cheese and three sepulchral bottles;
that on the kitchen shelf among the saucers
a pair of beetle-eyes would fix her own –
envoy from some village in the moldings …
Meanwhile, he, with a yawn,   15
sounded a dozen notes upon the keyboard,
declared it out of tune, shrugged at the mirror,
rubbed at his beard, went out for cigarettes;
while she, jeered by the minor demons,
pulled back the sheets and made the bed and found   20
a towel to dust the table-top,
and let the coffee-pot boil over on the stove.
By evening she was back in love again,
though not so wholly but throughout the night
she woke sometimes to feel the daylight coming   25
like a relentless milkman up the stairs.

The Roofwalker
for Denise Levertov

Over the half-finished houses
night comes. The builders
stand on the roof. It is
quiet after the hammers,
the pulleys hang slack.
Giants, the roofwalkers,
on a listing deck, the wave
of darkness about to break
on their heads. The sky
is a torn sail where figures
pass magnified, shadows
on a burning deck.

I feel like them up there:
exposed, larger than life,
and due to break my neck.

Was it worth while to lay –
with infinite exertion –
a roof I can't live under?
– All those blueprints,
closings of gaps,
measurings, calculations?
A life I didn't choose
chose me: even
my tools are the wrong ones
for what I have to do.
I'm naked, ignorant,
a naked man fleeing
across the roofs
who could with a shade of difference
be sitting in the lamplight
against the cream wallpaper
reading – not with indifference –
about a naked man
fleeing across the roofs.

Our Whole Life

Our whole life a translation
the permissible fibs

and now a knot of lies
eating at itself to get undone

Words bitten thru words   5

meanings burnt-off like paint
under the blowtorch

All those dead letters
rendered into the oppressor's language

Trying to tell the doctor where it hurts   10
like the Algerian
who walked from his village, burning

his whole body a cloud of pain
and there are no words for this

except himself   15

Trying to Talk with a Man

Out in this desert we are testing bombs,

that's why we came here.

Sometimes I feel an underground river
forcing its way between deformed cliffs
an acute angle of understanding
moving itself like a locus of the sun
into this condemned scenery.

What we've had to give up to get here –
whole LP collections, films we starred in
playing in the neighbourhoods, bakery windows
full of dry, chocolate-filled Jewish cookies,
the language of love-letters, of suicide notes,
afternoons on the riverbank
pretending to be children

Coming out to this desert
we meant to change the face of
driving among dull green succulents
walking at noon in the ghost town
surrounded by a silence

that sounds like the silence of the place
except that it came with us
and is familiar
and everything we were saying until now
was an effort to blot it out –
coming out here we are up against it

Out here I feel more helpless
with you than without you
You mention the danger
and list the equipment
we talk of people caring for each other
in emergencies – laceration, thirst –
but you look at me like an emergency

Your dry heat feels like power
your eyes are stars of a different magnitude
they reflect lights that spell out: EXIT
when you get up and pace the floor

talking of the danger
as if it were not ourselves
as if we were testing anything else.

Adrienne Rich

Diving into the Wreck

First having read the book of myths,
and loaded the camera,
and checked the edge of the knife-blade,
I put on
the body-armor of black rubber
the absurd flippers
the grave and awkward mask.
I am having to do this
not like Cousteau with his
assiduous team
aboard the sun-flooded schooner
but here alone.

There is a ladder.
The ladder is always there
hanging innocently
close to the side of the schooner.
We know what it is for,
we who have used it.
Otherwise
it's a piece of maritime floss
some sundry equipment.

I go down.
Rung after rung and still
the oxygen immerses me
the blue light
the clear atoms
of our human air.
I go down.
My flippers cripple me,
I crawl like an insect down the ladder
and there is no one
to tell me when the ocean
will begin.

First the air is blue and then
it is bluer and then green and then
black I am blacking out and yet
my mask is powerful
it pumps my blood with power
the sea is another story
the sea is not a question of power
I have to learn alone
to turn my body without force
in the deep element.

And now: it is easy to forget
what I came for
among so many who have always
lived here
swaying their crenellated fans
between the reefs
and besides
you breathe differently down here.

I came to explore the wreck.
The words are purposes.
The words are maps.
I came to see the damage that was done
and the treasures that prevail.   55
I stroke the beam of my lamp
slowly along the flank
of something more permanent
than fish or weed

the thing I came for: 60
the wreck and not the story of the wreck
the thing itself and not the myth
the drowned face always staring
toward the sun
the evidence of damage   65
worn by salt and sway into this threadbare beauty
the ribs of the disaster
curving their assertion
among the tentative haunters.

This is the place.   70
And I am here, the mermaid whose dark hair
streams black, the merman in his armored body
We circle silently
about the wreck
we dive into the hold.   75
I am she: I am he

whose drowned face sleeps with open eyes
whose breasts still bear the stress
whose silver, copper, vermeil cargo lies
obscurely inside barrels   80
half-wedged and left to rot
we are the half-destroyed instruments
that once held to a course
the water-eaten log
the fouled compass   85

We are, I am, you are
by cowardice or courage
the one who find our way
back to this scene
carrying a knife, a camera   90
a book of myths
in which
our names do not appear.

From a Survivor

The pact that we made was the ordinary pact
of men & women in those days

I don't know who we thought we were
that our personalities
could resist the failures of the race

Lucky or unlucky, we didn't know
the race had failures of that order
and that we were going to share them

Like everybody else, we thought of ourselves as special

Your body is as vivid to me
as it ever was: even more

since my feeling for it is clearer:
I know what it could and could not do

it is no longer
the body of a god
or anything with power over my life

Next year it would have been 20 years
and you are wastefully dead
who might have made the leap
we talked, too late, of making

which I live now
not as a leap
but a succession of brief, amazing movements

each one making possible the next

Power

Living   in the earth-deposits   of our history

Today a backhoe divulged   out of a crumbling flank of earth
one bottle   amber   perfect   a hundred-year-old
cure for fever   or melancholy   a tonic
for living on this earth   in the winters of this climate.

Today I was reading about Marie Curie:
she must have known she suffered   from radiation sickness
her body bombarded for years   by the element
she had purified
It seems she denied to the end
the source of the cataracts on her eyes
the cracked and suppurating skin   of her finger-ends
till she could no longer hold   a test-tube or a pencil

She died   a famous woman   denying
her wounds
denying
her wounds   came   from the same source as her power

SYLVIA PLATH
BIOGRAPHY

Sylvia Plath was born in Boston, Massachusetts, in October 1932. Her father Otto had emigrated to the US from Germany; her mother Aurelia was the daughter of Austrian emigrants. Otto Plath was a professor of entomology, the study of insects, and published an important scientific book entitled *Bumblebees and Their Ways* (a specialisation, perhaps, that influenced Plath's later interest in bee-keeping and poems such as 'The Arrival of the Bee Box'.) Plath seems to have had a happy childhood, and from the beginning it was clear that she was extremely bright and academically gifted. When she was eight years old, however, her father died of a diabetes-related illness. Plath would come to regard the period prior to her father's death with great nostalgia – as a perfect, idyllic time.

Plath's interest in literature began at an early age, and she published her first poem, in the *Boston Herald*, when she was only eight years old. At high school, Plath excelled academically and became involved in a wide range of social and extra-curricular activities. She had set her sights on becoming a writer, and devoted much of her spare time to reading and to writing poems and stories, a number of which were published in the school magazine.

In 1950 she won a scholarship to the prestigious Smith College, where her budding literary career continued. A major breakthrough came for her when one of her stories won first prize in a competition organised by the popular *Mademoiselle* magazine. She spent the summer of 1952 in New York working for *Mademoiselle* as a 'guest editor'. Despite these successes, however, Plath was a highly sensitive individual prone to depression and violent mood swings. As any reader of her *Journals* will note, her self-obsession was matched only by her craving for literary success.

On her return from New York, Plath discovered she had been rejected for a creative writing class she had applied for (conducted by the Irish writer Frank O'Connor). The rejection sent her into a black depression. She underwent a course of electroconvulsive therapy (ECT), attempted suicide by overdosing on sleeping pills, and spent four months in a psychiatric institution. Plath recovered from this setback, however, and returned to Smith College, from where she graduated in 1955. Her academic performance, as usual, was exceptional, and earned her a two-year Fulbright scholarship to Cambridge University.

Plath loved Cambridge but remained something of a tortured soul, and continued to endure bouts of depression and self-loathing. In January 1956 she met the young poet Ted Hughes, who was as hungry for literary success as her. The two promptly fell in love and were married, in virtual secrecy, only four months later. The young couple spent 1957 to 1959 in America, where Plath attempted to balance her literary ambitions with the necessity of making a living. She taught for a while at her old college, Smith College, and did part-time secretarial work. By this stage, she had decided against a career as a full-time teacher, believing that this would interfere too much with her own writing. Her marriage to Hughes was turbulent, and she suffered from depression and bouts of writer's block, but continued to produce poetry, including 'The Times Are Tidy' and 'Black Rook in Rainy Weather'. In 1959 she attended a writing class with the great American poet Robert Lowell, and, with Hughes, spent time at the famous artists' colony at Yaddo in New York State, two developments that greatly contributed to her maturation as a writer.

Plath and Hughes returned to England at the end of 1959, and moved to London, where Plath gave birth to her first child, Frieda. 'Morning Song' dates from this London period. In the autumn of 1961 the family relocated to what Plath described as her 'dream house' in the Devon countryside. Here, the couple wrote and shared the responsibility of looking after their baby daughter. Many of Plath's most important poems were written in Devon. That autumn she wrote 'Finisterre' and 'Mirror'. The following spring brought 'Elm' and 'Pheasant'.

Plath gave birth to a second child, Nicholas, in January 1962, but by that summer her marriage was in terrible trouble. Hughes had become involved with another woman. Plath's anguish at this development is evident in 'Poppies in July'. The two separated that autumn, leaving Plath alone in Devon with her two children. This was an extremely difficult period in Plath's life, and she became profoundly depressed. She continued to write powerful poetry, however, including 'The Arrival of the Bee Box'. In December, Plath left behind the isolation of Devon and returned to London with her children. The following February, she took her own life.

As we have seen, Plath had from an early age been prone to depression and suicidal tendencies. It seems that in February 1963 the strain simply became too much. She was greatly troubled by the failure of her marriage, and by the stresses and responsibilities of bringing up two young children alone. She had always found British winters particularly depressing, and the winter of 1962–63 was one of the coldest on record. January in London was particularly bleak, as power and other services failed. Illness was rampant and the suicide rate soared. Plath continued writing until the very end. 'Child' was written on 28 January, just two weeks before her death.

For many readers, the poetry of Sylvia Plath will always be overshadowed by the fact of her suicide. It is tempting to view Plath's work as a protracted suicide note, a record of her psychological and spiritual decline. Much of Plath's mental anguish stemmed from the fear that her poetic gifts would desert her, that she would never again feel sufficiently inspired to write another poem. It is perhaps ironic, therefore, that she produced the majority of her most famous poems when she was at her lowest psychological ebb. In the weeks and months before her suicide, in particular, she was extremely prolific, writing a poem, or even two, a day.

The Times Are Tidy

Unlucky the hero born
In this province of the stuck record
Where the most watchful cooks go jobless
And the mayor's rôtisserie turns
Round of its own accord.   5

There's no career in the venture
Of riding against the lizard,
Himself withered these latter-days
To leaf-size from lack of action:
History's beaten the hazard.   10

The last crone got burnt up
More than eight decades back
With the love-hot herb, the talking cat,
But the children are better for it,
The cow milks cream an inch thick.   15

[4] **rotisserie:** *a rotating spit used for cooking whole animals*
[11] **crone:** *witch*

COMPREHENSION

1. Consider the title of the poem. What do you think it means to say that 'The Times Are Tidy'? Does it seem a positive statement?
2. In the first stanza the poet speaks of 'this province of the stuck record'. What does this description suggest to you? Who suffers in such a place?
3. What sort of person would you usually associate with riding out 'against the lizard'? Consider the kind of world where such actions take place.
4. Why, according to the second stanza, does such activity no longer take place? What does it mean to say that 'History's beaten the hazard?'
5. The final stanza talks of the last time someone was burnt as a witch. What was lost and what was gained, according to the poet, when such activity ended?
6. How would you characterise the tone of the last two lines? Does the poet appreciate the way the world has changed?

PERSONAL RESPONSE

1. The poem contrasts two very different times. Write a paragraph about each period according to your interpretation of the poem. Which time period is more appealing to you?
2. Does the poem reflect the way you feel about the world? Consider both the events in the world today and the opportunities that are presently available to you when you finish school. Is the modern world predictable? Have we 'beaten the hazard?' Perhaps you might think of some of the natural disasters that have occurred in very recent times.

IN CONTEXT

Although many of Plath's poems reveal a personal anguish and despair, she was acutely aware of how wonderful the world can be when we open up our imaginations. However, we are not always free to appreciate and be inspired by the world. Consider how the poems 'The Times Are Tidy', 'Black Rook in Rainy Weather', and 'Child' refer to the possibilities and values of the imagination, whilst highlighting the restrictions that life and living often place upon this faculty.

Black Rook in Rainy Weather

On the stiff twig up there
Hunches a wet black rook
Arranging and rearranging its feathers in the rain.
I do not expect a miracle
Or an accident   5

To set the sight on fire
In my eye, nor seek
Any more in the desultory weather some design,
But let spotted leaves fall as they fall
Without ceremony, or portent.   10

Although, I admit, I desire,
Occasionally, some backtalk
From the mute sky, I can't honestly complain:
A certain minor light may still
Lean incandescent   15

Out of kitchen table or chair
As if a celestial burning took
Possession of the most obtuse objects now and then –
Thus hallowing an interval
Otherwise inconsequent   20

By bestowing largesse, honor
One might say love. At any rate, I now walk
Wary (for it could happen
Even in this dull, ruinous landscape); skeptical,
Yet politic; ignorant   25

Of whatever angel may choose to flare
Suddenly at my elbow. I only know that a rook
Ordering its black feathers can so shine
As to seize my senses, haul
My eyelids up, and grant   30

A brief respite from fear
Of total neutrality. With luck,
Trekking stubborn through this season
Of fatigue, I shall
Patch together a content   35

Of sorts. Miracles occur,
If you care to call those spasmodic
Tricks of radiance miracles. The wait's begun again,
The long wait for the angel,
For that rare, random descent.   40

[8] **desultory:** *haphazardly; randomly*
[10] **portent:** *omen, a sign of things to come*
[15] **incandescent:** *glowing, incredibly bright*
[19] **hallowing:** *making holy or sacred*
[19] **interval:** *a period of time*
[20] **inconsequent:** *unimportant*
[21] **largesse:** *generosity*
[25] **politic:** *prudent, crafty*
[31] **respite:** *a period of relief*
[37] **spasmodic:** *fitful, occasional, unpredictable*

COMPREHENSION

1. Where is this poem set? What is happening?
2. 'nor seek/ Any more in the desultory weather some design,/ But let spotted leaves fall as they fall,/ Without ceremony or portent'. As a group, discuss these lines and rewrite them in everyday English.
3. Why do you think the leaves are described as 'spotted'?
4. The speaker says she 'can't honestly complain'. Why is this?
5. According to the speaker, every 'now and then' light seems to burst from 'obtuse objects' such as kitchen tables and chairs. Do you think she really sees light emanate from these ordinary household objects? Is she hallucinating or is she using this 'minor light' as a metaphor for some other kind of experience?
6. She claims that this 'minor light' transforms an ordinary time into a 'hallowed' or holy moment. How does it do this?
7. The speaker walks warily through the landscape 'for it could happen'. What does she feel might occur?
8. She claims that an angel may suddenly 'flare' at her elbow. What do you think this angel represents?
9. According to the speaker, the sight of the rook on the branch seizes her senses and staves off the threat of 'total neutrality'. What do you think she means by 'total neutrality'?
10. What do you think is the 'content' the speaker aims to patch together?
11. *Class Discussion:* This poem has a hidden rhyme scheme. Can you identify it?

PERSONAL RESPONSE

1. Throughout the poem a number of different images are used to depict inspiration. Make a list of them. Which, in your opinion, is most effective? Why do you think this?
2. In the poem's opening stanza, the speaker claims that she no longer expects or longs for the 'accident' of inspiration. Based on your reading of the poem as a whole, do you think she has honestly given up on the possibility of being inspired?
3. *Group Discussion:* This poem is structured around opposites: heaven and earth, light and darkness, inspiration and total neutrality. Discuss this issue with your group and write a few lines describing how these ideas are developed throughout the course of the poem.
4. 'One of this poem's themes is chaos, the belief that events occur randomly, without order or design. Yet the poem's carefully concealed rhyme scheme suggests that a hidden pattern or order actually exists behind the apparent chaos of the world's events. It's Plath's way of suggesting that things happen for a reason after all, even though the plan mightn't immediately be obvious to us'. What do you think of this statement? Does it seem like a plausible understanding of the poem?

IN CONTEXT

1. This poem can be compared to 'Pheasant' – another poem where Plath is moved and inspired by the sight of a bird. It can be neatly contrasted with 'Elm' and 'Poppies in July', where the sight of nature fills the poet with rage, terror and disgust. Write a short essay comparing 'Black Rook in Rainy Weather' to these poems.
2. Plath once said: 'Oh, satisfaction! I don't think I could live without it. It's like water or bread, or something absolutely essential to me. I find myself absolutely fulfilled when I have written a poem, when I'm writing one. Having written one, then you fall away very rapidly from having been a poet to becoming a sort of poet in rest, which isn't the same thing at all. But I think the actual experience of writing a poem is a magnificent one'. Write a few lines relating these comments to 'Black Rook in Rainy Weather'.

Morning Song

Love set you going like a fat gold watch.
The midwife slapped your footsoles, and your bald cry
Took its place among the elements.

Our voices echo, magnifying your arrival. New statue.
In a drafty museum, your nakedness   5
Shadows our safety. We stand round blankly as walls.

I'm no more your mother
Than the cloud that distills a mirror to reflect its own slow
Effacement at the wind's hand.

All night your moth-breath   10
Flickers among the flat pink roses. I wake to listen:
A far sea moves in my ear.

One cry, and I stumble from bed, cow-heavy and floral
In my Victorian nightgown.
Your mouth opens clean as a cat's. The window square 15

Whitens and swallows its dull stars. And now you try
Your handful of notes;
The clear vowels rise like balloons.

COMPREHENSION

Lines 1–9

1. How is the child's vulnerability conveyed in the first two stanzas?
2. How do the parents respond to the birth of the child?
3. Consider Plath's choice of words in the opening stanzas (e.g. 'elements', 'echo', 'drafty museum', 'nakedness'). What sort of world has the child come to exist in?
4. How would you describe the mother's attitude to her new role?

Lines 10–18

5. Look at the metaphors and images that are used in the fourth stanza ('moth-breath', 'flat pink roses', 'far sea'). How do these differ from the ones used in the first two stanzas?
6. In the second stanza, the poet spoke of how she and her husband stood 'blankly as walls' around the newborn child. How does the fifth stanza highlight a change in attitude?
7. The poem is full of vivid images and metaphors. Compare and contrast those used in the first three stanzas with those used in the last three.

PERSONAL RESPONSE

1. How did you respond to the poem's description of the birth of a child in the first three stanzas? Did you appreciate the honesty and lack of sentimentality?
2. The first word of the poem is 'Love'? Do you think that this is ultimately a poem about parental love and affection?

IN CONTEXT

Consider how 'Morning Song' and 'Child' expose the terrible anxieties that can come with the responsibility of being a parent. How do the poems compare?

Mirror

I am silver and exact. I have no preconceptions.
Whatever I see I swallow immediately
Just as it is, unmisted by love or dislike.
I am not cruel, only truthful –
The eye of a little god, four-cornered. 5
Most of the time I meditate on the opposite wall.
It is pink, with speckles. I have looked at it so long
I think it is part of my heart. But it flickers.
Faces and darkness separate us over and over.

Now I am a lake. A woman bends over me, 10
Searching my reaches for what she really is.
Then she turns to those liars, the candles or the moon.
I see her back, and reflect it faithfully.
She rewards me with tears and an agitation of hands.
I am important to her. She comes and goes. 15
Each morning it is her face that replaces the darkness.
In me she has drowned a young girl, and in me an old woman
Rises toward her day after day, like a terrible fish.

COMPREHENSION

1. What are the characteristics of the mirror? What does the mirror mean when it claims that it is 'exact'? Do you think more than one meaning of this word might be intended here?
2. The mirror says that it 'swallows' whatever it sees. What do you think it means by this? Do you think it is fair to say that in this context the word 'swallow' has negative or sinister connotations?
3. The mirror describes how its days are spent. Write a couple of lines describing its daily routine.
4. The mirror compares itself to a lake. Do you think this is a good or accurate comparison? What similarities, if any, are there between a mirror and a lake?
5. The second stanza describes the 'relationship' between the mirror and the woman. Write a couple of lines summarising this relationship.
6. The mirror claims it is 'important' to the woman. In what ways might a mirror be important to an individual? Consider here psychological as well as purely practical factors.
7. What do you think the mirror means when it says 'In me she has drowned a young girl'? Is more than one possible meaning here? What does the 'terrible fish' represent?

PERSONAL RESPONSE

1. 'Mirror' has been described as 'a poem of images'. Pick out three different images from the poem. In the case of each image, say whether or not you think it is convincing and effective.
2. 'Mirror' is not a poem with a sustained argument. Instead, it communicates its meaning by subtle shifts in tone'. Would you agree that the mirror's tone changes over the course of the poem?
3. Imagine you are the woman in the poem. Write a few lines describing your daily routine, your mental state and your attitude towards the mirror.
4. 'Mirror' is commonly regarded as a poem of despair and desperation. How did reading it make you feel? Do you think there is any hope for the woman the poem describes?

Finisterre

This was the land's end: the last fingers, knuckled and rheumatic,
Cramped on nothing. Black
Admonitory cliffs, and the sea exploding
With no bottom, or anything on the other side of it,
Whitened by the faces of the drowned.　　　　　　　　　　　　　　5
Now it is only gloomy, a dump of rocks –
Leftover soldiers from old, messy wars.
The sea cannons into their ear, but they don't budge.
Other rocks hide their grudges under the water.
　　　　　　　　　　　　　　　　　　　　　　　　　　　　　10
The cliffs are edged with trefoils, stars and bells
Such as fingers might embroider, close to death,
Almost too small for the mists to bother with.
The mists are part of the ancient paraphernalia –
Souls, rolled in the doom-noise of the sea.
They bruise the rocks out of existence, then resurrect them.　　　15
They go up without hope, like sighs.
I walk among them, and they stuff my mouth with cotton.
When they free me, I am beaded with tears.

Our Lady of the Shipwrecked is striding toward the horizon,　　　20
Her marble skirts blown back in two pink wings.
A marble sailor kneels at her foot distractedly, and at his foot
A peasant woman in black
Is praying to the monument of the sailor praying.
Our Lady of the Shipwrecked is three times life size,
Her lips sweet with divinity.　　　　　　　　　　　　　　　　25
She does not hear what the sailor or the peasant is saying –
She is in love with the beautiful formlessness of the sea.

Gull-colored laces flap in the sea drafts
Beside the postcard stalls.　　　　　　　　　　　　　　　　　30
The peasants anchor them with conches. One is told:
'These are the pretty trinkets the sea hides,
Little shells made up into necklaces and toy ladies.
They do not come from the Bay of the Dead down there,
But from another place, tropical and blue,
We have never been to.　　　　　　　　　　　　　　　　　35
These are our crêpes. Eat them before they blow cold.'

[3]　**Admonitory:** *warning*
[10]　**trefoils:** *a plant having threefold leaves or an ornament like a threefold leaf*
[13]　**paraphernalia:** *personal belongings*
[36]　**crêpes:** *a light, thin pancake*

COMPREHENSION

Stanza 1

1. This stanza depicts a seaside landscape. Write a short paragraph describing the main features of this scene in your own words.
2. What do the words 'admonitory' 'knuckled' and 'rheumatic' suggest about the appearance and condition of the cliffs at Finisterre? (Look these words up in a dictionary if necessary.)
3. The speaker suggests that the ocean has 'no bottom' and that 'there is nothing on the other side' of it. Does she really think that this is the case? If not, why does she make this claim?
4. What do you think the speaker has in mind when she mentions the 'faces of the drowned'? Are there really drowned bodies visible from the cliff top where she stands or is she using this phrase metaphorically?
5. What words and phrases does Plath use to portray the violence and danger of the sea?
6. 'Other rocks hide their grudges under the water'. What does Plath mean by this? How is it possible for rocks to have grudges?

Stanza 2

7. What metaphor is used to describe the mists that drift up from the sea?
8. The speaker claims that the mists briefly 'bruise the rocks out of existence'. What does she mean by this?
9. *Group Discussion:* Why does the speaker claim to be beaded with tears? Is this phrase open to more than one interpretation?

Stanza 3

10. Why, according to the speaker, does Our Lady of the Shipwrecked ignore the sailor and the peasant?

Stanza 4

11. What do the peasants offer the speaker?

PERSONAL RESPONSE

1. 'Finisterre' has been praised for its vivid metaphors. Find four metaphors in the poem. Say which you think is most effective and which is least effective. Give reasons for your answer.
2. While composing 'Finisterre', Plath was deeply concerned about the possibility of a global nuclear conflict that would destroy the human race. How does this concern colour her description of the personal experience of visiting Finisterre?
3. Examine each of the poem's four stanzas. In the case of each, list the adjectives that in your opinion best describe the stanza's atmosphere and the speaker's tone of voice.
4. *Group Discussion:* What is the significance of the shifts in tone from stanza to stanza? How do they contribute to the poem's overall meaning?
5. What do you think is the poem's attitude toward religion? Is it significant that the peasant woman prays to the monument of the sailor praying rather than directly to God or Our Lady? Why do you think Our Lady of the Shipwrecked is said to be in love with the 'beautiful formlessness of the sea'?
6. In what ways does the final stanza differ from the rest of the poem? How, if it all, does it alter your response to what has gone before?

IN CONTEXT

The sea is a regular presence throughout Plath's work. In 'Elm', too, it has dark associations. In 'Morning Song', however, the mention of a gentle 'far sea' echoes the peasants' comments about the tropical and blue waters that exist far from the Bay of the Dead. Write a short essay about the depiction of the sea in Plath's poetry.

Pheasant

You said you would kill it this morning.
Do not kill it. It startles me still,
The jut of that odd, dark head, pacing

Through the uncut grass on the elm's hill.
It is something to own a pheasant,   5
Or just to be visited at all.

I am not mystical: it isn't
As if I thought it had a spirit.
It is simply in its element.

That gives it a kingliness, a right.   10
The print of its big foot last winter,
The trail-track, on the snow in our court –

The wonder of it, in that pallor,
Through crosshatch of sparrow and starling.
Is it its rareness, then? It is rare.   15

But a dozen would be worth having,
A hundred, on that hill – green and red,
Crossing and recrossing: a fine thing!

It is such a good shape, so vivid.
It's a little cornucopia.   20
It unclaps, brown as a leaf, and loud,

Settles in the elm, and is easy.
It was sunning in the narcissi.
I trespass stupidly. Let be, let be.

[14] **crosshatch:** *criss-cross pattern*

[20] **cornucopia:** *A mythical horn, perpetually full of flowers and fruit; a symbol of abundance*

COMPREHENSION

1. The poem begins in a dramatic and urgent fashion. Who do you think the speaker of the poem is addressing?
2. The speaker comes up with numerous reasons why the pheasant ought to live. Read through the poem and list these reasons.
3. The speaker first considers the pleasure and pride the bird gives her. However, she soon considers the bird to have its own value and significance. Where does this occur in the poem?
4. Stanza 4 introduces the notion of royalty and rights. What is it that gives the bird 'kingliness'? How does the 'print of its big foot' further the idea of royalty?
5. 'It unclaps, brown as a leaf, and loud'. What is the speaker describing here?

PERSONAL RESPONSE

Like many of Plath's poems, 'Pheasant' is full of rich, vivid images. Which ones did you find particularly pleasing and memorable?

IN CONTEXT

'I am not mystical: it isn't/ As if I thought it had a spirit'. Plath was very sensitive to the natural world without being sentimental about it. Compare and contrast her descriptions and use of nature in such poems as 'Pheasant', 'Black Rook in Rainy Weather' and 'Poppies in July'.

Elm

I know the bottom, she says. I know it with my great tap root:
It is what you fear.
I do not fear it: I have been there.

Is it the sea you hear in me,
Its dissatisfactions?
Or the voice of nothing, that was your madness?

Love is a shadow.
How you lie and cry after it
Listen: these are its hooves: it has gone off, like a horse.

All night I shall gallup thus, impetuously,
Till your head is a stone, your pillow a little turf,
Echoing, echoing.

Or shall I bring you the sound of poisons?
This is rain now, this big hush.
And this is the fruit of it: tin-white, like arsenic.

I have suffered the atrocity of sunsets.
Scorched to the root
My red filaments burn and stand, a hand of wires.

Now I break up in pieces that fly about like clubs.
A wind of such violence
Will tolerate no bystanding: I must shriek.

The moon, also, is merciless: she would drag me
Cruelly, being barren.
Her radiance scathes me. Or perhaps I have caught her.

I let her go. I let her go
Diminished and flat, as after radical surgery.
How your bad dreams possess and endow me.

I am inhabited by a cry.
Nightly it flaps out
Looking, with its hooks, for something to love.

I am terrified by this dark thing
That sleeps in me;
All day I feel its soft, feathery turnings, its malignity.

Clouds pass and disperse.
Are those the faces of love, those pale irretrievables?
Is it for such I agitate my heart?

I am incapable of more knowledge.
What is this, this face
So murderous in its strangle of branches?—   40

Its snaky acids hiss.
It petrifies the will. These are the isolate, slow faults
That kill, that kill, that kill.

[15] **arsenic:** *a deadly poison*
[18] **filament:** *a fine or thinly spun thread, fibre or wire*
[24] **scathe:** *to harm or injure, especially by fire*
[35] **irretrievables:** *things that never be regained*

COMPREHENSION

1. Who is speaking in this poem?
2. Who is being addressed?
3. What does the elm mean when it claims to 'know the bottom'? What is this 'bottom' that the elm knows? On the other hand, how might a person know the bottom?
4. According to stanza 3, what difficulties does the woman in the poem appear to be facing?
5. How does the elm describe the sound made by its branches in lines 9 and 10?
6. 'Till your head is a stone, your pillow a little turf/ Echoing, echoing'. What do you understand by these lines? What does it mean for someone's head to be a 'stone'?
7. In stanzas 5–7, the elm mentions three different torments it is forced to endure. What are these?
8. 'How your bad dreams possess and endow me'. What does this suggest about the relationship between the elm and the woman?
9. Would you agree that in stanzas 10 and 11 it is difficult to determine who is speaking – that these lines could be spoken either by the elm or by the woman?
10. 'I am inhabited by a cry … I am terrified by this dark thing/ that sleeps in me'. Assume that these lines are spoken by the elm tree. What might the 'dark thing' be? Now assume they are spoken by a human being. What 'dark thing' might it now be?
11. Would you agree that the poem's last three stanzas seem to be spoken by the woman rather than by the elm tree?
12. How is love presented in stanza 12?
13. Describe, in your own words, the poem's final image.

PERSONAL RESPONSE

1. 'Elm' is an intensely visual poem and contains many powerful images. Identify one image from the poem that you found memorable or vivid, and explain why you found it compelling.
2. In 'Elm', Plath's mastery of sound effects is at its greatest. Read the poem again and identify one example of each of the following: assonance, alliteration, cacophony, rhyme and repetition. Say how each contributes to the poem.
3. When Plath was composing 'Elm', she was very concerned about the possibility of a nuclear conflict between Russia and the United States. How is this fear of impending apocalypse evident in the poem? Choose three words that best describe the poem's atmosphere.
4. Read the poem aloud. How would you describe its tone? Describe how the tone alters as the poem progresses.
5. 'This poem has elements of a horror or fantasy story, featuring a bizarre "psychic link" between a woman and an elm tree growing in her garden. The elm somehow shares the woman's bad dreams. It seems to be the woman's "dark double", embodying the unpleasant, dangerous and hidden aspects of her personality.' Do you find this reading persuasive? Give reasons for your answer.
6. Bearing the above questions in mind, write a few brief paragraphs outlining your personal response to this poem.

The Arrival of the Bee Box

I ordered this, this clean wood box
Square as a chair and almost too heavy to lift.
I would say it was the coffin of a midget
Or a square baby
Were there not such a din in it.   5

The box is locked, it is dangerous.
I have to live with it overnight
And I can't keep away from it.
There are no windows, so I can't see what is in there.
There is only a little grid, no exit.   10

I put my eye to the grid.
It is dark, dark,
With the swarmy feeling of African hands
Minute and shrunk for export,
Black on black, angrily clambering.   15

How can I let them out?
It is the noise that appalls me most of all,
The unintelligible syllables.
It is like a Roman mob,
Small, taken one by one, but my god, together!   20

I lay my ear to furious Latin.
I am not a Caesar.
I have simply ordered a box of maniacs.
They can be sent back.
They can die, I need feed them nothing, I am the owner.   25

I wonder how hungry they are.
I wonder if they would forget me
If I just undid the locks and stood back and turned into a tree.
There is the laburnum, its blond colonnades,
And the petticoats of the cherry.   30

They might ignore me immediately
In my moon suit and funeral veil.
I am no source of honey
So why should they turn on me?
Tomorrow I will be sweet God, I will set them free.   35

The box is only temporary.

[22] **Caesar:** *title used by several Roman emperors*
[29] **laburnum:** *a tree with yellow flowers*
[29] **colonnade:** *a structure composed of columns placed at regular intervals*
[32] **moon suit and funeral veil:** *here these refer to the beekeeper's protective clothing*

COMPREHENSION

Stanzas 1–2

1. Briefly describe the bee box in your own words.
2. What is the speaker's initial response to the bee box? (Is she surprised, delighted, worried?)
3. Why is the box described as 'dangerous'?
4. Why do you think the speaker has to 'live with it overnight'?
5. Though the speaker thinks the box is 'dangerous', she is unable to 'stay away from it'. Why do you think this is?

Stanzas 3–4

6. Describe in your own words what the speaker sees when she puts her eye to the box's grid.
7. What most unusual image is used to describe this?
8. 'How can I let them out?' Why do you think the speaker is reluctant to release the bees?
9. Describe the speaker's reaction to the sound emanating from the bee box.
10. What simile is used to describe this racket?

Stanza 5

11. In this stanza, what metaphor is used to describe the bees' buzzing?
12. What does the speaker mean when she says she is 'not a Caesar'?
13. Why do you think she characterises them as 'maniacs'?
14. What options does she feel she has with relation to this box that frightens her so much?

Stanzas 6–7

15. The lines about turning into a tree are a reference to the Greek myth of Daphne, who was pursued by Apollo. She pleaded with the gods to help her and they responded by transforming her into a tree. Why do you think the speaker makes this reference to Greek mythology?
16. Why does she feel the bees will not turn on her if she releases them?
17. What does she finally decide to do with the box?

PERSONAL RESPONSE

1. Like much of Plath's best work, this poem is intensely visual. Identify two images from the poem that struck you as vivid or memorable, and say why.
2. *Class Discussion*: It has often been suggested that the bee box in this poem has a symbolic value. What do you think it represents?
3. 'In this poem, Plath seems to forecast her own tragic death. She envisages herself slipping away from this human life, transforming into a tree, wearing a funeral veil like a dead person, or a "moon suit" like an astronaut ready to depart this world'. Do you agree with this reading? Give reasons for your answer.
4. How would you characterise the tone of the poem?
5. Both 'The Arrival of the Bee Box' and 'Elm' are imbued with elements of terror and horror. Would you agree, however, that the tone of these poems is very different?
6. Do you think it is fair to say that this poem is about confronting and mastering one's fears? Would you describe it as an optimistic or pessimistic piece?

IN CONTEXT

Plath once said: 'I believe that one should be able to control and manipulate experiences, even the most terrific, like madness, being tortured, this sort of experience, and one should be able to manipulate these experiences with an informed and an intelligent mind'. How does this statement effect your understanding of the poem?

Poppies in July

Little poppies, little hell flames,
Do you do no harm?

You flicker. I cannot touch you.
I put my hands among the flames. Nothing burns

And it exhausts me to watch you   5
Flickering like that, wrinkly and clear red, like the skin of a mouth.

A mouth just bloodied.
Little bloody skirts!

There are fumes I cannot touch.
Where are your opiates, your nauseous capsules?   10

If I could bleed, or sleep! –
If my mouth could marry a hurt like that!

Or your liquors seep to me, in this glass capsule,
Dulling and stilling.

But colorless. Colorless.   15

[10] **opiates:** *drugs that dull feelings and induce sleep*

COMPREHENSION

1. What does the speaker expect from the flowers in the first eight lines of the poem? Why do the flowers frustrate her so much?
2. In the opening lines of the poem, the poppies are linked with fire. What is fire often associated with? What might the poet's desire to be burnt represent?
3. The redness of the poppies is linked vividly with the colour of flesh, 'the skin of a mouth'. Once again, the speaker introduces a startling reference to violence. Do the first eight lines ultimately tell us more about the speaker's own state of mind than they do about the flowers?
4. 'Where are your opiates?' Consider how the last seven lines express a desire for some form of oblivion. How do the speaker's wishes in the latter part of the poem compare with the sentiments expressed in the first eight lines?
5. 'If I could bleed or sleep!' The poem expresses a frustrated desire for two very different conditions. How would you describe each?
6. 'If my mouth could marry a hurt like that!' What do you think the speaker means by this? Why do you think the speaker needs to feel 'hurt'?
7. What does the 'glass capsule' mentioned in line 13 represent? Why do you think that the speaker would want the 'liquors' to be 'colorless'?

PERSONAL RESPONSE

1. Did you find the intensity of this poem disturbing? Surprising?
2. Could you sympathise with the speaker of the poem? Did you find the use of the flowers to convey violent anguish effective?

IN CONTEXT

In 'Pheasant', Plath looks out upon her garden and discovers something beautiful and valuable in nature, whereas in 'Poppies in July' and 'Elm' she finds only representations of her own troubled mind. Consider how nature functions in different ways for Plath.

Child

Your clear eye is the one absolutely beautiful thing.
I want to fill it with color and ducks,
The zoo of the new

Whose names you meditate –
April snowdrop, Indian pipe, 5
Little

Stalk without wrinkle,
Pool in which images
Should be grand and classical

Not this troublous 10
Wringing of hands, this dark
Ceiling without a star.

COMPREHENSION

1. How does the speaker of the poem perceive the child? Why does she chose to focus on the 'eye'?
2. Why does the speaker of the poem want to fill the child's eye with 'color and ducks'? What do we normally associate such things with?
3. 'April snowdrop, Indian pipe'. What do these objects suggest to you? Why has the speaker mentioned them?
4. Look at the language that the poet uses in the first nine lines of the poem. How would you describe the tone and mood of this part of the poem?
5. Plath uses two metaphors to describe the child. Can you identify them? What do they suggest about the child?
6. Lines 8 and 9 mention 'images' that ought to 'be grand and classical'. Are these images of a different kind to 'color and ducks'? What do you think the speaker intends by 'grand and classical' images?
7. The last three lines introduce a dark and unsettling twist to the poem. Explain in your own words what is happening here.
8. What would you normally associate the 'Wringing of hands' with?
9. The final image of the poem is particularly bleak. What does the 'dark/ Ceiling' represent? What is the significance of it having no stars?

PERSONAL RESPONSE

1. How did this poem make you feel? Does the poem allow for anything positive, or is it a poem of absolute despair?
2. 'Although the title of the poem is "Child", the poem is really about the mother.' Discuss this statement.
3. What issues does this poem raise with regard to motherhood?
4. The poem characterises the child as pure and innocent, and the mother wants to do all she can to protect these qualities. However, the end of the poem introduces the troubled and complex world of the adult. Discuss the view of the world that the poem gives.

DEREK MAHON
BIOGRAPHY

Derek Mahon was born in Belfast in 1941, the only child of Ulster Protestant parents. Like many only children, Mahon had to make his own fun. He became something of a solitary dreamer, comfortable with his own company but intensely aware of the physical world around him. Certain objects in his parents' house seem to have been especially important to him – for example, an old 1940s radio set. These objects, he claims, were his 'best friends' during childhood, acting as spurs for his youthful imagination. Mahon's status as an only child was important to his development as a poet: 'I had time for the eye to dwell on things, for the brain to dream about things.' In his poem 'Courtyards in Delft' he describes himself, famously, as 'a strange child with a taste for verse'.

This 'strange child' attended Skegoneil Primary School and then the Royal Belfast Academical Institution ('Inst.') – famous, among other things, for its rugby team. It is difficult to know whether Mahon's school days were happy or miserable. In an interview with the *Paris Review*, he presents himself as something of a teenage misfit: 'I started moping, brooding; I didn't go in for sport.' Elsewhere, however, he claims to have been a decent rugby player (a 'mean scrum-half'). What *is* certain is that Inst. played an important role in the growth of Mahon's poetic gift. Here, he encountered what he describes as other 'young sophisticates' – fellow students who shared his interest in poetry and literature. His English teacher, 'Basher' Boyle, was familiar with the Dublin literary scene and with the circle of the great Irish poet W.B. Yeats. From Boyle, Mahon acquired his lifelong fascination with Yeats' work: 'his idea of teaching five hundred years of English literature was to race through Shakespeare and the rest in the first term and spend the remaining two terms on a close study of Yeats.' Inst. also had a well-produced school magazine, to which Mahon contributed poems that according to the critic Hugh Haughton were 'fluent and extraordinary' for one so young.

Mahon's youth was shaped by his Protestant cultural background – what Haughton describes as the 'Protestant house-proud ethos', which involved a sober emphasis on hard work and religion above all else. His family was tied to industrial Belfast, with his father and grandfather both working in the famous Harland and Wolf shipyard, while his mother had worked at the York Street flax mills. As time went by, Mahon developed a negative, or at least ambivalent, attitude toward both his home town and his Protestant cultural inheritance. In 'Ecclesiastes', for instance, Belfast is presented as a grim, industrialised wasteland, with its 'shipyard silence' and 'dark doors', while its Protestant inhabitants are dismissed as 'puritan' and a 'credulous people'. Even in a poem as bitter as 'Ecclesiastes', however, Mahon acknowledges that his Protestant upbringing is an important part of his identity. As Haughton puts it, 'that Protestant world is crucial to him though it's one that he could be seen to be in flight from, to some extent, in his later work'.

Mahon, then, seems to have been glad to leave behind what an early poem describes as 'this desperate city' and relocate to Dublin to study at Trinity College. The move to Dublin was important in expanding Mahon's horizons. As the poet Gerald Dawe puts it: 'It was a move from a city which was highly industrialised, full of the work ethic and an intense environment … to the more open, cosmopolitan atmosphere of Trinity'. Here, Mahon began to mature as a poet. Though he admits that he 'didn't go to lectures much', he had a good social life and formed friendships with many now well-known writers, including Michael Longley, Eavan Boland and Brendan Kennelly. In 1960s Dublin, according to Dawe, he became intensely aware of the world beyond Ireland: 'They were picking up on a vibe that was coming from America and they found that very liberating.' Trinity College provided him with a link to European culture – something that was to be of huge importance to Mahon as a writer and as a person: 'it was a kind of bridgehead into Europe through the writers who'd gone before him, like Beckett.'

The poems selected for this course were written in the twenty years between his departure from Trinity in 1965, and the publication of his collection *Antarctica* in 1985. During this time, Mahon led something of a nomadic existence. He studied for a year in Paris, worked his way through Canada and the US, taught for a while in Dublin, and spent many years in London as a freelance journalist. It is not surprising, then, that Mahon is regarded as one of the great poets of place and travel, and that place names feature in the titles of so many of his poems. Throughout his wanderings, however, Mahon's Northern Protestant upbringing continued to exert a powerful pull on his work. Several of his poems are influenced – usually indirectly – by the Troubles that dogged Northern Ireland from the late 1960s.

Mahon eventually settled in the Republic of Ireland, and his recent work seems to identify more and more with the Southern state rather than with the Ulster of his birth. The US, too – especially New York – has loomed large in some of his recent poetry. In the past ten years, Mahon has emerged as a fierce critic of contemporary life, of the shallowness, greed and stupidity he sees everywhere in today's society. As Hugh Haughton puts it: 'These recent poems take on New York, homelessness, dereliction, and the new Celtic Tiger metropolis in Dublin'. He currently lives in Kinsale.

Derek Mahon

Grandfather

They brought him in on a stretcher from the world,
Wounded but humorous; and he soon recovered.
Boiler-rooms, row upon row of gantries rolled
Away to reveal the landscape of a childhood
Only he can recapture. Even on cold   5
Mornings he is up at six with a block of wood
Or a box of nails, discreetly up to no good
Or banging round the house like a four-year-old –

Never there when you call. But after dark
You hear his great boots thumping in the hall   10
And in he comes, as cute as they come. Each night
His shrewd eyes bolt the door and set the clock
Against the future, then his light goes out.
Nothing escapes him; he escapes us all.

[3] **gantries:** *overhead structures with a platform supporting a travelling crane, used in the building of ships*

COMPREHENSION

1. What is your general impression of the grandfather after reading the poem?
2. The first two lines are intriguing. What sort of incident do you think the grandfather was involved in (consider, in particular, the word 'Wounded')? Who do you think 'They' refers to?
3. Where did the grandfather work?
4. What do lines 3–5 say about the grandfather's memory?
5. In what manner does the grandfather resemble a child?
6. The grandfather is a man much given to secrecy. Consider how this is conveyed throughout the poem. Why do you think he acts this way?
7. The grandfather is said to resemble 'a four-year-old', yet the poem ultimately reveals that he is far from naive or innocent. Consider how the poem presents the grandfather as a more complex character than might first be supposed.
8. How might the grandfather be considered a 'larger-than-life' individual?
9. What do you think it means to 'set the clock/ Against the future'? What does the poem reveal about the grandfather's attitude to both the past and the future?

PERSONAL RESPONSE

1. Do you consider this poem to be nostalgic?
2. Does the poem reveal an endearing character or do you find the grandfather's secrecy a little unsettling?

IN CONTEXT

'Grandfather' is very close to the sonnet in form. 'Antarctica' uses the formal structure of the villanelle. How do these forms correspond with the themes of the poems?

Derek Mahon

Day Trip to Donegal

We reached the sea in early afternoon,
Climbed stiffly out; there were things to be done,
Clothes to be picked up, friends to be seen.
As ever, the nearby hills were a deeper green
Than anywhere in the world, and the grave   5
Grey of the sea the grimmer in that enclave.

Down at the pier the boats gave up their catch,
A writhing glimmer of fish; they fetch
Ten times as much in the city as here,
And still the fish come in year after year –   10
Herring and mackerel, flopping about the deck
In attitudes of agony and heartbreak.

We left at eight, drove back the way we came,
The sea receding down each muddy lane.
Around midnight we changed-down into suburbs   15
Sunk in a sleep no gale-force wind disturbs.
The time of year had left its mark
On frosty pavements glistening in the dark.

Give me a ring, goodnight, and so to bed …
That night the slow sea washed against my head,   20
Performing its immeasurable erosions –
Spilling into the skull, marbling the stones
That spine the very harbour wall,
Muttering its threats to villages of landfall.

At dawn I was alone far out at sea   25
Without skill or reassurance – nobody
To show me how, no promise of rescue –
Cursing my constant failure to take due
Forethought of this; contriving vain
Overtures to the vindictive wind and rain.   30

[6] **enclave:** *a part of one country surrounded by another or an enclosed community that is distinct from the rest of society*
[29] **vain:** *futile, useless; can also mean proud and conceited*
[30] **vindictive:** *cruel, spiteful, vengeful*

COMPREHENSION

1. Where and when is this poem set?
2. What everyday tasks have the speaker and his friends come to accomplish?
3. Describe the Donegal landscape in your own words. What contrast is drawn between land and sea?
4. What is happening at the pier? Why are the fish usually brought to the city?
5. What is the speaker's attitude to the dying fish? Give reasons for your answer.
6. Consider the phrase 'changed-down into suburbs'. Do you think this phrase could have more than one meaning?
7. How are the suburbs presented in the poem? What time of year is it?
8. What happens that night when the speaker goes to bed?
9. 'At dawn I was alone far out at sea'. What does this mean? Is he really 'out at sea'?
10. How does the speaker attempt to calm the rain and wind?
11. *Class Discussion:* The speaker claims he has constantly failed to 'take due/ Forethought for this'. What eventuality has the speaker neglected to prepare for? Would you agree that this phrase is open to more than one interpretation? Give reasons for your answer.

PERSONAL RESPONSE

1. Mahon has declared: 'It's practically my subject, my theme: solitude and community; the weirdness and terrors of solitude; the stifling and consolations of community. Also, the consolations of solitude.' In what sense could this poem be considered an investigation of solitude?
2. Identify four examples of alliteration in this poem, and say how they contribute to its atmosphere.
3. *Class Discussion:* Consider the different meanings of the word 'trip'. Would you agree that the speaker experiences a 'night trip' as well as a 'day trip' in this poem? Do you think the speaker actually wakes up to find himself far out at sea, or is he experiencing some form of vision or nightmare?
4. What link, in your opinion, is there between the fish dying on the pier and the strange experience the speaker undergoes that night?
5. Would you agree that 'Day Trip to Donegal' could be considered an environmentalist poem?
6. *Class Discussion:* Several critics have suggested that this poem somehow reflects the difficult political situation in Northern Ireland. Do you think that such a reading is realistic or far-fetched? Bear in mind that the speaker travels from Belfast in Protestant-dominated Northern Ireland to Donegal, which lies in the mainly Catholic Republic.

IN CONTEXT

1. 'Like many of Mahon's poems, "Day Trip to Donegal" features a mind at the end of its tether, a person facing into hellish circumstances.' With this statement in mind, write a paragraph comparing the present poem to either 'Antarctica' or 'After the *Titanic*'.
2. 'Both "Day Trip to Donegal" and "A Disused Shed in Co. Wexford" involve an intense sensitivity toward the non-human.' Write a paragraph responding to this statement.

After the *Titanic*

    They said I got away in a boat
And humbled me at the inquiry. I tell you
    I sank as far that night as any
Hero. As I sat shivering on the dark water
    I turned to ice to hear my costly   5
Life go thundering down in a pandemonium of
    Prams, pianos, sideboards, winches,
Boilers bursting and shredded ragtime. Now I hide
    In a lonely house behind the sea
Where the tide leaves broken toys and hatboxes   10
    Silently at my door. The showers of
April, flowers of May mean nothing to me, nor the
    Late light of June, when my gardener
Describes to strangers how the old man stays in bed
    On seaward mornings after nights of   15
Wind, takes his cocaine and will see no one. Then it is
    I drown again with all those dim
Lost faces I never understood, my poor soul
    Screams out in the starlight, heart
Breaks loose and rolls down like a stone.   20
    Include me in your lamentations.

Titanic: *the Titanic was built in Belfast. It sank on its maiden voyage to the US, with the loss of 1,500 lives. The speaker of the poem is Bruce Ismay. He was the manager of the White Star Line for which the Titanic sailed. He was one of few men who survived the tragic sinking of the ship, and was later criticised heavily for neglecting to help drowning passengers.*

[6] **pandemonium:** *chaos, confusion, mass disorder. The name of the place where the demons gathered after they were exiled from Heaven in John Milton's Paradise Lost.*

[8] **ragtime:** *a type of jazz music*

COMPREHENSION

1. How was the speaker treated by the 'inquiry' that was set up after the tragedy?
2. Why does the speaker feel that he ought to be treated with as much sympathy as 'any/ Hero'?
3. What do you think the speaker means when he refers to his 'costly' life?
4. How is assonance and alliteration used in lines 6 to 8 to convey the destruction of the ship?
5. The speaker mentioned the 'costly' life he led in line five. How does the life he now leads compare with his former life?
6. How does the sea serve as an effective metaphor for the memories that continue to haunt the speaker?
7. Why do you think that the speaker refers to those who died as 'Lost faces I never understood'?
8. Consider the description of human suffering in the closing lines. How does the poet use alliteration and assonance to heighten the emotional impact of these lines?

PERSONAL RESPONSE

9. Write a brief account of Ismay's life based on the poem. Do you think that the speaker is a tragic individual deserving of our sympathy or do you think he deserved to suffer for his actions?
10. Consider Mahon's economic use of language in describing the enormous tragedy of the Titanic. How effective did you find his portrayal of the incident? Consider lines 5 to 8 in particular.

Ecclesiastes

God, you could grow to love, it, God-fearing, God –
    chosen purist little puritan that,
for all your wiles and smiles, you are (the
    dank churches, the empty streets,
the shipyard silence, the tied-up swings) and 5
    shelter your cold heart from the heat
of the world, from woman-inquisition, from the
    bright eyes of children. Yes, you could
wear black, drink water, nourish a fierce zeal
    with locusts and wild honey, and not 10
feel called upon to understand and forgive
    but only to speak with a bleak
afflatus, and love the January rains when they
    darken the dark doors and sink hard
into the Antrim hills, the bog meadows, the heaped 15
    graves of your fathers. Bury that red
bandana and stick, that banjo; this is your
    country, close one eye and be king.
Your people await you, their heavy washing
    flaps for you in the housing estates – 20
a credulous people. God, you could do it, God
    help you, stand on a corner stiff
with rhetoric, promising nothing under the sun.

Ecclesiastes: *a book of the Bible, can also refer to a prophet or preacher*
[2] **purist:** *one who practices or urges strict correctness, especially in the use of words*
[2] **puritan:** *one who lives in strict accordance with Protestant precepts, especially one who regards pleasure or luxury as sinful*
[5] **tied-up swings:** *in Northern Ireland the public playgrounds would be closed on a Sunday and the swings would be tied up, and it was considered sinful to have fun on the sabbath*
[10] **locusts and wild honey:** *in the Bible this is the diet of prophets such as John the Baptist*
[13] **afflatus:** *divine inspiration*
[18] **close one eye and be king:** *a reference to the old proverb that 'In the land of the blind the one-eyed man is king'*
[21] **credulous:** *gullible*
[23] **rhetoric:** *the art of public speaking or of persuading by means of argument. This word is often associated with dishonesty.*

COMPREHENSION

1. Who is speaking in this poem?
2. To whom are his words addressed?
3. How does this addressee present himself to the people around him?
4. According to the speaker, what kind of person is he really?
5. The speaker claims that the addressee could 'grow to love it'. What do you think it is that the addressee could come to love?
6. Read lines 4 and 5 carefully. What city is being described here? What day of the week is it?
7. What must an Ecclesiastes 'shelter' himself from? Why do you think this is?
8. According to the speaker, what kind of lifestyle must an Ecclesiastes adopt?
9. What kind of mindset and emotional outlook must accompany this lifestyle?
10. The speaker says an Ecclesiastes must come to love a certain landscape. Describe this landscape in your own words. Do you find it appealing?
11. What, in your opinion, is symbolised by the 'red bandana and stick'?
12. The speaker tells the addressee that he can 'close one eye and be king'. What does this suggest about the people over whom he would rule?
13. Consider the phrase 'promising nothing under the sun'. Can you suggest two different meanings for this phrase?

PERSONAL RESPONSE

1. What features does the speaker associate with Belfast and its surrounding landscape? Make a list. What kind of atmosphere, in your opinion, does this description conjure?
2. Suggest three adjectives that might describe the tone used by the speaker in this poem.
3. Repetition plays a very important role in this poem. What effect does the speaker's repetition of key terms have?
4. Do you think the speaker really believes it would be a good idea for the addressee to 'close one eye and be king' of the Belfast Protestants, or do you feel he is being ironic and sarcastic?
5. 'In this poem, Mahon is actually talking to himself. The speaker and the addressee are the same person. Mahon considers the possibility of giving up poetry and becoming a political preacher. He realises that the poet and the preacher have much in common. Both attempt to cast a spell by means of language'. Do you agree with this assessment of the relationship between the speaker and the addressee?
6. Do you think this is a realistic portrayal of the similarities between the poet and the preacher's role? Give reasons for your answer.
7. What view of Belfast and the religion of Northern Irish Protestants is put forward in this poem? Based on your own knowledge and experience, do you think it is a fair and accurate depiction?

Derek Mahon

As it Should Be

We hunted the mad bastard
Through bog, moorland, rock, to the starlit west
And gunned him down in a blind yard
Between ten sleeping lorries
And an electric generator.   5

Let us hear no idle talk
Of the moon in the Yellow River;
The air blows softer since his departure.

Since his tide-burial during school hours
Our children have known no bad dreams.   10
Their cries echo lightly along the coast.

This is as it should be.
They will thank us for it when they grow up
To a world with method in it.

[7] **the moon in the Yellow River:** *a play by Denis Johnston dealing with the Irish response to modernisation. In the play, a revolutionary tries to blow up an electric generator and is shot.*
[9] **tide-burial:** *old burial ritual where the body is floated out to sea*

COMPREHENSION

1. How would you describe the tone in the opening lines of the poem?
2. What sort of person do you think is speaking here?
3. What aspect of Ireland is portrayed in the second line? How does this differ from the location of the killing?
4. The speaker dismisses 'idle talk' and wishes to hear no more of it. What sort of talk is he referring to here?
5. Why do you think the speaker uses the term 'tide-burial' to describe the disposal of the body?
6. Do you find the speaker's claims in lines 10–11 to be reasonable or irrational?
7. 'This is as it should be'. What sort of world does the speaker wish to live in?

PERSONAL RESPONSE

1. What is your reaction to the poem's speaker? Do you respect his point of view?
2. What images in the poem did you find most striking?
3. What do you think this poem has to say about the troubled history of Ireland?
4. Do you think that the kind of attitude the poem describes is of the past, or do you think that such attitudes still prevail in modern Ireland?

A Disused Shed in Co. Wexford

Let them not forget us, the weak souls among the asphodels
Seferis, Mythistorema

(for J.G. Farrell)

Even now there are places where a thought might grow —
Peruvian mines, worked out and abandoned
To a slow clock of condensation,
An echo trapped for ever, and a flutter
Of wild flowers in the lift-shaft, 5
Indian compounds where the wind dances
And a door bangs with diminished confidence,
Lime crevices behind rippling rain-barrels,
Dog corners for bone burials;
And in a disused shed in Co. Wexford, 10

Deep in the grounds of a burnt-out hotel,
Among the bathtubs and the washbasins
A thousand mushrooms crowd to a keyhole.
This is the one star in their firmament
Or frames a star within a star. 15
What should they do there but desire?
So many days beyond the rhododendrons
With the world waltzing in its bowl of cloud,
They have learnt patience and silence
Listening to the rooks querulous in the high wood. 20

They have been waiting for us in a foetor
Of vegetable sweat since civil war days,
Since the gravel-crunching, interminable departure
Of the expropriated mycologist.
He never came back, and light since then 25
Is a keyhole rusting gently after rain.
Spiders have spun, flies dusted to mildew
And once a day, perhaps, they have heard something —
A trickle of masonry, a shout from the blue
Or a lorry changing gear at the end of the lane. 30

There have been deaths, the pale flesh flaking
Into the earth that nourished it;
And nightmares, born of these and the grim
Dominion of stale air and rank moisture.
Those nearest the door grow strong –   35
'Elbow room! Elbow room!'
The rest, dim in a twilight of crumbling
Utensils and broken flower-pots, groaning
For their deliverance, have been so long
Expectant that there is left only the posture.   40

A half century, without visitors, in the dark –
Poor preparation for the cracking lock
And creak of hinges; magi, moonmen,
Powdery prisoners of the old regime,
Web-throated, stalked like triffids, racked by drought   45
And insomnia, only the ghost of a scream
At the flash-bulb firing-squad we wake them with
Shows there is life yet in their feverish forms.
Grown beyond nature now, soft food for worms,
They lift frail heads in gravity and good faith.   50

They are begging us, you see, in their wordless way,
To do something, to speak on their behalf
Or at least not to close the door again.
Lost people of Treblinka and Pompeii!
'Save us, save us,' they seem to say,   55
'Let the god not abandon us
Who have come so far in darkness and in pain.
We too had our lives to live.
You with your light meter and relaxed itinerary,
Let not our naive labours have been in vain!'   60

[14] **firmament:** *the sky*
[20] **querulous:** *given to complaining*
[21] **foetor:** *stench*
[22] **Civil War Days:** *the Irish civil war (1922–23)*
[24] **expropriated:** *dispossessed or stolen from*
[24] **mycologist:** *an expert on mushrooms and other fungi*
[43] **magi:** *the Three Wise Men who visited Jesus in Bethlehem; can also refer to sorcerers or wizards*
[45] **triffids:** *a plant-like species from another world that invades earth in the classic science-fiction tale Day of the Triffids by John Wyndham*
[54] **Treblinka:** *a Nazi concentration camp in Poland where thousands of Jews were put to death*
[54] **Pompeii:** *a city in Italy that was destroyed after the eruption of Mount Vesuvius in 79 BC*
[59] **light meter:** *a device used in photography to measure brightness*

COMPREHENSION

1. Having read the poem, why do you think Mahon chose to include the epigraph by Seferis? What bearing does this quotation have on the poem as a whole?
2. *Class Discussion:* What is the significance of the poem's opening line? To what extent does it suggest the themes that the poem goes on to explore? Does it make the reader want to continue reading?
3. List the various places mentioned in the first stanza. What do each of these places have in common?
4. Describe the environment in which the 'thousand mushrooms' have survived. How long have they existed in this place?
5. 'What should they do there but desire?'. What do you think the mushrooms have desired for all this time?
6. What have the mushrooms been able to 'see' and 'hear' over this period? What role does the keyhole play for them?
7. 'the gravel-crunching interminable departure/ Of the expropriated mycologist./ He never came back'. Who is being referred to here? Why do you think the mycologist 'never came back'?
8. Describe, in your own words, the various horrors the mushrooms have been forced to endure over their years of confinement.
9. What happens at the beginning of stanza 5? What do you understand by the phrase 'flash-bulb firing-squad'? How do the mushrooms respond to this?
10. The speaker uses a variety of comparisons to stress the strange appearance of the mushrooms. List the various things he compares them to. Do you find these comparisons effective or outlandish?
11. What condition are the mushrooms in when the speaker discovers them? Is it too late for the mushrooms to be 'rescued' from the shed in which they have been imprisoned?
12. According to the speaker, the mushrooms are 'begging' him to 'do something'. What action or actions do they want him to take?

PERSONAL RESPONSE

1. *Class Discussion:* This poem uses a technique called 'personification' whereby non-human creatures are presented as having human characteristics. In this instance, a group of mushrooms experience insomnia, desire, terror and good faith. What effect do you think the poet hoped to achieve by presenting the mushrooms in this way? Do you think his use of this technique is effective or is it simply silly and over the top?
2. The mushrooms are identified with 'Lost people of Treblinka and Pompeii'. What do they have in common with these 'lost people' from history?
3. *Group Discussion:* How would you describe the tone of the speaker throughout the poem? Would you agree that his tone changes at several points? What effect do these shifts in tone have?
4. 'In this poem the speaker realises the importance of speaking out on behalf of the voiceless. The true tragedy of history's "lost people" is not the "darkness" and "pain" they endure but the fact that their suffering is forgotten about. That is why the mushrooms plead with the poem's speaker to remember them.' Do you find this interpretation of the poem plausible?

IN CONTEXT

'A preoccupation with the tragedies of history can be found throughout Mahon's work'. Write a couple of paragraphs comparing 'A Disused Shed in Co. Wexford' to 'Rathlin', 'After the *Titanic*' and 'As it Should Be' in light of this statement.

Derek Mahon

The Chinese Restaurant in Portrush

Before the first visitor comes the spring
Softening the sharp air of the coast
In time for the first seasonal 'invasion'.
Today the place is as it might have been,
Gentle and almost hospitable. A girl   5
Strides past the Northern Counties Hotel,
Light-footed, swinging a book-bag,
And the doors that were shut all winter
Against the north wind and the sea-mist
Lie open to the street, where one   10
By one the gulls go window-shopping
And an old wolfhound dozes in the sun.

While I sit with my paper and prawn chow mein
Under a framed photograph of Hong Kong
The proprietor of the Chinese restaurant   15
Stands at the door as if the world were young,
Watching the first yacht hoist a sail
– An ideogram on sea-cloud – and the light
Of heaven upon the hills of Donegal;
And whistles a little tune, dreaming of home.   20

Portrush: *seaside town in north Antrim*
[18] **ideogram:** *a character symbolising the idea of a thing without indicating the sounds used to say it, as used in Chinese writing*

COMPREHENSION

1. The 'spring' plays an important role in readying the town for the arrival of the tourists. What does it achieve?
2. 'Today the place is as it might have been'. What do you understand the speaker to mean by this?
3. How would you characterise the attitude of the girl described in lines 5–7? What might she represent?
4. How would you describe the general atmosphere in the town? How does it differ to the way the place appears in winter?
5. How would you characterise the tone and mood of the last eight lines?
6. What do you think is the significance of the reference to eating 'prawn chow mein/ Under a framed photograph of Hong Kong' in the remote town of Portrush?
7. The proprietor of the restaurant 'Stands at the door as if the world were young'? What does this mean?

PERSONAL RESPONSE

Do you think the poem is a subtle commentary about the troubled history of Northern Ireland? Consider the poet's use of the word 'invasion' and the remark that 'Today the place is as it might have been'. Could the wolfhound be considered a symbol for violence that is presently absent? Or do you think that it is perhaps problematic to presume too easily that any poem about the North must be about the Troubles?

Rathlin

A long time since the last scream cut short –
Then an unnatural silence; and then
A natural silence, slowly broken
By the shearwater, by the sporadic
Conversation of crickets, the bleak   5
Reminder of a metaphysical wind.
Ages of this, till the report
Of an outboard motor at the pier
Shatters the dream-time and we land
As if we were the first visitors here.   10

The whole island a sanctuary where amazed
Oneiric species whistle and chatter,
Evacuating rock-face and cliff-top.
Cerulean distance, an oceanic haze –
Nothing but sea-smoke to the ice-cap   15
And the odd somnolent freighter.
Bombs doze in the housing estates
But here they are through with history –
Custodians of a lone light which repeats
One simple statement to the turbulent sea.   20

A long time since the unspeakable violence –
Since Somhairle Buí, powerless on the mainland,
Heard the screams of the Rathlin women
Borne to him, seconds later, upon the wind.
Only the cry of the shearwater   25
And the roar of the outboard motor
Disturb the singular peace. Spray-blind,
We leave here the infancy of the race,
Unsure among the pitching surfaces
Whether the future lies before us or behind.   30

Rathlin island: *a bird sanctuary off the Antrim coast, which was the site of a terrible massacre in 1575*
[4] **shearwater:** *a type of seabird*
[4] **sporadic:** *occasional*
[6] **metaphysical:** *immaterial; incorporeal, supernatural*
[9] **dream-time:** *the time of the creation of the world in Australian Aboriginal mythology: 'Aboriginal myths tell of the legendary totemic beings who wandered across the country in the Dreamtime … singing the world into existence'. Bruce Chatwin.*
[12] **oneiric:** *having to do with birds*
[14] **cerulean:** *azure, sky-blue*
[16] **somnolent:** *drowsy, sleepy*
[19] **a lone light:** *a reference to the lighthouse on Rathlin island*
[22] **Somhairle Buí:** *a Scots Irish chieftain whose main castle on Rathlin island. In 1575 the Earl of Essex, who was Queen Elizabeth's viceroy in Ireland, captured the castle and massacred its inhabitants, including the women and children. At the time, Somhairle Bui and his troops were trapped on the mainland and could only look on as his people were slaughtered. According to contemporary accounts, he went mad with grief.*

COMPREHENSION

1. What is the 'last scream' referred to in line one?
2. What do you think the speaker means by an 'unnatural silence'? Suggest why this unnatural silence had fallen upon Rathlin island? Why might it have been followed by a more 'natural' silence?
3. What kind of place is Rathlin?
4. How does the speaker arrive there?
5. What is meant by the phrase 'metaphysical wind'? Why do you think this strange wind is said to have haunted the island?
6. *Class Discussion:* What does the term 'dream-time' usually refer to? How might Rathlin island be said to have inhabited such a 'dream-time'? What does the speaker mean when he claims that the arrival of his boat 'shatters' this state of affairs?
7. Write a few lines describing the island's landscape and wildlife as they are depicted in stanza two. What three adjectives would you most readily associate with this place?
8. What contrast is drawn between Rathlin and the world beyond the island? In what different ways does the island seem to be a 'sanctuary'?
9. *Class Discussion:* The phrase 'through with history' is one that Mahon uses in several different poems. What does this phrase mean? In what sense is Rathlin through with history?
10. What is the unspeakable violence referred to at the beginning of stanza three?
11. What do you understand by the phrase 'the infancy of the race'?
12. Where is the speaker at the conclusion of the poem?

PERSONAL RESPONSE

1. What kind of atmosphere is created in stanza two? How does Mahon accomplish this? Would you agree that this atmosphere is shattered at the beginning of stanza three?
2. Write a couple of lines describing Mahon's use of rhyme in this poem.
3. Would you agree that this poem contrasts two different worlds? Give reasons for your answer.
4. 'On Rathlin the speaker discovers a place that is 'through with history', an island sanctuary that has been untouched by history's bloody hand'. Do you agree with this statement?
5. As the speaker leaves Rathlin he is unsure if the 'future lies before him or behind', if the future is represented by the island he is leaving or the mainland to which is headed. What kind of future is represented by the mainland? What kind of future is represented by Rathlin?
6. Do you feel that this is an optimistic poem? Give reasons for your answer.

IN CONTEXT

'Rathlin can be usefully compared to 'Antarctica', 'As it Should Be' and 'After the *Titanic*'. Each of these poems mourns the victims of various tragedies from history, and remembers their passing in a moving way'. Write a couple of paragraphs responding to this statement.

Antarctica

(for Richard Ryan)

'I am just going outside and may be some time.'
The others nod, pretending not to know.
At the heart of the ridiculous, the sublime.

He leaves them reading and begins to climb,
Goading his ghost into the howling snow; 5
He is just going outside and may be some time.

The tent recedes beneath its crust of rime
And frostbite is replaced by vertigo:
At the heart of the ridiculous, the sublime.

Need we consider it some sort of crime, 10
This numb self sacrifice of the weakest? No,
He is just going outside and may be some time –

In fact, for ever. Solitary enzyme,
Though the night yield no glimmer there will glow,
At the heart of the ridiculous, the sublime. 15

He takes leave of the earthly pantomime
Quietly, knowing it is time to go.
'I am just going outside and may be some time.'
At the heart of the ridiculous, the sublime.

In 1912 Captain Robert Scott and his crew succeeded in reaching the South Pole and were making their way back to the ship. Lawrence Oates, a member of the expedition, was suffering badly from frostbite and felt that he was slowing the others down. Having decided to leave the tent to walk to his death, his last recorded words were: 'I am just going outside and may be some time.'

[3] **sublime:** *of such grandeur and beauty as to inspire awe*
[7] **rime:** *frost formed from cloud or fog*
[13] **enzyme:** *a protein in the body that brings about change but remains unchanged itself*

COMPREHENSION

1. Who is speaking in the opening line? Who is he addressing?
2. How do you understand the response of the rest of the men in the tent to Oates' statement? Why do you think they pretend 'not to know'?
3. The poem repeats the point that at 'the heart of the ridiculous' is 'the sublime'. What do you understand the word 'sublime' to mean?
4. Comment on the poet's use of assonance and alliteration in line 5. How do these sound effects contribute to the atmosphere of the poem?
5. Do we respond differently to the poem's refrain each time it is used? If so, how?
6. What is the poet's response to Oates' 'self-sacrifice'?
7. Why do you think the poet refers to life as 'the earthly pantomime'?

PERSONAL RESPONSE

1. What is your reaction to the self-sacrifice of Oates? Do you think that the poem reveals 'the sublime' at the 'heart of the ridiculous'?
2. Do you think this poem celebrates the human spirit? Or is the poem a criticism of a certain mindset that does not allow for expression of emotion in the face of death?

Kinsale

The kind of rain we knew is a thing of the past –
deep-delving, dark, deliberate you would say,
browsing on spire and bogland; but today
our sky-blue slates are steaming in the sun,
our yachts tinkling and dancing in the bay   5
like racehorses. We contemplate at last
shining windows, a future forbidden to no one.

Kinsale: *a prosperous seaside resort in Co. Cork. Kinsale was the site of an important battle in 1601 between English forces and the Gaelic chieftains Hugh O'Neill and Hugh O'Donnell. A Spanish expeditionary force was also involved. The defeat of the 'two Hughs' signalled the end of Gaelic rule in Ireland, and the English began to establish a firmer foothold in the country, especially in Ulster.*

COMPREHENSION

1. *Class Discussion:* Has any member of the class ever visited Kinsale? What kind of place is it?
2. What do you know about Kinsale's history?
3. Describe, in your own words, the scene depicted in this poem.
4. What is the weather like?
5. Would you agree that 'browsing' is a somewhat unusual verb to describe the action of rain falling? What do you picture when you think of rain 'browsing' on a landscape?
6. Mahon uses the words 'we' and 'our' throughout this poem. What group of people do you feel he is referring to?
7. What kind of lifestyle do you associate with yachts and racehorses?
8. Think of the phrase 'shining windows'. Why are the windows in the poem shining? How might the world look when we gaze at it through 'shining windows'?
9. What do you understand by the poem's final phrase?
10. Identify two examples each of assonance and alliteration in this poem and say how they contribute to its atmosphere.

PERSONAL RESPONSE

1. Which of the poem's images did you find most effective or memorable? Say why.
2. What kind of building do you associate with a spire? Do you think the inclusion of a spire in this poem has any broader significance? Bear in mind Kinsale's particular history and the violence that has marred Ireland's recent past.
3. *Class Discussion:* It has been suggested that in this poem Mahon finally believes we can be 'through with history', that the violence and bitterness of the past need not continue into the future. Do you think this is an accurate summation of the spirit of this poem?
4. Do you feel that Mahon's apparent optimism is well placed, that the future will actually be forbidden to no one?

IN CONTEXT

Write a couple of paragraphs that compare and contrast 'Kinsale' with either 'Rathlin' or 'Ecclesiastes'. Try to identify three separate points of contrast or comparison.

NOTES

WILLIAM SHAKESPEARE

THEMES

ART

Shakespeare was much concerned with the passage of time. In many of his sonnets he meditates upon the terrible thought that everything that exists is destined to wither and die. Time is depicted as a cruel tyrant who destroys all that comes before him. Shakespeare was desperate to find something that could resist or overcome time. He knew that there was no possibility that he would live forever, but he thought that his works stood some chance of achieving immortality.

'Like as the waves' (Sonnet 60) is one of several poems where the poet suggests that his verses can resist the passage of time. The poet suggests that his poetry will be around 'to times' – for now and for all times to come. He suggests that as long as human history continues, people will continue to read his lines. Though everything else might fade away, his poetry will 'stand' against the ravages committed by time's 'cruel hand'. It will do so 'in hope', as a symbol or beacon of hope to all of us, as an indication that time's depredations can sometimes be resisted.

In 'Shall I compare thee' (Sonnet 18) the suggestion is made that as long as human beings exist his work will be read: 'So long as men can breathe and eyes can see/ so long lives this'. His poetry is one of the few things – perhaps the only thing – that will remain invulnerable to time's ravages. His lines will be 'eternal'.

Because these poems will last forever, so will the 'worth' of the Fair Youth. In ages to come, people will read these sonnets and will find his qualities and beauty recreated in their imaginations. The Fair Youth will never lose the fair qualities he presently possesses: 'Nor lose possession of that fair thou owest'. The 'summer' of the Fair Youth's beauty will be 'eternal' and will 'never fade'. As time 'grows' or moves forward through the centuries so shall the Fair Youth's beauty move forward with it: 'to time thou growest'.

In 'As an unperfect actor' (Sonnet 23) the poet expresses a similar confidence in his own work. He believes that it is his poems that best express his feelings. They are the 'dumb presagers of his speaking breast'. Whereas in speech many words are used, in a poem the words are so carefully selected that less of them are needed to convey what needs to be said. The poet's work pleads for love more effectively than the tongue that uses more words to express itself: 'plead for love … More than that tongue that more hath more express'd'.

LOVE

The power of love

'When in disgrace' (Sonnet 29) emphasises the deep love the poet has for the Fair Youth. All the poet has to do is 'think on' the Fair Youth and his despair lifts immediately. His almost unbearable despair is replaced by an equally intense joy, by a sense of euphoria wonderfully captured in the image of the lark rising from 'sullen earth' at daybreak and soaring into the dawn sky. Remembering the Fair Youth's love brings the poet such a wealth of happiness that he wouldn't swap places with a king. He wouldn't swap these thoughts or memories, and the joy they bring him, for all the earthly goods and power a king has at his disposal.

In 'When to the sessions' (Sonnet 30) it is again the poet's love for the Fair Youth that raises him out of his despair. Though he has called to mind countless woes and grievances, just thinking about his 'dear friend' for a while cancels out all the pain and misery he feels.

The pains of love

'As an unperfect actor' (Sonnet 23) describes how nerve-wracking and discombobulating love can sometimes be. The poet is overcome with nerves and incapable of expressing himself in his beloved's presence. He seems to get tongue-tied and lose all eloquence of speech. In this regard he is like a poor or under-rehearsed actor who is incapable of saying his lines.

Love can be an overpowering experience. We can feel so much love for someone that we are rendered incapable of expressing that love. The poet compares this experience to that of a warrior who is so enraged he is incapable of acting effectively. There is a suggestion here that emotions can sometimes be so overpowering that they render us weak or useless. Both love and rage are two such emotions.

In 'When to the sessions' we get a sense of the pain and misery that love can bring. The poet speaks of the 'woe' of love and says that though he has moved on from whatever it was that caused him grief he is still able to shed tears over the hurt he suffered. He tells us that his woe is 'long since cancell'd', but the tears that he sheds seem to tell a different story.

We might guess that it is the Fair Youth who caused the poet to suffer in the past. Calling the Fair Youth his 'dear friend' suggests not only that the youth is very precious to him but that he is also perhaps emotionally costly. The poet has 'paid before' for the love he feels, but is all the time ready to pay again ('new pay'). The poet's love for the Fair Youth is, therefore, at once a source of restoration and of loss.

The sonnets suggest that the poet is the weaker party in the relationship that he describes, and it is he that ultimately suffers most. 'They that have power' is a perfect description of this unequal relationship. The friendship between the poet and the Fair Youth is unequal because the Fair Youth is younger, better looking, wealthier and from a higher social class. This inequality is reinforced by the Fair Youth's icy personality: he is one of those people who exhibits a high degree of psychological self-control, who is 'as stone/ Unmoved, cold'. It is even further reinforced by the poet's fear that the Fair Youth is about to abandon him, to forget the promises he has made him in the past.

The poem is a portrait of a relationship where one party distinctly has the upper hand and has 'the power to hurt' the other. The poet's response to this situation is to point out the consequences of the Fair Youth's actions. If the Fair Youth hurts him, if he exercises this 'power to hurt', his soul and personality will become foul and corrupt. However, if he doesn't exercise this power, if he refrains from hurting the poet, then he will join the ranks of the truly blessed, he will 'rightly inherit heaven's graces'. There can be little doubt, however, that the poet is acting from a position of extreme weakness within the context of the relationship.

The nature of love

'Let me not to the marriage of true minds' (Sonnet 116) considers what ideal or 'true' love should be. True love never changes no matter how much the world or those who love change. If love 'alters' or 'bends' then it is 'not love'. Love is something permanent, an 'ever-fixed mark' that is always there. It remains steadfast even through the roughest times: 'looks on tempests and is never shaken'. However, love is ultimately not something we can ever hope to completely understand. It is something mysterious, like the stars in the sky. The poet says that its 'worth's unknown'.

In 'As an unperfect actor' the poet suggests that there are long established rituals or ceremonies that lover's must follow. The poet is eager to get it right, to 'say/ The perfect ceremony of love's rite', but finds that he cannot express himself adequately in his beloved's presence. He is overcome with nerves, and loses the ability to speak coherently.

Comparing a tongue-tied lover to an 'unperfect actor' suggests that the ritual of love involves a certain amount of acting. The lover must perform a role and convince his beloved that his feelings are true just as an actor must convince his audience. Love is essentially a 'rite' or ceremony that involves common formal or traditional acts and rituals.

Such a comparison, however, raises the problem of honesty. An actor is someone who pretends to be something that he is not, whereas the lover needs to represent what he actually is or feels. There is always the danger that those we love may only be acting and not hold us in genuine affection. The poet seems to raise such a fear in line 5 when he mentions his 'fear of trust'.

'That time of year' (Sonnet 73) suggests that pending death ought to make us more appreciative of those we love. The poet says that the end of his life is drawing near and so his time is limited. He calls on the Fair Youth to appreciate this fact and to love him all the more because soon enough they will be parted by death: 'love that well which thou must leave ere long'.

William Shakespeare

Love & physical beauty

'Shall I compare thee' is one of many poems in which the poet praises the qualities of the Fair Youth he holds in such deep affection. The poet praises the Fair Youth's looks, associating his beauty with summer, usually considered the most glorious time of year: 'thy eternal summer'. Yet according to the poet, the youth is in fact 'more lovely' than summer days generally tend to be. After all – as the poet so skilfully points out – summer days can all too often be disappointing.

The poet also celebrates the restraint, evenness and balance of the youth's personality by stressing how 'temperate' he is. The poet wittily emphasises these fine qualities by suggesting that the Fair Youth is in fact more temperate than a summer itself.

'They that have power' (Sonnet 94) is another poem where the poet celebrates the Fair Youth's beauty and other fine qualities. The Fair Youth's beauty is suggested in the description of him as a 'sweet' summer bloom: 'The summer's flower is to the summer sweet'. This echoes the comparison of the Fair Youth to summer in Sonnet 18 ('Shall I compare thee'). 'They that have power' also praises the Fair Youth's personality, celebrating the high degree of psychological self-control he exhibits, how he is 'Unmovèd, cold and to temptation slow'. In this regard, it resembles Sonnet 18 ('Shall I compare thee'), another poem that praises the Fair Youth's self-restraint, and which says how 'temperate' he is.

In 'They that have power', however, the poet also comes very close to actually criticising the Fair Youth. We see this in line 10, where we're told that the summer flower exists only for itself: 'Though to itself it only live and die'. The implication is that while the Fair Youth is a beautiful person, he 'lives and dies' only for himself. It suggests that he has a self-absorbed, self-contained and possibly even selfish existence, that other people tend to be beneath his attention or even his notice.

TIME

There are several sonnets where Shakespeare emphasises how quickly and relentlessly time passes us by. In Sonnet 60 ('Like as the waves'), for instance, he compares the minutes of our lives to waves powering towards the shoreline. Each minute disappears into nothingness just as each wave fizzles away upon the pebbles of the beach. Each minute of our lives is immediately followed by the next into extinction: 'Each changing place with that which goes before'. Minute follows minute in an endlessly consecutive or 'sequent' process, like the waves crashing relentlessly onto the beach.

'When I do count' (Sonnet 12) makes a similar point. There are occasions when the poet becomes very conscious of how quickly and relentlessly time passes us by. This happens when he hears bells chiming the hour ('When I do count the clock that tells the time'), when he watches night draw in ('the brave day sunk in hideous night'), and when he watches seasons change and flowers wither.

The poem suggests how rapidly time goes by and how summer's end seems to come around so quickly. Trees that once sheltered cattle suddenly stand 'barren of leaves'. The wheat and barley that once stood fresh and green in the fields now lie in bundles on the carts 'with white and bristly beard'. This reminds us of Sonnet 18 ('Shall I compare thee'), which also emphasises how summer exists for all too short a time before it must give way to autumn: 'Summer's lease hath all too short a date'. It also brings to mind Sonnet 116 ('Let me not'), which laments how quickly life's 'brief hours and weeks' pass by.

Shakespeare often emphasises how nothing is immune to time's ravages. In Sonnet 60 ('Like as the waves') he stresses how 'nothing stands but for his scythe to mow', while Sonnet 12 ('When I do count') reminds us that 'nothing 'gainst Time's scythe can make defence'. Nothing can stand up to time's terrible scythe. The passage of time will cause everything on earth to be destroyed or fade away.

'Since brass, nor stone' (Sonnet 65) is particularly powerful in its depiction of time as a destructive force. Nothing is strong enough to resist the passage of time. Even brass, steel and stone will eventually succumb to time's passage. Even the mightiest fortresses will eventually crumble: 'rocks impregnable are not so stout,/ Nor gates of steel so strong'. The poet compares time to a heartless tyrant who destroys and conquers without reason, and to a relentless army that lays 'wreckful' siege to a town it is hell-bent on destroying. Time's weapons are 'days', which are likened to battering rams no defences can resist.

'Fear No More the Heat o' the Sun' also reminds us that time is an indifferent and destructive force. Every living person will eventually die and turn to dust. It does not matter if you are rich like the 'Golden lads' or poor like a 'chimney-sweeper'. It does not matter if like a king you possess great earthly power or if like a scholar you possess great learning. Time's passage treats everyone the same. Nothing can resist its implacable march.

Shakespeare is keenly aware of how time destroys beauty, especially the good looks we possess when young. Sonnet 60 ('Like as the waves'), for instance, depicts time as a brutal tyrant who destroys beauty with his 'cruel hand'. He gives us the gift of youthful beauty, for it is time that turns us from infants into mature but youthful adults. Yet he also cruelly takes that gift away, transforming us from youthful adulthood to withered old age. Time is depicted as piercing beauty's 'flourish' with a weapon, digging lines into the foreheads of beautiful people, and feasting on the rare specimens of human beauty that nature produces. This notion of time as the destroyer of youthful beauty is present in several other poems:

- Sonnet 12 ('When I do count') stresses how things that are sweet and beautiful will eventually lose their sweetness and beauty: 'sweets and beauties do themselves forsake'. Even the Fair Youth's beauty will not be spared: 'thou among the wastes of time must go'.
- Sonnet 18 ('Shall I compare thee') laments how everything beautiful is eventually stripped or 'untrimm'd' of its beauty: 'And every fair from fair sometime declines'. This line means that everything fair or beautiful in this world must eventually 'decline' as its beauty slips away.
- Sonnet 65 ('Since brass, nor stone'), too, stresses how beauty is particularly vulnerable to the passage of time. Things made of stone and steel can withstand time for centuries though they will eventually decay. But physical beauty is more fragile, being 'no stronger than a flower'.
- Sonnet 116 ('Let me not') warns how the 'rosy lips and cheeks' of young lovers will be ravaged by time's 'bending sickle'.
- 'Fear No More the Heat o' the Sun' tells us 'golden lads and girls' and 'the lovers young' must eventually 'come to dust'.

DESPAIR

In 'Tired with all these' (Sonnet 66) the poet has been plunged into despair by all the wrongs he sees around him. He is 'Tired with all these', exhausted by the unfairness and injustice of this life. He is simply fed up of living in a world like this:

- A world where good people are condemned to poverty simply by an accident of birth.
- A world where it is extremely difficult to maintain integrity and sexual purity.
- A world full of lies and hypocrisy, where the chaste are branded unchaste, where those who do the right thing are 'unjustly disgraced', where those who tell uncomfortable truths are branded idiots.
- A world where the undeserving always seem to get ahead.
- A world where weak and foolish people run society at the expense of those with vigour, intelligence and ability.
- A world where good dominates evil.

The poet is so depressed by all this that he longs for death: 'Tired with all these, for restful death I cry'. He wants to die, leaving the wrongs and injustices of this world behind: 'Tired with all these, from all these would I be gone'. He imagines that death will be a pleasant, 'restful' experience, a sweet release from the hardships of this life.

'Fear No More the Heat o' the Sun' is similar in this regard. Several critics have suggested it presents human existence as grim, horrible and brutal, an endless series of trials and tribulations from which death is the only escape.

Sonnets 29 ('When in disgrace') and 30 ('When to the sessions') depict a more personal form of despair. In Sonnet 29 the poet has been struck by a period of bad luck or ill fortune. He has fallen into disgrace with his fellow men, and has become some kind of pariah or social outcast. Perhaps worst of all, the thing that usually brings him most joy in life now brings him only misery. He finds himself at an extremely low psychological ebb:

- He 'beweeps', or laments, his situation.
- He contemplates his life, and 'curses' the series of events that brought him to this sorry state.

- He cries out futilely to God for help.
- He desperately envies other men their good fortune.
- He has come dangerously close to hating himself.

In Sonnet 30 ('When to the sessions') the poet continues to feel utterly miserable. But the focus has shifted from the present to the past. As the poet sits in silent thought, he decides to call to mind all the heartache and misery he has experienced in times gone by. The poet thinks about the friends who have died and the pain that love has caused him. He thinks about all the things he wanted but never got and of all the things he had and then lost. In the process he makes himself perfectly miserable. Though he has already suffered enough in the past, calling these grievances to mind causes him to suffer still more. He compares the fresh bewailing of old woes paying a debt that has already been settled: 'I new pay as if not paid before'.

DEATH

There are several instances in the sonnets where death is presented as something dark, alien and terrifying. In Sonnet 18 ('Shall I compare thee'), for instance, Shakespeare presents death as a threatening figure or presence. He suggests that when we die we wander in death's 'shade'. This is a perhaps unpleasant and discomforting image, suggesting that when we die we wander aimlessly in some shadowy realm governed by this bragging, menacing figure. Or perhaps it suggests we wander forever in the shadow this grim giant casts upon the ground.

Sonnet 30 ('When to the sessions') is similar in this regard. The poet thinks of good friends who have passed away: 'I drown an eye … For precious friends hid in death's dateless night'. In death, these friends now dwell in an eternity of darkness, lost to those who continue to live. Death is like a night without end or beginning. Because it is eternal it cannot be measured in time: 'dateless night'.

Sonnet 73 ('That time of year') continues the theme, likening death to the darkness of night. Night is a form of death: 'Death's second self'. Just as the night eliminates the day's light, so death consumes our lives totally. And just as the night's darkness surrounds us when we sleep, sealing us up 'in rest', so the darkness of death will engulf us when we die. The poet also compares death to the extinguishing of a fire. He says that the bodies that sustain our existence must eventually be consumed just as the fire's fuel will eventually be consumed by the fire it feeds.

In Sonnet 18 ('Shall I compare thee') the poet seems confident that his poetry can overcome death. He suggests that the Fair Youth will never die: 'Nor shall Death brag thou wandr'st in his shade'. The poet's verses will continue to exist as long as the human race does. And every time a person reads these sonnets the Fair Youth will come to life in their imaginations. In a sense, therefore, the Fair Youth will continue to live in these 'eternal lines' long after his physical body has passed away: 'So long lives this and this gives life to thee'. Sonnet 73 ('That time of year'), on the other hand, seems more accepting of death's inevitability. The poet does not attempt to defeat death but looks instead to make the most of the time that remains to him.

In 'Fear No More the Heat o' the Sun' death is presented as a release from the evils and difficulties of this world. Now that Imogen has passed away, she need no longer worry about the trials and tribulations of this life:

- Nature can no longer harm her with its heat, blizzards, of winter, meteorites or lightning.
- Other people cannot harm her, whether they be angry cruel tyrants, people who gossip maliciously, or people who unfairly criticise others.
- She need no longer worry about material survival, (food, clothes and other worldly goods).
- She will no longer suffer from psychological or emotional upheaval.

Death, then, is presented almost as a welcome release from the trials and difficulties of living. In this regard, the poem echoes Sonnet 66 ('Tired with all these') where the poet is 'Tired with all these' – with all the wrongs and injustices of this corrupt and evil world – and longs to die so he can move beyond their reach. In both of these poems, death is also presented as something peaceful and soothing – a pleasant and calming experience that awaits us after we have worked to accomplish our 'worldly task'. In 'Fear No More the Heat o' the Sun', its rest is depicted as the 'wages', or reward, we receive for labouring in this life. In Sonnet 66 ('Tired with all these') it is depicted as 'restful', suggesting that it is an easeful slumber awaiting us once we are through with the trials and tribulations of this life.

Sonnet 12 ('When I do count')

William Shakespeare

LINE BY LINE

When the poet thinks about time and the passage of time he realises that nothing lasts forever. Time destroys everything: 'nothing 'gainst Time's scythe can make defence'. Evidence of this is all around the poet: day turns to night, hair that was once dark is now grey, flowers wilt and trees lose their leaves.

The ravages of time are particularly evident at the end of summer. This is when the wheat and barley are harvested. The harvest that once was green is now white and 'bristly'. It is cut and bound together with string and carried away on carts. The poet mentions the 'brier' upon which the harvest is borne away. A brier was also used for the conveyance of coffins and so the image of 'summer's green' upon the brier is suggestive of death.

When the poet sees the effect that time has on the light of day, on hair, flowers, trees and the harvest, he begins to think about his beloved's beauty. This too must eventually be destroyed by time. His beloved must die and his beauty vanish. The only way that his beloved can preserve his beauty against the ravages of time is to procreate. He will die but his beauty will live on in his children, or 'breed'.

THEMES

Time

This sonnet is concerned with the passage of time. There are occasions when the poet becomes very conscious of time passing. The chiming of bells signalling the hour draws his mind to this ('When I do count the clock that tells the time') as does the onset of night: 'the brave day sunk in hideous night'. The changing seasons also remind the poet of the fact that time is always flowing. The withering of flowers and the trees shedding their leaves are vivid reminders of the fact that time is passing him by.

The poem suggests how rapidly time goes by. The end of summer comes about so quickly. Trees that once shaded cattle with their leaves suddenly stand 'barren of leaves'. The wheat and barley that once stood fresh and green in the fields now lie in bundles on the carts 'with white and bristly beard'.

This sonnet also states that everything that is beautiful will be destroyed by time. The poet says that things that are sweet and beautiful must eventually lose their sweetness and beauty: 'sweets and beauties do themselves forsake'. The violet that once was pretty is now 'past prime'. Knowing this to be true, the poet must acknowledge that his beloved's beauty will also be destroyed: 'thou among the wastes of time must go'.

Of course, it is not just beautiful things that time destroys. The poet says that nothing can stand up to 'Time's scythe'. Everything will perish with time: 'nothing 'gainst Time's scythe can make defence'.

The poem considers how sweet and beautiful things ('sweets and beauties') do not last forever. Beauty will vanish over time. The 'brave day' will turn into 'hideous night', and the hair that was once black will become 'all silver'd with white'.

With such examples of lost beauty in mind, the poet begins to question the permanence of his beloved's beauty. Since his beloved is mortal and so must decline and decay ('among the wastes of time must go'), and since beauty will eventually 'forsake' everything to which it adheres, then the beloved's beauty must be lost over time.

This thought troubles the poet and he looks to find a way of ensuring the survival of his beloved's beauty. The solution to the problem lies in procreation. Beauty appears in something as quickly as it disappears in another. If the beloved procreates then, as his beauty vanishes, it will re-emerge in the children he creates.

This is Poetry · 157

William Shakespeare

LANGUAGE

Form
Like all Shakespearean sonnets, this one has fourteen lines divided into three quatrains and a closing couplet. It has the ABAB CDCD EFEF GG rhyme scheme used in all but one of the sonnets.

It is interesting that this sonnet, which deals with time, is number twelve in the sequence. Perhaps twelve is meant to reflect the number of hours on the clock.

Tone
The tone of the sonnet is sombre as the poet deals with the passage and destruction of time. Unlike some of the other sonnets that deal with the same theme (for example, Sonnets 60 ('Like as the waves') and 65 ('Since brass, nor stone')) there is not much of a change in tone at the close of the poem. The final line does offer a solution to the destruction of the Fair Youth's beauty at the hand of time, but the tone is barely uplifting or hopeful.

Figures of speech
The poet personifies the wheat when he describes its awn in terms of a 'white and bristly beard'. The wheat is like an old man who has died and is being taken away on a funeral cart: 'Bourne on the bier with white and bristly beard'. Time is also personified: it is depicted as a person with a scythe that cuts down all that stands before him.

Imagery
Shakespeare uses images connected with the end of summer to illustrate the passage of time and the fact that all living things must age and die. The violet, a symbol of spring and new growth, is said to be 'past prime'. The trees that would have shaded the cattle on hot summer days are now 'barren of leaves'. The image of the harvest being carted away is funereal and tells of the swift passage of time. Only a few months before, this wheat was young and green; now it is 'girded up in sheaves' and has a 'white and bristly beard'.

Sonnet 18 ('Shall I compare thee')

LINE BY LINE

The poet considers writing a poem that compares the Fair Youth to a fine day in summer time. However, he decides that this is not an appropriate comparison. There are several reasons for this decision. Firstly, he feels that such a comparison would not do the Fair Youth's beauty justice. The Fair Youth, we are told, is 'more lovely' than any summer's day.

Secondly, he feels that the Fair Youth's personality is too 'temperate' for such a comparison. The word 'temperate' suggests that the youth's personality is gentle and restrained, that his temperament is even and balanced, that he avoids excesses of emotion. According to the poet, he is far more 'temperate' than the days of summer, which can often exhibit excessive, unsettled conditions:

- Sometimes in early summer there can be a hard wind, shaking the blooms that have burst – or that are bursting – into flower: 'Rough winds do shake the darling buds of May'.
- Another problem with summer is that sometimes the sun can actually be too hot: 'Sometime too hot the eye of heaven shines'.
- On the other hand, there are also many times when the 'gold complexion' of the sun is made dim by cloud cover: 'And often is his gold complexion dimm'd'.

The Fair Youth also differs from summer because that season's beauty is over far too quickly. Just as a tenant occupies a rented property only for a fixed period – known as a 'lease' – so summer fills the world only for a predetermined portion of the year. Summer's 'lease' on the world is 'all too short', and its expiration date all too quickly upon us: 'summer's lease hath all too short a date'.

The Fair Youth's beauty, on the other hand, will exist forever. He will keep forever the qualities of fairness and beauty he currently possesses: 'Nor lose possession of that fair thou owest' (in this line, 'that fair thou owest' means the fair qualities you own). The summer of his beauty will be 'eternal' and will never fade away: 'thy eternal summer shall not fade'. This is because the poet's verse will capture the Fair Youth's beauty for all the succeeding ages. The poet's lines will be 'eternal'. They will be read as long as the human race continues: 'So long as men can breathe and eyes can see'. As long there are human beings in existence, they will read this poem – along with others by the poet – and experience the Fair Youth's beauty.

The poet declares that the Fair Youth's beauty will 'grow' with time: 'When to time in eternal lines thou growest'. Here, the word 'grow' seems to suggest 'advance' rather than expand. As time advances relentlessly through the ages, so will the Fair Youth, for he will continue to live in men's imaginations due to the poet's eternal lines.

THEMES

Time

This is one of the many sonnets that deal with the passage of time. Shakespeare emphasises how quickly and relentlessly time passes us by. Summer exists for all too short a time before it must give way to autumn. Sonnet 60 ('Like as the waves') also addresses this theme with its depiction of how the minutes of our life race away from us like waves toward the shoreline. Sonnets 12 ('When I do count') and 116 ('Let me not') are others that emphasise how quickly our lives rush to their conclusion.

This poem also emphasises how time is a destroyer: 'And every fair from fair sometime declines'. This line means that everything fair or beautiful in this world must sometime 'decline' as its beauty slips away. Everything beautiful is eventually stripped, or 'untrimm'd', of its beauty. Sometimes, beautiful things are 'untrimm'd' by random events, by chance or accident. Sometimes, they are 'untrimm'd' by preordained and predictable natural processes: 'By chance or nature's changing course untrimm'd'. But eventually, with the passage of time, all beauty is destroyed.

There are several other sonnets where Shakespeare presents time as a destroyer of beauty. Sonnets 12, 60 and 116 are similar to the present poem in that they show time destroying beauty. Sonnet 12 has the poet dreading how the Fair Youth's beauty might be ruined by the 'wastes of time', while Sonnet 60 laments how time gives the gift of youthful beauty but also takes it away. Sonnet 116, meanwhile, shows time eliminating the 'rosy lips and cheeks' of young lovers with his 'bending sickle'.

Art

This is one of several poems where the poet declares that his poetry can resist or overcome time. He suggests that as long as human beings exist, people will continue to read his lines. Everything else might be destroyed, die or fade away but his poems will continue to exist: 'So long as men can breathe and eyes can see/ so long lives this'. His poetry is one of the few things – perhaps the only thing – that will remain invulnerable to time's ravages. His lines will be 'eternal'.

Because these poems will last forever, so will the Fair Youth's beauty. In ages to come, people will read these sonnets and will find his qualities and beauty recreated in their imaginations. The Fair Youth, therefore, will never lose the fair qualities he presently possesses: 'Nor lose possession of that fair thou owest'. The 'summer' of the Fair Youth's beauty will be 'eternal' and will 'never fade'. As time 'grows' – or moves forward through the centuries – so shall the Fair Youth's beauty move forward with it: 'to time thou growest'. Sonnets 18 ('Shall I compare thee') and 65 ('Since brass, nor stone') also stress how the poet's skill and effort will preserve the Fair Youth's qualities for centuries to come.

Death

This is one of several poems where Shakespeare presents death as a threatening figure or presence. He suggests that when we die we wander in death's 'shade'. This is, perhaps, an unpleasant and discomforting image, suggesting that when we die we wander aimlessly in some shadowy realm governed by this bragging, menacing figure. Or perhaps it suggests we wander forever in the shadow this grim giant casts upon the ground.

However, the poet suggests that the Fair Youth will never die: 'Nor shall Death brag thou wandr'st in his shade'. Of course, the poet does not mean this literally: the Fair Youth's physical body will die and rot just like everyone else's. Yet, as we have seen, the poet's verses will continue to exist as long as the human race does. And every time a person reads these sonnets, the Fair Youth will come to life in their imaginations. In a sense, therefore, the Fair Youth will continue to live in these 'eternal lines' long after his physical body has passed away: 'So long lives this and this gives life to thee'.

Love
This is one of many poems in which the poet praises the qualities of the Fair Youth he holds in such deep affection. The poet praises the Fair Youth's looks, associating his beauty with summer, usually considered the most glorious time of year: 'thy eternal summer'. Yet according to the poet, the youth is in fact 'more lovely' than summer days generally tend to be. After all – as the poet so skilfully points out – summer days can all too often be disappointing

As we have seen, the poet also celebrates the restraint, evenness and balance of the youth's personality by stressing how 'temperate' he is. The poet wittily emphasises these fine qualities by suggesting that the Fair Youth is in fact more temperate than a summer itself. The present poem, then, bears comparison to Sonnets 12 ('When I do count') and 65 ('Since brass, nor stone'), which also praise the Fair Youth's beauty and admirable qualities.

LANGUAGE

Form
Like all Shakespearean sonnets, this one has fourteen lines divided into three quatrains and a closing couplet. It has the ABAB CDCD EFEF GG rhyme scheme used in all but one of the sonnets. Like many, but not all, of the sonnets, it has a volta – or change of direction – in line 9: the poet goes from describing the ravaging effects of time to describing how the Fair Youth will be spared these effects thanks to the poet's work.

Tone
The tone of this poem is often declared to be confident, poised and brash. The poet seems absolutely convinced that his lines will be 'eternal', that as long as there are human beings they will read his words. He has no doubt that because of his work's durability the youth will never die and will never lose the beauty he currently possesses. This brashness is perhaps also evident in his declaration that the Fair Youth is both more temperate and more lovely than even a summer's day.

Imagery
There are several notable images in this poem. The image of wind 'shaking' the budding or recently budded flowers is one of the most famous in English poetry. The image of the sun's 'eye' looking down on the world, and its 'complexion' being dimmed by cloud cover is also memorable. Perhaps less pleasantly so is the image of death as a type of person, as a sinister and menacing figure 'bragging' that certain individuals have entered his shadowy realm.

Figures of speech
In line 5 Shakespeare uses a wonderful metaphor to describe the sun, referring to it as the 'eye of heaven', and we can imagine how the sun might be thought of as Heaven's eye looking down on us from above. There is another fine metaphor in line 8 where beauty is compared to a garment or a suit of clothing. Beautiful things only get to wear this garment for a certain period of time before it is stripped or 'untrimm'd' from them by the passage of time. In another metaphor, the Fair Youth's physical beauty is compared to summer. This makes sense because summer is often thought of as the most beautiful time of year. Furthermore, summer – like youthful beauty – lasts only for a fixed period of time.

An unusual feature of this poem is Shakespeare's use of legal language to describe how summer fills the world only for a certain portion of the year. Summer, we are told, 'leases' the world only for a fixed and pre-determined period, just as a tenant leases a rented property.

The poet uses a number of 'personifications' in this poem. In each case, a thing or an idea is presented as if it were a person:

- Death is presented as a person, as a threatening and menacing figure who seems to brag about the beautiful people forced to wander in his shadowy realm.
- In line 6 it could be argued that the sun is presented

as a male person whose face has a 'gold complexion' and looks down on us from the skies above.
- It could also be argued that the idea or concept of summer is personified. It is depicted as renting the world like a human tenant rents a property. It is given the quality of temperance, one we usually associate with human beings. Human beings are said to be temperate when they avoid extremes of emotion. Summer, it could be argued, is temperate when it avoids extremes of temperature and weather.

Sound effects

This is a poem marked by an absolute profusion of broad vowels sounds throughout. This gives the verse a slow, sonorous and stately movement appropriate to the poet's overwhelming confidence and poised belief that his lines will live forever. There is a great deal of assonance:

- Note for instance the repeated 'a' and 'u' sounds in 'Rough winds do shake the darling buds of May'/ And summer's lease hath all too short a date'.
- Note the repeated 'o' and 'i' sounds in 'And often is gold complexion dimm'd'
- Note the repeated 'o' sounds in 'Nor lose possession of that fair thou owest'.
- Note the repeated 'a' sounds in 'Nor shall death brag thou wandr'st in his shade'.

In each case, this assonance creates a euphonious effect, a pleasant stately music suited to this poem where a master celebrates his own mastery.

Sonnet 23 ('As an unperfect actor')

LINE BY LINE

The poet wants to tell his beloved how he feels. He wants to do this in an eloquent and appropriate way: 'to say/ The perfect ceremony of love's rite'.

However, when the poet is in his beloved's presence he is unable to speak. There are two reasons for this:

- He lacks confidence and does not trust himself to say what he wants to say: 'for fear of trust'. In this regard he is like an ill-prepared actor who does not have confidence in his own performance and is, therefore, unable to perform his part when on stage: 'As an unperfect actor on the stage/ Who with fear is put beside his part'. (By 'fear of trust' might also mean that he is not completely sure of his beloved's feelings for him. He is, therefore, afraid to express the love that he feels because he does not yet have trust in the relationship.)
- The love that he feels is so intense and powerful that it overwhelms him and renders him incapable of behaving as he would like. In this regard he is like 'some fierce thing' whose rage debilitates him, clouding his judgement and preventing him from acting as he might wish.

The poet, therefore, asks that his beloved accept his poems as an expression of his love. These works contain the eloquence that his nervous speech lacks: 'O, let my books then be the eloquence'. They 'plead' with the beloved for love and look for reciprocation: 'look for recompense'. The words 'plead' and 'recompense' are suggestive of court proceedings where one pleads a case and looks for compensation or 'recompense'. According to the poet, his poems manage to present a better case than the tongue possibly could. His poems also achieve this using fewer words: 'More than that tongue that more hath more express'd'.

When he writes, it is his heart or 'breast' that speaks clearly and without interference. The works that he produces are, therefore, the representatives, or 'presagers', of his heart. They silently convey the heart's message to his beloved: 'dumb presagers'. The poet, therefore, dearly wishes that his beloved will read his poems, which were composed in silence but express his love: 'O, learn to read what silent love hath writ'. He tells his beloved that when someone is in love they ought to be able to 'hear' what has not been spoken but is there for the eyes to see. Such an ability belongs to love: 'To hear with eye's belongs to love's fine wit'.

THEMES

Love

The sonnet describes how nerve-wracking and discombobulating love can sometimes be. The poet is overcome with nerves and incapable of expressing himself in his beloved's presence. He seems to get tongue-tied and lose all eloquence of speech. In this regard, he is like a poor or under-rehearsed actor who is incapable of saying his lines.

Love can be an overpowering experience. We can feel so much love for someone that we are rendered incapable of expressing that love. The poet compares this experience to that of a warrior who is so enraged he is incapable of acting effectively. There is a suggestion here that emotions can sometimes be so overpowering that they render us weak or useless. Both love and rage are two such emotions.

The comparison of the lover with the 'unperfect actor' suggests a number of things. Firstly, it suggests that perhaps the ritual of love involves a certain amount of acting. The lover must perform a role and convince his beloved that his feelings are true, just as an actor must convince his audience. Love is essentially a 'rite' or ceremony that involves common formal or traditional acts and rituals. The poet knows what is expected of him but is unable to perform the act or say the appropriate thing: 'to say/ The perfect ceremony of love's rite'. It is not clear what exactly this 'perfect ceremony' entails but it does call to mind the ceremony of marriage. In order to express his feelings, the poet, therefore, needs to be a perfect actor.

Such a comparison, however, raises the problem of honesty. An actor is someone who pretends to be something that he is not, whereas the lover needs to represent what he actually is or feels. There is always the danger that those we love may only be acting and not hold us in genuine affection. The poet seems to raise such a fear when he says that in line 5 when he mentions his 'fear of trust'.

The poem suggests that love is ultimately built on trust. It is possible to understand the poet's 'fear of trust' to mean that he is unsure of the Fair Youth, that he is as yet unable to trust him. It is impossible to speak our true feelings to those we cannot trust. Perhaps he fears that the Fair Youth will not trust him when he speaks of his feelings. It is, of course, also possible that the poet does not trust himself to speak as he would wish because of nerves.

Art

In this sonnet the poet expresses confidence in his own work. He believes that what he writes is eloquent and capable of expressing what he feels. What he writes represents his true feelings. His books are the 'dumb presagers of his speaking breast'. The sonnets are a plea for love and look for some form of a response. The poet believes that in his finely crafted poems he is capable of saying a lot using only few words. Whereas in speech many words are used, in a poem the words are so carefully selected that so less are needed to convey what needs to be said. The poet's work pleads for love more effectively than the tongue that uses more words to express itself: 'plead for love … More than that tongue that more hath more express'd'.

LANGUAGE

Form

Like all Shakespearean sonnets this one has fourteen lines divided into three quatrains and a closing couplet. It has the ABAB CDCD EFEF GG rhyme scheme used in all but one of the sonnets.

A 'turn' or change of focus occurs in the ninth line. The poet moves from considering his inability to speak or act to considering his work as an expression of his love.

Tone

The tone of the first two quatrains is apologetic and somewhat remorseful as the poet admits his inability to express himself adequately. However, there a shift in tone in the third quatrain when the poet begins to speak about his work. Here, the tone becomes more confident and assured.

Figures of speech

The poem contains two central similes. The poet compares his inability to express his love in speech to an actor who cannot say his lines. He also likens the overwhelming and debilitating effect to love to the effect that rage can have on a fighter or warrior. Both love and rage are powerful emotions that can impede and impair those who experience them.

The poet also uses a metaphor to describe his poems. They are 'dumb presagers', the poet's representatives who travel before him and deliver his message of love.

The sonnet contains a number of paradoxes. The notion that the poet's heart or 'breast' speaks but cannot communicate whilst his poems cannot speak but do communicate is paradoxical. The fact that the poet's love is so strong that it weakens him is also paradoxical.

Imagery

Like a number of sonnets, this one contains legal imagery or terminology. The poet's work is likened to someone who will represent him in court and 'plead' his case for love. This representative will also seek 'recompense' from the Fair Youth.

Sonnet 29 ('When in disgrace')

LINE BY LINE

LINES 1–4

The poet is in a bad way:

- He has experienced a period of bad luck: he is 'in disgrace with fortune', meaning that his luck has deserted him.
- For some unstated reason the poet has become disgraced in the opinions of his fellow men: he is 'in disgrace with … men's eyes'.
- The poet has become something of a pariah or social outcast: he has been left 'all alone' and in an 'outcast state'.

The poet responds to this state of affairs by lapsing into a mental state of complete anguish. He laments, or 'beweeps', the fact that he has become such a social outcast. He contemplates his life and curses the fact that it is his fate to endure such isolation: 'I … look upon myself and curse my fate'.

The poet prays to God for relief. Perhaps he wants God to soothe the feelings of despair that grip him. Or perhaps he wants God to change the circumstances that led to this sorrow in the first place. He imagines his 'cries', or pleas, rising up towards God in Heaven. But he says that Heaven is 'deaf', meaning that God pays no attention to his prayers. His cries, therefore, are 'bootless' – meaning they are useless or futile.

LINES 5–8

The poet finds himself envying those he regards as being in a better situation than himself:

- He wishes he was like one particular man he knows who is 'rich in hope' – a man who has a great deal to look forward to in life.
- There is another man whom he envies for his good looks or features. The poet wishes he was 'featured like him'.
- There is another man whom the poet envies for his friends: 'Wishing me … like him with friends possessed'. This man, it seems, has many friends while the socially outcast poet has none. Or perhaps the poet would like the type of friends that this man has; maybe friends who are popular, influential or simply fun to be with.
- There is another man he envies for his knowledge and intelligence – or 'art' – and yet another whom he envies for his 'scope' – for the wide range of his intellect and mental ability: 'Desiring this man's art and that man's scope'.

At present, the thing the poet normally most enjoys in life is tormenting him: 'With what I most enjoy contented least'. Perhaps the thing the poet 'most enjoys' is writing poetry.

Perhaps he is going through a period of writer's block; a period when poetry, usually a source of pure delight, brings him only tension and frustration.

Or perhaps the thing the poet 'most enjoys' is his relationship with the Fair Youth. Perhaps the two have had a falling-out, and now this relationship – one that usually fills him with the greatest joy – brings him only sorrow and misery.

LINES 9–14

All in all, then, the poet is in a pitiful state. He is in such a negative state of mind that he almost 'despises' or hates himself: 'in these thoughts almost myself despising'. Yet there is a way out of the poet's misery. Sometimes, almost by chance, he finds himself thinking of the Fair Youth, and his despair gives way to happiness: 'Haply I think on thee' ('Haply' means by chance, by a happy stroke of luck).

Thinking of the Fair Youth fills the poet with euphoria. He uses a fine simile to describe this ecstatic joy. His mind, he says, resembles a lark soaring into the air as the sun comes up. The lark has spent the night resting on the gloomy, or 'sullen', earth. But 'break of day' sees it 'arising' into the dawn sky, singing as it does so.

Line 12 is somewhat ambiguous in that it is not clear exactly who or what 'sings hymns at heaven's gate'. Does this phrase refer to the lark or to the poet's 'state' of mind? If it refers to the lark then we can imagine 'heaven's gate' as the sky into which the lark rises singing in the morning. If it refers to the poet's state of mind then we imagine 'heaven's gate' as a condition of total emotional euphoria, only one step removed from the bliss of being in Heaven itself.

When the poet remembers the Fair Youth's love it brings him 'wealth'. He does not mean literal wealth, as in gold or precious stones; instead, he means a kind of psychological wealth, referring to the great abundance of happiness he enjoys at such moments. Remembering the Fair Youth makes the poet so happy that he would not swap places with a king: 'Then I scorn to change my state with kings'. He wouldn't exchange these joyous thoughts for all the riches and power that a king commands.

THEMES

Despair

This is one of several sonnets that depict the poet in a state of misery and despair. He has been struck by a period of bad luck or ill fortune. He has fallen into disgrace with his fellow men, and has become some kind of pariah or social outcast. Perhaps worst of all, the thing that usually brings him most joy in life now brings him only misery.

The poet finds himself at an extremely low psychological ebb:

- He 'beweeps', or laments, his situation.
- He contemplates his life and 'curses' the series of events that brought him to this sorry state.
- He cries out futilely to God for help.
- He desperately envies other men their good fortune.
- He has come dangerously close to hating himself.

The poem, then, resembles Sonnet 30 ('When to the sessions') and Sonnet 66 ('Tired with all these'), which also depict the poet in a state of intense mental anguish.

Love

The poem's final six lines emphasise the deep love the poet has for the Fair Youth. All the poet has to do is 'think on' the Fair Youth and the despair described above lifts immediately. His almost unbearable despair is replaced by an equally intense joy, by a sense of euphoria wonderfully captured in the image of the lark rising from 'sullen earth' at daybreak and soaring into the dawn sky.

As we have seen, merely remembering the Fair Youth's love brings him such a wealth of happiness that he would not swap places with a king. He would not swap these thoughts or memories and the joy they bring him for all the earthly goods and power a king has at his disposal. The poem is similar in this regard to Sonnet 30 ('When to the sessions'), another poem where the poet's feelings of sorrow are immediately ended by the thought of the Fair Youth. It also brings to mind Sonnet 66 where the despairing poet decides to go on living because death would mean separation from the Fair Youth he loves so much.

As we noted above, there is a sense in this poem that the poet's relationship with the Fair Youth may have hit something of a rocky patch. The poet claims that the thing that usually brings him most joy in life now brings him only misery. Perhaps he is referring to their relationship, which usually delights him but in the present circumstances only causes him sorrow. The fact that the poet is 'all alone' also suggests that the relationship is at least temporarily on hold. This is also hinted at by line 13 where the poet remembers the Fair Youth's 'sweet love', perhaps suggesting that for the moment at least their relationship is in the past tense.

LANGUAGE

Form

Like all Shakespearean sonnets this one has fourteen lines divided into three quatrains and a closing couplet. Like many, but not all of the sonnets, it has a volta – or change of direction – in line 9: the poet goes from lamenting his miserable state to rejoicing in thoughts of the Fair Youth's love.

However, this sonnet does depart a little from the Shakespearean norm in terms of rhyme scheme. Lines 2 and 4 rhyme not only with each other but also with lines 10 and 12. The poem therefore has an ABAB CDCD EBEB FF rhyme scheme where normally the third quatrain would rhyme EFEF. This is the only time Shakespeare departs from the standard rhyme scheme used throughout the rest of the sonnets.

Tone

This poem is marked by two very distinct tones. In the first eight lines the tone is one of lament and sorrow, perhaps even self-pity, as the poet bewails his 'outcast state'. In the final six lines, however, the tone changes to one of ecstatic joy as the poet is moved to what borders on euphoria by thoughts of the Fair Youth's love.

Imagery

Perhaps the most striking image in this poem is that of the lark soaring into the sky at 'break of day' from where it has spent the night on the dark and 'sullen' earth: night giving way to morning and the flight of a songbird are two concepts we tend to associate with joy.

Figures of speech

It has been suggested that there is an element of personification in line 1, where the poet claims he is in 'disgrace with fortune' – meaning bad luck that has befallen him. Here, the concept of luck or fortune is presented almost as if it were a person – one who has recently formed a low opinion of the poet and withdrawn her help from him.

There are two instances of metonymy in this poem. Metonymy occurs when instead of calling something by its own name we call it by the name of something closely associated with it. We see this in line 3 where the poet declares that instead of praying to God he prays to Heaven, something closely associated with God.

We also see this in line 1. Instead of declaring that he is disgraced in the opinion or judgement of his fellow men, he says he is disgraced with their 'eyes'. It could be argued that eyes are closely associated with the faculty of judgement, being one of the main ways we assess other people and the world around us.

There is an instance of paradox in line 8. A paradox is a statement that initially seems to contradict itself. In this instance it seems contradictory that the thing the poet most enjoys makes him least happy. However, as we noted above, when we think a little about this statement we can see how it might make sense.

There is a most memorable simile in lines 10–12 where the poet compares his mental state to a lark. When he is in despair his mind resembles a lark resting on the dark earth throughout the night. Yet when he thinks of the Fair Youth and experiences intense joy, his mind resembles a lark soaring into the air at daybreak.

The phrase 'heaven's gate' in line 12 is a metaphor. As we have seen, it may be a metaphor for the sky into which the singing lark rises – in which case it is easy to imagine the sky as a kind of door or gateway, a layer separating the heavens above from the earth below. It may also be a metaphor for the poet's state of mind. The poet experiences such a state of complete happiness that he compares himself to someone standing outside the gates of Heaven. The implication is that the euphoric bliss he feels when thinking about the Fair Youth is only marginally less intense than the joy experienced by those in Heaven itself.

Line 12 is somewhat ambiguous in that it is not exactly who or what 'sings hymns at heaven's gate'. Does this phrase refer to the lark or to the poet's 'state' of mind? If it refers to the lark, then we can imagine 'heaven's gate' as the sky into which the lark rises singing in the morning. If it refers to the poet's state of mind, then we imagine 'heaven's gate' as a condition of total emotional euphoria, only one step removed from the bliss of being in Heaven itself.

Several critics have suggested that there is an element of hyperbole in this poem, that the poet exaggerates both his deep misery and almost euphoric joy for dramatic effect. Would the poet really refuse to swap places with a king? Or is he merely exaggerating to emphasise the strength of his emotions? The word 'When' at the very beginning of the poem might also give us pause. Is the poet describing a situation he is currently experiencing or has experienced in the past? Or is he presenting the Fair Youth with a hypothetical and exaggerated scenario in order to illustrate how much he values the youth's 'sweet love'?

Sound effects

The opening four lines of the poem features a plethora of long broad-vowel sounds that slow the pace of the verse, giving it a mournful, melancholic feel appropriate to the despair it describes. The poem's closing lines feature assonance and alliteration. We see alliteration with the repeated 'l' sound in 'Like to the lark' and with the repeated 'h' sound in 'hymns at heavens'. Assonance, meanwhile, occurs with the repeated 'a' sounds in line 11 and also the repeated 'e' sounds in line 12. It is also present through the repeated 'i' sound in 'sings hymns'. In these lines, assonance and alliteration combine to create a pleasant euphonious effect, reflecting the intense joy the poet experiences.

Sonnet 30 ('When to the sessions')

LINE BY LINE

There are times when the poet likes to think in silence. He considers such moments, or 'sessions' of silent contemplation, to be enjoyable or 'sweet'. However, on some such occasions he calls to mind events from the past. When the poet thinks about the past he becomes deeply melancholic.

- He thinks about all the things that he wanted but never got: 'I sigh the lack of many a thing I sought'.
- He laments the time he has wasted trying to get these things: 'wail my dear time's waste'.
- He thinks of good friends who have passed away. In death, these friends now dwell in an eternity of darkness, lost to those who continue to live in the world of time: 'precious friends hid in death's dateless night'.
- He recalls the hurt, or 'woe', that love has caused him in the past. Though he has long gotten over the heartache and misery ('long since cancell'd woe'), when he calls to mind events that broke his heart he can weep once again: 'weep afresh'.
- He thinks about the emotional cost of all that he has lost: 'moan the expense of many a vanish'd sight'.
- He calls to mind old grievances or complaints from the past: 'grieve at grievances fore-gone'.

He does not often cry but when he thinks of such things he can shed a great many tears: 'Then can I drown an eye (unused to flow)'. The regrets or grievances that the poet thinks about on such occasions are 'old' but he is capable of crying over them again: 'with old woes new wail'. These are 'fore-bemoaned' grievances for which he has already suffered. Yet he sadly ('heavily') goes through each of these gripes, or 'moans', in detail, recounting what happened: 'from woe to woe tell o'er/ The sad account'. By doing so, he 'pays' for them again with fresh tears and moans as though he had not already paid for them with tears and moans in the past: 'I new pay as if not paid before'. However, if on such occasions the poet calls to mind the Fair Youth, all his grief is cancelled out and his sorrow is brought to an end: 'if the while I think on thee (dear friend)/ All losses are restored and sorrows end'.

THEMES

Passage of time

The sonnet suggests that even with the passage of time, the grievances we suffer are not forgotten nor is the pain diminished. The poet weeps 'afresh' over heartache that he thought was 'long cancell'd', and grieves at 'grievances fore-gone'.

Time is also considered something precious, or 'dear', and the poet is particularly aggrieved when he thinks of the time he has wasted. He is perhaps especially pained by the time he spent trying to get things that he never got. It is likely that unrequited love is at the fore of his mind on this occasion.

Despair

The poet has not emerged from the misery and despair described in the preceding sonnet ('When in disgrace …'). In Sonnet 29 ('When in disgrace') he lamented his ill luck and the fact that he has become something of a social outcast. In Sonnet 30 ('When to the sessions') the poet continues to feel utterly miserable. But the focus has shifted from the present to the past. As the poet sits in silent thought, he decides to call to mind all the heartache and misery of the past. He thinks about the friends who have died and the pain that love has caused him. He thinks about all the things he wanted but never got, and of all the things he had and then lost. In the process he makes himself perfectly miserable. Though he has already suffered enough in the past, calling them to mind causes him to suffer still more. There is a sense in which the poet is wallowing in his misery and making little effort to snap himself out of it.

Love

Yet again, it is the poet's love for the Fair Youth that raises him out of his despair. Though he has called to mind countless woes and grievances, just thinking about his 'dear friend' for a while cancels out all the pain and misery he feels. In this regard, the sonnet resembles Sonnets 29 ('When in disgrace') and 66 ('Tired with all these') where, again, thoughts of the Fair Youth bring an end to the poet's sorrow.

However, we might imagine that the Fair Youth was also a contributor to the poet's misery. The 'woe' of love that the poet says he has 'long since cancell'd' no doubt involved the very friend that now helps him to forget the heartache of the past. Calling the Fair Youth his 'dear friend' suggests not only that the youth is very precious to him but that he is also perhaps emotionally costly. The poet has 'paid before' for the love he feels but is all the time ready to pay again ('new pay'). The poet's love for the Fair Youth is, therefore, at once a source of restoration and of loss.

LANGUAGE

Form

Like all Shakespearean sonnets this one has fourteen lines divided into three quatrains and a closing couplet. It has the ABAB CDCD EFEF GG rhyme scheme used in all but one of the sonnets.

Tone

Though the tone of the opening lines are relaxed, the sonnet quickly descends into misery as the poet laments all the hurt he has suffered in the past. Unlike Sonnet 29 ('When in disgrace') where a change of tone occurs in line 9, here no such 'turn' takes place. The tone remains dejected until the last two lines, where the despair lifts.

Figures of speech

The poet uses a metaphor when describing his friends who have died. He compares death to an endless night, a period of darkness that cannot be measured by time: 'death's dateless night'. The poet also describes his grievances or woes in terms of debts that have been paid but which still retain their effect: 'I new pay as if not before', 'weep afresh love's long since cancell'd woe'.

The poet makes use of anaphora (the repetition of a word or a sequence of words at the beginnings of neighbouring clauses to create emphasis) to emphasise the presence of ancient and ineradicable grief. Lines 4 and 9 begin with the same words – 'Then can

I …' – suggesting the familiarity of the experience. This is something that the poet has gone through on numerous occasions. The fact that three lines of the poem begin with the word 'And' adds further emphasises to the repetitive nature of the woe.

Repetition also features in the sonnet. In lines 9–11 the poet repeats the word 'woe' and the prefix 'fore'. He also uses words that share the same roots, such as 'grieve at grievances' and 'fore-bemoaned moan'.

Sound effects
The sonnet features some examples of alliteration. In the opening line the poet uses a number of words beginning with 's' to establish a relaxed tone: 'to the sessions of sweet silent thought/ I summon'. Line 4 features a series of words beginning with 'w'. Combined with the long 'a' and 'o' sounds, this line creates a melancholic effect in keeping with the poet's despair: 'with old woes new wail my dear time's waste'.

Imagery
The sonnet is rooted in legal and accounting imagery. The poet compares the times of silent thought to 'sessions', or the sittings, of a court. It is as though he has been called before the court to give an account of his expenses. To 'summon up' can mean both call to mind and to appear before a court to answer a charge or give evidence. Some of the expenses that the poet summons up have already been 'cancell'd'. Again, this is a term used in relation to legal documents that have been annulled or rendered void. Yet the poet must 'new pay' these 'as if not paid before'. The phrase 'tell o'er' can mean in accounting to sum up, and so at the end of the poem the poet totals the debt of his woe. However, thinking a while of the Fair Youth balances the debt.

Sonnet 60 ('Like as the waves')

LINE BY LINE

The waves resemble minutes
The poet describes how waves 'make towards' or move in the direction of the coastline: 'waves make toward the pebbled shore'. When a wave reaches the shoreline it disappears – dissipating and fizzling out among the pebbles. This process just goes on and on, each wave following the next and meeting its end upon the shoreline: 'Each changing place with that which goes before'.

Line 4 emphasises how the waves move 'forwards' to the shore consecutively, one after another, in a 'sequent' fashion. The poet declares that they 'toil' and 'contend' forwards, suggesting that their journey toward the shoreline is a struggle, that they must force their way onward towards their own destruction.

According to the poet, the minutes of our lives resemble the waves. Each minute of our lives passes quickly, like a wave racing to the shoreline. It disappears into nothingness like a wave dissolving among the pebbles. Minute follows minute in a relentless march into extinction, just as wave follows wave toward dissipation on the beach.

The progress of each human life
These lines describe the progress of each person's life. Before we are born we exist in 'the main of light', in a vast expanse of luminosity, in an ocean of pure illumination ('main' used to mean the ocean or the open sea). The poet seems to have in mind some mystical state of being our soul or consciousness occupies while waiting to be born. At the hour of our births we exit this light-filled realm and begin our human existences in the state of 'nativity' or infancy.

We then gradually move ('crawl') to 'maturity'. The poet seems to have the period between twenty and thirty in mind here. This is the time of life when we are fully physically developed. We are at our strongest, fittest and healthiest. For many people, this is also the period when they are at their most physically attractive. According to the poet, we are 'crowned' with the maturity we have achieved: 'wherewith being crowned'. This suggests that maturity is the highest and most glorious stage in man's development.

However, no sooner have we achieved this stage of development than 'crooked eclipses' emerge to 'fight' against us, to destroy the 'glory' we have attained: 'Crooked eclipses 'gainst his glory fight'. The phrase 'Crooked eclipses' means something like 'evil fortune'. This is because in Shakespeare's time eclipses of the sun and moon were associated with bad omens and ill luck. The phrase suggests the misfortunes that enter every life as we grow older and that rob us of the glory we enjoyed at our maturity; misfortunes such as ill health, physical frailty, mental and bodily slowness.

Time's ravages

These lines depict the ravaging effects of time upon the human body:

* Time gave us the gift of maturity, transforming us from helpless infants into powerful young adults. However, time also takes this gift away, transforming us from young adults into frail old pensioners: 'And Time that gave doth now his gift confound'. The word 'confound' here suggests that Time destroys, overturns or reverses the gift of maturity he once gave us.
* When we are in the phase of youthful maturity, we wear our good looks like a decoration – a 'flourish' that has been placed or 'set' upon our bodies. (We might think of beauty as a fancy accessory, a cape or hat the young are fortunate enough to wear.) Time, however, destroys this flourish. He 'transfixes' it, meaning that he runs it through with a lance, sword or similar weapon.
* Time ruins the smooth foreheads of beautiful youths, lining them with wrinkles: 'delves the parallels in beauty's brow'. Time is depicted as 'delving', or digging parallel lines, into the brows of good-looking young adults.
* Time feeds upon, or 'devours', those rare specimens of human beauty that reveal nature at its truest and most magnificent: time 'Feeds on the rarities of nature's truth'.

THEMES

Time

This is one of the many sonnets where Shakespeare emphasises how quickly and relentlessly time passes us by. The minutes of our lives race away from us like waves powering toward the shoreline.

Each minute disappears into nothingness just as each wave fizzles away upon the pebbles of the beach. Each minute of our lives is immediately followed by the next into extinction: 'Each changing place with that which goes before'. Minute follows minute in an endlessly consecutive, or 'sequent', process, like the waves crashing relentlessly onto the beach.

The poem also stresses that no sooner have we attained the crowning glory of 'maturity' than we begin to lose it. We have only a brief time to enjoy our youthful maturity – this period when we are at our fittest, healthiest and most attractive. It all too quickly comes under attack from various misfortunes that transform it gradually into old age.

Sonnet 18 ('Shall I compare thee') also addresses this theme with its depiction of how summer exists for all too short a time before it must give way to autumn. Sonnets 12 ('When I do count') and 116 ('Let me not') are others that emphasise how quickly our lives rush to their conclusion.

This poem also emphasises how time is a destroyer of youthful beauty. Time is depicted as a vicious tyrant with a 'cruel hand' who mercilessly wields his scythe. He gives us the gift of youthful beauty, for it is time that turns us from infants into mature yet youthful adults. Yet he also cruelly takes that gift away, transforming us from youthful adulthood to withered old age. Time is depicted as piercing beauty's 'flourish' with a weapon, digging lines into the foreheads of beautiful people, and feasting on the rare specimens of human beauty that nature produces.

There are several other sonnets where Shakespeare presents time as beauty's enemy. Sonnets 12, 18 and 116 are similar to the present poem in that they show beauty being laid waste by time's relentless march. Sonnet 12 has the poet dreading how the Fair Youth's beauty might be ruined by the 'wastes of time', while Sonnet 18 laments how everything beautiful is eventually

William Shakespeare

stripped, or 'untrimm'd', of its beauty by time's passage. Sonnet 116, meanwhile, shows time eliminating lovers' 'rosy lips and cheeks' with his 'bending sickle'.

This poem also emphasises how nothing is immune to time's ravages: 'And nothing stands but for his scythe to mow'. The passage of time will cause everything on earth to be destroyed or fade away. Sonnets 12 ('When I do count') and 65 ('Since brass, nor stone') are very similar in this regard. Sonnet 12 stresses that 'nothing 'gainst Time's scythe can make defence'. Sonnet 65 declares that even the strongest things, like 'gates of steel' and the oceans themselves, will eventually succumb to time's destructive force.

Art
This is one of several poems where the poet suggests that his verses can resist or overcome time. The poet suggests that his poetry will be around 'to times', for now and for all times to come. He suggests that as long as human history continues, people will read his lines. Though everything else might fade away, his poetry will 'stand' against the ravages committed by time's 'cruel hand'. It will do so 'in hope' – as a symbol or beacon of hope to all of us, as an indication that time's depredations can sometimes be resisted.

Because these poems will last forever, so will the 'worth' of the Fair Youth. In ages to come, people will read these sonnets and will find his qualities and beauty recreated in their imaginations. Therefore, due to the poet's skill and efforts, the Fair Youth's worth is one of the few or only things that will be spared time's ravages.

Sonnets 18 ('Shall I compare thee') and 65 ('Since brass, nor stone') also stress how the poet's writings will preserve the Fair Youth's qualities for centuries to come. However, it could be argued that the poet seems less confident in the present poem in his ability to stand firm against time's effects than he does in those others. In this poem, time is presented as such an all-consuming and irresistible force that the poet's boast in the last two lines just does not ring true. We are perhaps less convinced than we are in other sonnets of his work's ability to withstand time's ravages forever.

LANGUAGE

Form
Like all Shakespearean sonnets this one has fourteen lines divided into three quatrains and a closing couplet. It has the ABAB CDCD EFEF GG rhyme scheme used in all but one of the sonnets. Many of the sonnets have a 'turn' in line 9. This one, however, only exhibits a change of thought of feeling in its final two lines: the poet goes from lamenting the devastation caused by time to describing how his own poetry will somehow resist time's ravages. It is almost certainly not a coincidence that Shakespeare placed this sonnet that deals with hours and minutes as number 60 in his sequence: after all, there are sixty minutes in an hour.

Tone
Like many of Shakespeare's sonnets this is marked by two very distinct tones. In the first twelve lines the tone might be described as sorrowful, as the poet laments how quickly time passes us by, how youthful beauty swiftly fades, and how it seems 'nothing' whatsoever can withstand time's ravages.

However, we can imagine the final lines being spoken in a quiet tone of determination as the poet defiantly declares that his verse will withstand time's ravages and serve as a beacon of hope. Yet, as we noted above, this boast is perhaps delivered with less confidence in this sonnet than it is in several others on the course.

Imagery
One of the more obvious images in this poem is that of the waves rolling relentlessly 'forwards' toward the shoreline, one after another in an endlessly 'sequent' or consecutive fashion. Sea imagery also features in line 5. As we have seen, the poet suggests that before we are born we exist in 'the main of light', a vast expanse or ocean of light out of which we are plucked to take our place in this world. This image, in particular, has attracted a lot of praise from scholars and critics.

There is something militaristic about the waves' unceasing march towards the 'pebbled shore', as if they form an army assaulting the coastline. This sense is reinforced by the fact that in Shakespeare the word 'contend' often means to fight, while the word 'toil' is often associated with the physical exertions of battle and combat. This military imagery is continued with the mention of 'parallels', which were defensive trenches, in line 10. We also see it with the mention of 'transfix', meaning to pierce with a weapon, in line 9. The implication is that time is engaged in an endless and destructive war against us.

There is something almost cinematic about the imagery in lines 5–7 – almost as if were watching a film in fast-forward. We can visualise a baby crawling forward and turning into a mature and strong individual before our very eyes, only for that strength to decay under time's assault. Also potent in this poem is the image of time as a great destroyer – destroying youthful beauty and mercilessly wielding the dreaded scythe that nothing in this world can stand against.

Figures of speech

There are several personifications in this poem. The most vivid of these is the personification of time. Time is depicted as a 'cruel' tyrant, one who gives us the gift of mature strength but also brutally takes that gift away. He wields a scythe nothing in this world can stand against. He relentlessly destroys youthful beauty: he pierces it with his weapon and even 'feeds on' or devours it. He 'delves' deep lines into the smooth brows of beautiful people.

In line 5 the concept of nativity is personified. We visualise it as a baby, crawling along the floor. In line 6, meanwhile, the concept of maturity is personified. We are inclined to visualise it as a powerful and strong individual, one 'crowned' with its own strength. As noted above, an interesting feature of these lines is the way we visualise the personification of nativity transforming into that of maturity. Furthermore, in lines 9 and 10 the concepts of youth and beauty are personified. Youth has his 'flourish' pierced by one of time's weapons, while beauty has deep lines dug into its brow. There are several other figures of speech in this poem:

- There is an example of simile in lines 1–2 where the waves dissolving on the shore are compared to the minutes of our lives slipping away.
- There is an example of metaphor in line 6 where physical maturity is compared to a crown worn by those who have attained that state.
- There is arguably another metaphor in line 9 where beauty is described as a 'flourish' that is set on the young. Here, beauty seems to be compared to a fancy accessory, a cape or hat that the young are fortunate enough to wear.
- There is yet another metaphor in line 10 where the wrinkles on our foreheads are compared to 'parallels', which were trenches or ditches used in time of war.

There is an example of synecdoche in line 14 with the phrase 'time's cruel hand'. Synecdoche occurs when part of something is used to represent the whole. In this instance, time's hand is used to represent the entirety of this dreaded personification.

Sound effects

An interesting feature of this poem is the sense of 'drive', or forward momentum, we get in the opening four lines. Shakespeare masterfully lends these lines a fast pace and a strong rhythm that suggests the relentlessly consecutive, or 'sequent', march of the waves toward the shoreline.

Line 5 is rich in assonance, the repeated '*a*' and '*i*' sounds creating a pleasant musical effect appropriate to the wonderful image of 'the main of light'. Assonance also occurs with the repeated broad-vowel sounds in lines 8 and 12. Yet, in these instances it creates a sad, slow and melancholy effect – one appropriate to lines that lament time's passage.

There are several instances of cacophony in this sonnet:

- We see this in line 7 with its repeated, hard and clashing '*g*' and '*k*' sounds.
- We see a similar effect it in line 9 with its repeated '*t*', '*f*' and '*s*' sounds.
- A similar effect is also arguably created by the repeated '*b*', '*p*', and '*l*' sounds in line 10.

In each instance, these clashing consonants create a harsh musical effect – one appropriate to lines that describe time's relentless destruction.

William Shakespeare
Sonnet 65 ('Since brass, nor stone')

LINE BY LINE

If brass, stone, earth and sea are incapable of holding out against time, how can something as fragile as beauty hope to survive? Brass and stone are some of the strongest materials, yet they will rust and crumble over time. The earth and the sea are also long-lasting, and with their vastness ought to be able to resist time's ravages. But 'mortality' has greater power than they have: 'But sad mortality o'er sways their power'.

Time is described as something full of fury and 'rage', a force that destroys all before it. It is like a heartless tyrant or someone who has gone berserk with rage and cares not for what it destroys. Facing 'this rage', how can 'beauty' hope to defend itself: 'How with this rage shall beauty hold a plea'? Beauty is fragile and tender. It is like a 'flower' that can be all too easily trampled underfoot. It has no more substance than the sweet-smelling summer air: 'summer's honey breath'. How can such a fragile thing stand up against a force as powerful and brutal as time?

Against a tyrant, there are two possible defences. One can make a legal case and hope that the law and those who enforce the law will come to your aid. Or one can build a mighty fortress and hope that the tyrant will not be able to gain access. But time is such a powerful and terrible force that neither law nor mighty walls of rock can prevent him conquering and destroying.

In a legal case, beauty's 'action' would have no more strength than a 'flower' against such 'rage'. And were beauty to build walls to defend itself, time would lay siege. Time's days are like powerful battering rams that will smash open all defences and destroy everything within. How, the poet wonders, can something as fragile as beauty hope to survive such a 'wreckful siege' when mighty walls of rock that cannot be scaled and 'gates of steel so strong' are incapable of holding out: 'rocks impregnable are not so stout,/ Nor gates of steel so strong'.

These thoughts about time's indiscriminating power to destroy everything horrifies the poet. It is frightening to think that everything beautiful must perish: 'O fearful meditation!' Thinking about beauty's fragility at the hand of time makes the poet fearful for the Fair Youth and his beauty. He thinks that the Fair Youth is the most precious thing in the world: 'Time's best jewel'. He wonders how the Fair Youth can possibly hide from time and so avoid ageing and death.

The poet compares the Fair Youth to a 'jewel', and time to a pirate or thief who wishes to take the jewel and bury it in a chest ('Time's chest' could also be

considered in terms of a coffin): 'where, alack,/ Shall Time's best jewel from Time's chest lie hid?' Time is like a thief, and the beautiful things in the world are like jewels that he steals and buries. How, the poet wonders, can we stop time from getting his hands on the jewels of the world? Who can possibly stop time from stealing these beautiful objects: 'who his spoil of beauty can forbid?' ('spoil' means stolen goods). Is there anything strong enough to stop such a 'swift' and powerful thief?

The poet's immediate answer is that there is no hand strong enough to restrain time, no one powerful enough to prevent him acting as he wishes. But there is the smallest possibility that the Fair Youth's beauty and the poet's love for the Fair Youth might be preserved forever in the poet's work: 'That in black ink my love may still shine bright'. It would be a 'miracle' if the poet's work should survive the passage of time, if it had the strength or 'might' to endure, but it is his only hope.

THEMES

Time

Time is seen as something destructive. It is a brutal force that destroys everything. The poet likens the passage of time to a blind 'rage' that sweeps away everything in its path. It is like a heartless despot or tyrant who destroys and conquers without reason. It lays siege to towns and its weapons are its 'days', which are likened to battering rams that break down all defences no matter how strong. This army is not just interested in entering the town but in destroying the town upon entry. Its siege is 'wreckful'.

Nothing is strong enough to resist the passage of time. Even brass, steel and stone will eventually perish. The mightiest fortresses can be built but they will eventually crumble: 'rocks impregnable are not so stout,/ Nor gates of steel so strong'.

Beauty is particularly vulnerable to the passage of time. Things made of stone and steel, though they eventually will be destroyed, can abide for centuries. But physical beauty is fragile, 'no stronger than a flower'. Time will destroy it quicker than it will brass or stone. It can do little to defend itself.

There are several other sonnets where Shakespeare presents time as beauty's enemy. Sonnets 12 ('When I do count'), 18 ('Shall I compare thee') and 116 ('Let me not') are similar to the present poem in that they show beauty being laid waste by time's relentless march. Sonnet 12 has the poet dreading how the Fair Youth's beauty might be ruined by the 'wastes of time', while Sonnet 18 laments how everything beautiful is eventually stripped, or 'untrimm'd', of its beauty by time's passage. Sonnet 116, meanwhile, shows time eliminating lovers' 'rosy lips and cheeks' with his 'bending sickle'.

Love

The poet's love for the Fair Youth is again evident in this sonnet. When he reflects on the passage of time, it is the Fair Youth's death that most troubles him. He wants to do all he can to preserve his love from the ruins of time.

Art

This is one of several poems where the poet suggests that his verses can resist or overcome time.

LANGUAGE

Form

Like all Shakespearean sonnets this one has fourteen lines divided into three quatrains and a closing couplet. It has the ABAB CDCD EFEF GG rhyme scheme used in all but one of the sonnets.

The beginning of the third quatrain in a number of the sonnets brings about a 'turn', or shift in focus or tone. In this sonnet the poet uses the first two quatrains to consider time's power to destroy, and in the third quatrain thinks specifically of the Fair Youth.

Tone

There is a certain desperation and urgency to the tone of this sonnet. Three lines begin with 'O', signalling the poet's despair. The sonnet's three quatrains are composed of questions to which the poet desperately seeks a response. The final two lines of the sonnet offer something of a solution, and the tone is hopeful even though the poet is well aware that a miracle is required to defeat the force of time.

William Shakespeare

Figures of speech

The poet uses personification to depict time. He describes times 'swift' foot and wonders who or what can possibly trip him up or hold him back. Time is depicted as a thief who steals valuable jewels and hides them in a 'chest', and also as a despot who attacks and destroys towns.

A number of metaphors are at play in this sonnet to describe time and the destructive effects of time. As mentioned, the poet compares time to a wicked tyrant who cannot be reasoned with. Time is also compared to an army that lays siege to towns. Time's days are its battering rams, and these powerful weapons can destroy walls of rock and 'gates of steel'.

Beauty is compared to a flower and also to the sweet-smelling summer air. Both the flower and the perfumed air are weak and insubstantial, and suggest the vulnerability of beauty to the passage of time. The Fair Youth is described metaphorically as 'Time's best jewel'. He is like a precious stone that time longs to take and bury in his chest.

The last line features a paradox. The poet hopes that the 'black ink' with which he writes will allow his love to 'shine bright'.

Imagery

Like Sonnet 30 ('When to the sessions'), this sonnet contains legal imagery. The term 'o'er-sway' can mean to rule over or govern. To 'hold a plea' can mean to successfully present a legal case. The word 'action' can refer to a legal process. The poem likens the fragility of beauty to a weak individual who must face the wrath of a tyrant in court. Such a case, the poet says, stands no chance of victory.

The sonnet also contains military imagery. The poet compares time to an army laying siege to a town. The term 'hold out' in line 4 means to maintain resistance. The passing days are likened to battering rams. The 'rocks impregnable' suggests the walls around a town, and the 'spoil of beauty' suggests the spoils or goods taken from an enemy or a captured city in time of war.

Sound effects

The poem features euphony and cacophony. The fifth line is composed of soft, euphonious 'h' and 's' sounds when describing the summer air, and contrasts with the more grating, cacophonous 't' and 'k' sounds of the sixth line where the poet describes the destructive force of time. This reflects the subject of the sonnet, which considers beauty to be fair and fragile and time to be ugly and destructive.

Sonnet 66 ('Tired with all these')

LINE BY LINE

The poet uses a series of 'personifications' in this poem. Throughout, its qualities or ideas are depicted as if they were people. When the poet looks at the world he sees only wrong-doing, corruption and unfairness. He lists a number of these wrongs. The word 'As' in line 2 means 'As in the following', and is used to introduce this catalogue of woe.

Good people suffer

Everywhere the poet looks he sees good people suffering. He sees 'desert' – the quality of deservingness – being born as a beggar. This suggests how decent and worthwhile people are born into poor families and struggle to survive.

He sees 'purest faith' – the quality of integrity and good faith – being 'forsworn'. The word 'forswear' can mean to renounce something or to lie under oath. This line might suggest that society encourages people to renounce or give up their integrity and principles.

However, it might also suggest that society encourages honest people to traffic in lies and untruths.

He sees 'maiden virtue' – the quality of chastity or purity – being 'strumpeted' or prostituted. This might suggest that chaste people are forced or encouraged by society to become unchaste. It might also suggest that chaste people are often wrongly branded as being unchaste by society at large.

He sees 'right perfection' – the quality of moral goodness – being unjustly 'disgraced'. This suggests that those who do right are wrongly accused of doing evil, and are branded a disgrace by the society in which they live.

He sees the quality of 'simple truth' being wrongly branded 'simplicity', which in Shakespeare's time meant stupidity or idiocy. This suggests that those who dare to tell society truths it does not want to hear are denounced as being simple-minded, mad or foolish.

The undeserving get ahead

The undeserving, meanwhile, seem to get ahead in life. He sees the quality of 'needy nothing' dressed in fine, frivolous and ornamental clothes, being 'trimm'd in jollity'. This suggests people who might be described as nonentities – people who have 'nothing' in their personalities to recommend them, who are 'needy' or lacking when it comes to admirable qualities. The poet sees such people attaining worldly success and treating themselves to the most fashionable finery.

He sees 'Gilded honour shamefully misplaced'. The phrase 'gilded' or golden honour suggests promotion to positions of high office, power and authority. According to the poet, these honours have been 'shamefully misplaced'; they have been giving to individuals who do not deserve them.

The wrong people control society

The wrong people seem to be in charge of the society in which the poet lives:

* He sees the quality of 'strength' being 'disabled' by the quality of 'sway' or power. Those with energy and vigour are prevented from acting by the weak or 'limping' people who hold sway in this society.
* He sees the quality of 'art' being silenced or 'tongue-tied' by the quality of 'authority'. This suggests that those with knowledge and wisdom are prevented from sharing their expertise by those in power.
* He sees the quality of 'folly' or foolishness controlling the quality of 'skill', suggesting that people with real knowledge and ability are forced to carry out the bidding of the foolish.

The poet, then, depicts a society controlled by weak and foolish people who keep the genuinely talented down. Some critics see a hint of generational conflict in these lines. Perhaps the poet feels that the present leaders of society have held onto power too long; that they are now old, weak and mentally feeble; that they should make way for a younger and more vigorous generation.

The poet declares that the quality of 'good' has been captured by the quality of 'ill' or evil. 'Good is depicted as 'attending' ill, meaning that it has been forced to become ill's servant. The poet, then, feels he lives in a world where evil is the dominant force and good is powerless.

It is possible that line 9 refers to censorship. In Shakespeare's time, books and (especially) plays would sometimes be banned by the authorities because they were deemed to have an inappropriate moral or political message. The image of art being 'tongue-tied by authority' may represent the poet's resentment at this restriction by the state of artistic expression. It should be noted, however, that in Shakespeare the word art usually refers to general knowledge, intelligence and ability rather than to creative activities such as writing and painting.

THEMES

Despair

The poet has been plunged into despair by all the wrongs he sees around him. He is 'Tired with all these', exhausted by the unfairness and injustice of this life. He is simply fed up of living in a world like this:

* A world where good people are condemned to poverty simply by an accident of birth.
* A world where it is extremely difficult to maintain integrity and sexual purity.
* A world full of lies and hypocrisy, where the chaste

are branded unchaste, where those who do the right thing are 'unjustly disgraced', where those who tell uncomfortable truths are branded idiots.
* A world where the undeserving always seem to get ahead.
* A world where weak and foolish people run society at the expense of those with vigour, intelligence and ability.
* A world where good dominates evil.

The poet is so depressed by all this that he longs for death: 'Tired with all these, for restful death I cry'. He wants to die, leaving the wrongs and injustices of this world behind: 'Tired with all these, from all these would I be gone'. He imagines that death will be a pleasant, 'restful' experience, a sweet release from the hardships of this life. Sonnets 29 ('When in disgrace') and 30 ('When to the sessions') also depict the poet in an intense state of sorrow and despair.

Love
As we have seen, the poet longs to die, longs for what he sees as death's sweet release. The only thing preventing him from killing himself is his love of the Fair Youth: 'Save that to die I leave my love alone'. If he dies he will be separated from this young man he holds in such incredible esteem. If he dies he will be denied the Fair Youth's company and the Fair Youth will be denied his. In this regard, too, the poem bears comparison to Sonnets 29 and 30. In those earlier poems, the thought of the Fair Youth lifted the poet from despair into happiness. In the present poem, thinking of the Fair Youth might not relieve the poet's misery but at least it prevents him acting on his self-destructive urges.

Death
There are several instances in the sonnets where death is presented as something dark, alien and terrifying. We see this tendency in Sonnet 30 ('When to the sessions') with its reference to the poet's friends who have been lost in 'death's dateless night'. It is also present in Sonnet 18 ('Shall I compare thee') where death is presented as a menacing and threatening figure, bragging about those who have been forced to wander in its shadowy realm.

In the present poem, however, death is presented as a release from the wrongs and injustices of this corrupt and evil world. It is described as 'restful', suggesting that it as an easeful slumber that awaits us once we are through with the trials and tribulations of this life. In this regard, the present poem echoes 'Fear No More the Heat o' the Sun' – another poem that presents death as a release from suffering.

LANGUAGE

Form
Like all Shakespearean sonnets, this one has fourteen lines divided into three quatrains and a closing couplet. It has the ABAB CDCD EFEF GG rhyme scheme used in all but one of the sonnets. Many of the sonnets have a 'turn' in line 9. This one, however, only exhibits a change of thought of feeling in its very final line: the poet goes from lamenting the lies and hypocrisies of the world to describing how only the thought of the Fair Youth prevents him from taking his own life.

It is, perhaps, no coincidence that Shakespeare placed this as the sixty-sixth in his sequence of sonnets. In the Bible's Book of Revelation the number 666 is associated with the devil and, in particular, with a period before the end of the world when the devil's influence will hold sway over all the earth. Perhaps the number 66 is meant to echo 666, just as this sonnet describes an evil time not unlike that predicted in the Bible.

Tone
The tone in this poem is one of extreme world-weariness. The poet seems disgusted and horrified at the injustices he sees around him. Yet his response is not one of rage or fury; instead, he comes across as simply tired and worn out by the world's endless wrongs. Living in such a world has left him so wearied and exhausted that he longs for the 'rest' his death will bring him. The repetition of the phrase 'Tired with all these' in lines 1 and 13 emphasises just how world-weary the poet has become.

Figures of speech
Perhaps the most notable feature of this poem is the large amount of personifications deployed throughout. Various abstract qualities are presented as if they were human beings. The qualities of 'maiden virtue', 'strength', 'art' and so on are all presented as human beings capable of suffering various unfortunate fates in the unjust world the poet describes.

It should be noted that the phrase 'gilded honour' is perhaps not a personification' instead, it brings to mind the golden items we might associate with awards, honours and positions of power: medals, sceptres and chains of office.

Also noteworthy is the description of folly as being 'doctor-like'. In Shakespeare's time, the word 'doctor' was applied more to learned scholars than to medical professionals. The phrase therefore refers to what was the traditional personification of folly as a pompous professor in fully academic gown and regalia. This depiction of folly is to be found in the work of Erasmus and in that of other prominent writers of the period.

An important feature of this poem is its use of anaphora. Anaphora occurs when a number of neighbouring lines each begin with the same word or phrase. In this instance there is something very effective about the way each item in the poet's list of wrongs beings with the word 'And'. We get the impression that this catalogue of injustices might just go on and on, relentlessly moving from one evil to the next: 'And … And … And'. The technique powerfully conveys the poet's low opinion of the society in which he lives.

Sonnet 73 ('That time of year')

LINE BY LINE

This sonnet is a reflection of growing old. The poet compares his ageing condition to the autumn season, the onset of night, and the dying flames of a fire.

The poet says that you may see in him the time of life that is much like the start of winter. The leaves that remain on the trees are yellow. Some trees are all but stripped of their leaves, whilst others stand completely bare. The branches are battered by the cold wind and 'shake' against it. The birds that recently ('late') stood upon the branches singing have departed: 'where late the sweet birds sang'. The poet compares the branches to 'choirs'. The choir is the part of a church given over to singers. The branches are, therefore, like abandoned choirs that have fallen into a state of ruin: 'Bare ruin'd choirs'.

In the ageing poet you will see the day's end: 'the twilight of such day'. The sun is setting and darkness is slowly replacing the light of day. The night's darkness is slowly taking the day's light away: 'Which by and by black night doth take away'. The night is akin to death: its darkness 'seals up' all who sleep.

The poet finally likens his ageing condition to a fire that is almost burnt out. He compares his body to the fuel that nourishes the fire. The fire itself is the life force or vitality that consumes the fuel. As we live we consume our bodies just like a fire consumes its fuel. A youthful body is, therefore, like a log that is in perfect condition. As we live, this log is slowly consumed until only ashes remain.

The poet says that he has burnt up his youth and now has very little fuel remaining: 'In me thou seest the glowing of such fire/ That on the ashes of his youth doth lie'. When the fire has completely burnt out, only ashes will remain. The poet compares this bed of ashes to 'the death-bed' upon which his life 'must expire'. The fire of life will eventually be choked by the very fuel that once nourished it; the log of youth having turned completely to ash, the fire will be extinguished.

Since the poet is moving towards death and has little time left, he hopes that the Fair Youth's love will be strengthened by this fact. As he will not be around for much longer, he hopes that in the time remaining he will be loved all the more, and will be considered precious: 'This thou perceiv'st, which makes thy love more strong,/ To love that well which thou must leave ere long'.

THEMES

Time

The poet uses three metaphors to describe his ageing self. He says that he is like the winter trees that are barren of leaves and from which the song birds have flown. Such a comparison suggests the loss of beauty as the body withers and decays. The shaking of the branches against the cold suggests the weakening and vulnerability that comes with age. The 'Bare ruin'd choirs' and the absence of the 'sweet birds' tells, perhaps, of the poet's loss of joy and inspiration.

The passage of time is again evident in the second metaphor, where the poet compares his time of life to the evening. He is drawing close to the end of his life just as the day is nearing night. The comparison suggests that he has little time left before he is engulfed in death's darkness.

The final metaphor suggests that with the passage of time our bodies are consumed by the very life it enables, just as the fuel of a fire is consumed by the very fire it feeds. The passage of time is, therefore, not kind. Our lives are a progression towards decay, decrepitude and death.

Death

The sonnet likens death to the darkness of night. Night is a form of death: 'Death's second self'. Just as the night eliminates the day's light, so death consumes our lives totally. And just as the night's darkness surrounds us when we sleep, sealing us up 'in rest', so the darkness of death will engulf us when we die. The poet also compares death to the extinguishing of a fire. He says that the bodies that sustain our existence must eventually be consumed, just as the fire's fuel will eventually be consumed by the fire it feeds.

There are several instances in the sonnets where death is presented as something dark. We see this tendency in Sonnet 30 ('When to the sessions') with its reference to the poet's friends who have been lost in 'death's dateless night'. It is also present in Sonnet 18 ('Shall I compare thee') where death is presented as a menacing and threatening figure, bragging about those who have been forced to wander in its shadowy realm.

Unlike a number of sonnets that describe death as something terrifying, here the poet seems to be more accepting of the fact. He does not attempt to find a way to defeat death but, rather, looks to make the most of the time he has left.

Love

The sonnet suggests that pending death ought to make us more appreciative of those we love. The poet says that the end of his life is drawing near, and so his time is limited. He calls on the Fair Youth to appreciate this fact and to love him all the more because soon enough they will be parted by death: 'love that well which thou must leave ere long'.

There is a sense in which the poet is pleading here for love. He seems to be exaggerating his pending demise in order to gain his beloved's affections.

LANGUAGE

Form

Like all Shakespearean sonnets, this one has fourteen lines divided into three quatrains and a closing couplet. It has the ABAB CDCD EFEF GG rhyme scheme used in all but one of the sonnets.

Tone

The tone of the sonnet is rather plaintive, contemplating as it does the end of life. Yet the final two lines sound more positive as the poet calls on his beloved to love him all the more strongly in the time that he has remaining.

Figures of speech

The sonnet is constructed around three metaphors, each describing the poet's ageing self and his advancement towards death. He is like the autumn, the season in which trees shed their leaves and birds depart for warmer climates. Just as the year is advancing towards its end, with winter near at hand, so the poet is advancing towards his life's end, with death near at hand. The second metaphor for his time of life is the day that draws towards night. The dwindling light of day represents the poet's dwindling life, and the coming night corresponds with death. The final metaphor again suggests the pending expiration of the poet's life. He is just like the fire that has nearly consumed all its fuel.

The poet also uses a metaphor to describe the branches

that the birds and leaves have deserted. He compares them to 'choirs' – the place in a church where the singers assemble. The trees are therefore like abandoned buildings that have fallen into disrepair: 'Bare ruin'd choirs'.

The sonnet also features anaphora. The poet begins both the second and the third quatrain with the same words, 'In me thou seest …'.

The notion that the very bodies which sustain us also in the end consume us is paradoxical: 'Consumed with that which it was nourished by'.

Sonnet 94 ('They that have power')

LINE BY LINE

The Fair Youth has provided the poet with a great deal: friendship, intimacy that may or may not be of a sexual nature, access to a world of wealth and influence, psychological support and, perhaps, even financial support for his writing. He has promised the poet that this relationship will continue into the future. Now, however, the poet feels that the Fair Youth is on the verge of abandoning him. In the sonnets leading up to this one, he reveals his suspicion that the Fair Youth is about to betray the promises he has made. This is the context in which the poem must be understood.

The poet praises a certain type of blessed person. These people are defined by three characteristics: they are highly attractive to others, they exhibit a high-degree of psychological self-control, and they have the power to cause emotional harm to others but choose not to do so. These blessed people seem to be highly attractive to those around them. We get this impression from the poet's description of them 'moving others'. This suggests that their beauty caused others to fall in love with them – to experience intense and overwhelming emotion. These blessed people exhibit a high degree of psychological self-control:

* They are described as resembling 'stone' and as being 'cold'. They keep their emotions in check and do not allow their feelings to influence their acts, choices and decisions.
* They are the 'lords and owners' of their own faces. They are totally in command of their outward appearance – of their facial expressions and body language – revealing only what they want to reveal about their inner selves.
* They are described as being 'to temptation slow', suggesting that they are completely in control of their needs and desires. They do not experience or give in to temptation in the way normal people do.
* While they move others, they remain 'unmoved' themselves. Their beauty causes others to experience emotional turmoil, yet they remain totally in control of their own inner state.

These blessed people have the 'power to hurt' others in the context of love, romance and relationships. However, they choose not to do so. They do not deliberately cause others emotional harm: 'They that have power to hurt and will do none' (in this line, the word 'none' means 'no hurt'.) They do not do the thing that they look most likely to do: 'That do not do the thing they most do show'. Though we expect them to hurt those around them, they avoid doing so.

The poet hopes that the Fair Youth will turn out to be one of these blessed people. The Fair Youth already has the physical attractiveness and emotional self-control that such people require. Yet it is not clear that the Fair Youth will avoid causing emotional harm to those around him. The poet, of course, is thinking about himself here. He is urging the Fair Youth not to harm him, not to betray him by breaking the various promises he has made to him in the past. If the Fair

Youth avoids causing this type of hurt he will become one of the blessed people described above:

- He will justly receive God's blessing: 'They rightly do inherit heaven's graces'.
- He will belong to a group considered far greater than other men: 'Others [are] but stewards of their excellence'.
- He will belong to a special group of individuals responsible for 'husbanding' or carefully managing 'nature's riches'.

However, if the Fair Youth does end up causing this type of hurt to the poet and, presumably, to others, his soul and personality will become corrupted. The Fair Youth has been born with a moral and noble temperament. Yet when such natural-born moral people go bad, they go incredibly bad: 'For sweetest things turn sourest by their deeds'. They actually become more evil than those born with a naturally wicked character. The poet uses a metaphor to describe this. He mentions a sweet flower of the summertime: 'The summer's flower is to the summer sweet'. Yet when such a beautiful bloom is infected by a parasite, it becomes fouler than even the lowliest or 'basest' weed: 'But if that flower with base infection meet,/ The basest weed outbraves his dignity'. The basest weed will outdo or 'outbrave' it in terms of dignity and splendour. After all, a sweet lily that 'festers' or rots smells far worse than any weed.

Note 1: The line 'Others but stewards of their excellence' can have two meanings, depending on how we interpret the word 'their' in line 8. Does the word 'their' refer to the blessed ones or does it refer to the 'others'? The first reading suggests that the blessed are served by the rest of us, that we function as their 'stewards' or servants.

The second reading suggests that the blessed ones are permanently great while we enjoy whatever greatness we might possess in only a temporary and uncertain fashion. They own their greatness the way a lord owns a manor, while we only possess greatness briefly, like a steward administering a kingdom on behalf of its owner.

Note 2: The phrase 'husband nature's riches from expense' can also have two meanings. It might suggest that this blessed few are somehow given power and control over the riches of the natural world, and are given the task of preventing these riches from going to waste. However, it is difficult to visualise precisely what the poet means by this.

The line might also suggest sexual self-control: these blessed ones are themselves 'nature's riches' and must have sexual intercourse only sparingly and with fitting partners who are worthy of them. They must ensure their precious genes do not go to waste but are passed on appropriately to the next generation.

THEMES

Love: unequal love

This poem is a masterful study of an unequal relationship. The friendship between the poet and the Fair Youth is unequal because the Fair Youth is younger, better looking, wealthier and from a higher social class. This inequality is reinforced by the Fair Youth's icy personality: he is one of those people who exhibit a high degree of psychological self-control, who is 'as stone/ Unmoved, cold'. It is further reinforced by the poet's fear that the Fair Youth is about to abandon him, to forget the promises he has made to him in the past.

The poem, then, is a portrait of a relationship where one party distinctly has the upper hand and has 'the power to hurt' the other. As we have seen, the poet's response to this situation is to point out the consequences of the Fair Youth's actions. If the Fair Youth hurts him, if he exercises this 'power to hurt', his soul and personality will become foul and corrupt. However, if he does not exercise this power, if he refrains from hurting the poet, then he will join the ranks of the truly blessed, he will 'rightly inherit heaven's graces'. However, there can be little doubt that the poet is acting from a position of extreme weakness within the context of the relationship.

Criticism of the Fair Youth?

This is one of many poems where the poet celebrates the Fair Youth's beauty and other fine qualities. The Fair Youth's beauty is suggested in the description of him as a 'sweet' summer bloom: 'The summer's flower is to the summer sweet'. This echoes the comparison of the Fair Youth with summer in Sonnet 18 ('Shall I compare thee'). It also brings to mind celebrations of the Fair Youth's beauty in Sonnets 12 ('When I do count') and 65 ('Since brass, nor stone').

This poem also praises the Fair Youth's personality, celebrating the high degree of psychological self-control he exhibits, how he is 'Unmovèd, cold and to temptation slow'. In this regard it resembles Sonnet 18, another poem that praises the Fair Youth's self-restraint, describing how 'temperate' he is.

In this sonnet, however, the poet also comes very close to actually criticising the Fair Youth. We see this in line 9 where we are told that the summer flower exists only for itself: 'Though to itself it only live and die'. The implication is that while the Fair Youth is a beautiful person, he 'lives and dies' only for himself. It suggests that he has a self-absorbed, self-contained and possibly even selfish existence – that other people tend to be beneath his attention or even his notice.

Furthermore, the poet declares that when moral and noble people such as the Fair Youth become wicked, they become extremely wicked. Therefore, if the Fair Youth betrays the poet, he will sink to depths of evil: 'the sweetest things turn sourest by their deeds'. The Fair Youth may retain the outer beauty celebrated in this and so many other sonnets but on the inside his soul and personality will become foul and corrupted. His inner self will 'fester' or rot like a beautiful lily afflicted with a 'base infection'.

There is also an implication that the Fair Youth has not been entirely honest with the poet. This is perhaps hinted at in line 2, which some critics interpret in the following way: the Fair Youth has 'shown' himself in a certain light to the poet, making him great promises and earning his trust. Yet now he will not act in the way he has suggested he will act. He will 'do' nothing about keeping the promises he has made. It has been suggested that line 7, too, implies the Fair Youth's dishonesty. As we have seen, this line praises the youth's command over his outward appearance. Yet it perhaps also suggests that he is not truly trustworthy, that his outward demeanour disguises what he really thinks and intends.

Also noteworthy in this regard is the description of the Fair Youth in lines 3–4. Superficially, as we have seen, these lines are intended as praise of the Fair Youth's great restraint and self-control. Yet is there not also an element of criticism in these lines? There is something a little unpleasant about the idea of someone who 'moves' others while remaining unmoved himself. Similarly, the idea of someone being 'cold' and 'like stone' also has negative connotations.

Even the thought that the Fair Youth is 'slow to temptation' can be interpreted in a negative light, as suggesting that the Fair Youth lacks the normal human desires and inclinations. All in all, then, these lines can be read as suggesting that the Fair Youth is cold-hearted, emotionless and callously indifferent to his impact on those around him.

Chastity

An alternative reading of the poem interprets it in light of sexual chastity. They suggest that the Fair Youth is on the verge of some affair or sexual promiscuity. On this reading, line 2 suggests the following: the Fair Youth 'most shows' – really looks like – he is about to engage in such an affair. By doing so he will cause the poet deep and terrible emotional 'hurt'.

The poet urges him not to exercise this 'power to hurt', not to have the affair he so looks like having. He urges him to resist 'temptation', to remain 'cold', 'unmoved' and 'as stone' in the face of his desires. By doing so he will become one of the blessed, inheriting 'heaven's graces' and becoming more excellent than other men.

The Fair Youth is himself one of 'nature's riches'. By exhibiting such sexual self-control, he will 'husband' or manage himself in an appropriate fashion. By having sexual intercourse only sparingly and with fitting partners who are worthy of him, he will ensure his precious genes do not go to waste but are passed on appropriately to the next generation. However, if the Fair Youth fails to exhibit such self-control, his personality will become debased and corrupted. His soul will rot, or 'fester', like a beautiful lily infected with a parasite.

LANGUAGE

Form

Like all Shakespearean sonnets this one has fourteen lines divided into three quatrains and a closing couplet. It has the ABAB CDCD EFEF GG rhyme scheme used in all but one of the sonnets. Like many of the sonnets, it has a volta (change of direction); this occurs in line 9. The poet goes from discussing fairly abstract characteristics and personality traits to describing the highly vivid image of the summer flower.

Tone
It is extremely difficult to determine the precise tone of this poem. Do we imagine the poet speaking in a desperate and pitiful tone, as if he is urgently pleading with the Fair Youth not to abandon him? Or do we imagine him speaking in a bitter, sarcastic and recriminatory tone – criticising the Fair Youth for thinking about breaking the promises he has made? Alternatively, perhaps we imagine the words being spoken in a preachy and superior tone, as if the poet is lecturing the Fair Youth on what proper behaviour actually is.

Imagery
The opening eight lines of this poem are rather abstract and philosophical, and contain little in the way of imagery. However, this is made up for by the intensely vivid images of rotting and corruption in lines 9–14. We are presented with a 'sweet' summer flower being corrupted by a 'base infection' until it becomes fouler than even the ugliest weed. We are presented with lilies that 'fester' or rot until they give off a stench worse than any weed.

Figures of speech
There is an example of simile in line 3 where those who are emotionally self-controlled are compared to things made out of stone.

There is another example of simile in lines 9–14 where the Fair Youth's potential behaviour is compared to that of a flower. If the Fair Youth behaves in this inappropriate manner, his inner self will become foul and corrupted, just as a summer flower decays and 'festers' when it meets with infection.

There is an example of metaphor in line 7 where those who control their demeanour and facial expressions are described as being 'lords and owners' of their own faces.

There is arguably an example of metonymy in line 5. Metonymy occurs when we call something by the name of a thing associated with it rather than by its own name. In this instance, the poet is talking about graces that come from God. Yet he substitutes the term 'heaven' for the word 'God' because the two terms are closely associated.

Sound effects
Assonance occurs in lines 5–8 where the repeated broad-vowel sounds create a pleasant musical effect:

- We see it in the repeated 'u', 'a' and 'e' sounds in 'husband nature's riches from expense'.
- We see this with the repeated 'a' and 'o' sounds in 'They are the lords and owners of their faces'.
- We see it with the repeated 'e' sound in 'Others but stewards of their excellence'.

This plethora of assonance creates a solemn and stately music, appropriate to the noble, blessed individuals it describes.

By contrast, the poem's final six lines contain several instances of cacophony. We see this with the repeated clashing 'b', 'd' and 't' sounds in line 12. We see it with the repeated 's', 't' and 'd' sounds in line 13. We also see it with the repeated 'l', 'f' and 's' sounds in line 13. These repeated clashing consonants create a harsh, grating and unpleasant musical effect suitable to the images of rotting and corruption contained within these lines.

William Shakespeare

Sonnet 116 ('Let me not')

LINE BY LINE

This sonnet describes what love should ideally be. True love, the poet states, should have no 'impediments'. If two people are honestly in love, their love should last forever and nothing should be able to impede or destroy it.

Love should not change just because circumstances change. If the love between two people alters when they or their circumstances change, then it is not true love: 'Love is not love/ Which alters when it alteration finds'. Nor should love yield or change direction when the loved person ceases to love: 'Or bends with the remover to remove'. Again, if love 'bends' or shifts whenever someone changes or departs, then it is 'not love'.

True love is like something that never alters or moves. It is like a sea mark, a prominent navigational feature for the guidance of ships: 'an evèr-fixed mark'. In the days before lighthouses, mariners used well-known prominent features on the land as a guide to fix their position at sea. The spires of coastal churches, towers, or outcrops of rock of a particular shape or colour were obvious sea marks. Such marks stand firm in storms ('tempests'), and are always there to guide the ships when needed. They are never 'shaken' or destroyed no matter how bad the conditions they must weather: 'an evèr-fixed mark/ That looks on tempests and is never shaken'.

In a similar regard, true love is like a star that remains static in the night sky and so serves as a fixed point of reference. The poet would seem to have the Pole Star (or North Star) in mind here. In the northern hemisphere, it always appears to be unmoving in the northern sky, while all the other stars circle around it. Such a star is an invaluable guide to every ship that is 'wandering' or possibly lost: 'It is the star to every wandering bark'. Although we can measure the distance from the earth to the stars (or measure its position relative to the horizon), we cannot place a value on a star: 'Whose worth's unknown, although his height be taken'. Love is also something whose 'worth' or value cannot be known.

Love is not effected by the passage of time. It does not age or wither. In this regard, it does not have to adhere to or bend to time's rules: 'Love is not time's fool'. Those who are in love, however, are at time's mercy. Lovers must age, wither and die, their 'rosy lips and cheeks' wrinkle and decay, but the love they feel should never alter. Mortal beauty will be destroyed over time, cut down by time's 'sickle'. Beauty is within time's range or 'compass', but love exists beyond it and does not change with the passage of time: 'Love alters not with his brief hours and weeks'. Love can bear the passage of time, can abide right up until the end of time or the last day of the world: 'But bears it out even to the edge of doom'.

The poet says that if he is mistaken in his belief that love is eternal and it can be proved that he is wrong ('If this be error and upon me proved'), then he has never written anything and no man has ever loved: 'I never writ, nor no man ever loved'. The suggestion here seems to be that if love is not as the poet has described, then it does not actually exist. If this is the case, then all that the poet has written about love would have no substance or meaning, and it would be as though he had never written anything.

THEMES

Time
This sonnet again considers the passage of time. Time is described as a destroyer, someone who wields a sickle and cuts down all before it. It is especially cruel to beautiful things. The poet mentions the 'rosy lips and cheeks' of young lovers, and says that these will be ravaged by time. However, love is not ruled by time. Unlike the lover's 'rosy lips and cheeks' that are at time's mercy, love exists beyond its realm or 'compass', and so avoids having to become time's slave, or 'fool'. True love is something eternal and so cannot be effected by time.

Love
The sonnet considers what ideal or 'true' love should be. True love never changes no matter how much the world or those who love change. If love 'alters' or

'bends', it is 'not love'. Love is something permanent, an 'ever-fixed mark' that is always there. It remains steadfast even through the roughest times: 'looks on tempests and is never shaken'.

Love is not something we can ever hope to completely understand. It is something mysterious, like the stars in the sky. The poet says that its 'worth's unknown'.

The opening words 'Let me not' can be understood in different ways. The poet could be saying that he refuses to admit to any barriers to true love. It is as if someone is arguing with him and saying that there are obstacles to true love. The poet is basically saying that he will not allow this argument to stand. In other words, he is saying 'I will not grant you the possibility of there being impediments to the course of true love.'

Alternatively, the poet could be saying that neither he nor anyone should be allowed to become an impediment to the union of two true-minded individuals. If two people are genuinely in love and want to be together, nothing should prevent this from happening. In other words, he is saying 'Do not let me introduce impediments to your union.'

LANGUAGE

Form

Like all Shakespearean sonnets this one has fourteen lines divided into three quatrains and a closing couplet. It has the ABAB CDCD EFEF GG rhyme scheme used in all but one of the sonnets.

The sonnet contains a slight shift in emphasis in line 9 where the poet considers love in terms of time. This change, or 'turn', is a common feature of the Shakespearean sonnet.

Fear No More the Heat o' the Sun

William Shakespeare

LINE BY LINE

This poem features in *Cymbeline*, act 4, scene 2. A character called Imogen has apparently died and is being laid to rest. Two other characters, Guiderius and Arviragus, make this speech over her body.

Guiderius stresses that Imogen has done what she was put on this earth to do: 'Thou thy worldly task hath done'. She has now gone 'home' – to some kind of restful afterlife. There, she will be rewarded for having lived in a good manner. As Guiderius wittily puts it, she has gone to the next life where she will receive her wages for having lived well in this one: 'Home art gone, and ta'en thy wages'.

Guiderius and Arviragus emphasise that nothing can hurt Imogen anymore. In death, she passed beyond all harm. They mention a number of the torments of this life, stressing that Imogen need no longer have any fear of such things:

- She need no longer fear the sun's heat.
- She need no longer fear the icy storms and blizzards of winter: 'the furious winter's rages'.
- She need no longer fear that meteorites (known in Shakespeare's time as 'thunder-stones') or bolts of lightning might strike her: 'Fear no more the lightning flash,/ Nor the all-dreaded thunder-stone'.
- She need no longer fear the wrath of cruel lords for she is now beyond the reach of their power: 'fear no more the frown of the great/ Thou art past the tyrants' stroke'.
- She need no longer fear 'slander', having her good name attacked, or being unfairly and overhastily criticised by others: 'Fear not slander, censure rash'.
- She need have no more worries about where her clothes, food and other goods will come from: 'Care no more to clothe and eat'.
- She need no longer fear emotional turmoil: 'Thou hast finished joy and moan'.

Imogen is in a place where strength and weakness no longer matter. To her, strength (symbolised by the oak) is the same as weakness (symbolised by the reed).

Guiderius and Arviragus stress that everyone in this life will eventually die and turn to dust. This will happen to wealthy young people: to 'Golden lads and girls'. It will also happen to poorer young people – for example, those who work as 'chimney-sweepers'. No one will be spared this fate: not kings ('sceptre'), not scholars ('learning'), not medical doctors ('pyhsic'), and not all the world's young lovers. All will eventually follow Imogen. All will 'consign to', or join, her in the process of dying and turning to dust.

Guiderius and Arviragus hope that Imogen will have a 'quiet consummation', that her body will be blended or consummated with the earth in a peaceful and uninterrupted fashion. They pray her rest will not be disturbed by evil forces: 'Nothing ill come near thee!' They pray that sorcerers ('exorcisers'), witches and ghosts will leave her grave alone:

No exorciser harm thee!
Nor no witchcraft charm thee!
Ghost unlaid forbear thee!

There is a sense here that the exorcisers and witches might use their dark arts to disturb Imogen's rest, perhaps by summoning or 'charming' her spirit or her body back to life. Guiderius prays that ghosts will 'forbear' or avoid the temptation to interfere with Imogen's grave. The ghost is described as 'unlaid' because it has not been subjected to the rites or ceremonies that will allow it to find peace once more.

Guiderius and Arviragus conclude their speech by wishing that Imogen will continue to be remembered after her death: 'Renowned be thy grave'. They want her fame or renown to live on among those who knew her though she herself has passed away.

THEMES

Time

Like many of the sonnets, this poem emphasises just what a powerful destroyer time is. Every living person will eventually die and turn to dust. It does not matter if you are rich like the 'Golden lads' or poor like a 'chimney-sweeper'. It does not matter if, like a king, you possess great earthly power, or if, like a scholar, you possess great learning. Time's passage treats everyone the same. Nothing can resist its implacable march. Sonnets 12 ('When I do count'), 60 ('Like as the waves') and 65 ('Since brass, nor stone') also depict time as an all-powerful destructive force nothing can stand against.

There is a sense in which this poem particularly laments the damage time does to youthful beauty, in how all the 'Golden lads and girls' and 'the lovers young' must eventually 'come to dust'. In this regard, too, the present poem echoes several of the sonnets on the course: in Sonnet 60 ('Like as the waves') we are told how time gives us the gift of youthful beauty only to cruelly take that gift away again, while Sonnet 12 ('When I do count') has the poet dreading how the Fair Youth's beauty might be ruined by the 'wastes of time'. Sonnet 18 ('Shall I compare thee') laments how everything beautiful is eventually stripped, or 'untrimm'd', of its beauty by time's passage. Sonnet 116 ('Let me not') shows time eliminating lovers' 'rosy lips and cheeks' with his 'bending sickle'.

Death

There are several instances in the sonnets where death is presented as something dark, alien and terrifying. We see this tendency in Sonnet 30 ('When to the sessions') with its reference to the poet's friends who have been lost in 'death's dateless night'. It is also present in Sonnet 18 ('Shall I compare thee') where death is presented as a menacing and threatening figure, bragging about those who have been forced to wander in its shadowy realm.

In the present poem, however, death is presented as a release from the evils and difficulties of this world. Now that Imogen has passed away, she need no longer worry about the trials and tribulations of this life:

- Nature can no longer harm her with its heat, blizzards of winter, meteorites or lightning.
- Other people cannot harm her, whether they be angry cruel tyrants, people who gossip maliciously or people who unfairly criticise others.
- She need no longer worry about material survival (obtaining food, clothes and other worldly goods).
- She will no longer suffer from psychological or emotional upheaval.

Death, then, is presented almost as a welcome release from the trials and difficulties of living. In this regard the poem echoes Sonnet 66 ('Tired with all these'), where the poet is 'Tired with all these', with all the evils of this world, and longs to die so he can move beyond their reach.

Death is also presented as something peaceful and soothing, a restful experience that awaits us after we have worked to accomplish our 'worldly task'. Its rest is depicted as the 'wages', or reward, we receive for labouring in this life. In this regard, too, the present poem resembles Sonnet 60 ('Like as the waves') with its depiction of death as a 'restful' slumber.

Despair

Several critics have identified an element of despair in this poem. They suggest it presents human existence as grim, horrible and brutal, an endless series of trials and tribulations from which death is the only escape. On this reading, the poem once again resembles Sonnet 66 ('Tired with all these'), which depicts this world as a place of wrongs, evils and injustices that causes the poet to despair and cry out for the release of 'restful death'.

LANGUAGE

Form

Though this piece is spoken by two individuals, it forms a perfect poem of four stanzas of six lines each. Each of the first three stanzas rhymes ABABCC, while the fourth rhymes AABBCC. The first three stanzas each conclude with a rhyme between 'dust' and 'must', creating an effect not unlike that of a song's chorus or refrain.

Tone

Because this poem is a kind of funeral song, we can imagine it spoken in a solemn and sombre tone of voice. We can imagine a sorrowful tone of lament perhaps tinged with a faint note of uplift, for while Imogen may be dead, there is at least the consolation that she has moved beyond the hardships and worries of this life, that nothing in this world can hurt her any more.

Imagery

This poem brings an amazingly wide array of images flashing before the mind's eye: everything from winter blizzards to blazing sunshine, from chimney-sweeps to frowning kings, from lightning and meteorites to witches and ghosts. None of these images is described in great detail, yet each flashes vividly and briefly before us before making way for the next.

Figures of speech

There is an example of metonymy in line 11 (when we call something by the name of a thing closely associated with it rather than by its own name): in this instance, instead of saying 'kings', 'scholars' and 'doctors', the speaker says 'sceptre, learning, physic'. This is because kings are closely associated with sceptres, scholars with learning, and doctors with 'physic', an old name for the science of medicine.

Metonymy also occurs in line 7 where instead of saying Imogen need no longer fear the displeasure or anger of great man, we are told she need no longer fear their 'frowns'. This is because frowns are closely associated with anger and displeasure. Similarly, in the poem's final line, instead of saying 'May you be renowned', the speaker says 'May your grave be renowned'. This is because a grave is closely associated with the person buried in it.

There is an element of personification in line 2. The season of winter is depicted almost as a human being, as a 'furious' person who is prone to 'rages'. We can imagine the winter as such an angry, aggressive person, with storms, blizzards and inclement weather as its 'rages'.

There are two symbols in line 9. The reed, one of the most fragile of plants, is often used to symbolise frailty and weakness. The stout and sturdy oak, meanwhile, is often used as a symbol of strength.

The phrase 'chimney-sweeper' involves a pun or play on words. On one level, the speaker is simply declaring that rich and poor alike must eventually die. Yet the lines also refer to dandelions. In Warwickshire, where Shakespeare came from, 'chimney-sweeper' was a slang name for a dandelion when it has gone to seed. It is possible to imagine how the head of a gone-to-seed dandelion might resemble a sweep's brush. Thus, dandelions are 'Golden lads and girls' when they are yellow and in bloom, then go to seed and become 'chimney-sweepers' before floating away as dusty particles on the breeze.

Sound effects

Perhaps the most notable sound pattern in this poem is that of repetition.

- Each of the first three stanzas begins with the expression 'Fear no more'.
- Each of the first three stanzas closes with a rhyme between 'dust' and 'must'.
- Furthermore, each line in the final stanza begins with the word 'no' and concludes with the word 'thee'.

All this repetition creates a prayer-like, meditative ambience, well suited to a funeral poem. The repetition also creates emphasis, stressing over and over that Imogen has nothing to fear any more, and that every living person must eventually 'come to dust'.

There is a plethora of broad-vowel sounds throughout this piece. The following are just a number of examples:

- We see this with the repeated 'ea' and 'o' sounds that dominate the opening line: 'Fear no more the heat o' the sun'.
- We see it with the repeated 'ea' and 'o' sounds in line 4: 'Home art gone, and ta'en thy wages'.
- We see it with the repeated 'o' and 'a' sounds in 'Fear no more the tyrant's stroke'.
- We see it with the repeated 'e' and 'a' sounds in 'Fear nor slander, censure rash'.

The effect of all this assonance is to create a sombre but pleasant musical effect – one appropriate for a poem that deals with such weighty themes. It also slows the pace of the verse, giving it a stately feel appropriate to a funeral poem.

Alliteration also contributes to this effect. We see this with the repeated 'g' sound in 'Golden lads and girls', in the repeated 'f' sounds in line 7 and 13, and in the repeated 's' sound in 'fear not slander, censure rash'.

It has been suggested that there is an element of cacophony in lines 2, 13 and 14. In each instance, clashing, hard-vowel sounds create a harsh and unpleasant musical effect – one appropriate to the horrors these lines describe.

WILLIAM WORDSWORTH
THEMES

THE BEAUTY OF THE NATURAL WORLD

Wordsworth was a great lover of the natural world. His greatest pleasure was to spend time alone out in nature. He felt that the natural world enriched his body and soul. In 'Tintern Abbey' he says that nature brings 'quietness and beauty' into our lives and fills our minds with 'lovely forms' and 'sweet sounds and harmonies'. The poet's great passion for nature is evident in so many of his poems:

'Skating' describes a beautiful winter scene: the ground covered with 'polished ice' that reflects the starlight, leafless trees and echoing hillsides, the stars sparkling in the east as the orange sunset slowly fades. The only sign of human habitation in this winter wonderland are the lights in 'cottage windows that blazed' through twilight gloom. Wordsworth takes great delight ('rapture') in careering through this icy paradise.

In 'The Solitary Reaper', the poet provides several memorable descriptions of nature at its most beautiful: a shady oasis in the Arabian desert, the bleak and silent outer Hebrides in springtime, and the 'Vale profound' through which he walks listening to the reaper's song.

'Lines Composed Upon Westminster Bridge' celebrates the peace, light and freshness of morning.

'Tintern Abbey' records the many 'beauteous forms' of the natural world. Wordsworth speaks of the towering cliffs, the lush greens of the countryside, the rushing waters of the river and the 'deep and gloomy wood' that stands before him. He also mentions grand aspects of nature, the 'light of setting suns,/ And the round ocean and the living air'.

NATURE AS RESTORATIVE POWER

Wordsworth often describes the natural world as something of a tonic, a restorative power that rejuvenates the mind and body. At one point in 'Tintern Abbey', he refers to Nature as his 'nurse'. When he is feeling tired and low he only has to think about some of the beautiful places he has visited, and he begins to feel restored.

In 'Tintern Abbey', the poet thinks about how his memories of the landscape surrounding the abbey have given him strength and helped him over the five years he has been absent:

I have owed to them
In hours of weariness, sensations sweet,
Felt in the blood, and felt along the heart;
And passing even into my purer mind,
With tranquil restoration

In 'To My Sister', the poet urges his sister to join him on a walk in the woods. He says that their 'minds shall drink at every pore/ The spirit of the season'. Wordsworth suggests that the body and the soul thirst for contact with the natural world, and that we need to spend regular time outdoors in order to be healthy and happy.

NATURE AS MENTOR

An important theme in Wordsworth's poetry is the idea of nature as a kind of mentor to the young poet. Nature, he felt, taught him lessons, guiding his moral and personal development. In *The Prelude*, Wordsworth declared that he was 'Fostered alike by beauty and by fear'. Sometimes nature taught him harsh lessons, what he described as 'severer interventions', lessons that were filled with 'pain and fear'. More often, however, nature was a gentle mentor, educating him through its profound beauty.

In 'Skating', nature encourages the young poet's personal development. The landscape fills him with serenity and inspiration. As readers, we sense the young poet's artistic talents begin to take shape.

In 'Tintern Abbey', the poet says that nature is his 'guide', and the 'guardian' of his 'moral being'.

In 'To My Sister', the poet tells his sister that their 'hearts' will make 'silent laws' if they allow themselves time to enjoy the beautiful spring weather. Yet again, Wordsworth associates time spent enjoying nature with moral growth.

In 'It is a beauteous evening', the poet is perhaps a little disappointed that his daughter does not share his sensitivity to the natural world. However, he says that being a child, she is perfectly innocent and good.

THE SUBLIME IN NATURE

Nature also offers the poet a glimpse or intimation of something powerful at play in the world. He senses something spiritual in nature, a 'presence' or 'motion' that exists in or works through all living things. It is there in 'the light of setting suns,/ And the round ocean and the living air,/ And the blue sky, and in the mind of man'. The natural world gives the poet a sense that there is something greater to life than what we merely perceive with our senses.

In 'It is a beauteous evening', the poet makes reference to the existence of some sublime power. Listening to the waves continuously crashing onto the beach, the poet calls on us to behold the presence of something powerful and eternal. He calls on his daughter to 'Listen' and behold 'the mighty Being'. However, his daughter seems oblivious to the force that the poet senses operating through the movements of the ocean.

In 'The Stolen Boat', the mountain that rises up over the lake seems to have a 'purpose of its own' and is said to be 'like a living thing'. This terrifying phenomenon again suggests the existence of some strange – and in this instance, frightening – force that is beyond our ability to fathom and explain.

In 'To My Sister' the poet speaks about the 'blessed power that rolls/ About, below, above'. Wordsworth can't say exactly what this force is, he can only sense its presence. However, there are times when he seems to gain a higher understanding of this spiritual realm. In 'Tintern Abbey', he describes moments when deep in some form of meditation he 'sees into the life of things'. It is almost as though his soul becomes free of the body for a short time, and rises above the realm of day-to-day reality.

ONENESS WITH NATURE

Another recurring theme in Wordsworth is the notion of oneness with nature:

In 'The Solitary Reaper', the 'highland lass' is at one with the landscape that surrounds her. She is a single figure in an isolated rural landscape, cut off from the wider world. She works closely with the natural world, cutting and binding the grain.

In 'She Dwelt Among the Untrodden Ways', Lucy is depicted as a young woman who lives in an isolated rural community, and seems at one with the beautiful landscape that surrounds her.

In 'A Slumber Did My Spirit Seal', the girl becomes literally one with nature as her dead body mingles with the rocks, stones and trees.

In 'To My Sister', the poet says that with the arrival of spring, love is now spreading from 'earth to man, from man to earth'. The poem suggests a strong connection between people and their natural surroundings. Wordsworth calls on his sister to live according to the 'living calendar' of nature and enjoy herself when the weather is so good.

In 'Tintern Abbey', the very force that moves through the natural world 'impels/ All thinking things'. Wordsworth does not see humanity as other to nature, but instead as essentially linked to the natural world.

William Wordsworth

'THE STILL, SAD MUSIC OF HUMANITY'

A recurring feature of Wordsworth's poetry is the strange pleasure he takes in sorrow, melancholy and lonesomeness:

In 'Skating', he describes how the sounds of children at play echoes from the distant hills as what seems to be a strange and sorrowful lament, an 'alien sound/ Of melancholy'. (To Wordsworth and his fellow Romantic poets, melancholic music was the most beautiful. And it seems no sound was truly sublime unless it had a sorrowful quality to it).

This focus on melancholy sounds is also present in 'The Solitary Reaper'. The reaper seems mesmerised by the sadness and strangeness of the highland lass' song.

There is something eerie and melancholic about the echoes created by the poet as he rows across the lake in 'The Stolen Boat.'

In 'Tintern Abbey', the poet describes how as he has grown older he has become more aware of the 'still, sad music of humanity'. Spending time alone in nature allows the poet to experience this plaintive sound.

SOLITUDE

Solitude played an important role in Wordsworth's life and in his poems. In Wordsworth's poetry solitude is generally presented in a positive light, as a source of joy, creativity and inspiration. It is through solitary contemplation that we best experience nature's beauty, peace and inspiration.

Wordsworth describes his love of solitude in 'Skating'. Although he takes great pleasure in playing on the ice with his friends, the poet regularly feels the need to take off on his own. Sometimes he rests or 'retires' alone in a 'silent bay'. Sometimes he just skates alone for a while across the ice.

A similar positive view of solitude is evident in 'The Solitary Reaper', where the poet praises the song the reaper sings to herself. The reaper's solitude is emphasised again and again. She is 'single' in the field, she is 'solitary', she is 'alone', she is 'singing by herself'.

We also see it in 'The Stolen Boat' where Wordsworth takes great pleasure in rowing alone across the lake.

In 'Composed Upon Westminster Bridge' the poet delights in the silence and emptiness of early morning London. It is the poet's solitude that makes the city beautiful. He relishes the calm silence before the city wakes and the daily hustle and bustle begins.

In 'She dwelt among the untrodden ways', Lucy is so attractive to the poet because she lives an isolated and solitary existence. She is hidden among the untrodden ways, far from the eyes of the wider world. It is precisely because she is 'unknown' and 'half-hidden' that he praises her so much.

'Tintern Abbey' also contains many references to solitude and isolation. The 'secluded scene' that the poet observes inspires feelings and thoughts of 'more deep seclusion'. He thinks of 'some Hermit's cave where by his fire/ The Hermit sits alone'. The poet also mentions his sister's 'solitary walk' and prays that her 'solitude' be accompanied by pleasant thoughts of nature. However, the poem also makes reference to the loneliness that can be experienced in crowded environments, the 'lonely rooms' in the midst of noisy 'towns and cities'.

CHILDHOOD

In his poetry, Wordsworth celebrates childhood as a time of innocence and openness. We see this in 'It is Beauteous Evening'. The child does not have the solemn thoughts that occupy the poet's mind, but this very innocence and naivety make the child very special in the eyes of God. 'Skating' also emphasises the innocence of childhood in its depiction of the childish skating games enjoyed by the young Wordsworth and his companions in the winter. It could be argued that childhood innocence also features in 'She dwelt Among the Untrodden Ways' with its depiction of the young maid Lucy, who lives hidden from the civilised society, at one with nature by the banks of the River Dove. 'The Stolen Boat' also describes a formative experience of childhood or early youth.

William Wordsworth

Lines Composed a Few Miles Above Tintern Abbey, on Revisiting the Banks of the Wye During a Tour. July 13, 1798

LINE BY LINE

LINES 1–22: *Setting the scene*

Five years have gone by since the poet last visited this very place. He stands 'a few miles above Tintern Abbey' and takes in the surrounding landscape. The place seems little changed since the poet was last here.

The poet listens to the soft, soothing sounds of the 'mountain-springs'. He observes the steep, towering cliffs and thinks how they make the place feel even more secluded: 'That on a wild secluded scene impress/ Thoughts of more deep seclusion'. The tall cliffs also draw the eye upwards towards the sky: they 'connect/ The landscape with the quiet of the sky.'

After five long years the poet is glad to be back resting beneath the shade of a 'dark' sycamore tree. From this vantage point he can observe the cottages on their small plots of land. He sees clusters of apple trees 'with their unripe fruits' almost lost in the surrounding dense greenery. He sees chaotic 'little' hedgerows, not planted in any orderly fashion, but left to 'run wild'.

The green of the countryside runs right up to the doors of farm dwellings and smoke can be seen rising silently above the trees. This smoke causes the poet to think of 'vagrant dwellers', travellers living out in the open, lighting fires in the woods. He also thinks of a 'Hermit's cave, where by his fire/ The Hermit sits alone'.

LINES 22–57: *How the landscape has remained with the poet over the five years*

The poet never forgot about these wonderful features of the landscape. Images of the place remained with him throughout the five years he was absent. These memories were of great benefit to the poet over the years. He describes three ways that they impacted his life:

1. They made him feel good. Whenever he was feeling lonely, tired or low, thinking about the beautiful features of this landscape restored him physically and mentally:

   … I have owed to them
   In hours of weariness, sensations sweet,
   Felt in the blood, and felt along the heart;
   And passing even into my purer mind,
   With tranquil restoration

2. They made him act in a kind and loving manner. The pleasure that he got from this beautiful landscape stayed with him and influenced his behaviour, inspired him to be kind and thoughtful towards others.

3. They enabled him to experience the world in a special way. The poet says that at times he has been able to distance himself from his everyday concerns and enter some tranquil meditative state in which he gains a deeper insight into 'the life of things'.

The poet realises that he may be going too far when he states that this beautiful landscape allows him to access some spiritual realm. However, the landscape has undoubtedly made him feel much better whenever life has gotten too much for him. 'In darkness' and during stressful days when nothing seems to work the poet has thought about this wonderful place and felt much better.

LINES 58–111: *How the poet has changed over five years*

The poet's memories of this place had faded over the last five years. However, as he looks around at the landscape he has flashes of recollection, 'gleams of half-extinguished thought', and much of what he sees seems dimly familiar: 'With many recognitions dim and faint'. As he stands once again before the landscape, it all starts to come back to him: 'The picture of the mind revives again'.

The poet is very happy to be here again. He knows that what he is now experiencing will stay with him for years to come. And yet the moment is tinged with a sadness. For it is not only memories of what he saw five years ago that now return to the poet; he also remembers how he was back then. When he last visited this valley he was five years younger.

When the poet last visited the area, he was beginning to become a man. He says that his boyish days with their thoughtless games were 'all gone by'. But he was still full of youthful energy and he 'bounded' over the mountains like a 'roe' or deer. He was impulsive and went 'Wherever nature led' him.

The poet doesn't know what motivated him back then. It was more like he was running away from something he feared than towards something he loved.

Nature meant everything to him: 'For nature then … To me was all in all'. It had a profound and immediate effect upon him. The sound of the waterfall troubled him like some desire or emotion he could not ignore or forget. The atmosphere of the landscape with its 'tall rock' and mountain rising above 'deep and gloomy' woods suited his mood, satisfying some hunger that existed deep within him.

The poet's response to what he saw as a younger man was emotional, and he felt no need to understand it on a deeper level nor attach any greater significance to it: 'a feeling and a love,/ That had no need of a remoter charm,/ By thought supplied'.

The poet no longer feels like this. He does not experience life with the same intensity. The 'aching joys' and 'dizzy raptures' that he felt five years previous are now a thing of the past. But this does not sadden him. He has learned to see nature differently. He no longer rushes through the landscape with 'thoughtless' passion and fervour. He is more considerate, and takes time to contemplate the natural world that surrounds him. The result is that he now gets something from nature that he never got as a younger, more passionate man, and this more than compensates for the loss of youthful ecstasy and joy.

How the poet experiences nature as an older man

The poet is still as much 'a lover of the meadows and the woods,/ And mountains' as he was when he was younger, only now he experiences nature differently:

Wordsworth says that when he looks upon nature now, he gets a sense of the sadness of life. He describes it in terms of 'hearing' the 'still, sad music of humanity'. This comes to him softly (it is not 'harsh nor grating') but it has a powerful effect upon him.

He also gets a sense of something mysterious, 'a spirit' or 'presence' that is impossible to fully comprehend but is nevertheless 'felt' as something real and present in all that surrounds him. It is there in 'the light of setting suns,/ And the round ocean and the living air,/ And the blue sky, and in the mind of man'. It is like some mysterious energy that 'rolls through all things'. It is a force that 'impels/ All thinking things, all objects of all thought'.

Nature also somehow serves the poet as a 'guide', giving him moral instruction and protecting him. It is his 'nurse' and 'guide, the guardian of [his] heart, and soul/ Of all [his] moral being'.

The poet is still a lover of nature, because it offers him all these things. He also no longer sees himself as being detached from nature. He is now aware of man's oneness with nature, and feels that the energy that he perceives flowing through the natural world also flows through and 'impels' man.

LINES 111–59: *The poet addresses his sister*

Even if the poet did not have this understanding of nature, this profound relationship with the world around him, to bolster his heart and guide him through life, his spirits would not suffer. The reason for this is that his sister is with him now and this gives him great pleasure.

The poet's sister is younger than him. He listens to her speaking joyfully about the landscape. Her words remind him of himself when he was younger, possibly how he was five years before, when he rushed through the area in high excitement: 'in thy voice I catch/ The language of my former heart, and read/

My former pleasures in the shooting lights/ Of thy wild eyes'. He is delighted to catch a glimpse of his former self in her.

The poet describes the great things that 'Nature' offers us:

- She brings continuous joy into our lives.
- She teaches us important things.
- She introduces calm and beauty into our lives.
- She gives us a sense of something great and profound.

All these things serve to protect us from the harsh and unpleasant elements of life: 'evil tongues', the 'sneers of selfish men', false people, and the 'dreary' conversations that form part of 'daily life'. With the power of nature, the poet and his sister will be protected from these nasty things, and their 'cheerful' faith will remain intact.

Knowing that nature is such a benevolent force, the poet prays that it will be of service to his sister throughout her life. He prays that the moon will shine on her and the 'misty mountain-winds' blow freely against her as she makes her 'solitary walk'. He also prays that when she is older and these wonderful moments have become fond memories, should she ever feel lonely, sad or afraid, she will remember him and his encouraging words.

Finally the poet asks that his sister remember him. Should she ever be far from him, he prays that she remember how they stood together on the banks of 'this delightful stream' and that he, as a 'worshipper of Nature' came there with great energy and love. He asks that she never forget how after five years absence from the area, he returned, and felt a greater love for the place because she was with him.

THEMES

Solitude & the 'sad music of humanity'

The poem contains many references to solitude and isolation. The 'secluded scene' that the poet observes inspires feelings and thoughts of 'more deep seclusion'. He thinks of 'some Hermit's cave where by his fire/ The Hermit sits alone'. He mentions his sister's 'solitary walk', possibly a reference to the fact that his sister was not married, and prays that her 'solitude' be offset by pleasant thoughts of nature. The poem also makes reference to the loneliness that can be experienced in crowded environments, the 'lonely rooms' in the midst of noisy 'towns and cities'.

This awareness of loneliness seems to stem from the poet's greater awareness of the sadness that pervades life. He speaks of how, as he has matured, he has become more aware of the

world and the difficulties of humanity. He is sensitive to the quiet sufferings of people, what he terms the 'still, sad music of humanity'. Spending time in nature has somehow made him aware of this sadness, consequently sobering and subduing his spirits.

The beauty of the natural world

The poem records the many 'beauteous forms' of the natural world. Wordsworth speaks of the towering cliffs, the lush greens of the countryside, the rushing waters of the river, and the 'deep and gloomy wood' that stands before him. He mentions grand aspects of nature – the 'light of setting suns,/ And the round ocean and the living air' – and also 'the meadows and the woods,/ And mountains'. Spending time in nature fills the poet's mind with 'quietness and beauty'.

Nature as restorative power

Wordsworth speaks throughout the poem about the health benefits of nature. At one point in the poem he refers to Nature as his 'nurse'. When he is feeling tired and low he only has to think about some of the beautiful places he has visited, and he begins to feel restored. His previous trip to the area surrounding Tintern Abbey provided him with many wonderful memories which he carried with him over the five subsequent years. These memories gave him pleasure and restored his spirits whenever he was feeling low:

> I have owed to them
> In hours of weariness, sensations sweet,
> Felt in the blood, and felt along the heart;
> And passing even into my purer mind,
> With tranquil restoration

Nature as mentor

The natural world also acts somehow as a 'guide' to the poet. Nature both inspires him to be a better person and instructs him. It is what grounds him and keeps him on the right track in life: 'The anchor of my purest thoughts'. He says that his small acts of kindness, the 'little, nameless, unremembered, acts/ Of kindness and of love', are the result of the pleasure he has experienced when out in nature. Nature makes him feel good, and he in turn acts with greater kindness and love towards others.

The sublime in nature

Nature offers the poet a glimpse or intimation of something powerful at play in the world. He senses something spiritual in nature, a 'presence' or 'motion' that exists in – or works through – all living things. It is there in 'the light of setting suns,/ And the round ocean and the living air,/ And the blue sky, and in the mind of man'. Wordsworth can't say exactly what this force is, he can only sense its presence. However, there are times when he seems to gain a higher understanding of this spiritual realm. He describes moments when deep in some form of meditation he 'sees into the life of things'. It is almost as though his soul becomes free of the body for a short time, and rises above the realm of day-to-day reality. Nature gives the poet a real sense that there is something greater to life than what we merely perceive with our senses.

City life

The poem contrasts the beauty and serenity of the natural world with the noise and confusion of the city. Wordsworth describes frustrating and stressful days spent "mid the din/ Of towns and cities'. In these environments he seems to feel lonely and agitated. There is much fretting and worrying, but it all seems to result in nothing of importance. The poet describes the 'joyless daylight; when the fretful stir/ Unprofitable'. City life wears the poet down. He feels the troubles of the world sit heavily 'upon the beatings of [his] heart'. It is in such places that he has to endure the false words and 'sneers' of others. The natural world offers him a much-needed break from the stresses and strains of urban living.

Youth & maturity

The poem records how the poet has changed over the years since he last visited the area. He remembers how when he first came here as a younger man he was full of energy and passion, racing over the hills and hardly stopping to think about what he was seeing. Nature meant everything to him and it seems he did give much consideration to the greater world of man. The poet speaks of experiencing 'aching joys' and 'dizzy raptures', such was his passion and excitement.

The poet feels a 'sad perplexity' when he recalls this. He has since lost this youthful passion and energy. He is more contemplative and considerate now, and his passions have been tempered by his greater experience of the world. Although Wordsworth is sad to think that the man who came to this part of the world five years previous is no more, he tries to comfort himself with the notion that maturity has brought other gifts to replace those lost with age. He is now more sensitive, both to the natural world and the world of man. Nature provides him with a keen sense of the sadness of life, but it also gives him a intimation of something great and powerful at work in the world: 'I have felt/ A presence that disturbs me ... a sense sublime/ Of something far more deeply interfused'.

So although age has sobered his passions and tempered his emotions, it has brought him greater insight and knowledge. The poet feels that he has been more than compensated for what he has lost. But there is still a sense in which he is mournful for what he has lost. Towards the end of the poem he observes his sister and sees something of his younger self in her. He asks her to pause a while, so he can remember what he was like.

Oh! yet a little while
May I behold in thee what I was once

Memory

The theme of memory is central to this poem. The area around Tintern Abbey is not only a place visited by the poet, it is a place remembered. He was in this very place five years before, and throughout the poem Wordsworth recalls again the memories that he cherished during the years when he was absent.

The poem reveals how central to our lives memories are. The poet says that all the time he has been away from the area, the 'beauteous forms' have remained with him. He owes a lot to these memories. The poem describes how pleasant memories can sustain us through hard times: 'I have owed to them/ In hours of weariness, sensations sweet'. The poet seems to have needed to call upon this resource of memory often in the intervening years: 'How oft, in spirit, have I turned to thee'. As he stands before the landscape once again, he thinks about what a store of memories he will be creating for future years: 'in this moment there is life and food/ For future years'. He tells his sister that she too will benefit from all that she sees in this wonderful place:

... thy mind
Shall be a mansion for all lovely forms,
Thy memory be as a dwelling-place
For all sweet sounds and harmonies

However, the poem also highlights how memories can fade with time. Wordsworth speaks of how his mind's picture of the place had broken down into 'gleams of half-extinguished thought' and that what he sees on his second visit to the area only dimly and faintly strikes him as familiar: 'With many recognitions dim and faint'. The poet tries also to remember the person that he was five years before, but has to admit that he 'cannot paint/ What then [he] was'.

The poet's attempt to recall his youthful self leads him to feel 'sad' and perplexed. He is sad to think that this younger man is no more, and that he has become older and less energetic and passionate. He attempts to re-connect with his younger self by observing his sister. In her excited response to the landscape, he perceives something of what he once was:

in thy voice I catch
The language of my former heart, and read
My former pleasures in the shooting lights
Of thy wild eyes

William Wordsworth
She Dwelt Among the Untrodden Ways

LINE BY LINE

Lucy lived near the source of the river Dove in Yorkshire. This is an isolated part of England, a place where very few people visit. The speaker describes its 'ways' or paths as 'untrodden' because so few people walk on them. Lucy was known and loved only by the 'very few' people with whom she shared this remote corner of the world.

The poet regarded Lucy as very beautiful. He compares her to a flower and star. Lucy is hidden away from the wider world. The poet compares her, therefore, to a half-hidden flower. Lucy is also unique. The poet compares her, therefore, to a single star shining in the sky.

Lucy lived a quiet, isolated existence. She was completely 'unknown' to the wider world. Only her few neighbours among the untrodden ways noticed when she died: 'She lived unknown, and few could know/ When Lucy ceased to be'. Yet though Lucy was an obscure and unimportant person, her death left the poet devastated, making a huge and negative difference to his life: 'But she is in her grave and, oh,/ The difference to me!'

LANGUAGE

Ballad form
This poem is written in ballad form: it has four-line stanzas and an ABAB rhyme scheme. It has four stresses in the first and third line of each stanza, and three stresses in the second and fourth lines. The poet uses simple, everyday language, and few long or complicated words. This is appropriate for a poem that celebrates the simple, uncluttered life of a girl in an isolated, rural community.

Metaphors
There are two fine comparisons in the second stanza. The first is a metaphor whereby Wordsworth compares Lucy to a violet that is 'half-hidden'. Lucy is like a half-hidden violet because she is beautiful and hidden away from the wider world in her isolated untrodden ways. The second is a simile whereby Wordsworth compares Lucy to a single star shining in the evening. This comparison stresses both Lucy's beauty and her uniqueness.

Tone
It could be argued that the poem's tone is one of mingled sorrow and celebration. in the last two lines the poet movingly laments the difference Lucy's death has made to his life. Yet the poem also celebrates her beauty and the innocent simplicity of the life she led.

Assonance & alliteration
Alliteration occurs in line 6 with the repeated 'h' sound in 'half' and 'hidden' and in line 8 with the repeated 's' sound in 'shining' and 'sky'. Assonance occurs in line 5 with the repeated 'o' sounds in 'violet', 'mossy' and 'stone'. We also see it in line 7 with the repeated 'a' sounds in 'fair' as a 'star'.

THEMES

The beauty of the natural world
Like so many of Wordsworth's poems this poem celebrates the beauty the natural world, with Wordsworth praising the beauty of stars and flowers. Similar praise for nature's splendour occurs in practically every poem by Wordsworth on the course.

Oneness with nature
To a large extent Lucy is so beautiful and important to the poet because she is one with nature. She lives in harmony with the natural world among the 'untrodden ways' far from the eyes of the wide world. She resembles the highland lass in 'The Solitary Reaper' who is lost in her work among the fields in the isolated Scottish highlands.

This theme of oneness with nature is one that recurs throughout Wordsworth's poetry. We see it in 'To My Sister' where love is described as flowing from 'earth to man, from man to earth'.

It could be argued that the young Wordsworth experiences a similar sensation of oneness with nature in

both extracts from *The Prelude*, as he skates on the ice and rows his boat across the lake in the quietness of evening. In 'A Slumber Did My Spirit Seal', Lucy literally becomes one with nature after her death, her body dissolving into the earth.

Solitude

This poem also touches on the notion of solitude, another recurring theme in Wordsworth's work. Lucy is so attractive to the poet because she lives an isolated and solitary existence. She is hidden among the untrodden ways, far from the eyes of the wider world. It is precisely because she is 'unknown' and 'half-hidden' that he praises her so much.

A similar positive view of solitude is evident in 'The Solitary Reaper', where the poet praises the song the reaper sings to herself, and in 'Skating', where the poet finds poetic inspiration when he skates away from his companions. We also see it in 'The Stolen Boat' where Wordsworth hopes to take pleasure in rowing alone across the lake, and in 'Westminster Bridge' where he delights in the silence and emptiness of early morning London. In each of these poems solitude is associated with beauty, peace and creativity.

Poetry

Wordsworth says that there was no one to 'praise' Lucy in her isolated and sparsely populated rural community. He seems to be suggesting that the 'few' who knew her among the untrodden ways were simple country folk who lacked the education and poetic training to adequately 'praise' her beauty. It takes a true poet like Wordsworth to 'praise' Lucy, something he accomplishes in the second stanza in particular, with its beautiful comparisons. The poem, then, could be taken as a celebration of poetry, in particular of the poet's ability to adequately 'praise' that which is beautiful.

William Wordsworth
A Slumber Did My Spirit Seal

LINE BY LINE

The poet is sleeping. His mind has been enfolded or 'sealed' by slumber. As the poet sleeps, he dreams about Lucy, who has passed away. She is now only a corpse, no longer capable of seeing or hearing. She is an inanimate object, a 'thing' that has no 'force' or 'motion'.

Now that Lucy is dead she can no longer be altered by the passage of time. The passing of 'earthly years' can no longer 'touch' or change her: 'She seemed a thing that could not feel/ The touch of earthly years'. The poet no longer has any reason to worry about Lucy: 'I had no human fears'. In death she has moved beyond 'human' concerns such as pain and suffering. Nothing can hurt her now.

Her buried body has decayed and has been absorbed into the earth. It has mingled with the 'rocks and stones and trees'. The earth revolves or 'rolls around' every twenty-four hours ('diurnally'). Lucy's remains, because they are now part of the earth, also 'roll around' every twenty-four hours. She is 'rolled round in earth's diurnal course'.

LANGUAGE

Assonance & alliteration
Alliteration occurs in line 1, with its repeated 's' sound. Assonance occurs in line 5 with the repeated 'o' sound in 'No', 'motion', 'now' and 'course'. We also see assonance in line 7, due to the repeated 'o' sound in 'rolled' and 'course' and due to the repeated broad-vowel sound sin 'earth' and 'diurnal'.

Ballad form
This poem, like 'She dwelt among the untrodden ways', is written in ballad form: it has four-line stanzas and an ABAB rhyme scheme. It has four stresses in the first and third line of each stanza and three stresses in the second and fourth lines. The poet uses simple, everyday language. (The only unusual word is 'diurnal' in line 7). This simplicity is appropriate for a poem that celebrates the simple, uncluttered life of a girl in an isolated, rural community

Tone
The tone of this poem mingles happiness and sorrow. The poet is obviously sad that his beloved Lucy has passed away. Yet there is also a note of relief or celebration that Lucy will in a sense exist forever, her substance having been absorbed into the earth.

THEMES

Oneness with nature
Lucy had died and yet she lives on. Her body has become one with the earth, mingling with the rocks, stones and trees. Her remains will revolve eternally with the earth as it turns through space. Now that Lucy is one with nature she cannot be altered by the passage of time. The poet has no need to fear for her or worry about her. She is now beyond the 'human' difficulties that effect the living.

This theme of oneness with nature is one that recurs throughout Wordsworth's poetry. In 'She Dwelt Among the Untrodden Ways' the living Lucy is depicted as living a life in tune with the natural world in her isolated, rural community. It is fitting, therefore, that in this poem Lucy literally becomes one with nature after her death, her body dissolving into the earth.

A similar focus on oneness with nature is evident in 'To My Sister' where love is described as flowing from 'earth to man, from man to earth'. It could be argued that the young Wordsworth experiences a similar sensation of oneness with nature in both extracts from *The Prelude*, as he skates on the ice and rows his boat across the lake in the quietness of evening. In 'A Slumber Did My Spirit Seal'

To My Sister

William Wordsworth

LINE BY LINE

The poet is keenly aware that spring has arrived. Excited and inspired by the change of season, he urges his sister to forget her household chores and join him for a walk.

What the poet sees & senses

Spring has arrived. The weather is milder. The poet listens to a robin ('redbreast') singing in a tree 'that stands beside' his door. He looks out over the countryside at the 'bare trees, and mountains' and the 'grass in the green field' and is excited by the arrival of spring. Every minute he says is more delightful than the one before.

The poet senses something special in the air, a 'blessing,' something that transforms the countryside before his eyes. This 'blessing' appears to be bringing 'a sense of joy' to the 'bare trees, and mountains bare'. The poet also senses 'Love' in the world around him. Love is everywhere, silently spreading from person to person. A bond seems to have been established between earth and man, and from each to each love is 'stealing'. On this day the poet senses an openness and a sympathetic feeling in the world: 'It is the hour of feeling'.

A plea to his sister

The poet urges his sister to forego her morning chores and join him for a walk in the sun: 'Make haste, your morning task resign;/ Come forth and feel the sun'. There is an urgency and excitement to his request, he tells her to 'make haste' and to 'Put on with speed' the dress that she wears when out walking in the woods. It seems that the poet's sister is feeling a little less spontaneous than the poet. We can imagine her saying, 'But what about Edward?' and 'But I must change my clothes!' The poet, however, will allow nothing to interfere with his 'wish' and tells her that 'Edward will come with you' and to change quickly.

Whereas the sister is concerned with day-to-day matters, the poet has no regard for routine. He is determined that nothing, even long-established practices and responsibilities, should restrict them today. He wishes to be spontaneous and act according to his instincts. Disregarding the 'joyless' demands of duty he boldly states that they act in accordance with the natural, 'living' world. Therefore, since nature seems to be starting afresh after winter, the poet thinks that they also ought to consider this day to be the 'opening of the year'.

The benefits of nature

The poet speaks about the benefits that will come from seizing the day and enjoying time outdoors. He suggests that a few moments spent out in nature will make you wiser than years spent studying books: 'One moment now may give us more/ Than years of toiling reason'. Out in the natural world the mind soaks in ideas and lessons, naturally and effortlessly.

Nature somehow causes the poet to have thoughts and ideas that help him to live a better life. He intuits moral 'laws' from the natural world: 'Some silent laws our hearts will make,/ Which they shall long obey'.

Nature instructs and guides, teaching the poet the right temperament: 'We for the year to come may take/ Our temper from to-day'.

Nature is a force that runs through all things. It is a 'blessed power that rolls/ About, below, above'. This force can have a significant impact on our lives. The poet suggests that we can attune our 'souls' to this force, achieve a oneness with nature. Nature is a benevolent force, and if we allow it to influence us we will be better people. If we attune our souls to the 'blessed power' of nature we 'shall be tuned to love'.

THEMES

The beauty of the natural world

The poet is inspired by the beauty and magnificence of the natural world. He revels in the simple details, deriving much pleasure from the song of the redbreast and the 'grass in the green fields'. Yet again we see how much nature meant to Wordsworth. He is overjoyed at the arrival of spring and keenly anticipates the time he will spend out in the open air.

Nature as mentor

Wordsworth considers nature to be a force that can guide us and influence our lives. Wordsworth associates nature with 'love' and he says that the coming spring is spreading love throughout the world. It is a benevolent force, something that the poet feels can teach us how to lead better lives. If we spend time in nature and attune ourselves to this special force we will derive great benefit. The spirit or force that Wordsworth detects in the natural world will somehow inspire and guide us. It will help us to formulate laws by which we will live: 'Some silent laws our hearts will make'.

The Stolen Boat

BACKGROUND & INTRODUCTION

This poem is an extract from *The Prelude*, which is generally considered to be Wordsworth's greatest poem. *The Prelude* is a long and detailed autobiographical work that records the poet's childhood, adolescence and early adulthood. In this extract, the poet describes an occasion in his youth when he borrowed a boat without permission in order to go rowing on a lake.

LINE BY LINE

Taking the boat

The young poet is out walking on a summer evening by the lake shore. He comes upon a boat tied to willow tree in a cave: 'I found/ A little boat tied to a willow tree/ Within a rocky cave, its usual home'. The phrase 'led by her' in line 1 refers to nature. Wordsworth thought of nature as a kind of living force with a mind of its own. In this instance nature has 'led' the young poet to the tied-up boat.

Impulsively, Wordsworth releases the boat from its moorings, gets in, and sets out across the lake: 'Straight I unloosed her chain, and stepping in/ Pushed from the shore'. In this instance 'Straight' means immediately, without delay.

The act of 'borrowing' the boat is one of 'stealth/ And troubled pleasure'. It is an act of 'stealth' because there is an element of sneakiness involved. He wants to set out on the boat as quickly and quietly as possible, perhaps fearful that its owner might suddenly appear and catch him in the act of 'borrowing' it. Taking the boat is an act of 'pleasure' because the Wordsworth enjoys rowing. His pleasure, however, is 'troubled'. Despite his enjoyment he feels guilty for taking the boat without the owner's permission.

A skilful rower

Wordsworth rows 'lustily', taking pleasure in the physical effort of moving the boat across the lake. He is proud of his skill in being able to row in a perfectly straight line:

like one who rows
Proud of his skill, to reach a chosen point
With an unswerving line.

Wordsworth uses a fine simile to capture the grace and smoothness with which the little craft moves, saying that the boat 'went heaving through the water like a swan'. He accomplishes this smooth, straight movement by keeping his gaze fixed on one particular point, 'the summit of a craggy ridge'. This summit is the highest point in the vicinity: 'the horizon's utmost boundary'. Above it there is only the fading sky of evening, where the stars have already begun to appear: 'for above/ Was nothing but the stars and the grey sky'.

A tranquil evening

The evening is particularly calm and peaceful. The sound of Wordsworth's oars echoes against the surrounding mountains: 'nor without the voice/ Of mountain echoes, did my boat move on'. The ripples created by the dipping oars shimmer in the moonlight: 'Small circles glittering idly in the moon'. Lines 6–20, then, provide us with a romantic portrayal of nature at its most idyllic: the evening quiet, the stars appearing in the sky, the still lake water in which the moon's reflection is disturbed only by the splashing oars, the young boy rowing skillfully and vigorously across the water as his boat glides with swan-like grace.

A terrifying vision

In line 21, however, this tranquillity is abruptly shattered. Suddenly a mountain peak appears behind the craggy ridge on which Wordsworth has been focusing in order to steer his boat: 'from behind that craggy steep ... a huge peak ... upreared its head'.

Wordsworth is terrified by this mountain that has seemingly appeared out of nowhere:

- He says that it has a dark and sinister appearance, calling it 'black' and a 'grim shape'.
- He emphasises its enormity by repeating the word huge: 'a huge peak, black and huge'.
- He says that the mountain grows larger and larger until it eclipses the stars: 'And growing still in stature the grim shape/ Towered up between me and the stars'.
- He says that the mountain began to move toward him like a living thing: 'with purpose of its own/ And measured motion like a living thing/ Strode after me'.
- He says that the mountain possesses 'voluntary power instinct', that it has a mind of its own.

Not surprisingly, Wordsworth turns his boat around and heads for shore in an attempt to escape from this monstrosity. His hands tremble as he does so: 'With trembling oars I turned,/ And through the silent water stole my way/ Back to the covert of the willow tree'. He leaves the boat where he found it. The sudden apparition of the huge, black mountain has clearly disturbed him, and he is upset as he makes his way home through the meadows: 'And through the meadows homeward went, in grave/ And serious mood'.

The aftermath

This frightening incident lingers in his mind for 'many days'. His mind grapples with deep and heavy thoughts (lines 35–7). His mood remains dark and troubled: 'o'er my thoughts/ There hung a darkness, call it solitude/ Or blank desertion'. His imagination is filled with weird, disturbing images: 'huge and mighty forms'.

These 'huge and mighty forms' resemble the towering mountain peak that appeared so suddenly at the lakeside. They move but are not 'alive' in any conventional sense: they 'do not live/ Like living men'. These disturbing 'mighty forms' occupy Wordsworth's thoughts during the day: 'moved slowly through the mind/ By day'. At night they haunt his dreams: 'and were a trouble to my dreams'.

What exactly is the apparition by the lakeside?

There are at least three possible answers to this question:

- The young Wordsworth has a guilty conscience about taking the boat. He is also completely alone amidst the eerie silence of the lake. These factors cause him to hallucinate or imagine that a giant mountain rears up out of the ground and starts walking toward him.
- Wordsworth believed nature to be a kind of living force with a mind of its own that 'mentored' him throughout his youth. It is possible that nature caused Wordsworth to have this frightening hallucination in order to teach him a lesson for stealing the boat.
- It is also possible that Wordsworth was not hallucinating, and that nature actually caused the giant mountain to come after him in order to teach him a lesson for stealing the boat.

THEMES

The beauty of the natural world

In 'The Stolen Boat', as in so many of his poems, Wordsworth celebrates the beauty of nature. We see this especially in the middle of the poem with its memorable description of the young boy rowing 'lustily' across the lake through the perfectly still evening with the moonlight reflecting in the lake's placid water. The poet's love of the natural world is also evident toward the end of the poem when he mentions the 'familiar shapes' of tress and fields that normally fill his imagination.

The critic F.W. Bateson argues that the apparition by the lakeside represents the young poet's dread of the urban, industrialised world. Bateson claims that this episode took place when Wordsworth was returning from his beloved Hawkshead Free School to spend the summer at his Uncle's draper shop in the drab provincial town of Penrith. Wordsworth hated the time he was forced to spend in the draper's shop, regarding it as a miserable, oppressive prison.

The young Wordsworth would often attempt to avoid thoughts of this industrial world he dreaded by fleeing into nature. On this occasion, however, his attempt at escapism is unsuccessful. The knowledge that he must return to Penrith haunts him in the form of an hallucination by the lakeside and in the form of the dark images that trouble his thoughts and dreams for 'many days' afterwards.

Nature as mentor

An important theme in Wordsworth's poetry is the idea of nature as a kind of mentor to the young poet, governing his moral and personal development. This notion is summarised in 'Tintern Abbey' when Wordsworth declares nature to be:

The anchor of my purest thoughts, the nurse,
The guide, the guardian of my heart, and soul
Of all my moral being

Elsewhere in *The Prelude* Wordsworth says he was 'Fostered alike by beauty and by fear'. Sometimes nature was a gentle mentor, educating him through its profound beauty (this is hinted at in the 'Skating' episode). Sometimes nature thought him harsh lessons, what he described as 'severer interventions', lessons that were filled with 'pain and fear'.

It is possible to read this extract as describing one of these 'severer interventions'. Wordsworth has misbehaved, taking a boat without the owner's permission. Nature, in its role as the poet's mentor, intervenes. It punishes him for his 'act of stealth' by giving him a terrible fright, a fright that lingers in mind for days afterwards. By doing so it reinforces his sense of right and wrong, and encourages him to respect other peoples' property in future.

It has also been suggested that nature teaches Wordsworth another even deeper lesson. The apparition at the lake not only punishes the young Wordsworth for his bad behaviour, but also introduces him to strange, dark thoughts that haunt his mind, thoughts that deal with 'unknown modes of being'. For days afterwards Wordsworth grapples with these 'dim' notions he could neither understand nor properly express: 'my brain/ Worked with a dim and undetermined sense'.

It's also important to note that in the first line Wordsworth declares that nature 'led' him to the boat's resting place in the rocky cave. It's almost as if nature wanted Wordsworth to take the boat and sail out across the lake so it could teach him these important lessons.

Poetry

Some of *The Prelude*'s most famous passages recount what Wordsworth referred to as 'spots of time', moments when the budding poet was suddenly struck by the majesty and splendour of the natural world. These moments of heightened experience made him aware that he possessed a special sensitivity toward nature, and contributed his sense of his destiny as a poet. They contributed to the 'growth of a poet's mind'. In 'The Stolen Boat' the speaker has these moments of heightened experience when he rows across the lake and also when the giant, black mountain rears up in front of him.

'Skating' also describes one of these 'spots of time', recounting the young poet's joy in playing with his friends, but also the serenity he experiences when he slips off on his own. It could be argued that similar moments of heightened experience are described in 'The Solitary Reaper', 'Tintern Abbey' and 'Lines Composed Upon Westminster Bridge'. For Wordsworth, the ability to experience these intense moments was intimately linked with the ability to write great poetry.

Solitude

This poem also touches on the notion of solitude, another recurring theme in Wordsworth's work. Wordsworth takes great pleasure in rowing alone across the lake, enjoying the silence, peace and tranquillity of the evening. Similarly In 'Skating' the poet finds nature to be most beautiful and inspiring when he skates away from his companions and pauses alone in some 'silent bay'

In 'She dwelt Among the Untrodden Ways' Lucy is so attractive to the poet because she lives an isolated and solitary existence. She is hidden among the untrodden ways, far from the eyes of the wider world. It is precisely because she is 'unknown' and 'half-hidden' that he praises her so much. A similar positive view of solitude is evident in 'The Solitary Reaper', where the poet praises the song the reaper sings to herself. and in 'Westminster Bridge' where he delights in the silence and emptiness of early morning London. In each of these poems solitude is associated with beauty, peace and creativity.

William Wordsworth
Skating

This is an extract from *The Prelude*, Wordsworth's long poem describing his boyhood, youth and early manhood. It describes a winter's evening when the young poet went skating with his friends.

LINE BY LINE

The opening lines present us with a picturesque winter landscape, like one we might find on a Christmas card. It is an evening in winter ('the frosty season'). It is six o' clock and the sun has set. The lights in cottage windows can be seen through the winter dusk: 'The cottage windows blazed through twilight gloom'. Wordsworth ignores the 'summons' of the cottage windows. He is happier to stay outside skating rather than retreat into the warmth and comfort represented by the windows' glow.

Wordsworth feels like a proud, powerful workhorse that delights ('exults') in physical activity and has no need of rest:

I wheeled about,
Proud and exulting like an untired horse
That cares not for his home

Wordsworth and his young friends play a game of chasing on the ice. Wordsworth describes this in terms of hunting in a woodland: their play is 'imitative of the chase/ And woodland pleasures'. Some of the children act as hunters with a 'pack' of hounds and a 'resounding' hunting horn. Others play the role of the 'hunted hare'.

The children shout and screech as they play: 'So through the darkness and the cold we flew,/ And not a voice was idle'. The din they make 'smites' or strikes the surrounding cliffs and returns to them as an echo: 'with the din/ Smitten, the precipices rang aloud'. When this racket strikes the nearby hills and trees it produces what seems to be pleasant 'tinkling' echoes. The trees and peaks, we're told, 'Tinkled like iron', as they reflected the noise of the children's games. However, when this racket strikes the 'far distant hills' it produces sad, strange echoes that Wordsworth describes as 'an alien sound/ Of melancholy'.

The young Wordsworth regularly slips away from his companions and their games. He leaves the 'uproar' of this noisy or 'tumultuous' gang behind: 'Not seldom from the uproar I retired … leaving the tumultuous throng'. Sometimes he would rest alone in a 'silent bay'. Sometimes he suddenly changes direction ('sportively glance sideways') and skates off across the ice on his own.

Wordsworth uses a vivid image to describe the speed with which the children skated, saying that they 'had given their bodies to the wind'. The notion of 'giving away' one's body suggests the feelings of recklessness and excitement the children experienced as they whizzed along the ice, moving so fast that they were almost out of control. As they skated, the banks on either side seemed to sweep toward him out of the gloom. It was as if the banks and not the skaters were moving: 'And all the shadowy banks on either side/ Came sweeping through the darkness'.

The poem concludes with Wordsworth braking sharply by stepping back on his heels: 'then at once/ Have I, reclining back upon my heels,/ Stopped short'. He is dizzy having travelled so quickly and the cliffs appear to continue to fly past him:

yet still the solitary cliffs
Wheeled by me-even as if the earth had rolled
With visible motion her diurnal round!

To Wordsworth in his dizziness it's as if the daily rotation of the earth (its 'diurnal round') had speeded up to the extent that its motion is visible to humans. Wordsworth stands there waiting for this spinning sensation to fade. When it does he experiences a feeling of the most intense tranquillity: 'I stood and watched/ Till all was tranquil as a dreamless sleep'.

LANGUAGE

Metaphor & simile

Wordsworth uses several memorable comparisons to describe the act of skating. Firstly, he compares himself to a horse: 'I wheeled about,/ Proud and exulting like an untired horse'. This simile conveys the energy, vigour and athleticism Wordsworth experiences as he skates across the ice. The comparison with the horse is reinforced by the metaphor in line 9, where Wordsworth describes himself and his friends as being 'shod with steel'. This metaphor compares the blades of the children's skates to the steel shoes of horses. Wordsworth also uses a metaphors to describe the pace and exhilaration of the children's flight across the ice. Next, he says they have 'given our bodies to the wind'.

Wordsworth also uses metaphor and and simile to describe three 'optical illusions' he experiences while skating quickly across the ice. In lines 28–31 he uses a metaphor to describe how when we are travelling quickly it can seem that the landscape is passing us by rather than us passing the landscape. In lines 35–7 he uses a simile to describe his dizziness after braking suddenly: it seems as if the earth's rotation has become suddenly visible.

Perhaps the most memorable example of this technique occurs in lines 26–8 which describe a star's reflection on the ice. Wordsworth attempts to skate across this 'reflex' or reflection. Yet no matter how quickly he skates the reflection will always seem to be in front of him. Wordsworth uses a wonderful metaphor to describe this optical effect, declaring that the reflection 'fled' away from him across the ice.

Assonance & onomatopoeia

The conclusion of the poem, in particular, is rich in assonance. We see this in 'shadowy banks' with its repeated 'a' sound, 'solitary cliffs' with its repeated 'i' sound, 'diurnal sound' with its repeated broad vowels and in 'dreamless sleep' with its repeated 'e' sounds. This profusion of assonance creates a pleasant and euphonious verbal music appropriate to the moments of tranquillity the poem's conclusion describes.

There are also several instances of onomatopoeia in the poem. The phrase 'hissed along the polished ice', for instance, seems to almost mimic the scraping noise of the children's skates. Similarly the phrase 'tinkled like iron' suggests the cheerful noise of the children's echoing against the nearby hillsides.

THEMES

The beauty of the natural world

Like so many of Wordsworth's poems 'Skating' celebrates the beauty of nature. The poem describes a beautiful winter scene: the ground covered with 'polished ice' that reflects the starlight, leafless trees and echoing hillsides, the stars sparkling in the east as the orange sunset slowly fades. The only sign of human habitation in this winter wonderland are the lights in 'cottage windows that blazed' through twilight gloom. Wordsworth takes great delight ('rapture') in careering through this icy paradise. A similar celebration of nature can be found in practically every one of Wordsworth's poems.

Nature as mentor

An important theme in Wordsworth's poetry is the idea of nature as a kind of mentor to the young poet. Nature, he felt, taught him lessons, guiding his moral and personal development.

Elsewhere in *The Prelude*, Wordsworth declares that he was 'Fostered alike by beauty and by fear'. Sometimes nature thought him harsh lessons, what he described as 'severer interventions', lessons that were filled with 'pain and fear'. More often, however, nature was a gentle mentor, educating him through its profound beauty.

It could be argued that in this extract nature encourages the young poet's personal development. The landscape fills him with serenity and inspiration. As readers we sense the young poet's artistic talents begin to take shape.

Solitude

This poem also touches on the notion of solitude, another recurring theme in Wordsworth's work. While the poet takes great pleasure in playing on the ice with his friends he regularly feels the need to take off on his own. Sometimes he rests or 'retires' alone in a 'silent bay'. Sometimes he just skates alone for a while across the ice. This emphasises the importance solitude played in Wordsworth's life and in his poems. It is through solitary contemplation that we

William Wordsworth

best experience nature's beauty, peace and inspiration.

A similar positive view of solitude is evident in 'The Solitary Reaper', where the poet praises the song the reaper sings to herself. We also see it in 'The Stolen Boat', where Wordsworth takes great pleasure in rowing alone across the lake and in 'Lines Composed Upon Westminster Bridge' where he delights in the silence and emptiness of early morning London. In each of these poems solitude is associated with beauty, peace and creativity.

Poetry

Some of *The Prelude*'s most famous passages recount what Wordsworth referred to as 'spots of time', moments when the budding poet was suddenly struck by the majesty and splendour of the natural world. These moments of heightened experience made him aware that he possessed a special sensitivity toward nature and contributed his sense of his destiny as a poet. They contributed to the 'growth of a poet's mind'.

'Skating' also describes one of these 'spots of time'. It recounts several moments of heightened experience: the young poet's joy in playing with his friends, the peacefulness of slipping off on his own, the intense feeling of tranquillity he gets when he brakes suddenly at the poem's conclusion. It could be argued that similar moments of heightened experience are described in 'The Solitary Reaper', 'Tintern Abbey' and 'Composed Upon Westminster Bridge'. For Wordsworth the ability to experience these intense moments was intimately linked with the ability to write great poetry.

Yet we also that Wordsworth's poetic gifts somehow set him apart from his companions. He is more sensitive than his friends to the charms of this twilit winter evening. While these hours of skating were a 'happy time' for Wordsworth's friends, for the poet himself they were filed with rapture or ecstasy: 'for me/ It was a time of rapture!' The need to leave behind the 'uproar' of the games also sets Wordsworth apart from the other children: he has a desire for solitude and introspection that his companions seem to lack. The young Wordsworth, therefore, comes across as a 'special' child, blessed with poetic gifts that need to be nurtured by private contemplation of the icy landscape.

The still, sad music of humanity

A recurring feature of Wordsworth's poetry is the strange pleasure he takes in sorrow, melancholy and lonesomeness. In this poem he describes how the sounds of children at play echoes from the distant hills as what seems to be an strange and sorrowful lament, an 'alien sound/ Of melancholy' To Wordsworth and his fellow Romantic poets melancholic music was the most beautiful. And it seems no sound was truly sublime unless it had a sorrowful quality to it.

This focus on melancholy sounds is also present in 'The Solitary Reaper', where he seems mesmerised by the sadness and strangeness of the highland lass' song. It could be argued that there is also something eerie and melancholic about the echoes created by the poet as he rows across the lake in 'The Stolen Boat.' Similarly, in 'Tintern Abbey' the poet describes himself as being captivated by the 'still, sad music of humanity' rising up from the valley below him. In each of these in instances beauty and pleasure are mixed with sorrow and strangeness.

The Solitary Reaper

William Wordsworth

BACKGROUND & INTRODUCTION

This poem was inspired by a trip Wordsworth made to the Scottish Highlands in 1803. It was harvest time. Wordsworth and his friends saw several fields where a lone worker was busy at the task of bringing in the harvest: As his sister Dorothy wrote in her diary: 'It was harvest time, and the fields were quietly – might I be allowed to say pensively? – enlivened by small companies of reapers. It is not uncommon in the more lonely parts of the Highlands to see a single person so employed'.

LINE BY LINE

STANZA 1

The poet passes a 'lass' or girl working by herself in a field: 'Behold her single in the field/ yon solitary Highland lass'. She is busy harvesting the crop: 'she cuts and binds the grain'. As she works she sings to herself. The poet describes the sadness of her song, referring to it as a 'melancholy strain'. (A 'strain' is a little piece of music). According to the poet her singing fills the entire deep valley ('Vale profound') in which she works: 'the Vale profound/ Is overflowing with the sound'.

STANZA 2

The poet praises the beauty of the girl's singing by using two unusual comparisons. Firstly, he mentions a nightingale's song heard by travellers in Arabia. The nightingale's music is extremely 'welcome' to the travellers because it signals they have reached an oasis (a 'leafy haunt') among the 'sands' of the Arabian desert. Yet the reaper's song is even more 'welcome' to the poet than the nightingale's song is to these travellers.

Secondly, the poet mentions a cuckoo's song heard in the outer Hebrides. This is a particularly 'thrilling' sound because it signals spring is coming to these bleak and isolated islands that suffer incredibly harsh winters. Yet the reaper's song is more 'thrilling' to the poet than the cuckoo's song is to the people of the 'farthest Hebrides'.

STANZA 3

The girl, it seems, is singing in Scots Gaelic and the poet cannot understand her. He is desperate, however, to know the meaning of her words: 'Will no one tell me what she sings?'

* He wonders if her sad song (her 'plaintive numbers') has to do with tragic events lost in the mists of time: 'old, unhappy, far-off things'.
* He wonders if her sad song has to with ancient defeats in war: 'battles long ago'.
* He wonders if her sad song (her 'lay') has to do with more 'humble' or everyday things: 'Familiar matter of today'. He imagines that she is singing about ordinary difficulties that occur again and again in life: 'Some natural sorrow, loss. or pain/ That has been and may be again?'

STANZA 4

To the poet it seems that this 'Maiden's' song will go on forever: 'the Maiden sang/ As if her song could have no ending'. The poet listens intently to her singing before finally going on his way: 'I listened motionless and still/ And, as I mounted up the hill'. Yet the reaper's singing stayed with the poet even after he had travelled out of earshot. He says that her singing stayed with him for a long time. He carried it in his mind and in his heart long after he had left the valley behind: 'That music in my heart I bore/ Long after it was heard no more'.

LANGUAGE

Poetic form

This poem is written in four eight-line stanzas, each rhyming ABCBDDEE.

Imagery

This poem features several memorable images:

* The image of the highland lass singing in the isolated valley.
* An image of the leafy oasis in the Arabian desert.
* There is the image of the cuckoo singing in the outer Hebrides in springtime.

These last two images could be described almost as 'opposites' to one another. Both feature what to Wordsworth would have been exotic, inhospitable landscapes: the icy, freezing Hebrides, and the scorching sands of the Arabian dessert.

It has been suggested that there is an element of metaphor about the poet's description of the reaper's song 'overflowing' the valley. Her music is compared to a liquid substance flooding the entire surrounding landscape.

It could also be argue that there is an element of hyperbole, or poetic exaggeration, in the poet's description of the reaper's song. Does the poet really believe that the lass' singing is more 'welcome' than that of the nightingale which signifies shelter in the desert, and more thrilling that of the cuckoo which signifies the start of springtime? It has been suggested that the poet is playfully exaggerating here in order to emphasise the beauty of the reaper's music.

Addressing the reader directly

In the first stanza Wordsworth addresses the reader directly, asking us to 'Behold' the singing girl and urging us to 'Stop here, or gently pass!' This creates a powerful impression of immediacy, giving us the sense that we are actually walking through the highland landscape with the poet.

THEMES

The beauty of the natural world

In 'The Solitary Reaper', as in so many of his poems, Wordsworth takes great delight in depicting the natural world. The poet provides several memorable descriptions of nature at its most beautiful: a shady oasis in the Arabian desert, the bleak and silent outer Hebrides in springtime, and the 'Vale profound' through which he walks listening to the reaper's song.

A similar delight in the natural world can be found in practically every poem by Wordsworth on the course, arguably even in 'Lines Composed Upon Westminster Bridge', which though set in an urban context, celebrates the peace, light and freshness of morning.

Oneness with nature

Another recurring theme in Wordsworth is the notion of oneness with nature. It has often been argued that in this poem the 'highland lass' is at one with the landscape that surrounds her. She is a single figure in an isolated rural landscape, cut off from the wider world. She works closely with the natural world, cutting and binding the grain. (It could also be argued that as an agricultural worker, she is in tune with the changing seasons and with the rhythms of the nature.

The depiction of the reaper can be compared to that of Lucy in 'She Dwelt Among the Untrodden Ways'. Lucy is also depicted as a young woman who lives in an isolated rural community and seems at one with the beautiful landscape that surrounds her. In 'A Slumber Did My Spirit Seal'; she becomes literally one with nature as her dead body mingles with the rocks, stones and trees.

Solitude

An important theme in this poem is that of solitude. The reaper's solitude is emphasised again and again. She is 'single' in the field, she is 'solitary', she is 'alone', she is 'singing by herself'. In Wordsworth's poetry solitude is generally presented in a positive light, as a source of joy, creativity and inspiration. In this poem the reaper's solitude is linked to her beautiful and moving singing that 'overflows' the entire valley.

A similar positive presentation of solitude is found in 'She Dwelt Among the Untrodden Ways', where it is Lucy's solitary and singular existence that makes her so beautiful and special to the poet. Both 'The Stolen Boat' and 'Skating' present moments of solitude that are linked to the young poet's developing sense of creativity. In 'Lines Composed Upon Westminster Bridge', it is the poet's solitude that makes the city beautiful. He relishes the calm silence before the city wakes and the daily hustle and bustle begins.

Poetry

It could be argued that this poem, like many poems by Wordsworth, comments on the nature of poetry and the role of the poet. The solitary reaper, singing to herself in the field, sums up Wordsworth's idea of what a poet should be:

- The reaper sings her song alone. Similarly, the poet must write his poems alone, at a remove from society.

(This is suggested in 'Tintern Abbey', 'The Stolen Boat' and 'Skating', where the growth of poetic creativity is liked to solitude and isolation).
- The reaper is happy to sing to herself. She doesn't care if she has an audience or not. Similarly, the poet must be happy to compose poetry for himself. He must not be concerned with fame or audience expectations.
- Good poems should remain in the reader's heart and mind, the way the lass' song will carried in the heart and mind of the poet long after he has left the vale behind.
- Finally, poets, like the reaper, should be close to nature.

The still, sad music of humanity

A recurring feature of Wordsworth's poetry is the strange pleasure he takes in sorrow, melancholy and lonesomeness. In this poem he seems mesmerised by the sadness and strangeness of the highland lass' song. (It is strange to him because he does not understand the language in which she sings). In stanza 3 he seems to take great delight in imagining the sorrowful circumstances that might have inspired the song, revelling in thoughts of old defeats in battle, ancient tragedies and more 'familiar' everyday sorrows.

In 'Skating' he describes the echo of the children's play creating a similarly sad and strange music. Wordsworth describes it as a 'melancholy' and 'alien' sound. It could be argued that there is also something eerie and melancholic about the echoes created by the poet as he rows across the lake in 'The Stolen Boat.' Similarly, in 'Tintern Abbey' the poet describes himself as being captivated by the 'still, sad music of humanity' rising up from the valley below him. In each of these in instances beauty and pleasure are mixed with sorrow and strangeness.

Lines Composed Upon Westminster Bridge, Sept. 3, 1802

LINE BY LINE

The poet is travelling across Westminster bridge heading into the city of London. It is very early in the morning, and the city is silent. The poet is amazed at how beautiful the city looks at this time of day. He cannot imagine of a more beautiful place, and thinks that somebody would have to be dull of spirit to pass such a magnificent sight and not be moved: 'Dull would he be of soul who could pass by/ A sight so touching in its majesty'.

In this early light the city looks its finest. The early morning light and the crisp morning air cover the city like fine clothing: 'this city now doth like a garment wear/ The beauty of the morning'. The city appears to be at one with the natural world. All its elements, from the ships docked on the river Thames to the towering buildings, seem 'open' to the fields and sky. At this hour of the morning the air is clean and everything seems shiny new, 'bright and glittering' in the sunlight.

The morning is illuminating the city in an a magnificent way. In fact, the poet thinks that the morning sun has never before illuminated any landscape so beautifully: 'Never did the sun more beautifully steep/ In his first splendour, valley, rock, or hill'. Without all the hustle and bustle of activity the city is peaceful. The poet says that he has never experienced such 'calm' before: 'Ne'er saw I, never felt a calm so deep'.

The river, uninterrupted by the activities of sailors and merchants, is free to move as it wishes: 'The river glideth at his own sweet will'. Without the coming and going of their inhabitants the 'houses seem asleep'. For now this 'mighty' city of London is 'lying still'.

The last line hints at the energy that is contained in the city, all of the life that is set to spring into action when the city starts to wake. The 'mighty heart' might be a reference the inhabitants of London, the very people that bring life to the place. It might also refer to something more mysterious, the power or force that moves through all things.

THEMES

The beauty of the natural world

Whereas many poems by Wordsworth set the beauty and calm of the natural world against the squalor and stress of the city, this sonnet embraces the city of London and considers it a beautiful spectacle. Basking in the gentle morning light and crisp clean air, the city, as yet undisturbed by hustle and bustle, strikes the poet as something very special. This man-made environment seems to sit so perfectly in the midst of green fields, beneath the clear morning sky. Everything seems to be in harmony and there is a wonderful tranquillity to the setting. The city at this hour of the morning is so peaceful that the poet feels certain he has 'never felt, a calm so deep!' The river, unimpeded by traffic is free to 'glideth at his own sweet will'.

LANGUAGE

This is a Petrarchan sonnet with a rhyming scheme of ABBAABBA CDCDCD.

The poem features an interesting simile where Wordsworth compares the fall of the morning light over the city to a 'garment' resting upon a body. The simile serves to suggest the beauty and tenderness of the morning and how the city, still and peaceful, possesses a natural, almost human, beauty in such light. The word 'bare' in the fifth line suggests a nakedness, a kind of Eden-like naturalness and innocence.

The poem also uses personification to great effect. The city is said to 'wear' the 'garment' of the morning and the sun and river seem to be alive and operating according to their own 'will'.

It is a Beauteous Evening, Calm and Free

LINE BY LINE

It is evening. The poet is taking a walk with a young girl, possibly his daughter. He is overawed by the beauty and tranquillity of the world that surrounds him. The evening is 'free' of the concerns and troubles of the day. The poet considers the time to be sacred and special. He compares the serenity of the evening to a 'Nun' deep in prayer. The sun is slowly setting. It appears 'broad' on the horizon, peacefully sinking. The skies are linked with 'heaven', gently and lovingly sitting over the 'Sea': 'The gentleness of heaven broods o'er the Sea'.

The continuous rolling of the waves crashing onto the beach sounds 'like thunder'. The noise suggests to the poet the existence of some 'mighty Being' or God who is eternally present in nature. He calls on the young girl to 'Listen!' and witness this magnificent presence.

However, it seems that the young girl is not quite as sensitive to her surroundings as the poet. She is not struck with the kind of notions that the poet is as she walks beside him this evening. But the poet tells her not to worry if she does not sense the existence of some special 'Being' in the world. This, he tells her, does not make her any less holy or special: 'If thou appear untouched by solemn thought,/ Thy nature is not therefore less divine'.

Though she may be untroubled by religious thoughts,

her childish innocence ensures that she remains special in the eyes of God. She is said to lie 'in Abraham's bosom all the year', meaning that God holds her dear and looks after her. And just by being her young innocent self she in turn worships God: 'And worshipp'st at the Temple's inner shrine'. God is with her, though she does not realise it or give it any thought.

THEMES

The beauty of the natural world

This sonnet once again demonstrates the poet's love of the natural world. He describes the perfect tranquillity of the evening as the 'broad sun' sets and the sky 'broods' over the sea. The scene is one of absolute calm and the poet is deeply moved by what he sees. His senses are alive and he is open to the sights and the sounds that surround him. He listens to the waves rolling on to the shore and thinks about the power of the natural world.

The sublime in nature

Wordsworth's poems often speak of some powerful force or presence evident in the natural world. In 'Tintern Abbey' for example, he spoke about a 'presence' in nature, a sense of 'something far more deeply interfused' in all that he perceives. In 'It is a beauteous evening' the poet once again makes reference to the existence of some sublime power. Listening to the waves continuously crashing onto the beach calls on us to behold the presence of something powerful and eternal:

Listen! the mighty Being is awake,
And doth with his eternal motion make
A sound like thunder – everlastingly.

Although the poem contains much religious imagery and suggests that this time of day is 'holy', the poet does not explicitly link the 'mighty Being' with a defined religious concept of God, such as perhaps Christianity might offer. But the presence that Wordsworth senses in the movement of the waves is certainly God-like, an eternal presence that works in a mysterious manner and is the force behind all living things.

Childhood

The poet is accompanied on his evening stroll by a young girl, widely regarded as his daughter. The poem's exhortation to 'Listen!' to the sounds of the waves and experience 'the mighty Being' are addressed to this young girl. However, because of her age or her character, the girl seems to take a less serious interest than the poet in her environment. She is 'untouched by solemn thought'. The poet may have been disappointed to find out that his daughter did not share his deep interest in the mystery of the natural world, but he does not register his disappointment here. Instead he celebrates the child's innocence and says that God holds her dear. He suggests that her innocence allows her occupy a special and serene place which he likens to 'Abraham's bosom'.

LANGUAGE

This is a Petrarchan sonnet with an ABBAABBA CDECED rhyming scheme.

It features much religious imagery. The poet compares the evening to a 'nun' in devoted and ecstatic contemplation of the divine. This simile suggests that the evening is somehow sacred and introduces a spiritual element to the poem, preceding the mentioning of the 'mighty Being' in the sixth line. The poem also makes reference to 'heaven'. The sky is personified and said to 'brood' over the sea. In the sestet of the poem, the poet introduces a biblical reference, saying that the young child 'liest in Abraham's bosom', and mentions the 'Temple's inner shrine'. Both of these serve as metaphors for the sacredness of childhood innocence. There is also a mention of God in the last line of the poem. These religious references ultimately give the poem a solemn tone and suggest the depth of the poet's own adoration of the natural world.

GERARD MANLEY HOPKINS
THEMES

NATURE

Perhaps the first thing to strike readers of Hopkins' poetry is his intense love of the natural world. His inspired and ecstatic response to nature can be summed by his declaration in 'Spring' that it the thrush's song strikes him 'like lightning'. Hopkins seems literally 'electrified' by the beauty of the natural world.

He exults in 'Spring' as time of fertility; of 'lushness', 'richness', growth and abundance. It is a time of gambolling lambs, blue skies and wildflowers shooting through the soil. He regards Spring as a time when nature can offer us a cleansing sense of personal rebirth and renewal. (This is evident when Hopkins describes his ears being 'rinsed' and 'wrung' dry by the thrush's song). All in all, for Hopkins spring is such magical time of year that it brings to mind the garden of Eden. In springtime the world is no less than a kind of paradise.

A similarly ecstatic response to the natural world can be found in 'The Windhover', where Hopkins lovingly describes the flight of a falcon, its 'riding of the rolling-level-underneath-him steady-air'. To Hopkins the falcon something majestic, a prince or 'dauphin' of the 'kingdom of daylight'. He seems moved to tears by the sight of this bird in all its majesty: 'My heart in hiding wept for a bird, the achieve of the mastery of the thing'.

A perhaps more restrained appreciation of nature is evident in 'Inversnaid' and 'Pied Beauty'. 'Inversnaid' delights in the sights and sounds of a 'burn' or brook crashing down a slope in the Scottish Highlands:

This darksome burn, horseback brown,
His rollrock highroad roaring down,
In coop and in comb the fleece of his foam

'Pied Beauty', meanwhile, celebrates the beauty of 'dappled things', sights that have a complex visual pattern, such as a trout's speckled skin, finches' wings and a landscape divided into many different fields and 'plots'.

There are also instances where Hopkins displays what might almost be described as an environmentalist attitude toward nature. in 'Inversnaid', for instance, he seems worried that the wild places of natural beauty like Inversnaid be consumed by urbanisation and industrialisation: 'What would the world be, once bereft/ Of wet and of wildness?' He concludes the poem hoping that such continue to exist long into the future: 'Long live the weeds and the wilderness yet'.

A similar attitude is evident in 'God's Grandeur'. Mankind, the poem maintains, has lost contact with the earth. This is symbolised by the fact that our feet are 'shod' and no longer touch the soil nor can foot feel, being shod'. Our industry and cities have had a devastating effect on the natural world, stripping the soil bare: 'And all is seared with trade; bleared, smeared with toil … the soil is bare now'. Yet Hopkins believes that the Holy Spirit guards the earth, keeping it fresh and new and undoing the damage done by man.

GOD & NATURE

Hopkins was an extremely religious man and his poems rarely just enjoy nature for its own sake. More often than not, in Hopkins' poetry thoughts of nature lead to thoughts of God:

In 'Spring', for instance, the earth in springtime reminds Hopkins of the Garden of Eden, which in turn leads him to think about sin. Specifically he thinks about children, who are sinless and innocent as Adam was before he ate the apple.

In 'The Windhover' the sight of the soaring falcon causes Hopkins to think about Christ's role as our redeemer.

In 'As kingfishers catch fire' considering nature's variety leads him to think about the 'just man', who 'justices' or lives in a just way and keeps himself in state of grace with God.

In 'Pied Beauty' a celebration of 'dappled things' leads Hopkins to praise God: 'Praise Him'.

Hopkins was keenly aware of God as the creator every living thing we see around us. This is evident in 'Pied Beauty', where he describes God as the force that gives birth to the wonders of the natural world, to everything that is 'original', 'spare' and 'strange'. God, he said, 'fathers forth' every thing we see around us in nature.

A similar point is made in 'God's Grandeur', where Hopkins describes God's energy flowing through all living things. It is like an electric 'charge' or current that pulses through everything in creation: 'The world is charged with the grandeur of God'. God's energy sustains the natural world, keeping it alive, fresh and new: 'nature is never spent;/ There lives the dearest freshness deep down things'. The holy spirit protects and shelters the world like a bird 'brooding' over the eggs in its nest.

'As kingfishers catch fire' also focuses on God's presence in the natural world. God, the poem suggests, has given everything in the world a unique spiritual essence. This essence 'dwells' inside each creature and object: 'that being indoors each one dwells'. We can think of it as a 'spiritual spark' or soul that resides within. Each creature and object reveals its unique essence to the world through its actions and appearances: the way it looks, the sounds it makes, the things it does. Everything acts in such a way that it spells out or expresses the essence God has placed within it: 'Selves-goes itself; *myself* it speaks and spells'.

Hopkins' outlook in these poems is influenced by the philosopher Johannes Duns Scotus who argued that God was present in every living thing, in every aspect of His creation. Dun Scotus was a major influence on Hopkins, who encountered his writings in 1872 while in training for the priesthood. His teachings allowed Hopkins to reconcile his intense appreciation of natural beauty with his devotion to God.

MAN'S RELATIONSHIP WITH GOD

The sinful nature of mankind

Hopkins was keenly aware that mankind was sinful. In 'God's Grandeur', for instance, he laments that humankind goes against God's will, smearing and despoiling the beautiful world he has given us. Hopkins despairingly asks why man fails to 'reck' or obey God's will: 'Why do men then now not reck his rod?'

'Spring', too, is highly conscious of sin. Hopkins celebrates the innocence of the young, claiming that 'innocent mind' and 'Mayday' exist in every child: 'Innocent mind and Mayday in girl and boy'. (To Hopkins 'Mayday' is associated with purity and innocence, perhaps due to the fact that May is traditionally regarded as the month of the Virgin Mary). Yet Hopkins is all too aware that as children grow older their innocent minds will be corrupted by sin: 'before it cloy … Before it cloud … and sour with sinning'.

Redemption through Christ

The speaker calls on Jesus to preserve the innocence of these children, requesting Christ to 'Have' and 'get' each boy and girl, to take them to him before their innocence is destroyed: 'Have, get … Christ, lord … Innocent mind and Mayday in girl and boy'. The conclusion of 'Spring', however, is a little vague. It is unclear exactly how Hopkins wants Christ to preserve the innocence of each child. Does the speaker want Jesus to keep the children young forever, to preserve them from the guilts and complications of adulthood? It is more likely that Hopkins wishes the children might grow up to be adults but remain 'childlike' in that they will be somehow free of sin.

There are several other poems where Christ is depicted as overcoming sin. In 'Felix Randal', for instance Hopkins claims that Christ, through communion, is our 'reprieve and ransom', the thing that saves us from sin and death. When Hopkins gives Felix communion his heart becomes 'heavenlier'. His soul becomes cleansed of sin and more fit to enter heaven. In 'The Windhover' Christ is depicted as a knight or 'chevalier' who does battle on our behalf against the forces of sin. Christ opposes sin like a knight riding into battle against an enemy army or the falcon battling against the 'big wind'.

'As kingfishers catch fire' also focuses on the notion of sin and redemption. The poem calls on us to 'justice', to behave as 'just men', to turn away from sin and live in a good or 'graceful' fashion: 'the just man justices;/ Kéeps gráce: thát keeps all his goings graces'. When we behave in such a fashion we resemble Christ. There is a sense in which by 'justicing', by behaving in a just fashion, we resemble Christ and make him present in the world. God sees Christ in eyes, limbs and faces of just men.

MENTAL SUFFERING

Hopkins' earliest mention of despair comes in 'Inversnaid'. He describes a little whirlpool in the highland brook as a black hole of despair. It has a black and 'fell' or evil look about it:

Of a pool so pitchblack, féll-frówning,
It rounds and rounds Despair to drowning.

This little black whirlpool of despair suggests Hopkins' unhappiness at the time. When he wrote 'Inversnaid' he was ministering in the slums of the great Northern English industrialised cities. Hopkins, who never enjoyed good health, found this work mentally and physically exhausting. This whirlpool image ominously suggests the despair into which the poet would later sink. 'Felix Randal' also seems to prefigure the poet's own suffering. The sick blacksmith's mind begins to 'ramble' as his sanity slips away, suggesting the madness-inducing torment that would soon grip the poet himself.

The 'terrible sonnets' describe this descent into mental torment. They were written over the last few years of the poet's life when he was working in University College Dublin. During this period Hopkins was in poor mental and physical health. He found his duties exhausting and unrewarding. Furthermore, he was lonely and miserable in Ireland, a country where he found it difficult to fit in and had few friends. As he put it in a letter these 'terrible sonnets' were the product of a 'continually jaded and harassed mind'.

'No worst there is none' could be described as a howl of mental torment. The poet has been 'pitched past pitch of grief'. He is experiencing a mental state that is far beyond ordinary grief or sorrow. Hopkins' mental torment is more or less unrelenting, with only the briefest of pauses between one bout of suffering and the next. His torment also keeps getting worse. To Hopkins it seems that his sufferings will keep increasing in intensity forever, that there is 'no worst', no rock-bottom for him to hit. It is hardly surprising, therefore, that the poet thinks of himself as a pitiful 'wretch', crying out in agony over and over again. His only 'comfort' is the oblivion offered by sleep or death.

'I wake and feel the fell of dark' which powerfully describes 'black hours' of mental distress that the poet, unable to sleep, must suffer through long 'black hours' of misery before the morning light arrives. He conveys this suffering by describing himself in terms of 'gall', 'heartburn' and bitterness. He compares himself to the 'lost', the souls of the damned 'sweating' in the furnaces of hell.

'Thou art indeed just, lord' is perhaps less intense than the other three. Here Hopkins presents his suffering in a more rational, restrained and subtle fashion. However, his despair and mental torment still resonate throughout the poem. It powerfully conveys Hopkins' desperate and 'straining' attempts to make something of his life and his sense of failure and disappointment when these attempts come to nothing. Hopkins feels completely barren, that he is incapable of 'building' or producing anything worthwhile. The only element of hope in the poem is Hopkins' desperate plea for God to do something to relieve his situation.

RELIGIOUS DOUBT

We first encounter religious the them of religious doubt in 'Felix Randal', where the powerfully built blacksmith curses God for allowing him to become ill: 'Impatient he cursed at first'. However, Felix 'mended' his ways when Hopkins 'anointed' him and gave him the secrets. Felix, it seems, became reconciled with God and somehow learned to accept his illness as part of God's plan.

'I wake and feel the fell of dark' and 'No worst there is

none' explore intense states of emotional and religious doubt. Hopkins is in a terrible state and calls out to God for help. God, however, fails to answer. Hopkins, then, feels abandoned by God in his time of greatest need. As he puts it in 'No worst': 'Comforter, where, where is your comforting?/ Mary, mother of us, where is your relief?' In 'I wake and feel the fell of dark' God is presented as somewhat distant and uncaring. He 'lives alas! away' and fails to respond to the speaker's 'laments'. The speaker, therefore, describes his pleas for comfort as 'dead letters', comparing his prayers to mail that has been posted to an abandoned or false address.

Hopkins most powerful statement of religious doubt comes in 'Thou art indeed just, Lord'. In it Hopkins asks an age old question: if God is good why does he let wicked men triumph and sinners get ahead in life? Furthermore, why does he let his faithful servants suffer? Hopkins has sacrificed so much for God yet nothing in his life succeeds. Meanwhile sinners who have sacrificed nothing, who are the slaves or 'thralls' of lust, get ahead in life. Hopkins, like many other people through history, wonders why God allows this to happen. There is a strong sense of frustration, perhaps even anger, in this poem. Everything Hopkins tries to do ends in disappointment and failure. He cannot understand why God allows this to happen, especially when Hopkins has served him so faithfully. Hopkins almost suspects that God has turned against him and is actually his enemy rather than his friend.

It has also been suggested that in this poem Hopkins expresses doubts about his religious vocation, especially his vow of celibacy. Hopkins sacrificed the sexual side of his nature for God. He also gave up his ability to 'breed', to father children. But in this poem he suggests that God has given him little or nothing in return. There's a sense in which he regrets these huge sacrifices, referring to himself in an almost demeaning fashion as 'Time's eunuch'. It's as if he envies those sinners who are 'thralls of lust', who are slaves to sexual passion.

It is tempting, then, to view Hopkins' poetry as a journey from faith into doubt. The early poems focus on God's kindness and mercy, presenting Him as the merciful redeemer of sinful, faithless mankind. The later 'terrible' sonnets, however, seem to doubt God's fundamental goodness. God, it appears, has turned his back on his faithful servant in his hour of greatest need.

HOPKINS' POETIC STYLE

Inscape & Instress

Inscape and instress are two terms permanently associated with the poetry of Hopkins, in particular with his nature poetry. Hopkins was convinced that everything in nature was unique. His term for the individuality of each thing, for the qualities it and it alone possessed, was inscape. Everything, he believed, from the tiniest pebble to a soaring falcon to the mind had its own inscape, or set of unique qualities. This view is evident in 'As kingfishers catch fire, dragonflies draw flame' which suggests that each object and living thing has its own unique inner essence and expresses this essence through its behaviour in the world.

Hopkins' poetry is driven by the desire to grasp the inscapes of the natural world, to capture in words the unique individuality of each bird and flower he described. Again and again, he sets out to capture the inscape of various natural objects by stretching language to its very limits. Very often Hopkins uses sound effects in an attempt to capture the uniqueness and character of a natural phenomenon. He was master, in particular, of assonance and alliteration. 'Spring' provides an good example of alliteration, the repeated soft 'l' sounds capturing the season's lushness and abundance: 'shoot long and lovely and lush;/ Thrush's eggs look little low heavens'.

Both assonance and alliteration, meanwhile, are deployed in 'Inversnaid' to capture the power and energy of the flowing stream. Line 2 is a good example of this, with its repeated 'r' and broad-vowel sounds: 'His rollrock highroad roaring down'. Hopkins also uses unusual metaphors and similes to capture the inscape of a particular phenomenon. In 'Pied Beauty', for example, the appearance of the sky is compared, bizarrely yet effectively, that of a cow: 'skies of couple-colour as a brinded cow'.

Another tactic used by Hopkins in his quest to capture the world's various inscapes is the invention of new words (known as 'neologisms' or 'coinages'). We see this in 'Inversnaid' where Hopkins coins the verb 'twindles' to describe vapour emanating from the foot of a waterfall. ('Twindles' combines the verbs 'twist', 'twitch' and 'dwindle'). Another, very famous, departure from standard English usage occurs in 'The Windhover', where the entire phrase 'rolling level underneath him steady' becomes an adjective, describing the air the falcon soars through.

Instress is another important term in Hopkins' work. According to Hopkins instress was God's divine energy, a force that flowed through everything like electricity and preserved the natural world in all its variety and beauty. 'God's Grandeur', in particular, explores the theme of instress. In this poem 'instress' is represented as an electrical charge that emanates from God and crackles through the universe, maintaining the beauty and individuality of each living thing.

Sprung Rhythm

Hopkins greatest contribution to English poetry was his concept of 'sprung rhythm'. The theory of sprung rhythm can be difficult to grasp, and has been the subject of many scholarly articles (including Hopkins' own almost incomprehensible 'Preface'). The best way to understand 'sprung rhythm', however, is to compare it to standard English verse. In traditional English poetry each line had a set amount of 'stressed' and 'unstressed' syllables. This creates a predictable rhythmic effect, something you could tap your foot to. A good example is the rhythm of the following lines from Wordsworth's 'The Solitary Reaper':

Will no one tell me what she sings?-
Perhaps the plaintive numbers flow
For old, unhappy, far-off things
And battles long ago:

Hopkins, however, changes the rules by focusing only on 'stressed' syllables. Each line has a set amount of 'stressed' syllables, but can have any amount of 'unstressed' syllables. The effect created by sprung rhythm will be obvious if the following passage from Hopkins is compared to the one above from Wordsworth:

As a skate's heel sweeps smooth on a bow-bend:
the hurl and gliding
Rebuffed the big wind. My heart in hiding
Stirred for a bird,-the achieve of the mastery of the thing!

The difference between standard rhythm and sprung rhythm, then, is that standard rythym has set amount of both stressed and unstressed syllables in each line, whereas sprung rhythm has only a set amount of stressed syllables in each line and can have any amount of unstressed. The only way to really understand sprung rhythm, however, is to read Hopkins' poems aloud. The technique generates a powerful, unpredictable music, which, while it may lack the regular pulse of traditional poems like the 'The Solitary Reaper', can bring the movement of natural phenomena, a falcon or a roaring stream, vividly to life in the mind of the reader. To Hopkins sprung rhythm was 'the least forced, the most rhetorical and emphatic of all possible rhythms, combining opposite and, one would have thought, incompatible excellences'.

As Kingfishers Catch Fire, Dragonflies Draw Flame

LINE BY LINE

LINES 5–8
This is the thinking behind the poem:

- God has given everything in the world a unique spiritual essence.
- This essence 'dwells' inside each creature and object: 'that being indoors each one dwells'. We can think of it as a 'spiritual spark' or soul that resides within.
- Each creature and object reveals its unique essence to the world through its actions and appearances: the way it looks, the sounds it makes, the things it does.

Therefore the actions and appearances of each creature and object are like a cry declaring its unique spiritual essence: 'Crying *What I do is me: for that I came*'. Every single thing 'came' into the world to express the unique essence God has placed within it: 'Each mortal thing does one thing and the same'. Everything acts in such a way that it spells out or expresses its essence: 'Selves-goes itself; *myself* it speaks and spells'.

LINES 1–4
Hopkins gives us several examples of creatures and objects expressing their unique inner essence. Firstly, he describes kingfishers and dragonflies. These creatures express their essence through their beautiful appearance, especially through the way they look when sunlight strikes their bodies. So bright are kingfishers and dragonflies that when the sunlight hits them they blaze with colour, appearing almost to go up in flames: 'As Kingfishers Catch Fire, Dragonflies Draw Flame'.

Even humble, ordinary stones have a unique essence that dwells within them. They express this essence through the sounds they make when they are thrown ('tumbled') into wells: 'As tumbled over rim in roundy wells/ Stones ring'. (Many readers find this phrase difficult because Hopkins plays around with the usual order of the words. We would ordinarily put it like this: 'Stones make a ringing sound when they are thrown over the rims or edges of roundy wells.')

Finally, Hopkins describes a string on a musical instrument and a church bell. A string 'tells', or expresses its essence, through the note it produces when plucked: 'each tucked string tells'. ('Tucked' is an old word for plucked.) Similarly, a church bell expresses its essence through the sound it makes when somebody rings it. The 'hung bell' dangles from the church tower, and when it is 'swung' its chime ring out.

LINES 9–14
In the poem's final six lines, Hopkins focuses on 'the just man', a man who lives in a just and righteous manner: 'I say more: the just man justices'. He is someone who 'keeps grace', who lives in accordance with God's law and stays free of sin. All the just man's activities (referred to here as his 'goings') are carried out in a decent and sinless way: he is someone 'that keeps all his goings graces'.

Christ is present in each of us when we live according to God's law, when we act like the 'just man'. Christ, therefore, is present all over the world wherever someone is doing the right thing: 'Christ plays in ten thousand places'. He is present in the limbs, eyes and faces of each just man:

*Lovely in limbs, and lovely in eyes not his
To the Father through the features of men's faces.*

(The eyes of the just man are not Christ's eyes. They are 'not his'. And yet Christ can be seen in them each time the just man does good.) When God looks down from heaven, He sees Jesus in the appearance and actions of just men, and to Him that is a 'lovely' sight.

THEMES

Nature
Like much of Hopkins' work, this poem emphasises the beauty of the natural world. It conjures up the fiery colourful beauty of kingfishers and dragonflies. The poem suggests that even something as humble and ordinary as the noise of stones dropping down a well deserves to be celebrated. Hopkins also celebrates

the beautiful sounds made by certain manufactured objects: strings on musical instruments and church bells. While these human-made objects are not technically part of the natural world, they blend with it in the poem's celebration of life's rich tapestry.

A similar celebration of nature can be found in 'Pied Beauty', 'Inversnaid', 'Spring' and 'The Windhover'. In each of these poems, Hopkins focuses on the uniqueness, or 'inscape', of each creature and object, devising complex and original poetic lines to capture that uniqueness. 'Kingfishers' is arguably Hopkins' greatest expression of this individuality. Everything, the poem suggests, acts in a way that expresses or spells out the unique essence that exists within it.

God & nature

'Kingfishers' also refers to another of Hopkins' central themes: the presence of God in nature. God has placed a unique essence inside each creature. Each creature expresses this essence through its actions and appearances. Therefore, God is present in every creature and object that makes up the natural world. A similar theme is evident in 'God's Grandeur', where Hopkins claims that the whole world is 'charged', or electrified, with God's presence.

In this poem, Hopkins draws a moral or religious lesson from his contemplation of the natural world. A similar move is made in 'Spring', 'God's Grandeur' and 'The Windhover'. In each of these poems, Hopkins moves from a meditating on nature's beauty to thinking about the sinfulness of man and the possibility of being saved from sin through God's grace. An interesting exception to this might be 'Thou Art Indeed Just, Lord', where the sight of the riverbanks becoming 'thick' with leaves makes Hopkins actually question God's fairness and justice.

Man's relationship with God

This poem emphasises the distinction between humanity and the rest of God's creations. Non-human creatures and objects come into this world with a simple purpose: to express through their actions and appearances the essence God has placed within them. Human beings have a higher purpose: to make Christ present in the world by behaving as a 'just man'.

Non-human creatures fulfil God's plan for them automatically, simply by existing. They have no choice in the matter. Human beings, on the other hand, have been given free will. We can choose to go against the purpose God has in mind for us by living in a sinful rather than a just manner.

The poem, therefore, calls on us to turn away from sin

and live in a 'just' and 'graceful' fashion. We will fulfil God's plan for us. We will make Christ present in the world through our good deeds. We will seem 'lovely' in the eyes of God as we remind Him of his son.

This preoccupation with sin and redemption can be found throughout Hopkins' poetry. It also evident in 'Spring', where Hopkins calls on God to preserve the innocence of children against the ravages of sin. We see it in 'The Windhover', where Hopkins celebrates the possibility of salvation through Christ. We also see it in 'God's Grandeur', where Hopkins calls on men to 'reck' God's laws and treat the world He has created for us with respect.

LANGUAGE

The sonnet form
'As Kingfishers Catch Fire' is a perfectly formed Petrarchan sonnet. It has the typical Petrarchan rhyme scheme: ABBAABBA CDCDCD. It is divided into an octet (eight lines) and a sestet (six lines). There is a shift in focus between the octet and the sestet. In the octet, Hopkins discusses how every creature and object expresses its inner essence through its actions and appearances. The sestet, on the other hand, deals with issues of morality. These defining features of the Petrarchan sonnet are also evident in 'Spring' and 'God's Grandeur'.

Metaphor
Hopkins uses a metaphor to describe the effect of sunlight striking the dragonflies' and kingfishers' bodies. It appears, he says, that these beautiful creatures have caught fire. Hopkins also uses a wonderful metaphor to describe the sound of the bell ringing, declaring that the bell is shouting out its name. The bell, he suggests, 'flings' its name throughout the surrounding countryside: 'each hung bell's/ Bow swung finds tongue to fling out broad its name'.

Sound effects
Like many Hopkins poems, 'As Kingfishers Catch Fire' is rich in assonance and alliteration. In the sestet, for instance, alliteration occurs with the repeated 'g' sound ('goings' and 'graces'), the repeated 'pl' sound ('plays' and 'places'), the repeated 'l' sound ('lovely' and 'limbs') and the repeated 'f' sound ('father', 'feature' and 'faces'). Assonance also occurs in these lines due to their repeated broad-vowel sounds. This combination of assonance and alliteration lends the verse a pleasant verbal music.

Hopkins believed one of the main purposes of poetry was to describe an object's 'inscape', or unique qualities. In this poem, and in many others, he uses a series of complex sound effects in an attempt to capture the qualities of the objects he describes:

- In line 1, Hopkins uses assonance and alliteration to create a pleasant verbal music, reflecting the colourful splendour of kingfishers and dragonflies. Assonance is present through the repeated broad 'a' sound in 'dragonflies draw flame'. Alliteration, meanwhile, features through the repeated 'f' sound in 'fire', 'flies' and 'flame'.
- It could be argued that there is an 'onomatopoeic' quality to lines 2 and 3. The large number of broad-vowel sounds and the alliteration of 'rim into roundy', with its repeated 'r', create a hollow, echoing music that mimics the sound of a stone falling down a well.
- Onomatopoeia also occurs in lines 3–4. The repeated 'b' sound in 'bell' and 'bow', and the rhyme between 'swung' and 'tongue' gives these lines a loud, booming quality, suggestive of the ringing bell they describe.

Nouns & verbs
One of Hopkins' favourite poetic techniques was to use a noun as a verb. In line 7, the noun 'self' is transformed into the verb 'to self', meaning to be oneself or express one's inner qualities. In line 9, the noun 'justice' is transformed into the verb 'to justice', meaning to live in a just and righteous fashion according to God's law.

Gerard Manley Hopkins

God's Grandeur

INTRODUCTION

This sonnet celebrates the greatness of God. It marvels at the magnificence of His creation and wonders why people no longer care for the world. Hopkins laments the damage that we are doing to the planet, but believes that, despite our appalling behaviour, nature can never be destroyed.

LINE BY LINE

LINES 1–3

The world is full of God's magnificence. It energises the world and fills it with vitality. It is like an electrical current that flows through all things.

The second line can be understood in different ways. This magnificent force erupts from the world, exploding in all directions like light reflecting off silver foil that is shaken: 'It will flame out, like shining from shook foil'. Perhaps this is a reference to the varied blossomings in nature, the flowers and trees with their magnificent displays of colour and vitality. However, the line could also be a description of the sun which warms and energises the world with its 'shining'. Thus, God's energy flames out from the sun and brings forth life on earth.

The glory of God manifests itself in many individual instances – in the various plants and animals that inhabit the earth for example. But all these instances of God's grandeur come together to reveal His singular 'greatness'. Hopkins compares this to the oil from many individual olives coming together to create a single jar of olive oil.

LINES 4–8

The fourth line of the poem begins with the word 'Crushed'. Though this word completes the previous line, the way that it stands alone at the beginning of the fourth line gives it greater significance. Followed immediately by a full stop, the word 'Crushed' brings about an abrupt stop. It signals a change in focus and introduces the environmental damage that the next five lines describe, the crushing of the beauty of the world by man. The word 'Crushed' might also represent the disappointment that the poet feels when he looks at the beauty of nature and the damage that man inflicts. His sense of wonder is in a sense 'crushed' by the disgraceful behaviour of his fellow man.

If God's greatness is so apparent in the world, why do people not take any notice of God? 'Why do men then now not reck his rod?' By 'rod' he might mean a stick used to inflict punishment. The question then is why do people no longer fear God's punishment. Or perhaps the 'rod' is a reference to a stick or staff that symbolises authority. The question then is why do people not acknowledge God's supremacy and power.

The poet suggests that for generations, people have moved across the world without any regard for its magnificence. The word 'trod', repeated three times, suggests mindless, ignorant movement. The world is damaged by human commercial activity. Man's desire to profit from the world's resources has resulted in a tarnishing of its natural beauty. Everything is 'seared' or scorched because of industry. The surface of the world has been damaged and messed up: 'Bleared, smeared with toil'.

Hopkins suggests that man is a somewhat disgusting creature that spoils the natural beauty of the world. The world now 'wears man's smudge and shares man's smell'. Over the course of our time on the planet, we have worn down the surface of the earth and exhausted it with our labours: 'the soil/ is bare now'. And all the time we have been distancing ourselves from nature. We are no longer sensitive to the world that we inhabit. Hopkins says that we have destroyed the ground, but we no longer feel close to it because our feet are 'shod' or covered in footwear.

LINES 9–14 *(the sestet of the sonnet)*

Following a rather depressing analysis of man's behaviour, the sestet of the poem introduces great hope. Despite man's lack of regard and the damage he inflicts on the world, 'nature' can never be exhausted or destroyed. This is because something very special exists deep within everything, something that cannot be destroyed or touched by man. This 'dearest freshness' allows for continuous renewal in the world. Hopkins illustrates this with a wonderful description of the sun setting in the west only to rise again in all its glory in the east:

And though the last lights off the black West went
Oh, morning, at the brown brink eastwards, springs –

The last two lines of the poem describe the presence of 'the Holy Ghost' lovingly watching over the world. The poet likens the Holy Ghost to a bird warming and protecting its young with its wings. It is over the 'bent' world that the Holy Ghost sits. The word 'bent' can be understood to mean different things. Perhaps it is a reference to the curved nature of the globe. However, the world 'bent' can also mean corrupt or morally crooked and so might be describing the activities of man. The poem, then, though critical of man and his treatment of the planet, ends with a sentiment of hope and love. No matter what we do to spoil the beauty of the planet, the natural world will survive and prosper.

THEMES

God & nature

The poem describes the powerful presence of God in the world. His greatness or 'grandeur' is everywhere evident, running through the planet like a powerful electrical current. This energy erupts in a magnificent display of dazzling beauty: 'It will flame out, like shining from shook foil'. And everything on the planet combines to reveal the singular 'greatness' of God.

Because of God's presence in the world, nature cannot be destroyed. Though the surface of the world can be damaged and tarnished, there exists something fresh – 'deep down things' that ensures that they will continue to abide. The world is cared for by the 'Holy Ghost' who protects God's creation lovingly with her 'warm breast' and 'bright wings'.

Man's relationship with God

The poem expresses astonishment at the fact that people no longer seem to be aware of God and His magnificent presence in the world. God's magnificence is all around us and yet we seem oblivious to it. Worse than that, we appear hell-bent on destroying it with our commercial activities. It seems that we no longer acknowledge God as a force in the world.

The poem, therefore, describes a breakdown in the relationship between man and God. God's existence is everywhere evident in the world, but we no longer take any notice. However, though we may have forgotten God and are blind to the magnificence of His creation, God has not forgotten us. Though we may be corrupt and reckless, the 'Holy Ghost' still sits lovingly over us and the world.

LANGUAGE

Form

Like many of Hopkins' poems, this is a perfectly formed Petrarchan sonnet. It has the typical Petrarchan rhyme scheme: ABBAABBA CDCDCD. It is divided into an octet (eight lines) and a sestet (six lines). It could also be argued that there is a shift in focus between the octet and the sestet. These defining features of the Petrarchan sonnet are also evident in 'Spring', 'As Kingfishers Catch Fire, Dragonflies Draw Flame' and 'I Wake and Feel the fell of Dark'.

Imagery

The poem uses images of light to describe the powerful presence of God in the world. His magnificence is said to erupt brilliantly in many individual rays of light, 'like shining from shook foil'. The 'Holy Ghost' that broods lovingly over the world protects it with 'bright wings'. The poem also features a wonderful description of the rising sun, used to illustrate the potential the world has for renewal. Hopkins suggests that man is doing everything he can to dull and smudge God's sheen and brilliance.

Sound effects

The poem derives its intense energy from Hopkins' extensive and highly original use of assonance and alliteration. In the phrase 'ooze of oil' for example, with its onomatopoeic quality, we can almost hear the oil slicking and flowing.

The sestet, however, is dominated by a gentler, more soothing – though still energetic – word music. The assonance of the phrase 'dearest freshness', with its repeated '*e*' sounds, for example, lends it a pleasant musical feel. A similar euphonious effect is created by the alliteration in 'last lights' with its repeated 'l' sound.

The poem's concluding lines, which describe the redemptive qualities of the Holy Spirit, are particularly rich with alliteration, generated by the repeated 'b' sound in 'bent', 'brood', 'breast' and 'bright', and the 'w' sound in 'world', 'warm' and 'wings'. Assonance is also present with the repeated 'i' sound in 'bright wings' and the repeated 'o' sound in 'World broods'. This surfeit of assonance and alliteration lends the poem's conclusion a sweet, soothing music, reflecting the kindness and gentleness of the Holy Ghost it describes.

Internal rhyme & repetition
An unpleasant harshness is created by the close proximity of the internally rhyming 'bleared' and 'smeared', the ugliness of the sound reflecting the environmental damage caused by man. The repetition of the phrase 'have trod' also contributes to the poem's verbal energy, emphasising the relentlessness and monotony of man's industrial endeavours.

The poet describes seeing a falcon in flight. He is amazed by the strength and skill of the bird. The bird inspires him to think of Christ.

The Windhover

LINE BY LINE

What did the bird do?
The bird was seen flying above the 'rolling' hills: 'riding/ Of the rolling level underneath him'. The falcon then flew high up into the sky ('striding/ High there') before spiralling downwards: 'how he rung upon the rein of a wimpling wing'. The bird then went sweeping away into the wind, gliding smoothly as it turned: 'then off, off forth on swing'. Finally, the falcon charges into the wind: 'Rebuffed the big wind'.

How did the bird appear?
The poet tells us that he 'caught' the bird. By this, he means that he caught sight of the bird, but there is also a sense in which the poet has captured the bird in language. Hopkins uses a number of metaphors and similes to describe the bird.

The poem opens with two descriptions of the bird:

* 'morning's minion' – the darling or favourite of the morning.
* 'kingdom of daylight's dauphin' – the prince of the kingdom of daylight.

The word 'dauphin' gives the bird a regal quality. This idea of royalty is also suggested by the word 'kingdom' being split so that the word 'king-' is left hanging at the end of the first line. The falcon is 'dapple-dawn-drawn'. This could mean that the bird has been drawn out or attracted by the dawn, which is dappled. The word 'dapple', which means having patches of colour, might equally refer to the falcon's feathers.

The bird is likened to a horse. The verbs that Hopkins uses to describe the bird's movements are more appropriate to a horse – for instance, 'riding' and 'striding'. The bird also uses his wings to control his speed and movement much like a horse rider uses the reins to control a horse. It is said to have 'rung upon the rein of a wimpling wing'. The falcon moves in rings or spirals. As it does so, it appears as if it is circling around some central point, as though his wing were connected to a rein around which he moves.

Hopkins finally compares the bird to an ice skater. He likens the arc of the falcon's flight to an ice skate sweeping across the ice as the skater makes a turn: 'As a skate's heel sweeps smooth on a bow-bend'.

What did the poet feel?
The poet was deeply moved by the bird's display of strength and skill. He was impressed both with what the bird accomplished and the masterful way it executed its moves: 'the achieve of, the mastery of the thing!' The poet seems particularly excited by the way the falcon took on the wind. This is seen as a great achievement. The small falcon hurls himself against the might of the 'big wind' and is said to rebuff or repel it.

The poet hints at the fact that he has been suffering from some sort of anguish ('my heart in hiding'), but that witnessing the falcon in all its glory has lifted his spirits.

What does the bird come to represent?
In the sestet of the poem, the image of the falcon fuses in the poet's mind with the idea of Christ. The very characteristics that the poet so admired in the bird – its beauty, strength, bravery and action – come together or 'Buckle' to reveal the greatness and glory of Christ. Just as the bird bravely 'Rebuffed the big wind', so Christ bravely fought against sin and the injustices of the world. The poet, therefore, sees Christ as a warrior riding heroically into battle to save mankind: 'O my chevalier!'

However, Christ achieved His most glorious triumph when he was crucified. Broken on the cross, Christ achieved something 'a billion/ Times told lovelier, more dangerous'. Dying, he took on the great burden of man's sin and opened up the way for redemption and eternal life.

The poet is not surprised that such beauty and strength could come at the very moment Christ was at his most exposed, weakened and near death: 'And the fire that breaks from thee then, a billion/ Times told lovelier'. Hopkins thinks of how earth that is broken and exposed by the plough is made to 'Shine' when the metal blades rub against it: 'sheer plod makes plough down sillion/ Shine'. Similarly, the dying embers of a fire reveal great inner beauty when they are smashed and broken: 'and blue-bleak embers … Fall, gall themselves, and gash gold-vermillion'.

The earth is made to shine because of the sheer hard work of the farmer: 'sheer plod makes plough down sillion shine'. And the burning embers in the fire glow magnificently when they break open. Both can be taken to represent different aspects of Christ's existence. Though the son of God, Christ lived the life of an ordinary man. He laboured hard during His life to spread the word of God. In this sense, He resembles the farmer whose sheer hard work makes the earth shine. And when He was crucified, He achieved His greatest glory. In this sense, He resembles the dying ember, which is at its most beautiful when gashed and broken.

THEMES
Nature
Like many of Hopkins' poems, 'The Windhover' reveals the poet's love of the natural world. However, unlike 'Pied Beauty' and 'Spring', for example, the poem is a celebration of a single moment of natural wonder rather than a celebration of nature itself. The poet is captivated by the magnificent flight of a falcon. He revels in the strength of the bird, watching breathlessly as it flies into the 'big wind' and skillfully sweeps and soars.

The poem gives high praise to the bird. Hopkins stands in awe of the falcon's skill and strength. He uses grand terms to describe the creature: 'daylight's dauphin', 'morning's minion'. He admires the bird's ability to control its movements. The falcon seems to possess great command of the environment it inhabits. He speaks of the falcon's steadiness and its 'achieve of, the mastery of the thing'. And greatest of all is the bird's strength and bravery, its willingness to fly into the wind, to tackle such a great force. The poet is inspired and deeply moved by this awesome spectacle.

God & nature
Once again, Hopkins is inspired by the natural world to think of God. The poet fuses the falcon with Christ in the poem's sestet. Here, the falcon's strength, bravery and beauty are linked with Christ's noble battle against sin and death. The poem describes Christ as a great hero. He is seen as a heroic warrior, a knight riding into battle. Just like the bird, Christ is considered beautiful and powerful ('Brute beauty'). And just as the bird took on the might of the wind, so Christ fought against the forces of evil in the world.

Gerard Manley Hopkins

LANGUAGE

Form
The poem is written in the form of a Petrarchan sonnet. It has the typical Petrarchan rhyme scheme: ABBAABBA CDCDCD. It is divided into an octet (eight lines) and a sestet (six lines). There is a shift in focus between the octet and the sestet. In the octet, the poet is concerned with the falcon. In the sestet, however, the focus shifts to Christ.

Sound effects
Hopkins uses incredible word play to relay his joy and excitement, and also to express the action of the bird. Taking even the first three lines, the music of the poem is evident. It opens with the soft alliteration of 'm's and 'n's and with the assonance of the 'o's. This is followed by a succession of 'i's – 'this morning morning's minion'. This fluid movement, broken by a comma, is succeeded by the alliteration of 'd's in a similar fashion: 'king-/ dom of daylight's dauphin, dapple-dawn-drawn Falcon'.

The alliteration and controlled use of commas in the first five lines work to give a sense of excitement. They also enrich the image of the bird as a noble horseman, which develops throughout the poem, and you can feel the clip-clop of a horse in the staccato rhythm. This eases as the flight of the bird takes hold. Smooth 's's and rolling 'r's begin to dominate, set against 't's. The lines reveal both the falcon's majestic mastery of the air and the poet's breathless admiration.

In the last two lines of the poem, Hopkins again uses alliteration to great effect. The soft 's' sounds of 'sillion/ Shine' works perfectly when describing the smooth beauty of the earth. And the slightly harsher 'g' sounds of the final line enhances the description of the embers as they fall and break.

Imagery
The poem uses a number of powerful images to illustrate the falcon's flight. There is the metaphor of the 'rein' illustrating the controlled flight of the bird as it spirals in the air. The poem also features the wonderful simile of a 'skate's heel' sweeping smoothly across the ice. Again, the image is one of masterful control and elegance.

The bird itself ultimately becomes a powerful metaphor for Christ and His noble actions. Hopkins fuses the falcon and Christ in the sestet of the poem. He then uses some wonderful imagery to reveal the magnificent beauty of Christ. Both the image of the earth rubbed smooth by the plough's blades and the embers exploding in dramatic colour are so wonderfully and vividly described.

Pied Beauty

LINE BY LINE

In this poem, Hopkins marvels at the variety of the natural world. In particular, the poem praises God for the existence of things that are 'dappled'. If something is dappled, it means that it has spots or patches of colour. The poet lists some dappled things that impress him:

- Skies that contain a variety of colours ('couple-colour'). These skies are compared to a 'brinded cow'. Brinded means having a grey or brownish streak or a patchy colouring. So Hopkins is likely thinking of skies with streaks of clouds of different shades.
- The rose-coloured 'moles' or spots that feature on the skin of the trout. These rose-coloured moles are dotted all over the trout ('in stipple').
- Chestnuts that fall and crack open to reveal their inner colours. These are compared to coals freshly taken from the fire, black and glowing red.
- The variety of colours that feature on 'finches' wings'.
- The different forms of land that make up the landscape. Hopkins thinks of the way the countryside is divided up into plots of farmland, with different plots being used for different things. He thinks of the 'fold' or enclosure for animals. (A 'fold' could also be a hill.) He also mentions 'fallow' land, land that has been ploughed and left unseeded.
- Finally, the poet speaks of all the 'trades' that people have and the variety of equipment and clothing they use: 'And all trades, their gear and tackle and trim'.

In the last five lines of the poem, Hopkins marvels at the incredible variety of God's creation. He wonders how it is possible for God to do what He has done: '(who knows how?)'. God has created such a variety of things and yet each thing is perfectly beautiful and unique.

God creates or 'fathers-forth' things that contrast ('counter'), are unique, rare ('spare') and 'strange'. He brings into existence all that is capable of sudden change ('fickle') and everything that is 'freckled'. There are fast things, slow things, things that are 'sweet' and things that are 'sour'. There are things that glow and sparkle ('adazzle'), and there are things that are dull and 'dim'.

Every individual thing is perfectly beautiful and requires no alteration: 'whose beauty is past change'. For all this God should be praised.

THEMES

Nature
The poem praises the great diversity and beauty of the natural world. Hopkins celebrates the wonderful colours and textures that are to be found in nature. Everything from the sky to the fields, from the smallest detail on the wing of a finch to the varied plots of farmland are included. In contrast to 'God's Grandeur', the poet even celebrates the manifold work that man does: 'And all trades, their gear and tackle and trim'. 'Pied Beauty' does not set man apart from nature and criticise him for his lack of care. Instead, Hopkins celebrates all that exists on the planet and marvels at the wonderful variety.

God & nature
Once again, Hopkins perceives the work of God in the natural world and celebrates His greatness. He marvels at God's creation '(who knows how?)', and glories in the act that there is such variety in the world. However, though the world is full of change and contrast, God remains unchanged. He creates many things that are are 'fickle' but is Himself 'past change'.

LANGUAGE

Sound effects
There is a joyous word music to 'Pied Beauty', reflecting the poem's lighthearted atmosphere of celebration. Typically, Hopkins makes extensive use of assonance and alliteration, lending the poem a pleasant euphonious effect. Line 9 provides a wonderful example of alliteration, with its repeated 's' sounds – 'swift, slow, sweet, sour' generating a pleasant sound. A similar musical effect is created by 'Fresh-firecoal' and 'fathers-forth', with their repeated 'f' sounds.

Gerard Manley Hopkins

Assonance features in lines 3 and 4 in phrases such as 'rose-moles', with its repeated 'o' sound, and 'finches-wings', with its repeated 'i' sound. The phrase 'couple-colour' in line 2 employs both assonance and alliteration, with its repeated 'c' sound and its repeated broad vowels: 'couple-colour'. A similar effect is created by the playful combination of 'fickle' and 'freckled' in line 8, with their repeated 'f' and 'ck' sounds.

This feast of assonance and alliteration reflects the joy with which Hopkins responds to nature's variety. The poem's music, however, is also intended to help us imagine the beauty of 'dappled things'. In conjunction with the vividness of Hopkins' descriptions, it is intended to bring their vividness and uniqueness to the mind of the reader.

Tone
The tone of the poem is quite light in comparison to Hopkins' other work. Much of this is down to the use of particular words and images. The word 'dappled' is itself quite playful, as is the image of the multicoloured cow being compared to the sky. The 'rose-moles' are 'all in stipple' on trout. 'Stipple' mimics the sound of 'dappled', maintaining this light feeling.

This lightheartedness is also evident in the word 'fickle', which is used in an unusual way in line 8. This term generally refers to a person who cannot make their mind up, and is generally not used as a compliment. Here, fickleness is seen as a characteristic in objects, animate and inanimate. It is representative of the random characteristics of things. The word also plays off 'freckled'.

The curtal sonnet form
'Pied Beauty' is an example of what Hopkins termed the 'curtal sonnet'. The curtal sonnet is a form invented by Hopkins and used in three of his poems. It is an eleven-line (or, more accurately, ten-and-a-half-line) sonnet. The first six lines replace the traditional octet, and the last four-and-a-half lines replace the sestet. It is essentially a reduced Petrarchan sonnet.

Spring

Gerard Manley Hopkins

This sonnet is a celebration of spring, which was Hopkins' favourite season.

LINE BY LINE

LINES 1–8

The poem's first eight lines focus on the delights of springtime, celebrating various features of the season:

- The poem begins by celebrating 'weeds'. It is probable that Hopkins has wildflowers such as daisies or dandelions in mind here. To Hopkins, these 'weeds' are not a pestilence or an irritation but have a beauty of their own that deserves to be praised. They are 'long and lovely and lush'.
- The poem also celebrates the beauty of a thrush's eggs: 'Thrush's eggs look little low heavens'. The eggs' surfaces are so clear and shiny that they function like a mirror, reflecting the sky (the 'heavens') above them. The eggs, therefore, look like 'little low heavens'. (They are 'low' because they are near the ground.)
- The poem also celebrates the thrush's song, which floats through the forest, echoing from the trees' wooden boughs. It moves, as Hopkins puts it, 'through the echoing timber'. To Hopkins, then, the thrush's music is a thrilling feature of the springtime. He uses an unusual simile to describe this, comparing the notes of the thrush's song to lightning bolts: 'it strikes like lightnings to hear him sing'.
- Hopkins next focuses on a pear tree, which is starting to put out leaves and blossoms: 'The glassy peartree leaves and blooms'. (The tree is described as 'glassy' because its fruit and leaves are shiny and glistening with morning dew.)
- The trees' branches seem to 'brush' against the blue sky: 'they brush the descending blue'. To Hopkins, the sky's blue has a deep, rich texture: 'that blue is all in a rush with richness'.
- Finally, Hopkins describes the newborn lambs that are racing about the place: 'The racing lambs too have fair their fling'. The lambs, it seems, are having a 'fling', a wild and happy time.

Spring, then is a beautiful time of year: 'Nothing is so beautiful as spring'. It is a time of lovely wildflowers, glistening fruit trees, of bird song and blue skies.

These lines emphasise the 'fertility' of springtime. Spring is depicted as a time of birth: newborn lambs gambol in the meadow and the thrush's nest is full of eggs from which chicks will soon emerge. It is a time of growth: wildflowers 'shoot', or burst, from the soil and blossoms grow on the pear tree. It is a time when the natural world seems full of 'richness', 'lushness' and abundance.

For Hopkins, spring seems to a time of renewal and regrowth. This is evident in his description of the thrush's music. The thrush's song, he says, cleanses the ears of those who hear it, just as one might clean a garment or a towel. Firstly, it 'rinses' our ears, washing away the noise and babble we have to put up with on a daily basis. Then it 'wrings' them, squeezing out any unpleasantness that might remain.

LINES 9–14

Hopkins considers the meaning of spring, this time of abundance and beauty, of juice and joy: 'What is all this juice and all this joy?' Because spring is a time of freshness and newness, it makes Hopkins think of the earth's early days, bringing to mind the time when God had just made the world and man was still living in the garden of Eden: 'a strain of earth's sweet being in the beginning/ In Eden garden'.

These thoughts of Eden lead Hopkins to consider children who are sinless and innocent, as Adam was before he ate the apple. Hopkins claims that 'innocent mind' and 'Mayday' exist in every child: 'Innocent mind and Mayday in girl and boy'. (To Hopkins, 'Mayday' is associated with purity and innocence, perhaps due to the fact that May is traditionally regarded as the month of the Virgin Mary.)

The speaker calls on Jesus to preserve the innocence of these children. He requests Christ to 'Have' and 'get' each boy and girl, to take them to Him before their innocence is destroyed: 'Have, get … Christ, lord … Innocent mind and Mayday in girl and boy'. Jesus, he says, must move to claim these children 'before' their innocent minds are corrupted by sin: 'before it cloy … Before it cloud … and sour with sinning'.

According to the speaker, the majority of these children are 'worthy the winning'. They are worth the effort it would take for Christ to 'win' them, to take them to Him and preserve their sinless nature: 'Most, O maid's child, thy choice and worthy the winning'. (Jesus is referred to as a 'maid's child' because he was given birth to by a maid, or virgin.)

THEMES

Nature

Hopkins was extremely sensitive and responsive to the natural world, and like many of his poems, 'Spring' celebrates the delights of nature. It celebrates deep-blue skies, the cleansing music of a thrush's song, glistening eggs and pear trees. A similarly ecstatic response to nature's beauties can be found in 'As Kingfishers Catch Fire', 'The Windhover' 'Pied Beauty' and 'Inversnaid'.

Perhaps above all else, spring is depicted as a time of fertility: of birth, growth and abundance. It is a time when nature can offer us a cleansing sense of personal rebirth and renewal. (This is evident when Hopkins describes his ears being 'rinsed' and 'wrung' dry by the thrush's song.) All in all, for Hopkins spring is such a magical time of year that it brings to mind the Garden of Eden. In springtime, the world is no less than a kind of paradise.

God & nature

As is so often the case in Hopkins' poetry, thoughts of nature lead to thoughts of God. In many of his poems, Hopkins draws a moral lesson from the natural world. In this instance, the beauty of spring causes him to think about childhood innocence, an innocence that is so easily 'soured' and corrupted by sin. A similar move is made in both 'The Windhover', 'Pied Beauty' and 'As Kingfishers Catch Fire, Dragonflies Draw Flame'. In 'The Windhover', the sight of a soaring falcon causes Hopkins to think about Christ's role as our redeemer. In 'As Kingfishers', the unique beauty of each natural thing causes Hopkins to think Christ's presence in each just man. In 'Pied Beauty', the glories of the natural world lead him to 'praise' God.

Man's relationship with God

Hopkins' poetry is greatly concerned with sin and redemption. In this poem he calls on Christ to preserve the innocence of each girl and boy, to take these children to Him before sin can corrupt their perfect natures. The notion of Christ as our redeemer, the one who saves us from sin and damnation, is also present in 'Felix Randal' and in 'The Windhover'. In 'Felix Randal', Hopkins refers to Christ as that which 'reprieves' or 'ransoms' us from sin. In 'The Windhover', Christ is depicted as a knight, or 'chevalier', who does battle on our behalf against the forces of sin.

The conclusion of 'Spring', however, is a little vague. It is unclear exactly how Hopkins wants Christ to preserve the innocence of each child. Does the speaker want Jesus to keep the children young forever, to preserve them from the guilts and complications of adulthood? Yet surely Hopkins realises that everyone must grow up eventually, that we cannot spend our lives in the blissful ignorance and naiveté of childhood. It is more likely that Hopkins wishes the children might grow up to be adults but remain 'childlike' in that they will be somehow free of sin. It is this remarkable and miraculous task that Hopkins calls on God to undertake.

NOTE

Spring, Hopkins claims, is a 'strain' of the earth's early days. This word 'strain' can be read in a number of ways: in this instance, however, it can be best interpreted as a remembered snatch of melody, or a piece of song. Springtime, then, is a kind of 'faint echo' of the way the world was in its early Eden-like state. It reminds the speaker of a time before Adam defied God's will and ate the apple, before sin and wickedness entered the world.

LANGUAGE

The sonnet form

Like many of Hopkins' poems, this is a Petrarchan sonnet. It has the typical Petrarchan rhyme scheme: ABBAABBA CDCDCD. It is divided into an octet (eight lines) and a sestet (six lines). There is a shift in focus between the octet and the sestet. In the octet, Hopkins discusses the beauty and joy of springtime.

The sestet, on the other hand, deals with issues of innocence and sin. These defining features of the Petrarchan sonnet are also evident in 'Spring' and 'God's Grandeur'.

Imagery

Hopkins uses an interesting metaphor to describe the weeds in line 2, referring to them as 'wheels'. It is possible to imagine the central portion of the wildflower as the wheel's 'hub' and its petals as the 'spokes'. A powerful simile, meanwhile, is used to describe the thrush's song, with Hopkins declaring that it strikes the ear like lightning. Perhaps the most beautiful image in the poem is that of the thrush's eggs reflecting the sky above them. Hopkins memorably refers to their reflective surfaces as 'little low heavens'.

'Spring' is full of images of movement in which Hopkins uses verbs that capture the freshness and energy of springtime. The weeds, we're told, 'shoot' out of the earth. The thrush's song 'strikes', 'rinses' and 'wrings'. Lambs 'race' through the meadows. Even the blue sky is depicted as being full of movement. It is 'descending … in a rush' as if it were pouring down from heaven.

Sound effects

In this sonnet, Hopkins sets out to write lines that are as breezy and energetic as the springtime itself. Assonance and alliteration contribute to the poem's pleasant or 'euphonious' musical effect. We see alliteration in lines 2 and 3, with their repeated '*l*' sounds (long, lovely, lush, little and low). The repeated '*r*' sound in 'rinse and wring' is also pleasantly alliterative. A similar effect is created in lines 7 and 8, with their repeated '*r*' and '*f*' sounds ('rush' and 'richness', 'fair' and 'fling'). Alliteration also occurs in line 9, with its repeated '*j*' sound.

Assonance also features widely. We see this in the repeated '*ee*' sound in the phrase 'weeds, in wheels' and the repeated '*i*' sound in 'strikes like lightnings'. Assonance also features in 'racing lambs', with its repeated '*a*' sound. All this assonance and alliteration generates a rich, euphonious music, suggesting the lushness and abundance of springtime. It gives the verse a rhythmic pulse, reflecting the energy of plants and animals in springtime.

Hopkins uses a number of musical effects to capture the power and energy of the thrush's song. The phrase 'echoing timber', for instance, has a strangely onomatopoeic quality, in which we can almost hear the thrush's singing echoing from the tree trunks. The use of powerful monosyllabic verbs such as 'rinse', 'wring' and 'strike' capture some of the energy Hopkins hears in the thrush's singing. It has also been suggested that the phrase 'sour with sinning' is onomatopoeic, the repeated '*s*' sounds bringing to mind the hissing of the snake in the Garden of Eden.

The poem's abundance of assonance, alliteration and other sound effects is related to Hopkins' theory of 'inscape'. Hopkins believed that every object and creature was unique. He referred to each object's uniqueness as its 'inscape'. In his poetry, Hopkins set out to capture something of each object's uniqueness through complex and musical combinations of language.

'Spring' is full of these attempts at 'inscaping', as the poet's rich word music struggles to reflect the singing of the thrush, the lushness of the weeds and the energy of the newborn lambs.

Nouns & verbs

One of Hopkins' favourite poetic techniques was to use nouns as verbs. (We see this in 'As Kingfishers Catch Fire', where the nouns 'justice' and 'self' are used as verbs.) In lines 6–8 of 'Spring', the nouns 'leaves' and 'blooms' are transformed into verbs. These unusual verb choices lend the line a curious power, suggesting the forceful movement of the foliage as it comes bursting out of the pear tree.

Gerard Manley Hopkins

Felix Randal

BACKGROUND & INTRODUCTION

This poem was written in the early 1880s when Hopkins was working as a priest in various parishes between Liverpool and Manchester. Hopkins was horrified by the circumstances of the poor in those industrial cities, which were polluted, dirty and ridden with disease. This poem was inspired by the death of one his parishioners, a thirty-one-year-old blacksmith. (The real-life blacksmith was called Felix Spencer. It is unclear why Hopkins felt compelled to use a different name in his poem.)

LINE BY LINE

LINES 1–4

As part of Hopkins' priestly duties, he tended to the sick. One man he tended to was Felix Randal, a 'farrier' or blacksmith. Hopkins had heard the news of Felix's death: 'Felix Randal the farrier, O he is dead then?' Hopkins' duty of care to Felix is now at an end: 'My duty all ended'.

Hopkins recalls Felix growing ill. The blacksmith was a big, strong and handsome man: ' big-boned and hardy-handsome'. Yet as his illness progressed, he began 'pining', or wasting away. Hopkins describes Felix's body as his 'mould of man', suggesting that it was manufactured in the same mould as that of all other men, crafted by God according to His likeness.

By the end, Felix was desperately sick in both mind and body. His powers of reasoning failed and his mind began to ramble: 'reason rambled'. Four different diseases, each of them 'fatal', had infected his body: 'some fatal four disorders, fleshed there'. Hopkins describes how the different diseases 'contended' or competed with one another to finish Felix off.

The strong and big-boned blacksmith was destroyed by illness: 'Sickness broke him'.

LINES 5–8

At the beginning of his illness, Felix cursed God for making him sick: 'Impatient, he cursed at first'. However, when Hopkins anointed him as part of the Last Rites, he mended his ways and made his peace with God: 'but mended/ Being anointed and all'. Hopkins would come to Felix's house and give him communion: 'since I had our sweet reprieve and ransom/ Tendered to him'. Because of this, in the months before his death the blacksmith's heart became more 'heavenly' or cleansed of sin. He began to focus in his heart and mind upon God and the next life: 'a heavenlier heart began some/ Months earlier'.

LINES 9–11

Hopkins thinks about the relationship between priests and the sick people they visit. The sick person becomes close ('endeared') to the priest, but the priest also becomes close to the sick person: 'This seeing the sick endears them to us, us too it endears'. Hopkins had a positive effect on Felix, comforting him as he lay weeping in agony. But Felix also had an effect on Hopkins. The sight of the blacksmith crying touched the poet in a deep and meaningful way: 'thy tears that touched my heart'.

LINES 12–14

Hopkins thinks of Felix in his prime, in the years before he became ill. In these years, Felix was more 'boisterous'. He was loud, rough and noisy. He was as physically powerful as any of his 'peers' – as any other blacksmith in the area. Hopkins thinks of him working at his forge, 'fettling' or shaping a horseshoe for a workhorse:

When thou at the random grim forge, powerful amidst peers
Did fettle for the great grey drayhorse his bright and battering sandal!

Felix's forge is described as 'random' because like a dry-stone wall, it is made from uncut, irregular stones. In those years of strength and health Felix never predicted or 'forethought' that he would end up broken by sickness, that he would spend his last days weeping in agony as he wasted. All such thoughts of sickness and death were 'far' from the mind of this powerfully strong and handsome blacksmith.

LANGUAGE

Sonnet form

Like many of Hopkins' poems, this is a Petrarchan sonnet. It has the typical Petrarchan rhyme scheme: ABBAABBA CCDCCD. It is divided into an octet (eight lines) and a sestet (six lines). There is a shift in focus between the octet and the sestet. In the octet, Hopkins describes the course of Felix's illness. It could be argued that in the sestet he meditates on the significance of these events. These defining features of the Petrarchan sonnet are also evident in 'Spring', 'God's Grandeur' and 'As Kingfishers Catch Fire'. Note, however, that this sonnet has longer lines and a slightly different rhyme scheme in the sestet.

Assonance, alliteration & onomatopoeia

Like most Hopkins poems, 'Felix Randal' is littered with assonance and alliteration. We see alliteration in 'mould of man', with its repeated '*m*' sound, in 'big-boned and hardy-handsome', with its repeated '*b*' and '*h*' sounds, in 'fatal four', with its repeated '*f*' sound, in 'reprieve and ransom', with its repeated '*r*' sound, and in 'bright and battering', with its repeated '*b*' sound.

Examples of assonance include 'four disorders', with its repeated '*o*' sound, 'fleshed there, all contended', with its repeated '*e*' sound, 'heavenlier heart', with its repeated '*ea*' sound, and 'great grey drayhorse'. It could be argued that onomatopoeia occurs in the poem's final two lines, where the powerful movement of the verse and the clashing consonants bring to mind the sound of the blacksmith's hammer clashing against an anvil.

Unusual words & phrases

Hopkins was a great lover of language and delighted in using unusual words in his poetry. In line 8 the poet asks God to grant Felix his rest in the next life, whatever offences he might have committed in this one. Hopkins uses the phrase 'all road ever', which was a Lancashire term meaning 'whatever'. It has also been suggested that 'sandal' was a Lancashire slang term for horseshoe.

Hopkins also uses some terms that had all but disappeared from English is his own day: 'farrier' for blacksmith, 'fettle' for shape and 'random', which means built from uneven blocks. It could also be argued that he uses the word 'boisterous' in its medieval sense – meaning huge or massive – in reference to the youthful Felix's big-boned physique. 'Heavenlier', on the other hand, is a neologism, a word Hopkins has made up himself.

Hopkins, therefore, uses words that are ancient, words that are brand new, and words that are unique to a single geographical area. His use of these strange words indicates not only his intense delight in language, but also his burning desire for accuracy, his need to find the exact descriptive term for each object and situation.

THEMES

Physical & mental suffering

This poem provides a moving portrayal of mental and physical suffering. There is something horrific about the description of four terrible diseases taking root in Felix's flesh and 'contending' with each other for the right to finally kill him. Felix suffers mentally, too. As his illness progresses his mind slips into insanity and his 'reason rambles'. 'I Wake and Feel the Fell of Dark' and 'No Worst, There is None' also depict suffering, though in those poems the suffering is perhaps more mental than physical. Felix's tears are reminiscent of Hopkins' 'cries' in these two terrible sonnets. Like Hopkins in the later poems, it could be said that Felix goes through 'black hours' of unimaginable suffering.

The poem movingly depicts how serious illness can make the strongest of us weaker than a little child. Felix, once a 'powerful', 'big-boned' and 'hardy-handsome' worker, is reduced to weeping like a baby: 'child, Felix, poor Felix Randal'. He is comforted by the priest's words and touch the way a child might be comforted by its mother: 'My tongue had taught thee comfort, touch had quenched thy tears'. The poem also makes the point that when we are young and strong we seldom think about illness. We give no 'forethought' to the difficulties that may await us. Perhaps the message here is that we shouldn't take health for granted and should make the most of it while we have it.

Gerard Manley Hopkins

Man's relationship with God

An important theme in Hopkins' poetry is man's relationship with God. In poem after poem, Hopkins stresses that it is only through Christ that we can be cleansed of sin and enter heaven. In this poem, Felix, like all men, is a sinner. Yet when Hopkins gives him communion his heart becomes 'heavenlier'. His soul becomes cleansed of sin and fit to enter heaven. Christ, through communion, is our 'reprieve and ransom', the thing that saves us from sin and death.

A similar view of sin and redemption is evident in 'Spring', where the poet calls on Christ to preserve the innocence of each girl and boy, to take these children to him before sin can correct their perfect natures. The notion of Christ as our redeemer, the one who saves us from sin and damnation, is also present in 'The Windhover', where Christ is depicted as a knight, or 'chevalier', who does battle on our behalf against the forces of sin.

Religious doubt

Another recurring theme in Hopkins is that of religious doubt. In 'I Wake and Feel the Fell of Dark' and 'No Worst, There is None', the poet begins to doubt God, feeling that his prayers, cries and desperate requests for comfort are going completely unheeded. In 'Thou Art Indeed Just, Lord' the poet feels that God has turned against him and is treating him like an enemy.

Similarly, in this poem, Felix begins to doubt God's goodness, cursing Him for making him ill. Felix's doubts are overcome when Hopkins administers the sacraments and he 'mends' his relationship with God. In the later sonnets, however, there is no such easy answer to the poet's doubts.

Inversnaid

INTRODUCTION

'Inversnaid' was written at a time when Hopkins was on the verge of the depression and despair that would characterise the last period of his life. The poem looks forward to Hopkins' 'terrible sonnets' such as 'No Worst, There is None' and 'I Wake and Feel the Fell of Dark', in which he explores personal feelings of incredible despair and devastation.

LINE BY LINE

STANZA 1

The opening stanza describes the movement of the stream, or 'burn', as it flows down the hillside to the lake below. Its water is dark brown, the colour of horsehair: 'The darksome burn, horseback brown'. The stream, we're told in line 2, goes 'roaring down' the slope, suggesting the power and force with which it thunders to the lake below. The course of the stream is described wittily by Hopkins as its 'highroad', reflecting the poem's Scottish setting. This 'highroad' is said to be 'rollrock': it twists and rolls; changing directions constantly as it is deflected by the obstacles in its path.

There are places on the burn's twisting course where it is 'cooped', hemmed in and restrained by rocks and boulders. There are other sections, however, where the water is not cooped up but flows freely. This surging water 'combs' through the stones and rocks on the stream's banks, breaking into 'foam' as it smashes against the rocks that line its banks. Hopkins compares this froth to a sheep's fleece: 'In coop and comb the fleece of his foam'.

The water 'Flutes' before it enters the lake that is its home and final destination. The word 'flute', in this instance, is open to two different interpretations:

- We can interpret 'flute' in terms of the musical instrument. On this reading, Hopkins is suggesting that the sound of the roaring water is more pleasant and enjoyable than the music of a flute or any other instrument.
- 'Flute' can also be taken as describing the shape of the stream's course. It is like an upside-down pint glass, thinner at its source way up on the hillside, broader at its bottom where it enters the lake.

STANZA 2

In this stanza, Hopkins continues his description of the foam that forms on the stream's surface. He depicts the froth as the stream's cap or 'bonnet': 'A windpuff-bonnet of fawn-froth'. (The froth, it seems, is somewhat brownish or 'fawn' in colour.) Hopkins' attention now focuses on a kind of 'mini-whirlpool' that has formed midway down the stream's path. In the air above this pool, the foam sprays in a kind of spiral pattern. In Hopkins' words, it 'Turns and twindles'. ('Twindles' is a verb that Hopkins made up himself, meaning to 'twist', 'twinkle' and 'dwindle' at the same time.)

The sight of this apparently harmless little pool seems to fill the poet with negative emotions. The water that gathers in it is depicted as a kind of 'black broth': 'the broth/ Of a pool so pitchblack'. The description of the pool brings to mind a witch's cauldron, in which a sinister brew might simmer. This black water is described as 'fell-frowning'. The fact that it is 'frowning' suggests its depressing, gloomy appearance. The word 'fell' is a word that can be understood in several different ways. In this instance, however, it is best to interpret 'fell' as meaning malevolent or evil.

To Hopkins, then, this little whirlpool that goes 'round and round' is a bleak and terrible place. Its gloomy pitch-black waters are associated with cruelty, sin and the devil. The sight of it fills the poet with 'Despair'. His spirit, it seems, is drowning in sorrow as it is sucked deeper and deeper into this despair, just as a little woodland creature might become trapped in the whirlpool before drowning in its black waters.

STANZA 3

Hopkins shifts his attention from the doom and gloom of the whirlpool to the beauty of the stream's banks, or 'braes'. The banks are sprinkled, or 'degged', with dew. When light shines on the dew-covered grass it creates a multicoloured or 'dappled' effect: 'Degged with dew, dappled with dew/ Are the groins of the braes that the brook treads through'.

Lines 11 and 12 focus on some of the plant life that blooms beside the stream, and that its waters nourish and sustain. Hopkins mentions packs or clusters of heather ('heathpacks'), and tufts ('flitches') of fern and ash trees: 'Wiry heathpacks, flitches of fern,/ And the beadbonny ash that sits over the burn'. The description of the ash tree as 'beadbonny' reflects the fact that it is covered with beautiful berries. The berries hang like beads or precious stones among its branches.

STANZA 4

The poet pleads that places like Inversnaid be left alone, with their streams wilderness and plant life. He asks: 'What would the world be, once bereft/ Of wet and wildness?' The answer to the question Hopkins puts, of course, is that the world would be a terrible place without 'wet and wildness', without unspoilt countryside and unpolluted rivers. 'Let them be left,/ O let them be left', he declares, pleading that the untouched countryside be left alone. The poem's last line, therefore, is a defiant cry for the wilderness to survive long into the future: 'Long live the weeds and the wilderness yet'.

THEMES

Nature

Once again, Hopkins reveals the beauty and splendour of the natural world. He captures the colours and the textures of the burn as it courses over the rocks. The water is 'horseback brown' and the foam a 'windpuff-bonnet'. We get a sense of the power and energy of nature as the water roars and falls. As in 'The Windhover', the poet uses images of a horse to capture the brute strength of nature.

However, unlike poems such as 'The Windhover' and 'Pied Beauty', which also describe the beauty and magnificence of the natural world, 'Inversnaid' contains a darkness that is lacking in both. The 'pool' is 'so pitchblack' and it 'rounds and rounds Despair to drowning'. Though the poet can admire the landscape that he observes and make a heartfelt plea for its preservation, there is a darkness at the centre of the poem, something disturbing in the description of the water that was absent in earlier poems such as 'Pied Beauty'. The poet has discovered a darkness lurking within the natural world that seems to chime with his own inner despair.

Mental suffering

The poem looks forward to Hopkins' 'terrible sonnets' such as 'No Worst, There is None' and 'I Wake and Feel the Fell of Dark' in which he explores personal feelings of incredible despair and devastation. Though stanzas 1 and 3 praise nature's splendour, it is a celebration that is tinged with sadness.

The burn is fertile and productive, its waters nourishing the plant life that grows around it. (Hopkins presents the brook's role of 'fertilising' the soil around it in explicitly sexual terms, saying it treads through the 'groins' of its banks.) Hopkins, on the other hand, considered his life barren and infertile. This infertility takes three forms:

* Firstly, he was sexually infertile, kept by his priestly vows from having children or a loving sexual relationship. (Hopkins' feelings on this subject are evident in 'Thou Art Indeed Just, Lord', where he refers to himself as 'Time's eunuch'.)
* Secondly, he was artistically infertile. The heavy workload of his clerical duties left him little time or energy to write his poetry, and cut him off from nature – his chief source of inspiration.
* Finally, he felt that this life as a whole was barren and empty, as the parish and teaching work that consumed so much of his resources left him frustrated and unfulfilled. There is something almost mocking about the beauty and fertility of the Inversnaid landscape, then, as it seems to taunt Hopkins with the very things he longs for so much but are denied him.

'Inversnaid' was written at a time when Hopkins was on the verge of the depression and despair that would characterise the last period of his life. He had sacrificed an incredible amount for God and had served His Church faithfully only to be rewarded with mental anguish and physical illness. (The doubts and inner turmoil this inspired are movingly documented in 'Thou Art Indeed Just, Lord' and the other 'terrible sonnets'.)

Perhaps the poem's central image, then, is 'the pool so pitchblack' – the little whirlpool in the brook's path that fills Hopkins with such horrified fascination. It's as if staring into its murky 'fell-frowning' depths gives him some premonition of the personal abyss into which he soon will fall, the despair in which he will soon find himself drowning.

LANGUAGE

Sound effects

As with so many of Hopkins' poems, 'Inversnaid' is rich with musical effects. The poem's first stanza pulses with a powerful rhythm, capturing the freshness and energy of the brook as it rushes down the slope. Alliteration predominates in this stanza. We see this with the repeated 'r' sounds in line 2: 'rollrock highroad roaring down'. Line 3, also, is rich in alliteration with the repeated 'c' sound in 'coop and in comb', and the 'f' sound in 'fleece of his foam'.

This preponderance of alliteration contributes to the vibrancy of the stanza's music, as does the internal rhyme in line 3 between 'comb' and 'foam'. A similar vibrancy is evident in stanza 3. Once again, alliteration is used extensively. We see it in the repeated 'd' sound in 'Degged with dew, dappled with dew', the 'br' sound in 'braes of the brook', and the 'f' sound in 'flitches of fern'.

Each stanza of 'Inversnaid' deals with a different theme. The poem twists and turns from subject to subject like the meandering river it describes. The opening stanza describes the power and energy of the brook as it rushes down the hill. The second stanza, meanwhile, focuses on a dark whirlpool that interrupts the river's flow. The last line of this stanza, with the repetition of 'rounds' and repeated 'o' sounds, mimics the swirl of the water. The third stanza marks another change of direction, celebrating the fertility the brook brings to the wilderness around it. The sprightly rhythm used in these lines reflects this life and energy. With the final stanza, the poem's focus shifts yet again as it becomes a desperate environmentalist plea for the wilderness to be left alone. The poet's use of a rhetorical question and repetition reveal his concern and desperation.

No Worst, There is None

Gerard Manley Hopkins

BACKGROUND & INTRODUCTION

This sonnet is a stark and pitiful cry for help. It is a desperate howl of abandonment from a man whose mind appears to be at the end of its tether. The speaker appears to be on the verge of a nervous breakdown, feeling abandoned by the God for whom he has sacrificed so much. This 'terrible sonnet' is a moving and honest account of psychological distress.

The poem was probably written in 1885 toward the end of the poet's life when he was working in University College Dublin. At the time, Hopkins was in poor mental and physical health. He found his duties exhausting and unrewarding. Furthermore, he was lonely and miserable in Ireland, a country where he found it difficult to fit in and had few friends. As he put it in a letter, these and the other 'terrible sonnets' were the product of a 'continually jaded and harassed mind'.

LINE BY LINE

A cry of despair

The poem's first eight lines are a cry of complete and total mental torment:

- Hopkins declares that he has been 'Pitched past pitch of grief'. His torment occupies a place on the scale of suffering that is beyond ordinary 'grief'. He is close to complete despair and possibly even to madness.
- Furthermore, his mental torment keeps getting worse. Each new pain he experiences has learned from earlier pains how best to make him suffer. He describes each new 'pang', therefore, as having been 'schooled' by the pangs that went before ('forepangs'). Each new pain 'wrings' his mind in a way that is 'wilder' and more violent than the last.
- Hopkins, therefore, feels that there is no limit to his torment. There is no such thing as rock bottom, no 'worst' possible situation for him to be in. No matter how badly he's suffering, new and more vicious pains will come along.
- The poet says his mind is being 'wrung' like a damp dishcloth. This image conveys the extreme nature of his suffering. His psyche is being choked and mangled by the mental torment that afflicts him.
- The poet says his mind is being beaten on an anvil, the 'age-old anvil' of mental torment. This image also powerfully conveys the extreme nature of his suffering. Mental torment makes the poet 'wince' in pain and 'sing' out in agony.

The poet cries out in torment and distress. His 'cries heave': we can imagine his chest heaving as he moans and groans in despair. His cries are 'long' and drawn-out and there are a great number ('herds') of them.

Religious issues

Hopkins, then, is in a terrible state. In the face of such torment, he calls out for help to Jesus, his 'comforter', and to the Virgin Mary: 'Comforter, where, where is your comforting?/ Mary, mother of us, where is your relief?' On this occasion, however, no relief appears to be forthcoming. The poet seems to have been abandoned by the God he has served so faithfully.

The poet's torment is caused not only by his own miserable circumstances but also by some universal problem, some great sorrow that affects the entire world: 'a chief woe, world-sorrow'. Hopkins doesn't describe the precise nature of this 'world-sorrow'. Some critics feel that Hopkins is referring to the tragedy of sin, that the great 'sorrow' he has in mind is mankind's failure to obey God's law. However, Hopkins could also be referring to the apparent distance between God and man. On this reading, the 'world-sorrow' is God's apparent unwillingness to answer our prayers and his apparent willingness to let evil men triumph.

No real relief from suffering

There seems to be a brief interval or 'lull' in the poet's torment when his sufferings pause ('leave off'): 'Then lull, then leave off'. However, this reprieve is only momentary. No sooner has one bout of suffering ended than the next one begins. There will be no real let-up in the poet's mental agony.

The poet personifies his mental torment as one of the Furies – the terrifying demons from Greek mythology whose purpose was to drive their victims mad. The furies were 'fell', or malevolent, beings who constantly tormented their victims, never allowing them a moment's rest. These beasts had no interest in pausing or 'lingering'. They wanted to be 'brief', to be quick, to drive their victims into insanity in as short a time as possible. The poet thinks of his mental torment as a Fury because it is constant and relentless. He feels that there will be no real let-up until he has finally been driven insane.

Despair's abyss

Hopkins comes up with yet another powerful image to describe his mental torment, comparing himself to a man hanging off the edge of a mountain: 'O the mind, mind has mountains'. He says he's dangling from the edge of a steep and jagged ('sheer') cliff above a terrifying drop: 'cliffs of fall/ Frightful, sheer'. Beneath him lurks an abyss so deep that no one has ever managed to 'fathom' it, to explore or comprehend it fully.

The poet seems aware that most people simply won't comprehend or appreciate the kind of suffering that he is forced to put up with. Only those who have 'hung there' above despair's abyss can fully understand what he's going through: 'Hold them cheap/ May who ne'er hung there'. The rest of us who have never (ne'er) dangled above this chasm will 'hold [his words] cheap'. We will not understand his complaints or take them seriously.

A crumb of comfort

The poet maintains that human beings are simply not cut out for the kind of mental torment he's going through. The human mind, he claims, is a weak and fragile thing with limited powers of endurance ('small durance'). It cannot deal with the 'steep' cliffs and 'deep' abyss that form the landscape of despair: 'Nor does long our small/ Durance deal with that steep or deep'. We cannot cope with this kind of extreme suffering for very long without simply falling apart.

Yet there is some comfort for the beleaguered poet, some shelter from the storm that has engulfed his mind: 'Here! Creep,/ Wretch under a comfort serves in a whirlwind'. Though his existence is miserable, he can take comfort from the fact that his life will one day be over: 'all life death does end'. Death will bring a final halt to his trials and sufferings. Furthermore, there is the comfort of sleep. When the poet is sleeping, it seems, his sufferings disappear or are at least diminished. The poem's conclusion, then, is a shocking indication of the extent of the poet's misery: his only relief comes from death or unconsciousness.

THEMES

Mental suffering

This poem could be described as a howl of mental torment. The poet has been 'pitched past pitch of grief'. He is experiencing a mental state that is far beyond ordinary grief or sorrow. Hopkins uses a number of very powerful images to describe the extraordinary torment he suffers:

- His mind is being violently 'wrung' like a piece of cloth.
- His mind is being beaten on an anvil.
- He personifies his suffering as a Fury, a malevolent demon from Greek mythology.
- He thinks of himself as dangling from a mountain above a seemingly bottomless pit of despair.
- He compares his mental torment to a violent 'whirlwind'.

Hopkins' mental torment is more or less unrelenting, with only the briefest of pauses between one bout of suffering and the next. His torment also keeps getting worse. To Hopkins, it seems that his sufferings will keep increasing in intensity forever, that there is 'no worst', no rock-bottom for him to hit. It is hardly surprising, therefore, that the poet thinks of himself as a pitiful 'wretch', crying out in agony over and over again. His only 'comfort' is the oblivion offered by sleep or death.

A similarly bleak portrayal of mental torment is evident in 'I Wake and Feel the Fell of Dark', which powerfully describes 'black hours' of mental distress. We also see it in 'Thou Art Indeed Just, Lord', where the poet bitterly laments the barrenness, frustration and disappointment that have consumed his life. Mental torment is also portrayed in 'Felix Randal', when the sick blacksmith's reason or sanity begins to slip away.

Religious doubt

This poem powerfully deals with what is arguably Hopkins' darkest theme: his sense of abandonment by God. In the throes of mental torment, Hopkins calls out to God and the Virgin Mary for comfort and relief. God, however, is unable or unwilling to help him. Hopkins, who was a loyal and devoted priest, seems to have been abandoned by the God he has served so faithfully.

A similar sense of abandonment is evident in 'I Wake and Feel the Fell of Dark', where Hopkins describes his prayers to God as 'dead letters' that will never reach their destination. We also see it in 'Thou Art Indeed Just, Lord', where Hopkins accuses God of 'thwarting' him and treating him like an enemy while allowing sinners to get ahead in life. This theme is arguably also present in 'Felix Randal', where the dying Felix curses God for making him ill.

NOTE

There is some disagreement about what is beaten on the 'age-old anvil' in line 6. Grammatically, it is the speaker's 'cries' that 'wince and sing' on the anvil: 'My cries heave … huddle … wince and sing'. Yet this seems to make little sense. How, after all, can 'cries' be beaten on an anvil? As the critic Norman White suggests, it makes more sense to read this as the poet's soul or mind being hammered on an 'age-old anvil', suffering mental torment as thousands have before throughout the ages. (It also been suggested that the poet's soul 'sings' God's praises even as he suffers.)

Hopkins enjoyed using words that have multiple meanings. This is evident in his use of the word 'pitched' in the opening line: 'Pitched past pitch of grief'. This phrase can be interpreted in at least three different ways:

- To 'pitch' is to throw or hit an object. Hopkins' mind has been thrown beyond grief into some new and even more terrible emotional state.
- To 'pitch' something can also mean to blacken it, to roll it round in wet tar. Hopkins' mind has been blackened by suffering. It is now more 'pitch' black than the blackness we associate with grief and mourning. It has entered a new kind of darkness.
- The word 'pitch' also suggests the notes on a musical scale. On this reading, Hopkins is suggesting that there is a 'scale' of suffering just as there is a scale of musical notes. As you go up the musical scale the pitch of the notes becomes higher and higher, each note having a more intense effect upon the ear than the last. Similarly, as you go up the scale of mental suffering, each new torment has a higher 'pitch', each degree of suffering has a more intense effect on the soul than the one that came before it.

Hopkins probably intended the word 'pitched' to be understand simultaneously in these three ways. Yet the phrase has a clear meaning. Hopkins has moved beyond mere grief into a darker emotional state.

LANGUAGE

The sonnet form

Like many of Hopkins' poems, this is a perfectly formed Petrarchan sonnet. It has the typical Petrarchan rhyme scheme: ABBAABBA CDCDCD. It is divided into an octet (eight lines) and a sestet (six lines). It could also be argued that there is a shift in focus between the octet and the sestet. These defining features of the Petrarchan sonnet are also evident in 'Spring', 'God's Grandeur', 'As Kingfishers Catch Fire, Dragonflies Draw Flame' and 'I Wake and Feel the Fell of Dark'.

Hopkins' short-hand technique

There are several examples in this poem of what we might describe as Hopkins' 'shorthand' style. We see this in the following phrase: 'Hold them cheap/ May who ne'er hung there'. A more conventional writer might express a similar sentiment like this: 'Those who have never hung from those terrible cliffs may well hold my words cheap and not take them seriously'. Entire words are left out as Hopkins compresses this sentence into a short, powerful poetic phrase.

A similar effect is created by the phrase 'herds-long'. This combines two distinct pieces of information about the poet's cries. The cries are 'long' and drawn-out and there are a great many ('herds') of them. We also find this technique in line 8, where 'Force' is a shortened version of the old word 'perforce', meaning 'it is necessary'.

Gerard Manley Hopkins

Imagery

In this poem, Hopkins uses several powerful images to describe his mental torment. He compares it to an anvil on which he is beaten and to a whirlwind that blasts him with its force. Perhaps most memorably he compares himself to a man dangling from a 'sheer' cliff above a vast and seemingly bottomless chasm.

The image of 'herds of cries' in line 5 is surreal and peculiar. The poet's cries are presented almost as living things, as poor bewildered beasts that 'huddle' together like cattle on a freezing winter evening. The comparison of the cries to living animals may seem weird and outlandish, but it successfully conveys the poet's distress, suggesting that he finds himself in a debased and animalistic state. His self-respect and dignity have been stripped away.

In line 7 we see an example of personification, The poet uses the image of the Fury to represent the mental torment that threatens to overwhelm him. There is something compelling about this depiction of the poet's inner suffering as a Fell, or malevolent being, from Greek mythology. This technique, whereby an idea or emotion is represented by a person or a mythological character, is known as 'personification'.

Sound effects

This sonnet is dominated by an unpleasant verbal music, reflecting the intense despair it describes. The opening lines, in particular, are marked by a jarring cacophony. This cacophonous effect is largely down to Hopkins' use of repetition. The repetition of the word 'pitch' in line 1, and the close proximity of 'pangs' and 'forepangs' in line 2, lend the opening a jerky, grating quality. This is reinforced by the alliteration in the first line, where the repeated '*p*' sound in 'Pitched past pitch' creates a harsh musical effect. The assonance and alliteration in 'wilder wring' with its repeated '*w*' and '*i*' sounds is also far from easy on the ear. A similarly unpleasant effect is created by the repeated '*h*' sound in line 5: 'My cries heave, herds long huddle in a main'. This repetition is almost onomatopoeic, suggesting the speaker's gasps and cries as he laments his suffering.

The poem also features several examples of internal rhyme. We see this in line 6, where 'woe' rhymes with 'sorrow', and in line 12, where 'steep' rhymes with 'creep' and 'deep'. Internal rhyme also occurs between the lines. We see this in lines 7 and 8, where there is a half-rhyme between 'shrieked' and 'brief', and in lines 10 and 11, where 'sheer' rhymes with 'there'.

It could be argued that in this context the abundance of internal rhyme contributes to the poem's cacophonous effect.

There is something particularly desperate about the poet's repetition of the word 'where' in line 3. In this repetition we can almost hear the poet's sighs. This is similar to the repetition of the word 'hours' in line 2 of 'I Wake and Feel the Fell of Dark'.

I Wake and Feel the Fell of Dark

Gerard Manley Hopkins

LINE BY LINE

'Black hours'

The poet has woken in the middle of the night and is now unable to sleep. As he lies awake in bed he feels the weight of darkness around him. If he was capable of a healthy night's sleep he would be waking to the light of day. Instead, he 'feels the fell of dark'. The word 'fell' can be interpreted in different ways:

* The poet is comparing the dark that surrounds him to the skin or hide of a dead animal ('fell' is another term for 'hide').
* The darkness of the night has fallen around him.
* The word also has a dark theological significance, suggesting Satan and the other wicked angels who rebelled against God and 'fell' from heaven. It also brings to mind the notion of sin, because of which man 'fell' from grace with God.

The time that the poet has spent awake has been deeply unpleasant. He describes the 'hours' through which he has lain awake as 'black hours'. His heart has suffered with him through the night. He reminds his heart of the terrible visions and struggles that they have had to endure. But the night is not over and the poet knows that there is still time before the morning light will arrive. Both he and his heart will have to endure yet more dreadful moments until then: 'And more must, in yet longer light's delay'.

When the speaker describes despair and anguish he speaks with great experience: 'With witness I speak this'. He has endured this kind of grief for a long time – in fact, all his life: 'But where I say/ Hours I mean years, mean life'. The poet has expressed his anguish in cries over the years, so many that he has lost count. He has cried out 'countless' times to his beloved God, 'dearest him'. But his cries are never heard or answered. God exists so far away and the poet's laments are like 'dead letters', letters that can neither be delivered nor returned to the sender.

Self-disgust

In the sestet of the poem – the last six lines – the poet considers his body. He is full of self-disgust and finds his physical self loathsome. He says that he is 'gall' and 'heartburn'. Both words convey how wretched and bitter the poet feels. Gall is the bitter fluid secreted by the liver that aids digestion. It is also another term for bitterness or resentment. 'Heartburn' is the burning sensation brought on by indigestion. Again, it is an unpleasant term suggesting bitterness and physical discomfort.

The poet believes that it was God's deepest wish or command that he would experience such bitterness in his life: 'God's most deep decree/ Bitter would have me taste'. And this bitterness that he experiences is due to his physical body: 'my taste was me'.

Hopkins considers the creation of his body to be a 'curse'. He describes the stages of his own creation, the stages of assembly that led to the 'curse' of his wretched existence. His bones were assembled and then filled with flesh before the blood was poured in to complete his cursed life: 'Bones built in me, flesh filled, blood brimmed the curse'.

Hopkins uses a baking metaphor to illustrate how his physical body ultimately interferes with and impedes his spirit. His spirit is like yeast, the cooking agent that causes bread to rise and become light and fluffy. His body is likened to a heavy dough that spoils this yeast and prevents it from rising: 'Selfyeast of spirit a dull dough sours'. So the poet considers his body to be an impediment or burden to his spirit.

The body is considered something that we are burdened with as punishment. It is our 'scourge', that which causes us misery. The 'lost' – possibly those who do not share the poet's faith – are also burdened with 'sweating' bodies. They must suffer the same punishment as him. However, he considers their burden to be 'worse' than his. Perhaps he considers their bodies to be more vile than his, or maybe it is that they must suffer more because of their sinning ways.

THEMES

Mental & physical suffering

The poem describes the terrible mental anguish that Hopkins endured for so much of his life. Troubled by religious doubts and depression, the poet is unable to sleep and must suffer through long 'black hours' of misery before the morning light arrives. This torturous night is not, however, an isolated incident of restlessness and suffering. The poem is ultimately about the despair and anguish that the poet has been living with all his life: 'But where I say/ Hours I mean years, mean life'. The root cause of this anguish is the poet's relationship with God. He feels isolated from God, abandoned and alone. He cries out to God but he does not receive any answer or relief.

The poem also describes an intense discomfort with the physical body. Hopkins speaks of his body as a curse from God, something torturous and unpleasant that he must endure: 'Bones built in me, flesh filled, blood brimmed the curse'. He says that his body tastes 'bitter' to him and compares his flesh to a 'dull dough' that sours his 'spirit'. He must share the same physical form as the 'lost', those who are condemned to an eternity in hell for their sins. The poet says that their 'scourge' or punishment, like his own, is to inhabit 'sweating' bodies. However, their situation is 'worse' than the poet's, for they must forever sweat in their bodies in the fires of hell, while he stands a chance of leaving behind his earthly form and enjoying an eternity in heaven.

Man's relationship with God

Once again, Hopkins speaks of the difficult relationship he has with God. God is the most important person in his life and he loves Him dearly. But he feels abandoned and alone. He cries out to God but never receives any reply. Comparing his cries to unanswered letters, the poet puts himself in the position of the heartbroken lover.

The poet has devoted his life to God. He considers God to be a great and benevolent being. And yet God does not offer him any relief or comfort. Worse than that, Hopkins says that it was God's will that he should suffer. He believes that his physical body is a curse, a punishment ('scourge') from God: 'God's most deep decree/ Bitter would have me taste'. The poem, therefore, offers a problematic view of the relationship between God and man. Though the poet obviously loves God, he can find precious little evidence of God's love for him. God remains a distant and unknowable being. He offers the poet no comfort in his agonising hours of sleeplessness. He has even worked to make the poet suffer by trapping his spirit in a 'sweating' body.

LANGUAGE

Form

The poem is composed in the form of a Petrarchan sonnet. It has the typical Petrarchan rhyme scheme: ABBAABBA CDCDCD. It is divided into an octet (eight lines) and a sestet (six lines). There is a shift in focus between the octet and the sestet.

Repetition

The poem uses repetition to express despair and anguish. In the second line, Hopkins conveys the terrible nature of the time he has spent awake when he says: 'What hours, O what black hours'. He also emphasises the extent of his suffering in the seventh line through the repetition of the word 'cries'.

Sound effects

The poem features plenty of assonance, frequently using long-vowel sounds to express despair. This despair is evident in the first line, which features long 'a' and 'e' sounds. The drawn-out sounds of the second line continue this, the 'o' sounds in particular expressing the poet's suffering. It is also evident in the long 'a' sounds of 'alas! away'. Alliteration, too, features to express the poet's discomfort. In line 11, the repeated 'b' and 'f' sounds express the bitterness that the poet is experiencing: 'Bones built in me, flesh filled, blood brimmed the curse'.

Metaphors & similes

The poem also contains some interesting metaphors and similes. The poet likens his severe discomfort to indigestion, saying that he is 'gall' and 'heartburn'. He compares the negative impact his body has on his spirit with 'dull dough' that interferes with the yeast that seeks to rise in the baking of bread. His unanswered cries to God are compared to letters that cannot be delivered.

Thou Art Indeed Just, Lord ...

Gerard Manley Hopkins

BACKGROUND & INTRODUCTION

In this poem, Hopkins expresses his doubts about the goodness and justice of God. It was written toward the end of Hopkins' life when his personal circumstances were dire. He was both depressed and suffering from intense bouts of physical illness. Years of difficult work as a priest had left him exhausted. Hopkins found the teaching duties that occupied the last few years of his life particularly exhausting. To make matters worse he was stationed at the time in Ireland, a country where he felt lonely, out of place and had few real friends.

LINE BY LINE

Hopkins complains to God

As a priest, Hopkins must believe that God acts in a just way. After all, religion teaches us that God is a being of complete goodness. Yet he cannot avoid having certain doubts. He cannot avoid feeling that some of God's actions are actually unjust. He 'contends' – or argues – with God, expressing these doubts:

- Why does God let evil men succeed in life?
- Hopkins is a loyal and dutiful priest, one of God's faithful servants. Why, then, does everything he attempts to do end in disappointment?
- Why does God persistently 'defeat' and 'thwart' him?
- Hopkins is God's friend but God treats him very badly. (Hopkins can't imagine getting worse treatment even if he was God's enemy.)
- Why do sinful men, who are enslaved by drink and sex, 'thrive' much more than Hopkins, who spends his life loyally serving God's 'cause'?

God may well be the most 'just' being in existence. But Hopkins feels that there is also justice to his own 'pleas' or complaints about God's actions and inactions: 'but, sir, so what I plead is just'.

The barrenness of Hopkins' life

Hopkins describes the richness and fertility of the natural world. He depicts river banks and woods ('brakes') becoming 'thick' with leaves, as life returns to them after the winter. Each spring the banks and hedges become 'laced' again with delicate and complexly interwoven parsley plants ('fretty chervil').

Yet while the natural world is fertile, Hopkins himself is completely barren:

- He is barren in the sense that as a priest he can have no children. (In this regard he compares himself to a 'eunuch', a man who has been castrated.)
- Hopkins also feels creatively barren. He 'strains' and struggles but can create no 'works that wake', no good poems that have any life in them.
- Hopkins also felt professionally barren. His priestly duties were exhausting and repetitive, and involved no worthwhile projects of lasting value.

Birds are busy building nests in the trees but Hopkins is incapable of 'building' anything worthwhile. He can produce no children, no poems and nothing of lasting value in his professional life.

Hopkins asks God to give him relief from this barrenness: 'O thou lord of life, send my roots rain'. He presumably wants God to send him poetic inspiration or improve the circumstances of his working life.

THEMES

Mental suffering

This poem is one of Hopkins' 'terrible' sonnets – poems in which Hopkins describes mental anguish. Other poems in this group include 'No Worst, There is None' and 'I Wake and Feel the Fell of Dark'. 'Thou Art Indeed Just, Lord' is perhaps the least intense of the three. Here, Hopkins presents his suffering in a more rational, restrained and subtle fashion.

However, the poet's despair and mental torment still resonate throughout the poem. It powerfully conveys Hopkins' desperate and 'straining' attempts to make something of his life, and his sense of failure and disappointment when these attempts come to nothing. Hopkins feels completely barren, that he is incapable of 'building' or producing anything worthwhile. The only element of hope in the poem is Hopkins' desperate plea for God to do something to relieve his situation.

Religious doubt

This is a powerful poem of religious doubt. In it, Hopkins asks an age-old question: if God is good why does He let wicked men triumph and sinners get ahead in life? Furthermore, why does He let his faithful servants suffer? Hopkins has sacrificed so much for God yet nothing in his life succeeds. Meanwhile, sinners who have sacrificed nothing – who are the slaves or 'thralls' of lust – get ahead in life. Hopkins, like many other people through history, wonders why God allows this to happen.

There is a strong sense of frustration, perhaps even anger, in this poem. Everything Hopkins tries to do ends in disappointment and failure. He cannot understand why God allows this to happen, especially when Hopkins has served Him so faithfully. Hopkins almost suspects that God has turned against him and is actually his enemy rather than his friend.

A similar sense of abandonment is evident in 'I Wake and Feel the Fell of Dark', where Hopkins describes his prayers to God as 'dead letters' that will never reach their destination. We also see it in 'No Worst, There is None', where Hopkins calls out in vain for God's comfort. This theme is arguably also present in 'Felix Randal', where the dying Felix curses God for making him ill.

It has also been suggested that in this poem Hopkins expresses doubts about his religious vocation, especially his vow of celibacy. Hopkins sacrificed the sexual side of his nature for God. He also gave up his ability to 'breed', to father children. But in this poem he suggests that God has given him little or nothing in return. There's a sense in which he regrets these huge sacrifices, referring to himself in an almost demeaning fashion as 'Time's eunuch'. Is it possible that Hopkins slightly envies those sinners who are 'thralls of lust', who are slaves to sexual passion?

God & nature

In many of his poems Hopkins draws a moral message from the natural world. The beauty of nature leads him to contemplate God's goodness. In 'The Windhover', the sight of a soaring falcon causes Hopkins to think about Christ's role as our redeemer. In 'As Kingfishers', the unique beauty of each natural thing causes Hopkins to think that Christ's presence is in each just man.

In this poem, however, the beauty of nature seems to tie in with Hopkins' angry questioning of God's justice. Each spring the riverbanks grow thick with leaves while God lets Hopkins' life remain barren and empty. Hopkins' only hope is that God will make his

life fertile and fulfilling, just as He sends rain to water the plants on the riverbank. Hopkins, therefore, calls out desperately for God to 'send my roots rain'.

LANGUAGE

The language of the courtroom
An interesting feature of this poem is the way Hopkins uses legal phrases and terminology that we might associate with a courtroom setting. Hopkins has certain issues with the way God has treated him, but he doesn't express himself in an angry or emotional fashion. Instead, he 'pleads' his case rationally like a lawyer in a courtroom. He addresses God in a respectful manner, the way a lawyer would a judge, calling Him 'Sir' and being careful to declare at the beginning of his 'plea' that God is just and right.

Puns
A recurring feature of Hopkins' poetry is his use of words that have different shades of meaning, a technique that adds to the texture and complexity of his work. The word 'contend' in line 1 can mean to offer an argument. Yet it also means to struggle, leaving us with the sense that Hopkins is struggling with God, desperately trying to convince the Almighty that his complaints are justified.

A similar ambiguity occurs in line 8, where Hopkins describes sinners 'thriving'. In one sense, this means that the sinners are succeeding and getting ahead in life. Yet it also suggests that the sinners are breeding and reproducing, something Hopkins himself cannot do due to his vow of celibacy. In the same line, Hopkins describes himself 'spending' his life on God's cause. In one sense, this simply means that Hopkins has passed his time in God's service. Yet the word 'spend' can also mean to waste, lending the line a suggestion that Hopkins has somehow wasted his life by devoting it to Christ.

There is also something punning about the phrase 'endeavour end'. The phrase highlights the presence of the word 'end' at the beginning of endeavour, suggesting that everything Hopkins attempts is ended as soon as it's begun.

Shifting syntax
The poem's opening is relatively simple in terms of syntax. We are presented with more or less straightforward sentences in which it is reasonably easy to work out what's going on. As the poem goes on, however, the syntax becomes more cluttered, difficult and convoluted. This is evident in lines 5–9, where most readers require several readings of the text in order to properly follow the poet's meaning. There is a sense in which this contorted word order reflects his confused and angry state of mind. At the beginning of the poem he speaks rationally and his intense emotions are kept in check. As the poem goes on, however, his confusion, bitterness and frustration come bubbling to the surface and are reflected in the increasingly difficult and tortured syntax.

Sound effects
This poem is not as rich in sound effects as some other Hopkins' poems. However, assonance and alliteration do occur in lines 9–11. We see assonance in the repeated 'b' sounds ('banks' and 'brakes', 'birds' and 'build'), in the repeated 'l' sound ('leaves' and 'lace') and in the repeated 'fr' sound ('fretty' and 'fresh'). Assonance also occurs in these lines due to their repeated broad-vowel sounds. The phase 'fretty chervil', in particular, creates a pleasing euphonious effect. These lines are typical of Hopkins in that he uses intense and musical language in order to describe the natural world in an effort to capture the uniqueness, or 'inscape', of each natural thing he depicts.

ELIZABETH BISHOP
THEMES

MOMENTS OF INSIGHT

Dawning awareness

Many of Bishop's poems are marked by moments of awareness – moments when a person suddenly realises something profound and important about themselves or about the world.

In 'First Death in Nova Scotia', the poem's narrator is a very young girl who seems to be unaware of the reality of death. While she may have heard the word mentioned, she has little or no real understanding of what death is or what it actually means for something to die. Now, however, her young cousin Arthur has passed away and his body has been laid out in the parlour of her house. The poem concludes with the speaker on the verge of awareness of what death really means.

In 'Sestina', it is the awareness of the loss of her parents that begins to dawn on the child. Just as with 'First Death in Nova Scotia', we get a sense that the child lacks the experience and mental capacity to fully comprehend the tragedy that has taken place. It seems that the child is protected from sorrow by her innocence, by her childlike lack of understanding. And just like in 'First Death in Nova Scotia' we get a sense that this innocence will not be enough to stave off the new and terrible awareness that is dawning upon the child.

'In the Waiting Room' is another poem that describes a dawning awareness of uncomfortable truths. Exposure to some strange images in a magazine along with a shocking realisation that she sounds just like her aunt throws the young girl into turmoil. She begins to realise that she is not quite as unique as she once thought. She is part of the human race and in many regards is just like all the other people who inhabit the planet: 'you are one of them'.

Epiphanies

Many of Bishop's poems are marked by moments of epiphany, moments when a person suddenly realises something profound and important about themselves or about the world. In 'The Prodigal', it could be argued that the prodigal experiences such moments on certain evenings in the pigsty. He is touched by moments of 'insight' that he cannot 'control' or stave off. He realises with a shudder the true horror of his existence in the farmyard. The prodigal's moments of insight are linked to his awareness of the bats' 'uncertain staggering flight' above him through the night sky. His awareness of the bat reminds him that he, too, can make an 'uncertain and staggering' journey home.

In 'The Fish', the poet's epiphany occurs after she has seen the five hooks lodged in the fish's mouth. The fish has been caught five times before, and each time he has managed to break the line and free himself. He is a survivor, someone who has struggled and lived. The poet suddenly establishes a connection with the fish. She can identify with him as she, too, has struggled and survived.

In 'Filling Station', the poet observes a 'dirty' filling station. She is appalled at the state of the place and the condition of the men working there. Everything is 'greasy' and soaked in oil. But in the midst of this filthy masculine environment, certain peculiar features stand out. Upon the porch 'behind the pumps' is a set of wickerwork furniture. The furniture is 'crushed' and soaked in grease, yet upon the 'taboret' is a 'doily' and a large begonia plant. The doily has been embroidered 'in daisy stitch/ with marguerites'. Such delicate decorative touches in this rough and dirty place appear most strange: 'Why, oh why'. The poet suddenly realises that somebody is making an effort to beautify the filling station. 'Somebody embroidered the doily./ Somebody waters the plant'. Someone actually cares how this filthy place looks. The poem concludes with the realisation that someone 'loves us all'.

MAN & NATURE

Fascination with the natural world

The natural world features in a number of Bishop's poems. The poet is fascinated by it and appreciative of its beauty. In 'At the Fishhouses', she describes the 'beautiful herring scales' that line the 'big fish tubs' and speaks of the fish's scales being its 'principal beauty'. In 'The Fish', she is fascinated by the large fish she has caught, and wants to capture its every detail in language. She admires the 'mechanism of his jaw' and 'shapes like full-blown roses' on its skin.

In 'Questions of Travel', the poet thinks that it would surely be a pity not to have experienced the 'trees along this road,/ really exaggerated in their beauty' and 'robed in pink'.

Correspondences with nature

In 'The Bight', the messy bay area the poet observes seems to somehow correspond with her own life. The chaotic bay area that she describes can easily be read as a metaphor for the poet's life at the time. The 'torn-open, unanswered letters' mentioned in the poem might be a reference to the poet's own desk and her neglect of certain affairs. Perhaps there are many people who have written to her to whom she has yet to reply. The broken boats that have yet to be salvaged 'from the last bad storm' might represent emotional hurt that the poet has experienced and from which she has yet to recover.

Nature as alien & familiar

In a number of Bishop's poems, the natural world is presented as something both alien and familiar. There are aspects of nature that we are comfortable with and make us feel at home, and there are other aspects of the natural world that are less familiar and even hostile to us. In 'At the Fishhouses', for example, the poet seems very much at ease on the land. The 'emerald moss/ growing on [the] shoreward walls' of the fishhouses and the 'sparse bright sprinkle of grass' on the 'little slope behind the houses' are pleasant and familiar. The sea, in contrast, is something alien. It seems to have an existence all of its own. It is described as 'swelling slowly as if considering spilling over'. There is a sense in the poem that we should keep our distance from the sea. It is an 'element bearable to no mortal'. The sea is presented as something harmful to us, something that will 'burn' our hands and tongue, and cause our body to 'ache' should we enter it.

'The Fish' also suggests how alien the natural world can be. The poet tries to establish a connection with the fish but it proves all but impossible. Bishop attempts to render the fish familiar. She uses domestic objects to describe the fish. The skin is like wallpaper, the fish's eyes seem to be packed with 'tinfoil', the swim-bladder is like a 'big peony'. But the fish is just not like us, and the phrases that we use to describe people do not quite work when applied to it: 'his lower lip/ – if you could call it a lip'. The fish is a creature of the water, and the oxygen that the poet breathes naturally is 'terrible' to it. She looks into the fish's eyes but their is no recognition there. They do not return her stare but 'tip' away from her.

Man's indifference to nature

'The Armadillo' can be read as an environmentalist poem, as a lament for mankind's careless indifference to nature. The fire balloons cause great destruction to wildlife when they come crashing down to earth. There is a sense in which the poem's final stanza seeks to speak on behalf of the armadillo, and perhaps – by extension – the 'baby rabbit', owls and other creatures effected by the 'falling fire'. She expresses the feelings of anger and incomprehension that they are unable to, articulating their reaction to the human carelessness and selfishness that has brought them so much harm. She gives voice to the armadillo's rage, condemning on its behalf the annual ritual that visits such destruction on the local wildlife: 'Too pretty, dreamlike mimicry!/ O falling fire and piercing cry/ and panic'

CHILDHOOD

'First Death in Nova Scotia' is one of several poems where Bishop wonderfully captures the childhood mentality of her young speaker. The speaker's child-like innocence comes across when she compares Arthur's corpse to a doll 'that hadn't been painted yet' and his coffin to 'a little frosted cake'. The speaker's childhood innocence is also conveyed by her response to death. She seems to fully grasp what death actually means. She does not fully grasp what death is, or understand that dead people and animals never go around walking and talking. We also see this innocent ignorance of death in the way the speaker believes, or almost believes, the stories about Jack Frost and about Arthur being summoned to be the 'smallest page at court'.

'Sestina' also wonderfully depicts the mentality of childhood. We see this in the description of the granddaughter staring at the kettle as it comes to boil and ignoring her grandmother's declaration that it is time for tea. Childhood mentality is also artfully portrayed in the depiction of the granddaughter drawing a house with her crayons. She draws in the typically 'rigid', over-deliberate fashion of children everywhere. She approaches the task with an innocent and childish dedication, 'carefully' sketching a flower bed and showing the finished picture 'proudly' to the grandmother.

'In the Waiting Room' is another poem that captures the childhood mentality of its speaker. The language is often simple and childlike, and reveals the young girl's innocence: 'It was winter. It got dark/ early'. The speaker of the poem is six and feels that she is special and unique. But her sense of who she is is suddenly rattled by the disturbing images she views in the magazine, and by the sudden realisation that she sounds just like her aunt. Just like in 'First Death in Nova Scotia' and 'Sestina', we get the impression that the speaker's childhood is coming to an end, and an adult understanding of the world is breaking through.

ADDICTION

Bishop struggled all her life with alcohol addiction, and the theme of addiction features in a number of her poems. In 'The Prodigal', she movingly and honestly confronts the issue of addiction. The poem emphasises how difficult it is for an addict to leave addiction behind, even when he realises the damage it is causing him. The theme of addiction arguably also features in 'The Armadillo' and in 'Questions of Travel'. 'The Armadillo' depicts what can only be described as compulsive behaviour. The local population know the fire balloons they release each evening at this time of year are illegal and that they cause great destruction to property and to wildlife, yet still they insist on releasing them. 'Questions of Travel' also touches on the area of compulsive behaviour. Bishop and other compulsive travellers are depicted as being caught up in a never-ending quest for the next destination, for the 'high' or 'rush' of the next new country.

EXILE & HOMELESSNESS

The notion of homelessness is one that occurs several times in Bishop's poetry. We see this in 'Questions of Travel', which concludes with the haunting and enigmatic question: 'Should we have stayed at home,/ wherever that may be?' These lines indicate Bishop's own sense of 'homelessness'. She is uncertain as to where her 'home' is, or if she even has one. A similar notion of homelessness is evident in 'The Prodigal'. Though the prodigal lives and works in absolutely dreadful conditions, he could end his misery simply by returning home. Yet for a very long time he refuses to do so.

A similar theme is evident in 'At the Fishhouses', where the speaker returns to the Nova Scotia of her childhood to find the place changed radically: the population is in decline and her grandparents have long since died. The poem suggests the transience and impermanence of places we might consider 'home'. 'At the Fishhouses' also touches on the notion of 'homelessness' in what might be described as an evolutionary sense. The sea, the ancient mother of our race, is an element that will no longer bear us ('bearable to no mortal'), and is a place to which we can never really return.

TRAVEL

In 'Questions of Travel', Bishop makes several devastating criticisms of travel and tourism.

Tourism is depicted as childish and silly running around. The poem stresses the superficiality of tourism: tourists give the things they see barely a single glance before declaring them 'delightful' and moving on to the next attraction. The poem also emphasises how travellers and tourists can become jaded or bloated from sightseeing: 'have we room/ for one more folded sunset, still quite warm?'

Travel is also criticised as a form of voyeurism where we watch strangers live their lives as if they were performers in a play put on for our amusement: 'Is it right to be watching strangers in a play/ in this strangest of theaters?' This point is perhaps also raised in 'In the Waiting Room' where the magazine read by the young girl contains images of 'A dead man slung on a pole', 'Babies with pointed heads' and 'black, naked women with necks/ wound round and round with wire/ like the necks of lightbulbs'. Is it right that images of 'black, naked women' should feature in magazines, most likely without their permission, to satisfy our curiosity? Is there not perhaps something pornographic about photographing the naked and the dead in this manner, of objectifying them and presenting them as something alien and exotic for shock value and entertainment?

Ultimately, Bishop refuses to state whether travel is a good or bad thing. There seem to be two reasons for this refusal to either condemn or approve of travel, to answer the poem's central question of 'Where should we be today?' Firstly, she suggests that we are not completely free to choose where we want to be: 'Continent, city, country, society:/ The choice is never wide and never free'. Secondly, she suggests that many people are unable to stay at home because they do not really know where home is – there is nowhere they really feel they belong: 'Should we have stayed at home,/ wherever that might be?'

An outsider's view

There are several instances where the speaker comes across as a detached, neutral observer of the communities and landscapes she describes. We see this in 'Questions of Travel' where she notes the various sights encountered on her journey in a dispassionate, almost journalistic, manner: the 'really exaggerated beauty' of the pink trees, the 'grease-stained filling station floor', the ornate cage and the crude wooden clogs. A similar detachment is evident in the 'The Armadillo' when the speaker acknowledges the beauty of the fire balloons when they drift smoothly into the distance but condemns the damage they cause when they fall to earth with a splat. Similarly, in 'Filling Station' the speaker surveys the scene with an outsider's eyes, meditating upon its features in a way that those who live in the area are never likely to.

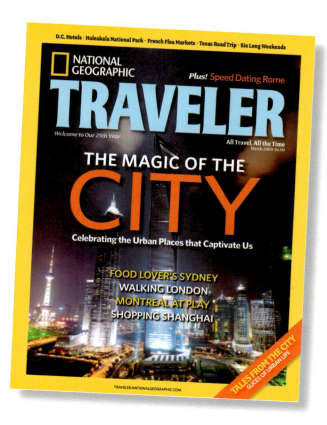

Travel & imagination

'Questions of Travel' makes the unusual point that travel represents a failure of the imagination. The poet suggests that it might be better to remain at home imagining our destination rather than actually travelling to see it – that it is better to stick with our imagined idea of a place rather than see how it really is. We get the impression that Bishop regards her persistent travelling as a sign of imaginative weakness and, therefore, of her weakness as a writer. Yet perhaps Bishop is being too hard on herself here – after all, her experiences of travel provided material for a number of her most memorable poems. Sights and sounds like those described in 'Questions of Travel' and 'Filling Station' fuelled her imagination, allowing her to create some of her best work.

Elizabeth Bishop
The Fish

LINE BY LINE

The poet catches an enormous fish
The poet has caught an enormous – or 'tremendous' – fish, and she holds him 'beside the boat/ half out of the water' so that she can observe him. The fish is held by the hook that is caught 'fast in a corner of his mouth'. It is of considerable weight and it makes a grunting sound as it hangs alongside the boat: 'He hung a grunting weight'. Considering it is such a large fish, the poet is surprised that it put up no resistance when it was caught: 'He didn't fight./ He hadn't fought at all'.

The fish's appearance
The fish is old ('venerable'), ugly ('homely') and worn or damaged ('battered') in appearance. The fish's skin is brown and it hangs off him in places 'in strips', much like strips of 'ancient wallpaper'. There are also 'darker brown' patterns on the fish, like patterns on wallpaper that have become 'stained' and faded over time: 'shapes like full-blown roses/ stained and lost through age'. The fish is 'speckled with barnacles', small shelled creatures that have attached themselves to the fish's body. The barnacles form white, rose-shaped patterns: 'fine rosettes of lime'. The fish's skin is also 'infested with sea-lice'. Seaweed hands down in rags underneath the fish.

The movement of the fish's gills draws the poet's attention to the fact that the fish is out of his natural environment and that the air he breathes is 'terrible oxygen' to him. The sharp, blood-filled gills that move as he breathes are 'frightening' to the poet, and she thinks how they 'can cut so badly'. While the fish is breathing in the 'terrible oxygen', the poet imagines the fish's internals:

- She thinks of the 'coarse white flesh' and how it is tightly 'packed in' and overlapped like a bird's plummage: 'like feathers'.
- She thinks of the fish's 'big bones and the little bones'.
- She imagines the 'dramatic reds and blacks/ of his shiny entrails'.

She pictures the 'pink swim-bladder', which she imagines looking like a 'big peony'.

The fish's eyes are 'far larger' than the poet's but they are 'shallower, and yellowed'. It is as if there is dulled tinfoil packed in behind and around the irises: 'the irises backed and packed/ with tarnished tinfoil'. The lenses covering the eye look like they are made from old 'isinglass' that has been 'scratched'. Isinglass is a transparent, almost pure gelatin prepared from the inner membrane of the swim bladder of the sturgeon and certain other fishes. It is used as an adhesive and a clarifying agent.

As the poet stared at the fish's eyes they 'shifted a little', but they do not move to look at her. It is as if the eyes are drawn or tilt naturally towards the light: 'like the tipping/ of an object toward the light'. The fish's face is gloomy, or 'sullen'. The poet admires the structure and arrangement of the parts of the fish's jaw: 'the mechanism of his jaw'. The fish's 'lower lip' is 'wet, grim and weaponlike'.

The five hooks in the fish's jaw
It is while she is examining the fish's jaw that she suddenly notices there are 'five big hooks' lodged firmly in the fishes 'lower lip'. The hooks have been lodged there for some time and have 'grown firmly into his mouth'. Attached to the hooks are pieces of line and wire that would have once connected the hooks to the rod. One of the lines is green and 'frayed', or ravelled, 'at the end/ where he broke it'. Two of the lines are 'heavier', and one is 'a fine black thread/ still crimped', or curled, 'from the strain and the snap/ when it broke and he got away'. The 'wire leader' is a piece of wire that would have run between the hook and the line. The hooks with their ragged lines and wire are like 'medals with their ribbons/ frayed and wavering'. The five threads that hang from the hooks resemble 'a five-haired beard of wisdom/ trailing from his aching jaw'.

The epiphany
Seeing the hooks with their broken lines lodged in the fish's jaw has a profound effect on the poet. She realises that she is looking at something remarkable, a creature that has been caught five times but each time has fought for and won his freedom. She stares and stares at the fish and gets an overwhelming sense of

'victory'. The world around her suddenly seems transformed by this fact. She says that 'victory filled up/ the little rented boat'.

The sense that something marvellous has just occurred is heightened by the colours that surround the poet in the boat. Oil has seeped into the pool of water that lies at the bottom of the boat ('the pool of bilge'), and this has created a multicoloured effect around the engine of the boat that resembles a rainbow. The poet says that the 'oil had spread a rainbow/ around the rusted engine'. The 'rusted engine' and the 'bailer rusted orange' add to the vivid colours that surround the poet, and they seem to somehow enhance the sense of 'victory' that the fish has inspired.

For a brief moment the world around the poet seems beautiful and joyous: 'everything/ was rainbow, rainbow, rainbow!' The little boat that she sits in is old, worn and dirty. The boat's engine and bailer are rusty, and the 'thwarts' are dry and cracked from the sun. But the fish that the poet stares at has momentarily transformed the space she inhabits and everything is suddenly seen in a wonderful new light. What the poet's intentions were when she initially caught the fish were never made clear, but having seen how it has fought for its freedom and won five times, the poet decides that she will release it: 'And I let the fish go'.

LANGUAGE

Form
The poem is written in free verse. It does not have any regular or formal rhyming pattern or metre.

Tone
At the start of the poem the poet expresses her excitement and pride at catching a 'tremendous fish', but the fact that the fish did not struggle leaves her feeling somewhat surprised or perhaps even disappointed. The initial tone of pleasure quickly gives way to a matter-of-fact tone as the poet focuses on the fish's every detail. The tone changes towards the end of the poem when the poet realises how the fish has struggled and survived. The poem closes with the poet feeling inspired by the fish, and the tone is one of almost ecstatic happiness.

Figures of speech
The poem features a number of similes. The fish's skin is compared to wallpaper decorated with roses that is peeling: the shapes on the fish's skin are 'like full-blown roses/ stained and lost through age'. The fish's flesh is 'packed in like feathers'. Its 'pink swim-bladder/ like a peony'. The eyes move 'like the tipping/ of an object toward light.' The lines attached to the fish's jaw are 'Like medals with their ribbons/ frayed and wavering'. The fish's jaw is 'weaponlike'.

The poet also uses a number of metaphors to describe the fish's appearance:

The irises are 'backed and packed/ with tarnished tinfoil', and the lenses are 'old scratched isinglass'. The lines resemble 'a five-haired beard of wisdom'.

THEMES

Man & nature
The poem suggests how alien the natural world can be. The poet tries to establish a connection with the fish, but it proves all but impossible. The fish is a creature of the water, and the oxygen that the poet breathes naturally is 'terrible' to it. She looks into the fish's eyes but there is no recognition there. They do not return her stare but 'tip' away from her. The eyes are 'shallower' than her own, and because they are 'yellowed' and 'tarnished', the poet cannot penetrate them.

The poet attempts to render the fish familiar. She uses domestic objects to describe the fish. The skin is like wallpaper, the fish's eyes seem to be packed with 'tinfoil', the swim-bladder is like a 'big peony'. The barnacles on the fish's skin form 'fine rosettes of lime'. But the fish is just not like us, and the phrases that we use to describe people do not quite work when applied to it: 'his lower lip/ – if you could call it a lip'. The fish's face seems 'sullen', like a person's, but 'the mechanism of his jaw' is strange and 'weapon-like'. The poet considers the fish's 'frightening gills' and thinks of how they can 'cut so badly'. The fish, therefore, remains something other, something alien and strange.

Moments of insight
The poet's epiphany occurs after she has seen the five hooks lodged in the fish's mouth. The fish has

been caught five times before, and each time he has managed to break the line and free himself. He is a survivor, someone who has struggled and lived. The poet suddenly establishes a connection with the fish. She can identify with him as she, too, has struggled and survived.

Perhaps the poet's 'victory' is also her understanding of the fish. She has managed to catch him in words, establish a correspondence with the fish. Her exuberance might be that of the artist's, the moment of inspiration having arrived. The poet gains a 'victory' in a sense that she has wrested a symbolic meaning from the fish.

The Bight

LINE BY LINE

The scene

The poet is standing before a 'bight'. A 'bight' is another word for a bay or a recess in the coast. It is the ideal location for docking boats because it is sheltered by the headlands or emerging land on either side. The poem is likely a description of a bay in Key West, Florida.

The poet observes the dock, or pier, where boats are moored. The dock is constructed using pilings: long wooden poles that are driven into the seabed. 'There is a fence of chicken wire along the dock/ where … the blue-gray shark tails are hung up to dry/ for the Chinese-restaurant trade'. The shark tails glint 'like little plowshares'. At the end of the dock, 'a little ocher dredge' is 'at work' removing soil or 'marl' from the seabed. It makes a clicking noise as it brings up each 'dripping jawful of marl'.

A recent storm has piled some of the smaller boats up 'against each other'. Some of these 'little white boats' have been damaged and they 'lie on their sides', their timber bodies crushed ('stove in'). Nobody has bothered to come to reclaim or recover these boats, and the poet wonders 'if they ever will be' salvaged. She compares the damaged, abandoned boats to 'torn-open, unanswered letters'. She says that the 'bight is littered with old correspondence'.

Because the tide is out, it is possible to see 'marl' or sedimentary rock jutting up out of the water. The poet likens the protrusion of the marl to 'ribs' emerging through skin. Man-of-war birds soar above the water and pelicans dive to catch fish.

All this time, 'sponge boats keep coming in'. Sponges are sea creatures that are used for the purpose their name suggests. Though most of the sponges we use today are synthetic, some are still manufactured from sea sponges. The boats are messy, or 'frowsy'. Bishop likens them to obedient hunting dogs: 'obliging air of retrievers'. The boats are full of long, thin wooden poles ('jackstraw gaffs') and the 'hooks' used for collecting the sponges. Bishop likens the effect of all these poles standing erect to the bristles on a hedgehog: 'bristling with jackstraw gaffs and hooks'. The boats are 'decorated' with 'bobbles', or tufted balls of sponge. The place is far from pretty but it does have a pleasant atmosphere: 'awful but cheerful'.

How does the poet describe the water?

Because it is low tide, the water seems very 'sheer', or transparent, to the poet. It is more like a 'peculiar gas' than a liquid. Bishop says that it is the 'color of the gas flame turned low as possible', and that she can 'smell it turning to gas'. It does not seem to be behaving as water ought to behave. The 'water in the bight doesn't wet anything'. Instead of being absorbed into the wooden boats and pilings, the water seems to be 'absorbing' the objects in the bight: 'Absorbing, rather than being absorbed'.

How does the poet describe the birds?
The birds seem larger than normal: 'The birds are outsize'. The diving pelicans plunge into the water in a violent manner: 'crash/ into this peculiar gas unnecessarily hard … like pickaxes'. They 'rarely' come up 'with anything to show' for their activity. As they fly away, they jostle each other in a playful manner: 'going off with humorous elbowings'.

The man-of-war birds 'soar/ on impalpable drafts/ and open their tails like scissors on the curves/ Or tense them like wishbones, till they tremble'. These birds seem to be lifted by 'drafts' of wind that are impossible to perceive: 'impalpable drafts'. As they fly, they 'open their tails like scissors' and 'tense them like wishbones, till they tremble'.

The reference to Baudelaire
The French poet Charles Baudelaire had a theory that it was possible to discover correspondences or analogies between the external world and the soul. For Baudelaire, the natural world was a special place full of symbols. He believed that the natural world was in communication with man.

Baudelaire also had a synaesthetic ability (synaesthesia occurs when one type of stimulation evokes the sensation of another, as when the hearing of a sound produces the visualisation of a colour). Bishop makes a humorous reference to the French poet's special talent: 'if one were Baudelaire/ one could probably hear it turning to marimba music'.

LANGUAGE

Form
'The Bight' is a lyric poem of thirty-six lines. It has no formal structure or rhyme scheme.

Tone
The poem is written in a natural and spontaneous tone. There is a relaxed feel about the poem, and the poet introduces some light-hearted touches such as the reference to Baudelaire.

Sound effects
The poet uses onomatopoeia when she describes the 'Click. Click' sound of the dredge.

Cacophony is used to suggest the rather violent behaviour of the pelicans crashing into the water. Bishop uses 'p' and 'c' sounds to convey the harsh, unpleasant activity: 'Pelicans crash/ into this peculiar gas unnecessarily hard,/ it seems to me, like pickaxes'.

Metaphor, simile, personification
There are a number of metaphors in the poem. Bishop compares the marl protruding through the water to 'ribs'. The sponge boats are compared to 'obliging' dogs.

The poet uses a simile when she compares the pilings to matches: 'the pilings dry as matches'. The pelicans are 'like pickaxes' when they dive 'unnecessarily hard' into the water. The man-of-war birds' tails are compared to scissors and wishbones. The shark tails shine like 'little plowshares' in the sun. The broken boats are 'like torn-open, unanswered letters'.

The poet uses personification when she says that the dredge 'brings up a dripping jawful of marl' like some animal eating.

THEMES

Man & nature
The natural world in the poem is messy and chaotic. Things appear odd and do not seem to function quite as they should. The water is like 'peculiar gas' that is 'Absorbing' rather than being absorbed', and the birds are 'outsize'. The creatures in the poem act or appear like tools and machines, whilst the machines behave like creatures. The pelicans are 'like pickaxes', and the man-of-war birds are like 'scissors'. The shark tails are 'like little plowshares'. The boats are like dogs, or 'retrievers', and the dredge seems to have the jaws of some beast: 'brings up a dripping jawful of marl'.

Bishop says that the bight is 'littered with old correspondences', and refers to the French poet Baudelaire's poem entitled Correspondences' that describes the natural world as full of 'symbols' that somehow correspond with our souls. Bishop does not suggest that the natural world is in communication with her soul, but there is a sense in which the bight corresponds with her own life. This is further suggested by the fact that the poem was written on the poet's birthday, a time of year when one tends to take stock of one's life.

The messy bay area, full of different chaotic activity, might therefore correspond with the poet's own life. Perhaps she considers her life to be a somewhat messy affair, disorganised and not quite coming together in any harmonious manner. The 'torn-open, unanswered letters' might be a reference to the poet's own desk and her neglect of certain affairs. Perhaps there are many people who have written to her to whom she has yet to reply. The broken boats that have yet to be salvaged 'from the last bad storm' might represent emotional hurt that the poet has experienced and from which she has yet to recover.

The poem ultimately suggests that life is anything but neat and orderly. It is a somewhat 'untidy' affair that we can never wrap up nicely. But the poet seems accepting of this fact. She is content to observe and record all the 'untidy activity' – in fact, she is, on the whole, rather 'cheerful'.

At the Fishhouses

LINE BY LINE

The scene

The fishhouses that Bishop writes about were probably situated on the islands of Nova Scotia. In the old days, the fishermen used these small timber houses or sheds to repair their nets and other fishing gear and also for storage. In the area that the poet observes, there are five fishhouses, each constructed in a similar manner.

The five fishhouses have steeply peaked roofs
and narrow, cleated gangplanks slant up
to storerooms in the gables
for the wheelbarrows to be pushed up and down on.

These simple one-room dwellings 'have peaked roofs' that allow for attic space. The attic space is reached from outside by means of a ramp that runs from the ground up into the gable (the gable is the triangular aspect of the wall formed by the sloping roof). The wooden ramp is 'cleated' – meaning that it has strips

of wood running across it at intervals for support. The 'shoreward walls' of these buildings (the sea-facing wall) are covered in green moss: 'the small old buildings with an emerald moss/ growing on their shoreward walls'.

Long ramps run from the fishhouses down to the water's edge. These ramps are used for bringing the boats up out of the water. The boats are pulled over thin tree trunks that act as rollers. The tree trunks 'are laid horizontally/ across the gray stones, down and down/ at intervals of four or five feet'.

There is a 'little slope' up behind the fishhouses that is covered in a 'sparse bright sprinkle of grass'. An 'ancient wooden capstan' lies in the grass. A capstan is a device used aboard ships to haul in ropes. It consists of a central shaft into which long wooden handles are inserted in order to turn it. The capstan that the poet observes is very old and has 'cracked'. The wooden handles are 'bleached' from the sun and the 'ironwork has rusted'. The rust from the ironwork has stained some of the wood; the stains look 'like dried blood' and lend the capstan a sad or melancholic appearance.

The whole place seems to be silver: 'All is silver'. The surface of the sea is silver and 'opaque', or non-transparent. The sea seems full and 'heavy'. It is 'swelling' and looks as if it is 'considering spilling over'. The 'benches,/ the lobster pots, and masts' that are 'scattered/ among the wild jagged rocks' are also silver. But in contrast with the sea's murky silver surface, the silver of these objects appears translucent.

The 'big fish tubs' and the wheelbarrows are 'completely lined/ with layers of beautiful herring scales'. The scales that cover the surfaces of the tubs and wheelbarrows are 'creamy' and display a spectrum of colours that shimmer ('iridescent'). They cover the surfaces like 'coats of mail'. Small flies that are coloured like the scales ('iridescent flies') crawl over the tubs and wheelbarrows.

The old man
The poet observes one of the fishhouses. It is 'a cold evening' and it is beginning to get dark. An old man sits by the fishhouse repairing his net: 'an old man sits netting'. The net is very hard to see because of the increasing darkness of the evening: 'his net, in the gloaming almost invisible'. The word 'gloaming' is another word for twilight or dusk. The net is 'a dark purple-brown'. The 'shuttle' that the man uses is 'worn and polished' from use. A 'shuttle' is a spool or reel on which thread of the net is wound.

The old man is waiting 'for a herring boat to come in'. The poet approaches him and offers him a cigarette, which he accepts: 'The old man accepts a Lucky Strike'. They start talking and the poet discovers that the fisherman was a friend of her grandfather. They talk of the 'decline in the population' of the area and 'of codfish and herring'.

There are 'sequins' of fish scales on the man's vest and on his thumb. Sequins are shiny circular decorations usually used on clothing. The old man has fish scales on his vest and thumb from scraping the scales off countless fish. The poet considers the fish's scales to be the most beautiful aspect of the fish: 'the principal beauty'. The old man uses a 'black old knife' to scrape the scales off the fish, 'the blade of which is almost worn away' from use.

The alien nature of the sea
The final section of the poem emphasises how difficult it is to describe or comprehend the sea. The poet has seen the sea many times in her life but it is difficult to capture this huge moving entity in words. Twice she begins describing the sea but gives up in face of the difficulty this task poses. On one occasion she begins to talk about a seal that she has seen instead and on another occasion she starts talking about Christmas trees. In line 65 she finally commences to give a sustained description of the sea but we get the impression that she is almost forcing herself to do so.

The poet's initial attempts to describe the sea used simple basic language, stressing how it is 'Cold' 'dark' 'clear' and 'deep'. Yet even these simple phrases emphasise the sea's complex and paradoxical nature. The sea can seem dark when we look at it from a distance, yet when we hold some of its water in our hands it seems clear. As if to accommodate this complexity, from line 65 on Bishop begins to use stranger, more poetic language in her attempt to capture the sea's nature.

Bishop goes to some lengths to describe how hostile and alien the sea is to us:

- It is 'bearable to no mortal'.
- If you touched it your hand would begin to 'ache' and then 'burn'.
- If you were to taste it, it would 'surely burn your tongue'.

The alien nature of the sea is also emphasised when Bishop likens it to a strange form of fire: 'a transmutation of fire'.

We are inclined to take the sea for granted but here Bishop uses heightened, exaggerated language to convey what an alien element it actually is.

The alien nature of the sea is further emphasised in Bishop's description of how it is detached and disconnected from the land: 'The water seems suspended/ above the rounded gray and blue-gray stones'. The phrase 'above the stones' is repeated no less than four times, stressing again and again the sea's separatedness from the land. It swings in and out over the land freely and 'indifferently' as if the land can present no constraint or obstacle to its flow.

The sea is also presented as a threatening, sinister presence – one that threatens to swamp or flood the entire world. In lines 14–15 the poet describes the 'heavy surface of the sea,/ swelling slowly as if considering spilling over'. In line 70 she imagines that the tide's progress will not stop at the stones on the shore but will continue to flow on over the world.

The sea as a point of origin

In ancient times people believed that there were four basic elements from which every other substance emerged: earth, air, fire and water. In this poem the sea is presented as some kind of primal fundamental force. It is linked to the other fundamental forces of fire and earth. It is described as being a 'transmutation' of fire, or fire that has almost magically taken on another form. It is also linked to the element of earth. It is described as being 'derived' or 'drawn' from rocks, flowing out like milk from a breast. It is also depicted as feeding on stones to fuel its own survival. The sea is described as a primordial force locked in a dance with these other primordial forces, a series of processes from which all creation emerges.

The poem also reminds us how the origin of the human species lies within the sea. Our ancient ancestors were sea-dwelling creatures that evolved over millions of years into the human beings we know today. The sea is presented as a kind of mother figure to the human race. Yet the descriptions of this primordial mother as 'cold', 'hard' and 'rocky' tells of how far we have developed from this and how alien it now seems.

The permanence of the sea

When the poet observes the landscape around her, everything seems to be decaying and disappearing: the local population is in 'decline', the old man's shuttle is 'worn', his blade is 'almost worn away', the ironwork of the capstan is 'rusted', and the fir trees will soon be cut down for Christmas. The sea, in contrast, seems to be a stable and constant presence: 'the same sea, the same'. It cannot be altered in the same way the human world can.

However, the more closely we examine the sea, the more we realise that it, too, is in a constant state of flux – it is only the same sea 'slightly'. It may not undergo the changes that we see in the landscape and amongst human society. Yet it is permanently shifting and flowing and changing. It is 'moving, utterly free … flowing and drawn'.

The sea & knowledge

Bishop likens the sea to 'knowledge'. Like the sea, water knowledge can be 'clear'. It can also be 'dark' or unclear. Sometimes, knowledge can be bitter and unpleasant, like the taste of salt water.

Our knowledge of the world comes through our senses. We suck knowledge from the world like a baby sucking milk from its mother's breast – like the way Bishop imagines the sea water been drawn up from the 'rocky breasts' deep below.

The world around us is constantly changing. Therefore, our knowledge of the world is changing, too, as our senses provide us with new information. Like the sea, our knowledge is 'flowing', 'moving' and 'utterly free'.

Because the world is constantly changing, our knowledge is constantly going out of date. Some things, like the temperature in the room, change second to second. Other things, like the identity of the US president, take longer to change. The information we have about certain things will remain relevant for only a certain amount of time before the situation changes again and our knowledge becomes 'historical'. Therefore, our knowledge needs to be constantly updated.

The seal & the fir trees

Bishop twice interrupts her attempts to describe the sea: once by describing a seal that she has 'seen here evening after evening', and on the second occasion by looking back at the trees above the fishhouses. The seal that the poet describes provides the poet with a comfortable link to the alien and sinister sea. Whilst the sea remains 'opaque' and sinister, the seal is friendly and familiar, interacting with the poet and observing her as she observes him: 'He was curious about me'. The poet relaxes in her description of the seal. She tells us that she sings him songs and suggests that he is 'interested in music'. The songs that she sings are 'Baptist hymns'. Baptists believe that when someone is baptised, they should have their whole body immersed in water (as opposed to just sprinkling water over the forehead). They also believe that baptism should take place in adulthood when someone is old enough to be a believer. The poet jokes that the seal is – like her – 'a believer in total immersion'.

The poet also turns her attention to the fir trees that stand up behind the fishhouses. The tall trees seem to be 'dignified'. In the fading light, they appear 'Bluish', and they seem to be blending or 'associating with their shadows'. The poet uses hyperbole to cover the great number of fir trees in the area: 'a million Christmas trees'. The trees seem to be 'waiting for Christmas'. Like the seal, these trees are familiar to the poet: they are representative of Christmas – a time of year that the poet might well associate with her past. Again, the trees can be contrasted with all that the sea represents.

LANGUAGE

Form

The poem is written in free verse and does not have any formal rhyming pattern.

Tone

Like many of Bishop's poems 'At the Fishhouses' features a somewhat relaxed, detached and matter-of-fact tone. The poet strives for accuracy and seeks to capture as honestly as possible what she sees and senses around her. There is a certain intimacy to the opening lines, a sense that the poet is slowly drawing us into the scene. The dense opening description – deliberately slow for fifty lines of the poem – is intended to subject us to the scene, to draw us deeply into it – to immerse us in the scene. There is a melancholic feel to these lines as the poet describes a world that seems to be slipping away.

The second half of the poem – though broken by a touch of humour with the description of the seal – adopts a somewhat more edgy and uncertain tone as the poet grapples with complex ideas of knowledge and origin.

Figures of speech

The poem features anaphora (the repetition of certain words or phrases): 'the *same* sea, the *same*,/ … swinging *above the stones*,/ icily free *above the stones*,/ *above the stones* and then the world'.

THEMES

Exile & homelessness

The fishhouses that Bishop describes are situated in Nova Scotia, a place where she spent much of her childhood. This is where her grandparents lived. But the place has changed since then: the population is in decline and her grandparents have passed away. The only human connection to her family that remains is the old man mending the net. He was a friend of the poet's grandfather.

The poem, therefore, suggests the impermanence of 'home'. There is a sense in which the place that the poet visits is slowly fading away, gradually becoming lost in evening darkness: 'in the gloaming almost invisible'. The objects that the poet observes – such as the capstan and the old man's blade – are rusting and wearing away. We get the feeling that it is only a matter of time before the place vanishes once and for all. We can return to the places we associate with our childhood, but as these places change and the people we knew pass away, it becomes more and more difficult for us to consider them our home.

'At the Fishhouses' also suggests how we as humans

have become alienated from our original primal mother, the sea. In the poem's closing lines, the poet describes the 'cold hard mouth' and the 'rocky breasts' of the world. There is a suggestion here of our origins as a species in the sea. However, we have evolved far beyond this, and no longer bear any connection to it. It is an element that will no longer bear us ('bearable to no mortal'), a place to which we can never return.

Man & nature
The poem presents the natural world as something both familiar and alien to us. There are aspects of the natural world that we know and are comfortable with, and then there are aspects of the natural world that are unfamiliar and disturbing. The poet seems very much at ease on the land. The 'emerald moss/ growing on [the] shoreward walls' of the fishhouses and the 'sparse bright sprinkle of grass' on the 'little slope behind the houses' are pleasant and familiar. The 'dignified tall firs' are, likewise, part of the world that the poet knows well. These firs are associated with Christmas: 'a million Christmas trees'.

The sea, in contrast, is something alien. It seems to have an existence all of its own, somewhat set apart from the 'bright' grass and 'emerald moss'. It is described as 'swelling slowly as if considering spilling over'. The sea seems to be disconnected from the rest of the world: 'The water seems suspended/ above the rounded gray and blue-gray stones'. The poet has seen the sea on many occasions but it remains alien to her – its otherness is always evident. It is also described as something threatening and dangerous. There is a sense in the poem that we should keep our distance from the sea. It is an 'element bearable to no mortal', something that will 'burn' us and cause our body to 'ache' should we enter it.

Knowledge
The poem deals with what knowledge is, and draws comparisons between it and the sea. Knowledge of the world around us is gained through our senses. But as the world is in a constant state of flux, our knowledge is forever changing. Bishop speaks of the fading light, the 'gloaming' and of objects rusting and wearing away – like the old capstan and the fisherman's blade. There is a sense in the poem that things are forever slipping beyond our grasp, 'moving' and 'flowing'. We apprehend things but only for a brief moment.

There is much about the world that we do not know and that we cannot comprehend. Certain things remain 'opaque', 'dark' and impossible to grasp. At times, we think we know something but it turns out to be false or different than we imagined. What we see is sometimes only of an 'apparent translucence'.

The Prodigal

LINE BY LINE
This poem can be read as an updating of the well-known parable from the Gospel of St Luke. Jesus tells how a son asks for his inheritance from his wealthy father. The son heads off to a foreign country, squandering his money on drink, gambling and other vices. Eventually, his funds run out and he ends up working in a pigsty. For a long time, he endures labouring in the muck and dung as he is too ashamed to return home with his money spent and in such a lowly condition. Eventually, he can take no more, and he returns to his father, who forgives him and welcomes him with open arms.

STANZA 1
This poem describes an alcoholic farm labourer who not only works in but also sleeps in a pigsty. He is employed on a farm that is a long way from home. He is a voluntary 'exile', who would rather work in the pigsty than return to where he came from. The pigsty can only be described as unpleasant:

- The floor is 'rotten'.
- The walls are covered with dung: 'The sty was plastered halfway up with glass-smooth dung'.
- One female pig, we are told, consistently devours her

- own children: 'the sow that always ate her young'.
- It has been suggested that there is something unpleasant or even slightly sinister about the way the pigs' eyes follow the prodigal around the barn: 'the pigs' eyes followed him, a cheerful stare'
- The foul stench of the place closes in around the prodigal in a way that is swamping and claustrophobic.

The odour has so overpowered the prodigal's sense of smell that he can no longer 'judge' it; he no longer notices its foulness: It 'was too close … for him to judge'. Unsurprisingly, the prodigal finds himself disgusted, or 'sickening', in this foul environment.

Like many alcoholics, the prodigal is secretive about his drinking, hiding pint bottles of rum or whisky behind the pigsty's planks of wood: 'he hid the pints behind a two-by-four'. It seems that he often gets drunk early in the morning: 'sometimes mornings after drinking bouts'.

On such mornings he watches the sunrise in a drunken state, struck by the beauty it brings to the farmyard. The mud and puddles of the yard reflect the colour of the sunrise. The puddles seem to 'burn' and the mud is described as being 'glazed' with red. This beautiful sight seems to 'reassure' the prodigal, making him feel his life in the barn is worth living: 'the burning puddles seemed to reassure'. In such moments, he feels he can continue to put up with the filth and squalor of the pigsty for at least another year rather than returning home to where he came from: 'And then he thought he almost might endure/ his exile yet another year or more'. (Of course, this sense of 'reassurance' might also stem from the alcohol he has just consumed.)

STANZA 2

This stanza describes an evening in the farmyard. It is getting dark. The sun is 'going away' and the 'first star' has appeared in the sky. The prodigal completes what are presumably his last tasks of the day: 'Carrying a bucket along a slimy board'. His employer 'shuts the cows and horses in the barn' and returns to his farmhouse by the light of a lantern. As he walks away, his lantern casts an 'aureole', or halo of light, upon the farmyard's mud. This aureole seems to 'pace' along with him as he returns to the farmhouse: 'The lantern – like the sun, going going away –/ Laid on the mud a pacing aureole'.

If the prodigal's mornings are sometimes filled with hope and reassurance, then his nights seem truly miserable. He views the 'first star' as a warning to him that night is on its way, suggesting that his night-time hours are highly unpleasant. We can imagine his nights being filled with guilt and self-loathing caused by his addiction and by the fact that he has ended up living and working in such a squalid environment.

The prodigal's circumstances are contrasted to those of the farmer and the farm animals. Each evening, the cows and horses are 'shut up' snugly in their barn, 'safe and companionable' as the animals in Noah's Ark. The pigs, meanwhile, snore contentedly: 'the pigs stuck out their little feet and snored'. The farmer, having seen to the cows and horses, returns to the warmth and comfort of his farmhouse.

This contrast emphasises the misery of the prodigal's sleeping arrangements. While the farmer and his animals are comfortable, he must sleep amid the filth and discomfort of the pigsty. It also emphasises the intense loneliness of his situation. The animals sleep in a 'companionable' togetherness while the prodigal is completely alone. Our sense of his loneliness is reinforced when the farmer returns to his farmhouse for the night, leaving the prodigal behind in the pigsty.

The image of the farmer's lantern receding into the distance is almost unbearably sad, powerfully emphasising the prodigal's isolation. These lines also emphasise the intense loneliness of the prodigal's nights. On evenings like this – as darkness is drawing in and he prepares for another night alone in the barn – the prodigal's mind is struck by moments of insight: 'He felt … shuddering insights, beyond his control,/ touching him'. He becomes aware of the full grimness of his situation, and shudders in horror at the awfulness of his life in the pigsty. These moments of horrified insight are 'beyond his control'. He may find these thoughts unwelcome or unpleasant but there is nothing he can do to avoid them. He cannot fend them off with drink, or with reassuring thoughts about the sunrise.

These 'shuddering insight' seems related to the prodigal's awareness of the bats that fly above the barn: 'he felt the bats' uncertain staggering flight'. It has been suggested that these bats flying blindly through the night serve as a metaphor for the prodigal's situation. Just as they stumble and fumble through the air, so the prodigal staggers and lurches through life, uncertain of how he should live. Yet the bats, though blind, possess a 'homing instinct' that allows them to navigate safely. The prodigal, too – it is implied – possesses such a 'homing instinct', some inner drive or intuition that will eventually cause him to leave the pigsty behind and return to his father's house.

Surprisingly, however, these moments of 'shuddering insight' do not cause the prodigal to immediately change his life. Although he realises the misery of his situation, it is a long time before he can find it in himself to leave the pigsty behind and return home: 'But it took him a long time/ finally to make up his mind to go home'.

THEMES

Addicton

'The Prodigal' is a moving and honest portrayal of an addict. The prodigal, as we have seen, suffers from severe alcohol addiction. He drinks even in the mornings, hiding his bottles of spirits behind planks of wood. Like the character in the Bible story, his vices have brought him to a terrible situation. He spends his days amid the filth and squalor of the pigsty. Even worse, he spends his nights there, too. He also suffers from terrible loneliness. Furthermore, we get the impression that his nights are racked by guilt and self-loathing.

The poem, then, paints an unflinching picture of the misery addiction brings. Yet it also highlights how addicts takes comfort and solace in their own condition. Addiction may be a miserable way of life but it is one they understand and are familiar with. We see this in the way the pigsty's foul odour no longer offends the prodigal. Even the 'glass-smooth' dung caked on the walls is presented as being somewhat attractive. The pigs, too, are depicted as having a certain curious attraction with their 'light-lashed' eyes and 'cheerful stare'. They offer the prodigal a strange kind of companionship, which is evident as he leans down to scratch the sow's head.

The poem also emphasises how difficult it is for an addict to leave addiction behind even when he realises the damage it is causing to his life. The prodigal seems torn about changing his life. In the evenings, there are moments of 'shuddering insight' when he realises the full horror of his situation. His awareness of the bats flying through the sky reminds him that he can follow his instincts and return home, leaving his addiction and the pigsty behind. However, in the mornings – as he drunkenly watches a sunrise – he feels 'reassured' that he can endure his miserable way of life for at least another year. In the end, it takes the prodigal 'a long time' to finally decide to give up his addictions and return to his father's house.

It should perhaps be pointed out that there is a strong autobiographical element to this poem. From Bishop's college days, she had been a problem drinker. After leaving college she spent a period attempting to break into New York's literary scene, during which she quickly developed into a full-blown alcoholic. According to her biographers, she drank to combat feelings of low self-esteem and depression. As is so often the case, however, drinking only made these feelings worse. Her struggle with alcohol was lifelong, and was fought with varying degrees of success.

Exile & homelessness

A notable feature of this poem is the prodigal's refusal to return to his father's house. Though he lives and works in absolutely miserable conditions, he could end all this simply by returning home. Yet for a very long time he refuses to do so – he decides to 'endure' his self-imposed 'exile' rather than return to his family. We get a sense, then, that the prodigal feels he does not really have a home to go to anymore, that he is simply not welcome any longer in his father's house. The word 'home' is the only end-word in the poem that does not have a full rhyme, perhaps suggesting the difficulty the 'concept' of home causes to the prodigal.

This notion of homelessness is one that occurs several times in Bishop's poetry. She lost her parents when she was very young, and her early years were spent being shifted from place to place and from guardian to guardian. In her later years, she remained something of a wanderer, dogged by feelings of restlessness and rootlessness, uncertain if there was anywhere she could really call home. We see this in 'Questions of Travel': the speaker expresses uncertainty regarding where, if anywhere, she belongs. A similar theme is evident in 'At the Fishhouses' where the speaker returns to the Nova Scotia of her childhood only to find the place radically changed. The place she once thought of as her home no longer really exists. In Bishop's poetry, then, the journey 'home' is not an easy one to make.

Moments of insight

Many of Bishop's poems are marked by moments of epiphany, moments when a person suddenly realises something profound and important about themselves or about the world. In this poem, it could be argued that the prodigal experiences such moments on certain evenings in the pigsty. He is touched by moments of 'insight' that he cannot 'control' or stave off. He realises with a shudder the true horror of his existence in the farmyard. A similarly uncomfortable moment of insight strikes the young speaker in 'In the Waiting Room'. It could be argued that the speakers of 'The Fish' and 'Filling Station' experience more pleasant or more uplifting moments of epiphany.

Man & nature

An interesting feature of this poem is the way the prodigal's moments of insight are linked to his awareness of the bats 'uncertain staggering flight' above him through the night sky. His awareness of the bats reminds him that he, too, can make an 'uncertain and staggering' journey home. This brings to mind several instances in Bishop's poetry where human beings gain insight from the natural world. We are reminded of 'The Fish' where the speaker seems to stare stubbornly at the hooked creature until she has gained some insight from it. It arguably also recalls 'The Bight' where the speaker sees in the shoreline landscape a metaphor for her own life and mind on the occasion of her birthday.

LANGUAGE

Form

This poem can be described as a 'double sonnet'. It consists of two fourteen-line stanzas. In each stanza one line rhymes with one other line. The first stanza has an ABAC DBCE DFEF GG rhyme scheme, while the second stanza rhymes ABAC DBEC FEDE GG. All of the rhymes are full rhymes, with the exception of the half-rhyme between 'time' and 'home' at the poem's conclusion.

Imagery

Bishop is well known as a poet of rich and detailed description. We especially see this in her depiction of the pigsty's horrible stench. Interestingly, Bishop describes the sty's smell in visual terms, declaring that the odour is 'brown' and 'enormous'. She also appeals to our sense of hearing and of touch in depicting this stink, referring to the odour's 'breathing' and its 'thick hair'. Here, Bishop uses a poetic technique known as synaesthesia, whereby an experience associated with one sense is described in terms of another. In this instance, Bishop describes the pigsty's odour as having colour, size and thick hair – things we usually associate with other senses than the sense of smell. Her description, however, successfully conveys the overpowering nature of this disgusting aroma.

Also memorable is Bishop's description of the pigs with their 'light lashes' and 'moving snouts'. Her depiction of the pigs' facial expressions as 'self-righteous' and 'cheerful' accurately captures how happy and self-satisfied pigs often seem to look. In her description of the dung on the pigsty's walls, Bishop skilfully appeals to the sense of touch, describing it as 'glass-smooth'. Another fine piece of description occurs in lines 8–9, which describes how the reflection of the farmer's lantern 'paces' alongside him as he returns to the farmhouse.

Light, it is important to note, plays an important role in this poem. In the first stanza the blazing sunrise fills the prodigal with 'reassurance', with the feeling that he can continue in his miserable existence. Stanza 2, however, depicts the light fading out. Both the sun and the glow of the farmer's lantern are 'going away'. Darkness is settling in, making a sharp contrast to the beauty of the sunrise depicted in stanza 1. Whereas sunrise filled the prodigal with reassurance, the coming darkness offers him a warning.

Metaphor

There are also several fine metaphors in this poem. The hay packed above the animals in the barn's hayloft is compared to 'clouds', and we can imagine it as cloudy golden puffs above the sleeping cows and horses. In line 11 the red light of sunrise is compared to a 'glaze' that is spread over the mud of the farmyard. The red glow of its reflection on the puddles is compared to fire: 'the burning puddles'.

Sound effects

Line 1 is rich with assonance due to its repeated broad-vowel sounds: 'the brown enormous odor'. Here the repeated 'o' sounds slow the movement of the line.

It has been suggested by one critic that the profusion of assonance 'clogs or overpowers' the movement of the verse, suggesting the claustrophobic and overpowering odour of the pigsty.

Bishop deploys assonance in order to emphasise the beauty of the sunrise. We see this in line 11 with its repeated 'a' sound ('glazed the barnyard') and in line 12 with its repeated 'u' sound: 'burning puddles'. This profusion of assonance creates a pleasant musical effect, reflecting the morning's beauty. The repeated 'a' sound in 'pacing aureole' creates a melancholic musical effect, suited to this mournful depiction of the lantern's glow disappearing into the distance. Assonance also features through the repeated broad-vowel sounds in 'glass-smooth dung'. Alliteration, too, features, in these lines with the repeated 'l' sound in 'light-lashed'. This assonance and alliteration generates a pleasant and euphonious musical effect, emphasising that the prodigal manages to find life in the pigsty more bearable than we might think.

Questions of Travel

This poem is set in Brazil and is based on Bishop's experiences as a tourist in that country. (Bishop would later live in Brazil for many years.)

LINE BY LINE
LINES 1–12

The opening lines describe what seems to be a spectacular landscape of mountains with waterfalls running down their sides. The mountains are so high that their tops pierce the cloud cover and streams of cloud pour down their upper reaches. To the speaker, it seems that the weight of the cloud mass causes it to be pressed onto the peaks, forcing these billows of cloud down the mountainsides: 'the pressure of so many clouds on the mountain tops/ makes them spill over the sides'. These streams of crowd resemble 'slow-motion' waterfalls as they flow down the mountain: 'turning to waterfalls under our very eyes'. The poet imagines that over time these cloud streams will turn into actual waterfalls through some unspecified geological process: 'For if those streaks … aren't waterfalls yet,/ in a quick age or so, as ages go here,/ they probably will be'.

It must be noted that while this landscape seems to be spectacular, the poet does not seem particularly taken with it. We see this in the unpleasant comparisons she uses. The streams of cloud spilling down the mountainside are described as 'streaks' and 'tearstains'. The mountains themselves are described as the slimy hulls of capsized ships. The whole scene is presented in terms of pressure, haste and crowdedness:

- There are 'too many' waterfalls and 'so many' clouds.
- The streams of the waterfalls are 'crowded' together and they move 'too rapidly down to the sea'.
- As we have seen, the mass of clouds in the sky seems to exert 'pressure' on the mountaintops.
- The clouds and streams are always 'traveling, traveling' – the repetition emphasising the pace and relentlessness of their movement.

Even time itself seems to be in a hurry. The age it takes the cloud streams to become waterfalls will be a 'quick one'.

The poet's tone is one of weariness – as if she has seen and experienced too much on her travels. We get the impression that she is bored by sights like this one, that no mountain range, no matter how spectacular, can thrill her now.

LINES 13–30

In these lines the poet mentions what she regards as several problems with the activity of travel and tourism.

'Think of the long trip home', she says, suggesting that the experiences we have when we travel abroad are not worth the hassle.

She describes the impulse to travel as a form of 'childishness'.

She questions the morality of tourism, regarding it as a voyeuristic intrusion into another people's landscape and culture: 'Is it right to be watching strangers in a play/ In this strangest of theaters?'

The poet depicts travel as a form of consumerism. Tourists, she suggests, rush around trying to squeeze in as many exotic sights as possible. They consume attractions like fast food until they are bloated and can take no more: 'And have we room/ for one more folded sunset, still quite warm?'

Yet they make little effort to understand or appreciate the things they see. Sights such as 'inexplicable old stonework' are taken in with a single glance and declared in a clichéd meaningless response to be 'delightful': 'instantly seen and always, always delightful'.

One of the poet's objections to travel is particularly unusual. We often have a dream of travelling to a particular place. However, the poet wonders if it might not be better for us not to travel, not to make these dreams a reality: 'Oh, must we dream our dreams/ and have them, too?' She suggests that it might be better to remain at home imagining our destination rather than actually travelling to see it: 'Should we have stayed at home and thought of here?' The poet seems to feel it is better to stick with our imagined idea of a place rather than see how it really is. This objection may seem strange to us but we can envisage how it might make sense to a writer like Bishop – someone for whom the notion of 'imagination' held great value.

LINES 31–69

In these lines the poet describes certain experiences she had during her time in Brazil. These experiences seem to revolve around a road trip into the Brazilian countryside where she stopped for 'gas' (petrol) at a filling station and was forced to listen to two hours of monsoon-like rain.

It would have been a pity 'not to have seen the trees along this road' she has driven down. The trees are pink and possess a 'really exaggerated' beauty.

She heard the sound made by the home-made clogs of the man in the filling station. The poet is taken with the fact that each of the man's two clogs strikes a different note on the filling-station floor. In another – perhaps more developed – country the clogs would be mass-produced, and would each produce the same tone when their wearer walked around in them: 'in another country the clogs would all be tested./ Each pair there would have identical pitch'.

She heard the singing of the 'fat brown bird' who resides in a cage above a 'broken gasoline pump' in the filling station. Its music, she says, is less primitive (and perhaps more pleasant) than the two-note tune produced by the man's clogs.

She had the chance to 'ponder' the connection between the clogs and the birdcage. The clogs are very basic: 'the crudest wooden footwear'. The cage, on the other hand, is very elaborate. It has been carved, or 'whittled', out of bamboo in a 'careful and finicky' manner. It is described as baroque, meaning complex and elaborate. Perhaps the poet wonders why over the centuries the people of rural Brazil have continued to carve such intricate birdcages while at the same time carving only the most basic footwear for themselves.

She had a chance to wonder what the birdcage can tell her about Brazilian history. The cage reminds her of a particular episode in Brazil's past: the coming of the Jesuit missionaries from Europe. This is because the cage resembles a church built in the 'Jesuit baroque' style, a type of architecture the missionaries brought with them to South America. She describes the elaborate patterns of the cage's wooden bars as 'calligraphy' – as if they were a piece of writing that might tell her something about Brazil's past.

She heard the 'sudden golden silence' that came after two hours of listening to monotonous heavy rainfall.

On the surface, these six experiences seem like positive ones. Yet it would be wrong to say that the poet is completely positive about any of them. The pink trees may be beautiful but there is something overstated or vulgar about their splendour. She describes their beauty as 'exaggerated' and compares them to the performers in a pantomime, suggesting there is something silly or over the top about their appearance. The poet may be taken with the fact that the man in the filling station's clogs are home-made rather than factory-produced, but the sound made by the clogs is still a 'sad' one. An air of desperation seems to cling to their wearer as he goes 'carelessly clacking' over the 'grease-stained' floor of the filling station. Similarly, though the fat brown bird sings sweetly, it is a prisoner, caged in this miserable filling station with its broken pump and its grease-stained floor. Furthermore, the 'golden silence' she enjoys so much is special only because it has come after two hours of listening to the monotonous sound of rainfall.

The poet attempts to understand Brazil's past by contemplating the birdcage and the wooden clogs. But she has pondered only 'blurr'dly and inconclusively'. Her speculations have been blurred rather than clear, and they have been inconclusive, leading to no real answers. The cage may be a form of 'calligraphy' that conveys a message about Brazil's past, but it is a 'weak' one and can ultimately tell her little of substance.

The speaker declares that 'surely it would have been a pity' not to have had these six experiences. As we have seen, however, the poet's description of each one is highly qualified – each having a negative as well as a positive aspect. Would the poet really have regretted missing out on these experiences? Or is she merely trying to convince herself that her time in Brazil was worthwhile?

THEMES

Travel
Good or bad?
This poem makes several devastating criticisms of travel and tourism. Tourism is depicted as childish and silly running around. It is criticised as a form of voyeurism where we watch strangers live their lives as if they were performers in a play put on for our amusement. It is depicted as a form of consumerism whereby we rush around 'doing' as many sights as possible as quickly as possible. To make matters worse, tourists engage with the countries they visit on only the most superficial of levels. They barely give the things they see a second glance before declaring them 'delightful' and moving on to the next attraction.

The poem also emphasises how difficult it is to really experience a foreign country. As visitors, the things we see are as artificial as a performance in a theatre. The only way to experience the 'real' culture of a place is by participating in it. The only way to 'know' a country is by actually living there for a reasonable period of time. Interestingly, after the experiences recorded in this poem, Bishop did go on to live in Brazil for many years.

The poem also stresses how difficult it is for us to really understand the significance of what we see when we travel. The old stonework will always be 'inexplicable' and 'impenetrable' to the casual tourist. The speaker attempts to understand the significance of the fact the people in the filling station make fabulously ornate birdcages but only the most basic wooden footwear. She wonders what this might say about Brazil's past, but her thoughts are blurred and inconclusive, revealing no real answers.

The poem also emphasises how travellers and tourists can become jaded or bloated from sightseeing. As Bishop so memorably puts it: 'have we room/ for one more folded sunset, still quite warm?' We see this at the beginning of the poem where the speaker has such a negative reaction to what seems to be a spectacular landscape of mountains and waterfalls. She describes this vista in terms of pressure, haste and crowdedness, referring to the streams of cloud as 'streaks' and 'tear-stains' and to the mountains as 'slime-hung'. We get the impression that the speaker has become jaded by travel and sightseeing. She can now respond to even the most spectacular views with boredom and weariness.

Yet despite all these objections and criticisms, Bishop cannot help wondering if travel might still be justifiable or even necessary. The French writer Blaise Pascal famously stated that 'all the evil in the world comes from man's inability to sit quietly in his room'. Yet the poet cannot help hoping that Pascal might have been wrong, or at least 'not entirely right', when he gave this advice: 'Or could Pascal not have been entirely right/

about just sitting quietly in one's room?' In lines 30–59 she mentions several vivid memories of her travels in Brazil, declaring that 'surely it would have been a pity' not to have experienced these things. Yet as we noted above, even her depiction of these seemingly pleasant memories of travel is tinged with negativity.

So finally, then, does the poet feel that travel is a good or a bad thing? Should we be 'here, or there'? Should we be travelling or 'Should we have stayed at home'? Ultimately, Bishop refuses to answer this question – simply declaring 'No'. There seem to be two reasons for this refusal to either condemn or approve of travel, to answer the poem's central question of 'Where should we be today?':

Firstly, she suggests that we are not completely free to choose where we want to be: 'Continent, city, country, society:/ The choice is never wide and never free'. Some of us, she seems to suggest, are compelled by reasons beyond our control to travel, and others are compelled to stay at home. Yet neither group can really be praised or blamed for their actions.

Secondly, she suggests that many people are unable to stay at home because they do not really know where home is, that there is nowhere they really feel they belong: 'Should we have stayed at home,/ wherever that might be?'

The poem, then, concludes on a note of uncertainty, with Bishop flatly declaring that she is either unable or unwilling to answer its central question. Yet we are left in no doubt that Bishop regards the activities of travel and tourism with a deeply critical and sceptical eye.

Travel & imagination
Perhaps the poem's most unusual criticism of travel is that it represents a failure of the imagination. As we noted above, the poet suggests that it might be better to remain at home imagining our destination rather than actually travelling to see it, that it is better to stick with our imagined idea of a place rather than see how it really is. Perhaps it is only a lack of imagination, therefore, that causes us to actually visit the places we dream about: 'Is it only lack of imagination that makes us come to imagined places?'

We get the impression that Bishop regards her persistent travelling as a sign of imaginative weakness and therefore of her weakness as a writer. Perhaps a great writer would be content to 'stay at home' and imagining her destination, constructing an image of it in her head, or, better still, in a book. In these lines, therefore, Bishop seems to regard her own restless existence as a sign of artistic frailty, as a betrayal of her imaginative resources. Yet perhaps Bishop is being too hard on herself here. After all, her experiences of travel provided material for a number of her most memorable poems. Sights and sounds like those described in 'Questions of Travel' fuelled her imagination, allowing her to create some of her best work.

An outsider's view
This is one of several poems by Bishop where the speaker presents herself as something of an outsider in the community she describes. We see this in her use of the phrase 'as ages go here' in line 8, which suggests that she is a visitor or immigrant rather than a native inhabitant. The speaker presents herself as a somewhat detached, neutral observer, noting the 'really exaggerated beauty' of the pink trees, the 'grease-stained filling station floor', the ornate cage and the crude wooden clogs.

Our sense of the speaker as an outsider is reinforced by her inability to understand the significance of what she sees. She ponders what the clogs and cage might tell her about Brazilian history, but can do so only in a blurred and inconclusive manner. 'Filling Station' and 'The Armadillo' are other poems by Bishop where the speaker is an outsider in the landscape she describes.

Exile & homelessness
As we noted, the poem concludes with a haunting and enigmatic question: 'Should we have stayed at home,/ wherever that may be?' These lines indicate Bishop's own sense of 'homelessness'. Bishop's father died when she was only eight months old and her mother was institutionalised when she was still a child. In the years that followed, she was shunted around from place to place, from guardian to guardian. Due to this traumatic and restless childhood, Bishop felt she had never been given the opportunity to settle anywhere. She is uncertain, therefore, as to where her 'home' is, or if she even has one.

Addiction

'Questions of Travel' also suggests the restlessness and rootlessness that characterised Bishop's adult life. Throughout her life, Bishop travelled a great deal and lived in a number of different locations, almost as if she was searching for a place where she could finally belong. The poem is quite critical of this behaviour, presenting it almost as a form of addiction: 'What childishness is it that …' Bishop and other compulsive travellers are depicted as being caught up in a never-ending quest for the next destination, for the 'high' or 'rush' of the next new country. The poet seems to realise that it is silly or childish, though we get the impression that she cannot control her compulsion to keep moving. Addiction is also touched on in 'The Prodigal', which describes a chronic alcoholic, and arguably also in 'The Armadillo', which describes a religious compulsion to launch dangerous fire balloons into the night sky.

LANGUAGE

Form

The poem is written in loose and irregular free verse with no consistent rhyme scheme. There is a neat twist at the poem's conclusion. In line 59 we are told that the speaker writes something in her notebook during the 'golden silence' after hours of rainfall. In lines 60–7 we are actually presented with this jotting. The jotting is like a poem within a poem. It is divided into two 4-line stanzas, each rhyming AABA.

Tone

Throughout most of the poem, the speaker's tone is that of a detached and neutral observer. The poet simply describes the things she sees and hears without a great deal of fuss or emotion. If anything, as we noted above, her tone is one of boredom and weariness, as if she is jaded by too much travelling and sightseeing. The tone is perhaps more critical in lines 13–29 where the speaker lays out the problems with travel and describes the silly, superficial behaviour of tourists. It is important to note, however, that this criticism is aimed as much at herself as at anyone else.

Imagery

This poem is very rich in imagery. The opening twelve lines are like a landscape painting, with their vivid depiction of mountaintops with waterfalls and streams running down them. Also memorable is the depiction of the filling station with its 'grease-stained floor', its 'broken gasoline pump' and its owner 'clacking' around in crude wooden clogs. Other images include the 'inexplicable old stonework', the 'tiniest green hummingbird in the world', the pink trees along the road and the 'fat brown bird' in its ornate bamboo cage.

An unusual image is that of the 'folded sunset, still quite warm'. In a sense, this suggests that our memories of travel are like photographs. We fold each one away immediately in our memory banks like photos in an album until our minds are full and can take no more. Yet it also likens experiences of travel to items of food, perhaps bringing to mind folded sandwiches like crêpes or burritos. The poem suggests that we stuff our minds with sights and experiences just as we stuff our stomachs with food until we are full and have 'room' for no more.

Metaphor & simile

This poem is notable for the memorable metaphors Bishop deploys:

- In line 6 the streams of cloud running down the mountainside are compared to 'mile-long, shiny, tearstains'.
- In line 45 the bamboo cage is compared to a church.

In line 54 the cage's ornate design is described as a form of 'calligraphy' or handwriting that might contain a message about Brazil's past: 'the weak calligraphy of songbirds' cages'.

There are also several fine similes in this poem:

- In line 11 the mountains are compared to 'the hulls of capsized ships/ slime hung and barnacled'.
- In line 56 the monotonous sound of the rain is compared to the monotonous sound of droning political speeches: 'rain/ so much like politicians' speeches:/ two hours of unrelenting oratory'.

In line 34 the pink trees are compared to performers in a pantomime: 'noble pantomimists, robed in pink'.

Line 34 also features an element of personification. The trees are described in human terms, as 'gesturing' and as performers in a pantomime. There is also an element of oxymoron about the expression 'noble pantomimists' because we do not usually associate pantomimes with higher values like nobility. (An oxymoron occurs when a noun is described by an adjective that contradicts or is not usually associated with that noun.)

Sound effects

Assonance occurs in a number of places throughout the poem: in line 34 the repeated '*o*' and '*i*' sounds in 'noble pantomimists robed in pink' creates a pleasant musical effect, suggesting the beauty of the pink trees along the road.

It could be argued that the profusion of broad-vowel sounds in lines 45–7 also creates a pleasant verbal music, suggesting the singing of the caged bird.

There is a series of half-rhymes and repeated broad-vowel sounds in lines 16–17 that create an interesting musical effect: 'Is it right to be watching strangers in a play/ in this strangest of theaters?'.

A perhaps less pleasant musical effect is created by the repeated slender-vowel sounds in 'mile-long shiny tear stains'.

The repeated broad-vowel sounds in the phrase 'hulls of capsized ships,/ slime-hung and barnacled' dramatically slows the pace of the verse, suggesting the static and motionless mountains.

Alliteration occurs in the phrase 'spill over the sides in soft slow-motion', where the repeated sibilant '*s*' sound suggests the noise of moisture pouring down the mountainside. Onomatopoeia occurs in lines 36–9: in these phrases we can almost hear the sound of the filling station owner 'clacking' around the floor in his crude wooden clogs.

The Armadillo

LINE BY LINE

'The Armadillo' is set in Brazil, where Bishop lived for many years. Every June her neighbours commemorated their local saint by releasing fire balloons into the night sky:

This is the time of year
when almost every night
the frail, illegal fire balloons appear

She describes the fire balloons drifting up toward the top of a nearby mountain, toward a statue of the saint they are meant to honour: 'Climbing the mountain height,// rising toward a saint/ still honored in these parts'.

Like many fireworks, the balloons are dangerous and illegal. Every year they were responsible for damage to property and to the surrounding countryside. Bishop even installed a sprinkler system in her own home for fear of the destruction the fire balloons might cause. But these risks did not stop the locals from celebrating their ritual.

What really comes across in the poem's opening eighteen lines is the balloons' mysterious beauty. Fire pulses 'like hearts' within their paper spheres: 'the paper chambers flush and fill with light/ that comes and goes, like hearts'. The balloons float away slowly and gracefully, 'solemnly/ and steadily', seeming to drift through the constellations of the night sky: 'if it's still they steer between/ the kite sticks of the Southern Cross'. The poet describes how observers are 'forsaken' by the fire balloons, as if they feel abandoned by the balloons' grace and beauty once they float out of sight.

The remaining lines, however, emphasise not the

balloons' beauty but the threat they pose to the surrounding area. On windy nights, the movement of the balloons is not so graceful. They 'flare and falter, wobble and toss' in the breeze. Sometimes, a current of air from the mountains takes them dangerously close to people and to buildings: 'in the downdraft from a peak,/ suddenly turning dangerous'.

The previous night a balloon actually crashed into the ground behind the poet's property: 'Last night another big one fell … against the cliff behind the house'. The crashed balloon set alight the vegetation on the cliff side, causing great destruction. The flames destroyed an owls' nest, sending its terrified occupants flying into the night sky. They shrieked in fear and pain, the 'bright pink' glow of the flames reflected on their bellies as they whirled away: 'whirling black-and-white/ stained bright pink underneath'.

A startled rabbit leaped from the burning vegetation on the cliff, its ears burned away by the flames: 'short-eared to our surprise'. The rabbit's eyes are 'ignited', burning with fear. It stares directly ahead in a 'fixed' fashion, as rabbits often do when in a panicked state. We can imagine it almost hypnotised by the flames that threaten to destroy it.

A single armadillo also fled the chaos. Its leathery armoured shell was 'rose-flecked' from the flames. It is unclear whether the armadillo is actually on fire or whether its shell is simply covered with pieces of burning material. Its head and tail are described as being 'down', as if it is cowering in fear in a desperate attempting to protect itself.

According to the poet, these balloons, released in honour of a saint, are a form of 'mimicry', or imitation. Perhaps they are intended to mimic how the saint's soul ascended to Heaven and became one with God. They do this by drifting into the night sky and by seeming to merge with the stars above. Or perhaps the balloons are meant to mimic the act of prayer. The balloons drift upwards toward the stars and the other 'heavenly bodies' in the night sky just as our prayers are directed upward towards God and the saints in Heaven. Yet this religious ritual, this attempt to mimic oneness with God, all too often has disastrous consequences. For as we have seen, the fires caused by crashed balloons bring pain, death and panic to the local wildlife: 'O falling fire, and piercing cry/ and panic'.

The poet describes the reaction of the armadillo at this destruction. It raises its clenched fist against the sky in a traditional gesture of anger and defiance (the armadillo's fist is described as 'mailed' because of the leathery armour that covers its body). However, the creature's rage is futile. It is 'weak' and 'ignorant'. It cannot comprehend the destruction that has been visited upon its home or do anything about it: 'a weak mailed fist/ clenched ignorant against the sky!'

A notable feature of the poem is the fact that the final stanza is set apart from the others by being printed in italics. We get a sense that this is because the poet is speaking for the armadillo, is attempting to articulate this dumb animal's reaction to the human carelessness that has destroyed its home. When she condemns the fire balloons for their 'Too pretty, dreamlike mimicry!', we get the impression she does so on behalf of the armadillo and of the other animals burned or terrified by the 'falling fire'. She is expressing the feelings of anger and incomprehension that they are unable to.

The balloons are also described as 'pretty' and 'dreamlike'. This suggests that the sight of the fire balloons mingling with the stars is like something from a beautiful dream. Yet the speaker suggests that the balloons are too beautiful, 'too pretty'. Presumably this is because these beautiful objects all too often cause destruction to the surrounding landscape.

THEMES

Religion

This poem focuses on a religious ritual. 'This is the time of year', we are told, when 'almost every night' the fire balloons are released in honour of a local saint.

As we have seen, the balloons are a form of 'mimicry' designed to imitate oneness with God. They seem to merge with the stars like saints rising to Heaven and becoming one with the divine.

The balloons are a 'pretty' and 'dreamlike' form of mimicry. There is something extremely beautiful about them: about the light that 'comes and goes' within their fragile paper chambers, about how they 'solemnly' and 'steadily' float into the night sky, 'receding' and 'dwindling' among the stars. Yet the wind can cause the balloons to 'suddenly' become dangerous. The poet describes how one 'splattered' into the cliff behind her house, bringing 'fire and piercing cry/ and panic' to the creatures that live there. A baby rabbit's ears are burned off, terrified owls fly off in panic, and an armadillo's skin is left 'rose-flecked' from the flames.

Perhaps the poem, then, emphasises that religion can be both a good and a bad thing. The religious impulse, the desire to mimic or imitate the saints, can lead to great beauty, to acts of virtue, humanity and kindness. But it can also find itself 'suddenly turning dangerous'. For the desire to imitate the saints, to find oneness with God, had also lead to incredible violence and suffering throughout the ages: to holy wars, discrimination, massacres and terrorism.

We get the impression that the speaker regards the ritual of the fire balloons as a primitive, almost pagan, form of Christianity. This is, perhaps, indicated by the fact that the balloons are as likely to merge with the planets named after ancient pagan gods – Venus and Mars – as they are to steer towards the Southern Cross – a name derived from Christianity.

The phrase 'receding, dwindling, solemnly/ and steadily forsaking us' is an interesting one. As we have seen, it describes the balloons drifting away into the night sky. Yet in a sense it could also apply to the Southern Cross, suggesting perhaps that the speaker feels Christianity is on the wane in the modern era. Perhaps the religion represented by the Southern Cross is 'forsaking' this world and will one day 'recede' and 'dwindle' like the ancient Roman religion the planets are named after. The local saint is 'still' honoured in these parts, but perhaps one day that devotion will be no more.

Travel
The speaker presents herself as something of an outsider in the community she describes, as a visitor or immigrant rather than as a native inhabitant. We see this in her use of the phrase 'in these parts' in stanza 1. The speaker presents herself as a detached, neutral observer. She acknowledges the beauty the fire balloons possess when they drift smoothly into the distance, but condemns the damage they sometimes cause when they fall to earth with a bang. We perhaps get a sense that the speaker regards the launching of the fire balloons as a quaint and primitive custom, an

almost pagan ritual designed to remember a saint 'still honoured' only in 'these parts'. A similarly detached, neutral point of view is evident in 'Filling Station' and 'Questions of Travel'.

Man & nature
'The Armadillo' can be read as an environmentalist poem, as a lament for mankind's careless indifference to nature. The fire balloons cause great destruction to wildlife when they come crashing down to earth. The local population presumably know the balloons lead to this 'falling fire and piercing cry/ and panic'. They know the balloons are illegal. Yet each year they still celebrate their ritual. In one sense, then, the poem can be read as an attack on human selfishness and short-sightedness, condemning how we continue to indulge in unnecessary activities even when we know they damage the natural world.

As we have noted, there is a sense in which the poem's final stanza seeks to speak on behalf of the armadillo, and perhaps – by extension – the 'baby rabbit', owls and other creatures effected by the 'falling fire'. Bishop expresses the feelings of anger and incomprehension that they are unable to, articulating their reaction to the human carelessness and selfishness that has brought them so much harm. She gives voice to the armadillo's rage, condemning on its behalf the annual ritual that visits such destruction on the local wildlife: 'Too pretty, dreamlike mimicry!/ O falling fire and piercing cry/ and panic'.

Addiction
This is one of several poems where Bishop describes people who are caught up in what can only be described as compulsive behaviour. The local population know that the fire balloons are illegal. They know that the balloons cause great destruction to property and to wildlife. And yet still they insist each year on releasing them. They are compelled by their devotion to their local saint to continue in this dangerous activity. It is perhaps not too outlandish to regard this religious impulse as a form of addiction, a compulsion that people brought up in this tradition are powerless to resist or control. In this regard, the poem resembles 'The Prodigal' with its portrayal of a chronic alcoholic, and 'Questions of Travel', which touches on the notion of the compulsive traveller.

Poetry
It is also possible that the balloons symbolise poetry itself. The balloons are described as 'paper chambers'. This brings to mind that poems are written on paper and are often divided into stanzas – an Italian word originally meaning chambers. We are told that fire balloons are filled with light that 'comes and goes, like hearts', just as we often think of a poem as containing something of the poet's heart. Perhaps the description of the balloons as 'frail' even brings to mind how we tend to regard poetry as something fragile, weak and useless in the modern world. Poems, like the fire balloons, can be things of great beauty. Perhaps, in the right conditions, a poem can steer its way between the stars and assume a place alongside the great works by people like Shakespeare and Yeats.

In other conditions, however, even something as 'frail' and beautiful as a poem can be dangerous. This, Bishop believed, was particularly true of the work of Robert Lowell, her friend and fellow poet, to whom she dedicated 'The Armadillo'. Bishop was very critical of Lowell for publishing poems in which he revealed extremely personal details about his wife and family, especially around the time of the break-up of their marriage. Bishop felt Lowell should never have written, or at least published, these poems, because of the great anguish they caused his wife and others close to him. In situations like this, poems, like fire balloons, are capable of causing great damage.

LANGUAGE

Form
The poem consists of ten four-line stanzas, each rhyming ABCB.

Tone
In the poem's first nine stanzas, the poet's tone is one of neutrality and detachment. While she describes the fire-balloon ritual – mentioning the balloons' beauty and recounting the destruction caused by the 'big one' that fell 'last night' – she does not directly reveal her feelings on the matter. The final stanza, however, is a direct outpouring of emotion. Her distress at the plight of the armadillo prompts an emotional outburst of anger and condemnation, shattering the normally serene surface of her verse. As we noted, there is also a sense in this stanza that the poet is attempting to speak on 'behalf' of the armadillo, to articulate the rage and incomprehension it feels toward the human carelessness that led to the destruction of its home. It is perhaps fitting, therefore, that the final stanza is set apart from the others by being printed in italics.

Imagery
Particularly memorable in this poem is the image of the fire balloons' serene flight into the night sky, the image of these frail objects 'solemnly' and 'steadily' drifting upwards until they become indistinguishable from the moon and planets or float away into the distance, seeming to steer between constellations like the Southern Cross.

Also noteworthy is the image of the crashed fire balloon 'splattering' against the cliff side so that 'The flame ran down'. Perhaps the most powerful images in the poem, however, are those of the destruction caused by the fire balloons: the owls reeling away in panic with flame reflected on their bellies, the armadillo's skin 'rose-flecked' from the fire, the terrified baby rabbit's 'fixed, ignited' eyes.

Metaphor & simile
Bishop uses a fine simile to describe the light coming and going within the balloons' paper chambers. The coming and going of this light, she says, resembles the

regular beating of the human heart: 'with light/ that comes and goes, like hearts'.

Another fine simile compares the crashed fire balloon to an egg that has fallen on the floor: 'It splattered like an egg of fire'.

An equally memorable metaphor is used to describe the Southern Cross constellation. The crossed poles of the constellation are compared to 'kite sticks', and we can imagine how they might be said to resemble the sticks of a diamond-shaped kite.

In another metaphor, the pink reflection of flames on the owls' bellies is described as a stain: 'stained bright pink underneath'.

Sound effects

Lines 15–18 feature a profusion of broad-vowel sounds. This slows the pace of the verse, giving it a 'solemn' and 'steady' movement appropriate to this depiction of the balloons' graceful flight.

In contrast, line 14 has a jerky, uncertain sound appropriate to how the wind causes the balloons to 'wobble and toss' in an ungainly fashion.

Cacophony occurs in the poem's final stanza where the profusion of clashing '*p*', '*k*', '*f*' and '*t*' sounds creates a harsh and unpleasant musical effect appropriate to the destruction these lines depict.

Mention should perhaps also be made of the onomatopoeic word 'splattered', in which we can almost hear the ugly sound of the balloons' impact against the cliff side.

Sestina

LINE BY LINE

The poem is set in the kitchen of what might be a farmhouse. It is a rainy evening in September. The kitchen is occupied by a grandmother and her granddaughter. They sit by the stove on which a kettle is boiling, the grandmother reading jokes aloud from an almanac.

Almanacs, once extremely popular in rural America, are like diaries in that they had a page for every day of the year. Each page contained jokes and folk sayings as well as horoscopes, weather predictions and agricultural advice. Almanacs were often attached to a piece of string that would be looped around a hook on the farmhouse wall.

It seems that the family has been struck by some terrible sorrow. In line 6 we are told that while the grandmother might talk and laugh at the jokes in the almanac, she does so only 'to hide her tears'. This great sorrow is 'known only to a grandmother'. The child's mental capacity is not developed enough for her to fully grasp or comprehend the tragedy that has taken place. We get the impression that the grandmother 'hides her tears' in an attempt to shield the child from awareness of this terrible event.

The kettle makes a whistling noise as its water reaches boiling point: 'The iron kettle sings on the stove'. The grandmother declares that tea is ready, and she begins to slice some bread. The granddaughter, however, is distracted by the moisture running down the kettle's sides:

*but the child
is watching the teakettle's small hard tears
dance like mad on the hot black stove*

To the granddaughter, the moisture on the kettle resembles 'small hard tears'. Perhaps this indicates that on some level she is aware that a great sorrow has struck her family though she may be too young to fully grasp the tragedy that has taken place.

The grandmother clears up after tea and returns the almanac to its hook. At this point, the poem becomes bizarre, dreamlike and sinister. The almanac begins to fly around the kitchen, like a kite on the end of its string: 'Birdlike, the almanac/ hovers half open above the child/ hovers above the old grandmother'. In line 22 we are presented with the strange and haunting image of the grandmother's teacup being 'full of dark brown tears' rather than tea. The stove and the almanac are depicted as having a conversation about the tragedy that has struck the family: 'It was to be, says the Marvel Stove./ I know what I know, says the almanac'.

Throughout the poem the almanac is presented in a distinctly sinister light. The grandmother believes the family tragedy was somehow 'foretold' by its horoscopes and predictions. There is something almost conceited about the almanac's declaration of 'I know what I know' — as if it is proud of the fact that it predicted the family's loss. Furthermore, there is something ominous about the way it hovers above the child and her grandmother. Tellingly, at this point the grandmother 'shivers'.

The granddaughter draws a house with her crayons. We can imagine this as a typically happy and simple childish drawing, one composed of 'rigid' lines featuring a flower bed, a winding path and a man standing in the garden. The child shows this drawing 'proudly' to her grandmother.

Once again, however, the almanac is depicted in a sinister light. It hovers above the child's drawing. Little moons fall out of its pages, presumably from its star charts and horoscopes, and tumble into the child's picture. These little moons 'fall like tears', dropping into the flower bed she has drawn. The almanac declares that it is 'Time to plant tears'. There is something unsettling about the notion of these tears somehow taking root among the flower beds of the granddaughter's drawing.

THEMES

Childhood

Like 'First Death in Nova Scotia' and 'In the Waiting Room', 'Sestina' wonderfully depicts the mentality of childhood. We see this in the description of the granddaughter staring at the kettle as it comes to boil, and ignoring her grandmother's declaration that it is time for tea. We can imagine a young girl being mesmerised by the sight of 'tears' running down the kettle's side, and thinking how these drops must resemble the rain on the farmhouse roof.

Childhood mentality is also artfully portrayed in the depiction of the granddaughter drawing a house with her crayons. She draws in the typically 'rigid', over-deliberate fashion of children everywhere. She approaches the task with an innocent and childish dedication, 'carefully' sketching a flower bed and showing the finished picture 'proudly' to the grandmother.

Throughout the poem there are moments when Bishop skilfully inhabits a child's point of view. This phrase 'clever almanac', for instance, has a distinctly childish ring to it. The child, presumably, is aware from observing the adults around her that the almanac contains predictions and folk wisdom. Therefore, in an amusingly babyish phrase, she refers to it as 'clever'. Similarly effective is the description of the stove as 'marvellous'. We can imagine that this is how the granddaughter might refer to the stove. To this innocent and childish girl, the stove is a wondrous and fascinating object. She therefore confuses the brand name 'Marvel' with the word 'marvellous'.

As we have seen, the poem's second half is full of strange and bizarre occurrences. We get the impression, however, that these weird events are not 'real' but merely take place in the granddaughter's imagination. She imagines that the almanac hovers around the kitchen with a mind of its own and sends a rain of moons into her picture, that her grandmother's cup contains tears rather than tea, that the stove and the almanac have a brief conversation.

The grandmother notices none of these events. She goes about her business as if nothing strange is happening, reinforcing our sense that these bizarre occurrences take place only in the imagination of the child. This sense is further reinforced when the almanac sows moons 'secretly' in the child's drawing, somehow unnoticed by the grandmother as she 'busies herself about the stove'. The poem then wonderfully captures how a child's imagination can run riot, viewing even simple household objects as living things and as a source of fear and wonder.

Moments of insight

It is difficult not to regard 'Sestina' in terms of Bishop's biography. Bishop's father died when she was only eight months old and when Elizabeth was only five years old her mother suffered a mental collapse and was institutionalised. Following these tragic events, young Elizabeth went to live with her maternal grandparents. The tragedy that has struck the family is 'known only to a grandmother'. The child is still too young to fully comprehend the terrible events that have occurred.

Yet we get the impression that awareness of this tragedy is slowly dawning on the child:

The moisture running down the sides of the kettle reminds her of tears.

Similarly, she imagines that the grandmother's cup contains tears rather than tea.

To the child, the drops from the kettle seem to 'dance like mad', perhaps suggesting that on some level she is aware her mother was institutionalised.

She imagines the stove and almanac talking about the tragedy: 'It was to be, says the Marvel Stove./ I know what I know, says the almanac'. This suggests that she is aware on some level that something terrible has befallen her even if she cannot verbalise exactly what 'it' is.

We get an impression that the child attempts to shield herself from sorrow by drawing houses. It is as if she tries to create in her imagination an ideal house, an alternative world where the tragedy that struck her never occurred. Interestingly, the house is described as 'rigid', suggesting it is a tough and solid safe haven. The man in the drawing presumably represents the father she so tragically lost. Yet the fact that the man's buttons are like 'tears' suggests that even in the idealised world of her drawing, the child cannot escape the dawning awareness of sorrow.

The child may be protected from sorrow by her youthful inability to fully comprehend the tragic events that occurred, but this defence will only last for so long.

The almanac hovers in an ominous manner above the granddaughter as if it represents awareness of this tragedy waiting to descend upon her. We see this when the almanac 'plants tears' in the child's drawing, letting moons spill like tears from its pages and take root in the picture's flower bed.

We get the impression, however, that tears have also been 'planted' in the child's life and will soon bear fruit. At present, she lacks understanding to fully comprehend what it means to have lost her parents. That understanding, however, and the tears that accompany it will come soon enough.

'Sestina' bears close comparison to 'First Death in Nova Scotia'. Both poems involve a child confronted with a family tragedy; the death of cousin Arthur in 'First Death' and the loss of the child's parents in 'Sestina'. In both poems, we get a sense that the child lacks the experience and mental capacity to fully comprehend the tragedy that has taken place. In both poems, it could be said that the child is protected from sorrow by her own lack of understanding. Yet in each case we get a sense that an awareness of tragedy and a deep sense of sorrow is slowly dawning upon the child. 'In the Waiting Room' is another poem that depicts the awareness of an uncomfortable truth slowly dawning on a little girl.

LANGUAGE

Form

The sestina is a notoriously difficult poetic form, one that few English-language writers have been able to employ successfully. In this poem, however, Bishop displays consummate command of the form, perhaps using its intense difficulty and rigid structure to contain the difficult childhood emotions she feels compelled to explore. The sestina consists of six six-line stanzas and a three-line section called an *envoi*.

The sestina employs six 'end-words' instead of rhymes – in this case 'house', 'grandmother', 'child', 'stove', 'almanac' and 'tears'. The same six end-words must be used in each stanza. The position of each end-word shifts from stanza to stanza. 'Home', for example, concludes the first line of stanza 1, the second line of stanza 2, the fourth line of stanza 3, the fifth line of stanza 4, the third line of stanza 5 and the last line of stanza 6. The other end-words shift in a similar fashion. The *envoi* must contain all six end-words: three at the end of its lines and three in the middle.

Tone & atmosphere

This poem conjures a melancholy autumnal atmosphere. It is September, signalling that summer is over and that winter, the dead season, is on its way. The poem is set at evening time, when the light is failing and the darkness gathers. The autumn cold slips in through the walls of the house: 'She shivers and says she thinks the house feels chilly'.

An important feature of the poem is its increasingly menacing descriptions of the rain. In the first line we are told that the rain is simply 'falling' on the house. By line 7, however, the rain 'beats' on the house, which suggests violence or assault. In lines 15 and 16 the child reckons the rain must be dancing 'like mad' on the roof of the house.

The rain, the cold, the time of year and the time of day all combine to conjure a haunting and melancholy atmosphere. The lonely atmosphere outside the house perfectly suggests the tragedy that has visited the people living within. The rain aggressively beating on the house suggests the sorrow that threatens to overcome the young girl but that – for the moment at least – is held in check by her inability to fully comprehend what has happened.

Imagery

One of the most notable features of this poem is the bizarre imagery Bishop deploys in its second half. As we have noted, the child imagines that the almanac hovers around the kitchen with a mind of its own and sends a rain of moons into her picture, that her grandmother's cup contains tears rather than tea, that the stove and the almanac have a brief conversation (particularly potent is the image of the grandmother's cup being 'full of dark brown tears', suggesting her intense sorrow). These surrealistic images powerfully convey how children see the world: as a place full of wonder, mystery and terror.

Figures of speech

There are several interesting similes and metaphors in this poem.

- In a fine metaphor, the drops of moisture on the kettle's side are compared to tears.
- In am equally fine simile, the buttons on the man in the child's drawing are compared to tears.
- In another simile, the moons falling from the almanac's pages are compared to tears, and we can imagine how the full, half and quarter moons depicted on the almanac's pages might resemble tears.
- In another fine simile, the almanac is compared to a bird: 'Birdlike, the almanac/ hovers half open above the child/ hovers above the old grandmother'. We can imagine the almanac's half-open pages resembling wings as it hovers about the kitchen.

Personification occurs in lines 15–16 where both the rain falling on the roof and the droplets falling on the stove are depicted as dancing (personification occurs when a non-human object is described as having human characteristics – in this instance, both the rain and the droplets are described as dancing, a very human activity).

Sound effects

For the most part, Bishop uses flat, everyday language in this poem. Yet there is a superb piece of word music in lines 15–16. There is an onomatopoeic quality to the lines: 'small hard tears/ dance like mad on the hot black stove' in which we can almost hear the rain rattling on the rooftop. Bishop achieves this unusual effect by using a lot of monosyllabic words, many of which feature hard consonants like 'd', 't' and 'k'. Also notable is the profusion of broad-vowel sounds in lines 33–4, which slows the pace of the verse, giving it a melancholy feel appropriate to the melancholy depiction of the moons falling into the child's picture.

First Death in Nova Scotia

Elizabeth Bishop

This moving poem dramatises a child's first encounter with the reality of death. It was inspired by an episode that occurred in Bishop's youth. Bishop spent the early part of her life in Nova Scotia, which is a Canadian territory.

LINE BY LINE
The speaker's young cousin Arthur has died and his corpse has been laid out in the parlour of the house. In the parlour, there is also a stuffed loon, which is a lake-dwelling bird, and a set of chromographs, which were an early type of colour photograph. The loon has been shot and stuffed by the speaker's uncle, the little dead boy's father: 'on the table/ stood a stuffed loon/ shot and stuffed by Uncle/ Arthur, Arthur's father'. The chromographs depict the British royal family, who are heads of state in Canada.

The speaker's attention is drawn to the stuffed loon. She emphasises the softness and whiteness of its feathers, how it 'was deep and white/ cold and caressable'. She compares the table on which it rests in death to the lake on which it rested in life: 'his white frozen lake,/ the marble-topped table'. She describes how its eyes have been replaced with pieces of red glass as part of the stuffing process. To the young speaker, these pieces of glass resemble gems, or precious stones: 'his eyes were red glass/ Much to be desired'.

The speaker's mother tells her to bid her cousin a final farewell. She is lifted up so that she is face to face with Arthur, and is given a flower to put in his dead hands: 'I was lifted up and given/ one lily of the valley/ to put in Arthur's hand'. She emphasises the smallness of Arthur's body and how pale he is in death: 'Arthur was very small. He was all white/ like a doll/ that hadn't been painted yet'.

The speaker explains Arthur's paleness to herself by referring to Jack Frost, a fairy-tale character. The speaker has been told that this mythical character is responsible for painting all the maple leaves in Canada their distinctive red colour: 'he always painted/ the Maple Leaf'. She imagines that Jack Frost was also supposed to paint Arthur's body, bringing colour to it: 'Jack Frost had started to paint him'. She tells herself that Jack Frost had only begun this process, painting Arthur's red hair, before being interrupted and abandoning it: 'Jack Frost had dropped the brush/ and left him white'.

The speaker imagines that the royal couples depicted in the chromographs have summoned Arthur to become one of their pageboys or courtiers, 'to be the smallest page at court'. This could be another childish fantasy concocted by the speaker herself. However, it could also be the kind of gentle lie an adult might tell a child to shield her from the truth about death. Perhaps her mother told her this fantastic story, wanting her to understand that Arthur will not be around anymore but also desiring to shield her from the harsher realities of dying.

At the poem's conclusion, however, we find the narrator questioning this fantasy. She seems to realise the absurdity of the stiff, immobile corpse marching off to take up a job at the court of King George:

But how could Arthur go,
clutching his tiny lily,
with his eyes shut up so tight
and the roads deep in snow?

Arthur's corpse, she seems to realise, is incapable of opening his eyes. How, therefore, could he make it to King George's court? Furthermore, even if he could see, how could a little boy travel alone through the snowy and icy roads?

THEMES
Moments of insight
The poem's narrator is a very young girl who seems to be unaware of the reality of death. While she may have heard the word mentioned, she has little or no real understanding of what death is or what it actually means for something to die. We see this when she mentions the silence of the stuffed loon. The speaker describes how the loon has been silent, has 'kept his own counsel', since her uncle shot him: 'Since Uncle Arthur fired/ a bullet into him,/ he hadn't said a word'.

The fact that this surprises the child, that she even considers it worth remarking on, indicates her lack of comprehension of the reality of death. She seems to have no understanding of what it means for a person or an animal to die. She does not understand that the dead no longer go around talking and walking.

Now, however, her young cousin Arthur has passed away and his body has been laid out in the parlour of her house. As the poem's title suggests, this will be a powerful moment of awareness for the young speaker. It will be her first confrontation with the reality of death, her first understanding of what dying actually means. Throughout the poem, however, she attempts to evade thoughts of bereavement, this strange and uncomfortable new reality she is encountering directly for the very first time:

- In stanza 2 she focuses on the stuffed loon instead of on her recently deceased cousin.
- Even when she is lifted up to give Arthur a flower, she tries to avoid contemplating his strange new state, preferring to focus on the stuffed loon opposite him and on the coffin in which he lies: 'Arthur's coffin was/ a little frosted cake/ and the red-eyed loon eyed it/ from his white frozen lake'.
- It is as if she attempts to avoid dealing with the true horror of death by thinking of it in innocent and homely terms: Arthur's coffin is compared to a 'little frosted cake' and his corpse is compared to a doll.
- She uses fantasy to avoid thinking about death, telling herself that Arthur is white only because Jack Frost forgot to paint him.
- Similarly, she tells herself that Arthur will not be around anymore not because he is dead but because he is heading off to the court of King George, where he will work as the 'smallest page'.

An interesting feature of the poem is the way in which the speaker describes the loon in terms that could be equally applicable to her cousin's corpse: mentioning how 'he kept his own counsel', how his breast 'was deep and white/ cold and caressable', and referring to it by using the pronouns 'he' and 'his' rather than 'it' and 'its' as we might expect. As we have seen, the speaker tries to focus on the loon rather than on her dead cousin. Yet the loon and Arthur seem to become blurred in her mind. Try as she might, then, the speaker cannot avoid thinking about her cousin and the strange new state his body occupies.

Furthermore, there is an air of menace in stanza 3, as if the speaker is becoming aware, at least on some level, of death's finality and horror. There is something sinister about the depiction of the 'red-eyed loon', which almost hungrily 'eyes' the dead boy in his coffin. Red eyes, it should be noted, are also associated with tears of grief and bereavement.

An important feature of stanza 3 is the way the word 'forever' is emphasised: by being bracketed off in line 33 and by being repeated in line 38. Despite the speaker's attempts to avoid thinking about death, she is becoming aware, on some level, that an eternal and unalterable change has taken place. Arthur has been transformed 'forever'. From now on he will be nothing but this white corpse: 'left him white forever'.

The poem concludes, then, with the speaker on the verge of awareness. We get the impression that the fantastic stories she tells herself – about Jack Frost and King George – are not capable of shielding her from the truth. She seems to know deep down that the story about Arthur going off to be a page at court simply cannot be true. Despite all her attempts to avoid this grim epiphany, she is about to understand what death is and what it means for a person to die; she is about to realise something strange and terrible and unalterable.

'First Death in Nova Scotia' bears close comparison to 'Sestina'. Both poems involve a child confronted with a family tragedy: the death of cousin Arthur in the present poem and the loss of the child's parents in 'Sestina'. In both poems, we get a sense that the child lacks the experience and mental capacity to fully comprehend the tragedy that has taken place. In both poems, it could be said that the child is protected from sorrow by her innocence, by her childlike lack of understanding. Yet in both poems we get the sense that this innocence will not be enough to stave off the new and terrible awareness that is dawning upon the child. 'In the Waiting Room' is another poem that depicts the awareness of an uncomfortable truth slowly dawning on a little girl.

Childhood

This is one of several poems where Bishop wonderfully captures the childhood mentality of her young speaker. 'Sestina' and 'In the Waiting Room' are two other poems where Bishop accomplishes this. In

'First Death in Nova Scotia', the speaker's childlike innocence comes across when she compares Arthur's corpse to a doll 'that hadn't been painted yet' and his coffin to 'a little frosted cake'.

It is also evident when she describes the loon's eyes as 'much to be desired'. Presumably, the stuffed bird's eyes have been replaced with cheap pieces of red glass. Yet the innocent speaker thinks of these as precious and highly valuable gemstones. It has also been suggested that the speaker's childhood mentality comes across in her somewhat peculiar use of the word 'forever'. The child thinks of Jack Frost painting the maple leaves, which in turn makes her think of the popular Canadian song 'The Maple Leaf Forever': 'the way he always painted/ the Maple Leaf (Forever)'.

The speaker's childhood innocence is also conveyed by her response to death. She mentions the fact that the dead loon has 'kept his own counsel' since it was shot. The fact that she considers this worth mentioning indicates her innocent lack of awareness of death. She does not fully grasp what death is or understand that dead people and animals never go around walking and talking. We also see this innocent ignorance of death in the way the speaker believes, or almost believes, the stories about Jack Frost and about Arthur bring summoned to be the 'smallest page at court'.

LANGUAGE

Form
The poem is written in five stanzas, each nine lines long. There is no regular rhyme scheme. However, the rhymes between 'cake' and 'lake' in stanza 3 and between 'go' and 'snow' in stanza 5 give a sense of powerful musical closure to the stanzas in question. It could be argued that this is also true of the half-rhyme between 'hair' and 'forever' in stanza 4.

Tone & atmosphere
The poem has a chilly, icy atmosphere, suitable to a poem that deals with the themes of death:

- In the very first line, we're told the parlour is 'cold, cold' – the repetition emphasising the room's frostiness.
- The loon's breast is described as being 'cold'.
- The marble-topped table is compared to a 'frozen lake'.
- The coffin is compared to a 'frosted' cake.
- There is reference to 'Jack Frost', a fairy-tale character associated with frost and coldness.
- The roads in the surrounding countryside are described as being 'deep in snow'.

The poem's final image is a particularly wintry one as the speaker imagines little Arthur, vulnerable and alone, wandering through the icy wastes.

Bishop's relentless references to whiteness also contribute to the icy atmosphere. The loon's breast is white, as is the table on which it rests. Arthur's coffin is also probably white, since it is described as a 'frosted cake'. Furthermore, the flower placed in his hands is a white lily. Perhaps the most notable occurrence of whiteness is that of Arthur's pale corpse, which is now 'white, forever'.

The only other prominent colour in the poem is red: there are the loon's fake red eyes, Arthur's hair, and the red clothes of the royal couples in the chromograph. The comfort of the people in the chromograph – 'warm in red and ermine' – makes a sharp contrast with the coldness of the scene in the parlour, especially with Arthur's, white frozen body.

Imagery
One notable feature of this poem is the almost fairy-tale imagery Bishop deploys. We see this in stanza 3 with its mention of Jack Frost, whose is responsible for painting all the maple leaves in Canada but was somehow interrupted halfway through painting cousin Arthur. It is also evident in stanza 5 with its description of Arthur being summoned to serve as 'the smallest page at court'. The image of the boy walking with his eyes shut tight through snowdrifts toward a king's court is like something from one of the darker tales of Hans Christian Andersen. These fairy-tale images, then, are not only innocent and childlike but are also haunting and even menacing.

Metaphor & simile
Bishop uses a fine metaphor to describe the table on which the loon rests, comparing it to a frozen lake: 'He kept his own counsel/ on his white frozen lake,/ the marble-topped table'. In another metaphor, Arthur's coffin is compared to a 'little frosted cake'. In a fine simile, Arthur's corpse is compared to a doll: 'He was all white, like a doll/ that hadn't been painted yet.'

Elizabeth Bishop

Filling Station

LINE BY LINE

The speaker of the poem stands before a filling station and describes what she sees. Behind the pumps is a concrete porch, and upon this porch is some 'wickerwork' furniture – a sofa and taboret are mentioned (a taboret is a type of armless and backless seat or stool). A 'doily' is draped over the taboret (a doily is a small piece of paper or cloth with a pattern of little holes in it, used as a decoration on a plate or under a cake). On top of the doily are some comic books. A dog lies on the sofa. The speaker also mentions a colourful plant, a large begonia that may be situated somewhere on the porch or even on the table. The cans of oil are arranged somewhere on the premises in such a manner that the word 'ESSO' is visible on the first and half the word visible on those lined behind it: 'ESSO–SO–SO–SO'.

The filling station is family-run: 'it's a family filling station'. The speaker can see the father and 'several' sons. The father wears a formal suit – or 'monkey suit' – that is a little too small for him and so 'cuts him under the arms'. His sons work quickly and are fond of making sexually-loaded jokes. Like everything else in the filling station, they are covered in grease: 'quick and saucy/ and greasy'.

The filling station is very messy. There is oil everywhere. The place is soaked in oil: 'oil-soaked'. Oil has seeped into everything and is present in every part of the filling station: 'oil-permeated'. The wickerwork is 'grease-/ impregnated'. The oil gives the place an 'over-all/ black translucency'. The oil makes everything black, but it is possible to see through the oil – it is translucent. The speaker even jokes that the plant is oiled rather than watered: 'Somebody waters the plant,/ or oils it, maybe'. The only objects that have not been coated in oil are the comic books. They 'provide/ the only note of color –/ of certain color'. Everything else is so coated in oil that it is no longer possible to say exactly what colour it is.

The filling station is a very masculine environment. The only visible people are men: the father and an indeterminate number of sons. Even the plant has a manly appearance: 'a big hirsute begonia'. The place is 'all quite thoroughly dirty'.

Yet, despite the fact that the place is run by a bunch of greasy men and is utterly filthy, the filling station has elements of decoration. The plant, the taboret and the doily on top of the taboret are all essentially decorative – their presence in such a male-dominated and dirty environment something of a mystery: 'Why the extraneous plant?/ Why the taboret?/ Why, oh why, the doily?' These are 'extraneous' items, superfluous to requirements. What is especially baffling to the speaker is the way that the doily has been embroidered 'in daisy stitch/ with marguerites … with gray crochet'. The doily has been decorated with flowers (marguerites are a type of daisy) and grey stitching. Such a pretty and delicate item is so out of keeping with the rest of the place.

As she stares in amazement at these curious items, the speaker has a moment of epiphany. Somebody has obviously taken time to beautify the place. Somebody had to have 'embroidered the doily' and 'water the plant'. Somebody also took the time to arrange the cans of oil so they all faced the same way. It can hardly have been any of the men. There must be another person, someone not present who bothered to do all these things. The speaker is amazed that such an effort was made in such a filthy place. It astounds her that evidence of care and love should be discovered here, that someone should bother to arrange the oil cans in an aesthetically pleasing manner, out of consideration for the highly-strung. The final line suggests that if love can exist in such a place, then it is possible for everyone to be loved: 'Someone loves us all'.

THEMES

Travel

The poet seems to have just come across the filling station that she describes. It does not strike us as a place that she regularly visits or passes. She stands before it as an outsider or tourist, fascinated by something she has not seen before, and alert to the features of the place that strike her as unusual or unique. She views the place with outsider's eyes, meditating upon its features in a way that those who live in the area are never likely to.

The poem, therefore, suggests that when we travel we are more keenly aware of what we experience and see. Travelling through strange places defamiliarises the world and allows the most banal things to become strange and fascinating. A filling station is nothing unusual, yet the poet finds this one remarkable, and she views it with a fascination she is unlikely to hold for the more familiar sights of home.

Moments of insight

The poet observes a 'dirty' filling station. She is appalled at the state of the place and the condition of the men working there. Everything is 'greasy' and soaked in oil. But in the midst of this filthy masculine environment, certain peculiar features stand out. Upon the porch 'behind the pumps' is a set of wickerwork furniture. The furniture is 'crushed' and soaked in grease, yet upon the 'taboret' is a 'doily' and a large begonia plant. The doily has been embroidered 'in daisy stitch/ with marguerites'. Such delicate decorative touches in this rough and dirty place appear most strange: 'Why, oh why'.

The poet realises that somebody is making an effort to beautify the filling station. 'Somebody embroidered the doily./ Somebody waters the plant'. Someone actually cares how this filthy place looks. The men who work there are concerned about getting the work done, but there is someone in the background who is concerned with how the place appears. The way the cans of oil have been arranged is particularly interesting. These have been stacked so that the word 'ESSO' is legible on the first and just the last two letters on the rest: 'ESSO–SO–SO–SO'. The effect is pleasing and soothing and seems to have been created for the benefit of the passing motorists.

The poet's moment of insight occurs at the end of the poem. The place shows her how love and beauty can survive in even the most filthy and ugly environments. The idea that 'Someone loves us all' can be read in two ways. Perhaps the poet is referring to the men who work in the filling station and is saying that if these people can be loved then anyone can be loved. However, it might be that the poet is thinking about the fact that someone is making an effort to beautify the filling station for the benefit of those who visit it. She is therefore saying that this person has all our interests at heart, that she 'loves us all'.

Elizabeth Bishop

In the Waiting Room

LINE BY LINE

It is winter in Worcester, Massachusetts. The poet is aged six. She accompanies her Aunt Consuelo on a visit to the dentist. While her aunt is in with the dentist, the child sits in the waiting room. The waiting room 'was full of grown-up people', winter coats ('arctics and overcoats'), 'lamps and magazines'. While the young girl waits for her aunt, she reads the *National Geographic* (she is proud of the fact that she could read at that age – 'I could read'). She carefully studies the photographs as she reads. Certain images grab her attention:

- There is a photograph of 'the inside of a volcano'.
- 'Osa and Martin Johnson/ dressed in riding breeches,/ laced boots, and pith helmets'. Osa and Martin Johnson were American explorers and adventurers who travelled to Africa and made documentary films about the wildlife and the people.
- 'A dead man slung on a pole/ – 'Long Pig', the caption said'. In the Polynesian islands in the South Pacific, human flesh was called 'long pig'.

'Babies with pointed heads/ wound round and round with string;/ black, naked women with necks/ wound round and round with wire'.

The poet is self-conscious as she sits by herself in the waiting room, and so she immerses her in the magazine to avoid having to look at the other people waiting. She reads the magazine 'straight through' because she is 'too shy to stop'. When she is finished reading the magazine she looks at 'the cover:/ the yellow margins, the date', anything but look at the other people around her.

Suddenly she hears 'an *oh*! of pain' coming 'from inside'. It is her 'Aunt Consuelo's voice'. The cry of pain is 'not very long or loud'. The young poet is not 'at all surprised' that her aunt would make this noise: 'even then I knew she was/ a foolish, timid woman'. However, the young girl is suddenly thrown into a state of confusion. The voice that she took to be her aunt's was also strangely her own voice: 'What took me/ completely by surprise/ was that it was *me*:/ my voice, in my mouth'. All of a sudden it is not so clear what occurred.

There are a number of possibilities here:

1. The aunt made an *oh*! sound from 'inside' the surgery. The young girl suddenly realises that her aunt's voice is the same as her own.
2. The young girl made the *oh*! sound but thought initially that it was her aunt because it sounded just like the aunt. In this case, the 'inside' refers to *inside* the young girl, i.e. the sound came from inside her. It sounded like 'Aunt Consuelo's voice' but is in actual fact the poet's own: 'it was *me*:/ my voice, in my mouth'.

The place from which the cry or voice originates is unclear. When Bishop says 'inside', we can understand this to mean inside the dentist's surgery where the aunt is or we can understand it to mean inside the young girl. Bishop intends this ambiguity, for at this moment she can no longer properly distinguish between herself and her aunt. Their voices are the same, and for a brief, unsettling moment their identities become fused in the young girl's mind.

The realisation that she shares traits with her 'foolish aunt' causes the young girl to feel dizzy. She feels as if she is 'falling', or, rather, that she and her aunt are falling since to the startled young girl they now seem to be one and the same person: 'I – we – were falling'. All the time she has her eyes 'glued to the cover' of the magazine, reading the name and date.

The young girl tries to steady herself by reminding herself that her birthday will be in three days. She latches on to this fact in an effort to 'stop/ the sensation of falling off/ the round, turning world/ into cold, blue-black space'. But thoughts about who and what she is keep coming, and she tries desperately to make sense of it all.

The young girl thinks about how she can define herself. She is an individual, an 'I'. But she is also 'an *Elizabeth*', one of many Elizabeths in the world. She is also a member of the human race, one member of a vast group, some of whom are gathered in the waiting room with her: 'you are one of *them*'.

For the first time in her life, the young poet seems to be thinking about the human race, the vast number of people inhabiting the planet. It seems that before this moment she did not give much or any thought to the collective group of people who occupy the world around her. She seems to have seen the world as composed of a multitude of individuals, each with their own separate identity and living their own unique lives. She does not seem to have given thought to the similarities between people, to the habits, experiences and traits that unite us. For the first time, she must acknowledge that she is 'one of them', one of billions of others not so unlike her who are living at the same time.

The idea that she is a member of the human race is immediately disturbing to the young girl: 'Why should you be one, too?' She can hardly bring herself to contemplate the group she must now acknowledge she is a part of: 'I scarcely dared to look/ to see what it was that I was'. But her curiosity gets the better of her, and she lifts her eyes a little and glances around the room. She cannot bring herself to look any higher than the legs of the other people in the waiting room, but it is enough to give her a sense of what people are: 'shadowy gray knees,/ trousers and skirts and boots/ and different pairs of hands'.

Having to acknowledge the similarities between people and realising that she is just one of billions of people inhabiting the planet leaves the young poet at a loss as to how she should think of herself as an individual: 'Why should I be my aunt,/ or me, or anyone?' And if it is hard to know what it is that defines us as individuals (that makes me *me* and not you), then what are the features or characteristics that bring us together and make 'us all just one'? Are they the 'boots, hands, the family voice' that the poet has just heard in her throat'? Even the terrifying image of the 'hanging breasts' in the magazine must now be understood in terms of shared traits that define and unite us.

The young girl is suddenly wrestling with complex notions of identity and the meaning of life. She wonders how she has 'come to be here', and what it is that makes her who she is. In such a short space of time, her way of thinking about herself and the world she inhabits has radically changed, and she knows that 'nothing stranger/ had ever happened, that nothing/ stranger could ever happen'. Her existence and that of the rest of the world suddenly seems like a fantastically strange idea, something terribly unlikely: 'How – I didn't know any/ word for it – how "unlikely" …'

All these unexpected and confusing questions overwhelm the young girl. The thoughts she is trying desperately to rationalise seem like great waves that rise above her and crash down upon her. She suddenly feels that the waiting room is 'bright/ and too hot', and that she is about to black out: 'It was sliding/ beneath a big black wave,/ another, and another'.

But just as she feels she is about to faint, she regains control and gets a grip. The panic ends and she finds herself 'back in' the everyday world. She steadies herself with the facts and the familiar, with a thought that though everything has changed, everything remains the same: 'The War was on. Outside in Worcester, Massachusetts,/ were night and slush and cold,/ and it was still the fifth/ of February, 1918'.

THEMES

Moments of insight

Many of Bishop's poems are marked by moments of epiphany, moments when a person suddenly realises something profound and important about themselves or about the world. 'In the Waiting Room' describes just such a moment in the young poet's life.

It seems that before her visit to the dentist with her aunt, the young girl had a simple but clear idea of who she is. She defines herself in terms of her age and her abilities ('I could read'). She can clearly see the differences between herself and the other people in the waiting room: 'The waiting room/ was full of grown-up people'. She is young, they are old. She is special because she is only six and can already read. Her understanding of the greater world is also secure and safely limited to certain facts: 'It was winter. It got dark/ early'.

But the content of the magazine in which she immerses herself in order to avoid contact with the others in the waiting room is strange and frightening. She is exposed to images of strange cultures and

Elizabeth Bishop

practices that horrify her: 'A dead man slung on a pole … Babies with pointed heads …. black, naked women with necks/ wound round and round with wire'. The exposure to all these bizarre images is terrifying and unsettling. The magazine reveals that the world is stranger and more alien perhaps than she ever imagined.

Just as her mind is reeling from these strange images, she hears a cry 'from inside'. It is her aunt's voice but it is also her own voice: 'it was me:/ my voice'. All of a sudden, her sense of who she is exploded. She realises that she resembles her 'foolish, timid' aunt. And if she shares similarities with her aunt, then perhaps she also shares similarities with the other people in the waiting room. She is part of the human race: 'you are one of them'. The notion that she is just one of countless people who share similar feelings, habits and characteristics is deeply unpleasant to the young girl who only moments before thought herself utterly unique. She is shocked that she is just 'one of them'.

The notion that she is part of the human race leads to the necessary conclusion that she shares similarities with the strange people in the magazine. The differences that she perceived between herself and the women in the magazine are not perhaps as great as she thinks. They are women and she also is a woman (or is soon to become a woman).

Travel

The magazine that the young girl reads contains images of people and practices from places remote from her home town of Worcester, Massachusetts. She gazes at 'A dead man slung on a pole' and at 'Babies with pointed heads' and 'black, naked women with necks/ wound round and round with wire/ like the necks of light bulbs'. Although the poem does not question the ethics of depicting other cultures in this manner, the young girl's experience does bring to mind the question that Bishop raises in 'Questions of Travel': 'Is it right to be watching strangers in a play/ in this strangest of theaters?'

Is it right that images of 'black, naked women' should feature in magazines – most likely without the permission of those photographed – to satisfy our curiosity? Is there not perhaps something pornographic about photographing the naked and the dead in this manner, of objectifying them and presenting them as something alien? The images in the magazine seem intended to shock and horrify. Yet, as the young girl begins to realise, we are not as different as we might sometimes imagine from the people living in these distant societies. Though the magazine presents them as strange and bizarre, perhaps we would do better to realise the similarities that exist between us all and think about what it is that holds 'us all together' and makes us 'all just one'.

THOMAS KINSELLA
THEMES

OLD AGE

Negative effects of ageing

Many of Kinsella's poems depict the ravages time inflicts on the human body. In 'Mirror in February', for instance, the poet is shocked at the sight of his own 'exhausted' and 'downturning' features. He is suddenly horrified to realise he is no longer young. This poem movingly deals with the ageing process, describing how the passage of time damages or 'mutilates' our bodies. The older we get the more our bodies waste and decay.

In 'Thinking of Mr D.' Kinsella describes the loneliness that sometimes comes with getting old. The final image in the poem of the ghostly Mr D. down on the wharfs, staring into the dark water, is intensely lonely. For all his gossiping and socialising in bars, it seems that Mr D. led a lonely, solitary life. 'Dick King' is another poem that suggests our later years can be difficult. Kinsella refers to the 'dread years' that lay ahead of his neighbour as he approached old age. Dick King is described making his 'wintry bed' through all the seasons of the year, suggesting that after his wife had died his days were intensely lonely.

'Thinking of Mr D.' also focuses on the 'pain' and 'bodily plight' of the elderly. The poet describes how Mr D.'s body would jerk with pain as he walked: 'turning …/ Quickly aside from pain'. In this regard the poem can be compared to 'Tear' where the poet describes the physical suffering that his grandmother had to endure upon her deathbed.

'His Father's Hands', too, touches on this theme, with its moving depiction of the poet's aged grandfather playing the fiddle. The old man seems weak and frail, his hands barely moving as he 'scrapes' at the instrument's strings. The grandfather is so deaf he has to slant his head and hold the fiddle close to his ears in order to hear the tune he's playing. We can almost imagine him slumped wearily by the fireside, humming weakly to himself as he plays.

Acceptance of growing old

It is understandable, 'Mirror in February' suggests, that we might flinch or 'quail' in the face of these unpleasant facts of human existence, or that we should regard the horrible reality of human ageing with 'distaste'. There is a tone of sadness and resignation about the poem's last lines: all we can do is accept that we are 'man' and that growing old is part of the human condition. But there is also an air of defiance here, a determination to face the mutilations of the ageing process with as much grace, courage and dignity as possible. 'Tear' also suggests that with ageing comes an ability to endure and handle whatever life brings. 'Old age', Kinsella writes, 'can digest/ anything'.

CHILDHOOD & YOUTH

Childhood mentality

Many of Kinsella's poems wonderfully capture the innocent world of the child. In 'Model School', for example, the poet describes the childish amusement that he and his classmates find in the fact that Mr Browne is actually quite brown and in the fact that some words in the Irish adding-up tables sound like Miss Carney's name.

In 'His Father's Hands' Kinsella depicts how he amused himself by hammering a pinch of sprigs into the grandfather's workbench. There is a sense in these lines that the young poet is imitating the grandfather, almost playing at being a cobbler like his cousins before him. The poem also features childhood memories of watching the grandfather cut tobacco for his pipe and of him playing the fiddle.

'Dick King' also evokes the world of the child. The image of the young boy sheltering against the older man's coat suggests vulnerability and a need for protection and reassurance. This act of nestling in against the clothing of an older person is also present in 'Tear' where the poet recalls burying his face in his grandmother's black aprons.

'Hen Woman' skillfully evokes a childhood mentality. The child seems mesmerised by the simple and trivial incident that plays out in front of him.

Youthful mentality

Some of the poems on the course also deal with the later adolescent years, the in-between period in life when we are no longer children but are not quite adults either. In 'Chrysalides' Kinsella wonderfully captures a lazy and listless adolescent mentality, depicting how the two boys meander through the countryside, keep odd hours and stay in bed till noon.

However, this time of life can also be difficult and unpleasant. In 'Tear', for example, Kinsella describes a harrowing and intensely awkward youthful encounter with his dying grandmother.

END OF INNOCENCE

Kinsella suggests that such encounters are ultimately important and necessary if we are to make the transition from childish innocence to adult awareness and understanding. In 'Tear', for example, having to face his dying grandmother forces the young poet to enter a dark and derelict place in his mind, a place that smells of ashes. This is a terrible place and seems to be representative of the young boy's sudden awareness of death.

'Model School, Inchicore' also describes how childhood innocence is inevitably lost. The young Kinsella gains knowledge in the Model School. As his mind becomes more knowledgeable and sophisticated his childhood innocence disappears.

'Chrysalides' describes the sexual change and awakening that occurs in adolescence. The young poet and his brother are at the stage in life where the hormonal changes associated with this period of life really start to kick in. They feel this 'strange wakefulness' within themselves. This sexual awakening makes the boys numb and 'insensitive'. Their instincts are 'blurred' and their hearts are 'dulled'. They seem too wrapped up in themselves, in their own altering bodies and minds, to really be aware of what's going on around them. They fail to notice how these precious summer days are slipping away, missing the 'unique succession of our youthful midnights'.

STRUGGLE FOR COMPREHENSION

Many of Kinsella's poems present us with speakers or characters who desperately attempt to make sense of the world around them. In 'Tear' the young poet finds the experience of visiting his dying grandmother to be overwhelming and he struggles to comprehend what he encounters: 'I was carried off/ to unfathomable depths'.

A desire for understanding and a struggle to comprehend is evident in 'Model School'. We see it when the young poet, eager for knowledge, declares that 'I am going to know everything'. It is also perhaps evident at the poem's conclusion, where the young poet sits alone in the bike shed, troubled and confused by the new knowledge he has gained. In 'Mirror in February' the older poet attempts to 'learn', to look into the mirror of his soul and understand himself. The poem shows him attempting to come to terms with the reality of ageing and bodily decay, but also with his own emptiness and lack of artistic fulfilment.

A struggle to comprehend the mystery of death is evident in 'Dick King'. Kinsella recalls his ageing neighbour 'naming the dead' and searching for a 'gate' by which to enter his own 'temperate ghosthood by'.

DEATH & MORTALITY

Elegy

A number of Kinsella's poems could be described as elegies, poems that remember and honour someone who has died. In 'His Father's Hands' the poet remembers his grandfather, lovingly depicting the old man cutting tobacco, working with leather and playing the fiddle. He describes the grandfather as a 'serene' and gentle person, referring to his 'peace', 'patience' and gentleness. 'Dick King' registers the poet's sadness at the fact that his neighbour no longer exists.

Yet Kinsella's elegies are not always straightforward celebrations of the dead. In 'His Father's Hands', for example, the poet unflinchingly depicts the difficulties his grandfather endures. 'Thinking Of Mr D.' is another poem that remembers a dead man in an honest manner. The poem is sympathetic to the sufferings that Mr D. endured in his later years but it does not suggest that the man was by any means a perfect saint. Kinsella describes the 'scathing' smile of Mr D. and his love of 'malicious' gossip.

Dawning awareness of death
'Tear' illustrates how as we grow older we come become more aware of death and gradually learn to accept it as a inevitable part of life. Through the recollection of his response to his infant sister's death and a later encounter with his dying grandmother, the poem describes the gradual awareness of death that accompanies childhood.

In 'Mirror in February', meanwhile, the poet's awareness of mortality is reinforced as he catches sight of his reflection in the shaving mirror. He realises that he is no longer young but also that unlike the trees he is 'not renewable'. He will eventually grow old and die.

MEMORY

Trivial memories
Several of Kinsella's poems deal with events that seemed unmemorable to the poet at the time of their occurrence but that nevertheless went on to haunt his memory for many years afterwards. This is probably true of the schoolroom incidents described in 'Model School, Inchicore' and of the times spent playing with nails in his grand father's workshop described so powerfully in 'His Father's Hands'. Furthermore, when the young poet stood alongside Dick King that day on James's Street it is unlikely that he would have considered the moment significant and memorable. Yet it has remained with him and when he thinks of it now it is with a great sense of poignancy.

'Hen Woman', too, describes a trivial and unimportant incident. Did the young poet think the incident of the lost egg memorable at the time it occurred?

In 'Chrysalides' the youthful poet wasn't overly moved by the sight of the dying ants. There is little sense that he considered this incident particularly memorable at the time of its occurrence. Similarly, 'Tear' shows how in his infancy he didn't find the sight of his father weeping for his dead little sister terribly significant, moving or memorable. Yet these events would find their way into his consciousness and recur there with 'lasting horror' for many years afterwards.

Description of the process of memory
In 'Hen Woman' Kinsella powerfully describes his view of how the process of memory takes place. Memories, he says, are stored or hoarded within our minds: 'there is no end to that which, not understood,/ may yet be hoarded in the imagination'. He uses a wonderful metaphor to describe this, suggesting that memories are stored at the centre of our being just as the yolk is contained at the centre of an egg. An equally powerful depiction of the memory process can be found in 'Tear', where memory is depicted as a vast vault in which the recollections of various events are stored.

Both 'Tear' and 'Chrysalides' illustrate how unpleasant memories from our past can be forgotten and suddenly found again. In 'Tear' the poet's memory of his infant sister's death had lain dormant within the 'vaults' of his mind for a number of years before been discovered at the moment when he sunk his face in his grandmother's aprons and closed his eyes. The memory of his father shedding tears over the infant's coffin is suddenly retrieved from the 'vaults of memory'. Similarly, in 'Chrysalides' the young poet seems to quickly forget the sight of the dying ants. The young poet and his brother are too numbed and 'dulled' by the changes taking place inside themselves to appreciate the horror of this sight. It is only much later that this event resurfaces in his memory, to recur there with 'lasting horror' for many years.

'Dick King', too, deals with the memory process, describing how the death of a loved one alters the significance of the memories we have of them.' The poem's opening lines describe 'death' roving 'our memories igniting/ Love'. When those who we care for die it is with great love that they are remembered. Memories that we have of particular moments take on a new significance when those who feature in them have passed away. To the poet the memory of Dick King standing by the fountain on James's Street speaking softly of the dead appears poignant and significant now that his neighbour has died.

How memories haunt us
'Hen Woman' powerfully shows how the memories of certain events haunt our minds. The memory of the falling egg is one the poet returns to again and again: 'I feed upon still as you see'. In his memory the egg is

still falling toward the grate and will continue to do so for the rest of his life: 'It still falls for me ... and will continue to fall, probably, until I die'.

There are many other Kinsella poems that illustrate how childhood memories continue to haunt us when we are older.

- In 'Dick King', for instance, the poet only knew Dick King as a child, yet he has never forgotten him. It seems that Dick King is almost a presence in the daily life of his psyche.
- 'Thinking of Mr D.' depicts another old man who has died yet continues to feature in the poet's consciousness.
- Similarly, in 'His Father's Hands' the poet seems haunted by the memory of his grandfather quietly playing the fiddle and singing to himself.
- 'Chrysalides', meanwhile, depicts how the memory of the wedding flight of ants returned to haunt the poet for many years.
- In 'Model School, Inchicore' the poet seems haunted by the memory of sitting alone in the school shed and being revolted by the ink's bitter taste.

HORROR & DESOLATION

Horrified reactions are a regular feature of Kinsella's poetry. 'Model School, Inchicore' presents us with the poet's horrified reaction to the pen's ink, showing how his mouth shrinks or recoils from its taste. In 'Mirror in February' the poet responds with shock and horror to his own reflection in the shaving mirror. He suddenly realises he is no longer young and is 'riveted' by the sight of his own care-worn face.

In 'His Father's Hands' the poet is filled with horror when he imagines the environment of prehistoric Ireland: 'I do not like this place ... It feels evil'. 'Chrysalides', meanwhile, deals with the speaker's belatedly horrified reaction to the sight of the dying ants. Kinsella wonderfully captures the disturbing nature of this sight, describing how the winged male ants drop out of the air and die an 'agonised' death on the roadside.

However, perhaps Kinsella's most memorable depiction of horror occurs in 'Tear'. The young boy experiences horror at the thought of touching or kissing his grandmother. He imagines her turning toward him and whispering for him to come 'bury' himself 'in her drying mud'.

It could be argued that there is also an element of horror or disgust in 'Hen Woman'. This is perhaps evident in the poet's description of the beetle pushing the ball of dung across the ground and in his description of the egg emerging from the orifice 'flecked wuth greenish brown oils'. It is important to note, however, that the poet does not explicitly state that he is horrified by these sights.

Kinsella's poetry is also marked by recurring scenes of bleakness and desolation:

- 'Model School, Inchicore' concludes with a grim scene in which the little boy sits alone in the bicycle shed contemplating God's judgement as scraps of paper blow about the place.
- 'The Familiar' is set in a cold, bleak and desolate environment. The poet looks out the window at 'sheets of frost/ scattered down among the rocks' of the hills. Two 'hooded crows high in the cold' fly 'up toward the tundra'.
- Similarly, 'Mirror in February' takes place in a harsh wintry scene of rain and 'dark' leafless trees that have been brutally 'hacked clean' and defaced.
- A scene of desolation also features in 'His Father's Hands', where Kinsella imagines the beginnings of Irish civilisation. In these lines Kinsella depicts a bleak and desolate landscape of boulders, dampness and freezing soil.
- 'Thinking of Mr D.' concludes with a scene of urban desolation, depicting the tortured figure of Mr D.'s ghost gazing into the patterns formed by oil on the surface of the canal.

Once again 'Tear' is particularly memorable. When the young boy sinks his face into the grandmother's aprons and closes his eyes, his mind is plunged into a dark psychological landscape, what we might term the 'vaults' of his mind. Kinsella describes the boys search through the vaults of memory in terms of a 'derelict' building that smells 'of ash'. The young boy feels his way through the pitch black, listening to the 'rustle' of 'unseen walls and roofs' and 'disturbing/ dead ashes' as he goes.

FAMILY & ANCESTRY

Ancestry & inheritance
In 'His Father's Hands' Kinsella traces his ancestry through the centuries and generations. The phrase 'Beyond that' recurs as Kinsella traces his family history further and further into the past.

The poem also focuses on how certain traits are handed on down through the generations from father to son. Kinsella describes how his grandfather's personality was marked by a 'blocked gentleness'. This gentleness was passed on to Kinsella's father in a different form. In the father this gentleness was 'modulated' or changed into seriousness and what might be a slightly aggressive tendency to repeat himself. Kinsella himself also inherited this gentleness only to have it modulated to 'offhandedness' and to a tendency to repress 'certain impulses'.

Also relevant to this theme is the poem's final image of the breaking workbench. It is difficult not to envisage the 'countless little nails' that slip from the block as a metaphor for Kinsella's own extended family. His ancestors have come 'squirming and dropping' from the black mass of Irish history over the centuries from the arrival of the first settlers to the present day.

Hardship
'His Father's Hands' powerfully chronicles the different hardships endured by Kinsella's family over the generations, as they lived through the chaotic series of 'dispersals and migrations' that makes up Irish history. The poet describes the miserable conditions endured by his earliest ancestors as they attempted to exist in the harsh landscape of Ireland after the Ice Age, as they attempted to survive in a land still damp and freezing from the 'long cold'.

Whereas 'His Father's Hands' deals with the hardships endured by the poet's relatives throughout history, 'Tear' suggests the hardships endured by his relatives in the more immediate past. It shows how Kinsella's parents and grandparents endured lives of hardship and struggle: 'lives bitter with hard bondage'. When the poet's infant sister died he momentarily became aware of the 'sad dullness and tedious pain' of his father's and grandparent's lives. However, it is only when he is somewhat older and visits his dying grandmother that he begins to properly understand the unhappy lives that these people lived: 'How I tasted it now'.

Isolation
The fact that Kinsella's parents and grandparents led such hard lives seems to have resulted in them becoming bitter and cold individuals. In 'Tear' for instance we find little evidence of love or affection, nor is their any sense of family solidarity. Everybody mentioned in the poem seems to be alone and isolated. 'His Father's Hands', too, features a powerful sense of isolation. The grandfather is portrayed as an isolated figure. He is a gentle person but cannot properly communicate that gentleness to those around them.

Yet there is also a sense in which both Kinsella himself and his father are also psychologically isolated. The father's personality is marked by seriousness and a tendency to repeat himself. We see this at the beginning of the poem when he stridently makes the same point over and over again: 'His finger prodded the air/ marring his point'. Yet these traits have an unfortunate tendency to 'mar' or spoil his point, undermining his ability to communicate with those around him.

KINSELLA & THE IDEAS OF CARL GUSTAV JUNG

At a certain point in his career Kinsella came under the influence of the psychologist Carl Gustav Jung. Different aspects of Jung's philosophy had an impact on Kinsella's poetry.

Jung believed that in order to become a complete person one had to go on a psychological journey. One had to encounter the 'shadow', the dark and negative aspect of your own psyche. One also had to encounter the 'anima'. This means that a man would have to encounter the female aspect of his personality whilst a woman would have to encounter the male aspect of her personality. Only by undergoing such an inner journey could a person gain self-knowledge, awareness and completeness.

Kinsella structured a series of poems called 'Notes From the Land of the Dead' around this theory. Both 'Hen Woman' and 'Tear' come from this sequence. Both poems show the young poet encountering old women that are taken to represent the 'anima'. In 'Hen

Woman', the hen and the egg, both associated with female fertility, also represent the 'anima'.

Both of these poems also contain references to the 'shadow', the hidden part of the psyche that contains our fears, doubts and other negative emotions. We see this in 'Tear' when the poet explores the dark recesses of his own mind, which he describes as a cavernous place full of ashes. It is also present in 'Hen Woman' where the grate in the yard hints at a dark, cavernous underground space. In both 'Hen Woman' and 'Tear' the poet emerges from these encounters with new knowledge and a new sense of self-awareness.

Jung believed that certain 'archetypes' or symbols represented important aspects of the human psyche. Several of these are present in 'Tear' and 'Hen Woman'. We have already mentioned the old woman, the egg and the shadowy cavern. Another Jungian symbol is the 'orus boris' where a snake eats its own tail, which in Jungian psychology is a symbol of eternal renewal. We see this in 'Hen Woman' which depicts memories feeding upon themselves until they are ready to be turned into a poem. This image also turns up in 'Model School, Inchicore' where the young poet makes a snake out of plasticine.

'His Father's Hands' was written a few years after 'Hen Woman' and 'Tear', yet stills contains the influence of Jung. Kinsella explores his relationship with his father, his father's father and all his male descendents right back to the time of Ireland's first settlers. It is a counterpoint to the earlier poems. Whilst they deal with femininity, 'His Father's Hands' deals with masculinity.

NUMEROLOGY

Kinsella believed that there were five stages in the evolution of the self. He associate each one with a number, from zero to four.

The number 0 was related to the earliest stages of the self's formation when our minds are raw, unfocused and almost blank. There are several zeros in 'Model School', a poem that deals with these earliest stages of mental development. The snake of plasticine that the boy weaves around his hand can be seen as a zero, so can the dot that the teacher draws on the board.

There are also several zeros in 'Hen Woman', a poem that also deals with the psyche's first stages of development. There is the 'black zero' of the hen's orifice and the white zero of the egg. The mention of the word 'one' at the end of 'Hen Woman' suggests that the poet is leaving behind this earliest stage of mental development and moving on to the next stage of development: 'It's all the one,/ there's plenty more where that came from'.

'His Father's Hands' deals with the next stage of development, the stage associated with the number 1. There are several references to this number in the poem. The grandfather's nails are described as 'silver units'. Furthermore, at the end of the poem the upright workbench could also be taken to look like a 1.

In Kinsella's poetry the 0 stage was associated with the feminine while the 1 was associated with the masculine.

It is not clear to what extent Kinsella actually believed in Jungian philosophy. However, for a certain time he was happy to use these concepts to provide a structure for his poetic projects. In recent years Kinsella has made less and less reference to these notions in his work.

Thinking of Mr D.

LINE BY LINE

The poet remembers Mr D., an old man familiar to him from his locality. He would often see Mr D. in pubs around the neighbourhood. He remembers Mr D. as an 'ageing' individual, no longer able to drink alcohol quickly. Yet Mr D. was still nimble and agile: 'A man still light of foot'. Though he was old he still took care of his appearance. His shoes were polished and the poet recalls him carefully 'tucking in his scarf'.

Mr D. was a terrible gossip. The stories he liked to tell and hear were slanderous, meaning they were malicious and damaged people's reputations. This is suggested when the poet refers to the 'stabbing little' tales that Mr D. would tell. He would murmur these malicious stories to his drinking cronies ('the right company') in the corner of the pub. Mr D. took delight in this vicious gossip: 'his quiet tongue/ Danced to such cheerful slander'.

Mr D. was not someone who suffered fools gladly. His smile was 'scathing' suggesting that he was a critical person. It was difficult to impress him or get him to agree with you. He might nod his head if you told him something, but it was obvious that he did not 'assent' or agree with you: 'His sober nod withheld assent'.

The poet claims to have seen Mr D. after he died. He claims to have seen Mr D. leaving a group of fellow-drinkers in the pub having just told one of his gossipy stories:

Once as he used retire
On one last murmured stabbing little tale
From the right company, tucking in his scarf.

He also claims to have seen Mr D. down by the riverbank, on the wharf where the boats would dock for unloading. He was walking through a patch of light cast by a streetlight, then into darkness, and then into another patch of light cast by a streetlight: 'Lamps that plunged him in and out of light'. As he walked he looked at the oily reflections in the river.

The speaker claims that Mr D. was in poor physical condition as he walked by the riverbank. He was 'wolfish-slim' and in a 'bodily plight'. His body would jerk as he experienced a stabbing pain: 'turning …/ Quickly aside from pain'.

THEMES

Old age: negative effects of ageing

Although the first ten lines of the poem describe a confident, well-dressed drinker, gossiping with his cronies in a bar, the last six lines describe an intensely lonely individual. There is something desperately sad about Mr D. walking alone by the riverbank slipping in and out of darkness as he gazes into the oil-stained water. Like 'Dick King' then, where Kinsella speaks

of his elderly neighbour making his 'wintry bed' following the death of his wife, the poem describes the loneliness that sometimes comes with old age.

'Thinking of Mr D.' also focuses on the 'pain' and 'bodily plight' of the elderly. The poet describes how Mr D.'s body would jerk with pain as he walked: 'turning … / Quickly aside from pain'. In this regard the poem can be compared to 'Tear' where the poet describes the physical suffering that his grandmother had to endure upon her deathbed.

Death & mortality

Like 'Dick King' this poem describes how those who have died continue to haunt the living. Both Dick King and Mr D. live on in the poet's mind and he is unable to forget them. In 'Thinking of Mr D.' the poet speaks of seeing Mr D. on two occasions after the man had died. It is possible that the poet's memories of Mr D. are so strong and vivid that the dead old man seemed to be standing in front of him once again. The power of memory is so strong that the poet almost hallucinates the presence of Mr D. The poem, therefore, suggests how vividly the dead remain in our memories even after they have gone.

However, like 'Dick King', the poem can be read as a testament to the existence of ghosts. Is Kinsella saying that the spirits of the dead continue to exist in the world after the physical body has gone?

If this poem is a ghost story then it is one that presents a very bleak view of life after death. Mr D. does not seem to have found peace beyond the grave. Instead his spirit seems to wander restlessly through the night in the darkness by the riverbank. He gazes mournfully in the dirty river water as his body is wracked with pain.

Perhaps the oily river is meant to remind us of the river Styx. In Greek myth this was the river that the souls of the dead had to cross in order to reach the next world. Mr D.'s spirit seems to be trapped on this side of the river. He is unable to cross and pass-over to what awaits him in the next life.

LANGUAGE

There is alliteration in the fourth line with the repeated 's' sound: 'He sipped and swallowed with a scathing smile'.

Assonance is used in the last line with the repeated 'i' sounds: 'To note the oiled reflections chime and swim'.

Rhyme is introduced in the final six lines where 'scarf' rhymes with 'wharf', 'light' with 'plight' and 'slim' with 'swim'.

The poet uses a metaphor to describe the delight with which Mr D. told his tales, saying his tongue 'danced' cheerfully as he spoke.

The poem's last line presents a vivid image. We can almost visualise the reflections forming and breaking apart as the oily water laps up against the riverbank.

Dick King

LINE BY LINE

Though dead a good many years, Dick King still haunts the poet and his ghostly presence teaches him something important about death. When he thinks of the dead man the poet experiences feelings of love. Death, therefore, is seen as a positive force at play in the minds of those who are still living. The poet personifies death and imagines it moving through our minds 'igniting/ Love'.

It seems that the poet cannot forget Dick King. He refers to him as a 'plague', something that constantly bothers him. When he appears to the poet it is as an old man, for the poet only ever knew him as such: 'You haunt with the taint of age'. And yet it is a benevolent ghost that haunts the poet: 'Kind plague'.

Dick King seems to have been a good and decent man and the poet suggests that a certain form of decency vanished from the world when he died: 'vanished good'. And so although he is fondly remembered and his memory inspires feelings of love, Dick King also reminds the poet of what has been lost from the world: 'Fouling my thought with losses'.

The poet has a distinct memory of being aged nine and with Dick King on James's Street. He remembers the 'rain on the cobbles' and how the falling rain caused ripples in the 'iron trough' used to provide water for horses. He remembers the horses with their faces 'dipped' in the trough beneath the 'Fountain'. The poet recalls how he nestled against Dick King's coat, feeling 'sheltered' and secure against his 'buttons'. This seems to have been a time when Dick King was in good condition, before things got hard for him: 'And your own dread years were to come'.

Standing on James Street by the Fountain with the young boy nestled against him, Dick King spoke softly of certain individuals who had died: 'And your voice, in a pause of softness, named the dead'. Naming the dead seems to have caused Dick King to reflect on his own mortality. He stands lost in thought seeking to discover 'A gate to enter temperate ghosthood by'. It is almost as if he is drawn to the land of the dead and searching for a way to pass over into the afterlife.

The young boy regains Dick King's attention by squeezing his hand. The older man eventually emerges from his meditation on death and again feels the poet's small hand 'hidden' in his own.

II

Dick King was a principled man who seemed to have a strong sense of what was right and wrong: 'Dick King was an upright man'. The poem states that he has been dead for 15 years: 'Fifteen he lies with God'. The description of him treading the 'dull stations underfoot' for sixty years might be referring to the fact that he worked at the railway station all his life. However, the word 'stations' might also refer to the 14 Stations of the Cross, a form of devotion for Catholics. The Stations involve making a spiritual pilgrimage of prayer, through meditating upon the chief scenes of Christ's sufferings and death.

Dick King grew up in Galway: 'By the salt seaboard he grew up'. He later left this rocky and wet landscape to move to Dublin: 'left its rock and rain'. The poet describes Dick King bringing the 'dying language' of Irish to Dublin: 'To bring a dying language east/ And dwell in Basin Lane'. He went to work for the Great Southern Railways company. It seems that he worked in 'the iron sheds', perhaps involved in making the rails. This was a very noisy place to work: 'the clangour of the iron sheds'.

Dick King's move to Dublin, working for the Railway, led to the beginning of a new life: 'His second soul was born'. It seems to have been a profitable existence, at least enough for a man to perhaps buy a house and start a family: 'By the Southern Railway he increased'. However, he married a sickly or disabled woman: 'An invalid he took to wife'. She seems to have spent much of her time praying: 'She prayed her life away'. The poet describes her whispering her prayers in the 'whitewashed yard' of the house 'Until her dying day'.

The last two stanzas of the poem suggest that Dick

King's later years were rather bleak and unhappy. The bed in which he slept is described as 'wintry', suggesting coldness and loneliness. This 'wintry bed' he made 'season in, season out'. He followed the same routine each day, walking to the 'turnstile' of the station 'Morning and night till he was dead'.

It seems that Dick King died in South Dublin Union Hospital, now called St James's Hospital. In a ward in this hospital he could hear the bell of St James's Church. When he heard this bell he would clasp his hands in prayer: 'He clasped his hands in a Union ward/ To hear St James's bell'.

The poet seems to have visited Dick King just before he died. He says that he was 'The last to wish him well'. Perhaps Dick King's mind was not the best before he died. There is a suggestion in the second last line that the poet searched his eyes for recognition when he visited the old man: 'I searched his eyes though I was young'.

THEMES

Childhood
The poem also evokes the world of the child. The image of the young boy sheltering against the older man's coat suggests vulnerability and a need for protection and reassurance. This act of nestling in against the clothing of an older person is also present in 'Tear' where the poet recalls burying his face in his grandmother's black aprons.

Death & mortality
Though he has been dead for many years, Dick King is still present in the poet's life. The opening lines of the poem suggest that Dick King not only continues to live on in the poet's memory, but that his ghost or spirit actually haunts him. Kinsella suggests that the old man's spirit plagues or torments him, yet there is no malice in the ghost. He is described as 'Kind' and his presence inspires feelings of love.

The notion that we continue to have a ghostly existence after we die seems to be something that Dick King himself believed. The description of him naming 'the dead' in the third verse suggests that Dick King had a fascination with death and the afterlife. Kinsella describes him on this particular occasion being 'Bemused' or puzzled and suggests that the old man's meditation on the dead was a means of discovering a way to pass over into the afterlife and become a ghost: 'discovering/ A gate to enter temperate ghosthood by'. It is as if on this occasion Dick King is somehow preparing and readying himself for his own death.

Although 'Dick King' registers the poet's sadness at the fact that his neighbour no longer exists, by associating death with love the poem casts something of a positive light upon the experience. The dead man inspires the poet to see how remembrance of those who have passed away often generates fond memories. Kinsella personifies 'death' and imagines it moving through the minds of the living 'igniting/ Love'.

Old age
Negative effects of ageing
The poem suggests that Dick King's later years involved suffering. In the second verse we are told that when he stood with the young poet on James's Street his 'dread years' lay ahead of him: 'your own dread years were to come'. The word 'dread' can mean that Dick King greatly feared becoming old and sick, that this was a part of life he dreaded. The word dread might also mean that Dick King's later years were dreadful and full of suffering.

From the second part of the poem, where we are given some basic facts of Dick King's life, we get a sense that his later years were lonely and unhappy. His wife seems to have been a sickly woman and died before him. In the second last verse of the poem Kinsella describes Dick King making his 'wintry bed' through all the seasons of the year. The description of his bed as 'wintry' suggests great loneliness and coldness.

Memory
How memories haunt us
The poem illustrates how our childhood memories continue to haunt us when we are older. The poet only knew Dick King as a child, yet he has never forgotten him. It seems that Dick King is almost a presence in his daily life. In this regard the poem can be compared to 'Thinking of Mr D.' where the poet describes another man who has died yet continues to feature in the poet's life.

Vividness & detail

Kinsella recalls with great clarity a particular moment when he stood next to Dick King on James's Street. Although it is many years in the past he can still recall minor details from the scene. He speaks of the 'rain on the cobbles,/ Ripples in the iron trough, and the horses' dipped/ Faces'. As such the poem is a testament to the vividness of memory. In this regard we can compare the poem with 'Hen Woman' and 'Tear' where the poet also recalls scenes from his childhood in great detail.

The process of memory

When the young poet stood alongside Dick King that day on James's Street it is unlikely that he would have considered the moment significant and memorable. Yet the moment has remained with him and when he thinks of it now it is with a great sense of poignancy.

As such the poem illustrates how memory enables moments from our past to take on new meaning and significance in the future. To the older poet the memory of Dick King standing by the fountain on James's Street speaking softly of the dead appears poignant and significant now that his neighbour has died. Thinking about the moment sixteen years after Dick King has died, Kinsella gets the sense that his neighbour's naming of the dead was a means of 'discovering/ A gate to enter temperate ghosthood by'. Yet this is certainly not what the nine-year-old boy would have been thinking at the time.

In this regard the poem can be compared with both 'Hen Woman' and 'Tear'. In 'Hen Woman' the laying of the egg and the presence of the beetle become symbolic of something more profound, the act of artistic creation, in the mind of the older poet. In 'Tear' the young boy in the grandmother's room recalls a moment after his infant sister had died. Though his father shedding tears over his daughter's coffin struck the poet when a child as something strange and unpleasant, it is only as an older boy in the presence of his dying grandmother that he begins to understand the pain and misery that his father has had to endure.

The poem also describes the peculiar effect that death can have on the memories we hold. The opening lines of the poem describe 'death' roving 'our memories igniting/ Love'. When those who we care for die it is with great love that they are remembered. Memories that we have of particular moments take on a new significance when those who feature in them have passed away.

LANGUAGE

Like 'Thinking of Mr D.' this poem is an elegy for a man that the poet once knew. The poet recalls Dick King with great fondness and suggests that a form of decency or goodness was lost when he died.

The tone of the first part of the poem is particularly plaintive and the poet's recollection of the time he stood close to Dick King on James's Street is quite moving. Assonance and alliteration is used to good effect here. The lines are full of long, mellow vowels and soft consonants.

In the opening three lines the poet uses long 'o' sounds to create a haunting, melancholic effect: 'In your ghost Dick king, in your phantom vowels I read/ That death roves our memories igniting/ Love'. In the second verse he uses alliteration to create a soft and pleasant sound: 'I remember rain on the cobbles,/ Ripples in the iron trough'.

The second part of the poem is less personal and more matter-of-fact as the poet seeks to record the details of Dick King's life. The shorter lines and the ABAB rhyming scheme create a very different mood to the first part of the poem.

Thomas Kinsella

Chrysalides

LINE BY LINE

This poem is set during the poet's youth, probably when he was about thirteen or fourteen years old. Kinsella and his brother are staying with relatives in the countryside. The poet and his brother spend the summer cycling around the country. They visit various country towns in the locality, tracking the progress of their daytrips on a map.

There is a sense in which these are lazy and relaxed summer days. The two boys pedal 'slowly' and stop for picnics of chocolate and fruit. They 'moon about', meaning they mooch or wander listlessly through the countryside. Their journeys are 'vagaries', meandering trips without urgency or purpose.

At night they attend ceilís that take place in local barns where they watch farmers from the locality dance to accordion music. These countrymen 'twirl and leap' as they dance, their large boots crunching on the floor of the barn. The poet and his brother do not really participate in this barn dance. We get a sense that they merely watch form the wings as the country folk enjoy themselves.

The two boys go to bed late and sleep late in the morning: 'Sleeping too little or two much'. In fact they usually don't get up until noon. This causes them to be gently teased by the woman of the house in which they are staying. When they get up they head hungrily to her kitchen for breakfast: 'we awoke at noon/ And were received with womanly mockery into the kitchen'.

The two boys are tolerated by the world around them in a way they will never be again: 'Daily we strapped our saddlebags and went to experience/ a tolerance we shall never know again'. They are indulged or almost 'mollycoddled' by the people around them.

There is a sense in which society sill treats them as children. This, however, is the last summer in which they will experience such treatment. The two boys experience a change within themselves. They feel something new 'wake' and begin to come alive. This inner change has a peculiar effect on them, making them slow, lazy and listless: 'a strange wakefulness sapped our energies … our slow-beating hearts'.

This change makes them numb and 'insensitive'. It 'blurs' their instincts and 'dulls' their hearts, making them incapable of feeling strong emotion: 'It dulled our slow-beating hearts/ To the extremes of feeling'. The two boys seem wrapped up in this inner change and fail to really notice what is going on around them.

They fail to appreciate that the precious days of this youthful summer are slipping away. These days are special and unique and will never come again: 'insensitive alike to the unique succession of our youthful midnights'.

They also fail to be moved by the sight of a swarm of ants on its wedding flight. A wedding flight occurs when the young queen ants fly away from their colony pursued by a swarm of winged males. The males attempt to mate with the young queens as the swarm flies through the air. The thousands of male ants die during or shortly after the wedding flight. The pregnant young queens then move off to start new colonies.

This is what the boys encounter on the road before them. The swarm shimmers and glistens in front of them. They watch hundreds or even thousands of winged males drop from the air and die an agonised death on the roadside. The two boys, however, are in too numb and insensitive a state to appreciate the

LANGUAGE

There are several fine examples of assonance in this poem. The repeated broad-vowel sounds in the phrase 'unique succession of our youthful midnights' creates a pleasant verbal music. A similar effect is created by the phrase 'sapped our energies and dulled out slow-beating hearts' where the broad-vowel sounds slow the verse in a manner appropriate to the lazy state of mind the line describes. The phrase 'strapped our saddlebags' features both assonance with the repeated '*a*' sound and alliteration with the repeated '*s*' sound.

Onomatopoeia features in the description of the barn dance. In the phrase 'crunching boots of countrymen' we can almost hear the boots crunching as the men dance around the bar. Similarly, the phrase 'lurch of melodeon music' has about it something of the rhythm of an Irish jig, the type of music that might be played at such an occasion.

The poem features several interesting similes. The dancing countrymen are described as being 'weightless a shadows', capturing the energy and lightness with which they dance around the barn. The two boys are described as being like hungry calves poking their faces into the kitchen each morning as they go in search of breakfast.

Particularly powerful is the poem's concluding description of the ants wedding flight. The swarm of winged ants hovers in the air before the two boys. Kinsella uses a fine metaphor to describe this sight, saying that the swarm hovered like a hazy vapour or 'perspiration' in front of them. He also uses a simile, comparing the ants to 'drops of copper' that glisten in the air.

Kinsella uses a paradoxical phrase to describe the ants' mating process. The swarm contains thousands of winged males attempting to mate with at most a few young queens. The swarm is 'spawning' or breeding as some of the males impregnate the queen. Yet it is also dying as male ants fall from the air and perish on the roadside. The swarm, therefore, is 'spawning to its death'. Its wedding flight combines dying and the creation of new life in a single process.

THEMES

Childhood & youth

Before a caterpillar becomes a butterfly it first turns into a 'chrysalides', or 'pupa'. To be chrysalides, then, is to be in a transitional stage of development. It is to be in the process of transformation from one thing into another.

The poet and his brother are about fourteen years old. They are in the process of changing from children into fully fledged adolescents. Throughout this particular summer they are neither children nor proper teenagers. Instead they are in a peculiar in-between state. On one hand the two boys are allowed to act with the independence of teenagers. They are free to explore the countryside on their own, cycling to different towns. They are permitted to stay up late and attend a grown-up event like the barn dance

Yet there is also a sense in which the poet and his brother are still indulged, mollycoddled and treated like children. They are given chocolate and fruit for their picnics. Scones and jugs of milk are left out for them in their bedroom each night. They are allowed to behave in a manner that could be regarded as rude or inappropriate in an older person. They moon about their relatives' house at 'odd hours'. They only get up at noon but still 'poke' their faces into the kitchen expecting breakfast. Yet their behaviour is tolerated. The woman of the house 'receives' them into the kitchen and are feeds them. As Kinsella puts it they experience a 'tolerance' we only afford to children.

Yet this in-between state cannot last. Just as a pupa must eventually turn into a butterfly so the boys must eventually become fully fledged adolescents. This is their last 'free summer', the last time will completely free of the burdens and expectations of young adulthood. They shall never again experience the 'tolerance' we usually only afford to children. This is the last time they will be allowed to think that certain behaviours are 'licit' or appropriate just because they are 'familiar', just because they are used to getting way with them.

This is also a poem of sexual change and awakening. They are at the stage in life where the hormonal changes associated with adolescence really start to kick in. They feel this 'strange wakefulness' within themselves. As we noted above this change makes them slow, lazy and listless: 'a strange wakefulness sapped our energies … our slow-beating hearts'. This listlessness and lack of energy is evident in their daytrips through the countryside. The two boys pedal 'slowly' and stop for picnics of chocolate and fruit. They 'moon about', meaning they mooch or wander listlessly through the countryside. Their journeys are 'vagaries', meandering trips without urgency or purpose.

This theme of sexual awakening is reinforced by several images throughout the poem. Firstly, we have the personification of the moon as a virgin, as person at the beginning of her sexual life. ('This personification of the moon as a young and female virgin is something that recurs throughout literature). Secondly, we have the description of the swarm of ants, who are also at the beginning of their brief sexual lives. (The wedding flight will be their only sexual experience: the males will all die and the queen will not mate again).

This sexual awakening makes the boys numb and 'insensitive'. Their instincts are 'blurred' and their hearts are 'dulled'. They seem too wrapped up in themselves, in their own altering bodies and minds, to really be aware of what's going on around them. They fail to notice how these precious summer days are slipping away, missing the 'unique succession of our youthful midnights'. They are unmoved by the horrible sight of the ants dying by the roadside. (Though the memory of this event causes them 'lasting horror' when they think back on it in later years).

To recap, then, in 'Chrysalides', the two boys are on the verge of moving from an 'in between state' to what we might call young adulthood. There are two consequences of this transition. Firstly this is the last time they will be indulged or 'tolerated' by those around them. Secondly they experience a sexual awakening. The poem recalls 'Model School, Inchicore', 'Tear' and 'Mirror in February'. 'Model School, Inchicore' deals with the loss of the earliest childhood innocence. Both 'Tear' deals with the painful transition from childhood to youth. 'Mirror in February', meanwhile, deals with the equally distressing transition from late youth to early middle age.

In this poem Kinsella wonderfully captures a lazy and listless dolescent mentality, depicting how the two boys meander through the countryside, keep odd hours and stay in bed till noon. This relates it to 'Tear', 'Dick King', 'Model School. Inchicore', 'His Father's Hands' and 'Hen Woman', all of which to varying extents capture a childhood mentality.

Horror & desolation

Depictions of horror are common in Kinsella's poetry. We see such a response in 'Model School, Inchicore', for instance, when the speaker chokes at the taste of his pen's nib, and in 'Tear' when the young poet must kiss his dying grandmother. In 'His Father's Hands' the poet is filled with what we can only describe as horror when he contemplates this environment: 'I do not like this place … It feels evil'.

'Chrysalides', meanwhile, deals with the speaker's belatedly horrified reaction to the sight of the dying ants dying. Kinsella wonderfully captures the disturbing nature of this sight, describing how the winged male ants drop out of the air and die an 'agonised' death on the roadside. At the time the two boys were too numb too realise the horror of this sight. It was only some time afterwards when they felt the psychological impact of what they'd seen.

Memory

Like many of Kinsella's poems this describes how the memory of an event haunts the poet long after he has witnessed it. In this instance he describes how the ants' wedding flight stayed in his mind for years afterwards as a source of 'lasting horror'. 'Hen Woman', 'Dick King', 'Model School, Inchicore' and 'Tear' also deal with childhood memories that haunt the poet's consciousness and that he returns to again and again.

Several of Kinsella's poems deal with memories of events that seemed unmemorable to the poet at the time of their occurrence but that nevertheless went on haunt his memory for many years afterwards. In 'Chrysalides' the young poet and his brother are too numbed and 'dulled' by the changes taking place inside themselves to appreciate the horror of the sight of the dying ants. The event seems unmemorable to them at the time. It is only later that this event resurfaces in their memories to recur there with 'lasting horror' for many years. In this regard the poem recalls 'Model School, Inchicore', 'Dick King' and arguably 'Hen Woman', each of which deals with a trivial or seemingly unmemorable event that nevertheless lives on long afterwards in the poet's memory.

Typically In 'Chrysalides' the poet remembers the dying ants in vivid detail, recalling how they glistened like 'drops of copper' in the air before him before dying an agonising death on the roadside. Another recurring feature of Kinsella's poetry is this vividness and detail with which events are recalled. When he remembers hugging Dick King, for instance, he remembers not only the smell of the old man's clothes but also how the cobblestones were damp with rain and how water was rippling in the 'iron trough'. When he remembers his class being taken outside for lessons he remembers a bee buzzing and the light 'greeny gold' pouring through a tree.

Mirror in February

Thomas Kinsella

LINE BY LINE

Setting the scene

It is really early in the morning. The poet is shaving in his bedroom, using a shaving mirror. He is still only 'half-dressed'. The lamp in the bedroom is 'fading'. Its glow is becoming less pronounced or noticeable as the morning light outside gets stronger.

The poet describes the various smells in the bedroom. The air in the bedroom is musty, dry and stale, presumably because the windows have been closed during the night. The poet can also smell the rain, trees and soil outside his window.

The poet is daydreaming as he shaves. His brain, is 'idling', meaning it is functioning in a lazy or unproductive manner. His mind, he says, is filled with a 'fantasy'. This fantasy is 'compulsive'. It is something his mind returns to again and again. However, we are not told what the poet is fantasising about.

The poet realises he is no longer young

The poet is drying his face when he is suddenly struck by his reflection in the shaving mirror: 'I towel my shaven jaw and stop and stare'. He is stunned or 'riveted' by the sight of his own reflection. He suddenly realises how old-looking he has become: 'Riveted by a dark exhausted eye,/ A dry downturning mouth'. It is in this split second that the poet realises he is no longer young.

This realisation snaps the poet out of his fantasy or daydream. His mind returns to dealing with the real world: 'for the time being I return'. He feels that there is a lesson he must learn: 'It seems again that it is time to learn'.

The poet looks inside himself

The poet meditates, looking deep inside himself. As he memorably puts it, he looks into the 'mirror of his soul'. He sees that he is no longer young: 'I read that I have looked my last on youth'. He also sees that he is hollow and unfulfilled. His soul is empty, containing 'little more' than the realisation that his youth is past.

The poet contrasts himself with Christ

The poet contrasts himself with Christ. Christ was thirty-three years old when he was crucified. At that age Christ was 'made whole'. His purpose in life was fulfilled by dying for humanity's sins. The poet is also thirty-three years old. Yet he has not been 'made whole'. He has not yet fulfilled his purpose in life.

The poet contrasts himself with the trees

The poet also contrasts himself with the trees outside his window. The trees have been deformed or 'defaced'. Their branches have been pruned or 'hacked' away. This is so they will grow back even stronger in the summertime. The trees will have a better appearance or 'bearing' because they have been 'defaced' in this way. The hacking the trees must endure is brutal but necessary: 'suffering their brute necessities'.

Just as the trees have been mutilated by axes, so the poet's body has been mutilated by the passage of time. For each 'span' or period of time that passes he is mutilated more than the trees are: 'that span for span is mutilated more'. The passage of time has damaged his body. It has worn him out, leaving him with a 'dark exhausted eye'. It is unsurprising, therefore, that he 'quails' or loses heart.

Conclusion

The poem ends with a note of acceptance. The poet accepts that he is no longer young. He accepts that unlike the trees he is not renewable; he will not be born again each summer. He accepts that as a human being he will always be subject to the ravages of time. He is 'Not young and not renewable, but man'.

To the poet these harsh facts are unpleasant. He regards them with 'distaste'. Yet all the poet can do is carry himself with 'grace'. The only response available to him is to face the ravages of time with all the courage and dignity he can muster.

LANGUAGE

The first two stanzas have ABACBCD rhyme scheme. The final stanza has an ABACBCC rhyme scheme, the rhyme between 'span', 'can' and 'man' providing a satisfactory sense of closure. The poet makes use of several half rhymes, such as 'fantasy' with 'eye' and 'growth' with 'youth'.

Kinsella is a skilful writer and throughout the poem he uses assonance to create a pleasant musical effect. We see this in line 3 with the repeated 'a' sound in 'fading lamp', in line 5 with the repeated 'a' sound in 'shaven jaw', and in line 20 with the repeated 'o' sound in 'folded towel'.

Kinsella also makes interesting use of cacophony in this poem. Lines 6 and 7, for instance, create a harsh verbal music, suitable to the description of the poet's withered and ageing face. A similar cacophonous effect is evident in lines 16 and 17, where the repeated 'b', 'd' and 't' create a harsh verbal music appropriate to the description of the defaced trees.

In line 11 Kinsella uses an interesting metaphor to describe the act of introspection or examining one's own mind. To engage in such an act, he says, is to look into the mirror of our souls. The poem's title, then, has two meanings. Mirrors reflect and in this instance reflection refers not only to the physical reflection in the shaving mirror, but also to reflection in the sense of introspection, meditation and self-examination.

There is an interesting use of paradox in line 10, where Kinsella describes the world as a 'crumbling place of growth'. How can the world be both a place of growth and a place of crumbling and decay? This is because all around us we see plants, animals and people that are born and grow. Yet we also see things that are 'crumbling', that are dying and decaying. We see life continuing in an 'untiring' cycle of birth and death.

There is a sense in which personification occurs in the poem's final lines. The trees are depicted almost as human beings. They 'stand', 'awaken', 'suffer' and are 'defaced' just as human beings are.

THEMES

Old age

This poem movingly deals with the ageing process, describing how the passage of time damages or 'mutilates' our bodies. The older we get the more our bodies waste and decay. With every span or period of time that passes we are 'mutilated more'. The mutilating effects of the ageing process leave the poet with a 'dark exhausted eye' and a 'dry downturning mouth'.

The poem highlights an important difference between human beings and the plant life that surrounds us. Trees and plants are 'renewed' each spring and summer when they bloom again. Human beings, in contrast, are not 'renewable'. Once our youthful beauty passes it is gone forever.

It is understandable, 'Mirror in February' suggests, that we might flinch or 'quail' in the face of these unpleasant facts of human existence, or that we should regard the horrible reality of human ageing with 'distaste'. There is a tone of sadness and resignation about the poem's last lines: all we can do is accept that we are 'man' and that growing old is part of the human condition. (The phrase 'fold my towel' perhaps suggests the phrase 'throw in the towel, meaning to surrender). But there is also an air of defiance here, a determination to face the mutilations of the ageing process with as much grace, courage and dignity as possible.

The negative effects of ageing are a recurring theme in Kinsella's poetry, also featuring in 'Dick King', 'Thinking of Mr D.', 'Tear' and 'His Father's Hands'. In each of these poems Kinsella touches on the damage old age has done to an elderly person.

Horror & desolation

The poet responds with shock and horror to his own reflection in the shaving mirror. He suddenly realises he is no longer young and is 'riveted' by the sight of his own care-worn face.

Such horrified reactions are common in Kinsella's poetry. We see such a response in 'Model School, Inchicore', for instance, when the speaker chokes at the taste of his pen's nib, and in 'Tear' when the young poet must kiss his dying grandmother. 'Chrysalides', meanwhile, deals with the speaker's belatedly horrified reaction to the sight of dying ants. In 'His Father's Hands' the poet is filled with horror when he imagines the environment of prehistoric Ireland: 'I do not like this place … It feels evil'.

Like many of Kinsella's poems 'Mirror in February' takes place in a bleak and desolate landscape. It features a harsh wintry scene of rain and dark leafless trees that have been brutally 'hacked clean'. Similarly desolate landscapes are depicted in 'The Familar', and in 'His Father's Hands', both of which present barren, wintry scenes. A more urban desolation is present in 'Thinking of Mr D.', with its canal-bank scene and in 'Model School, Inchicore' with its lonely depiction of the empty school shed.

Death & mortality

In this poem the poet's awareness of his own mortality is reinforced by the sight of his own ageing reflection in the shaving mirror. He realises that he is no longer young but also that unlike the trees he is 'not renewable'. He will eventually grow old and die. This reinforced awareness of mortality links 'Mirror in February' to 'Tear' and 'Chrysalides' and 'Model School, Inchicore', each of which deals with the young poet's gradually dawning awareness of death.

Childhood & youth

This poem depicts how the effects of ageing can creep up on us. The poet catches a glimpse of his reflection in the shaving mirror and is suddenly shocked and mesmerised by how old-looking he has become. In a split second he realises that his youth is over: 'I read that I have looked my last on youth'. In this regard 'Mirror in February' recalls 'Model School, Inchicore', 'Tear' and 'Chrysalides'. 'Model School, Inchicore' deals with the loss of the earliest childhood innocence. Both 'Tear' and 'Chrysalides' deal with the painful transition from childhood to youth. 'Mirror in February', meanwhile, deals with the equally distressing transition from late youth to early middle age.

Art

This poem also touches on the notion of artistic fulfilment. The poet is thirty three, the age at which Christ fulfilled his purpose in life by being crucified. The poet is now thirty-three but has yet to fulfil his purpose in life. He therefore feels hollow, empty and fulfilled. There is little in his soul apart from the realisation that he is no longer young.

It is probable that the poet feels he must find fulfilment by writing great poetry, by making the most of the poetic talent he has been given. It is also probable that this is the 'compulsive fantasy' he daydreams about in the opening stanza. The poet's mind returns again and again to the fantasy of fulfilling his potential and becoming a great literary artist. We get a sense that it is only with difficulty that the poet can turn away from this fantasy and return 'for the time being' to the real world.

Struggle for comprehension

Like many of Kinsella's poems 'Mirror in February' deal with a figure struggling to make sense of the world or to come to terms with some aspect of the human condition. In this instance the poet attempts to 'learn', to look into the mirror of his soul and understand himself. The poem shows him attempting to come to terms with the reality of ageing and bodily decay, but also with his own emptiness and lack of artistic fulfilment.

Thomas Kinsella
Tear

LINE BY LINE

STANZAS 1–4
The young poet's grandmother is lying on her deathbed. He is instructed to visit her room and say 'goodbye to her'. His reluctance to do so is evident in the fact that he 'was *sent in* to see her'. The experience of having to enter this darkened room and say goodbye to a dying woman is something that he is not prepared for. When he goes into the grandmother's room he is entering the unknown and he finds it almost overwhelming: 'I was carried off/ to unfathomable depths'.

The entrance to the room is filled with 'hangings', lines of beads that stand in place of a door. The speaker pushes through them and as he does so they make a rattling noise, which sounds like voices chattering: 'A fringe of jet drops/ chattered at my ear'. The light in the room is poor and as the poet passes through the beads he feels the darkness surround him in an unpleasant manner: 'I was swallowed in chambery dusk'. The 'last watery light' of the day comes in through the window. The room smells horribly 'of disused/ organs and sour kidney'.

STANZAS 5–8
The grandmother is lying on the bed. She is 'propped high' with pillows. The covers are 'gathered close/ up to her mouth'. The poet observes that 'the lines of ill-temper still' remain around her mouth. The grandmother does not appear to notice her grandson in the room. She is 'distracted' and stares 'at the ceiling'. She is suffering from some form of intermittent attacks, which drain her energy and make breathing difficult.

The grandmother's 'grey hair' is not tied up and it lies 'loosened out like a young woman's/ all over the pillow'. Shadows are being cast across her face and along the pillow by the light from the window. The shadows, along with strands of loose hair, 'criss-crossing her forehead' form the appearance of a web 'tying down her head' to the pillow.

The strands of the web seem to be 'tangling down toward' the shadows on the floor. The poet imagines that these shadows are advancing toward him, devouring the floor as they approach: 'eating away the floor at my feet'.

STANZAS 9–14
When the speaker enters the room he is initially frozen with fear: 'I couldn't stir at first'. The room is eerie and frightening. The sight of his grandmother and the prospect of approaching her and touching her fills him with dread. He fears that if he attracts her attention she will coax him with 'some fierce wheedling whisper' to come and lie closely beside her: 'to hide myself one last time/ against her'. Perhaps this was something that the speaker used to do when he was much younger. However, he now finds the idea of snuggling up to the old woman revolting. He compares her withered and decaying body to 'drying mud'.

The speaker is confused about what he should do now that he is in the room: 'Was I to kiss her?' The thought of kissing the old woman disgusts him. He says that he would 'As soon/ kiss the damp that crept/ in the flowered walls/ of this pit'. But he feels that he ought to kiss her, that this is what is expected of him: 'Yet I had to kiss'.

He moves close to the bed and kneels down. The grandmother's 'black aprons' lie 'folded at the foot of the bed'. The speaker recalls how when he was younger he would 'bury' his face in these aprons. He rests his face upon the folded aprons and pushes down into the cold material: 'sank my face in the chill/ and smell of her black aprons'. The aprons smell of tobacco and acrid perfume: 'Snuff and musk'.

The smell and the feel of the aprons have the effect of transporting the speaker 'into a derelict place'. He imagines he is in some darkened place where the 'walls and roofs' are not visible. The place smells of 'ash' and he feels as though he is working through 'dead ashes' searching for 'any trace/ of warmth'. The speaker seems to be moving through the dark inner space of his mind. He does not know what he is searching for. Suddenly 'far off/ in the vaults' of his memories a sound is heard. It is the sound of a drop splashing.

STANZAS 14–18

The sound of the drop splashing provides the speaker with what he 'was looking for'. Burying his head in the aprons, he was not searching for 'heat nor fire,/ not any comfort'. Rather it seems that he was searching for a way of relating to the experience of his dying grandmother, of putting it in context with the rest of his life.

Suddenly he hears her voice, hears her as she spoke to someone shortly after her grandchild, the speaker's sister, died. The grandmother is describing how the poet's father wept uncontrollably for his daughter: 'God help him, he cried/ big tears over there by the machine/ for the poor thing'.

Kneeling beside his grandmother's bed with his face sunk in her aprons, the speaker has suddenly struck upon a memory that helps him to deal with the difficult situation he now faces. He recalls how he responded to the death of his 'infant sister'. His grief then was intense but short-lived. He was only a child and he wailed for a time but this 'child-animal grief/ was soon done'.

The death of his infant sister then offered the young child a momentary glimpse of the pain and hardship of life. But this 'early guess// at the sad dullness and tedious pain/ and lives bitter with hard bondage' was, as he says, only guessed at and not properly comprehended or understood. He was simply too young back then to really grasp the suffering that life can bring. However, now as he lies by his grandmother's deathbed witnessing her slow and painful dying, he gets a deeper sense of life's hardships and struggles: 'How I tasted it now –/ her heart beating in my mouth!'

STANZAS 19–22

The sound of the grandmother's difficult breathing, her tired shudder and her pushing at the bedclothes draws the speaker back to the room in which he kneels. He snaps out of his reverie and meditation upon grief and pain. He leaves the room 'promising' that he will get around to 'really' kissing his grandmother when she is 'really dead'.

The speaker's grandfather is seated at the fireplace in the room adjoining the grandmother's bedroom. He half looks up as the speaker emerges, gives a shrug and turns back 'with a deaf stare to the heat' of the fire. The speaker stands awkwardly in the room 'beside him for a minute' before going 'out to the shop' at the front of the house. It is still bright in the shop and he feels 'better able to breathe' there.

Stanzas 23–4

Witnessing his grandmother's dying and his grandfather's attitude when he emerged from the room, suggests to the speaker that 'Old age can digest/ anything'. The demise of the body, the 'struggle' that lies ahead of us all our lives, this 'commotion' is somehow silently accepted and endured by his grandparents. The experience reveals to the speaker just how 'long and hard' life can be. That is 'unless like' his infant sister, 'little Agnes/ you vanish with early tears'.

LANGUAGE

Light & darkness

The poem is full of images of light and darkness:

- The room is which the grandmother lies dying is described as being 'in chambery dusk'. Only weak 'watery light' comes in through the window.
- The speaker looks to escape from this murky 'pit' by shutting his eyes and burying his face in the 'black aprons'. Only in this total darkness can he begin to see some light and begin to think in a clearer way about what he is experiencing.
- With his face buried in the aprons he recalls the 'Bright// drops' of his father's tears upon the coffin of his infant sister.
- The 'watery light' of his grandmother's room is almost suffocating and it is only when he enters the 'still bright' shop that the poet is 'better able to breathe'.

Appeals to the senses

The poem contains many references to smells, sights, sounds, tastes and touch:

- The 'jet drops' on the hangings seem to chatter in the poet's ear as he enters the grandmother's room: 'A fringe of jet drops/ chattered at my ear'.
- He is immediately hit with 'the smell of disused/ organs and sour kidney' when he enters.
- The poet seeks to escape the horror of the room by sinking his face into the 'smell of her black aprons'. From the aprons he gets the scent of 'Snuff and musk'

- and he is transported to a place 'smelling of ash'.
- In this dark and strange place he remembers the time that followed the death of his infant sister and this enables him to 'taste' the bitterness and hardship of life: 'How I tasted it now'.

THEMES

Childhood & youth

The poem recounts the experience of a young boy, possibly in his early teens. He is not a child, but neither is he yet an adult. The poem describes the uncertainties and feelings of awkwardness that accompany this period in life.

The young boy must deal with a very difficult experience, but he is not at all sure how he should act. He is reluctant to go in and see his ailing grandmother and very unsure about what he should do when he enters the room. He feels that the appropriate thing to do is kiss her, but he finds the dying woman repulsive and cannot bring himself to do it. When he eventually emerges from his grandmother's room he is again at a loss as to what he should say or do. He stands fidgeting 'for a minute' beside his grandfather before heading 'out to the shop'.

End of innocence

The poem describes an encounter between a young boy and a very old woman. Although he finds the whole experience deeply uncomfortable and he is very unsure about how he should behave, having to face his dying grandmother forces the young poet to come to terms with some unpleasant truths about life. As such the poem recounts a tale of lost innocence. The young boy's encounter with his grandmother leads to an understanding of the world. In the grandmother's room he is exposed to certain truths about suffering and death, the exposure of which means that he can no longer exist in a state of childhood innocence. In this regard it is similar to both 'Model School' and 'Chrysalides'.

Having to encounter his dying grandmother forces the young poet to enter a dark and derelict place in his mind, a place that smells of ashes. This is a terrible place and seems to be representative of an awareness of death. Being in the same room as his dying grandmother also results in the unearthing of memories from his childhood, from a time shortly after his infant sister died.

The young boy suddenly remembers the tears his father shed over the young girl's coffin. However, the poet was too young then to fully fathom grief and tragedy and it is only now that a proper sense of his family's pain and the hardships they have had to endure become clearly apparent to him. His eyes are suddenly opened to the 'sad dullness and tedious pain' of life and he sees that his father and his grandparents have endured 'lives bitter with hard bondage'. This understanding, coupled with his newfound awareness of his mortality, is profoundly disturbing and shocking. He emerges from the grandmother's room.

The world of the child

The poem also offers us glimpses of the poet as a much younger child. He mentions how he used to bury his face in his grandmother's black aprons. This act of nestling in close against the clothing of an older person reminds us of the description of the nine-year-old boy seeking shelter against the buttons of his neighbour in 'Dick King'. Both poems tell of a child's need for comfort and protection. However, whereas in 'Dick King' it seems that the young child drew great comfort from being close to his neighbour, in 'Tear' we get little sense that the child was ever particularly fond of his grandmother.

'Tear' also gives us an account of how the child responded to the death of his infant sister. The poem suggests that the grief of the young child is akin to 'animal grief', meaning that it is instinctual, short-lived and hardly comprehended. The young child in the poem wailed momentarily with an instinctual sense of loss and sadness and with this his grieving was done.

Old age

The poem provides a vivid description of the suffering that some in their later years must endure. The poet's grandmother is close to death. She lies alone in a room, suffering from some form of attacks that drain her energy and make her breathing difficult. The poet's description of both the condition of the grandmother and the atmosphere in the room are shocking and unpleasant. He describes the almost unbearable 'smell of disused/ organs and sour kidney' as he enters the room. He cannot hide his own disgust at what he witnesses. He compares her decaying flesh to 'drying mud' and says that he would prefer to 'kiss the damp' upon the walls of the room than kiss his grandmother.

Acceptance of growing old
The poem also suggests that with ageing comes an ability to endure and handle whatever life brings. 'Old age', Kinsella writes, 'can digest/ anything'. Witnessing his grandmother's terrible and painful struggle upon her deathbed and his grandfather's silent presence outside the room suggests to the poet that these people are somehow better equipped to handle and accept the terrible realities of illness and dying. Visiting his grandmother brings home to the young boy the terrible 'commotion' that sometimes accompanies the end of a life, 'the struggle' that faces us when we grow old. Whereas such insights are overwhelming for the boy, they have been stoically accepted by his grandparents.

Death
The poem offers us different responses to dying and death. There is the response of the young child to the death of his infant sister. This response is instinctual and the poet compares it to the wail of an animal. Such a reaction to death is uncomprehending. The child is unable to fully grasp the reality of death and its response is therefore immediate and short-lived.

The young boy who enters the grandmother's room is somewhat older and is better able to understand the world. Yet the experience of being in the room of a dying woman is perhaps wholly new and the young boy finds it almost overwhelming. He is unsure about how he should act in the presence of his grandmother and struggles for a way to understand and respond to the difficult experience. Lying beside her bed with his face buried in her aprons, he begins to get a proper sense of the life's hardships and the pain that death brings. He begins to think about the way both his father and his grandparents have had to cope with life's difficulties and he senses the struggles that lie ahead. As such his experience of death marks a step on the boy's path to maturity and signals the end of childhood innocence.

The description of the father's reaction to the death of his infant daughter is one of immense grief. He is described shedding 'big tears' over the little girl's coffin. In contrast, both grandparents seem unemotional, hardened by a lifetime of pain and sadness. Both appear worn out with life, no longer capable of or needing to wail or shed 'big tears'. The grandmother silently endures her struggle with death while the grandfather sits silently before the fire, barely turning to acknowledge the speaker as he emerges from the dying woman's room. At the end of their long lives an acceptance of death seems to have occurred.

Family
'Tear' presents us with various generations of the poet's family and suggests that they endured lives of hardship and struggle: 'lives bitter with hard bondage'. When the poet's infant sister died he momentarily became aware of the 'sad dullness and tedious pain' of his father's and grandparent's lives. However, it is only when he is somewhat older and visits his dying grandmother that he begins to properly understand the unhappy lives that these people lived: 'How I tasted it now'.

The fact that his father and his grandparents led such hard lives seems to have resulted in them becoming bitter and cold individuals. There is little or no evidence of love or affection in the poem, nor is their any sense of family solidarity. Everybody mentioned in the poem seems to be alone and isolated. The grandmother lies alone upon her deathbed, struggling in solitary silence. The grandfather sits alone by the fire, barely turning to register the youth as he emerges from the grandmother's room. Even the description of the father crying over the coffin of his dead daughter suggests isolation. The grandmother describes how 'he cried/ big tears *over there* by the machine', suggesting that the father is apart from everyone in his grief.

Horror & desolation
'Tear' describes with great honesty the horror that the young poet felt when he had to visit the room of his dying grandmother. The atmosphere both inside and outside the room is creepy and unsettling:

- The dark beads that hang down in the doorway seem to come alive and chatter in the young boy's ear as he enters the room.
- The young boy feels that the darkness is devouring him: 'I was swallowed in chambery dusk'.
- He is immediately struck with the strong, unpleasant odours or decay: 'My heart shrank/ at the smell of disused/ organs and kidney'.
- The shadows that criss-cross the grandmother's face resemble a spider's web lashing her to the pillow.

This 'web of strands' appears to be alive and 'tangling down toward the shadow/ eating away the floor' at the boy's feet.

The young boy also experiences horror at the thought of touching or kissing his grandmother. He imagines her turning toward him and whispering for him to come 'bury' himself 'in her drying mud'. The grandmother is portrayed as some malevolent temptress seeking to manipulate the young boy: 'she might turn and tempt me/ (my own father's mother)'. The thought of kissing her is particularly odious to him. He says that he would sooner kiss the damp on the walls.

When the young boy sinks his face into the grandmother's aprons and closes his eyes, he enters another dark and desolate place, what we might term the 'vaults' of his mind. Kinsella describes the boys search through the vaults of memory in terms of a 'derelict' building that smells 'of ash'. The young boy feels his way through the pitch black, listening to the 'rustle' of 'unseen walls and roofs' and 'disturbing/ dead ashes' as he goes.

Struggle for comprehension
In 'Tear' the young poet is forced to deal with a very difficult experience. His grandmother is dying and he must enter her room alone. Having to do so brings the young boy into close contact with the terrible reality of old age, illness and death. The experience is overwhelming and he struggles to comprehend what he encounters: 'I was carried off/ to unfathomable depths'. Unlike his grandparents, who in their old age 'can digest/ anything', the young poet is ill-equipped to cope with and respond to the experience.

Only by shutting his eyes can the young boy begin to get a handle on the situation. The grandmother's struggle upon her deathbed suddenly ceases to be an isolated moment of suffering that the young boy cannot rationalise or contextualise. Recollecting the moment when his father stood in tears over the coffin of his infant daughter, the young poet begins to comprehend the difficult lives that his grandparent's and his father have lived. For the first time in his life his eyes are properly opened to the 'sad dullness and tedious pain' of their lives and he begins to see how their lives of labour and struggle have made them 'bitter': 'lives bitter with hard bondage'. Only now does he 'taste' the pain of their lives.

As such 'Tear' describes a moment of transition in the young boy's life. He is moving from the childish world of innocence into the more adult world of awareness and understanding. He must now acknowledge and start to comprehend that life can be 'long and hard' and that 'struggle' lies 'in store for you all your life'. The poem is similar to 'Chrysalides' in this regard. Both poems describe a transition from childhood to adulthood.

Memory
Like a number of Kinsella's poems, 'Tear' is very much concerned with memory and how memory works. The poem is a vivid recollection of a very traumatic moment from the poet's childhood. He recalls in clear detail visiting his grandmother as she lay upon her deathbed. The sights, sounds and smells of the room are all described with great clarity.

As such, the poem testifies to the power of memory, to the remarkable way in which details from our experiences remain with us long after we have encountered them. In this regard the poem is similar to both 'Hen Woman' and 'Dick King'. In both these poems the poet recollects tiny details from moments in the distant past. In 'Dick King', Kinsella recalls the 'rain on the cobbles' and the 'Ripples' in the water of the 'iron trough'. In 'Hen Woman' he recalls the movements of a beetle transporting a ball of dung.

'Tear' also illustrates how memories from our past can be forgotten and suddenly found. The poet uses the metaphor of a dark vault to describe the place where memories are held. The poet's memory of his infant sister's death had lain dormant within the 'vaults' of his mind for a number of years before being discovered at the moment when he sunk his face in his grandmother's aprons and closed his eyes. The memory of his father shedding tears over the infant's coffin is retrieved from the vaults and the moment is examined and suddenly understood in a way that it was impossible for the child to understand when it happened.

Hen Woman

Thomas Kinsella

LINE BY LINE

A hen lays an egg

This poem is based around one of Kinsella's childhood memories. The young poet is the yard of a whitewashed cottage. The weather is hot and humid, the kind of weather that suggests a thunder storm is on the way: 'The noon heat in the yard/ smelled of stillness and coming thunder'. The landscape is filled with stillness and silence. Yet this is a 'brooding' or menacing calm, the calm before the storm.

The young poet watches a hen scratch around near a 'shore' or drain. Suddenly the hen begins to lay an egg: 'It stopped, its body crouched and puffed out'. This brings the woman of the house running from the cottage 'in her slippers'. She is worried that the egg will fall down the drain. The possibility of losing the egg in this way seems to anger her: 'Her face dark with anger'. She picks up the hen and 'fumbles' in an attempt to catch the egg.

The young poet takes in this scene. Both the woman and the hen have their mouths open. The half-laid egg is visible in the hen's sphincter. The hen seems to be looking directly at the young poet. He wonders what the hen's eyes perceive when they look at the world around it, imagining it must see its environment as some kind of 'mad blur'.

To the young poet it seems that time has stopped: 'time stood still … Nothing moved'. Both the woman (who is 'fumbling' to catch the egg) and the hen (that is being 'fumbled' by the woman's hands) seem to be completely motionless. The young poet too seems to be motionless. Like the woman and the hen he is 'locked there' with his mouth open: 'locked there/ (as I must have been) gaping'.

The dung beetle

The only thing moving is a beetle at the poet's feet: 'There was a tiny movement at my feet'. The beetle is bronze-coloured and has a jagged, or serrated, head. Using its tarsi it pushes a little ball of dung across the yard:' was inching across the cement … a ball of dung bigger than its body'. The beetle makes only 'minute' or very slow progress in this enterprise: 'the dung ball advanced minutely'. As it does so it repeatedly raises and lowers its head. Little flecks of dung break away from the ball as the beetle continues to push it.

The egg falls

Suddenly time seems to speed up again: 'time not quite stopped'. Previously both the hen and the woman had been 'locked' in motionlessness. Now they begin to move once more. However, everything happens extremely slowly, almost as if the world around the young poet is moving in slow motion.

The egg is still in the hen's sphincter. It moves under the sphincter's 'torsion' or pressure. Then the 'mystery' of birth is complete and the egg is pushed free of the hen's orifice:

The black zero of the orifice
closed to a point
and the white zero of the egg hung free.

The egg begins to fall. The woman scrambles to catch it, her fingers spread or 'splayed' to bring it into her grasp. The woman manages to 'fuss with' or alter the egg's course as it falls but she cannot catch it. The egg 'floats outward' away from the hen's body and begins to fall toward the drain below, turning over as it does so. As we have noted to the young poet all of this seems to happen in slow motion, the event taking place with a 'dreamlike' slowness. As he puts it: 'Through what seems like a whole year it fell'.

The poet's theory of poetry

The poet speaks about how his memory of this event has nourished his imagination over the years: 'I feed upon it still, as you see'. He outlines his theory of how a poem gets created:

- The memory of some event is stored for years in the poet's imagination, at the very core of his or her psyche: 'in the yolk of one's being, so to speak' Even memories of events the poet doesn't understand can be stored or 'hoarded' in this way: 'that which, not understood,/ may yet be hoarded in the imagination'.

- While hoarded in the imagination the memory takes on a life of its own, growing and evolving: 'there to undergo its (quite animal) growth'.
- Eventually the poet finds a poetic structure suited to the memory. The memory can then be turned into a poem.
- There is a sense in which the memory is only half-alive while it is stored in the poet's imagination. It evolves 'blindly' or unconsciously, almost like a virus: 'dividing blindly, twitching, packed with will'. It is only when the memory finds its place within the structure of a poem that it is 'wakened' fully into life.

The memory of this event has stayed with the poet since he witnessed it as a boy all those years ago. He still remembers the egg falling toward the shore, the red gold of the yolk inside the 'silvery womb' of egg white. This event is still 'alive' in his memory. In his memory the egg continues to fall and will do so for the rest of his life: 'as it still falls, for me … As it will continue to fall, probably, until I die'.

Conclusion

The poet turns from these reflections on memory and imagination to conclude his depiction of what happened in the yard all those years ago. Time has slowed to a crawl. The egg has been falling for what seems like an eternity. Now, however, things speed up again: 'It was over in a comical flash'. The egg smashes against the shore's grating and disappears into the darkness below. Part of the shell clings to the grating 'a little while longer' before slipping down into the drain.

Initially the woman seems extremely irritated at the loss of this egg: 'She stood staring, in blank anger'. However, she quickly calms down and laughs off the incident: 'then her eyes came to life and she laughed'. She declares that the loss of the egg doesn't matter: 'It's all one'. After all, the hen will lay many more eggs: 'There's plenty more where that came from!'.

THEMES

Memory

Several of Kinsella's poems deal with events that seemed unmemorable to the poet at the time of their occurrence but that nevertheless went on haunt his memory for many years afterwards. This is true of the schoolroom incidents described in 'Model School, Inchicore' and arguably of the poet's childhood embrace of Dick King. In 'Chrysalides' the youthful poet wasn't overly moved by the sight of the dying ants. 'Tear' shows how in his infancy he didn't find the death of his little sister terribly significant or moving. Yet these events would find their way into his memory and recur there with 'lasting horror' for many years afterwards.

In many respects 'Hen Woman' describes a trivial and unmemorable incident. A hen begins to lay an egg near a drain or 'shore'. A woman runs from the house to stop the egg falling down the drain. She picks up the hen but the egg slips through her fingers, smashes on the grating and disappears. Kinsella has described this as a trivial episode, one that was 'comical' or even faintly ridiculous. Yet it was an incident that stayed with the poet for many years.

Yet did the young poet think the incident of the lost egg memorable at the time it occurred? He seems mesmerised by the trivial and slightly comical incident unfolding in front of him, he stands there 'locked' in motionlessness, watching open-mouthed as the egg is lost: 'locked there/ (as I must have been) gaping'. Time seems to slow and stop, suggesting that at least on some level the young poet found this event significant. Yet ultimately it is not clear if the young Kinsella realised at the time that this incident would be a part of his mental landscape for many years to come.

How memories haunt us

'Hen Woman' powerfully shows how the memories of certain events haunt our minds. This is a memory the poet returns to again and again: 'I feed upon it still as you see'. In his memory the egg is still falling toward the grate and will continue to do so for the rest of his life: 'It still falls for me … and will continue to fall, probably, until I die'.

Important in this respect is line 11: 'I had felt all this before'. We get a sense that the poem is just one more 'replaying' of this memory. Also perhaps relevant here is the fact time seems to stop or slow. It is possible that this was how Kinsella perceived the incident at the time. Yet it is also possible that he is simply replaying the memory in 'slow motion', carefully and almost lovingly going through every aspect of the remembered event.

Vividness & detail

A recurring feature of Kinsella's poetry is the vividness and detail with which events are recalled. When he remembers hugging Dick King, for instance, he remembers not only the smell of the old man's clothes but also how the cobblestones were damp with rain and how water was rippling in the 'iron trough'. When he remembers his class being taken outside for lessons he remembers a bee buzzing and the light 'greeny gold' pouring through a tree. 'Chrysalides' remembers the dying ants in agonising detail, recalling how they glistened like 'drops of copper' on the roadside.

'Hen Woman', too, is filled with incredibly detailed recollections. The poet vividly recalls the atmospheric weather conditions, the woman's cottage, tiny little details about the dung beetle, each stage of the egg-laying process and the egg's final tumble toward the grate. He even recalls the fact that the woman was wearing slippers when she ran out in her attempt to save the egg. However, particularly vivid is his memory of how the remains of the smashed egg slipped down into the shore: 'The soft mucous shell clung a little longer,/ Then drained down'.

The process of memory

In this poem Kinsella powerfully describes his view of how the process of memory takes place. Memories, he says, are stored or hoarded within our minds: 'there is no end to that which, not understood,/ may yet be hoarded in the imagination'. He uses a wonderful metaphor to describe this, suggesting that memories are stored at the centre of our being just as the yolk is contained at the centre of an egg. An equally powerful depiction of the memory process can be found in 'Tear', where memory is depicted as a vast vault in which the recollections of various events are stored. 'Dick King', too, deals with the memory process, describing how the death of a loved one alters the significance of the memories we have of them.

Childhood & youth

Like many of Kinsella's poems 'Hen Woman' skillfully evokes a childhood mentality. The child seems mesmerised by the simple and trivial incident that plays out in front of him. He stands there stock still and gaping as the woman picks up the hen and attempts to save the egg it's laying. His childlike and innocent mind is fascinated by the little details of the yard, by the weather and the whitewashed cottage, by the beetle pushing its ball of dung across the ground, by the egg emerging like a 'clean new world' then falling and smashing against the grate.

This impression of the young poet's childhood mentality is perhaps reinforced by certain almost childish phrases such as 'The brooding silence seemed to say "Hush …"' and 'a clock murmured "Gong …"' It's as if the young poet's childlike imagination runs away with him and he envisages the silence and the clock as actually speaking. A similar depiction of childhood mentality occurs 'Model School, Inchicore', 'Dick King' and 'His Father's Hands'.

Horror & desolation

Horrified reactions are common in Kinsella's poetry. We see such a response in 'Model School, Inchicore', for instance, when the speaker chokes at the taste of his pen's nib, and in 'Tear' when the young poet must kiss his dying grandmother. 'Chrysalides', meanwhile, deals with the speaker's belatedly horrified reaction to the sight of dying ants. In 'His Father's Hands' the poet is filled with what we can only describe as horror when he contemplates this environment: 'I do not like this place … It feels evil'.

It could be argued that there is also an element of horror or disgust in 'Hen Woman'. This is perhaps evident in the poet's description of the beetle pushing the ball of dung across the ground and in his description of the egg emerging from the orifice 'flecked wih greenish brown oils'. It is important to note, however, that the poet does not explicitly state that he is horrified by these sights.

Art

In 'Hen Woman', as we have noted, Kinsella powerfully presents his view of the creative process, describing his theory of how a poem gets written. The memory of some event is stored for years in the poet's imagination, at the very core of his or her psyche: 'in the yolk of one's being, so to speak'.

While hoarded in the imagination the memory takes on a life of its own, growing and evolving: 'there to undergo its (quite animal) growth'. It evolves 'blindly' or unconsciously. Its growth resembles that of a virus replicating copies of itself or of a foetus slowly expanding cell by cell: 'dividing blindly, twitching, packed with will'. Eventually the poet finds a poetic structure suited to the memory and it can be turned into a poem.

There is a sense in which the memory is only half-alive while it is stored in the poet's imagination. It is only when the memory finds its place within the structure of a poem that it is 'wakened' fully into life.

An interesting feature of the poem is the various ways it links the creative process in with eggs:

- A poet's imagination 'feeds' upon memories the way one might deed upon the proteins and nutrients of an egg.
- In order to create a poem, the poet must store a memory at the centre of his being, just as the yolk is stored at the centre of an egg.
- We get a sense that Kinsella associates artistic production with the 'mystery' of birth, as if the poem emerges from the poet like an egg emerging from a hen.

In 'Hen Woman', Kinsella seems to associate creativity with femaleness and femininity, with both the 'hen' and 'woman' of the poem's title and with eggs. This links the poem to 'The Familiar', which shows poetic inspiration coming from an almost supernatural female muse figure.

It is also possible to view the dung beetle as a metaphor for the life of the artist. Kinsella views the true artistic life as one of constant, painstaking and often unrewarded toil as the artist spends year after year struggling to create a body of work. It could be argued that the labours of the dung beetle as it struggles to 'inch' and 'advance minutely' across the yard represent the arduous labours of the artist. Like the beetle the artist can only make slow or 'inching' progress as he or she struggles through a lifetime of repetitive creative toil. The beetle bows its head humbly. Similarly the artist must humble himself: he must bear his artistic gifts modestly, remain true to his inspiration, and 'sell out' for commercial gain, prizes or popular success.

Struggle for comprehension

There is a real sense in this poem that the young poet is baffled and confused by the sight fo the hen laying the egg. He stands there 'gaping', utterly motionless and locked in place. On one level he realises he is witnessing something important or significant. But on another he doesn't quite know what to make of this sight. The poem can be taken to describe a child's first full-on encounter with birth, in the form of the egg being laid, and with destruction, in the form of it smashing against the grating. It is his introduction to concepts he is too young to properly understand. However, for the rest of his life he will grapple with these issues and will return again and again to the time he first encountered them.

LANGUAGE

Atmosphere

One of the most noticeable features of this poem is the dense, thundery atmosphere Kinsella conjures up. There is a real sense of heat and humidity in the opening lines, the kind of weather that suggests a thunder storm is on the way: 'The noon heat in the yard/ smelled of stillness and coming thunder'. He describes the landscape as being filled with a 'brooding' or menacing silence, the calm before the weather breaks. It is not surprising that the young poet hears the 'mutter of thunder' far away in the distance.

Metaphor & simile

This poem is studded with fine metaphors and similes. There is an interestingly visual simile in line 27 where the brown beetle is compared to 'a bronze leaf'. It is perhaps less easy to visualise the metaphor in line 17 where the hen's eyes are compared to pebbles. Several memorable metaphors are used to describe the egg:

- As it emerges from the hen it is compared to a new planet: 'a clean new world'.
- Similarly, it is compared to the moon as it begins its drop toward the grate: 'it floated outward, moon-white,/ leaving no trace in the air'.
- It is also memorably described as a 'tender blank brain'. We can almost envisage the freshly laid egg as brain-like blob.
- Kinsella also compares the egg to an eye-ball and once again we can imagine the visual similarity: 'the yoke and white of my eye'.
- The egg is also compared to a womb, with the yolk imagined as a 'beating' embryo and the white as the silvery amniotic fluid: 'the red gold beating in its silvery womb'.

Detailed description

Above all else 'Hen Woman' is marked by Kinsella's fantastically detailed descriptions. We see this in lines 25–35 where he minutely describes the beetle and its ball of dung, mentioning the insect's 'serrated brow' and 'small tarsi' as well as the tiny flecks that come away from the dung ball.

We also see this attention to detail in his description of the egg. He describes the 'greenish brown' oils that cover it when it is freshly laid. In lines 46–50 he wonderfully captures its tumble toward the grate. We can almost visualise the egg falling in slow motion as Kinsella details every stage of its plunge. Finally, in lines 71–2 there is the lovingly detailed depiction of the smashed egg lingering on the grate for a moment before sliding into the drain.

There is an interesting visual similarity between the cottage and the hen. Both the hen and the white-washed cottage are white. The cottage door opens to reveal a black hole from which the woman appears just as the hen's orifice opens to reveal a black hole from which the egg emerges. There is also a playful pun on the word 'brooding' in line 5. The word can mean menacing or threatening but also refers to the process by which a hen warms eggs to make them hatch.

His Father's Hands

LINE BY LINE

Lines 1–8: *The poet drinks with his father*

The poet is drinking with his father, more than likely in a pub or bar: 'I drank firmly/ and set the glass down between us firmly'. The father is speaking in an argumentative or strident manner. He stabs the air repeatedly with his finger to emphasise the points he is making: 'Emphas-/ emphasemphasis' However, the poet feels that the father's overly forceful and argumentative manner only prevents him expressing himself clearly. It 'mars' or spoils his point.

Lines 9–39: *The poet thinks about his grandfather*

As the poet watches his father's hands 'prodding the air' he finds himself thinking about his grandfather: 'I have watched/ his father's hands before him'. He remembers the grandfather squeezing a lump of black Plug tobacco between his thumb and a small knife. The grandfather would carve little curvy strips ('curlicues') from this lump and roll them in his palms before smoking them.

The poet also remembers hanging around his grandfather's workshop as a child. The grandfather worked part time as a cobbler. He would cut into the leather with his knife to form a groove that he would hold open with his thumb. He would slip ('insinuate') sprigs ('little nails') into this groove and prepare to hammer them into place. The grandfather would store a number of these small nails in his mouth, slipping one out 'between his lips' when needed.

The poet would amuse himself by taking a 'pinch' of nails from the hole where they were stored and hammering them into the block that served as the grandfather's work bench. The poet's older cousins had amused themselves in the same way. Over the years 'hundreds' of nails had been driven into the workbench by the grandfather's young relatives. Many of these have 'gone black' with age. However, the heads of the new nails hammered in by the poet show as 'bright points' on the workbench's surface.

The poet also remembers his grandfather playing the fiddle, 'scraping' the strings with his bow and 'shifting' his left hand across them. The grandfather was almost deaf but played the fiddle anyway, slanting or 'inclining' his head so that his ear was right next to the instrument's sound-holes. The grandfather would sing or hum as he played, in a voice so low he was almost 'whispering'. The poet remembers his grandfather playing one song in particular: 'The Wind that Shakes the Barley'. Lyrics from this song are scattered throughout lines 30–39.

Lines 40–58: *The poet thinks about earlier generations of his family*

The poet finds himself thinking about earlier generations of his family, those who existed before or 'beyond' his grandfather's time. He has been thinking about 'The Wind that Shakes the Barley', a song inspired by the 1798 rebellion against British rule in Ireland. He now thinks about how his family lived during the period of that revolt:

- The family were originally from Tullow in Co. Carlow.
- They moved to Farnese where they were surrounded by a small community of settlers from Scotland or Northern Ireland.
- The poet remembers hearing how at that time his family worked as stonemasons or stonecutters while probably also doing a bit of farming.
- He remembers being told how his ancestors helped the Irish rebels (the 'Croppies') after they had been defeated by English forces (the 'Yoes' or Yeomen) in the 1798 rebellion.
- The poet's family sheltered the Lacey brothers who were among the rebellion's leaders and were later caught and hanged by the English.

Lines 59–69: *The poet thinks about the beginnings of Irish civilisation*

The poet now finds himself thinking about the very beginnings of Irish history. His thoughts drift back far 'beyond' the 1700's to a time just after the Ice Age when Ireland was first populated. He imagines himself in a bleak and desolate landscape that is littered with rocks or boulders: 'Littered uplands. Dense grass. Rocks everywhere'. The soil is wet from the freshly melted ice and is still cold: 'wet underneath, retaining memory of the long cold'.

A group of people seem to be constructing some kind of monument in this wasteland. They choose a 'prow' or prominent piece of land. They place wooden tracks on this hill. They drag huge boulders up the tracks and arrange them to create the monument. The boulders are stacked so that they support each other and remain upright, forming a stable dolmen-like shape: 'The boulders chosen/ and sloped together, stabilized'.

The poet thinks of the monument as a bleak and menacing presence in the landscape. Kinsella has written several poems that deal with dark gods and cults of human sacrifice in prehistoric Ireland. It is probable that the monument is a temple or altar where such grisly sacrifices were carried out. The poet thinks of this as an 'evil' place where 'terrible things happened'. It fills him with fear: 'I feel afraid here when I am on my own'. He believes that the people who lived in this landscape, in the shadow of the dark monument, were 'never happy'.

LINES 70–86

These early settlers with their human sacrifices are the ancestors of Kinsella, his grandfather and of every Irish person living today. The poet thinks about how these prehistoric people evolved and multiplied through the centuries to form the modern Irish nation. This was a random and chaotic process, a long series of 'evolutions and accidents' as the vast family tree of the Irish race grew from those earliest inhabitants. It was a process greatly effected by the events of Irish history, by 'dispersal and migrations' as different groups of people moved to, from and around the island.

Kinsella thinks of the blood or DNA of the Irish race flowing through the different generations. It 'advances' through the centuries, occupying different vessels or bodies as it does so: 'The blood advancing/ – gorging vessel after vessel'. This blood line 'gorges' or fills to bursting each Irish person it occupies. It is then passed on to the next generation in a slightly different or altered form.

This bloodline eventually gave rise to Kinsella's grandfather fiddling by the fireside. The poet thinks of his grandfather as a patient person who was peaceful and serene. He remembers the grandfather looking at him with kindness when as a child he hung around his workshop. Yet it seems the grandfather could not adequately express the peace and gentleness that was part of his personality. Kinsella refers to the grandfather's 'blocked gentleness', suggesting that his kindness remained somehow bottled up inside him.

The grandfather passed this gentleness on to Kinsella's father and on to Kinsella himself: 'Behold, that gentleness already/ modulated twice, in others'. The father inherited this gentleness only to have it altered or 'modulated' by his 'earnestness and iteration', by the fact that he was overly serious and had a tendency to repeat himself. (We see this at the beginning of the poem where the father is depicted as an argumentative person repeating his point over and over again). Kinsella himself also inherited this gentleness only to have it modulated by his 'offhandedness' and by his tendency to repress 'certain impulses'.

Lines 87–95: *Conclusion*

In these lines Kinsella remembers finding the rough block that had served as the grandfather's work bench. The block had been abandoned for years in a 'corner of the yard'. One day 'in sunlight after rain' the poet comes upon this 'wet and black' object from his childhood. He stands it up and runs his fingers over its surface. Over the years the wood has grown soft and rotten. When the poet touches it its 'soft flesh' breaks open and little nails come pouring out: 'countless little nails/ squirming and dropping out of it'. These are the nails Kinsella and his cousins drove into the block when they hung around the grandfather's workshop as children all those years ago.

THEMES

Family & ancestry

In this poem powerfully traces his ancestry through the centuries and generations. The phrase 'Beyond that' recurs as Kinsella traces his family history further and further into the past. His imagination moves from his father to his grandfather, to his ancestors who worked as stonemasons in Farnese and helped the Irish rebels in 1798, to their origins in Tullow. His imagination then drifts even further back in time to the very beginnings of Irish history. He envisages the country's first post-ice-age settlers, who are the ancestors not only of Kinsella's own family but of all modern-day Irish people.

Kinsella's depiction of these first settlers emphasises the link between them and the present day inhabitants of Ireland. Instead of simply describing this ancient environment Kinsella depicts himself as having been imaginatively transported into it, using phrases like 'I do not like this place', 'I feel afraid here when I am on my own'. It's as if the settlers' memories had somehow been transmitted through their DNA to Kinsella himself, their present-day descendant. This is what is sometimes referred to as the notion of 'race memory'.

Kinsella imagines the blood line of the Irish people stemming from these first prehistoric inhabitants as their descendants multiplied and occupied the island. Their blood surges through the centuries, occupying different vessels or bodies as it does so: 'The blood advancing/ – gorging vessel after vessel'. This blood line 'gorges' or fills to bursting each Irish person it occupies. It is then passed on to the next generation in a slightly different or altered form. Kinsella emphasises the random and chaotic process of 'evolutions and accidents' that leads from the stone-age settlers to his own family.

The poem also focuses on how certain traits are handed on down through the generations from father to son. Kinsella describes how his grandfather's personality was marked by a 'blocked gentleness'. This gentleness was passed on to Kinsella's father in a different form. In the father this gentleness was 'modulated' or changed into seriousness and what might be a slightly aggressive tendency to repeat himself. Kinsella himself also inherited this gentleness only to have it modulated to 'offhandedness' and to a tendency to repress 'certain impulses'.

Also relevant to this theme is the poem's final image of the breaking workbench. The imagery in these final lines is very masculine. The block standing erect in the yard brings to mind the male sexual organ. There is something sperm-like about the little nails that erupt from the 'wood's soft flesh'. When Kinsella wrote this poem he was under the influence of the psychologist C.G. Jung. The little nails squirming from the block suggest snakes, which in Jung's philosophy were associated with masculinity.

In this poem, where Kinsella deals with his male relatives, it is difficult not to envisage the 'countless little nails' that slip from the block as a metaphor for Kinsella's forefathers, for the countless male ancestors that have existed since the first people arrived in Ireland after the Ice Age. Over the centuries his ancestors have come 'squirming and dropping' from the black mass of Irish history. The image might also suggest the poet's male descendants who will exist in the future as the blood continues to advance through the generations.

Hardship

'His Father's Hands' powerfully chronicles the different hardships endured by Kinsella's family over the generations, as they lived through the chaotic series of 'dispersals and migrations' that makes up Irish history:

- He describes the miserable conditions endured by his earliest ancestors as they attempted to exist in the harsh landscape of Ireland after the Ice Age, as they attempted to survive in a land still damp and freezing from the 'long cold'. These people, he says, were 'never happy'.
- He suggests that these early ancestors lived in the shadow of a dark cult of human sacrifice, one that seemed to fill the entire landscape with evil.
- In the eighteenth century his ancestors were so poor they had to practice two trades in order to make a living; that of farmer and that of mason or stonecutters.
- The poem suggests how Kinsella's ancestors, along with the rest of the Irish nation, were conquered and oppressed by Britain, a foreign power. In 1798 his ancestors aided the 'Croppies' who rebelled against this alien rule.

'Tear' is another poem that deals with the sufferings undergone by Kinsella's family. Whereas 'His Father's Hands' deals with the hardships endured by the poet's relatives throughout history, 'Tear' suggests the hardships endured by his relatives in the more immediate past.

Isolation

There is a powerful sense of isolation in the poem. The grandfather is portrayed as an isolated figure. He is a gentle person but cannot properly communicate that gentleness to those around them. It is 'blocked' and confined within him. His inability to express his personality leaves him trapped in a social vacuum, a 'blocked void' of isolation from those around him. He exists in a private but lonely mental space, unable to communicate effectively with those around him: 'in privacy across a blocked void'. The image of the father playing and singing weakly to himself by the fireside powerfully reinforces the sense we get of his deep and tragic isolation.

Yet there is also a sense in which both Kinsella himself and his father are also psychologically isolated. The father's personality, as we have noted, is marked by seriousness and a tendency to repeat himself. We see this at the beginning of the poem when he stridently makes the same point over and over again. Yet these traits have an unfortunate tendency to 'mar' or spoil his point, undermining his ability to communicate with those around him.

There is a sense, too, in which the poet himself is depicted as a somewhat psychologically isolated person. Like the grandfather he 'blocks or 'represses' certain impulses inside himself. His personality is also marked by an 'offhandedness', a brusque or overly casual manner that might cause offence to those close to him. There seems to be psychological distance between himself and the father at the beginning of the poem. The father's point is 'marred', meaning they are not communicating properly. The poet puts his glass down between them 'firmly', almost as he was placing a barrier between them. Like 'Tear', then, 'His Father's Hands' is a poem where Kinsella unflinchingly captures the sense of isolation that existed between the members of his own family.

Death & mortality

Like many of Kinsella's poems 'His Father's Hands' is in some respects an elegy, a poem in which the poet remembers and honours someone who has died. In this instance the poet remembers his grandfather, lovingly depicting the old man cutting tobacco, working with leather and playing the fiddle.

He describes the grandfather as a 'serene' and gentle person, referring to his 'peace', 'patience' and gentleness. Kinsella remembers how the grandfather would tease him in a gentle way when he hung around the workshop. The grandfather would stop working, he would pause in 'slashing' his knife into the leather, and gaze in 'kindly mockery' at his grandson hammering little nails into the workbench.

Yet this is not a straightforward celebration of the dead grandfather. Instead Kinsella unflinchingly depicts the difficulties his grandfather endures. The grandfather's gentleness was 'blocked' within him because he was somehow unable to express this inner tenderness to those around him. Kinsella shows how the grandfather occupied a private but lonely mental space: 'in privacy across a blocked void'. The grandfather's psychological isolation is powerfully suggested by the image of him playing and singing weakly to himself by the fireside. Like 'Dick King', 'Tear' and 'Thinking of Mr D.' this is a poem that remembers the dead but does so in a brutally honest fashion. All four of these poems depict how the memories of the dead continue to haunt the living long after they have passed away.

Old age

Many of Kinsella's poems depict the ravages time inflicts on the human body. In 'Mirror in February', for instance, the poet is shocked at the sight of his own 'exhausted' and 'downturning' features. He is suddenly horrified to realise he is no longer young. Both 'Dick King' and 'Thinking of Mr D.' suggest the ravages of time on older men the poet knew growing up.

'His Father's Hands', too, touches on this age-old poetic theme, with its moving depiction of the poet's aged grandfather playing the fiddle. The old man seems weak and frail, his hands barely moving as he 'scrapes' at the instrument's strings. The grandfather is so deaf, he slants his head and holds the fiddle close to his ears in order to hear the tune he's playing. We can almost imagine him slumped wearily by the fireside, humming weakly to himself as he plays.

Childhood & youth

Kinsella is well known as a poet of childhood. In 'His Father's Hands', as in many of his finest poems, he finds inspiration in childhood memories. His imagination returns to what must be very early memories of hanging around his grandfather's workshop. The poem also features childhood memories of watching the grandfather cut tobacco for his pipe and of him playing the fiddle.

In this poem Kinsella reveals his skill at conjuring a childhood mentality, depicting how he amused himself by hammering a pinch of sprigs into the grandfather's workbench. There is a sense in these lines that the young poet is imitating the grandfather, almost playing at being a cobbler like his cousins before him. A similarly deft depiction of a childhood mentality takes place in 'Dick King', 'Hen Woman' a 'Model School, Inchicore'. It could be argued that a slightly older more 'youthful' mentality is depicted in 'Chrysalides' and 'Tear'.

Horror & desolation

Horror and desolation feature in lines 59–69, where Kinsella imagines the beginnings of Irish civilisation. In these lines Kinsella depicts a bleak and desolate landscape of boulders, dampness and freezing soil. Similarly desolate landscapes are depicted in 'Mirror in February' and 'The Familar', both of with present barren, wintry scenes. A more urban desolation is present in 'Thinking of Mr D.', with its canal-bank scene and in 'Model School, Inchicore' with its lonely depiction of the empty school shed.

The poet is filled with what we can only describe as horror when he contemplates this environment: 'I do not like this place … It feels evil'. This horrified reaction is provoked in particular by the monument the settlers are building on the prow of the hill. The poet associates this structure with 'menace', and, as we have seen, several scholars suggest it is linked to prehistoric cults of human sacrifice. We get a sense that this grim monument is linked to the evil that fills the landscape and to the fact that the people who lived there were 'never happy'.

Such horrified reactions are common in Kinsella's poetry. We see such a response in 'Model School, Inchicore', for instance, when the speaker chokes at the taste of his pen's nib, and in 'Tear' when the young poet must kiss his dying grandmother. 'Chrysalides', meanwhile, deals with the speaker's belatedly horrified reaction to the sight of dying ants.

Memory

In this poem the poet remembers in intense detail certain activities carried out by his grandfather many years ago. He remembers the grandfather cutting tobacco and playing the fiddle. There is a special clarity to his memories of the grandfather's workshop, as he recalls the grandfather holding nails in his mouth and the black heads of the nails beaten into the workbench by his cousins.

Kinsella's work often demonstrates how certain seemingly insignificant and unmemorable incidents can lodge themselves in our minds, to be remembered ever after. We see this in 'Dick King', 'Tear' and 'Model School, Inchicore' and arguably also in 'Hen Woman'. In 'His Father's Hands' the poet remembers with great clarity playing in his father's workshop, occasions that in themselves might be regarded as trivial and unmemorable.

Kinsella's poetry is keenly aware of how certain childhood memories can haunt us for the rest of our lives. In this poem we get a sense that the poet will be forever haunted by the image of his grandfather almost silently playing the fiddle and singing to himself: 'To his deaf, inclined head/ He hugged the fiddle's body'.

LANGUAGE

Free association
One notable feature of 'His Father's Hands' is the way the poet 'free associates', his mind jumping from topic to topic. The sight of his father's hands reminds him of his grandfather's hands. The memory of the grandfather playing 'The Wind that Shakes the Barley' reminds him of his family's activities during the 1798 rebellion. This in turn causes him to imagine what life must have been like for Ireland's first settlers. The phrase 'Beyond that' recurs as Kinsella's mind jumps from topic to topic.

An imaginative leap
A striking feature of this poem is the way the poet imagines himself in the landscape of prehistoric Ireland. Instead of simply describing this ancient environment Kinsella depicts himself as having been imaginatively transported into it, using phrases like 'I do not like this place/ I feel afraid here when I am on my own'. This technique adds greatly to the power and immediacy of the poem.

Quotation
Another interesting feature of this poem is the way it quotes from the old Irish song called 'The Wind that Shakes the Barley'. Phrases from this song take up most of lines 30–38. Kinsella, however, does not quote a continuous passage from the song's lyrics Instead he takes random phrases and scatters them throughout these lines. These snatches of song-lyric are interrupted by a phrase of Kinsella's own: 'in privacy, across a blocked void'. All in all, these lines have a jerky and uncertain movement as the reader is moved from phrase to random phrase. Quotation also features in lines 40–58 where Kinsella makes use of certain phrases from a letter written by his uncle.

Imagery
An important feature of this poem is the way different images associated with hands reoccur throughout:

- There is the image of the father stabbing the air with his finger to emphasise his point.
- There are the images of the grandfather using his hands to cut tobacco, work with leather and play the fiddle. These images are rendered with the vividness and attention to detail of Kinsella's best writing.
- There is the idea of Kinsella's ancestors working with their hands as stone cutters or masons.
- There is the image of Ireland's earliest settlers using their hands to construct the monumnet on the prow of the hill.
- Finally there is the image of the workbench breaking in the poet's own hands.

There are several other memorable images in the poem. We are presented with Ireland's first settler's building a monument in a bleak landscape of 'Littered uplands' and the blood line of the Irish nation 'gorging vessel after vessel' as it flows through the centuries. However particularly striking is the poem's final image of the grandfather's workbench breaking open.

We can almost see the block's soft and rotten flesh tearing and the rusty nails come squirming out of it.

Assonance
We see assonance in a phrase like 'dark of his palms' with its repeated 'a' sound, in 'insinuating little sprigs' with its repeated 'i' sound and 'wood's soft flesh broke open' with its repeated 'o' sound.

Euphony occurs in lines 27–9. A complex combination of broad and narrow-vowel sounds gives the verse a sweet but melancholy music, reminiscent perhaps of the sad air the grandfather used to play: 'To his deaf, inclined head/ He hugged the fiddle's body'. A similar effect is created by lines 25–6 with their repeated 'o' and 'a' sounds: 'Or his bow hand scarcely moving,/ scraping in the dark corner'.

from *Settings*: Model School, Inchicore

LINE BY LINE

LINES 1–19

In this poem Kinsella remembers his time in primary school. His first teacher was called Miss Carney and his second teacher was called Mr Browne. He remembers the first day Mr Browne began to teach the class decimals, drawing a 'white dot' or decimal point on the black board. The young poet was extremely eager to learn: 'I am going to know/ everything'.

He also remembers Miss Carney giving her class plasticine (commonly known as 'marla' or 'mála') to play with. The plasticine is obviously old because all the strips of different colours have been mashed together into a kind of brown blob. Kinsella remembers how his classmates would roll the plasticine on a piece of paper until it formed a long, snake-like cylindrical shape. They would keep applying pressure to this 'snake' until it split into two parts.

The innocent and childlike mentality of the poet and his classmates is evident in these lines. He seems taken with the fact that the teacher called Mr Browne actually looks a little brown, presumably having a dark or sallow complexion. He and his classmates are amused when they recite the 'adding-up tables in Irish' and come to words that sound like Miss Carney's name. Kinsella is probably referring to the table for the number 5:

- A cúig is a haon, sé
- A cúig is a dó, seacht
- A cúig is a trí, ocht
- A cúig is a ceathar, naoi

Here the words 'ceathar, naoi' sounds like 'Carney', causing the poet and his fellow pupils to 'titter' or laugh at one another.

LINES 20–37

In these lines the poet remembers being outside the classroom in the school's grounds. He remembers a sunny day in early summer when Mr Browne took them out into the grounds for their history lesson. Mr Browne sits in his chair under a tree and the children sit at his feet in two rows.

The young poet and his classmates are glad to be out of the classroom on this beautiful day. The sunlight is warm and flickering. A 'fat bee' buzzes around them. Under the tree all is green and gold, as the sunlight pours down through the leaves.

The poet also remembers playing in the school grounds during autumn time. He remembers how 'big chestnut leaves/ fell all over the playground'. He and his class mates would pile the leaves into heaps. The boys in his class would then engage in horseplay, racing around the schoolyard, jumping over the piles of leaves and falling into them.

LINES 38–50

In these lines the poet remembers sitting alone in the school's bicycle shed, watching bits of paper being blown about the place by the wind. The poet's class studied the old-style 'religious catechism' in school, meaning they learned by heart a series of questions about God along with the answers to those questions. A particular question and answer goes through the young poet's mind as he sits alone in the bicycle shed. This describes how God observes and judges 'even our most secret thoughts and actions', and will force us to account for all our deeds on the 'Day of Judgement'.

In the poem's last lines the poet remembers tasting the ink from the nib of his fountain pen. He describes how his mouth seemed to 'shrink' from the ink's unpleasant taste. This is a good description of how our mouths seem to almost spasm or recoil when we taste something extremely tart or acidic.

THEMES

Childhood & youth

In this poem Kinsella wonderfully captures the innocent mentality of childhood:

- The poet and his classmates find childish amusement in the fact that Mr Browne is actually quite brown and in the fact that some words in the Irish adding-up tables sound like Miss Carney's name.
- They take a simple delight in being allowed to have

their history class outside on a sunny day.
- The poet capture's the innocent pleasure they take in racing around the schoolyard among the autumn leaves.
- The young poet exhibits a child-like thirst for knowledge when he declares that 'I am going to know everything'.

A similarly effective depiction of a childhood mentality can be found in 'His Father's Hands', 'Hen Woman' and 'Dick King'. A slightly older more youthful mentality is depicted in 'Tear' and 'Chrysalides'.

Yet 'Model School, Inchicore' also describes how childhood innocence is inevitably lost. The young Kinsella gains knowledge in the Model School. As his mind becomes more knowledgeable and sophisticated his childhood innocence disappears. He learns about dark and disturbing concepts such as sin, death and divine judgement.

In lines 38–47 there is a distinct sense that this knowledge troubles the young poet, robbing his mind of its carefree childhood innocence. The poem's atmosphere changes from light-hearted and cheerful, with images of children playing in the schoolyard, to dismal and depressing, with the image of the boy sitting alone in the shed as scraps of paper blow about him. The poem seems to suggest that knowledge can only be achieved at the cost of losing innocence.

There is a sense in which the poem retells the story of the Garden of Eden. At the beginning of the poem the young poet is perfectly innocent, just as Adam and Eve were in the garden. However, like Adam and Eve the young poet thirsted for knowledge: 'I am going to know/ everything'. Adam and Eve acquired knowledge by eating fruit from a forbidden tree while the poet acquired knowledge by learning tables, decimals, history and catechism. Several images in the poem reinforce this similarity to the Bible story:

- The school yard in lines 20–37 is depicted as an idyllic place of almost perfect beauty, suggesting the Garden of Eden itself.
- The plasticine snake in the opening lines suggests the snake that tempted Adam and Eve in the garden.
- In lines 20–29 the children sit under a tree while learning, perhaps suggesting the tree of knowledge in the Bible story.
- In lines 48–51 the poet tastes his pen, a tool for acquiring knowledge, just as Adam tasted the apple from the tree of knowledge itself.

The poet's mouth shrinks or recalls from the taste of the pen's ink, suggesting that knowledge is a bitter thing. Adam and Eve's new knowledge brought them only misery, getting them ejected from the Garden of Eden. Similarly, the young poet's knowledge only brings him misery, leaving his mind troubled and robbing him of his childhood innocence. 'Tear' and 'Chrysalides' are other poems where Kinsella deals with loss of innocence.

Death & mortality

There is a sense in which this poem deals with the young poet's dawning awareness of his own mortality. As we have noted, the young boy's religion classes bring him face to face with disturbing concepts such as sin, death and divine judgement. The horror with which he reacts to this new awareness is evident in the poem's final lines as his mouth 'shrinks' in disgust. It could be argued that a dawning awareness of mortality also features in 'Tear' and 'Chrysalides'. In 'Mirror in February', meanwhile, the poet's awareness of mortality is reinforced as he catches sight of his reflection in the shaving mirror and suddenly realises how old looking he has become.

Struggle for comprehension

Many of Kinsella's poems present us with speakers or characters who desperately attempt to make sense of the world around them. We see it in both 'Hen Woman' and 'Tear', for instance, where the young poet is confused by the situation he finds himself in and is unsure how to react. This theme is also present in 'Mirror in February', where the poet attempts to come to terms with ageing and mortality, and in 'Thinking of Mr D.' where the old man's ghost, wracked with pain, seems to contemplates the canal water in a vain search for answers.

A similar desire for understanding is evident in this poem. We see it when the young poet, eager for knowledge, declares that 'I am going to know everything'. It is also perhaps evident at the poem's conclusion, where the young poet sits alone in the bike shed, troubled and confused by the new knowledge he has gained.

Horror & desolation

Horrified reactions are a regular feature of Kinsella's poetry. This poem demonstrates the poet's horrified reaction to the pen's ink, showing how his mouth shrinks or recoils from its taste. Similarly horrified reactions are evident in 'Mirror in February', 'Chrysalides', 'Tear' and 'His Father's Hands'.

Kinsella's poetry is also marked by recurring scenes of bleakness and desolation. This poem presents us with the grim scene of the little boy sitting alone in the bicycle shed contemplating God's judgement as scraps of paper blow about the place. This is reminiscent of 'Tear' where the speaker finds himself transported to a derelict place/ smelling of ash' and of 'His Father's Hands', where the speaker finds himself transported to a desolate and terrifying prehistoric landscape. 'Mirror in February' and 'Thinking of Mr D.' also feature figures lost in contemplation in a bleak and desolate landscape.

Memory

Like many of Kinsella's poems 'Model School, Inchicore' deals with the topic of memory. His work often demonstrates how certain seemingly insignificant and unmemorable incidents can lodge themselves in our minds, to be remembered ever after.

In this poem the poet seems to vividly remember seemingly trivial childhood events such as maths classes and playing in the school yard.;

A recurring feature of Kinsella's poetry is the vividness and detail with which events are recalled even many years later. There are several such detailed memories in this poem: the memory of the brown plasticine, of how the class tittered while learning tables, of Mr Browne's brown face and white teeth, of the fat bee, of schoolyard games in autumn.

Kinsella's poetry is keenly aware of how certain childhood memories can haunt us for the rest of our lives. In 'Model School, Inchicore' we get a sense that the poet will be forever haunted by the memory of sitting alone in the school shed and tasting the bitterness of the pen's ink as he watches papers being blown about by the wind. We also see this in 'Dick King', 'Tear' and 'His Father's hands' and arguably in 'Hen Woman'.

Art

The conclusion of 'Model School, Inchicore' suggests the hard years of devotion required by a career literature. Kinsella considers the writer's life to be one of patience, careful focus and unrelenting toil as he or she struggles to perfect his or her craft. The young poet sits surrounded by symbols of writing. 'Papers' flap in the breeze. He holds a pen in his hand. His mouth shrinks or recoils from the ink's taste, suggesting the bitter difficulty that a life of writing brings. It's as if the young poet already has some sense of his poetic vocation, and of the difficulty and sacrifice such a vocation involves.

LANGUAGE

Perhaps the standout feature of this poem is the skill with which Kinsella depicts the world from a child's point of view. (For more on this see the section on 'Childhood' in Themes).

The poem is also marked by a pronounced shift in tone and atmosphere. The tone in the opening part of the poem is light-hearted and carefree as the poet depicts his classmates' childish jokes and the simple pleasure they took from being out in the schoolyard. However, the tone becomes suddenly darker and sadder in line 38 where we find the speaker dealing with the consequences of his new knowledge.

An interesting feature of this poem is the way it moves through the different seasons. Lines 20–9 depict an idyllic summer scene. Lines 30–7 present us with an autumn scene. Lines 38–47 depict a bleak wintery scene. It is possible that this movement from summer to winter represents the young poet's move from innocence to knowledge.

Another interesting feature is the recurrence of the colour brown. The lumps of plasticine the children play with are brown. One of the teachers is called Mr Browne and he has a brown face. Presumably the autumn leaves in lines 30–37 are mostly brown. It has been suggested that the recurring use of the colour brown suggests the young poet's decaying innocence, brown being a colour often associated with decay.

Thomas Kinsella

from *The Familiar*: VII

LINE BY LINE

I

The speaker of the poem has risen early and has gone to the kitchen to make breakfast. It is a very cold morning and there is 'frost on the window'. He takes a mouthful of 'chilled grapefruit' and looks out the window. The landscape outside the house is rugged and frozen. There are rocky hills 'scattered' with 'sheets of frost'. There is a wood, above which fly 'two hooded crows high in the cold'. They are 'flying up toward the tundra, beyond the waterfall'. The 'tundra' is an area of land that is permanently frozen and upon which very little grows.

The kitchen is a little cosier than the outside world. The poet mentions a 'cat' that is curled up in the kitchen. Yet the cat seems to be ragged and somewhat nervous. It is described as 'Torn and watchful'.

The speaker prepares breakfast. He slices some tomatoes. He heats the kettle and prepares tea. He makes toast, remembering it just in time to save it from burning. An effort is made to arrange things in an orderly fashion, though the result is less than perfect. The damp 'thin discs' of tomatoes are arranged in 'sequence into their dish'. The toast is 'Arranged' in 'slight disorder around the basket'. Finally the speaker fixes two places at the table, 'one with the fruit/ and one with the plate of sharp cheese'.

Just before everything is complete the speaker rings a little bell to alert his partner to the fact that the meal is ready. He then stands next to the table with his arms stretched out over the meal, like a priest might extend his arms out over the altar above the bread and wine: 'extended/ over the sweetness of the sacrifice'.

A woman appears in the door of the kitchen. She is appreciative of the speaker's efforts. She tells him that he is 'very good' for making breakfast and that he 'always made it nice'.

II

The poem seems to describe a very normal domestic moment. The title itself appears to be a reference to that which is routine and comfortably recognisable, the 'familiar'. But on closer inspection the poem becomes a little strange and unsettling.

The cat is described as 'Torn and watchful'. This description fits uncomfortably into the tranquil domestic scene of a man lovingly preparing breakfast for his wife.

- The 'two hooded crows' are described as 'talking to each other'.
- The landscape itself is rather unusual. The speaker of the poem seems to be living in some terribly remote and rather inhospitable environment. The house is located near 'the tundra' by some woodland at the base of rocky hills down which a waterfall tumbles.
- The way the speaker stands 'with arms extended/ over the sweetness of the sacrifice' seems initially rather humorous, but in context with all the other elements of the poem begins to strike us as perhaps a little spooky.

Finally, and perhaps most significantly, the description of the woman is quite bizarre. Firstly, we are told that her 'shade' appeared in the door. This is an unusual way to describe somebody's appearance. Secondly, the way her voice is described makes it seem like it is separate from the 'shade', as though it is disembodied and independent of the form that appears in the door: 'Her voice responded'. Thirdly, it is strange that she says 'You always *made* it nice' when referring to the meal. Why does she say 'made' and not 'make'?

THEMES

Art

'The Familiar: VII' is the seventh and final part of a longer work by Kinsella. The first six sections describe an encounter with an unnamed female who visits the poet one evening. This woman, whom the poet refers to as 'Muse' in the third section of the poem, arrives at the door of his Baggot Street flat with a suitcase and an intention to stay: 'I lifted in her case./ It was light, but I could tell/ she was going to stay'. There then follows a description of the night spent together.

The night is at times intensely passionate, feverish and full of struggle: 'In my night sweat she was everywhere,/ feeding'. At times what the poet describes is dreamlike and surreal. However, as the night progresses the poet and the 'Muse' seem to relax in each other's company and a 'friendship' develops: 'I felt my way back afterwards/ along the landing, into my place./ Our legs locked in friendship'.

The final part of the poem, the part that features on the course, deals with either the morning immediately after or a morning some time in the future. In contrast with the rather intense activities of the night, the morning is tranquil and the relaxed. The speaker seems to be at ease as he makes breakfast and when the 'shade' appears at the door, he humorously extends his arms over the 'sacrifice' of the meal.

'The Familiar', therefore, deals with the poet and poetic inspiration. It suggests that this relationship can be a difficult one and that the poet needs to invest time and care in order to ensure that he remains inspired. The poem suggests that he might have struggled with inspiration in his early years but that in time he learnt how to work with the 'Muse' (In the first section of the poem Kinsella describes an unpleasant break-up: 'Remembering/ our last furious farewell/ – face to face, studying each other/ with a hardness like hate'.)

'The Familiar: VII' suggests that the poet must tend to the muse, to the source of his inspiration, in much the same way that a husband must tend to and nurture the relationship with his wife. The muse's comment when she sees the meal that he 'always made it nice' suggests that the poet has always treated her well and was attentive and considerate in his dealings with her.

Desolation

'The Familiar: VII' is set in a cold, bleak and desolate environment. The poet looks out the window at 'sheets of frost/ scattered down among the rocks' of the hills. Two 'hooded crows high in the cold' fly 'up toward the tundra'. We are reminded of Mirror in February where the poet contemplates the 'dark' and 'defaced' trees beyond his window on a cold winter morning. However, in contrast with 'The Familiar: VII', Mirror in February hints at the coming of spring and growth in the description of 'the awakening trees'.

from *Glenmacnas*: VI – Littlebody

LINE BY LINE

The poet is out walking in the hills of Glenmacnass. It seems to be a regular walk that he takes, walking 'as far as the sheepfold … and back'. On his return to his car he observes the 'black bog channels' and the 'white cottonheads/ on the old cuttings nodding everywhere'. Just as he approaches the car 'shining in the distance' he catches the sound of uileann pipes coming from 'behind a rock prow/ with the stones on top for an old mark'. The 'music of the pipes' is distant and clear.

He goes to see who is playing the music and, not wanting the player to hear his approach, climbs silently up the rocks. As he gets closer to the player the music stops for a moment, 'leaving a pagan shape in the air'. The player then takes a deep breath and recommences playing: 'a base growl,/ and it started again, in a gutteral dance'.

The poet looks 'around the edge' of the rock and catches sight of the player. It is 'Littlebody', a leprechaun, and he is 'hugging' the bag of his uileann pipes 'under his left arm' and playing music 'with his eyes closed'. The poet slips and Littlebody suddenly becomes aware that he is being observed. He looks at the poet before making a desperate scramble to get away. He is oddly shaped and runs in a humorous manner, 'elbows out and neck back'.

But the poet calls on him to stop, telling him that he has been found and must now pay the price: 'Stop, Littlebody!/ I found you fair, and I want my due'. Littlebody stops, drops his pipes and spreads his arms out, waiting to see what the poet will do next. The poet recites a verse instructing Littlebody to hand over his bag of gold: 'surrender your purse/ with the ghostly gold'. Littlebody obeys the command and takes out a 'fat purse' and places it 'on a stone'. In response he too recites a verse, telling the poet: 'You found me fair,/ and I grant your wishes./ But we'll meet again,/ when I dance in your ashes'.

Having gone through the necessary ritual Littlebody sits down and gets ready he play the pipes again. Looking dejectedly 'off to one side' he tells the poet that he thought he would be able to play his music without distraction and audience. He says that sometimes you have to play music just for the sake of the music and not for any other end. He bemoans the fact that he has often to play to please a crowd and put on the sort of performance that the crowd expects:

I thought I was safe up here.
You have to give the music a while to itself sometimes,
up out of the huckstring –
jumping around in your green top hat
and showing your skills
with your eye on your income.

He runs his fingers 'up and down the stops' and with a 'solemn' face gives the 'bag a last squeeze'. A 'slow air' drifts 'out across the valley'. The leprechaun is a skilled player and the poet appreciates how 'his fingertips fondled all the right places'.

The poet decides to leave him and does not take the 'purse': 'I left him to himself./ And left the purse where it was'. The poet feels that he has all he needs 'for the while I have left// without taking unnecessary risks'. He makes his way back 'down to the main road' and thinks about the next time that he will meet Littlebody: 'with my mind on our next meeting'.

THEMES

Art

Kinsella avails of the traditional Irish myths about leprechauns in order to say something about art. The poem suggests that true art is created for its own sake and not for money or fame. Littlebody suggests this when he says that 'You have to give the music a while to itself sometimes,/ up out of the huckstring'. However, the production of art draws attention to the artist. Littlebody is happy to be playing music by himself but the sound attracts the attention of the poet and his playing is interrupted. The leprechaun had thought that he was 'safe' where he was and is disappointed to have been found.

However, artists also have to make a living and are sometimes forced to commercialise their art for profit. The leprechaun speaks of having to 'jump around in your green hat/ and showing your skills/ with your eye on your income'. In other words, he must put on a performance that is tailored for the market. People expect and want to see leprechauns in green top hats and so Littlebody obliges them because it pays him to do so. The art that gives him the most personal satisfaction, however, is produced away from the crowds.

Death

The final lines of the poem suggest that the poet is no longer a young man. He is growing old and says that he has all he needs for 'the while I have left'. With his youth behind him and his thoughts turning toward the end of his life he is not willing to take 'unnecessary risks'. As he leaves Littlebody he says that his mind was 'on our next meeting'. This will be when he is dead and Littlebody will dance in his ashes.

from *Belief and Unbelief*: Echo

Thomas Kinsella

LINE BY LINE

This poem describes a couple making a pilgrimage to a 'holy well'. They go there to perform a ritual, to tell the well everything about themselves. The ritual seems more pagan than Christian in character. Ireland has many holy wells that were originally sites of pagan ceremonies. The Celts believed that gods and spirits dwelled within these springs.

The couples relationship began many years ago. On that distant day they promised that they would one day go to the well and conduct the ceremony. Now that days has come. The well is located in the centre of a woods. The gates to the woods is broken and overgrown with thorns, suggesting that the well is not visited very often. The man clears the thorns that block the entrance to the wood and they walk hand in hand to the centre.

When they reach the well they speak into it, telling it many things about their lives: they 'told their tales'. They also speak their names into the well. In pagan times there was a superstition that if people knew your true name they would have power over you.

They finish speaking and begin to leave the well. However, the woman turns back and whispers something into the well's depths: 'whispered/ a final secret/ down to the water'. We get the impression that the man can't hear this secret thing she whispers.

THEMES

Memory

Kinsella was very interested in Celtic mythology, in the rituals and legends of pre-Christian Ireland. This poem depicts two people conducting just such a pagan ritual. Furthermore, like pagans they are superstitious about revealing their true names. It is possible that the couple are living in modern times and go to the well to carry out a ceremony that has been long forgotten in Ireland. This is suggested by the fact that the gate is broken and the woods overgrown.

The couple are haunted by some vague memory of this distant Celtic religion and seek to reconnect with it. The ceremony that they conduct is like some faint echo of a pagan ritual that once dominated Ireland. In this sense the poem parallels 'His Father's Hands' where the speaker is also haunted by pagan practices in Ireland's pre-Christian past. It is also similar to 'Littlebody' where the speaker calls upon Irish mythology and personifies greed in the form of a leprechaun.

This poem comes from a series called 'Belief and Unbelief' where Kinsella examines the topic of religious faith. This ancient ceremony might now appear ridiculous to us, but it is no more ridiculous perhaps than Christian practices might seem to people in the future.

Romantic love

The poem also examines the theme of romantic love and marriage. The couple are committed to telling the well everything about themselves. However, there is a secret that the woman does not want to tell in front of her husband. She turns back and whispers into the well so that her husband doesn't hear. The poem suggests that no matter how long a couple are together and no matter how well they know one another, they will always have secrets. We can never completely know the people we spend our lives with.

LANGUAGE

This poem uses the plain and simple diction of a fairy tale. There are several images that would not be out of place in such a legend, such as the overgrown woods, the path and the well.

SYLVIA PLATH
THEMES

MENTAL ANGUISH

Inner turmoil
Many of Plath's poems express feelings of inner turmoil, describing a speaker who is haunted by raging storms of emotion. In 'Finisterre' the sea's violent fury is often taken to represent Plath's tumultuous mental state.

'The Arrival of the Bee Box' also depicts mental turmoil. The sight and sound of the locked box fills the speaker with dread: 'The box is locked, it is dangerous'.

'Mirror' is another poem that illustrates mental turmoil. The woman in the poem is gripped by a fit of loneliness or despair, examining herself in the looking glass as she cries and wrings her hands: 'She rewards me with tears and an agitation of hand'. We get a sense that much of the woman's turmoil stems from the fact that she has lost her way in life, has lost her sense of her own identity.

'Elm' is perhaps one of Plath's greatest poems of mental turmoil, one in which the poet powerfully reveals her own anguished mental state. The female speaker in the poem is in an intensely agitated and tumultuous state of mind. She suffers from 'bad dreams', she seems to have experienced bouts of madness and she fears hitting rock 'bottom', complete and total mental desolation.

Perhaps the most disturbing aspect of 'Elm' is the way it suggests that there is no limit or extreme to human suffering. The elm claims to have known the 'bottom'. It has experienced the most intense possible degree of mental anguish. It is 'incapable of more knowledge', of dealing with any more mental suffering. However, we are left with the impression that more knowledge must be borne, that more suffering must yet be undergone.

There is a slight note of hope in 'Finisterre' that this mental turmoil will come to an end and the speaker can enter a new and tranquil mental space. The peasants mention a peaceful place 'tropical and blue', far from the furious waters of the bay where they live. Yet as the poem concludes we are left with the impression that such inner peace is a distant prospect, as distant as the faraway waters the peasants have 'never been'. 'The Arrival of the Bee Box' also features a note of hope. The speaker can overcome her fear of the bees by releasing them, rather like someone who is afraid of flying stepping onto a plane. At present the speaker is controlled by her terror of the bees. By releasing them, however, she will conquer her fear and empower herself. She will go from being powerless ('no Caesar') to being powerful ('sweet God'). If the speaker can overcome this seemingly irrational fear of the bee box perhaps she can also overcome the deeper mental turmoil that effects her.

Feelings of inadequacy
Some of Plath's poems explore the feelings of inadequacy and uncertainty that she felt as a mother. In 'Morning Song' the poet describes how she struggled to feel a bond with her child when it was born. The child is described as a somewhat alien being, likened initially to a 'statue' and then to a pool of water that exists remotely from the cloud that created it. Both descriptions suggest that the poet is struggling to feel the natural maternal bond that we might expect a mother to feel towards her new-born child. This feeling of inadequacy as a mother is also present in 'Child' where Plath describes the anguish that she feels at being unable to offer her child the kind of joyful experiences it needs.

Feelings of inadequacy are also explored in 'Mirror'. The speaker looks at her reflection with 'tears and an agitation of hands'. She turns away to the soft glow of candles and the moon, as if she does not like what she sees in the mirror.

Feelings of self-doubt are powerfully dramatised in 'Elm'. Plath is inhabited by her own self doubts just as the elm is inhabited by a 'dark' clawed creature with a murderous face.

In a sense the terms 'feelings of inadequacy' or an 'awareness of failings and failures' are too weak to describe Plath's mental state in this poem. The term 'self-loathing' might be nearer to the mark. The creature that inhabits the elm seems to represent a dark and loathsome aspect of her own personality, one that is 'malign' or evil and fills her with disgust.

Self-destructive thoughts

There are several instances in Plath's poetry where the speaker expresses what might be described as self-destructive thoughts or desires. Many readers feel that these desires surface in 'The Arrival of the Bee Box'. When the speaker imagines herself wearing the protective garments of a beekeeper, she describes the face-covering as a 'funeral veil'. There is a sense here that she is anticipating her own demise or on some level even desiring it.

A similar desire to be erased from human consciousness is also present in 'Poppies in July'. In this poem the speaker sees only two ways out of her numbing depression: experiencing intense physical pain or slipping into a blissful drug-induced trance: 'If I could bleed, or sleep!' She is desperate to escape from her numbed and neutral existence. She looks at the poppies and thinks that they resemble 'bloodied' mouths. This makes her long for her mouth to 'hurt like that'. And if she cannot suffer such pain or injury she wishes to lapse into a coma-like existence where she will feel and experience nothing at all. The poem closes with the poet imagining herself within a 'glass capsule' into which she longs for opiates to 'seep'. These 'liquors' will dull and still her until total oblivion is reached and the world fades away.

Such desires are arguably expressed in 'Finisterre' when the speaker describes herself walking into the sea-mist. She describes how this mist 'erases' the rocks and yet she enters it. It's as if on some level she desires to be erased from existence herself. She imagines the mist being composed of dead souls and yet she enters it, as if on some level she desires to join them in death. Many readers feel that the description of the souls almost choking the speaker also reflects her self-destructive desires: 'They stuff my mouth with cotton'.

A fear of total neutrality

'Black Rook In Rainy Weather' touches on one of Plath's most recurring themes: the dread of 'total neutrality' or lack of poetic inspiration. To a large extent for Plath writing was everything. For her, creative neutrality meant not only artistic frustration and inspiration but also a grey, blank and passionless existence. She would be plunged into a limbo-like existence similar to that endured by the ghosts of the drowned in 'Finisterre'.

In 'Morning Song' Plath describes how she struggled with such feelings of neutrality when her child was born. The poem depicts the poet and her husband standing 'round blankly as walls' suggesting that they are somewhat numb and feel no strong emotion about the arrival of their child.

NATURE

To Plath nature was often a source of inspiration. We see this in 'Black Rook in Rainy Weather' where the bird's shining feathers aid the speaker in her attempts at poetic composition. The sight of the bird allows her to patch together 'a content of sorts', to engage in some form of artistic creation. It helps stave off the fear of 'total neutrality', the fear that she will never again be sufficiently inspired to write a poem. 'Pheasant' is also a celebration of nature. Once again the speaker is inspired and ennobled by the sight of a bird, of this 'fine' thing that visits her garden. The poem praises the 'kingliness' of the pheasant, of this bright bird that fills the speaker with 'wonder'.

'The Arrival of the Beebox' and 'Pheasant' are both concerned with the power that humans sometimes wield over the natural world. In 'Pheasant' the poet's husband has threatened to kill the bird and it is now up to her to convince him that the pheasant's life is worth preserving. In 'The Arrival of the Bee Box' it is the poet herself who entertains the possibility of killing the bees that are in her possession: 'They can die, I need feed them nothing, I am the owner'. But she cannot be so cruel. In the end she decides to be 'sweet God' and 'set them free'.

PSYCHIC LANDSCAPES

There are many poems where Plath creates what she described as 'psychic landscapes'. She uses a scene from nature or an element of the natural world in order to convey an inner state of mind. In 'Black Rook in Rainy Weather' the speaker's dull and uninspired state of mind is reflected in the 'dull ruinous landscape' she trudges through and in the rainy, grey and 'desultory' atmosphere that dominates the scene.

This tendency is particularly evident in both 'Elm' and 'The Arrival of the Bee Box'. The bee box serves as a metaphor for Plath's turmoil-filled mind. The box seethes with furious black bees 'angrily clambering' over one another in a chaotic fashion. Similarly her mind seethes with dark, angry and negative emotions. The elm undergoes various tortures, which serve as metaphors for Plath's turmoil-filled mental state. It is inhabited by a dark creature which serves as a metaphor for Plath's feelings of inadequacy and what might be described as the dark side of her personality. 'Poppies in July' does something similar. The description of the field of poppies corresponds with and illustrates the neutrality and numbness that the poet is experiencing:

'Finisterre' paints a particularly rich and suggestive psychic landscape. The sea's violent fury is often taken to represent Plath's tumultuous mental state. The ocean is presented as a terrifyingly vast 'exploding' force that 'cannons' into the coastline, making an endless and oppressive roaring sound; a 'doom-noise'.

POETIC INSPIRATION

A spiritual view of inspiration

'Black Rook in Rainy Weather' presents an almost spiritual view of poetic inspiration. Poetic inspiration, the poem suggests, is a holy or sacred phenomenon. It is described as a rare and miraculous event. It is associated with the descent of angels. It is associated with a 'celestial' or heavenly burning. It is even associated with 'backtalk' from the heavens above, as if being inspired meant being spoken to by God.

Inspiration is presented as inducing almost a religious ecstasy in those lucky enough to experience it. When we are inspired the things we look at seem to 'shine'. An 'incandescent' light world seems to lean out of them. The sight of them is 'set on fire' in our eyes. Our 'senses are seized' and we stand rapt and awestruck before the world. On the whole, then, inspiration is presented as a 'celestial' phenomenon, something that is sent down to us from some heavenly realm.

Yet 'Black rook in Rainy Weather' also stresses that inspiration is something that happens in a random, haphazard and unpredictable way. It is described as an 'accident' and as 'spasmodic'. It is not something we can actively seek out. Instead we can only wait for it to strike us, if we are lucky enough to be in the right place at the right time. The poet's role is presented as one of waiting. She must stubbornly wait for inspiration to strike, all the while remaining 'politic' or alert, careful not to miss the magic moment if it does occur.

Exploring the unconscious

Plath felt that in order to be a true poet one had to explore one's unconscious mind, delving into the darkest depths of the psyche. This theme is particularly evident in 'The Arrival of the Bee Box'. The bee box can be taken to represent hidden aspects of the mind, the dark and mysterious parts the true poet must explore. Like the bee box our unconscious mind is almost completely sealed: we cannot know what it contains until we begin to explore it.

In 'Elm' the tree reaches into the soil with its 'great tap root', claiming to have known the 'bottom', to have reached into the earth's very foundations. This can be taken as a metaphor for the work of the poet's task of probing the depths of his or her own psyche. There is also a sense in which 'Mirror' explores this theme. The woman looking into the mirror's depths can be taken as a metaphor for this kind of-self-exploration.

In 'Finisterre' the ocean is often taken as a metaphor for the unconscious mind. Yet just as the peasants venture into the ocean and extract little shells from it, so the true poet must venture into the depths of his or her own psyche. Just as the peasants produce little toys from the fruit of their explorations, so the poet might create a 'pretty trinket' from her own mental explorations – a trinket that would, of course, take the form of a poem.

Plath was keenly aware that such an inner journey was a dangerous business and involved encountering all kinds of inner demons, dark thoughts, traumas and negative emotions that are usually kept hidden in the mind's deepest recesses. Some critics see the 'terrible fish' at the conclusion of 'Mirror' as not only representing old age but also these inner demons. Similarly, 'Finisterre' depicts the ocean, representing the unconscious mind, as a place of great danger, as being furious and treacherous; with 'no bottom, or anything on the other side of it'

This notion is particularly powerfully explored in 'The Arrival of the Bee Box'. Just as the speaker is terrified and disgusted by the bee box, so Plath was nervous about exploring her unconscious mind and horrified by the demons that might lurk there. By opening up her unconscious she will unleash her inner demons, just as the speaker will release the bees. Yet just as the speaker can't stay away from the bee box, so Plath was drawn back again and again to probe around the edges of her unconscious, for she felt that only by exploring this hidden aspect of herself could she create great poetry.

Total neutrality

We must remember that for Plath, writing was everything. She was someone who simply couldn't function unless she had the time and space to work on her poetry and many of her diary entries and letters give the impression that literature mattered as much to her as friendship or family life.

There is a sense in which 'Black Rook in Rainy Weather' touches on this artistic insecurity. The speaker is completely uninspired and is 'skeptical' about the possibilities of such inspiration occurring. She dreads 'total neutrality', losing her poetic talent. For her, such creative neutrality meant not only artistic frustration but also a grey, blank and passionless existence. She would be plunged into a limbo-like state of being.

Many readers feel that 'Mirror' also touches on this anxiety, that it depicts a situation where the 'front' or 'facade' of the perfect housewife is in danger of choking the artist within. They suggest that the poem's speaker is in danger of forgetting about the artist she really is and gazes into the mirror's depths in a desperate attempt to reconnect with her own creativity. A similar note is struck by 'The Times Are Tidy'. The poem describes a society that has 'beaten the hazard', that has seen off all threats and enemies. Technological advances make life easy, producing an abundance of wonderful material goods. Such a safe and technologically advanced society might be a comfortable place to live but it will also be a dull and uninspiring place to live, especially if you are a poet.

ORDER & CHAOS

'Black Rook in Rainy Weather' presents the world as a random and chaotic place. It suggests that there is no pattern or meaning to the way that things happen. Everything happens randomly. The leaves fall haphazardly, not according to some 'ceremony' or hidden pattern. Studying events reveals no 'portent' no sign of deeper meaning. Inspiration, too, is random and chaotic. It is 'spasmodic', occurring in a way that is entirely haphazard and unpredictable.

In 'Finisterre' the sea is associated with chaos. Perhaps its key feature is its 'formlessness'. It is presented as a vast, shapeless void churning chaotically. Order, on the other hand, is represented by the solidity and stableness of the coastline. Similarly, in 'The Arrival of the Bee Box' the bees are a chaotic force, swarming hectically and frenziedly within their box. They are like a wild and disorderly mob. Only the box imposes order on them, containing their fury. Tellingly the poem's opening lines associate the box with order: 'I ordered this, this clean wood box'.

A similar attitude to order and chaos is evident in 'The Times Are Tidy'. This poem was written during the 1950s not long after the Second World War had ended. It was a decade of conformity and conservatism in America. There was a sense that the forces of evil had been destroyed and that the future was safe. However, to many artists of the time such a society appeared dull and materialistic. Plath characterises it as the 'province of the stuck record'. It is a tedious place of order and regularity where things happen mechanically in a perfectly predictable manner and there is no need for imagination or heroics. In fact, human input is barely required as things turn round of their 'own accord'.

There is a sense in which Plath feels that society needs a degree of fear and unpredictability in order to avoid becoming boring and complacent. She seems to feel that society needs 'hazards' or dangers. These could be the hazards of legend and superstition that terrified people in medieval times or they could be the all-to-real hazards that America had fought against in the world wars.

Sylvia Plath
The Times Are Tidy

LINE BY LINE

The poet considers the world in which she lives to be unexciting, predictable and dull. Plath refers to it as 'province of the stuck record'. Each day is the same and nothing new and exciting ever happens.

The world in which she is living is now too safe. Heroes are no longer needed because all threats have been eliminated: 'History's beaten the hazard'. The evil forces of old have 'withered … from lack of action'. The last witch or 'crone' was burnt over eighty years ago.

Everything is thought of in an ordered and rational manner. There is no longer a sense of wonder or magic in the world. When people stopped believing in witches they also stopped believing in magic potions ('love-hot herb') and talking cats.

Technological innovation means that skilled craftspeople are no longer needed. The 'most watchful cooks go jobless' because machines have been built to do the work that was once done by hand: 'the mayor's rotisserie turns/ Round of its own accord'.

Plath ends by saying that 'the children' are better off in this ordered and technologically advanced world. Dairy production is now greatly improved: 'The cow milks cream an inch thick'. But of course she does not believe this. The last lines of the poem are ironic and imply that children are actually worse off in such an unimaginative world. They lack excitement, magic and wonder.

THEMES
Order & chaos

This poem was written during the 1950s not long after the Second World War had ended. It was a decade of conformity and conservatism in America. There was a sense that the forces of evil had been destroyed and that the future was safe. To many artists of the time such a society appeared dull and materialistic.

In 'The Times Are Tidy' Plath characterises such a place as the 'province of the stuck record'. It is a tedious place of order and regularity. Things happen mechanically in a perfectly predictable manner and there is no need for imagination or heroics. In fact, human imput is barely required as things turn round of their 'own accord'. There is no 'hazard', chaos has been eliminated.

Plath contrasts this period with times gone by. She evokes a romantic and fantastic world of knights, dragons and witches. Such a world is full of adventure and heroics. The poem imagines the knight 'riding against the lizard' or dragon. This imagined world is chaotic and dangerous. Its inhabitants would never know what terrible events lay in store for them. In contrast with the world of the 'stuck record' it is a place fear and uncertainty.

Poetic inspiration

Of course, there never was a time when dragons existed and knights were called on to ride 'against the lizard'. But there was a time when people believed in the existence of such things as dragons and 'talking' cats. These were superstitious times, full of fear and uncertainty, but they were also times of great imagination.

'The Times Are Tidy', therefore, suggests that a society that has 'beaten the hazard' and become technologically advanced might produce wonderful material goods, such as cream that is 'an inch thick', but it will be a dull and uninspiring place to live, especially if you are a poet. Ultimately Plath favours a world of fear and unpredictability because it stimulates the imagination and prevents complacency. She feared nothing more than feeling neutral and uninspired. She needed a certain amount of chaos in her life in order to be able to write.

Black Rook in Rainy Weather

This is a poem about poetry, about the agonising wait for the inspiration that makes a poem possible. Throughout history poets have been inspired by nature, by birds, storms and sunsets. In this poem the speaker longs for nature to 'speak to her', to provide her with the inspiration for a poem.

LINE BY LINE

Setting the scene
It is late autumn or early winter, what Plath memorably describes as the 'season of fatigue'. The weather is 'desultory', suggesting that it is a dull and miserable day. It is raining and the falling leaves are 'spotted' with moisture.

The speaker trekking through a grim and depressing stretch of countryside: 'a dull ruinous landscape'. As she trudged stubbornly through this wintry scene she observes a rook perched on a branch: 'On the stiff twig up there/ Hunches a wet black rook'. The weather is so miserable that the rook sits 'hunched' upon its perch.

What is inspiration?
To be inspired is to experience a 'radiance', a strange optical illusion or trick of the light. It is to see the world in an intense and heightened way, as if everything around you was filled with light: it 'sets the sight on fire/ In [your] eye'.

She imagines what the rook would look like if she was to experience such a moment of inspiration right now. Its feathers would 'shine'. It would captivate her senses. Her eyelids would be 'hauled up', almost as if they were glued open. She would be unable to close her eyes or look away from the blazing bird.

The speaker thinks of artistic inspiration as a kind of religious experience, as something holy and spiritual:

- She refers to it on three separate occasions as a 'miracle'.
- She twice describes it as an angel, as if she thinks of it as a creature of fire and light descending from heaven and exploding into the artist's life: 'whatever angel may choose to flare/ Suddenly at my elbow'.
- She wittily describes it as 'backtalk' from the sky, as if being inspired meant being spoken to by God.

The arrival of inspiration is 'rare' and it is completely 'spasmodic' or unpredictable. It is something that happens randomly and accidentally. Therefore, the speaker is completely 'ignorant' as to whether she will be inspired or as to what form her inspiration might take.

The speaker's desire for inspiration
As she trudges through this wintry landscape we get the impression that the speaker has not experienced inspiration for some time. She longs to be inspired, to experience some of the 'backtalk' from the heavens mentioned above. Unfortunately, however, for her the sky is 'mute'. Furthermore, she does not really expect to be inspired any time soon: 'I do not expect a miracle/ Or an accident'. She is quite 'skeptical' about the possibility of such an event occurring.

Yet the speaker has not completely given up hope. She feels there is still a possibility that inspiration might strike her, even in a landscape as depressing as this one: 'for it could happen/ Even in this dull ruinous landscape'. She will therefore tread warily and be 'politic' or careful, determined not to miss the moment if it does occur.

The poem concludes on a note of defiance and grim determination. The speaker will be 'stubborn'. She is determined to endure the 'long wait' until the angel of inspiration descends blazing into her life: 'The wait's begun again,/ The long wait for the angel'.

The minor light
The speaker also describes a second and lesser type of inspiration. Proper inspiration is associated with angels, blazing lights and 'backtalk' from the heavens. This lesser inspiration is associated with only a 'minor light'. Proper inspiration is associated with nature while this lesser inspiration is associated with domestic scenes.

Sylvia Plath

The speaker describes what happens when this lesser inspiration strikes. Common household objects seem consumed by heavenly or 'celestial' fire and a blazing or 'incandescent' light pours out of them. 'light may still/ Lean incandescent// Out of a kitchen table or chair'.

This lesser inspiration can 'hallow' or make sacred a moment that would otherwise be completely unimportant: 'hallowing an interval/ Otherwise inconsequent'. It is presented, then, as a holy and benevolent force, associated with honour love and largesse (generosity).

The speaker desires proper inspiration and all that goes with it. Yet she feels she 'honestly can't complain' as long as she has this lesser inspiration and its 'minor light'. She will always long for proper inspiration but as long as this lesser inspiration is part of her life she will be able to get by.

Stanza 7, therefore, can be read in two ways. Perhaps the speaker is suggesting that if she's lucky proper inspiration will strike her and she will be able to create a poem: 'With luck … I shall/ Patch together a content of sorts'. However, she might also be suggesting that even in the absence of proper inspiration she will attempt to patch something together from the moments of lesser inspiration she has been lucky enough to experience.

THEMES

Poetic inspiration
A spiritual view of inspiration

'Black Rook in Rainy Weather' presents an almost spiritual view of inspiration. Poetic inspiration, the poem suggests, is a holy or sacred phenomenon. It is described as a rare and miraculous event. It is associated with the descent of angels. It is associated with a 'celestial' or heavenly burning. It is even associated with 'backtalk' from the heavens above, as if being inspired meant being spoken to by God.

Inspiration is presented as inducing almost a religious ecstasy in those lucky enough to experience it. When we are inspired the things we look at seem to 'shine'. An 'incandescent' light world seems to lean out of them. The sight of them is 'set on fire' in our eyes. Our 'senses are seized' and we stand rapt and awestruck before the world. On the whole, then, inspiration is presented as a 'celestial' phenomenon, something that is sent down to us from some heavenly realm.

As we have noted Plath discusses two different types of inspiration in this poem: proper inspiration and lesser inspiration. Proper inspiration is associated with angels, blazing lights and 'backtalk' from the heavens. Lesser inspiration is associated with only a 'minor light'. It seems that proper inspiration is associated with nature (with things like the rook perched on its branch) while lesser inspiration is associated with domestic scenes (with things like kitchen tables and chairs).

The randomness of inspiration
Yet it is equally important to note that inspiration is described as an 'accident'. It is 'spasmodic', something that happens in a random, haphazard and unpredictable way. It is not something we can actively seek out. Instead, we can only wait for it to strike us, if we are lucky enough to be in the right place at the right time.

The speaker, then, presents her role as one of waiting. She must stubbornly wait for inspiration to strike, all the while remaining 'politic' or alert, careful not to miss the magic moment if it does occur: 'The wait's begun again,/ The long wait for the angel,/ For that rare, random descent'.

Total neutrality
This poem powerfully depicts artistic insecurity. The speaker is completely uninspired. She is creatively neutral or unengaged. The sky is 'mute'. She hasn't experience any of the backtalk from the heavens associated with inspiration. She is 'skeptical' about such inspiration occurring. She is haunted by the fear of total creative neutrality, that her artistic gift will desert her completely preventing her from ever writing another poem.

Inspiration from the natural world
This poem echoes 'Pheasant' in that it shows how the natural world can provide poetic inspiration. In this poem the poet longs to be inspired by the rook 'Arranging and rearranging its feathers'. In 'Pheasant' the speaker is inspired by the 'kingliness' and 'wonder' of the pheasant that has roosted in her garden.

Order & chaos
'Black Rook in Rainy Weather' presents the world as a random and chaotic place. It suggests that there is no pattern or meaning to the way that things happen. Everything happens randomly. The leaves fall haphazardly, not according to some 'ceremony' or hidden pattern. Studying them reveals no 'portent' no sign of deeper meaning. Even inspiration is random and chaotic. It is 'spasmodic', occurring in a way that is entirely haphazard and unpredictable. The speaker, therefore, believes that things happen chaotically rather than according to God's plan. She therefore doesn't look for any sign of purpose or 'design' in the natural world around her. The speaker may think of inspiration in spiritual and almost religious terms but we are left with the distinct impression that her outlook on the world is atheistic.

Mental anguish
There is a sense in which this poem touches on one of Plath's most recurring themes: that of mental anguish. Plath dreads 'total neutrality', losing her poetic talent. We must remember that to a large extent for Plath writing was everything. She was someone who simply couldn't function unless she had the time and space to work on her poetry and many of her diary entries and letters give the impression that literature mattered as much to her as friendship or family life.

For her such creative neutrality meant not only artistic frustration and inspiration but also a grey, blank and passionless existence. She would be plunged into a limbo-like existence similar to that endured by the ghosts of the drowned in 'Finisterre', into the bank numbness endured by the speaker of 'Poppies in July'. A similar blankness is arguably described in 'Child', where the speaker compares her life to a 'dark/ Ceiling without a star'.

Psychic landscapes
There are many poems where Plath creates what she described as 'psychic landscapes'. She uses a scene from nature or an element of the natural world in order to convey an inner state of mind. This tendency is evident in 'Elm', 'Finisterre', 'The Arrival of the Bee Box' and 'Poppies in July'. In this poem the speaker's dull and uninspired state of mind is reflected in the 'dull ruinous landscape' she trudges through and in the rainy, grey and 'desultory' atmosphere that dominates the scene.

LANGUAGE

The poem, it is important to note, has a 'hidden' rhyme scheme in which the first lines of each stanza rhyme or almost rhyme ('there … fire … desire … chair') as do the second lines ('rook … seek … backtalk … took … walk') and so on. It has been claimed that the poem's unusual structure contradicts its argument that the world is a random and chaotic place.

It is possible, after all, that a hidden order lies behind the apparently chaotic and random events we see around us just as there is a hidden pattern behind the seemingly random arrangement of the poem's lines.

Plath skillfully conjures a rather depressing atmosphere. She depicts a 'dull ruinous landscape' of rain and falling leaves appropriate to the 'season of fatigue' that is late autumn or early winter, a time when nature itself seems tired and worn.

This poem features a great deal of assonance, in particular patterns of repeated broad-vowel sound. These slow our reading of the lines in a way that is appropriate to the rather depressing landscape the poem describes. The movement of the verse brings to mind the speaker trudging stubbornly through this grim winter scene. We see this in the following phrases:

- 'Arranging and rearranging its feathers in the rain'.
- 'Thus hallowing an interval/ Otherwise inconsequent'.
- 'Even in this dull ruinous landscape'.
- 'Trekking stubborn through this season/ Of fatigue'.

We see alliteration in lines 29–30 with their repeated 's' sounds and in line 40 with its repeated 'r' sounds. This creates a pleasant verbal music appropriate to the longed-for moment of inspiration the lines describe.

Another important feature of this poem is its use of personification. Inspiration, an abstract quality or concept, is depicted as a kind of person, a supernatural angel that can descend from heaven at any moment and appear like a burst of flame beside the speaker: 'whatever angel may choose to flare/ Suddenly at my elbow'.

Like several of Plath's poems, 'Elm' personifies an inanimate object, in this case an elm tree. The tree is given a voice and allowed to express its feelings. It talks to the speaker, who seems to live in a house right next to it. The speaker reports the words of the elm, telling us what it says to her.

Morning Song

Sylvia Plath

LINE BY LINE

LINES 1–9

The poem describes the poet's response to the birth of her child.

The parent's lovemaking set the child's life in motion. The poet likens the creation of life to the winding of a watch: 'Love set you going like a fat gold watch'.

What happens when the child is born?

When the child is born the midwife slaps its footsoles and it begins to cry. The parents express their enthusiasm at the birth. They 'magnify' the 'arrival' of the child and 'echo' each other's sentiments.

What sort of world is the child born into?

The world into which the child has been born seems cold and unsympathetic. It is unceremoniously greeted with a slap on the footsoles. The room in which it is born is unhomely and lacking in warmth: 'a drafty museum'. There is a sense in which the world is coldly indifferent to the child's existence. The child must take its place 'among the elements'. The word 'elements' might be a reference to the harsh weather that the child will have to endure or it might refer to the basic substances of earth, wind, fire and water. Either way, the world seems unwelcoming.

How is the child described?

The child is described as a 'New statue', perhaps because it is something to be observed and commented upon. It is also likened to a 'fat gold watch' in the opening line. Both descriptions are lacking in tenderness and warmth.

The child is also described as vulnerable. The poet refers to its 'nakedness' and its 'bald cry', and says that it must now take its place among the 'elements'.

How do the parent's respond to the birth of their child?

The child's birth unsettles the parents. They seem unsure about how to act: 'We stand round blankly as walls'. The child's vulnerability and need for protection makes them feel insecure: 'your nakedness/ Shadows our safety'.

How does the poet feel about becoming a mother?

The poet seems to feel unsure about her relationship with the child. Now that the child has been born she does not feel bonded to it. She says that she can no more be considered the mother of the child than a cloud can be considered the mother of the rain that it creates and which forms a mirror-like pool upon the ground: 'I am no more your mother/ Than the cloud that distills a mirror'. And just as the cloud's destruction or 'effacement' by the wind will be reflected in the pool it has created, so too will the poet's destruction with age be reflected in the child's eyes. The poet seems to be implying she has created something that will strengthen and grow while she begins to wither and fade with age.

Lines 10–18

In the second half of the poem the poet is at home with the child. It is night-time. The child is asleep in a room decorated with 'pink roses'. It breathes softly and rhythmically. Its gentle breath is likened to that of a moth. Its breathing sounds like the sea heard from a great distance: 'A far sea'.

The poet wakes 'to listen' to the child. The moment that the child begins to cry she gets up to feed it. She is wearing a 'floral' nightgown. Her tiredness is evident when she says that she 'stumbles from bed'. Her breasts are heavy with milk and she likens herself to a cow that needs to be milked: 'cow-heavy'. When she picks up the child its 'mouth opens clean as a cat's' ready to feed.

As she feeds the child the day breaks. Slowly the windows brighten and the stars disappear from the sky: 'The window square// Whitens and swallows its dull stars'. When the child has finished feeding it makes some happy vowel-like sounds: 'And now you try/ Your handful of notes;/ The clear vowels'.

THEMES

Femininity & motherhood

The poem shows how becoming a mother can be a difficult experience. When her child is born the poet experiences doubts and uncertainties about her role as a mother:

- She does not seem to know how to respond to the birth of her child. She and her husband 'stand around blankly as walls', not knowing what to do.
- She feels less secure now that the child has come into her life. She says that the child's 'nakedness/ Shadows' her own safety. Before the child was born she only had to worry about herself. Now, however, her sense of own sense of security has been overshadowed by the child's vulnerability.
- She initially feels distant from the child. She likens herself to a cloud that has shed its rain and no longer bears a connection to that which it once carried.

However, when the poet is at home with the child she begins to feel more at ease and comfortable about her role as a mother. The description of her rising during the night to feed the child is tender and suggests that the poet is less troubled by doubt and uncertainty. Her description of herself as 'cow-heavy' introduces a light-heartedness into the poem, as does the mentioning of her 'Victorian' floral nightgown.

Like 'Child' 'Morning Song' suggests that motherhood is not a straightforwardly joyous and natural experience. The responsibilty that comes with the role can be overwhelming and it can be hard to adjust to the fact that there is now another person in your life that needs your care and protection. However, unlike 'Child' this poem ends on a positive and rather joyous, uplifting note with the description of the child's 'notes' rising 'like balloons'.

Mental anguish: inadequacy

There is a sense in the first half of the poem that the poet does not feel adequate as a mother. Now that her child is born she no longer feels a bond with it. The child is described as a somewhat alien being, likened initially to a 'statue' and then to a pool of water that exists remotely from the cloud that created it. Both descriptions suggest that the poet is struggling to feel the natural maternal bond that we might expect a mother to feel towards her new-born child. This feeling of inadequacy as a mother is also present in 'Child' where Plath describes the anguish that she feels because she is unable to offer her child the kind of joyful experiences that a child ought to have.

Neutrality

When the poet's child is born both she and her husband struggle with their response to the birth. The description of them standing 'round blankly as walls' suggests that they are somewhat numb and feel no strong emotion about the arrival of their child. That their 'voices echo, magnifying' the arrival suggests that they feel the need to put on a show of joy in order to mask their lack of natural feeling. Because she does not experience immediate joy the poet is moved to say that she cannot be defined as the child's mother. However, the poem eventually shows how with time the poet comes to feel a bond with the child and by the end of the poem we sense that she is no longer feeling neutral about the experience.

LANGUAGE

The poem features a number of unusual similes and metaphors.

- The poet likens the child to 'a fat gold watch'. Perhaps this comparison is a reference to the description of God as watchmaker. It suggests the complexity of human life. The fact that the watch is gold suggests that the child is valuable. However, it is a rather cold and mechanical comparison and hints at the poet's struggle to come to terms with her new role as mother.
- She also describes the newborn child as a 'New statue'. This is an especially cold and lifeless comparison to make with a baby. It suggests that the poet feels detached from the child.
- She also compares her connection to the child to that of the connection between a cloud and the rain it has shed. Again this comparison highlights the poet's struggle to feel a bond with the child to whom she has just given birth.

Some of the poem's similes and metaphors are a little easier to grasp.

- She says that she and her husband 'stand round blankly as walls'.

- She likens the opening of the child's mouth as it begins to feed to that of a cat: 'Your mouth opens clean as a cat's'.
- She compares the sound of the child breathing to the sound of a distant sea and suggests that it is as faint and gentle, like the breathing of a moth.

The poem also features personification. Plath says that the window 'swallows' the stars as morning comes.

Mirror

LINE BY LINE

The mirror speaks

Like several of Plath's poems 'Mirror' gives voice to an inanimate object. The mirror is silver. (This may refer to a silver frame around its reflective surface. Alternatively the reflective surface itself may be made from polished silver). It is square or rectangular in shape, 'being four-cornered'.

It hangs opposite a pink speckled wall. The mirror claims to stare continuously at this wall, 'meditating' upon it: 'I have looked at it so long'. Every night it becomes too dark for it to see the wall opposite it. Furthermore, people regularly check their reflections in the mirror's surface, blocking its view of the wall: 'faces and darkness separate us over and over'.

The mirror has spent so long 'meditating' in this way that it now believes the pink wall is part of itself: 'I have looked at it so long/ I think it is a part of my heart'. These lines are oddly touching. We get the impression that the mirror has somehow fallen in love with the speckled wall opposite it.

The mirror stresses how accurate it is

The mirror stresses how accurately it reflects anything that is put in front of it. It is 'exact' and 'truthful'. It shows each person and object 'Just as it is'.

The mirror claims to 'swallow' all it sees. This is a metaphor for how mirrors create the illusion of depth. The reflection of a given object seems to be inside a double of the room we're standing in. As if it's been 'swallowed' or taken inside the mirror's world.

The mirror claims to have no feelings whatsoever toward those who examine themselves in its surface. It neither 'loves' nor 'dislikes' them and has no biases or prejudices toward them: 'I have no preconceptions'. It doesn't blur or alter reflections in order to flatter those it likes or hurt the feelings of those it hates. Everything it shows is 'unmisted by love or dislike'.

Very often people are disappointed by what they see when they look in the mirror. Most people want to look younger, thinner and sexier. The mirror, however, refuses to be blamed for any dismay or disappointment people might feel when they examine themselves in its surface. It is not 'cruel', having no interest in making them feel bad about themselves. It is simply being 'truthful', doing its job of reflecting the world as it really is: 'I am not cruel only truthful'.

The mirror as a kind of god

The mirror depicts itself as a kind of God: 'I am … the eye of a little god, four-cornered'. This comparison is not as strange as it might first sound. People, after all, pay an almost religious devotion to their reflections. We spend a great deal of time and energy in an effort to keep ourselves young and beautiful, and all in an effort to make sure the mirror is kind to us when we stare into it.

This description brings to mind the other meaning of the word 'exact' which is to demand payment. The mirror is a kind of God that exacts tribute or payment from those who worship it. The poem suggests that we are willing to pay a high price in sweat and money in order that the mirror will show us what we want to see: 'I am silver and exact'.

The mirror & its owner
Stanza 2 describes the relationship between the mirror and the woman who owns it. This woman seems to be mentally anguished. She is regularly gripped by fits of loneliness and despair that involve 'tears and an agitation of hands'. She spends a great deal of time staring in the mirror, gazing at her reflection in an attempt to understand herself.

The mirror needs the woman. We get the impression that it looks forward to her daily visits and would be lonely without them: 'Each morning it is her face that replaces the darkness'. The mirror acts almost like the woman's faithful servant, loyally continuing to reflect her back even when she turns away from it: 'I see her back, and reflect it faithfully'.

The woman also needs the mirror: 'I am important to her'. The mirror is important to the woman in a casual, everyday sense. (How else could she check her appearance before going out?). Yet it is also important to her in a psychological sense. She returns to the mirror again and again, gazing into it in an attempt to reach self-understating, to find out 'what she really is'.

An unequal relationship
We get a sense, however, that the relationship between the mirror and the woman is an unequal one. While the mirror is confined to one place the woman enjoys the freedom to move around: 'She comes and goes'.

The mirror describes the woman sitting in candlelight or gazing out her window at the moon: 'Then she turns to those liars, the candles or the moon'. There is a sense in these lines that it is jealous of the candles and the moon, resentful of the fact that the woman is looking at them instead into its own reflective glass.

The mirror, it seems, feels hurt and betrayed when the woman turns away from it. Yet even when she does so, it remains faithful to her, loyally reflecting her back: 'I see her back and reflect it faithfully'.

All the mirror gets in return for this loyalty is the opportunity to witness the woman's distress: 'She rewards me with tears'. According to several critics the tone here is one of bitterness and sarcasm, as if the mirror feels the sight of the woman's tears isn't much of a 'reward' for its faithful service.

A terrible fish
The mirror compares itself to a lake. The comparison between the mirror and a lake is obvious. Like a lake the mirror has a flat reflective surface. It is possible, on a calm day, to study one's reflection in a lake just as it is in a mirror.

The mirror has recorded the slow ageing of the woman. When the woman looks at herself in the mirror she can see traces of the child she once was. Those traces, however, become fainter and fainter as time goes on. The mirror uses a striking metaphor to describe this process, saying that the woman 'has drowned a young girl' in its depths.

Every day the woman wakes up and looks in the mirror and every day an older version of herself looks back. With each passing day she sees the old woman she will one day become is closer and closer. Another powerful metaphor is used to depict this process, the mirror declaring that old age is a fish swimming out the lake's depths and rising up toward her: 'in me an old woman/ Rises toward her day after day, like a terrible fish'.

THEMES

Mental anguish
Inner turmoil
Like many of Plath's poems this depicts mental turmoil. The woman in the poem is gripped by a fit of loneliness or despair, examining herself in the looking glass as she cries and wrings her hands: 'She rewards me with tears and an agitation of hand'. Similar emotional turmoil is depicted in 'Elm', 'The Arrival of the Bee Box' and 'Finisterre'.

We get a sense that much of the woman's turmoil stems from the fact that she has lost her way in life, has lost her sense of her own identity. She gazes into the mirror in an attempt to locate and reconnect with her true self. It's as if staring at her own reflection allows her to explore the depths of her own psyche and discover what really makes her who she is: 'Now I am a lake. A woman bends over me,/ Searching my reaches'.

Inadequacy
Several of Plath's poems touch on the notion of inadequacy and worthlessness. We see this in 'Child', 'Elm' and 'The Arrival of the Bee Box'. Such feelings are also explored in 'Mirror', where the speaker looks at her reflection with 'tears and an agitation of hands'. She turns away to the soft glow of candles and the moon, as if she does not like what she sees in the mirror. There are several possible reasons for these feelings of inadequacy:

- Perhaps she feels that her personal appearance does not measure up to the standards of beauty demanded by the fashion industry.
- Or perhaps when she looks into the mirror she is reminded of what she sees as the failings of her personality.
- Or perhaps seeing her own reflection reminds her that she is somehow living a lie, presenting a false impression of herself to the world.

The notion of inadequacy brings to mind the depiction of the mirror as something threatening and menacing: as something that swallows all it sees, as an exacting God, or as a lake with treacherous depths. Self-examination, the poem reminds us, can be a dangerous business, leading to all sorts of negative emotions.

Old age
The poem's last two lines mark another shift of direction, introducing the theme of old age and death. We get a sense that the woman is also troubled by the prospect of impending old age. There is something unsettling and disturbing in this depiction of old age as a 'terrible fish', as some monstrous creature of the deep that each of us will someday have to face.

Love
It is worth pointing out that the mirror itself also seems to feel psychological distress. This stems from its unequal relationship with the woman. As we have seen the woman can come and go but the mirror cannot. Even the woman is unfaithful the mirror continues to reflect her back faithfully. When the mirror declares that 'I am important to her' we almost get the feeling that it is trying to convince itself of this fact. 'Elm' is another poem that describes mental anguish arising from a failed relationship.

Poetic inspiration
Plath felt under pressure to conform to the ideal of the perfect 1950s American young woman: to marry, have children and be a successful mother and housewife. Yet she also harboured the burning ambition to be a great writer. She worried that these two goals were incompatible: 'Will I be a secretary – a self-rationalising housewife, secretly jealous of my husband's ability to grow intellectually & professionally while I am impeded – will I submerge my embarrassing desires &aspirations, refuse to face myself, and go either mad or become neurotic?'

Many readers feel that 'Mirror' touches on this anxiety, that it depicts a situation where the 'front' or 'facade' of the perfect housewife is in danger of choking the artist within. They suggest that the poem's speaker is in danger of forgetting about the artist she really is and gazes into the mirror's depths in a desperate attempt to reconnect with her own creativity.

Plath felt that in order to be a true poet one had to explore one's conscious mind, delving into the darkest depths of the psyche. There is a sense in which 'Mirror' explores this theme. The woman looking into the mirror's depths can be taken as a metaphor for this kind of self-exploration.

Plath was keenly aware that such an inner journey involved encountering all kinds of inner demons, dark thoughts and emotions that are usually kept hidden in the mind's deepest recesses. Some critics see the 'terrible fish' at the poem's conclusion as not only representing old age but also these inner demons. 'Elm', 'Finisterre' and 'The Arrival of the Bee Box' are other poems that deal with this topic.

Femininity & motherhood
It is also possible to read 'Mirror' as a comment on the pressure women feel to meet certain standards of beauty, pressure that comes from films, magazines and advertising. (Nowadays it could be argued that men are also subject to such pressure – unlike when Plath wrote the poem). We see this in the depiction of the mirror as a kind of God that exacts tribute or payment. Women, the poem suggests, will pay a

high price in order that the mirror will be kind to them. The psychological dangers associated with this pressure are suggested by the description of the mirror having treacherous depths and swallowing all it sees.

As we have seen 'Mirror' also touches on femininity in the way it can be taken to depict the conflict between Plath's desire to meet society's expectations of what a woman should be and her desire to be a great artist.

LANGUAGE

Personification

An interesting feature of 'Mirror' is its use of 'personification', where an inanimate object is given human characteristics. The mirror is presented as a 'thinking being', a character with thoughts, ideas and emotions. The poem endows the mirror with human traits such as truthfulness, faithfulness and jealousy. It even has a relationship, of sorts, with its owner, the rather disturbed woman on whose wall it hangs.

Tone

An important feature of this poem is the shifts in tone it contains. At times the mirror seems confident and assured. It is convinced of its accuracy and truthfulness. It thinks of itself as a kind of God. It even seems somewhat menacing: swallowing all it sees, exacting payment, having treacherous and hidden depths. It seems casually indifferent to the feelings of those who examine themselves in its surface: 'I am not cruel only truthful'.

Yet there are also moments when the mirror's tone is one of need and sorrow. There is something almost pathetic about the way it seems to have fallen in love with the piece of wall opposite it. A similar tone is evident when the mirror describes its jealousy of the candles and the moon. We also see this when it describes how it remains faithful to the woman even when she turns away from it, loyally reflecting her back: 'I see her back and reflect it faithfully'. When the mirror declares that 'I am important to her' we get the feeling that it is trying to convince itself. A more bitter sarcastic tone is evident in line 14. It's as if the mirror feels the sight of the woman's tears isn't much of a 'reward' for its faithful service.

Metaphor & simile

There are several interesting metaphors and similes in this poem:

- Using a fine metaphor the mirror compares itself to the 'eye of a little God'.
- The mirror compares itself to a lake and the woman to someone on the lake shore, staring into the water's murky depths.
- The mirror uses a striking metaphor to describe the process of getting older, saying that the woman 'has drowned a young girl' in its depths. Another powerful metaphor is used to depict this process, the mirror declaring that old woman is swimming out the lake's depths and rising up toward her: 'in me an old woman/ Rises toward her day after day'.
- In a final striking simile this swimming old woman is compared to a 'terrible fish'.

The fact that poem has two nine-line stanzas seems to reflect its title. There is a sense in which each stanza reflects or mirrors the other. Several critics have pointed out how the poem's opening stanza is like a child's riddle. If the poem was stripped of its title it would be a challenge to work out what object was speaking.

Finisterre

Finisterre, which means land's end, is the westernmost tip of Brittany, in north-west France. Plath visited Finisterre in 1960 with her husband, the poet Ted Hughes. Finisterre is a bleak and rugged headland frequently battered by high winds and stormy seas. The treacherous waters below it have caused so many shipwrecks and drownings that it is known as the bay of the dead.

LINE BY LINE

The land

Finisterre is depicted as a 'gloomy' place: It is a headland of grim, black cliffs. These cliffs are described as 'admonitory', meaning they seem to warn those who see them to stay away. All that grows on them are weak and withering 'trefoils', little three-leaved plants that are 'close to death'.

Rocky outcrops protrude from the water. They are worn and brittle, like the 'knuckled and rheumatic' fingers of an old man. Other large rocks lurk threateningly beneath the water's surface: they 'hide their grudges under the water'. Furthermore, many smaller rocks seem to have been 'dumped' into the ocean. These, too, contribute to the bay's gloominess: 'Now it is only gloomy, a dump of rocks'.

The sea

The ocean is presented as menacing and aggressive. It seems terrifyingly vast: 'With no bottom, or anything on the other side of it'. It is an 'exploding' force that 'cannons' into the coastline. It makes an endless and oppressive roaring sound, what Plath describes as a 'doom-noise'.

Its erosion of the land is depicted as a military campaign. It slowly reduces the cliffs to little rocks that litter the seascape like corpses, casualties of its endless assault on the coastline: 'Leftover soldiers from old, messy wars'. The description of the sea 'cannoning' and 'exploding' reinforces our sense of it as a hostile military force.

The poem's opening statement, 'This was the land's end', can be read in two ways. On one level it refers to the fact that Finisterre is one of continental Europe's

westernmost points. On another level, however, it can be read as stating that this was the end of the land's existence. The sea seems filled with such apocalyptic fury that it threatens to swallow the entire coastline.

The souls of the drowned

Plath is reminded of all the people who drowned off the coast of Finisterre. She imagines that the souls of these poor people remain somehow trapped in the bay long after their bodies have passed away:

- She imagines their souls being imprisoned forever in these bleak waters, bobbing and tossing on its raging waves: 'rolled in the doom-noise of the sea'.
- She imagines that patches of white surf on the ocean's surface are the faces of these drowned people: 'whitened by the faces of the drowned'.
- She imagines that the mist rising from the ocean is composed of these drowned souls.
- She imagines this mist of ghosts drifting sorrowfully aimlessly and hopelessly around the bay: 'They go up without hope, like sighs'.
- When the speaker walks into the mist she imagines the ghosts wrapping themselves around her in a kind of cocoon and penetrating her mouth: 'they stuff my mouth with cotton'.
- When she walks out of the mist she imagines the ghosts release her again: 'they free me'.

When she leaves the fog there are beads of water on her cheeks: 'I am beaded with tears'. This may simply be mist that has condensed on her face. However, it is also possible that the speaker is actually crying, weeping out of pity for those who have drowned over the years off Finisterre's deadly coast.

Our Lady of the Shipwrecked

There are a pair of large marble statues near the cliff side. One depicts the Virgin Mary. She is depicted with a serene and holy smile on her face: 'Her lips sweet with divinity'. She is depicted wearing a wind-blown pink dress and walking purposefully in the direction of the ocean: 'striding toward the horizon'.

The other statue depicts a sailor: 'A marble sailor kneels at her foot'. He is depicted kneeling before the Virgin and praying to her in a 'distracted' manner. In this instance 'distractedly' means desperately and despairingly rather than and casually and inattentively. A local woman has come to pray at the statues. However, she seems to focus her prayers more on the statue of the sailor than on the statue of the Virgin herself: 'A peasant woman in black/ Is praying to the monument of the sailor praying'.

Plath personifies the statues of the Virgin and the sailor, depicting them as real people capable of praying and answering prayers. The sailor prays to the Virgin. The Virgin, however, does not pay any attention to his prayers or to the prayers of the peasant woman: 'She does not hear what the sailor or the peasant is saying'.

The Virgin is sometimes referred to as 'Our Lady of the Shipwrecked' because she is believed to help sailors and those who have been lost at sea. However, Plath presents her as being more interested in admiring the ocean before her than in listening to the prayers of sailor and their families: 'She is in love with the beautiful formlessness of the sea'.

Gifts & postcards

The local peasants have stalls in the vicinity of the Finisterre headland, where they sell postcards and crepes to tourists. They urge the poet to eat some freshly prepared crepes before the sea wind cools them too much: 'These are our crepes. Eat them before they blow cold'. It is not clear whether the locals are attempting to sell the poet crepes or are offering them for free.

They also sell little trinkets, which are made by beading seashells onto lengths of lace: 'pretty trinkets … necklaces and toy ladies'. These shell-and-lace trinkets 'flap' in the stiff sea breeze and have to be weighed down with conches to stop them blowing away: 'Gull-coloured laces flap in the sea drafts … The peasants anchor them with conches'.

The peasants tell Plath about the shells used to manufacture these trinkets. They are found 'hidden' in the sea around Finisterre. However they originate in a faraway, tropical sea: they come 'from another place, tropical and blue,/ We have never been to'. We marvel at the thought of the ocean carrying the shells thousands of miles from some tropical paradise to the bleak shores of western Brittany.

THEMES

Mental anguish

Many of Plath's poems express feelings of inner turmoil, describing a speaker who is haunted by raging storms of emotion. In 'Finisterre' the sea's violent fury is often taken to represent Plath's tumultuous mental state. The ocean is presented as a terrifyingly vast 'exploding' force that 'cannons' into the coastline, making an endless and oppressive roaring sound; a 'doom-noise'. As we have seen, the images associating it with an invading army reinforce our sense of its violence.

It is also possible that the description of the peasants' trinkets in the final stanza suggest this mental turmoil. The speaker's mind is battered by gales of emotion just as the 'toy ladies' made by the peasants are blown about by the sea drafts from Finisterre. Such mental turmoil is also a feature of 'Elm', 'The Arrival of the Bee Box' and arguably of 'Child'.

There is only a slight note of hope in 'Finisterre'. The peasants mention a peaceful place 'tropical and blue', far from the furious waters of the bay where they live. This suggests that the speaker believes an end to her mental turmoil is possible, that she can enter a new and tranquil mental space. Yet as the poem concludes we are left with the impression that such inner peace is a distant prospect, as distant as the faraway waters the peasants have 'never been'. It could be argued that the 'The Arrival of the Bee Box' features a similar note of hope.

Some readers feel that 'Finisterre' expresses feelings of numbness rather than turmoil. The poem describes the ghosts of the drowned drifting eternally around the bay of the dead. They float endlessly and hopelessly: 'They go up without hope like sighs'. Their grey, limbo-like existence suggests the mental limbo and emotional deadness that Plath so dreaded.

It could also be argued that the landscape as a whole suggests a grey and blank emotional state. It is a 'gloomy' dump of rocks, a place of grim cliffs, wasting flowers, and brittle 'rheumatic' rocky outcrops. There are several poems where Plath expresses this emotional blankness. We see it for example in 'Poppies in July' where the speaker feels nothing, being locked in a state of complete emotional neutrality. It is also arguably present in 'Child' where the speaker compares her life to a 'dark/ Ceiling without a star'.

There are also several instances in Plath's poetry where the speaker expresses what might be described as self-destructive thoughts or desires. Such desires are arguably expressed in 'Finisterre' when the speaker describes herself walking into the sea-mist. She describes how this mist 'erases' the rocks and yet she enters it. It's as on some level she desires to be erased from existence herself. She imagines the mist being composed of dead souls and yet she enters it, as if on some level she desires to join them in death. Many readers feel that the description of the souls almost choking the speaker also reflects her self-destructive desires: 'They stuff my mouth with cotton'.

A similar tendency is evident in 'The Arrival of the Bee Box' where the speaker describes the protective garments of the beekeeper as a 'funeral veil'. There is a sense here that she is anticipating her own demise or on some level even desiring it. In the same poem the speaker imagines herself being transformed into a laburnum tree or cherry tree as if she wants to give up human consciousness and become an unthinking but beautiful piece of plant life. This desire to be erased from human consciousness is also present in 'Poppies in July' where the speaker imagines herself lapsing into an unconscious coma-like state.

Psychic landscapes

There are many poems where Plath creates what she described as 'psychic landscapes'. She uses a scene from nature or an element of the natural world in order to convey an inner state of mind. As we have seen this tendency is evident in 'Finisterre'. The description of the bay can be taken to suggest either a storm of emotional turmoil or a state of complete mental numbness or perhaps even both. This tendency is also evident in 'The Arrival of the Bee Box', where the box serves as a metaphor for Plath's turmoil-filled mind. 'Elm' and 'Poppies in July' are other poems where the natural world is used to convey troubled mental states.

Order & chaos

Many of Plath's poems deal with the notion of order and chaos. In this poem the sea is associated with chaos. Perhaps its key feature is its 'formlessness'. It is presented as a vast, shapeless void churning chaotically. Order, on the other hand, is represented by the solidity and stableness of the coastline.

The poem shows chaos slowly encroaching on order as the sea reduces the coastline to nothing. It breaks down the mighty cliffs of Finisterre till they're worn, rheumatic fingers, then little rocks, then only part of its formless drifting. Human beings, too, are reduced to nothing – or next to nothing – by the ocean. Those it drowns are left as wisps of fog, like lost, pathetic, ghosts.

In a sense this process is presented in a negative light. The speaker seems horrified by the violence and menace of the raging sea's assault upon the land. Yet there is also a sense in which the speaker finds the chaos represented by the ocean attractive and intoxicating. Its formlessness after all is described as a 'beautiful' formlessness. To Plath, then, chaos is simultaneously both horrific and attractive. A similarly complex response to chaos is evident both in 'The Times Are Tidy' and in 'The Arrival of the Bee Box'.

Femininity & motherhood
Many of Plath's poems deal with the difficulties of motherhood and touch upon the idea of mother's failing their children. We see this in both 'Child' and 'Morning Song'. It is also present in 'Finisterre' through the depiction of Our Lady of the Shipwrecked.

Our Lady is often thought of as the 'mother' of the human race. Yet in this poem she is certainly depicted as having failed her children. Despite her serene and beautiful smile, 'her lips sweet with divinity', she is cold, distant and uncaring. She no longer hears the pleas of those who pray to her, either of the despairing sailor or of the peasant woman. She is unmoved by the plight of the lost souls that drift around the place like mists (unlike the speaker who emerges from their fig 'beaded in tears').

Poetic inspiration
To write poetry, Plath believed, it was necessary to explore the darkest recesses of the mind, to explore the deepest reaches of the soul. Plath felt probing the unconscious mind was a business, for it risked disturbing all kinds of inner demons. In this poem the ocean is often taken as a metaphor for the unconscious mind. It is presented as a place of great danger, furious and treacherous; with 'no bottom, or anything on the other side of it'.

Yet just as the peasants venture into the ocean and extract little shells from it, so the true poet must venture into the depths of his or her own psyche. Just as the peasants produce little toys from the fruit of their explorations, so the poet might create a 'pretty trinket' from her own mental explorations – trinket that would, of course, take the form of a poem. In this regard 'Finisterre' echoes 'The Arrival of the Bee Box' and 'Elm', other poems where Plath touches on the unconscious mind and the demons that might wait there.

Religion
'Finisterre' presents a bleak and disillusioned view of religion. Traditionally, people have used religion to impose order and meaning on their lives. In this poem, however, religion seems to have failed. Our Lady no longer seems to care about those who beseech her, serenely ignoring their prayers. According to the speaker, she has fallen in love with chaos and formlessness, the very things religion is meant to oppose. The poem, then, suggests that religion no longer offers any compensation against the chaos of this life.

Yet there is also a sense in the poem that people have forgotten the real meaning of faith. The people in the poem pray publicly to a marble monument rather than privately to God. The marble sailor prays 'distractedly', perhaps suggesting that he is not really focused on his prayers. The peasant woman doesn't pray to God directly. In fact she doesn't even pray directly to the Virgin. Instead she prays 'to the monument of the sailor praying'. There is a real sense, therefore, that people have lost touch with God. Perhaps mankind has abandoned religion as much as religion has abandoned mankind.

LANGUAGE

Perhaps the most striking feature of 'Finisterre' is the powerfully grim atmosphere Plath manages to conjure. The bay is depicted in a truly 'gloomy' fashion, a place of black cliffs, raging waves and sorrowful mists.

The tone of the final stanza is quite different from that of the rest of the poem. The previous three stanzas employ heightened, dramatic phrases and violent imagery. The last stanza, however, is more relaxed in tone. It uses simple, childish vocabulary: 'pretty trinkets', 'Little shells', 'toy ladies'. In these lines the peasants reveal a different aspect of the ocean. It is more than just the gloomy, violent seascape visible from the headland of Finisterre. It is also a storehouse of beautiful shells, which can be made into harmless souvenirs.

There are several striking metaphors in this poem:

- The white surf on the sea's surface is compared to the faces of people who have drowned: 'whitened by the faces of the drowned'.
- Rocky outcrops protruding from the water are described as fingers: 'the last fingers, knuckled and rheumatic,/ Cramped on nothing'.
- Smaller rocks are described as dead or wounded soldiers: 'Leftover soldiers from old messy wars'.
- The mist the speaker walks into is compared to cotton: 'The stuff my mouth with cotton'.

In line 4 Plath describes how the ocean has 'no bottom, or anything on the other side of it'. Of course she isn't suggesting that the sea is literally bottomless or endless. Rather, she uses hyperbole, or poetic exaggeration, to convey its enormity.

There are several instances of personification in the poem. Personification occurs when we apply human qualities to inanimate objects or natural phenomena. In this poem large rocks are described as having 'grudges'. The mists are depicted as human souls drifting mournfully around the bay. The description of the cliffs as 'admonitory', as issuing a warning, is arguably another instance of personification.

Personification also occurs in the depiction of the statues. The Virgin is depicted as a real person. She strides toward the ocean. She is capable of ignoring and of answering prayers. She is enthralled by the sea's formlessness. The statue of the sailor, too, is personified, depicted as praying 'distractedly' to the Virgin.

An important feature of the poem is the depiction of the sea's assault on the land as a kind of military campaign. At the time of the poem's composition, war was an issue that greatly preoccupied the poet. She had been moved by the sight of wounded veterans of the Franco-Algerian war convalescing at the resort of Berck-Plage which was in the vicinity of Finisterre. Many of these soldiers had been horribly maimed. Seeing them brought home to Plath the horror of war.

Plath depicts the land and sea as being involved in an endless and brutal conflict: 'old messy wars'. The sea slowly reduces the cliffs to little rocks that litter the seascape like dead or wounded bodies, casualties of its endless assault on the coastline. The rocks that have been submerged by the ocean's advance bear 'grudges', like warriors who have suffered a bitter and humiliating defeat. The description of the sea 'cannoning' and 'exploding' reinforces our sense of it as a hostile military force.

The opening stanzas of this poem feature several instances of cacophony. Phrases such as 'Knuckled and rheumatic/ Cramped on nothing', 'Whitened by the faces of the drowned', 'a dump of rocks' and 'Leftover soldiers from old messy wars' all feature hard clashing consonants that produce a jarring and unpleasant verbal music. The rhyme between budge and grudges produces a similar effect. Plath uses this cacophony to suggest the furious sound of the raging sea.

Stanza 2 features a profusion of broad-vowel sounds which slow our reading of the verse and produce a mournful musical effect suitable to the depiction of the ghosts drifting around the bay. We see this in phrase such as 'beaded with tears' with its repeated 'ea' sound, in 'mouth with cotton', with its repeated 'o' sound, and in 'ancient paraphernalia' with its repeated 'a' sound. There is an element of onomatopoeia in the phrase 'Souls rolled in the doom-noise of the sea'. If we say it aloud we can almost hear the sea rolling and churning.

Pheasant

Sylvia Plath

LINE BY LINE

A Pheasant has settled in the poet's garden. The speaker's husband considers the bird to be a pest and has promised to kill it: 'You said you would kill it this morning'. But the speaker has become fond of the bird and asks her husband not to kill it. She gives a number of reasons why she considers the pheasant's life ought to be spared:

- The bird's appearance is startling and pleasant. The poet admires the movement of the bird's head: 'The jut of that odd, dark head, prancing// Through the uncut grass'. She considers the bird to have 'such a good shape' and thinks the 'green and red' colours of the feathers to be 'vivid', especially when set against the white of the snow: 'The wonder of it, in that pallor'.
- It is 'in its element' and therefore seems to have a certain 'right' to be in the garden. The bird is at home in the natural environment and the poet thinks that this gives 'it a kingliness, a right' to be there. The 'print of it's big foot' in the snow is like its royal mark or stamp, and the 'trail-track, on the snow' like its signature. It seems to be lord over the common 'sparrow and starling' that also appear in the garden.
- It is at ease in the garden, 'sunning in the narcissi' and settling 'in the elm'. It is even like the surroundings it inhabits: 'brown as a leaf'. The speaker in contrast feels awkward and out-of-place there: 'I trespass stupidly'.
- Such a bird is rare and it is 'something' to own one or just be visited by one at all.

The speaker does not wish to preserve the bird's life because she thinks it is in any way sacred: 'I am not mystical: it isn't/ As if I thought it had a spirit'. The bird just seems to offer so much. It is 'a little cornucopia' or plentiful source of pleasure. In fact, the speaker would be happy to have 'a dozen' or 'A hundred … Crossing and recrossing' on the hill before her house.

THEMES

Nature

The poem is a celebration of the beauty and wonder of the natural world. The poet describes the many wonderful features of a pheasant that has come to live in her garden. She focuses on the beauty of the bird and takes great pleasure in watching it move.

Like 'The Arrival of the Beebox' this poem deals with the power that humans sometimes wield over the natural world. The poet's husband has threatened to kill the bird and it is now up to her to convince him that the pheasant's life is worth preserving. However, there is a sense in which the bird will only survive as long as it continues to amuse the poet. When she says that it 'startles me still' there is an implication that when it ceases to do so it can be destroyed.

The poem ultimately suggests that the bird has a natural right to be in the garden and that it is human beings who are the intruders and trespassers in such places. In the end the poet pleads with her husband to let nature be. But the final entreaty does not read like a heartfelt plea for the preservation of the natural world. The repetition of 'Let be, let be' contains little passion and does not suggest great concern for the life of the pheasant.

Poetic inspiration

Like 'Black Rook in Rainy Weather' this poem suggests that the natural world is a rich source of inspiration to the poet. The sighting of a pheasant catches her eye and inspires her to describe the peculiar features and movements of the bird. Its appearance in her garden is something 'rare' and out of the ordinary and proves to be a 'a little cornucopia' or abundant source of inspiration.

Elm

Sylvia Plath

LINE BY LINE

The human speaker's state of mind
The human speaker seems to be in a distressed and agitated state of mind:

- According to the elm she fears the 'bottom', a mental state of complete desperation and loneliness: 'It is what you fear'.
- In line 6 the elm suggests that the speaker has previously endured episodes of madness.
- In line 27 the elm describes how the speaker has bad dreams.

At least part of the speaker's anguish appears to stem from the failure of a relationship. She seems to have been abandoned by her lover, or by love itself. The elm describes how her love has 'gone off, like a horse'. According to the elm she just lies there mourning her lost love: 'How you lie and cry after it'.

The elm taunts the speaker
A strange 'psychic link' seems to exist between the elm and the human speaker it addresses. According to the elm they somehow share the same dreams. The elm describes how it is 'possessed' by the speaker's nightmares: 'How your bad dreams possess and endow me'.

Yet the elm addresses the speaker in a cruel and mocking manner. Its words seem designed to torment the speaker in her anguished mental state. 'Love', the elm declares, 'is a shadow' a worthless and insubstantial illusion. The elm mocks the speaker's need for this illusion, and her distress at being abandoned by it: 'How you lie and cry after it'.

Her tone is also unsympathetic when she describes the speaker's fear of the bottom. The elm herself has no fear of the bottom, having already experienced and survived it: 'I know the bottom ... I do not fear it: I have been there'. (This also suggests that the elm's main root, her 'tap root', has reached down into the depths of the earth: 'I know the bottom, she says, I know it with my great tap root').

The elm appears keen to upset the speaker with the different noises it makes. It mentions three different disturbing or unsettling sounds:

- The wind in its branches will remind the speaker of the sea, something she associates with sorrow and dissatisfaction: 'Is it the sea you hear in me,/ Its dissatisfactions?'
- The wind in its branches will remind the speaker of the 'voice of nothing', something the speaker associates with her previous bouts of madness.
- If love is a horse then the noise made by the elm's branches is its hooves running away from the speaker.

The elm urges the speaker to 'Listen' to this last distressing sound. It wants this sorrowful noise to fill the speaker's head all night long, until her head feels like the stone struck by the horse's hooves, her pillow like the turf it gallops over: 'All night I shall gallop thus, impetuously,/ Till your head is a stone, your pillow a little turf'.

The elm describes the torments it has endured
The elm describes the rain has fallen down upon it: 'This is rain now'. The rain makes a shushing or hushing sound as it falls upon the elm's leaves: 'this big hush'. Yet this rain is toxic, a kind of acid rain. The noise it makes is 'the sound of poisons'. It causes the elm to bear strange almost mutant fruit: 'this is the fruit of it: tin-white like arsenic'.

The sun isn't particularly kind to the elm either. The sunsets it endures are brutal and violent: 'I have suffered the atrocity of sunsets'. They produce an unnatural heat, scorching the elm 'to the root'. Her branches ('filaments') are baked in the sun's heat until they're red, dry and lifeless: 'My red filaments burn and stand, a hand of wires'.

The wind, too, assaults the elm, breaking off bits of its branches: 'Now I break up in pieces that fly about like clubs'. The fact that the flying branches are compared to weapons ('clubs'), suggests the wind's violence. In response to such a violent onslaught, the elm has no choice but to cry out in agony: 'A wind of such violence/ Will tolerate no bystanding: I must shriek.'

The moon is another of the elm's tormenters: 'The moon, also, is merciless'. It burns the elm with its brightness: 'Her radiance scathes me'. It gets caught in the elm's branches, pulling and dragging them: 'she would drag me/ Cruelly'. The elm wonders if the moon is torturing it on purpose. Perhaps the elm is responsible for its own discomfort, having accidentally snared the moon in its branches: 'perhaps I have caught her'. This seems to be the case, for the elm releases the moon: 'I let her go, I let her go'.

The elm contemplates love
The elm contemplates the clouds forming and dissolving different shapes in the sky above her: they 'pass and disperse'. Once a given cloud formation breaks up it is 'irretrievable', it will never reconstitute itself.

She wonders if love and relationships are as fleeting and transitory as these cloud-shapes: 'Are those the faces of love, those pale irretrievables?' We are reminded of her earlier declaration that love is no more than 'a shadow', an insubstantial illusion.

Previously the elm mocked the speaker for caring about love, for allowing a failed relationship to distress her. Now, however, the elm admits that it too allows love to trouble it: 'Is it for such I agitate my heart?' It has allowed love, something no more substantial than a cloud or shadow, to 'agitate its heart'.

The presence in the elm's branches
The elm is tormented by a 'dark' presence that dwells within its branches. In many respects this presence is bird-like. It is 'feathery' and has 'hooks' or talons. It rests each day and each night it 'flaps out' of the elm to hunt. The elm is desperately frightened by this presence: 'I am terrified by this dark thing'. She thinks of it as 'malign' or evil. She seems horrified by the thought of this presence sleeping within it: 'All day I feel its soft feathery turnings, its malignity'.

The poem concludes with the elm staring this dark presence in the face. It lurks in a 'strangle' or tangle of the elm's branches. It's face bears a 'murderous' expression. Acid comes sizzling and hissing from its mouth: 'Its snaky acids hiss'. To look at this creature is to experience complete despair, to lose even the will to survive. Its gaze 'petrifies' or freezes the will to live.

THEMES

Mental anguish
Inner turmoil
'Elm' is one of Plath's great poems of mental turmoil, one in which the poet powerfully reveals her own anguished mental state. The female speaker in the poem is in an intensely agitated and tumultuous state of mind. As we have seen she suffers from 'bad dreams', she seems to have experienced bouts of madness and she fears hitting rock 'bottom', complete and total mental desolation.

Plath also uses the elm tree to embody or personify her own mental turmoil. The elm suffers different torments. It is lashed by poisonous rain, burned by the sun, whipped by the wind, then 'dragged' and 'scathed' by the moon. These torments serve as powerful metaphors for the Plath's own mental ordeals, reflecting the tortured state of mind she experienced around the time of the poem's composition. 'Finisterre' and 'The Arrival of the Bee Box' are other poems that deal with this kind of mental turmoil. It is arguably also present in 'Child'.

Perhaps the most disturbing aspect of 'Elm' is the way it suggests that there is no limit or extreme to human suffering. The elm claims to have known the 'bottom'. It has experienced the most intense possible degree of mental anguish. It is 'incapable of more knowledge', of dealing with any more mental suffering. However, we are left with the impression that more knowledge must be borne, that more suffering must yet be undergone.

Romantic love
'Elm' presents a bleak view of romantic love. It is worth noting that at the time Plath composed the poem her own marriage was in trouble. Much of the human speaker's turmoil seems to spring from the agony of a failed relationship. The elm mockingly describes how she lies there weeping over her lost love: 'How you lie and cry after it'. Yet the elm itself also 'agitates' its heart because of love. The poem grimly suggests that love is no more than a shadowy illusion, something no more solid or retrievable than a cloud. And yet we cannot help but agitate our hearts for it.

Feelings of inadequacy

Many of Plath's poems express what can only be described as feelings of inadequacy and worthlessness. Such feelings of failure are evident in 'Morning Song', where the speaker doubts her ability to be a good mother and in 'Child', where the speaker laments that she can only give her child the 'agitated wringing of hands'. It is also present in 'The Arrival of the Bee Box' where the speaker doubts her ability to control the swarm of bees once she releases them.

Such self-doubts are powerfully dramatised in 'Elm'. The 'dark' clawed creature with a murderous face represents Plath's feelings of failure and inadequacy. Plath is inhabited by these feelings just as the elm is inhabited by the creature:

- Plath is disgusted by the faults and failings that lie within her psyche just as the elm is disgusted by the 'soft feathery turnings' of the creature.
- The creature flies out each night looking for love, suggesting that Plath associated her need for love with weakness and failure.
- The creature drips acid from its mouth, suggesting how Plath's awareness of her own failings corrodes her mental health.
- The sight of the creature's face 'petrifies' the elm's will, suggesting how Plath's awareness of her own failings almost freezes her desire to go on living.
- The elm believes that this 'murderous' creature will be the death of it. Similarly Plath believes that her own failings will eventually be the death of her: 'These are the isolate slow faults/ That kill, that kill, that kill.'

In a sense the terms 'feelings of inadequacy' or an 'awareness of failings and failures' are too weak to describe Plath's mental state in this poem. The term 'self-loathing' might be nearer to the mark. The creature that inhabits the elm seems to represent a dark and loathsome aspect of her own personality, one that is 'malign' or evil and fills her with disgust.

Psychic landscape

There are many poems where Plath creates what she described as 'psychic landscapes'. She uses a scene from nature or an element of the natural world in order to convey an inner state of mind. As we have seen, this tendency is particularly evident in 'Elm'. The elm undergoes various tortures, which serve as metaphors for Plath's turmoil-filled mental state. The elm is inhabited by a dark creature which serves as a metaphor for Plath's feelings of inadequacy or the dark side of her personality. 'Finisterre', 'The Arrival of the Bee Box' and 'Poppies in July' are other poems where the natural world is used to convey troubled mental states.

Poetic inspiration

The elm reaches into the soil with its 'great tap root'. It claims to know the 'bottom', to have reached into the earth's very foundations. This can be taken as a metaphor for the work of the poet. Plath believed that the true poet needed to probe of the depths of his or her own psyche. Just as the elm delves into the soil, so the poet must explore the recesses of his or her unconscious mind. Plath was simultaneously fascinated by this type of mental exploration and afraid of what dark thoughts and feelings she might mind lurking in her unconscious. In this regard 'Elm' echoes 'The Arrival of the Bee Box', another poem where Plath touches on the topic of the unconscious mind and the demons that might wait there.

Femininity & motherhood

This poem has been described as a study of feminine suffering. It features three female presences, each of which suffers. The female speaker, as we have seen, endures mental turmoil. The elm is depicted as female and suffers all kinds of outlandish tortures. The third female presence that suffers is the moon, which is traditionally portrayed as female.

The moon is caught by the elm tree and is released in a 'flat' and 'diminished' state. It is possible that the moon is an aggressor in this encounter, attaching itself to the elm and 'dragging' it 'most cruelly'. She seems to torture the elm out of jealousy, envying the tree its fertility and fruitfulness. The moon, after all, is a completely barren and infertile place. It is also possible, however, that the moon has become innocently ensnared in the elm's branches: 'perhaps I have caught her'.

LANGUAGE

Personification

Perhaps the stand out feature of this poem is that the elm is personified or given human characteristics.

It is portrayed as being capable of emotion, speech and suffering. It is even capable of love. As noted above Plath uses this speaking elm to describe her own mental anguish. The elm's tortures represent Plath's own mental sufferings. The dark creature that inhabits its branches represents the negative and corrosive aspects of her personality: what she saw as her faults, failings and inadequacies.

Tone

At the beginning of the poem the elm's tone is cold and confident. She addresses the speaker in a cruel and mocking fashion, chiding her need for love. By the end of the poem, however, the elm's coldness and confidence seem to have vanished. Her tone becomes one of fear and agitation. She admits that she too has a need for love: 'Is it for such that I agitate my heart?'

At the poem's beginning the elm claims to have known the bottom, to have experienced the worst that can possibly be experienced. By the end, however, she seems to feel that even greater torments lie in store for her: 'I am incapable of more knowledge'.

Nightmarish imagery

It nearly goes without saying that 'Elm' is not a realistic or logical poem. The elm suffers a number of terrible tortures one after the other: poisonous rains, raging storms, a scorching sun. A bizarre bird-like being inhabits its branches and torments it. It even somehow snags the moon in its branches. The narrative of the poem follows its own crazed and surreal path, fading from grim image to the next with the logic of a nightmare.

Sources of imagery

The elm asks the speaker if the sound of the wind in its branches reminds her of the sea: 'Is it the sea you hear in me,/ Its dissatisfactions?' In Plath's poetry, the sea is often a menacing presence, associated with 'formlessness' and destruction. It tends to represent the dissolution of order into chaos, sanity into madness, meaning into meaninglessness, life into death. The sea is also portrayed negatively in 'Finisterre'.

The elm asks if the wind in its branches reminds the speaker of the 'voice of nothing that was your madness?' These lines owe something to Shakespeare's play *King Lear*, where Lear loses his mind and is left raging on a heath in an apocalyptic storm not unlike the one described by the elm. The mad kind is repeatedly referred to as 'nothing' in this scene.

At the time of this poem's composition Plath, along with the rest of the world, was very much concerned about the possibility of a nuclear conflict between USSR and United States. The intense, blazing heat endured by the elm suggests less a normal sunset than the red sky caused by a nuclear explosion, which could, of course, be regarded as the 'sunset' of the world. Similarly, the unstoppably violent wind that tortures the elm calls to mind the force of a nuclear blast. The poisonous rain that falls on it suggests the aftermath of a nuclear disaster or of a comparable environmental catastrophe.

There are several references to medical procedures in the poem. Lines 25–6 describe how the moon is left 'diminished and flat' as if it has had a breast removed in an operation. Plath described how the description of the trees branches being 'scorched to the root' in line 17 was inspired by her experiences of electroconvulsive therapy.

Metaphors

Plath uses a wonderful metaphor to depict the withering of the elm's branches, describing their parched, shrivelled forms as 'a hand of wires'. Using a simile, Plath compares the flying branches to weapons ('clubs'), suggests the wind's violence. We see metonymy in line 28. Metonymy occurs when a thing or concept is not called by its own name, but by the name of something intimately associated with that thing or concept. Instead of declaring 'I am inhabited by a creature', the elm declares that 'I am inhabited by a cry', the cry being something intimately associated with the creature. There is a great seal of cacophony throughout this poem. The harsh clashing sounds in phrases like 'My red filaments burn and stand' are appropriate to the torments they describe.

The Arrival of the Bee Box

Sylvia Plath

During the summer of 1962, while she lived with her husband in the Devon countryside, Plath experimented with bee keeping. This experience provided her with the inspiration for a number of poems about bees, one of which is 'The Arrival of the Bee Box'.

LINE BY LINE

A description of the box

In this poem the speaker has just received a 'clean wood box' that is full of bees. Tomorrow she will release the bees into the hive she has prepared for them. Tonight, however she must keep the box in her house: 'I have to live with it overnight'.

The box has the following features:

- It is square in shape: 'square as a chair'.
- It is heavy: 'almost too heavy too lift'
- It is 'locked' and its only opening in the box is a small grid or grille for ventilation: 'There are no windows … no exit'.

The bees inside it produce a loud 'din' of buzzing.

The speaker's reaction to the box

The speaker reacts to the box with a feeling of dread and horror. She thinks of it as 'dangerous'. She seems to associate it with death, referring to it as a 'coffin'. We get a sense in the opening line that she is regretful or even somehow surprised that she purchased the bees in the first place.

Yet though the box horrifies the speaker it also fascinates her. She feels compelled to stay near it: 'I can't keep away from it'. She puts her 'eye to the grid' or grille and attempts to peer into it. She lays her ear on its surface and listens to the bees buzzing within. The speaker's reaction to the box, then, is complex and contradictory. It seems to repulse her and attract her at the same time.

The speaker's reaction to the bees

The speaker reacts to the bees inside the box with what can only be described as fear and horror:

- Though the box's interior is 'dark, dark' when she looks through the grille she can just make out the bees scrambling and 'clambering' around within it. According to the speaker the bees look like the tiny shrunken hands of dead Africans.
- She finds the sound they make even more horrifying and upsetting than their appearance: 'It is the noise that appals me most of all'. She compares their buzzing to a strange language full of 'unintelligible syllables'. She associates the bees with rage and anger, thinking of them 'as a box of maniacs'. They clamber 'angrily' and the sound they make is 'furious'.

The speaker is highly conscious that a swarm of bees can pose a threat to a human being. In this regard she compares the bees to a rioting crowd in ancient Roman times: 'It is like a Roman mob'. On his own each member of a Roman mob was powerless. As a rioting group, however, they could threaten the stability of the entire city. Similarly, a single bee can do little harm to a human being. An entire swarm, however, could easily sting a person to death: 'Small, taken one by one, but my God together!'

The speaker fears that once released the bees will turn on her and overwhelm her: 'How can I let them out?' It took a powerful ruler like Caesar to master the mobs of Rome. Similarly it will take a skilled and confident beekeeper to control the bees once they have been released from the box. The speaker, however, feels she does not possess the qualities necessary to tame or control this raging swarm: 'I am no Caesar'.

What will the speaker do with the bees?

The speaker considers her options with regard to the bees. Firstly, she could return them to the shop she bought them from: 'They can be sent back'. Secondly, she could starve them and let them perish in their clean wood box: 'They can die, I need feed them nothing, I am the owner'. Finally, she could overcome her fear of the bees and release them in the morning as she had originally planned.

She wonders if the bees are hungry enough to attack her should she decide to release them: 'I wonder how

hungry they are'. She feels there is little real chance of this attack occurring: 'I am no source of honey/ So why should they turn on me?' The bees, in fact, will probably just ignore her if sets them free: 'They might ignore me immediately'.

The speaker has a God-like power over the bees; the power of life and death. She decides that tomorrow she will act like a 'sweet' or benevolent God. Instead of sending the bees back or letting them die she will set them free. Having concluded that they pose little threat to her she will release them into the garden: 'Tomorrow I will be sweet God, I will set them free.// The box is only temporary'.

THEMES

Mental anguish
Like many of Plath's poems 'The Arrival of the Bee Box' depicts mental turmoil. The sight and sound of the locked box fills the speaker with dread: 'The box is locked, it is dangerous'. Her dread is exacerbated by the fact that she can't see into it. On one level, of course, the speaker is simply afraid that the bees might escape and sting her.

Yet her intense reaction to the box seems to stem from more than this practical concern. She is 'appalled' by the noise of their buzzing and disgusted by what she can see of them through the grille. She associates them with rage, thinking of them as 'furious' maniacs 'angrily clambering' in the darkness. The dread she experiences seems to reflect her inner turmoil. She has such a strong reaction to the box because of the troubled and tumultuous mental state she is in when they arrive.

Such mental turmoil is also a feature of 'Elm', Finisterre' and arguably of 'Child'. Unlike those poems, however, 'The Arrival of the Bee Box' features a note of hope. The speaker can overcome her fear of the bees by releasing them, rather like someone who is afraid of flying stepping onto a plane. At present the speaker is controlled by her terror of the bees. By releasing them, however, she will conquer her fear and empower herself. She will go from being powerless ('no Caesar') to being powerful ('sweet God'). If the speaker can overcome this seemingly irrational fear of the bee box perhaps she can also overcome the deeper mental turmoil that effects her.

There are several instances in Plath's poetry where the speaker expresses what might be described as self-destructive thoughts or desires. Many readers feel that these desires surface in 'The Arrival of the Bee Box'. When the speaker imagines herself wearing the protective garments of a beekeeper, she describes the face-covering as a 'funeral veil'. There is a sense here that she is anticipating her own demise or on some level even desiring it.

This tendency is perhaps also evident when she imagines herself being transformed into a tree:

I wonder would they just forget me
If I just undid the locks and stood back and turned into
  a tree.
There is the laburnum, its blond colonnades,
And the petticoats of the cherry

There is a sense in which the speaker seems to desire this transformation, to leave behind the human condition with all its trials and tribulations. She wants to give up human consciousness and become an unthinking but beautiful piece of plant life. A similar desire to be erased from human consciousness is also present in 'Finisterre' and in 'Poppies in July'.

Many of Plath's poems express what can only be described as feelings of inadequacy and worthlessness. Such feelings of failure are evident in 'Morning Song', where the speaker doubts her ability to be a good mother and in 'Child', where the speaker laments that she can only give her child the 'agitated wringing of hands'. It is also present in this poem where the speaker doubts her ability to control the swarm of bees once she releases them: 'I am no Caesar'.

Poetic inspiration

'The Arrival of the Bee Box' is often regarded as dealing with the theme of poetry and the unconscious. To write poetry, Plath believed, it was necessary to explore the darkest recesses of the mind, to explore the deepest reaches of the soul. Yet this, she felt, was a dangerous business, for it risked disturbing all kinds of inner demons: various traumas and negative emotions the mind has covered up.

The bee box, according to many readers, represents the hidden aspect of mind, the dark and mysterious parts the true poet must explore:

- Like the bee box our unconscious mind is almost completely sealed: we cannot know what it contains until we begin to explore it.
- Just as the speaker is terrified and disgusted by the bee box, so Plath was nervous about exploring her unconscious mind and horrified by the demons that might lurk there.
- By opening up her unconscious she will unleash her inner demons, just as the speaker will release the bees.

Yet just as the speaker can't stay away from the bee box, so Plath was drawn back again and again to probe around the edges of her unconscious, for she felt that only by exploring this hidden aspect of herself could she create great poetry.

In this regard 'The Arrival of the Bee Box' echoes 'Elm', another poem where Plath touches on the unconscious mind and the demons that might wait there.

Psychic landscapes

There are many poems where Plath creates what she described as 'psychic landscapes'. She uses a scene from nature or an element of the natural world in order to convey an inner state of mind. This tendency is also evident in 'The Arrival of the Bee Box'. The box serves as a metaphor for Plath's turmoil-filled mind. The box seethes with furious black bees 'angrily clambering' over one another in a chaotic fashion. Similarly her mind seethes with dark, angry and negative emotions. 'Finisterre', 'Elm' and 'Poppies in July' are other poems where the natural world is used to convey troubled mental states.

Order & chaos

Many of Plath's poems focus on the distinction between order and chaos. In this poem the bees are a chaotic force, swarming hectically and frenziedly within their box. They are like a wild and disorderly mob. Only the box imposes order on them, containing their fury. Tellingly the poem's opening lines associate the box with order: 'I ordered this, this clean wood box'. However, once the box is opened order will be removed. The chaos represented by the bees will be free to make its way in the world.

The speaker finds this an unpleasant and perhaps even frightening prospect: 'How can I let them go?' In this poem, as in 'Finisterre', Plath seems to regard chaos with what can only be described as fear and horror. Yet also as in 'Finisterre' there is a sense in which chaos is presented as something alluring and attractive. We see this in the way the speaker 'can't stay away' from the bees' frenzy and in her decision at the end of the poem to release this 'box of maniacs' into the world.

Nature
In 'The Arrival of the Bee Box' the speaker has complete control over an aspect of the natural world. She owns the bees and can do what she wants with them: 'I am the owner'.

She can let the bees starve in their box, she can send them back to the shop or she can release them into the garden. The speaker has a God-like power over these insects and can choose to be a cruel, unforgiving God or a 'sweet' benevolent one. In a sense, then, the poem echoes 'Pheasant', where the speaker along with her husband has the power of life and death over the pheasant that has come to live in their garden.

LANGUAGE

Unusual imagery
This poem features the rich and unusual imagery that is typical of Plath's poetry. We see this in her description of the box as 'the coffin of a midget/ Or a square baby'. On one level of course, this description is outlandish and perhaps even slightly amusing. Yet there is also something unpleasant and unsettling about it. The description of the box as a coffin introduces the notion of death and suggests the speaker's desire for oblivion.

She uses a bizarre and somewhat disgusting metaphor to describe the bees, comparing them to the hands of dead African people that have been cut off, shrunken and exported back to Europe as souvenirs of the dark continent: 'African hands/ Minute and shrunk for export'. The image of thousands of tiny hands clambering around the box's dark interior is truly a disturbing one.

There is an interesting classical reference in limes 28–30 where the speaker imagines herself as Daphne, a doomed character from Greek myth who was transformed by the gods into a tree.

Similes & metaphors
Plath uses a fine metaphor to describe the sound of the bees' buzzing. She compares it to a strange language full of 'unintelligible syllables' such as Latin: 'I lay my ear to furious Latin'.

In another fine simile Plath compares the swarm to a rioting mob in Roman times: 'It is like a Roman mob'. As we noted a single Roman citizen was powerless. As a rioting group, however, they could threaten the entire government. Similarly, a single bee can do little harm to a human being. An entire swarm, however, could easily sting a person to death.

Plath extends this comparison with another metaphor, comparing a bee keeper to a roman emperor. Just as it took a powerful ruler like 'Caesar' to master the mobs of Rome so it will take a skilled and confident beekeeper to control the bees once they have been released from the box.

Metaphor also features in line 31 where Plath compares a bee-keeper's protective clothing to an astronaut's space suit. She also compares a bee-keeper's protective face mesh to a veil worn by a dead woman at her funeral: 'in my moon suit and funeral veil'.

Cacophony & euphony
We see cacophony in lines 13–15 where the repetition of hard 'b', 'r' and 't' sounds creates a harsh musical effect, appropriate to the disturbing image the lines describe. Euphony occurs in lines 32–36. The repeated broad-vowel sounds in 'source of honey', 'moon suit', 'funeral veil' and 'box is only' create a pleasant musical effect. So too do the repeated internal and external rhymes between 'honey', 'me', 'sweet', 'free', 'only' and 'temporary'. This pleasant verbal music is appropriate as the speaker imagines herself overcoming her fear and releasing the bees.

Poppies in July

LINE BY LINE

The speaker is looking at a field of poppies in the summer. She is in an extremely agitated state of mind. She uses several violent and disturbing comparisons to describe the poppies:

- The poppies intense redness reminds her of the fires of hell. The poppies are 'little hell flames'.
- The poppies remind her of mouths that are wounded and bleeding. They are 'wrinkly and clear red, like the skin of a mouth.// A mouth just bloodied.'
- She also compares them to skirts that are covered in blood: 'Little bloody skirts'.

The poet seems to be worn out and exhausted: 'it exhausts me to watch you'. She is gripped by feelings of numbness and emptiness. She longs to escape this numbness by experiencing physical pain. She wants the flames of the poppies to burn her: 'I put my hand among the flames'. She also longs to be brutally punched in the mouth: 'If my mouth could marry a hurt like that'. Her bleeding mouth would resemble the blood-red poppies.

Poppies produce opiates, drugs that put their users into a calm and blissful state of sleep. She wishes she could inhale the opiates by smelling the flowers. However, she knows that in reality the opiates reside within the flower, in buds or capsules: 'Where are your opiates, you nauseous capsules?' She imagines drinking the opiate in liquid form and feeling it move through her body. The opiate would put her into a sleep or a trance-like state. It would switch off her senses and fill her with an intense calm: 'Dulling and stilling'.

The poet imagines herself to be existing within a 'glass capsule'. Perhaps this is a reference to the fairy tale of 'Snow White'. In that story Snow White is given a poisoned apple. When she eats the apple she falls into a death-like sleep. The dwarves with whom she lives place her in a glass capsule and here she remains until a prince wakes her with a kiss. Plath suggests a longing for such a sleep in 'Poppies in July'.

The poem's last line could mean two different things. It is possible that the word 'colorless' belongs to the clear opiate potion that the speaker wants to drink. It could also refer to the trance-like state the speaker wants to enter. In this state she would no longer be aware of the sights and sounds of the world around. To her everything would be soundless and 'colorless'.

THEMES

Mental anguish

The speaker of the poem is exhausted and gripped by numbness and emptiness. The fact that she feels nothing causes her great mental anguish. Her utter neutrality makes her long for some form of extreme physical sensation. She reaches out to the poppies in the hope that they might 'harm' her. To her the flowers seem to be 'flames'. But she is incapable of feeling them, let alone being burnt by them. She is feeling so numb that she feels nothing at all: 'I cannot touch you./ I put my hands among the flames. Nothing burns'.

The speaker sees only two ways out of this numbing depression: experiencing intense physical pain or slipping into a blissful drug-induced trance: 'If I could bleed, or sleep!' She is desperate to escape from her numbed and neutral existence. She looks at the poppies and thinks that they resemble 'bloodied' mouths. This makes her long for her mouth to 'hurt like that'. And if she cannot suffer such pain or injury she wishes to lapse into a coma-like existence where she will feel and experience nothing at all. The poem closes with the poet imagining herself within a 'glass capsule' into which she longs for opiates to 'seep'. These 'liquors' will dull and still her until total oblivion is reached and the world fades away.

The use of the word 'marry' in line 12 brings to mind Plath's own marriage, which was in great difficulty at the time the poem was written. It is almost certain that the difficulties in her marriage contributed to the severe depression she describes so vividly in this poem.

Psychic landscapes

The landscapes that feature in the Plath's poems are often representations of her own inner mental state. She referred to such landscapes as 'psychic landscapes'. In 'Poppies in July' the description of the field of poppies corresponds with and illustrates the mental turmoil that the poet is experiencing:

- She is in a hellish place and describes the flowers as 'little hell flames'.
- But because her anguish stems from her neutrality and numbness, the flowers are incapable of being touched or of harming her in any way: 'I cannot touch you'.
- Her longing to experience pain as a means of escaping her neutrality is reflected in the description of the red petals as 'the skin of a mouth … just bloodied'.
- Her own self-disgust is evident in the description of the flowers as 'bloody skirts', a possible reference to menstruation.

LANGUAGE

This poem is marked by its vivid, nightmarish imagery. The speaker uses two metaphors and a simile to describe the poppies:

- She uses a metaphor when she compares them to 'little hell flames' and when she compares them to 'Little bloody skirts'.
- She uses a simile when she says they are 'like the skin of a mouth'.

The speaker uses short, choppy lines, skilfully suggesting the agitated mental state of someone in deep depression.

The poet's use of repetition also suggests her mental agitation. The word 'little' is repeated in the first line, the word 'colorless' in the last. The word 'capsule' is repeated in lines 10 and 13. There is also repetition between 'bloodied' and 'bloody' and between 'flicker' and 'flickering'.

Child

LINE BY LINE

The poet admires the beauty of her child's eye. Her child's eye is 'the one absolutely beautiful thing'. She considers it to be something pure and untainted. It is 'clear', just like a pool of water. She sees her child as something perfect, someone yet untarnished by experience: 'Little// Stalk without wrinkle'.

The child seems to be hungry to learn about the world. The poet describes the child meditating upon new words, possibly those of animals and flowers in a book. The poet mentions some exotic flowers that the child might be looking at: 'April snowdrop, Indian pipe'.

The poet wants to present her child with images that are fun and colourful: 'I want to fill it with 'color and ducks'. She also wishes to offer the child 'grand and classical images'. Such experiences will nourish the child's mind, allowing it to blossom and grow.

However, the poet seems to be suffering from some form of anguish or depression. She describes the 'troublous/ Wringing' of her hands. The world in which she exists appears to be dark and confined: 'this dark/ Ceiling without a star'. The last line may describe an actual room or it may be a metaphor for the way the poet views her own life. Ultimately it suggests a terrible lack of hope and despair.

THEMES

Femininity & motherhood

Like 'Morning Song' this poem illustrates how being a mother can be a very difficult and troubling experience. It suggests that a mother should fill her child's world with wonder and joy. The poet is conscious of the fact that her child is hungry for experience and knowledge. She wishes to give her child experiences that will nourish and preserve its beauty and innocence. That she cannot makes her feel that she is failing in her role as mother, and this leads to feelings of greater anguish and despair.

Mental anguish

This is ultimately a stark poem about mental anguish. To the poet the world seems a terribly dark place: 'dark/ Ceiling without a star'. Her description of the 'troublous/ Wringing' of her hands illustrates her inner mental suffering. Her child's innocence and her inability to provide it with bright and happy moments only heightens her sense of suffering. She is left feeling inadequate as a mother.

In this regard the poem can be compared to 'Morning Song' where the birth of poet's child leaves her feeling

numb and uncertain. However, in 'Morning Song' there is a sense in which the poet overcomes her feelings of inadequacy and doubt and relaxes into the role of being a mother. In 'Child' there is no suggestion that her feelings of inadequacy and despair are set to end.

LANGUAGE

Symbols

The flowers that the poet mentions are interesting: 'April snowdrop, Indian pipe'. It is quite possible that Plath meant them to represent something. The April snowdrop is a particularly beautiful flower, pure white in colour. Perhaps Plath meant this flower to represent the child who she considers perfectly beautiful and innocent.

The Indian pipe on the other hand is a less beautiful flower. It is said to exist in darkened forests and feeds on the decaying matter of other dead flowers. It may, therefore, represent the mother in the poem. She feels that she is living in a world without light, beneath a 'dark/ Ceiling without stars'. And perhaps she feels that in her despair and her inability to offer the child grand and beautiful images she is sucking the goodness out of it.

Metaphors

Plath compares her child to a 'Little// Stalk without wrinkles'. She also compares the child's eye to a 'Pool'. Both metaphors suggest the child's purity and innocence.

Imagery

The last three lines of the poem are powerful and convey so much to the reader. In twelve words Plath manages to convey the intensity of her anguish. She achieves this by focusing on two images: 'Wringing' hands and a 'dark/ Ceiling without star'. By focusing on the movements of her hands, the poet illustrates her inner turmoil. The image of the 'dark/ Ceiling without star' suggests that the speaker's world is closing in and that she is without hope.

DEREK MAHON
THEMES

COMPASSION

Mahon is a poet of compassion. He displays great feeling and understanding for those who have suffered throughout history. In 'After the *Titanic*', Mahon gives a voice to Bruce Ismay, a man that history has labelled a villain and a coward. The inquiry said that Ismay 'got away' the night of the disaster (when the *Titanic* sank) while leaving women and children to drown. Yet Ismay stresses that he has never been able to escape the horrific feelings of guilt and the terrible memories that have haunted him since the disaster. It is as though Ismay died and went to hell on the night of the disaster: 'I tell you/ I sank as far that night as any/ Hero'. By giving Ismay a voice, Mahon allows us to feel compassion and sympathy for a man the world would prefer to label a villain and to forget about.

In 'Antarctica', we are again presented with a man who finds himself in a dire situation and is faced with almost impossible choices. The image of Captain Laurence Oates walking out into the howling snow to die is intensely harrowing and heartbreaking. Mahon lauds the quiet dignity with which Oates departs the tent, declaring that he 'is just stepping outside and may be some time'. Mahon appreciates that there is something ridiculous about this 'stiff-upper-lipped' departure into the snow, and perhaps, too, about the entire expedition. But he also stresses that Oates' self-sacrifice to save his friends is a 'sublime' act of the human will.

There is a similarity between 'Day Trip to Donegal' and 'A Disused Shed in Co. Wexford'. Both poems show a deep compassion towards non-human creatures – fish in one case and mushrooms in the other. In 'Day Trip to Donegal', Mahon's compassion is evident in his description of the fishes' death throes. The fact that he describes their suffering in terms of human emotion – in 'attitudes of agony and heartbreak' – reinforces our sense of the compassion he feels for them. There is also real compassion in his depiction of the mushrooms' sufferings in the disused shed for fifty years. He mentions their nightmares and insomnia, their aching thirst, the shed's foul air, silence and darkness. His compassion also comes across when he describes the mushrooms warped and weakened state after a half-century of confinement.

'A Disused Shed' also displays compassion toward all those who have suffered throughout human history. The speaker associates the mushrooms with the 'Lost people of Treblinka and Pompeii', with all those who have suffered and died through natural disasters or through man's inhumanity to man. 'Rathlin' is another poem where Mahon reveals a deep compassion with those who have suffered throughout history. The poet is keenly aware of the 'unspeakable violence' that was visited upon Somhairle's people on the island in 1575, and of the horror and sorrow that must have that afflicted Somhairle as he listened to the women and children of his tribe being slaughtered.

ISOLATION

Many of Mahon's poems present us with individuals in extreme states of isolation. 'After the *Titanic*' describes how, as the *Titanic* sank, Bruce Ismay sat alone 'shivering on the dark water' in a small lifeboat. In the years following the disaster, the disgraced Ismay lives a life of seclusion: 'Now I hide/ In a lonely house behind the sea'. He suffers intense feelings of despair and psychological isolation, best captured by the powerful image of his 'soul' screaming out 'in the starlight'.

In 'Antarctica', the description of Oates as a 'Solitary enzyme' suggests the terrible isolation and loneliness of his predicament as he 'goads' himself out into the wilderness of 'howling snow'. It is harder to imagine a lonelier place on earth in which to die.

'Daytrip to Donegal' also presents us with a person in an extreme state of isolation. In his dream, the speaker find himself completely isolated on the ocean waves in the middle of a raging storm. He is utterly alone, lacking anyone to help, advise or even reassure him.

NATURE

Mahon is a poet keenly aware of the beauty of the natural world, and many of his poems contain wonderful nature imagery. 'The Chinese Restaurant in Portrush' highlights the beauty and tranquillity of the springtime with its soft air and pleasant, heavenly light 'upon the hills of Donegal'. Even the creatures in the poem are depicted as being playful and relaxed.

'Kinsale' offers a similar celebration of the natural world. Mahon lovingly describes the wet slates reflecting the sky, the damp windows shining in sunlight, the beautiful bay with its 'dancing' yachts.

In 'A Disused Shed in Co. Wexford', the mention of the rhododendrons and the rooks crying out in the 'high woods' powerfully contrasts nature's beauty outside the shed with the dismal environment inside. Similarly, 'After the *Titanic*' mentions the pleasures of springtime that no longer bring joy to the psychologically broken Ismay: 'The showers of/ April, flowers of May mean nothing to me, not the/ Late light of June'.

In 'Raithlin', Mahon celebrates Rathlin island as a serene 'sanctuary', a place where an unrivalled or 'singular' peace holds sway. He lovingly describes the noises made by the island's wildlife and the way the colours of sky and ocean meet at the faraway horizon: 'cerulean distance, an oceanic haze'.

However, Mahon is also well aware of the menace and danger of the natural world. Nature can be cruel and violent, and can sometimes display little regard for man. We see this in 'A Disused Shed', with the mention of Pompeii, the ancient town destroyed by a volcano. 'After the *Titanic*' reminds us how the supposedly unsinkable ship was sent 'thundering down' by its collision with the iceberg. Its mention of stormy weather in lines 15–16 also brings to mind nature's dangerous and menacing side.

The menacing power of the sea is highlighted in several poems. In 'Rathlin', there is a sense of threat and uncertainty as the poet and his friends leave the island, blinded by spray and tossed about on the 'pitching surfaces' of the 'turbulent sea'. In 'After the *Titanic*', the image of Ismay sitting alone upon the 'dark water' suggests the vastness and the indifference of the ocean. The conclusion of 'Day Trip to Donegal' makes a similar point: the speaker makes vain attempts to survive on the vastness of the storm-tossed ocean. 'Day Trip to Donegal' also emphasises how the 'grey' and 'grim' sea is consistently attacking the very land we stand on. The fishermen of Donegal may harvest the bounty of the sea, but the sea's power is steadily cutting the land from under their villages, until they collapse into the waves. It undermines the harbours and piers, the very places where its fish are brought ashore to die. The land is forced to forever futilely resist the sea's 'immeasurable erosions'.

Mahon is also aware that nature can sometimes be simply gloomy and depressing. In 'The Chinese Restaurant in Portrush', he mentions the sharp weather with its 'north-wind and the sea-mist' that force the people of the town to bolt their doors all winter. 'Ecclesiastes' depicts a bleak and oppressive environment, one of cold and hard January rain that darkens the landscape, of bogs littered with graves. The opening lines of 'Kinsale' are similar in this regard, with their depiction of dark rain 'browsing on spire and bogland'. 'Rathlin', though primarily a celebration of beauty, also suggests nature's gloomier side, with its mention of the 'bleak' wind that sometimes assaults the island.

THE NIGHTMARE OF HISTORY

The notion of history as an endless cycle of violence haunts several of Mahon's poems. His poetry tends to view human history as a vicious and bitter cycle of revenge, one in which each terrible act leads inexorably to the next. Irish history, in particular, is presented as a violent and tragic tale, as a senseless cycle of violence and bloodshed. This notion is evident in 'Rathlin'. The Rathlin massacre of the sixteenth century and the Northern Irish Troubles of the twentieth century are presented as being part of the same bitter and tragic story. The 'unspeakable violence' of 1575 leads to the 'bombs [that] doze in the housing estates' in the 1970s. 'A Disused Shed in Co. Wexford' touches on two episodes of Ireland's violent and troubled history: the civil war of the 1920s and the 'expropriation' of Protestant land by the new Catholic-dominated Southern state.

In 1601 the town of 'Kinsale' was the site of a bloody and decisive battle between Irish and English forces, one that led to many centuries of bitter conflict between England and Ireland and between the Catholic and Protestant communities within Ireland itself. In lines 1–3 of that poem, the dark, threatening rain falling endlessly on the dreary landscape symbolises these miserable centuries.

The imagery in 'The Chinese Restaurant in Portrush' also suggests Ireland's turbulent and bloody past. The 'old wolfhound' calls to mind the mythic character of Cú Chulainn, reminding us of the wars that were fought between Irish clans in ancient times. The description of harsh winter weather also seems symbolic of past violence, of invaders such as the Vikings coming across the sea to attack the town. The mention of the 'Northern Counties Hotel', meanwhile, reminds us that today Ireland remains a divided country.

'A Disused Shed in Co. Wexford' broadens its focus beyond Ireland, reminding us that human history as a whole can all too often be characterised as an endless series of bloody disasters. The mushrooms are associated with the victims of Treblinka and Pompeii, and by extension with all those who have suffered in natural disasters and cruel atrocities. We get the impression that it is too late to save the mushrooms. Yet they are presented as pleading with the poet to 'speak on their behalf'. If he speaks on their behalf, remembering how they lived and suffered, then their agonies, their 'naive labours', will not have been for nothing. Similarly, it is too late to save the 'lost people' of historical tragedies like Treblinka and Pompeii. Yet if we remember them, if we speak on their behalf and remember how they lived and suffered, perhaps their trials will not have been for nothing.

AN ESCAPE FROM HISTORY'S NIGHTMARE

In 'Rathlin', the poet imagines that Rathlin island is 'through with history', that the island is somehow outside Ireland's tragic and violent tale. He fantasises that the island is lost in a 'dream-time', a mystical and mythological period before history began. A similar notion is evident in 'Kinsale', which declares that 'the rain we knew is a thing of the past … We contemplate at last shining windows'. This new-found eternal sunshine is a metaphor for leaving history behind, of moving on from the cycles of bitter conflict that characterise Ireland's past. Whereas in the past, different factions and communities tried to deny one another a future, from now on the future will be 'forbidden to no one'. This impulse is also present in 'The Chinese Restaurant in Portrush'. On this spring day, Portrush seems a peaceful and relaxed place. It is 'Gentle and almost hospitable'. The 'invasion' that the town prepares itself for is no longer that of the Celts, Vikings or English, but, rather, one of tourists. The image of the 'old wolfhound' dozing in the sun also suggests that Ireland's days of war and bloodshed might just be behind it. However, such fantasies of escaping history cannot easily be sustained. In 'Rathlin', 'Kinsale' and 'The Chinese Restaurant in Portrush', we get the sense that Mahon cannot quite believe that the past is really left behind, cannot quite believe that the cycles of history are broken.

NARROW-MINDEDNESS

Many of Mahon's poems touch on the notion of narrow-mindedness, of individuals and communities who display a lack of tolerance, forgiveness and understanding toward others. This is evident in 'A Disused Shed in Co. Wexford'. The Protestant landowner who grew the mushrooms has his property 'expropriated' or confiscated by the new Catholic state that emerged after the Irish War of Independence. The mention of Treblinka in this poem brings to mind the Nazi's blind prejudice against the Jews and other minorities, an attitude that lead to millions of deaths in concentration camps.

In 'Ecclesiastes', the Protestants of Belfast are depicted as being extremely narrow-minded. They are presented as a 'God-chosen' community. 'As it Should Be' depicts a similarly narrow-minded attitude. The speaker and his companions mercilessly hunt the 'mad bastard' through the countryside before murdering him in a 'blind yard'. In 'Kinsale', however, Mahon dares to imagine that these fanatical and narrow-minded attitudes might be left in the past. He imagines a future 'forbidden to no one', that is open to and shared by all traditions, one in which no group forbids the others from partaking. A similar desire is hinted at in 'The Chinese Restaurant in Portrush'.

Grandfather

Derek Mahon

LINE BY LINE

The poem begins with a description of a time the grandfather was 'Wounded'. The details of the accident are vague. We are not told who brought the grandfather in on the stretcher, nor from where exactly he was brought. Saying that he was brought in 'from the world' gives us no clue as to his whereabouts when he was wounded. Perhaps Mahon says that the grandfather was brought in 'from the world' because the grandfather's movements are such a mystery to him that he cannot be more specific. As we read the poem, we get a sense that the grandfather is something of a secretive individual, someone the rest of the family find hard to keep track of ('Never there when you call', 'he escapes us all').

Though 'wounded', the grandfather remained in good spirits, and we are told that 'he soon recovered'. However, the injury, which may have been work-related, seems to have brought an end to his working life in the shipyard. The grandfather has probably worked in the shipyards since he was a young man. For many years, therefore, his weeks would have centred around the docks. The 'Boiler-rooms' and 'row upon row of gantries' would have been features of his daily professional life. When Mahon says that the boiler-rooms and gantries 'rolled/ Away to reveal the landscape of a childhood', he may mean two things:

- The grandfather's mind is deteriorating and the memories of his working years are slowly vanishing but those of his childhood remain strong.
- The grandfather's mind is still sharp but now that he is no longer working in the shipyards, he gives little thought to the place. It is as if the period spent working on the docks was a great block of time dividing him from his childhood. Now that he is no longer working, that part of his life can be put to one side and he can return to the world of his childhood, a time of freedom and no responsibility.

Despite the fact that he has retired, the grandfather maintains a routine of sorts. Perhaps the fact that he has been getting up early for work for so long accounts for the fact that 'Even on cold/ Mornings he is up at six'. But his daily routine now lacks the focus and discipline of his working years. He occupies himself with apparently random, aimless activities. He is like a mischievous child, 'discreetly up to no good/ Or banging around the house like a four-year-old'.

The grandfather answers to nobody. He comes and goes as he wishes, and feels no obligation to explain his movements. The fact that he is 'Never there when you call' suggests that he is out of the house most of the time, often only returning home 'after dark'. Though he makes no secret of his return – 'You hear his great boots thumping in the hall' – he reveals little about where he has been, possibly cleverly avoiding any questions regarding his whereabouts: 'in he comes, as cute as they come'.

Every night before he falls asleep, the grandfather's 'shrewd eyes bolt the door and set the clock/ Against the future'. What does it mean to say that the grandfather bolts the door and sets the clock with his 'eyes'? We might also wonder what it means to bolt the door and set the clock 'Against the future'. There are a number of possibilities here:

- The grandfather actually bolts the door and sets the clock every night. That Mahon says he does this with his 'shrewd eyes' may mean that the grandfather does this in a very conscious manner, carefully checking that it is done properly. The grandfather does not do these things to protect himself against the future. The poet thinks that his grandfather is afraid of the future, and he associates the grandfather's nightly actions with this assumed fear.
- The grandfather does not actually bolt the door and set the clock before he sleeps. The bolting of the door and setting of the clock are metaphors for the way the grandfather mentally deals with the idea of the future. It may be the idea of his own mortality that he fears, or just that he has no time for the modern world and wishes to live in the past. Each night before he sleeps, he blocks out all thoughts of what is set to come. Mahon is aware that his grandfather feels this way about the future, and uses the metaphor of the door and clock to illustrate the old man's fear or dislike of the future.

Whatever fears or misgivings the grandfather has about the future, the measures he takes seem to give him peace of mind. Once he has gone through the ritual of bolting the door and setting the clock (whether actually or metaphorically), he instantly falls asleep: 'his light goes out'.

The last line of the poem tells us of the grandfather's sharpness: 'Nothing escapes him'. He seems to notice everything. Though he behaves at times like a 'four-year-old' and is often absent from the house, it appears that the grandfather is very clued-in to what is going on around him. But if he has a solid grasp on the actions of the rest of the family, they are incapable of getting a firm grip on him: 'he escapes us all'.

THEMES

The grandfather

The poem is essentially a character sketch of the poet's grandfather. The grandfather seems to have retired from work after the injury mentioned at the start of the poem. We are not told anything about the accident that occurred but we might guess that the grandfather's injury was work-related and possibly due to his ailing mental or physical condition. He is getting old and is no longer as capable as he once was. The description of the shipyards rolling 'Away to reveal the landscape of a childhood' suggests that the grandfather's memory might be suffering and he may no longer be able to recall the place he worked at. His behaviour is also becoming somewhat childlike. He is described as being 'up to no good' and 'banging round the house like a four-year-old'.

Yet the grandfather remains a formidable individual. He remains in good spirits when he is injured, and recovers quickly from his injuries: 'he soon recovered'. We get the impression that the grandfather is a force to be reckoned with: 'You hear his great boots thumping in the hall'. He is a man used to hard work: 'Even on cold/ Mornings he is up at six'. Now, however, his days lack the focus and discipline of his working years. He busies himself with activities that probably have little purpose. The description of him working with 'a block of wood/ Or a box of nails' suggests that the poet finds it impossible to say what it is that the grandfather is doing with these items.

It seems that the grandfather is something of an enigma to the rest of the family: 'He escapes us all'. We get the impression that the grandfather likes to be discreet and feels no obligation to let others know of his whereabouts: 'Never there when you call'. Though he is behaving in a childlike fashion, he remains 'shrewd' and 'cute as they come'. He seems to be well aware of all that is happening around him: 'Nothing escapes him'.

Mahon hints at the grandfather's uncertainty or fear of the future. He seems to feel the need to shut what lies ahead out of his mind before he goes to sleep: 'Each night/ His shrewd eyes bolt the door and set the clock/ Against the future'. Perhaps it is thoughts of growing old and dying that the grandfather tries to ward off, or perhaps he has a lack of regard for the changing modern world.

Old age

When he stops working, the grandfather suddenly has his days completely to himself. The last time he had such freedom and independence was when he was a child. The grandfather's working life seems to have ultimately amounted to a lengthy interlude or break from a childhood that he resumes upon retirement. When he stops working at the shipyards, this part of his life seems to just vanish, or roll away, and reveal the world that he knew as a child: 'row upon row of gantries rolled/ Away to reveal the landscape of a childhood'. The grandfather's reversion to the world of his childhood may be a result of his weakening mental faculties.

The poem suggests that old age can be much like a second childhood. Upon retirement, the grandfather's behaviour seems to become childlike. He is described messing around 'with a block of wood/ Or a box of nails' and 'banging around the house like a four-year-old'. Though he continues to rise early – a habit from his working days – his activity now seems aimless, random and incomprehensible to the rest of the family. We get the impression that the grandfather may not be the easiest person to live with. He keeps to himself and seems to be a bit of a troublemaker: 'discreetly up to no good'.

But even if he behaves like a child, his age disallows the rest of the family from treating him like one. He comes and goes as he pleases, often disappearing without word to anyone: 'never there when you call'.

Derek Mahon

LANGUAGE

Form

The poem is written in the form of a sonnet. Like all sonnets, it has fourteen lines. The first eight lines (the octet) are separated from the last six (the sestet). However, Mahon does not strictly observe the conventions of the sonnet. Although some lines contain ten syllables, most contain more.

The poem features a lot of half-rhyme. Mahon rhymes 'world' with 'rolled', 'recovered' with 'childhood', and 'dark' with 'clock'.

Sounds

The third line features both assonance and alliteration: 'row upon row of gantries rolled'. Assonance occurs in the repetition of the 'o' sounds, and repeated 'r' sounds are an example of alliteration.

Day Trip to Donegal

LINE BY LINE

In this poem, the speaker and some friends make a trip from Belfast to a seaside village in Donegal. They arrive in the afternoon, their legs stiff from the car journey. They set about performing the errands that brought them there: 'there were things to be done,/ Clothes to be picked up, friends to be seen'. According to the speaker, the hills of Donegal are an incredibly rich green, a 'deeper green than anywhere in the world'. The view, however, is not entirely pretty, for the sea off the Donegal coast is particularly bleak and grey: 'the grave/ Grey of the sea the grimmer in that enclave'.

Fishing boats deposit their haul of fish at the village's pier. Dying fish writhe and squirm on the boats' decks. The speaker vividly depicts their death throes: 'Herring and mackerel, flopping about the deck/ In attitudes of agony and heartbreak'. To him, these dying fish seem to endure 'heartbreak', a very human type of anguish. The fact that he thinks of the fish having human emotions indicates his distress at their suffering.

After a few hours, the speaker and his friends return to Belfast. They drive through the countryside, the sea receding into the distance behind them: 'The sea receding down each muddy lane'. Eventually, they reach the suburbs of Belfast where the speaker lives. The speaker bids his friends goodnight, promising to phone them soon, and heads to bed: 'Give me a ring, goodnight, and so to bed'.

The suburbs are presented as a cosy environment, one where people sleep safely. This is a landscape far from the storms and rages of the sea: 'Sunk in a sleep no gale force wind disturbs'. However, the phrase 'changed-down into suburbs' suggests that this suburban landscape is somewhat dull or boring. This phrase refers to the driver putting the car into a lower gear as they enter the suburbs. However, it also suggests that suburban life represents a 'change down', or lowering in excitement and intensity. Life in the suburbs, it seems to imply, is simply duller and more mundane than life outside them.

That night, the speaker's rest is disturbed by a terrifying dream or hallucination. He dreams that he is almost completely immersed in sea water. He dreams that the seawater erodes his body with an incredible or immeasurable slowness: 'That night the slow sea washed against my head/ performing its immeasurable erosions'. He dreams that seawater comes pouring into his skull, presumably through his mouth, eyes and ears: 'Spilling into the skull'.

In the dream, the speaker is keenly aware of coastal erosion. The waves threaten to slowly erode the land from under the fishing villages, making them fall into the sea: 'Muttering its threats to villages of landfall'. It caresses the stones that form the backbone of the harbour until they are smooth as marble: 'Marbling the stones that spine the very harbour wall'. The effect of each wave upon the land is 'immeasurable'; it is too small to notice or be measured. Yet, over time the waves will reduce the coastline to nothing.

The nightmare enters a new phase. It is dawn and the speaker is floating on the ocean's surface. It is unclear if he is actually in the water or if he is aboard some kind of craft.

He is surrounded by a raging storm, lashed at by the wind and rain. He lacks the 'skill' or knowledge to deal with this situation. He is utterly alone. There is no one to reassure him, no one to rescue him, no one to teach him how to survive this ordeal: 'nobody/ To show me how, no promise of rescue'.

The speaker curses himself for failing to anticipate or prepare for this possibility: 'Cursing my constant failure to take due/ Forethought of this'. He pleads desperately with the wind and rain not to destroy him: 'Contriving vain/ Overtures to vindictive wind and rain'. His pleas, of course, are 'vain' – or futile – because the weather cannot listen.

THEMES

Compassion

Mahon's intense compassion comes across in many of his poems. In 'Day Trip to Donegal', this compassion is evident in his description of the fishes' death throes. The speaker appears to feel real sympathy for these creatures that writhe in 'attitudes of agony and heartbreak'. The fact that he describes the suffering of the fish in terms of human emotion reinforces our sense of the compassion he feels for them.

The poem stresses the fact that the fishermen are driven by commercial concerns. They make a living because city-dwellers are prepared to pay a lot of money for the fish they catch: 'they fetch/ Ten times as much in the city as here'. It has been suggested that the speaker seems to experience guilt because his fellow human beings are killing the fish for reasons of profit. Perhaps it is this mixture of guilt and compassion that prompts the nightmare or vision that overcomes him as he lies in bed that night.

A similar compassion is evident throughout Mahon's poetry: towards Captain Oates in 'Antarctica', towards Bruce Ismay and the 'dim/ Lost faces of the drowned' in 'After the *Titanic*', towards the hunted 'mad bastard' in 'As it Should Be'. There is a particular note of similarity between this poem and 'A Disused Shed in Co. Wexford'. Both poems show a deep compassion for non-human creatures: for fish in one case and for mushrooms in the other.

Nature

This is a poem that highlights the menace and danger of the natural world – specifically, the power and fury of the sea:

- The sea's menace is first suggested in stanza 1. The ocean is described as being 'grave', 'grey' and 'grim' – terms that suggest its dangerous and threatening nature.
- It is also referenced in stanza 3: the cosy inland suburbs are described as being spared the raging winds associated with the ocean: 'Sunk in a sleep no gale-force wind disturbs'.
- In stanza 4, we see it slowly but relentlessly consuming the harbours of the fishing villages: 'Muttering its threat to villages of landfall'. These processes of erosion may be too gradual too measure ('immeasurable'), but they are constantly occurring.
- Particularly unnerving is the speaker's dream that he is lying immersed up to his head in ocean water, the sea 'pouring' into his skull.
- Above all, the sea's menace is highlighted by the speaker's terrible nightmare of floating alone on the ocean's surface in the middle of a storm. There is something highly unsettling about the thought of being 'alone far out at sea/ without skill reassurance'.

Many readers see this poem as a depiction of an endless struggle between land and sea. In the first half of the poem, the land might be said to have the upper hand. We see land dwellers harvesting the ocean's inhabitants for commercial gain. Fishermen are depicted plundering the ocean's depths, knowing they can sell the mackerel they catch for a huge profit in the city.

In the second half of the poem, however, the power of the sea over the land is emphasised. The fishermen of Donegal may harvest the bounty of the sea, but the sea's power is steadily cutting the land from under their villages, until their villages collapse into the waves. The sea is slowly undermining the harbours and piers, the very places where its fish are brought ashore to die. The land is forced to forever futilely resist the sea's 'immeasurable erosions'.

At the beginning of the poem, it is the fish that struggle hopelessly to survive on land. At the end, it is the human speaker who makes vain attempts to survive on the vastness of the ocean. His desperate pleadings to the wind and rain can be compared to the futile writing of the fish in stanza 2. Like them, he is out of his natural element. Both the fish on the pier and the speaker on the vast ocean make vain attempts to survive in unspeakably alien and hostile environments.

The menace and power of the sea is also highlighted in 'Rathlin', where the speaker's boat is tossed among ocean's 'pitching surfaces' as he leaves the island behind. It is also present in 'After the *Titanic*', which depicts the 'pandemonium' that occurred in the wake of the liner's tragic collision with the iceberg. 'Antarctica', too, highlights nature's menace, depicting the deadly 'howling snow' of the frozen continent.

Isolation

Like many of Mahon's poems, this one presents us with a person in an extreme state of isolation. In his dream, the speaker find himself completely isolated on the ocean waves in the middle of a raging storm. As noted above, he is utterly alone, lacking anyone to help, advise or even reassure him. Similar terrible moments of isolation occur in 'Antarctica', where Captain Oates walks alone into the ice and snow, and in 'As it Should Be', where the 'mad bastard' is hunted alone through the countryside, and in 'After the *Titanic*', which describes how Bruce Ismay finds himself living a reclusive, isolated life.

The nightmare of history

This poem can also be subjected to a political reading. Significantly, the menacing sea is located in Donegal, a predominantly Catholic area. Donegal is presented as a Catholic 'enclave', as one Catholic county surrounded by the Protestant North. In the 1960s, when Mahon wrote the poem, Northern Catholics were greatly exploited and oppressed by the dominant Protestant majority, just as the sea's resources are exploited by the fishermen in the poem. Perhaps, therefore, the sea's night-time 'revenge' on the poet represents a Catholic backlash against this exploitation, a backlash that Mahon, as a Protestant, greatly feared, and which eventually materialised at the start of the Northern Irish Troubles in 1968. The Protestant majority, the poem suggests, should take 'due forethought' of their actions before it is too late and they are left making 'vain overtures' in an effort to halt terrible waves of violence.

This notion of history as an endless cycle of violence haunts several of Mahon's poems. His poetry tends to view human history – in particular Irish history – as a vicious and bitter cycle of revenge, one in which each bad or violent act leads inexorably on to the next. We see this notion in 'Rathlin', in 'Kinsale' and in 'The Chinese Restaurant in Portrush'. It is arguably also present in 'A Disused Shed in Co. Wexford'.

LANGUAGE

There are several instances of pathetic fallacy in this poem. This occurs when we attribute human emotions to non-human things. In stanza 2, for instance, the fish are described as experiencing 'heartbreak', a very human state of being. Similarly, in stanza 5 the wind and rain are described as 'vindictive', suggesting that they are deliberately trying to torment the speaker.

This poem is a masterpiece of atmosphere, a mood of fear and tension gradually building throughout. The first notes of unease are struck by the depiction of the sea's menacing greyness and of the fish suffering and dying. Though stanza 3 describes the cosiness of the suburbs, it still references the raging gales that lash the coastline. The ice on the footpaths remind us that the suburbs are by no means immune from nature's effects. The poem's final stanzas are particularly unnerving in tone and atmosphere, with their chilling descriptions of the speaker's nightmare.

An interesting feature of the poem is the way it moves from the realistic imagery of the opening stanzas – which depict a trip to visit friends and perform errands – to the bizarre and surreal imagery of the poem's conclusion. We move from straightforward narrative language ('We reached the sea in early afternoon … We … climbed stiffly out … We left at eight') to imagery that is nightmarish, weird and unsettling.

Particularly surreal is the phrase 'marbling the stones/ That spine the very harbour wall'. On one level, this refers to the ocean eroding the rocks and landmasses that form the foundations of the harbour. Yet we can also visualise the seawater washing against the speaker's head, pouring into his ear, flowing down the inside of his back and caressing the components of his spine. This strange and unnerving description is the stuff of nightmares.

'Day Trip to Donegal', like much of Mahon's poetry, makes extremely skilful use of sound effects:

- The alliterative repetition of the harsh 'gr' sound in 'grave', 'grey' and 'grimmer' generates a cacophonous musical effect, emphasising the ocean's bleakness and severity.
- The repeated sibilant 's' sound in the phrases 'slow sea', 'spilling into the skull' and 'stones that spine' mimics the sound of the sea washing against the coast.
- Assonance creates a sweet, euphonious effect through the repeated 'e' sounds in 'deeper green', suggesting the beauty of the hills.
- The phrase 'A writhing glimmer of fish' is arresting both visually and musically. We can almost visualise the fish squirming in agony on the pier. The repeated 'i' sound reinforces the power of the image, generating a sinewy, sensuous music.
- Onomatopoeia occurs in lines 11–12. The verse here has an uneasy, jumpy quality, in which we can almost hear the dying fish 'flopping about the deck'.
- A similar onomatopoeic effect is generated by the phrase 'performing its immeasurable erosions', in which we can almost hear the waves dissolving on the shoreline.
- It should also be noted that the poem has a strict AABBCC rhyme scheme.

After the *Titanic*

INTRODUCTION

The speaker of the poem is Bruce Ismay. He was the manager of the White Star Line, the company responsible for the *Titanic*. Ismay was aboard the ship on its tragic maiden voyage to America. Ismay stated that after the ship struck the ice, he helped for nearly two hours in clearing the starboard boats, helping women and children into them, and lowering them over the side. He claimed that when he got into the forward collapsible boat, there was nobody left for him to help. He also testified that as the *Titanic* broke apart and sank, he turned away, unable to watch his creation vanish beneath the waters of the North Atlantic. In view of the fact that more than 1,500 persons perished in the disaster, Ismay was the subject of criticism both in England and in America for his conduct in leaving the *Titanic* at all. His reputation was irreparably damaged, and he maintained a low public profile after the disaster.

LINE BY LINE
LINES 1–8

Ismay was humiliated, or 'humbled', at the inquiry established to investigate the sinking of the *Titanic*. He was accused of acting in a selfish and cowardly manner, of escaping in one of the few available lifeboats, leaving women and children to perish. 'They said I got away in a boat'.

The American press considered those men who sank with the ship heroes, and they labelled Ismay a coward for surviving. But Ismay says that he 'sank as far that night as any/ Hero'. Whereas the so-called 'heroes' sank to the bottom of the ocean, Ismay 'sank' in a metaphorical sense, possibly into the depths of despair.

Shivering in the small lifeboat 'on the dark water', Ismay 'turned to ice' as he listened to the 'costly' life he had established for himself crumble and sink beneath the water: 'I turned to ice to hear my costly/ Life go thundering down'. When he says that he 'turned to ice', he may be referring to how cold he felt upon the water. Ismay was so cold that he metaphorically 'turned to ice'. But the phrase is more likely a reference to his emotional condition as he watched all he had worked so hard to build crumble and vanish. Ismay suggests that he froze with shock and horror as he listened to the terrible sounds of the ship breaking. (We could also understand the phrase in terms of the ship's movements before it struck the iceberg. The *Titanic* turned towards ice and this resulted in the destruction of Ismay's 'costly life'.)

Ismay's life can be considered 'costly' in a number of ways:

* It was a life that entailed great financial cost. The building of such grand ships cost extraordinary amounts of money.
* As a highly successful businessman, Ismay's life was costly or lavish.
* His life was costly in that the disaster resulted in the loss of so many lives.

Lines 6–8 describe the deafening, chaotic sounds of the sinking ship. The word 'thundering' tells of the violent, explosive sound of the ship entering the water. The word 'pandemonium' suggests the mayhem as the boat rips apart and all kinds of object are thrown about, smashed and crushed: 'a pandemonium of/ Prams, pianos, sideboards, winches,/ Boilers bursting and shredded ragtime'.

LINES 8–20

Ismay is now an old man. He lives alone in a remote house somewhere by the sea. Here, he hides from the world: 'Now I hide/ In a lonely house behind the sea'. The word 'behind' suggests that Ismay is using the sea to shield himself, perhaps from the rest of the world.

Since the disaster occurred, Ismay lives an unhappy life. The changing seasons bring him no joy: 'The showers of/ April, flowers of May mean nothing to me, nor the/ Late light of June'. When he is feeling particularly bad. he 'stays in bed' all day and 'will see no one'.

Though many years have passed since the disaster, Ismay cannot forget about the tragedy. Thoughts of those who died, especially the women and children, continue to return and haunt him. The speaker uses a metaphor to describe the way these memories return. He says that the sea silently deposits 'broken toys and hatboxes' at his door. The 'broken toys' represent the children who died and the 'hatboxes' the women. Thoughts of these victims of the disaster continue to haunt the man who was accused of neglecting them when he 'got away' in one of the lifeboats. Ismay's suffering is most intense after stormy nights. After such 'nights of/ Wind', he stays in bed and takes cocaine to soothe his troubled mind. But the cocaine does not allow him to escape the nightmarish memories of the disaster. On such mornings, after he has taken his cocaine, Ismay imagines that he is drowning 'again' with the

many victims of the disaster: 'Then it is/ I drown again with all those dim/ Lost faces'.

Ismay imagines that he is once again sitting alone in the lifeboat on the night of the disaster. He imagines his 'soul' screaming out into a vast and indifferent universe: 'poor soul/ Screams out in the starlight'. He also imagines his heart breaking free from his body and sinking into the ocean: 'heart/ Breaks loose and rolls down like a stone'.

Ismay describes those who actually died that night as 'dim/ Lost faces I never understood'. The faces are 'dim' to Ismay because, perhaps, these are people he never knew well. Ismay would have only mingled with the first-class passengers on the ship and, therefore, never gotten to know the bulk of those travelling on the ship. Because of the class divisions of the time, the rich and poor led very separate existences, and so Ismay would have 'never understood' the lives of many of the people who drowned that night. Those who drowned are now 'Lost' deep beneath the ocean.

In one sense, Ismay feels that he also drowned or died the night the *Titanic* sank. Though he lives on, it is a life without joy, a hellish existence in which he is condemned to suffer again and again. He asks at the end of the poem that we consider him along with the dead and include him in our 'lamentations' for the victims of the *Titanic*.

THEMES

Compassion
In 'After the *Titanic*', Mahon presents us with a man that history has labelled a villain and a coward. Bruce Ismay has traditionally been cast as the selfish and heartless character in the tragic tale of the *Titanic*. There is much debate about what he did and did not do both before the ship hit the iceberg and after. But Mahon does not focus on this. He does not seek to judge Ismay in the poem. He gives Ismay a voice and allows him to speak of the suffering he endured the night the ship sank, and also of the suffering he has endured ever since.

Ismay was never able to leave the incident behind. Feelings of guilt and memories of the night the ship sank remained with him all his life. He tells us that he now lives a secluded life, hidden away from the rest of the world, no longer able to feel any pleasure at the beauty of the natural world around him: 'The showers of/ April, flowers of May, mean nothing to me'. On some mornings, the memories of the incident and, perhaps, feelings of guilt are so strong that he remains in bed, 'takes his cocaine and will see no one'.

It is as though Ismay died and went to hell the night the ship sank. Though the inquiry said that he 'got away' from the disaster, Ismay stresses that he has never been able to escape. In this regard, he perhaps has suffered as much, if not more, as any man who drowned that night: 'I tell you/ I sank as far that night as any/ Hero'. By giving Ismay a voice, Mahon allows us to feel compassion for his suffering and to sympathise with someone the world would prefer to cast as a villain and to forget.

Isolation
The poem describes the terrible isolation that Ismay experienced the night the *Titanic* sank. As the great ship broke apart and went 'thundering down' into the ocean, Ismay sat alone 'shivering on the dark water' in a small lifeboat. We might compare his ordeal to that of Captain Oates in 'Antarctica' – another man who became isolated in a very remote part of the world.

Following the disaster, Ismay was isolated by society. The press labelled him a coward and vilified him for his behaviour: 'They said I got away in a boat'. As a result, Ismay sought to hide himself away. He moved to 'a lonely house' and lived a life of seclusion: 'Now I hide/ In a lonely house behind the sea'.

Ismay's feelings of isolation are most intense after stormy nights. It is on such occasions that he vividly re-experiences the terrible night the *Titanic* sank. Shut away in his room, he 'takes his cocaine and will see no one'. It is then that he relives the horror of being alone upon the 'dark' water. Perhaps the most powerful description of isolation in the poem is that of Ismay's 'soul' screaming 'out in the starlight', a horrifying image of aloneness in a vast, indifferent universe.

We also get a sense of how the class structure of the time – particularly evident on the *Titanic* – meant that Ismay remained apart from many of the passengers on the ship. He hints at this divide when he refers to 'all those dim/ Lost faces I never understood'.

Nature

The poem presents us with two sides of the natural world. On the one hand, the natural world is something perilous and indifferent to the lives, dreams and ambitions of man. Ismay's whole world is sent crashing to the bottom of the ocean when the *Titanic* strikes the iceberg. The image of him sitting alone upon the 'dark water' suggests the vastness and the indifference of the ocean. The violent stormy nights that are mentioned in lines 15–16 cause Ismay to suffer greatly as he is reminded once again of the disaster.

The poem also reveals the softer and more beautiful side of the natural world. Mahon lists the pleasant features of the seasons that no longer bring joy to the broken Ismay: 'The showers of/ April, flowers of May mean nothing to me, not the/ Late light of June'.

LANGUAGE

Tone

The poem is a lamentation in which the speaker – Bruce Ismay – describes the suffering he has had to endure since the *Titanic* sank. The tone of the poem is predominantly melancholic. Although Ismay begins with an assertive tone at the beginning ('I tell you …'), the poem finishes with a broken and guilt-ridden man asking us to include him in our 'lamentations'.

Imagery

Like a number of other Mahon poems on the course, this poem contains images of the sea. Ismay describes the 'dark water' that he had to sit on as the *Titanic* broke apart and sank. There is also the image of the sea depositing 'broken toys and hatboxes' at the speaker's door.

Sound effects

The poem features a number of examples of alliteration. In lines 6–8 the repetition of hard consonant sounds reflects the unpleasant sound of the ship breaking apart: 'a pandemonium of/ Prams, pianos, sideboards, winches,/ Boilers bursting'. The combination of these harsh sounds provide us with a good example of cacophony.

Lines 18–19 use alliteration to a different effect, featuring a number of words beginning with 's': 'my poor soul/ Screams out in the starlight'. The repeated 's' sounds are good example of sibilance.

Lines 17–20 feature repeated 'o' sounds, a good example of assonance:

I dr*o*wn again with all th*o*se dim
L*o*st faces I never underst*oo*d, my p*oo*r s*o*ul
Screams *o*ut in the starlight, heart
Breaks l*oo*se and r*o*lls d*o*wn like a st*o*ne

The assonance in these lines, along with the repeated soft 's' sounds, creates a mournful effect that reflects the speaker's suffering.

The repeated 'a' sounds in lines 3 and 4 is another example of assonance: 'I sank as far that night as any/ Hero. As I sat shivering on the dark water'. Again, the effect of the long-vowel sounds is to slow the reader down and reflect the speaker's bleak situation.

Rhyme

The poem does not have any structured rhyming scheme. There is an example of internal rhyme in lines 11 and 12 where Mahon rhymes 'showers' with 'flowers'.

Ecclesiastes

Derek Mahon

LINE BY LINE

Who is speaking in this poem & who is being spoken to?

In this poem, an artist is being addressed by an unnamed speaker. The artist grew up in Belfast. We get the impression that he has been away from the city for a long time and has returned there only for a brief visit. The speaker urges the artist to become an 'Ecclesiastes', a kind of prophet or religious leader.

How does the poem depict the Protestant religion in Belfast?

This poem paints a very negative portrait of the Protestant religion as it is practised in Belfast:

- This type of religion is described as 'puritan', meaning it regards nearly all pleasure and luxury as sinful.
- It is described as 'God-fearing', suggesting that it depicts God as a terrifying, vengeful force rather than as a being of love.
- It is described as 'God-chosen': its adherents believe that they alone are chosen by God to be saved, that they alone know what it is to be righteous.
- It is presented as being suspicious of joy and fun: in Belfast, the swings in the public parks were tied up on Sundays because it was considered sinful to play on the Lord's holy day.

On the whole, this Belfast Protestantism is depicted as grim and joyless. It is associated with a series of dreary images: 'empty streets', 'dank churches', 'tied-up swings', 'dark doors', dark and hard January rain, with bogs that are littered with graves.

What kind of lifestyle is the artist currently living?

We get a sense that the artist enjoys a laid-back, somewhat carefree existence devoted to travel and art. His values are symbolised by the red bandana, the stick and the banjo. The stick, like a hiker's staff, symbolises his love of travel. The banjo suggests his love of music, literature and art. The red bandana was a fashion item associated with a liberal and non-conformist youth culture. It suggests the easygoing way of life associated with the hippy movement of the 1960s and 1970s.

What does the speaker urge the artist to do?

The speaker urges the artist to abandon his current carefree existence: 'Bury that red/ bandana and stick, that banjo'. He urges him instead to become an Ecclesiastes – a type of prophet or spiritual leader. An Ecclesiastes must behave in the following way:

- An Ecclesiastes must become 'cold'. He must leave behind feeling and emotion.
- He must deny himself contact with women and children.
- He must wear only black clothing.
- He must adopt the traditional diet of the Old Testament prophets, drinking only water and eating only 'locusts and wild honey'.
- He must learn to love the grim Antrim landscape: the dark hard January rains, the dark doors of Belfast city, the bleak hills and the boggy meadows filled with the graves of his ancestors.
- He must learn to speak with 'afflatus' – with inspiration and authority that comes directly from the heavens.
- He must not listen to the arguments, excuses or objections of others: he must 'not/ feel called upon to understand and forgive'. The only point of view that matters to an Ecclesiastes is his own.
- Such a lifestyle would 'nourish a fierce zeal' in the Ecclesiastes, strengthening his religious convictions and his belief in his own status as a prophet.

Perhaps the most disturbing item on this list is the depiction of women and children as a dangerous 'heat' that might damage the prophet's cold heart: 'shelter your cold heart from the heat/ of the world'. The phrase 'women-inquisition' suggests that women are an invasive and distracting presence. Children, too, are to be avoided: 'shelter your cold heart … from the bright eyes of children'.

Derek Mahon

What does the speaker say about the artist's personality?

The artist thinks of himself as a cheerful, liberated and light-hearted person, one full of 'wiles and smiles'. Yet according to the speaker, at heart he is still a 'God-fearing, God-/ chosen purist little puritan'. He is unable to shake off the influence of the extremely stern and puritan religion he grew up with.

Because the artist was so greatly influenced by Belfast's joyless brand of Protestantism, he could come to love the bitterly strict lifestyle of an Ecclesiastes: 'God, you could grow to love it'.

What role will the artist play if he becomes an Ecclesiastes?

By becoming an Ecclesiastes, the artist could make himself leader, or 'king', of Protestant Belfast. The speaker declares that the Protestants of Belfast are waiting for him, eager for him to assume the role of their spiritual leader: 'this is your country … your people await you'. They will greet him not with flags or palm branches but with laundry dangling on washing lines: 'their heavy washing/ flaps for you in the council estates'.

The artist could 'stand on a corner stiff/ with rhetoric' preaching to the Belfast faithful. According to the speaker, he would offer his people 'nothing under the sun'. This phrase might imply that he will offer them not the brightness and happiness we associate with the sun but only darkness and misery. However, it might also imply that he that he would promise his people nothing, that all his promises are false. (Rhetoric is the art of public speaking, of persuasive argument. However, it also suggests exaggeration, insincerity and false promises.)

The speaker concludes by emphasising once again that the artist could take the step of becoming an Ecclesiastes, of becoming Protestant Belfast's spiritual king: 'God, you could do it'. Yet the preacher seems to acknowledge that this is not an attractive move. His comment 'you could do it, God/ help you' indicates that he has a degree of pity for anyone who would assume the role of religious leader to these people.

What is meant by the phrase 'close one eye and be king'?

This phrase refers to an old proverb, coined by Erasmus: 'In the land of the blind, the one-eyed man is king'.

- At the moment, the artist is mentally 'fully sighted'; he is an intelligent, intellectually aware and open-minded young man.
- In order to become an Ecclesiastes or spiritual leader, he must give up some of this open-mindedness. He must 'Close one eye' in order to be 'king'.
- Yet he will never be as blinkered as the Protestant people of Northern Ireland. These people, it is implied, are completely intellectually blind.

Metaphorically speaking, the artist will be a 'one-eyed man' among the blind, and in a land of blind people even being able to see out of one eye leaves you in a privileged, powerful position. Therefore, by metaphorically closing 'one eye', Mahon could become leader, or 'king', of Protestant Belfast.

THEMES

A complex relationship with place

The speaker highlights the artist's complicated relationship with his home city of Belfast. The poem provides a scathing description of the city:

- In physical terms, it is grim and depressing: a city of empty streets, dank churches and dark doors. It is lashed by 'hard rain' and surrounded by hard hills and grave-filled bogs.
- Its people are depicted as intellectually blinkered and mentally limited. As we have seen, the speaker implies that Protestant Belfast is the 'land of the blind', a place filled with gullible or 'credulous' people.
- As we have seen, the religion practised there is depicted as being remarkably bleak: a stern and puritan creed that denies most of the pleasures in life.

Yet the speaker emphasises that this grim city is very much a part of the artist's mind and personality. On one level, the artist *is* the dank churches and the empty streets of Belfast: 'you are (the/ dank churches, the empty streets'). Because he grew up in Belfast, no matter how far he travels that city will be a part of his psychological make-up.

The people of Belfast may be intellectually blind but they are still his people: 'this is your country … your people await you'. This is the place where generations of his ancestors are buried: 'the heaped graves of your grandfathers'. He may have left Belfast behind but in an important sense he will always be a part of the Belfast community he grew up in.

The artist may think of himself as a carefree person full of 'wiles and smiles' but the stern and puritan religion of his childhood has had a major effect on his personality. Deep down, the poem suggests, he is still a 'purist, little puritan'.

In a sense, then, the poem reflects Mahon's mixed feelings about the city he grew up in. He left Belfast as a young man and never lived there for any sustained period throughout his adult life. Yet, in an important sense, the city and its people have continued to haunt the landscapes of his mind and of his poetry.

Narrow-mindedness
In this poem, the Protestants of Belfast are depicted as being extremely narrow-minded. They are a 'God-chosen' community, one that believes they alone have been chosen by God and know what is right. As we have seen, they are dismissed as a gullible and 'credulous' race, one that is mentally and intellectually blind.

If anything, an Ecclesiastes, as spiritual leader of these people, is required to be even more narrow-minded. He must express no forgiveness of others, no understanding of others' points of view. He must cultivate the 'fierce zeal' of an Old Testament prophet, an absolute certainty that he alone is right. He must convince himself that he speaks with 'afflatus', that his words have been directly inspired by God.

'As it Should Be' depicts a similar attitude. In that poem, the speaker and his companions display a similar narrow-mindedness, a similar lack of forgiveness and understanding, when they hunt the 'mad bastard' through the countryside before murdering him in a 'blind yard'. It could be argued that narrow-mindedness is also referred to in 'A Disused Shed in Co. Wexford'. In that poem, the Protestant landowner who grew the mushrooms has his property 'expropriated' or confiscated by the new Catholic state that emerged after the Irish War of Independence.

Religion
As we have seen, this poem is extremely critical of the type of Protestantism practised in Belfast. It is presented as being remarkably bleak, a faith associated with images of dank churches and empty city streets. It is a stern and puritan creed that denies most of the pleasures in life – so much so that swings must be tied up on Sundays. Its adherents associate God with fear as much as with love. They believe that they alone have been chosen by God to be righteous. They appear to have little interest in understanding or forgiveness, or at least do not require those qualities in their spiritual leaders.

This bleakness is particularly evident in the things required of an Ecclesiastes. In order to a be a leader of this religion, one's heart must be cold, one must deny oneself contact with women and children and – by extension – sex, love and family life. One must also avoid nice food, music and travel, and one must live an incredibly strict and miserable way of life. Yet is Mahon a little too hard on Ulster Protestantism? Several readers have criticised him for dismissing out of hand an entire community.

Nature
In many of his poems, Mahon celebrates the beauty of nature. 'Ecclesiastes', however, shows us what might be described as nature's darker side. It depicts a bleak and oppressive environment, one of cold and hard January rain that darkens the landscape, of bogs littered with graves. There is a sense in which the bleakness of the landscape around Belfast reflects the bleakness of the religion practised in the city and the narrow-mindedness of its inhabitants.

'Kinsale' is similar in this regard, also depicting dark rain 'browsing on spire and bogland'. In that poem, too, there is sense in which the grim weather seems to symbolise narrow-mindedness.

LANGUAGE

An interior dialogue?
In this poem, an unnamed speaker addresses an artist, urging him to give up his artistic lifestyle and become a spiritual leader of Protestant Belfast. However, 'Ecclesiastes' can also be read as a kind of 'interior dialogue' between two different aspects of

Mahon's character. On one hand, there is the artistic, carefree aspect which is full of 'wiles and smiles'. On the other, there is the part of him that is still a 'puritan', that still responds to the bleak, pleasure-denying Protestantism he knew when growing. Mahon, therefore, is torn between these two aspects of his personality, between continuing with his artistic lifestyle or embracing a way of life determined by the Protestant religion of his youth. He knows, of course, that becoming an Ecclesiastes would be a personal disaster for him. Yet maybe, just maybe, he could find himself taking this step.

It has also been suggested that there is an element of self-disgust in this piece. Mahon seems to regard his own life and personality with cold disregard:

- He presents himself as a liberated, modern individual but deep down he is still defined by the stern, puritan religion of his youth.
- He describes himself as a person of 'wiles and smiles', a 'wile' being a trick meant to fool, trap or entice. This suggests he does not think of himself as a truly honest and trustworthy person.
- The use of the word 'little' in line 2 suggests a large degree of self-contempt.

Mahon presents himself as someone dedicated to the artistic lifestyle symbolised by the red bandana, stick and banjo. He describes himself as a 'purist', one dedicated to rigidity and perfection in art. Yet according to several critics, we get a sense in this poem that Mahon fears his devotion to art might in reality be something shallow, silly and superficial.

Atmosphere

'Ecclesiastes' is also an intensely atmospheric poem. Mahon wonderfully captures the somewhat depressing atmosphere of the Belfast Sundays of his childhood, with their tied-up swings, miserable churches and the silence from the shipyards of the city which are empty and idle for the Lord's holy day.

Powerful, too, is the depiction of the rain falling on the city and its surrounding countryside, darkening the cityscape and lashing the hillsides and the bogs that are full of graves: 'the January rains when they/ darken the dark doors and sink hard/ into the Antrim hills, the bog meadows'. Even the washing on the lines of Belfast is described as 'heavy', reinforcing this bleak and haunting atmosphere.

Tone

The poem's tone, especially in the opening lines, is booming, like that of a preacher addressing a crowd. The constant repetition of key words and phrases, such as 'God' and 'you could', is a common tactic of those skilled in the arts of rhetoric or public speaking. There is a powerful sense of urgency throughout the poem. We can almost sense the speaker urging, pushing and prodding the artist into changing his way of life.

However, several critics have also detected an element of mockery or irony in the speaker's tone as if he does not really believe what he is saying, does not really believe the artist should give up his carefree existence and become an Ecclesiastes. We see this at the conclusion where the speaker says 'God help' anyone who would become such a spiritual leader. On this understanding, the poem's tone is one of bitter, mocking sarcasm.

Exaggeration

Becoming a modern-day prophet may not involve literally surviving on rations of insects, but it certainly involves denying oneself rich food and other pleasures of the flesh. In these lines, therefore, the dietary practices of the Old Testament prophets are used as a metaphor for the self-denial needed to become an Ecclesiastes.

As it Should Be

LINE BY LINE

The poem describes how a group of people pursued a man through the Irish countryside and shot him dead. The poem is based on an incident that occurred around the time the Irish state was being formed. A young man, in protest against the modernisation of the country, attempted to blow up a hydro-electric power plant and was shot. The tale provided the plot for a play called 'The Moon in the Yellow River'.

In 'As it Should Be', Mahon adopts the persona of one of those responsible for the man's execution. He describes the killing and says why he thinks it was justified. The speaker labels the man they shot a 'mad bastard'. He describes how they 'hunted' him through remote areas of the countryside: 'Through bog, moorland, rock'. They finally caught up with him somewhere in the west in a 'yard' with ten lorries and 'an electric generator'.

It was night when they cornered the man in the yard, and the stars were visible in the sky: 'the starlit west'. The man is utterly isolated and alone. Even the parked lorries are described as 'sleeping'. The yard offered the man no means of escape: 'a blind yard'. Trapped between these 'ten sleeping lorries/ And an electric generator', he was 'gunned' down. It seems that the body was then dumped in the sea the following day. In line 9 the speaker mentions 'his tide-burial' and says that this took place 'during school hours'.

The speaker of the poem is in favour of progress, of the technological advancement of the country. He considers those who are against the modernisation of the state to be 'idle' dreamers, useless idealists that stand in the way of practical action. He insists that there be 'no idle talk/ Of the moon in the Yellow River'. The moon's reflection in the river is only an illusion and to talk of such things is a waste of time.

According to the speaker, killing the 'mad bastard' has made the world a better place. He says that 'The air blows softer since his departure'. In lines 9–11 the speaker says that the children in the community have been much happier since the man was killed. They no longer have nightmares: 'Our children have known no bad dreams'. They also play happily and without fear. According to the speaker, the joyful cries of children can now be heard echoing 'lightly along the coast'. This, says the speaker, is how the world 'should be'. He believes in a 'world with method in it', a world of order and reason. The young children in the community would probably not understand how killing a man can be considered morally correct. But the speaker is sure that when they are older, they will appreciate the fact that such action was taken: 'They will thank us for it when they grow up/ To a world with method in it'.

THEMES

Compassion

Just like in 'After the *Titanic*', Mahon adopts the persona of someone else. In 'After the *Titanic*', it is Bruce Ismay who speaks, a man labelled a coward when he survived a disaster in which so many women and children perished. We feel compassion for Ismay because we see what a tortured and unhappy life he has lived since the disaster occurred. He displays a sense of remorse and guilt that is simply not evident in 'As it Should Be'.

If we feel compassion for anyone in the poem, it is the victim. Though he is labelled a 'mad bastard' at the start of the poem, it is the speaker of the poem who seems more deserving of such a description. The way the victim is hunted like an animal and 'gunned' down in 'a blind yard' is appalling. We can only imagine his fear and isolation as he was chased through the countryside and finally trapped.

It is impossible for us to feel compassion for the speaker of the poem. His absolute conviction that he knows what is in everybody's interest is frightening. He believes that it is justifiable to kill those members of society that hold different beliefs to his own. Claiming that the 'air blows softer since' the man was executed is simply ridiculous, as is the notion that children's bad dreams are cured with murder.

Derek Mahon

The nightmare of history
The poem is based on an event associated with the early years of the Irish Free State. This was a turbulent time when different people and groups had different ideas what was best for the country. There were those who believed in the preservation of rural tradition and the ways of the past. There were others who believed that Ireland needed to be modernised and other industries developed in order for the country to prosper. 'As it Should Be' gives us something of an insight into the mindset of some at the time. It suggests that violence and intolerance underpinned the foundation of the state. The recurrence of violence in Irish history is central to much of Mahon's writings on Ireland. We see examples of this in 'Rathlin', 'A Disused Shed' and in 'Kinsale'.

Narrow-mindedness
The speaker of the poem has certain ideas about what he thinks is best for society. He speaks about a 'world with method in it', a world governed by strict rules. His dismissal of the 'idle talk' of moons reflected in rivers suggests that he has little time for the imagination and idealism. He believes in rationality and practicality.

But it is not the speaker's political and social beliefs that are odious. He has every right to hold opinions and to express his point of view. What is deeply troubling is his absolute certainty that he is right and that those with different opinions need to be silenced and eliminated. The speaker of the poem tells us that 'This is how it should be', and is intolerant of those who think differently: 'Let us hear no idle talk'. 'As it Should Be' illustrates just how dangerous such narrow-mindedness can be.

LANGUAGE

Tone
The speaker of the poem adopts a somewhat unpleasant, cold and aggressive tone in explaining and justifying the murder, calling the victim a 'mad bastard' and demanding that no more be said of the 'moon in the Yellow River'.

Imagery
The poem features imagery connected both with the modernisation of the country and the romantic ideal that the victim was probably seeking to preserve. The lorries and electric generator are symbolic of the new technologies and represent a more industrialised society. The 'bog, moorland, rock' and the 'starlit west' are images of a landscape untainted by development.

A Disused Shed in Co. Wexford

INTRODUCTION
This poem deals with a group of mushrooms abandoned in a shed for fifty years. It is important to note that the mushrooms are depicted as having what can only be described as human characteristics. They are capable of seeing and hearing, of being patient, of hoping and of desiring. They suffer very human torments like nightmares and insomnia. They are depicted as speaking and even screaming. They even seem to have throats.

LINE BY LINE

What is the significance of the first stanza?
The poem does not focus on the mushrooms immediately. Its opening stanza presents a list of abandoned, forgotten places:

- An abandoned mine in Peru, where the only activity is condensation forming, a few flowers growing in a lift-shaft, and an echo rebounding endlessly against the walls of the mine.

- An abandoned compound in India, where the only activity here is the wind 'dancing', causing a door to slam.
- Crevices in walls of limestone houses behind barrels used to 'Lime crevices behind rippling rain-barrels'.
- Forgotten corners where dogs go to bury their bones: 'Dog corners for bone burials'.
- Finally, the speaker mentions the disused shed that is the focus of the poem.

Each of these places is abandoned, insignificant and forgotten. Yet according to the speaker, they are places where 'a thought might grow'. These silent forgotten places could serve as the starting point for thought or meditation. Despite their apparent insignificance, these abandoned locales might inspire us to think seriously about the world we live in.

Who is the speaker of this poem?
The speaker appears to be a tourist exploring the grounds of a 'burnt-out hotel' in County Wexford with some friends. He carries a camera and a light meter, a piece of photographic equipment. His travels follow a relaxed schedule, or 'itinerary'.

Where are the mushrooms?
The speaker comes upon the mushrooms in a disused shed, which is located in the grounds of the hotel. He randomly opens the shed door and discovers the mushrooms inside. As well as the mushrooms, the shed contains discarded household junk: 'bathtubs and washbasins', 'Utensils and broken pitchers'.

Who grew the mushrooms?
The mushrooms were grown in the 1920s by the person who owned the grounds at that time. He seems to have been an amateur mycologist who used the coolness and darkness of the shed to grow his specimens (a mycologist is someone who specialises in growing mushrooms and other fungi).

We get the impression that the mycologist was a member of the wealthy protestant Anglo-Irish class, who owned most of the 'Big Houses' in the country at that time. When Ireland was under British rule, this Anglo-Irish class had enjoyed great power. However, when the country became independent after the Irish War of Independence, many of their mansions and other properties were either burned down by the IRA or confiscated by the new Irish state. This seems to have been the fate of the mycologist in the poem. After the civil war of 1922–23, his lands were confiscated or 'expropriated' by the new Irish government. He was forced to leave his estate behind, abandoning the mushrooms in their shed. The mushrooms heard him walk down the gravel path outside their shed for the last time. His departure is described as endless, or 'interminable', suggesting he left very slowly and reluctantly. After that, he never returned to tend them: 'He never came back'.

How long have the mushrooms been abandoned in the shed?
The mushrooms have been in the shed for about fifty years: from 'the civil war days' of the 1920s to the day in the 1970s when the speaker discovers them. We are told that the mushrooms have spent a 'half century, without visitors, in the dark'. In all those years, not a single person has opened the shed door. When the speaker finally does so, the lock is cracked from fifty years of rust and the hinges creak: 'the cracking lock/ And creak of hinges'.

What were conditions like in the shed?
The conditions endured by the mushrooms over their fifty years of imprisonment are pretty hellish:

- They survive in almost complete darkness, the only illumination being the light that comes through the keyhole of the shed door.
- They survive in a deathly silence only occasionally interrupted by a noise from outside the shed: 'once a day, perhaps, they have heard something'.
- They survive in air that is stale and filled with a foul and putrid moisture: 'grim dominion of stale air and rank moisture'.
- They are surrounded by the 'foetor', or stench, of their own sweat: 'a foetor/ Of vegetable sweat'.
- They are 'racked' or tortured by drought. Their throats are so dry that they are filled with spider's webs: they are 'web-throated'.
- They suffer from insomnia and nightmares.
- They endure a claustrophobic, deathly silence that is broken only by an occasional, distant sound: 'And once a day perhaps, they have heard something'.
- Many mushrooms have died, their bodies decaying back into the very soil they grew out of: 'There have been deaths, the pale flesh flaking/ Into the earth that nourished it'.

The poem particularly emphasises the darkness the mushrooms must endure. In a striking metaphor, the keyhole is described as the only 'star' in the sky, or 'firmament': 'This is the one star in their firmament/ Or frames a star within a star'. According to the speaker, the mushrooms are 'crowding' towards this keyhole, desperate for the little light it provides.

The mushrooms lucky enough to be near the keyhole have become relatively big and strong, nourished by its feeble light. The speaker imagines these stronger mushrooms crowding out the weaker ones who are further from the light: 'Those nearest the door grow strong –/ 'Elbow room! Elbow Room!'

The misery of the mushrooms' predicament is contrasted with the freedom and beauty of the world outside. Beyond the shed's confines there are birds and flowers: 'So many days beyond the rhododendrons … Listening to the rooks querulous in the high wood'. The image of the planet earth dancing through the heavens is also one of beauty and freedom. All of this, however, is denied to the mushrooms. They exist 'beyond' the rhododendrons, in the squalor of the disused shed.

How have the mushrooms been affected by their ordeal?

It seems that the years of surviving in the darkness have left the mushrooms warped, mutated and unnatural-looking. They have 'Grown beyond nature now'. They are compared to 'moonmen' and 'triffids', suggesting how alien and otherworldly their appearance has become ('Triffids' were plant-like invaders in a famous science-fiction novel). The mushrooms are now so strange-looking that they might have originated in outer space. The description of them as 'magi', as sorcerers or wizards, also suggests there is something bizarre or otherworldly about their appearance.

The mushrooms have also been left in an incredibly weakened state by their ordeal: 'only the ghost of a scream/ At the flash-bulb firing-squad we wake them with/ Shows there is life left in their feverish forms'. These lines indicate the mushrooms' terrible state:

- They are sickened and 'feverish'.
- They are described as 'frail', 'soft' and 'Powdery', indicating how weak and flaky they have become. After their fifty-year ordeal, they are barely solid anymore.
- They are barely alive after so many years in the dark, dank shed. As the speaker puts it, they are little more than 'soft food for worms'.
- The speaker photographs the mushrooms but the camera flash is too much for them. In their sickened state, its light strikes them with the ferocity of 'a firing squad'. Yet they are so weak, they can barely scream in response to pain they feel at the flash of the speaker's camera when he photographs them: 'only the ghost of a scream'.

How did the mushrooms respond to their ordeal?

There was nothing practical the mushrooms could do to help themselves. Their only option was to wait there patiently, longing to be released: 'What could they do there but desire?' They have learnt to be patient. And because there was no use in calling out, they have learnt to be silent as well: 'they have learnt patience and silence'.

Yet throughout their years of misery, they have clung to the belief that they would eventually be rescued. There is something almost religious about their faith that they would some day be released from the shed's confines. Throughout their ordeal, they have 'been waiting', have been 'expectant' that 'deliverance' would one day come. They have come through fifty years of 'naive labours'; they have laboured to endure the shed's indignities in the naive or foolish hope that they would one day be set free.

What do the mushrooms ask the speaker to do?

The mushrooms beg the speaker and his companions to help them: 'They are begging us, you see, in their wordless way'. Somehow, despite their feverish weakness, they lift their 'frail heads' toward him. It is as if they are using the last of their energy to ask for his assistance, beseeching him for help in 'gravity and good faith', in a serious and honest fashion.

The mushrooms ask the speaker to do three things:

- Ideally, they want the speaker to save their lives; they beg him to 'do something', and to 'Save us, save us.'
- If this is not possible, they want the speaker to record their suffering, to tell their story for them: 'to speak on their behalf'.
- If the speaker refuses to do either of these things,

if he simply walks away, then they want him to at least leave the shed door open as he does so rather than confine them once more to the darkness: 'Or at least not to close the door again'.

To the mushrooms, after fifty years of almost complete darkness, the speaker seems to be a kind of god. He has total power over them. He can help them in some fashion or he can simply walk away and leave them in darkness once more. They beg this 'God' not to abandon them. If he does so, their years of naive labour, of enduring the shed's grim horrors in the foolish hope of rescue, will all have been for nothing: 'Let not our naive labours have been in vain!'

It seems that the speaker has turned up too late to save the mushrooms' lives. We get the impression that the mushrooms are beyond saving. 'A half century, without visitors, in the dark' is 'Poor preparation' for rescue. As we have seen, he finds them on the verge of death, little more than food for worms. There is still a chance, however, that even if the speaker cannot save the mushrooms' lives he will speak out on their behalf and tell their story for them.

THEMES

Compassion

Mahon's intense compassion comes across strongly in this poem. There is real humanity in the sympathetic way Mahon depicts their sufferings: the foul air they are forced to dwell in, their nightmares and insomnia, their aching thirst, the silence – perhaps above all the fifty years of endless darkness. His compassion also comes across when he describes the mushrooms' warped and weakened state after a half-century of confinement. These creatures have been left so deathly and feverish that they are barely able to scream or lift their heads.

'A Disused Shed' also displays compassion towards all those who have suffered throughout human history. The speaker associates the mushrooms with the 'Lost people of Treblinka and Pompeii'. Treblinka was a concentration camp in Poland where the Nazis murdered thousands of Jews. Pompeii was an ancient Roman city where thousands died when it was buried by lava after Mount Vesuvius erupted in AD 79. The poem, therefore, sympathises with all those who have suffered and died through natural disasters or through man's inhumanity to man.

This intense compassion is evident throughout Mahon's poetry: towards Captain Oates in 'Antarctica', towards Bruce Ismay and the 'dim/ Lost faces of the drowned' in 'After the *Titanic*', towards the hunted 'mad bastard' in 'As it Should Be', towards the victims of the massacre in 'Rathlin'.

There is a particular note of similarity between this poem and 'Day Trip to Donegal'. Both poems show a deep compassion towards non-human creatures – towards fish in one case and towards mushrooms in the other. The speaker appears to feel real sympathy for the fish that writhe in 'attitudes of agony and heartbreak' and for the mushrooms that are 'racked by drought and insomnia'. The fact that he describes these creatures suffering in terms of human emotion reinforces our sense of the compassion he feels for them.

Narrow-mindedness

Like many of Mahon's poems, 'A Disused Shed' touches on the notion of narrow-mindedness, of individuals and communities who display a lack of tolerance, forgiveness and understanding towards others. We see this in the reference to the 'expropriated mycologist'. As we have seen, he was a member of the Protestant minority in the new Irish state created after the War of Independence. Like many Protestant landowners, he found his lands confiscated by the government of this new state. It could be argued that in this instance the Catholic majority in the new state displayed little understanding or forgiveness towards their Protestant neighbours. The description of the mushrooms as 'Powdery prisoners of the old regime' reinforces this theme. The mushrooms were grown by one of the Anglo-Irish landowners, a member of the 'old regime' that once ruled the country but which was finally swept aside at the same time the mushrooms were imprisoned in the shed.

The mention of Treblinka brings to mind a much greater episode of narrow-mindedness, summoning up the Nazi's blind prejudice against the Jews and other minorities, an attitude that led to millions of deaths in concentration camps. This notion of narrow-mindedness also features in other poems by Mahon on the course.

- In 'Ecclesiastes', the Protestants of Belfast are depicted as being extremely narrow-minded. They are a 'God-chosen' community, one that believes they alone have been chosen by God and know what is right. An Ecclesiastes, as spiritual leader of these people, is required to be even more narrow-minded. He must express no forgiveness of others, no understanding of others' points of view.
- 'As it Should Be' depicts a similar attitude. In that poem, the speaker and his companions display a similar narrow-mindedness, a similar lack of forgiveness and understanding when they hunt the 'mad bastard' through the countryside before murdering him in a 'blind yard'.

Nightmare of history

Many of Mahon's poems deal with what might be termed the nightmare of history, viewing human existence as a vicious and bitter cycle of revenge, one in which each violent act leads inexorably on to the next. Irish history in particular is regarded in this light. 'A Disused Shed' touches on this theme when it mentions the Irish civil war and the confiscation of the mycologist's land by the new Irish state.

These are just two of the difficult events that make up Ireland's tragic tale, an endless sequence of struggles between Ireland and England, between Protestant and Catholic, in which each bloody deed generates the next. This notion of history as an endless cycle of violence haunts several of Mahon's poems. We see it in 'Rathlin', in 'Kinsale' and in 'The Chinese Restaurant in Portrush'. It is arguably also in 'Day Trip to Donegal'. Yet it must be noted that 'A Disused Shed' broadens its focus beyond Ireland. The mention of Treblinka and Pompeii reminds us that not only Irish history but human history as a whole can all too often be characterised as an endless series of bloody disasters.

As noted above, the mushrooms' plight is associated with the victims of disasters such as those at Treblinka and Pompeii. The victims of these tragedies are long dead. They cannot speak for themselves. They are voiceless and 'wordless'. Yet they long to be remembered in some fashion, for the story of their suffering to be told. They are imagined as beseeching the people of the present to tell their stories for them: 'They are begging us you see, in their wordless way'.

The poem's epigraph is a desperate appeal to be remembered. 'Let them not forget us' goes the plea, and this might be the motto not only of the mushrooms but also of all history's victims, who long for their lives to be remembered even if they themselves must die. As the mushrooms remind the speaker, 'We too had our lives to live'. If we speak on their behalf and remember their lives, their agonies, their 'naive labours', it will not have been all for nothing.

The poem, then, presents us with a powerful challenge. We get the impression that is too late to save the mushrooms, just as it is obviously too late to save the people of all the historical disasters such as Treblinka and Pompeii. Ye we can still 'speak on their behalf'. We can remember those ordinary people who died in those countless disasters in human history, both natural and man-made. It challenges us to remember all these 'lost people', and, as best we can, attempt to tell their stories.

It could be argued that this is a challenge Mahon rises to in many of his poems. In 'Rathlin', for instance, he remembers the victims of the 1575 massacre. In 'After the *Titanic*', he remembers not only those who drowned but also Bruce Ismay, the disgraced owner of the vessel. 'Antarctica' remembers Captain Laurence Oates, while 'As it Should Be' remembers the poor 'mad bastard' who is hunted through the fields before being gunned down.

Nature

Mahon is well known for his beautiful nature imagery. Though this poem is largely set in the confines of a dank and miserable shed, his eye for nature still comes through. The mention of the rhododendrons and the rooks crying out in the 'high woods' powerfully contrasts nature's beauty outside the shed with the dismal environment inside. A similar contrast is evident in line 5 where the wild flowers in the lift-shaft alleviate the bleakness of the abandoned Peruvian mine.

Mahon uses a wonderful, almost cosmic, metaphor to describe the planet earth travelling through space. The world, he says, is 'waltzing' as it moves in a circular orbit around the sun. It is held within a 'bowl of cloud', a semi-spherical layer of cloudy puffs.

Yet the mention of Pompeii brings to mind nature's more dangerous side. Nature, we are reminded, is not only beautiful but can also spring terrible natural disasters upon us. 'After the *Titanic*' deals with just such a natural tragedy, while 'Antarctica', 'Day Trip to Donegal' and 'Rathlin' are also all keenly aware of nature's treacherousness and ferocity.

LANGUAGE

Metaphor

There are several interesting metaphors in this poem:

- In line 3 the noise of the dripping condensation is compared to the ticking of a clock.
- In line 6 the movement of the wind is compared to a dance.
- In line 15 the keyhole is compared to a star.
- In line 18 the circular orbit of the earth is described as a waltz and the layer of cloud around it is compared to a bowl.

Atmosphere

In many respects, this poem is a masterpiece of atmosphere. Mahon wonderfully captures the eerie, empty atmosphere of the abandoned mine where an echo is trapped forever, the sound waves bouncing back and forth between its walls for all eternity. Similarly, the empty Indian compound is wonderfully evoked: a haunting landscape where the only sound is that of a banging door.

Yet the most powerful atmosphere in this poem is that of the shed itself. Mahon wonderfully realises this dark location filled with discarded dusty bric-a-brac, a place full of spiders' webs and dead flies that have turned to mildew: 'Spiders have spun, flies dusted to mildew'. He powerfully conveys the shed's putrid, claustrophobic air: 'the grim dominion of stale air and rank moisture'. Perhaps above all, he conveys the shed's endless darkness from which the only relief is the faint beam of light coming through the keyhole.

Nightmarish imagery

There are several instances of grim and almost disturbing imagery. We see this in lines 31–2 which describe the mushrooms dying and decaying in the shed's grim atmosphere: 'the pale flesh flaking into the earth that nourished it'. Also unsettling, perhaps, is the comparison of the mushrooms with Triffids, suggesting that they have mutated till their stalks are outlandishly long. The description of them as 'web-throated' is also nightmarish, suggesting their throats are so dry that spiders have spun webs in them.

SOUND EFFECTS

Onomatopoeia

There are several memorable instances of onomatopoeia in this poem. In line 3 the phrase 'slow clock of condensation' summons up the noise of condensation dripping in the empty mine. Similarly, in the wonderful phrase 'gravel-crunching interminable departure/ Of the expropriated mycologist' we can almost hear the sound of the landowner walking away down the gravel path.

We also see onomatopoeia in lines 42–3: 'the cracking lock/ And creak of hinges'. The repetition of the hard 'ck' sound in 'cracking lock' suggests the noise of the lock on the shed door breaking. The onomatopoeic 'creak', meanwhile, conjures up the sound it makes as it swings open on its rusty hinges. It could also be argued that onomatopoeia is present in line 47 where the phrase 'flash-bulb firing-squad' conjures the noise made by the flash of an old-style camera.

Euphony & cacophony

There are several instances of cacophony in this poem. In lines 44–6 the repeated hard-vowel sounds and jerky movement of the verse creates a harsh musical effect well suited to the mushrooms' terrible circumstance. A similar effect is created by lines 31–2: 'the pale flesh flaking into the earth that nourished it'. Euphony, meanwhile, occurs in lines 17–19 where the repeated broad-vowel sounds create a pleasant verbal music suited to the beautiful world beyond the shed's confines.

Rhyme

The poem has six stanzas of ten lines each. Each line rhymes with another line in the same stanza. However, there is no repeated pattern between the stanzas. Furthermore, many of these rhymes could be described as half-rhymes or even quarter-rhymes. For instance, 'dances' rhymes with 'confidence', 'barrels' rhymes with 'burials', and 'cloud' rhymes with 'wood'.

Personification

A feature that makes the poem stand out is the way the mushrooms are given human characteristics. As we noted above, they are depicted as suffering human torments like nightmares and insomnia, and are depicted as speaking and even screaming. They are capable of human emotions like patience, hope and desire.

Puns

The punning reference to light meter in line 59 is interesting. On the one hand, of course, this refers to a piece of photographic equipment the speaker is carrying. Metre (note the different spelling), however, also refers to poetic rhythm, suggesting how Mahon uses a 'light metre': a delicate and subtle blend of different rhythms characterise his poetic style. Similarly, the phrase 'relaxed itinerary' refers not only to the relaxed schedule of the poem's speaker but also to the easygoing lifestyle of the artist who has no other duty but to create art. This line, therefore, can also be interpreted as a direct plea from the mushrooms to the poet.

The mushrooms, therefore, beg the speaker to use his abilities as a poet to record their existence, to construct a monument to their sufferings. This is something the poet has accomplished, of course, in the writing of this famous poem.

The Chinese Restaurant in Portrush

LINE BY LINE

LINES 1–12

The poem offers us a snapshot of Portrush – a coastal town in north Antrim – at the beginning of spring. The town that has been 'shut all winter' is slowly opening its doors and preparing for the arrival of the tourists.

We get a sense that the winters in Portrush are harsh. The town is exposed to the winds and mists that blow in from the sea. During the winter season, the doors remain shut 'Against the north wind and the sea-mist'. However, spring brings a very different feel to the place.

- It softens 'the sharp air of the coast'.
- The doors that remained shut all winter 'Lie open to the street'.
- The gulls are humorously described as going 'window-shopping'.

The image of 'an old wolfhound' dozing 'in the sun' and the description of the girl striding 'Light-footed' and 'swinging a book-bag' past the Northern Counties Hotel further suggest the relaxed spring atmosphere in Portrush.

The 'softening' influence of spring comes just 'In time for the first seasonal "invasion"' of tourists. Mahon places the word 'invasion' in inverted commas because the word is most commonly used to describe the arrival of an enemy or harmful force. The modern variety of invasion that Mahon is referring to is of a different order to the invasions of the past. An invasion of tourists, as unpleasant as it may be, is nothing compared to the invasion of the Vikings or Anglo-Norman forces. Mahon places the word invasion in inverted commas to highlight awareness of the exaggerated, or hyperbolic, use of the word.

The pleasant atmosphere of the day allows the poet to imagine that Portrush is 'as it might have been,/ Gentle and almost hospitable'. When Mahon says that the town is 'as it might have been', he could mean two things:

- This is how the place might actually have been a long time ago, before the first settlers arrived.
- This is how the place might have been had not all the troubles of the recent past occurred.

Existing on the northern coast of Ireland, Portrush was never going to have been tropical. The best it could have been, the poet humorously suggests, is 'almost hospitable'.

LINES 13–20
The poet is sitting in a Chinese restaurant in Portrush reading a newspaper and eating a 'prawn chow mein'. Above him hangs a 'framed photograph of Hong Kong'. The owner or 'proprietor' of the restaurant 'Stands at the door' whistling 'a little tune'. Out upon the sea 'the first yacht' is hoisting a sail, and the light is shining 'upon the hills of Donegal'. The owner of the restaurant is Chinese. The poet imagines how the yacht's sail might seem to him an 'ideogram', a character used in Chinese script, against the white background of 'sea-cloud'. As he stands in the doorway whistling and watching Portrush come back to life, the poet imagines that the proprietor is 'dreaming of home' in Hong Kong.

THEMES

Escape from history's nightmare
The poem describes a town that has been shut against the 'north wind and the sea-mist' all winter. But the winter has passed and the spring has come, softening the 'sharp air of the coast'. There is a real sense of a new beginning or fresh start about the place. It is 'as if the world were young' and all the events of history had never occurred.

The wintery conditions that the poem describes might be symbolic of the conflicts and difficulties of the past. The 'sharp air of the coast' suggests a violent force attacking the town, and the description of the 'doors' being 'shut all winter' suggests a community that has been guarded and closed. But things have changed, a 'softening' has occurred, and the doors now 'Lie open to the street'. The 'invasion' that the town prepares itself for is no longer that of the Celts, Vikings or Anglo-Normans but, rather, an 'invasion' of tourists.

The fact that the poet is sitting beneath a 'framed photograph of Hong Kong' eating Chinese food in the remote Northern Irish town of Portrush tells of the multicultural modern world, a place where the peaceful co-existence of different nationalities and cultures is possible. Though the proprietor is from a distant country, he dwells happily amongst the other inhabitants of the town. He may be a little homesick but he seems content as he 'whistles a little tune, dreaming of home'.

The image of the girl striding confidently past the Northern Counties Hotel seems further evidence that things have changed. She seems carefree and safe, walking in a 'Light-footed' manner and casually 'swinging a book-bag'. The hotel that she 'Strides past', the 'Northern Counties Hotel', is a reminder of the political division in Ireland. That she 'Strides' past the place suggests a confidence and, perhaps, an escape from the burdens of an embittered social divide that have plagued and defined the area for decades.

The image of the 'old wolfhound' dozing 'in the sun' hints at the end of violence and conflict. The wolfhound suggests the mythic character of Cú Chulainn, often referred to as the 'Hound of Ulster'. Cú Chulainn was a violent and fierce warrior, and the fact that the 'wolfhound' is now 'old' and 'dozes in the sun' suggests that his fighting days are behind him.

On this spring day, Portrush seems a peaceful and relaxed place. Mahon describes it as 'Gentle and almost hospitable'. It seems almost blessed with the 'light/ Of heaven upon the hills'. There is a real sense of hope that the cycle of conflict and violence has ended.

The nightmare of history
The images in the poem hint at the turbulent events of the past, and of the many conflicts that have occurred

over the course of Irish history. The 'old wolfhound', calling to mind the mythic character of Cú Chulainn, reminds us of the wars that were fought between different clans many years ago. The mentioning of the 'Northern Counties Hotel' reminds us of the fact that Ireland remains a divided country. The description of the harsh winter weather ('the sharp air of the coast') also seems to be symbolic of the violence of the past, of invaders like the Vikings coming across the sea to attack the town.

We might wonder if the poem describes an escape from the conflicts of the past or just a brief interlude. The winter has gone but another will come. The 'sharp air of the coast' will soon be attacking the town, and doors will again be shut against the unpleasant weather. But the poem seems to suggest that things have permanently changed for the better, that a cycle of conflict has been broken. The presence of the Chinese restaurant owner in Portrush tells of the peaceful co-existence of different cultures, and the confident 'Light-footed' girl seems to represent a generation unburdened with the grievances of the past. On this spring day, as the poet eats his chow mein and gazes out upon the hills of Donegal, he certainly seems hopeful.

Nature
The poem highlights the beauty and tranquillity of spring. The air is soft and there is a pleasant, heavenly light upon the hills of Donegal. There is a playful and relaxed air about the creatures that feature in the poem. The gulls are humorously described as going 'window-shopping', while the 'old wolfhound dozes in the sun'.

However, the poem also gives us a sense of the unpleasant winter conditions that exist in Portrush. Mahon mentions the 'north-wind and the sea-mist' that force the citizens to bolt their doors all winter. The weather at this time of year appears like an enemy, its 'sharp' features like weapons that attack the town.

LANGUAGE

Form
The poem is split into two stanzas. The first stanza focuses on the town, whilst the second focuses on the poet who sits in a Chinese restaurant in Portrush. The poem does not have any formal rhyming scheme but it does feature some rhyme. Mahon rhymes 'mein' with 'sail', an example of oblique, or forced, rhyme. He also uses perfect rhyme when he rhymes 'one' with 'sun'.

Tone
The poem's tone is generally light-hearted and relaxed. Mahon humorously describes the gulls going 'window-shopping', and says that Portrush is preparing for the 'invasion' of tourists. The end of the poem is a little more melancholic as we get a sense of the restaurant owner's homesickness.

Sound effects
The opening lines feature repeated 's' sounds in keeping with the softening effect of spring: 'comes the spring/ Softening the sharp air of the coast'. Lines 10–12 feature repeated 'o' sounds: 'Lie open to the street, where one/ By one the gulls go window-shopping/ And an old wolfhound dozes in the sun'.

The repeated 'v' sounds and the alliteration of the 'h's creates a pleasant effect in lines 18–19 in keeping with the relaxed atmosphere: 'the light/ Of heaven upon the hills of Donegal'.

Personification
Mahon personifies the gulls when he suggests they are going 'window-shopping'.

Imagery & symbolism
The image of the town closed against the harsh elements of the wind and sea could be read metaphorically as a description of the North in recent times — insular, intolerant and indignant. We are reminded of the poet's descriptions of Belfast in 'Ecclesiastes' where he speaks of the 'dark doors' and the 'January rains'. The image of Portrush in winter is similarly bleak.

Reflecting the modern, youthful aspect of Portrush is the girl who 'Strides past the Northern Counties Hotel,/ Light-footed, swinging a book-bag'.

Mahon compares the yacht's sail against the sky with an 'ideogram on sea-cloud' — as though it were a Chinese character drawn onto the cloud.

Rathlin

Derek Mahon

INTRODUCTION

Rathlin is an island bird sanctuary off the coast of Antrim, and is renowned for its beauty. In 1575 over six hundred people – mostly women and children – were slaughtered in cold blood on Rathlin island. These were the people of Somhairle Bui Mac Ghonnaill, a Gaelic chieftain who resisted English rule in Ireland. To protect the families of his warriors, he installed them in a fortified castle on the island, believing Rathlin's isolation would keep them safe.

However, English forces under the Earl of Essex laid siege to the castle. The people inside were promised no harm would come to them if they surrendered peacefully. They accepted Essex's offer. However, when they gave themselves up, he had them massacred. Somhairle Bui himself helplessly observed the slaughter from the mainland. According to English spies in his camp, he was almost insane with grief and rage.

LINE BY LINE

The poet thinks about the massacre of 1575

The poet has come to visit Rathlin island with some friends. They arrive on a boat powered by an 'outboard motor' and dock at the island's pier. The poet thinks about the terrible massacre that took place there all those centuries ago:

- He imagines the horror of that night: 'A long time since the last scream cut short'.
- He imagines that the massacre was followed by an eerie, 'unnatural silence'; as if all the living things on the island were stunned into quietness by the terrible slaughter.
- He imagines that this unnatural silence was eventually replaced by a 'natural' one, in which the creatures of Rathlin could be heard again: 'the shearwater, by the sporadic/ Conversation of crickets'.
- He imagines that the wind howling onto Rathlin served as 'a bleak reminder' of the atrocity, echoing the screams of those murdered by Essex's men.

The poet thinks of the island as being outside history

The poet fantasises that he and his friends are the first people to set foot on Rathlin: 'As if we were the first visitors here'. The flocks of birds that occupy the island are 'amazed' at the arrival of their motor boat. They 'whistle and chatter' in startlement, and fly off from the surfaces they occupy: 'Evacuating rock-face and cliff-top'.

The poet imagines that Rathlin is lost in a 'dream-time', which in aboriginal mythology is a magical period before human history began. The island, he imagines, is a place that is 'through with history', that exists in some mystical, prehistoric state. The island is presented not only as a bird 'sanctuary' but also as a sanctuary from history itself.

The poet's descriptions of Rathlin contribute to this notion of the island as a dream-time place. The fact that everything is blurred by 'sea smoke' and 'oceanic haze' lends the place a dream-like atmosphere. The island's bird species are described as 'oneiric', which means having to do with dreams. Even the occasional passing freighters, he says, are drowsy, or 'somnolent'.

It is possible that the description of the lighthouse further reinforces the notion of Rathlin's existence outside historical time. The lighthouse repeats 'one simple statement' over and over, with none of the change, complication and messiness that characterises human history.

Beyond this dream-time island, history holds sway, an endless cycle of violence, bloodshed and human stupidity. In particular, the poet thinks of the violence taking place in Northern Ireland at that time: 'bombs doze in the housing estates'. Rathlin, however, seems to offer the speaker a refuge from all that, a haven uncorrupted by human history where he can step out of man's nightmarish tale.

The poet's fantasy is unsustainable

In stanza 3, however, the poet acknowledges that this notion of Rathlin as a dream-time island is only a fantasy. After all, nowhere on earth can truly be

free of human history. He thinks again about the 'unspeakable violence' that took place there in 1575: 'Somhairle Bui, powerless on the mainland,/ Heard the screams of the Rathlin women'. He accepts that far from existing outside history, the island has some very brutal history of its own.

The poet leaves the island
The speaker and his companions leave the island on their boat: 'Only the cry of the shearwater/ And the roar of the outboard motor/ Disturb the singular peace'. The trip back to the mainland is a disorientating one for the speaker. He finds himself 'Spray-blind' as foam from the ocean's surface flies into his eyes. As the turbulent water shifts violently beneath them, the speaker and his friends are suddenly unsure which way they are facing: 'Unsure among the pitching surfaces'.

THEMES

The nightmare of history
'Rathlin' presents the history of Ireland as a senseless cycle of violence and bloodshed. The poem views Irish history as a seemingly endless series of struggles between England and Ireland, between Protestant and Catholic, one in which each cruel deed sows the seeds of the next. The Rathlin massacre in the sixteenth century and the Northern Irish Troubles of the twentieth are part of the same bitter and tragic story. The 'unspeakable violence' of 1575 leads, however indirectly, to the 'bombs [that] doze in the housing estates' in the 1970s.

Escape from history's nightmare
The poet fantasises that Rathlin is 'through with history', that the island is somehow outside the grisly cycles of revenge discussed above. He fantasises that Rathlin has no human history because he and his friends are the first people to ever set foot on the island. He fantasises that the island is lost in a 'dream-time', a mystical and mythological period before history began.

However, this fantasy cannot be sustained. In stanza 3 the poet is forced to acknowledge that Rathlin has a bloody past and is very much a part of Ireland's tragic tale. The bloody cycles of history cannot so easily be escaped. The phrase 'through with history' reflects this notion. In one sense, as we have seen, this means that the island has nothing to do with history. Yet it can also be read as suggesting that the island is 'shot through' with history; that it is completely filled with history.

The phrase 'infancy of the race' is similarly ambiguous. This can be read as referring to a period of 'dream-time' human innocence, which the speaker imagined he had found on Rathlin and which he now regretfully abandons as he sails away. However, the phrase could also refer to the massacre of 1575. Perhaps the race's 'infancy' refers to the almost childish, pointless cruelty involved in the massacre of Somhairle's people.

The poet and his friends are blinded by spray as they leave the island. They become disorientated as their boat rocks and pitches on the surface of the ocean. These lines can also be read in a metaphorical sense. The human race is tossed on the choppy waters of history, leaving us blinded and confused. We are uncertain what the future holds: 'unsure among the pitching surfaces/ Whether the future lies before us or behind'.

Is the future represented by the mainland, which lies before the poet, or by Rathlin, which lies behind? Will the future be a time of violence characterised by the bombs that 'doze in the housing estates' of the mainland? Will it be a time characterised by mindless slaughter, such as that which took place on Rathlin in 1575? Or will it be a time of peace and tranquillity, reflecting the serenity of the island as it is today? The poem offers no definite answers. However, there can be little doubt that Mahon suspects the future will be filled not with peace but with conflict as the cycle of history turns bloodily on.

Nature
This is one of many poems where Mahon reveals his keen eye for the natural world and his appreciation of nature's beauty. He appreciates Rathlin as a serene 'sanctuary', a place of unrivalled or 'singular' peace.

He carefully describes the noises made by the island's wildlife: the chirping of the crickets, the 'cry' of the shearwater, the 'whistle and chatter' of the other species of bird that inhabit it. He describes the wind on the island as 'metaphysical' because it seems more than a merely physical phenomenon. It is a ghostly reminder of previous wrongs: 'the bleak/ Reminder of a metaphysical wind'.

The beautiful word 'cerulean' – meaning a deep or azure blue – probably applies to both the ocean and the sky, the two blending together in a haze at the faraway horizon: 'cerulean distance, an oceanic haze'.

Yet the poem's final lines suggest nature's darker side. There is a sense of threat and uncertainty as the poet and his friends leave the island, blinded by spray and tossed about on the 'pitching surfaces' of the 'turbulent sea'. We are reminded that nature is not only beautiful but can also be a deadly and menacing force. In this sense, Rathlin recalls 'Day Trip to Donegal', 'After the *Titanic*' and 'Antarctica'.

Compassion
This is one of the many poems where Mahon reveals a deep compassion with those who have suffered throughout history. The poet is keenly aware of the 'unspeakable violence' that was visited upon Somhairle's people in 1575. He remembers the horror and sorrow that must have afflicted Somhairle as he listened to the women and children of his tribe being slaughtered:

Since Somhairle Buí, powerless on the mainland,
Heard the screams of the Rathlin women
Borne to him, seconds later, upon the wind.

A similar sense of compassion for history's victims is evident in 'As it Should Be', 'Antarctica' and 'After the *Titanic*'. We also see it in 'A Disused Shed in Co. Wexford', where Mahon remembers the 'lost people of Treblinka and Pompeii'.

Place

A recurring feature of Mahon's poetry is the way he sets his poems in specific locations that are conjured up with great vividness in the imagination of the reader. In this poem, Mahon vividly conjures up the misty and dream-like landscape of Rathlin island with its 'oceanic haze' and its 'amazed,/ Oneiric species' of birdlife. A similarly vibrant sense of place is evident in poems such as 'The Chinese Restaurant in Portrush', 'Day Trip to Donegal', 'Kinsale' and 'Ecclesiastes'.

LANGUAGE

In 'Rathlin', each line rhymes with another line in the same stanza. For example, in the first stanza 'short' rhymes with 'report', and 'pier' rhymes with 'here'. However, the stanzas do not follow a regular pattern. For example, the first line in stanza 1 rhymes with the seventh line ('short' and 'report'), while the first line in stanza 2 rhymes with the fourth line ('amazed' and 'haze').

Furthermore, Mahon makes extensive use of half-rhyme throughout the poem: 'chatter' with 'freighter', 'shearwater' with 'motor', 'cap' with 'top', and 'mainland' with 'wind'. This approach to rhyme is typical of Mahon's poetry, and can also be seen in 'A Disused Shed in Co. Wexford'.

This poem sees Mahon's descriptive powers at their sharpest. The second stanza, in particular, captures the dreamlike, lazy atmosphere of Rathlin island:

- As we have seen, the description of the island being surrounded by a 'Cerulean distance, an oceanic haze' contributes to this effect.
- So does the description of the birds as 'oneiric', or dreamlike, and the description of the freighter moving in a 'somnolent', or drowsy, fashion.
- The description of the lighthouse that repeats 'one simple statement' over and over also contributes to our sense of Rathlin as a place of unchanging, timeless beauty.

Mahon uses assonance and alliteration to reinforce this dream-like atmosphere. The repeated 's' sound in phrases like 'Cerulean distance', 'oceanic haze' and 'sea-smoke' generate a pleasant, lulling music. Assonance creates a similar effect: the repeated broad-vowel sounds in lines 13–16 slows the pace of the verse, contributing to this laid-back, lazy mood.

There are also several instances of onomatopoeia in this poem. In the phrase 'whistle and chatter' we can almost hear the shrill noise of the birds as they take flight from the rocks and cliffs where they have been perching. It has also been suggested that the phrase 'report/ Of an outboard motor at the pier' captures the stuttering, mechanical sound of the boat's engine.

We see euphony in lines 11–16 in phrases such as 'Cerulean distance', 'oceanic haze', 'amazed/ Oneiric species' and 'sea-smoke to the ice-cap'. In each case, the repeated broad-vowel sounds and soft consonants create a pleasant verbal music suggesting the physical beauty of the island.

Cacophony occurs in lines 25–30. The repeated '*b*' and '*p*' sounds in the line 'Disturb the singular peace. Spray-blind' create a harsh, jagged sound. A similar harsh verbal music occurs in the phrases 'roar of the outboard motor' and 'unsure among the pitching surfaces'. In each case, the rough verbal music suggests the roughness of the 'turbulent sea' on which the boat rocks and pitches as it leaves the island. This is particularly true of line 29, which has a 'lurching', unsteady movement, suggesting the turbulent sea.

There are several instances of personification in this poem. The wind is given certain human qualities. It haunts the island like some ghostly presence, bringing with it a reminder of the terrible deed carried out there in 1575. The wildlife, too, is imbued with human qualities; the birds 'chatter' while the crickets are described as having a 'conversation'.

More menacingly, in line 17 we are told that 'bombs doze in the housing estates'. There is something unnerving and unsettling about this image. We are aware that the bombs are most 'half-asleep', and that they will soon 'awake' or explode and wreak their carnage.

Antarctica

Derek Mahon

BACKGROUND

In 1912 Captain Robert Scott and a crew of men that included Lawrence Oates set out on an expedition to reach the centre of Antarctica. Having reached the Pole only to discover that a Norwegian explorer had arrived before them – thus depriving them of the honour of being the first – Scott and his crew journeyed back disheartened to their ship. However, the conditions were much worse than they had anticipated. On March 2 Oates revealed that he was suffering badly from frostbite. Two weeks later, Oates realised that in his worsening condition he was slowing down his companions. Rather than remain a burden to them and put their lives at risk, he chose to walk from the tent to his death. His final recorded words were: 'I am just going outside and may be some time'.

LINE BY LINE

What does Captain Oates do?

Captain Oates is suffering terribly from frostbite. He is weak and knows that he can no longer continue on the long trek back to the ship. He feels that he is now only a burden to his fellow explorers, that he is slowing them down and putting their lives at risk. He has decided to end his life by leaving the tent and walking out into the blizzard. He will take leave of the group 'Quietly, knowing it is time to go'.

Oates does not tell the other men in the tent that he is going to walk out into the raging blizzard to die. Instead, he says that he is 'just going outside and may be some time'. He leaves the tent and steps outside into the 'howling snow'. He does this to perhaps spare the men's feelings of guilt or perhaps just to avoid protest.

Though he is weak and tired, Oates forces himself to 'climb' through the snow. He goads himself, or what remains of himself, to keep climbing through the blizzard: 'Goading his ghost into the howling snow'. The tent disappears behind him, hidden beneath a coating of frost and snow: 'The tent recedes beneath its crust of rime'. Oates is overcome with feelings of dizziness, or 'vertigo', as he climbs up the mountainous terrain of Antarctica, the sensation of which distracts him from the pain of his frostbite: 'And frostbite is replaced by vertigo'.

How do the others respond?
The other men in the tent pretend 'not to know' that Oates is leaving the tent to die. When he tells them that he is 'just going outside and may be some time', they just 'nod'. As he leaves, they choose not to look at him, and continue 'reading' their books. It is as if they do not want to acknowledge what is really happening. It is easier for them and perhaps for Oates if they pretend that he is really only 'going outside' for a while and will soon be back. Their lack of response, emotional or otherwise, can perhaps be considered in terms of the British tradition of maintaining a stiff upper lip.

The fourth stanza seems to bring us back inside the tent to where the other men have been left. They ask themselves whether they should think it 'some sort of crime' that the weakest of the group be allowed to kill himself in order that they be saved. They decide that what just took place is not a crime. After all, they say, 'He is just going outside and may be some time'. It is as if they wish to maintain the pretence that they do not know what Oates is doing, that they ought to take him at his word even though the notion that someone would just step out into a raging snow storm is in any way a reasonable thing to do.

How does the poet describe Oates?
The poet describes Oates as a 'Solitary enzyme'. An enzyme is a protein molecule that helps other molecules to change but does not itself change. Its actions can be considered, therefore, utterly selfless. It acts for the benefit of others. Like such an enzyme, Oates is acting alone. And what he is doing is for the benefit of others and not himself. He hopes that by sacrificing himself, others will live. He wishes to bring about a change in the lives of others but not benefit from the change himself. If he dies, his fellow explorers will have more food between them and will stand a greater chance of reaching the ship.

We are reminded of Christ carrying the weight of the cross on his back as he climbed to Calvary. Indeed, there is something Christ-like about Oates' act. Christ died in order that man might be saved. Similarly, Oates has chosen to sacrifice his life in order that the rest of the crew might survive.

What does Mahon think of the way Oates & his fellow explorers behaved?
Mahon considers the behaviour of Oates and his fellow explorers to be both ridiculous and sublime.

- It is ridiculous that Oates should say that he is 'just going outside and may be some time' when what he intends to do is walk to his death.
- It is even more ridiculous that the others should silently accept such an absurd announcement.
- What is perhaps most ridiculous is the group's effort to maintain the pretence that Oates is really just stepping out for a while after he has gone. This is evident in the fourth stanza when those left in the tent console their consciences with the words Oates spoke as he left: 'No,/ He is just going outside and may be sometime'.
- Mahon characterises the situation in terms of a 'pantomime', a farce in which people play ridiculous roles. (There is a hint of Macbeth's soliloquy in which life is considered a stage upon which man struts and frets in an ultimately meaningless way.)

But the moment is also extraordinary or 'sublime'. It is extraordinary that someone should choose to die so that others might have a better chance of living. It is equally extraordinary that this should be done in such a quiet and dignified manner. Oates displays no fear or emotion as he walks out into the darkness and the 'howling snow'. It is a sublime image – that of Oates, a man weak and tired with frostbite, 'Goading his ghost into the howling snow'. The idea of that solitary individual in one of the remotest places on earth battling against ferocious elements in order to bring some hope of survival to his fellow explorers is truly awe-inspiring and grand It is a 'sublime' act.

THEMES

Compassion

In a number of Mahon poems, we are presented with individuals who find themselves alone and having to endure terrible ordeals. In 'After the *Titanic*', for example, the speaker of the poem is Bruce Ismay, the manager of the company responsible for the *Titanic*. Ismay was on board the ship the night it sank. He managed to escape the sinking vessel in a lifeboat. Though he was heavily criticised for his behaviour, Mahon does not seek to judge him in the poem. Instead, he allows Ismay to speak, and enables us to feel compassion for the terrible suffering he had to endure both on the night the ship sank and for many years after the disaster.

In 'Antarctica', we are again presented with a man who finds himself in a dire situation and is faced with almost impossible choices. Stuck in one the most remote places on earth and suffering from frostbite, Oates has to face the fact that if he continues to try to make it back to the ship, he will endanger the lives of the whole team. The image of Oates walking out into the howling snow to die is intensely harrowing and heartbreaking. Mahon shows us what an extraordinary act of selflessness Oates performed in the harshest conditions.

Mahon displays great sympathy for the dignity with which Oates sets about his departure. In order to spare the feelings of his fellow explorers and perhaps to avoid interference with his decision, Oates says that he is just stepping out of the tent for a while. He takes his leave 'Quietly, knowing it is time to go'. Mahon appreciates how such a situation might seem ridiculous, but realises that what Oates ultimately demonstrates in the wilderness of Antarctica is the most 'sublime' act of the human will.

Nature

'Antarctica' describes one man's plight in one of the most remote places on earth. When we read the poem, we get a sense of the severe conditions that exist in the Antarctic. Mahon describes the 'howling snow' and the 'crust of rime' that quickly covers the tent. This mountainous continent of ice is a place where few life forms can survive. The poem reminds us that the natural world can be a terrifying and merciless place. When Oates leaves the tent, he steps out into a violent, vast and indifferent landscape.

Isolation

The description of Oates as a 'Solitary enzyme' suggests the terrible isolation and loneliness of Oates' predicament. The word 'enzyme' conveys the smallness of Oates in the midst of Antarctica. The word 'enzyme' also suggests just how inhospitable a place the Antarctic is, a place where few life forms can survive. There are few places on the planet as remote. When Oates takes leave of the tent, he leaves the small human shelter of his fellow explorers and enters a dark wilderness of 'howling snow'. It is harder to imagine a lonelier place on earth in which to die. Not only is Oates in a land remote from civilisation, in his quest to end his life he distances himself from the small group of people he is with. As he climbs up into the mountains of the Antarctic, he is about as isolated from mankind as it is humanely possible to be.

LANGUAGE

Form

The poem is written in the form of a villanelle. A villanelle is a nineteen-line poem with two repeating rhymes and two refrains. The form is made up of five tercets followed by a quatrain. The first and third lines of the opening tercet are repeated alternately in the last lines of the succeeding stanzas; then, in the final stanza, the refrain serves as the poem's two concluding lines.

Imagery

Mahon compares the isolated Oates to a 'Solitary enzyme'. The metaphor suggests that Oates is acting in an effort to bring about a change in the other explorers' lives, a change that he will not benefit from. The metaphor also draws attention to the smallness of Oates, a tiny dwindling life force in the midst of a vast continent of ice. The poem also compares the happenings on earth to a 'pantomime', suggesting that life is ultimately ridiculous.

Sound effects

The poem features an example of assonance. The repeated long 'o' sounds in 'Goading his ghost into the howling snow' reflects Oates' slow and painful struggle to climb up the mountain.

Derek Mahon
Kinsale

LINE BY LINE

The first three lines describe rain failing on a dreary and sombre landscape of bogs and church spires. The rain is presented as being grim and perhaps even a little threatening. It is 'dark' and hard, sinking deep into the ground it falls upon: 'deep-delving dark'. There is something ominous and unsettling about how it deliberately 'browses' the landscape, almost as if it was hunting for something or someone.

The poem's remaining four lines describe a very different scene, a pleasant moment in Kinsale, the harbour town in County Cork. A rain shower has ended and the sun has just come out, creating a beautiful effect:

- The rainwater on the roofs of the town reflects the colour of the sky, making the roof-slates seem 'sky blue': 'today/ our sky-blue slates are steaming in the sun'.
- Rainwater is also glistening on the windows of the town as it reflects the sunlight: 'We contemplate at last shining windows'.
- Yachts are moving gracefully and powerfully around the harbour: 'yachts tinkling and dancing in the bay like racehorses'.

The poem, then, sets up a contrast between the past on one hand, and the present and future on the other. The past is associated with darkness: with hard, dark and constant rain. The present and future, on the other hand, are associated with brightness: with the 'sun', with 'sky-blue slates', with 'shining windows'. The past is associated with a miserable landscape of bogs and spires. The present is associated with a pleasant landscape; a seaside town glittering in the sunlight after rain, with yachts 'tinkling' in the harbour.

THEMES

The nightmare of history
Many of Mahon's poems deal with what might be termed the nightmare of history, viewing human existence as a vicious and bitter cycle of revenge, one in which each violent act leads inexorably on to the next. Irish history in particular is regarded in this light. This theme is very much present in 'Kinsale'. In 1601 the town of Kinsale was the site of a bloody and decisive battle between Irish and English forces, one that led to many centuries of bitter conflict between England and Ireland and between the Catholic and Protestant communities within Ireland itself.

In lines 1–3 the dark, threatening rain falling endlessly on the dreary landscape symbolises these miserable centuries. The mention of the church spires suggests how, throughout this time, religious differences served as a source of strife. The mention of the bogland suggests how for centuries the Irish people became mired – or 'bogged down' – in the conflicts and issues of the past.

This notion of history as an endless cycle of violence haunts several of Mahon's poems. We see it in 'Rathlin' and in 'The Chinese Restaurant in Portrush'. It is arguably also present in 'A Disused Shed in Co. Wexford' and in 'Day Trip to Donegal'.

An escape from history's nightmare
Mahon seems to suggest that in the past it rained constantly: an endless, dark and miserable downpour. 'Today', however, thing are finally different. The downpour has just stopped forever: 'the rain we knew is a thing of the past'. Free from the rain we are 'at last' free to enjoy the brightness. We get the impression that Mahon believes this dry, bright spell will continue into the future: 'We contemplate at last shining windows/ A future forbidden to no-one'.

Mahon, of course, does not actually believe that it will never rain in Ireland again. This eternal sunshine is a metaphor for leaving history behind, of moving on from the cycles of bitter conflict that characterise Ireland's past. Whereas in the past different factions and communities tried to deny one another a future, from now on the future will be 'forbidden to no one'. (The mention of yachts and racehorses might suggest Mahon's hope that the future will be one of wealth and privilege after the centuries of miserable poverty that characterised Ireland's past.)

A similar impulse to somehow escape history is evident in other poems. In 'Rathlin', for instance, the speaker fantasises that he has found a 'dream-time' island, a place that is 'through with history', that is somehow untouched by history's nightmarish cycles. In 'The Chinese Restaurant in Portrush', he imagines that the vicious wolfhound of Irish history is safely sleeping. In each of these poems, however, we get the sense that Mahon cannot quite believe that the past is really left behind, cannot quite believe that the cycles of history are broken.

Narrow-mindedness
Several of Mahon's poems deal with a grim and fanatical mindset, a narrow-mindedness expressed by the speaker of 'As it Should Be' and associated with the Protestant population of Belfast in 'Ecclesiastes'. In 'Kinsale', however, he dares to imagine that these fanatical and narrow-minded attitudes might be left in the past. He imagines a future open to and shared by all traditions, one in which no group forbids the others from partaking. A similar desire is hinted at in 'The Chinese Restaurant in Portrush'.

Nature
In 'Kinsale', as in many of his poems, Mahon celebrates the beauty of nature. He lovingly describes the wet slates reflecting the sky, the damp windows shining in sunlight, the bay with the yachts 'dancing' in it. Similar celebrations of nature's beauty occur in 'The Chinese Restaurant in Portrush', 'A Disused Shed in Co. Wexford', 'Day Trip to Donegal' and 'Rathlin'.

Yet 'Kinsale' also shows us what might be described as nature's darker side. Its opening lines depict a bleak and oppressive environment, one of rain-lashed bogs and church spires (as noted above, there is something ominous or even threatening about the hard, deep-delving rain). This bleak landscape represents the troubled cycles of Ireland's history, while the sunny landscape depicted in lines 4–7 represents an escape from that bitter past.

There is also a sense in which the landscape depicted in the opening lines of 'Kinsale' suggests the fanatical narrow-mindedness that held sway throughout Ireland's troubled past. 'Ecclesiastes' is similar in this regard. That poem also depicts dark January rain falling on bogs and on 'dank churches'. There is a sense in which the bleakness of the landscape around Belfast reflects the bleakness of the religion practised in the city, and the fanatical narrow-mindedness of its Protestant inhabitants.

LANGUAGE

A notable feature of this poem is that it conjures two very different atmospheres. The atmosphere of the opening lines is depressing, brooding and perhaps even threatening, with their depiction of spires, bogs and menacing rain. The atmosphere in lines 4–7 is much more hopeful and uplifting, with its sunlight, shining windows, dancing yachts and slates reflecting the sky's blue.

In lines 1–3 assonance and alliteration are used to create a sombre and melancholy effect. Alliteration occurs through the repetition of the 'd' sound in 'deep-delving, dark, deliberate'. This slows down our reading of the line, creating a solemn effect. A similar technique is used in line 3 through the repetition of the 'b' sound in 'browsing' and 'bogland'. The repeated long broad-vowel sounds in these three lines slows the pace of the verse, creating a sad musicality.

A happier and more upbeat musical effect is created in lines 4–6. Alliteration is again used in line 4, the repeated sibilant 's' sound creating a pleasant musical effect. It also quickens the pace of the line, allowing our tongues to slip from one word to the next. We see assonance in line 5 where the repeated broad-vowel sounds create a pleasant or euphonious musical effect: 'our yachts tinkling and dancing in the bay/ like racehorses'. The assonance in the phrase 'shining windows' also contributes to the overall musical effect with its repeated 'i' sound.

It is also worth noting that the poem has the following rhyme scheme: ABBCBAC.

The simile in line 6, which compares the yachts to dancing racehorses, may seem outlandish but is strangely fitting. Yachts and racehorses are generally associated with speed, freedom, travel and privilege, a far cry from the 'spires and bogland' that characterise the past. The fact the yachts are depicted as 'dancing' further suggests their grace and power.

Quick Reference

WILLIAM SHAKESPEARE

	Passage of Time	Love	Despair	Art	Death
12 When I count the clock ...	Life rushes by: summer is all too short – Destroys beauty with its 'wastes of time – 'Destroys everything	Procreation only counter to time's ravages – Celebrates Fair Youth's beauty			
18 Shall I compare thee ...	Life rushes by: summer is 'all too short' – Destroys beauty' – 'untrims' everything that's fair	Celebrates Fair Youth's beauty and temperance		Defies time: Fair Youth's qualities will be preserved in verse – Defies death	Art defeats it: Fair Youth will never die because of this poem
23 As an unperfect actor ...		How overwhelming and nerve-wracking love can be – poet can't express himself		Allows poet to express what he's too nervous/overwhelmed to speak out loud	
29 When in disgrace ...		Thoughts of Fair Youth soothes poet's despair – turns it to joy – Abandonment by Fair Youth hinted at	Poet in state of despair: out of luck, disgraced and socially 'outcast', lamenting his faith		
30 When to the sessions ...		Thoughts of Fair Youth soothes poet's despair – turns it to joy.	Poet in state of despair: relives old woes and heartache		Friends lost in 'Death's dateless night'
60 Like as the waves ...	Life rushes by: minutes like waves – Destroys everything – Destroys beauty			Defies time: Fair Youth's qualities will be preserved in verse	
65 Since brass, nor stone ...	Destroys everything – Destroys beauty	Celebrates Fair Youth's qualities: 'time's best jewel'		Defies time: Fair Youth's qualities will be preserved in verse	
66 Tired with all these ...		Thoughts of Fair Youth soothes poet's despair – makes him continue living	Poet in state of despair: weary of life's wrongs and injustices – feels suicidal		Death as release from suffering
73 That time of year ...	Destroys everything	Impending death should make us love all the more			Night as 'Death's second self'
94 They that have power ...		Unequal relationship – Abandonment by Fair Youth hinted at			
116 Let me not to the marriage ...	Life rushes by: 'brief hours and weeks'. Destroys beauty, withers lovers	True love doesn't change over time			
Fear No More	Destroys everything – not even kings can stand against it – Destroys beauty of golden lads and girls		Element of despair at how hard life is		Death as release from suffering

WILLIAM WORDSWORTH

Quick Reference

	Beauty of the Natural World	Nature as Restorative Power	Nature as Mentor	The Sublime in Nature	Man's Oneness with Nature	'Still, sad music of Humanity'	Solitude
Tintern Abbey	Records the 'beauteous forms' of the natural world	Nature is the poet's nurse, restores his energy and spirit	Poet says nature is his 'guide' and 'guardian' of his mental well-being	Poet senses a 'presence' or 'motion that works through all living things.		As the poet gets older he becomes more aware of the sadness that exists in the world	The area inspires thoughts of seclusion.
She Dwelt	Praises the beauty of the stars and flowers.				Lucy seems to be at one with the landscape that surrounds her		Lucy is attractive to the poet because she lives an isolated and solitary existence
A Slumber					The girl's body becomes one with the natural world when she dies		
To My Sister	Celebrates the beauty that comes with the arrival of spring.	Spending time out in the natural world rejuvenates body, mind and soul	The natural world encourages us to be true and good.	Poet speaks of a 'blessed power' working through all things	The arrival of spring unites man and nature once again		
The Stolen Boat	Celebrates the calm, still beauty of the lake he rows across		Nature seems to teach the poet a sharp and severe lesson.	The mountain seems to have a 'purpose of its own'		Poet feels a melancholic yearning as he rows acorss the lake	Poet takes great pleasure in rowing alone across the lake
Skating	Celebrates the icy paradise through which he skates		Nature encourages the young poet's personal development and inspires him			The echoing sounds of the children at play seems an 'alien sound/ Of melancholy'	Poet regularly feels like spending time skating by himself
The Solitary Reaper	Several memorable descriptions of nature at its most beautiful				The 'highland lass' is at one with the natural world that surrounds her	The speaker is fascinated by the sadness of the lass' song.	The reaper is 'single', 'solitary' and 'alone'
Lines Composed	Records the peace, light and freshness of the morning.						Poet delights in the city that is empty in the early morning
It is a Beauteous	Celebrates nature's tranquility on this lovely evening			Poet calls on to recognise 'the mighty Being' that is present in the natural world			

Quick Reference

GERARD MANLEY HOPKINS

	Nature	God and Nature	Man's Relationship with God	Religious Doubt	Mental Suffering
God's Grandeur	Man has lost contact with nature and spoils it with his industry	Senses God's energy flowing through all living things, sustaining the natural world	Man goes against God's will, smearing the beautiful world he has given us		
As Kingfishers …		Senses God's presence in all living things. Nature's variety leads him to think of the 'just man' and of living in grace with God.	Calls on us to behave in a 'just' manner and turn away from sin		
The Windhover	The poet is inspired by the falcon	The falcon's strength inspires the poet to think of Christ	Describes the battle that Christ fought in order that man would be free of sin		
Pied Beauty	Celebrates the beauty of 'dappled things'	Describes God as the force that gives birth to the wonders of the natural world. Nature's beauty leads Hopkins to praise God.			
Spring	Poet exults in the beauty of springtime		Hopkins is keenly aware that innocence will be soured with sinning. Calls on Christ to preserve the innocence of each child		
Felix Randal			Christ, through communion, is our 'reprieve and ransom', saving us from sin and death	Felix curses God for allowing him to become ill	Felix in physical pain. Felix in mental torment – his mind wanders as his sanity begins to give way.
Inversnaid	Poet delights in the sights and sounds of a 'burn' or brook				The black whirlpool of despair suggests the poet's unhappiness
No worst …				Hopkins feels abandoned by God in his hour of greatest need	Poet 'pitched past pitch of grief' – experiences intense mental suffering
I wake and feel …				God is described as distant, uncaring and unresponsive: 'dearest Him who lives alas away'	Poet suffers through long 'black hours' of night. Describes himself in terms of 'gall' and 'heartburn'
Thou Art Indeed …				Why does God allow evil men to thrive? Why do those who live holy lives suffer?	Desperate and 'straining' attempts to make something of his life. Feels intense disappointment when these efforts come to nothing.

Quick Reference

ELIZABETH BISHOP

	Moments of Awareness	Nature	Travel	Childhood	Addiction	Exile/Homelessness
The Fish	Poet experiences epiphany when she sees hooks in fish's mouth	Poet's fascination with natural world. Natural world both familiar and strange.				
The Bight		Aspects of the bight correspond with the poet's life				
Fishhouses		Description: effort to understand the sea				Sense of homelessness – poet's home changed beyond all recognition. Human race evolved far from original home in sea.
Prodigal	Prodigal experiences epiphany in farmyard at night – realises horror of situation	The prodigal sees a correspondence between his own situation and the bats flying overhead			Compulsive behaviour – the prodigal's alcoholism	Prodigal's self-imposed exile. Unwilling to go home – unsure if he is welcome or belongs in his father's house.
Questions of Travel			Travel and tourism: good or bad? Travel and imagination. An outsider's view.		Compulsive behaviour – restless travel	Poet uncertain where home really is or what the concept even means
Armadillo		Poet exhibits concern about damage done to natural world by fire balloons	An outsider's view		Compulsive behaviour – locals continue to release dangerous fire balloons	
Sestina	The child's dawning awareness of the tragedy that has befallen her family			Wonderfully captures child's point of view		
First Death	The child speaker's dawning awareness of what death means			Wonderfully captures child's point of view		
Filling Station	Poet experiences moment of epiphany when she realises somebody cares about the filthy station – 'Somebody loves us all'		An outsider's view			
In the Waiting Room	Child's sudden realisation she sounds like her aunt. Dawning awareness that she is just like everybody else.		Is travel good or bad – exploitative pictures in magazine	Wonderfully captures child's point of view.		

This is Poetry · 391

Quick Reference

THOMAS KINSELLA

	Childhood/ Youth	Death/ Mortality	Old Age/ Ageing	Family/ Ancestry	Horror/ Desolation	Struggle for Comprehension	Memory	Art
Mr D.		Elegy for someone the poet knew. How the dead haunt the living.	Negative effects of ageing: Mr D.'s pain and loneliness		Desolation: canal-bank scene	Mr D. staring at the water of the canal	Memory of Mr D. haunts the poet	
Dick King	Captures childhood mentality: depiction of young poet with Dick King	Elegy for childhood neighbour. How the dead haunt the living. Preparation for death: Dick King 'discovering a gate'.	Negative effects of ageing: The 'dread years'. Dick King alone at the end of his life.			Dick King thinking about the dead and the afterlife	Memory of Dick King haunts the poet. Death ignites love in our memory.	
Mirror in February	Describes the 'end of youth'	Awareness of mortality: realises that he is not getting younger and won't be renewed like trees	Negative effects of ageing: poet's 'dry, exhausted eye'		Desolation: winter landscape, the defaced trees. Horror: poet's aged face.	Poet tries to come to terms with ageing		Artistic ambition. Lack of fulfilment.
Chrysalides	The boys' cycling trip: adolescent mentality. Changes occurring within them. Treated like children but this innocence is ending.	Dawning awareness of mortality caused by sight of dying ants			Horror: Dying ants		Memory of dying ants haunts the poet. Describes the processes of memory.	
Hen Woman	Captures the childhood mentality of the child watching the egg being laid				Horror: egg being laid?	Child struggles to comprehend significance of what he has seen	Memory of egg haunts the poet. An event that seemed insignificant stays with poet. Describes the processes of memory.	Description of artistic process: how memory yields a poem. Difficult life of the artist: beetle.
Tear	Youthful mentality of young poet in grandmother's room. Childhood mentality to poet responding to infant sister's death. End of innocence.	Elegy for poet's grandmother. Dawning awareness of death. Poem illustrates different responses to death: young child, father, grandparents. Preparation for death: grandparents.	Negatives effect of ageing: grandmother's desiccated body. Old age makes people tough and durable.	The hardship of grandparents' and parents' lives. Hardened by experience. Isolated from one another.	Horror: grandmother's room and appearance. Desolation: The ashes in 'vault' of mind.	Young poet struggles to make sense of grandmother's death and what it represents	Memory of dying grandmother and dead sister haunt the poet	
His Father's Hands	Depiction of childhood mentality, especially the boy in the grandfather's workshop	Elegy for grandfather. How the dead haunt.		Hardship of earlier generations. The hardship of grandparents' and parents' lives. Hardened by experience. Isolated from one another. Ancestry and race memory.	Horror: primeval landscape and monument. Desolation: Primeval landscape and monument.		Memory of the grandfather haunts the poet. An event that seemed insignificant stays with poet. Race memory.	
Model School	Depicts childhood mentality of schooldays and end of that innocence	Dawning awareness of mortality: scene in bicycle shed			Desolation: school shed scene. Horror: taste of ink.	Wants to 'know everything'	Memory of school days haunt the poet. An event that seemed insignificant stays with poet.	The difficult life of the artist
VI – Littlebody								Artistic integrity
VII								The muse
Echo						Race memory		

392 · This is Poetry

SYLVIA PLATH

	Psychic Landscape	Order & Chaos	Mental Anguish	Femininity & Motherhood	Poetic Inspiration	Nature
Black Rook in Rainy Weather	Speaker's dull, uninspired state of mind is mirrored in 'dull, ruinous landscape'	World presented as a random and chaotic place. No purpose to the natural world.	Fears a numb mental state of neutrality that comes with a lack of inspiration		A spiritual view of inspiration. Inspiration is random. Fear of losing it.	
The Times Are Tidy		Describes a tedious era of order and conformity. Contrasted with more chaotic but heroic times.			Describes a dull and uninspiring world. The poet needs chaos to write.	
Morning Song			A sense of neutrality. Feels nothing when child is born.	The difficult transition to motherhood.		
Finisterre	Description of storm suggests emotional turmoil. The ghost-like mist suggests numb mental neutrality.	Sea = chaos. Land = order. Chaos attracts and repulses.	Inner turmoil. Mental neutrality. Self-destructive urges.	Our Lady: idea of mother failing her children	Dangerous mental exploration necessary for poet	
Mirror			Inner turmoil. A sense of neutrality.	Comment on the pressure women feel to meet certain standards of beauty	Dangerous mental exploration necessary for poet	
Pheasant					Nature provides her with inspiration	A celebration of natural world. Life in the poet's hands (the pheasant).
Elm	Elm undergoes various tortures that serve as metaphors for Plath's turmoil-filled mind		Inner turmoil: elm's sufferings. Inadequacy: awareness of her own failings.	A study of feminine suffering	Dangerous mental exploration necessary for poet	
Poppies in July	Field of poppies illustrates the mental turmoil of poet		A sense of neutrality. Self-destructive urges.			
The Arrival of the Bee Box	The box seethes, like her mind, with dark, angry and negative emotions	The bees represent chaos. The box imposes order on them. Chaos attracts and repulses.	Depicts inner turmoil. Self-destructive thoughts or desires. Inadequacy.		Dangerous mental exploration necessary for poet	Life in the poet's hands (the bees)
Child			A sense of inadequacy in relation to her child. Captures inner turmoil.	Mother failing her children		

Quick Reference

DEREK MAHON

	Compassion	Violent Cycle of History	Escape from History	Narrow-mindedness	Nature	Isolation
Day Trip	Poet exhibits compassion for dying fish	Irish history as cycle of violence and revenge – Donegal as 'enclave'			Nature's beauty but also its darker, destructive side	Isolation of poet in nightmare or vision
After the *Titanic*	Poet exhibits compassion for Ismay's suffering. Also exhibits compassion for victims of the disaster.				Nature's darker, destructive side. Also nature's beauty.	Ismay's isolation upon the water and from society in his later life
A Disused Shed	Exhibits compassion for mushrooms' plight. Exhibits compassion for victims of Treblinka, Pompeii and other disasters.	Irish history as cycle of violence and revenge – reference to Irish civil war. History in general as horrific – Treblinka and Pompeii.			Nature's beauty (grounds of hotel), but also its darker, destructive side (Pompeii)	
Ecclesiastes				Narrow-minded attitude of Belfast Protestants. Narrow-minded attitude of Ecclesiastes figure.	Depressing and oppressive portrayal of nature	
As it Should Be	Poet exhibits compassion for the 'mad bastard' who is brutally killed			Narrow-minded attitude of speaker		Isolation of the victim as he is hunted through the countryside
Chinese Restaurant		Irish history as cycle of violence and revenge – reference to wolfhound and 'invasion'	Poet imagines new beginning free from the conflicts of the past	Poet imagines narrow-minded attitudes of past left behind	Nature's beauty, but also its darker, destructive side	
Rathlin	Poet exhibits compassion for victims of massacre	Irish history as cycle of violence and revenge – 1575 and the bombs 'dozing'	Poet imagines Rathlin as a 'dream-time' island untouched by the violence of history		Nature's beauty but also its darker, destructive side	
Antarctica	Poet exhibit's compassion for Oates' brave and lonely plight.				Nature's darker, destructive side – its indifference to human life	Oates' isolation as he walks out into the snow
Kinsale		Irish history as cycle of violence and revenge – Battle of Kinsale	Poet imagines new beginning free from the conflicts of the past	Poet imagines narrow-minded attitudes of past left behind	Depressing and oppressive portrayal of nature. Also reveals beauty of nature.	

EXAM PREPARATION

HOW TO ANSWER THE POETRY QUESTION

I've been asked to write an essay in response to the following statement: 'I like (or do not like) to read the poetry of Sylvia Plath.'

STAGE 1: PLANNING THE ANSWER

Establish a point of view
Firstly, I'm going to decide what my point of view is. I'm going to declare that I like the poetry of Sylvia Plath for the following reasons:

i   It is emotionally intense, and it deals with the darker aspects of the human psyche.
ii Her vivid and violent imagery linger in the mind long after we have read the poems.

This is one of the most important steps in the whole process. I have decided a point of view. I will not be rambling on vaguely about my attitude to Plath's poetry. Everything in my answer will now relate to this point of view.

Decide which poems to talk about
I am now going to decide which poems to talk about. It's good to talk about four to six poems in an answer. I'm going to talk about six: 'Elm', 'Poppies in July', 'The Arrival of the Bee Box', 'Morning Song', 'Black Rook in Rainy Weather' and 'Child'. I'm going to quickly jot down the titles of these poems along with a couple of quotations from each poem that will relate to my point of view.

Structure the essay
Now I'm going to structure my essay. I'm going to write six paragraphs.

- The first paragraph, the introduction, will clearly state my point of view.
- The second paragraph will deal with 'Elm' and 'The Arrival of the Beebox'. I will be discussing Plath's inner turmoil as exhibited in these poems.
- The third paragraph will discuss 'Black Rook in Rainy Weather' and 'Poppies in July'. I will discuss feelings of numbness or mental neutrality as exhibited in these poems.
- My fourth paragraph will discuss 'Child' and 'Morning Song'. I will discuss the feelings of inadequacy as a mother exhibited in these poems.
- My fifth paragraph will discuss vivid and memorable images in Plath's poetry. I will refer to a number of the poems mentioned above.
- The final paragraph will be the conclusion.

STAGE 2: WRITING THE ESSAY

Writing the introduction
I'm going to write my introduction. The first one or two sentences of my introduction will simply state the point of view I came up with in the planning stage:

> I really admire the poetry of Sylvia Plath because it is emotionally intense and it deals with the darker aspects of the human psyche. I also liked how her vivid and violent imagery linger in the mind long after we have read the poems.

I am now going to flesh this out in a few more sentences. It is good to make these sentences personal, if possible, to describe the impact the work had on you. In this instance, I am going to emphasise the impact Plath had on me by contrasting her with the other poets I have studied:

> I really admire the poetry of Sylvia Plath because it is emotionally intense and it deals with the darker aspects of the human psyche. I also liked how the vivid and violent imagery she uses lingers in the mind long after we have read the poems. Throughout my life I have always found poetry to be dull, boring and intellectual. The poets I read never really connected with me. However, this was definitely not the case with Sylvia Plath. This is poetry that came from the heart as much as from the head. Her work spoke to me immediately due to its raw and intense

emotional content and its unforgettably violent imagery.

Its obvious that the five sentences I have added here flesh out my point of view. The sentences are personal and show that I have really engaged with the work of the poet.

Writing the body paragraphs

I see from my plan that my first body paragraph will deal with the inner turmoil expressed in 'Elm' and 'Arrival of the Beebox'. So I'm going to start the paragraph with a topic sentence, a sentence declaring what the paragraph is going to be about:

> In 'Elm' and 'The Arrival of the Beebox' we see Plath expressing intense inner turmoil.

Every other sentence in this paragraph is going to relate to or expand on this topic sentence. If I find myself writing something that does not relate directly to this topic sentence, I know I've gone wrong.

To complete this paragraph I am going to write a couple of sentences about 'Elm' and 'The Arrival of the Beebox':

> In 'Elm' and 'The Arrival of the Beebox' we see Plath expressing intense inner turmoil. 'Elm' depicts a mind at the end of its tether. The poet is tormented by the dark emotions that dwell within her psyche: 'I'm terrified by this dark thing/ That sleeps in me'. The elm tree has been 'scorched' by the 'atrocity' of 'sunsets', has been lashed by poisonous rain and blasted by 'wind of such violence'. Yet we feel that these terrible sufferings are a metaphor for the mental turmoil the poet endures. 'The Arrival of the Beebox' is another poem that deals with mental turmoil. The beebox has thrown the poet into a state of confusion and distress. She is both frightened and fascinated by this object: 'The box is locked, it is dangerous./ I have to live with it overnight/ And I can't keep away from it'. She is disgusted by the sight of the bees through the box's grill: 'Black on black, angrily clambering'. She is even more upset by the sounds that are coming from the box: 'It is noise that appals me most of all'. As in 'Elm', we feel that there is an element of metaphor to this poem. The box serves as a symbol for the darker side of the poet's psyche, for the feelings of fear and inadequacy that she keeps locked inside her and that she fears will destroy her should she set them free.

Note how every sentence I have written relates to my topic sentence. I don't wander off the point by talking about Plath's marriage or about life in the 1950s when she wrote the poem.

Note how I don't fall into the trap of paraphrasing the poems, of telling the examiner everything that happened in each of them. I simple take two or three aspects that are relevant to my topic sentence.

Note also how I back up every point with a quote. The golden rule here is 'Always be quoting'!

Finally, note how at the end of my paragraph I link the two poems it discusses. This is a skill that can be acquired with practice.

I see that my next paragraph is going to deal with feelings of numbness or mental neutrality as exhibited in 'Black Rook in Rainy Weather' and 'Poppies in July'. Once again, I start off with a simple topic sentence:

> 'Black Rook in Rainy Weather' and 'Poppies in July' display a desperate state of mental neutrality and numbness.

Once again I am going to write a number of sentences that relate to this topic sentence. I'm going to make sure that nothing I write strays away from this topic.

> 'Black Rook in Rainy Weather' and 'Poppies in July' display a desperate state of mental neutrality and numbness. In 'Black Rook in Rainy Weather', the poet expresses her 'fear/ Of total neutrality'. In one sense, this suggests her fear of writer's block, the fear that she will never again be visited by 'the angel' of inspiration, by that 'rare, random descent'. However, the mention of 'total neutrality' calls to mind the intense numbness or emptiness experienced by those suffering from depression. The grey, desolate landscape in which the poem is set serves as a metaphor for this state of 'total neutrality'. The 'desultory weather' and the 'season/ Of fatigue' calls to mind the dead inner emptiness the poet fears. In 'Poppies in July', this fear seems to have

been realised. The poet is gripped by a feeling of numbness and emptiness. She longs for physical pain just so she can feel something: 'If I could bleed, or sleep! –/ If my mouth could marry a hurt like that'. She wishes the 'flames' of the poppies could burn her in order to return some sensation of feeling to her life.

Note again how every sentence I have written relates to my topic sentence.

I don't fall into the trap of paraphrasing the poems, of telling the examiner everything that happened in each of them. I simple take two or three aspects that are relevant to my topic sentence.

I back up every point with a quote.

Note how the two poems are linked in the middle of the paragraph. Again, this is a skill that comes with practice.

The remainder of the body paragraphs will follow the same format outlined above.

Writing the conclusion

The idea here is to sum up what I have said in the essay without repeating myself too much. I am going to bring the point of view I established in the introduction back in again. I am going to try and get personal.

The first thing I am going to do is rewrite my point of view in slightly different language.

> For me, then, Plath's poetry stands out because of its sheer emotional power.

Now I am going to add a sentence that contains a phrase like 'In the poems discussed above' or 'As I have outlined above' or 'As I have discussed'. This sentence will refer back to the essay I have just written.

> For me, then, Plath's poetry stands out because of its sheer emotional power. In poems like those discussed above, there is an emotional intensity like nothing else I have come across in poetry.

Now I am going to add two or three more sentences that flesh out this point. I am going to try to make these as personal as possible.

> For me, then, Plath's poetry stands out because of its sheer emotional power. In poems like those discussed above, there is an emotional intensity like nothing else I have come across in poetry. Reading Plath's poetry, I felt she was really talking to me, that she was describing dark emotional states that I and every other human being will experience at some time. The powerful imagery, like that of the elm, the beebox and the disturbing field of poppies, will remain with me for the rest of my life.

Note how the conclusion is short and does not ramble on and on repeating the points made in the essay.

Note how the conclusion describes a personal response.

Note how the conclusion is tied into the point of view established at the start of the essay.

If you are good at English, it can be good to finish with a flourish. This might involve using a memorable phrase, a quote from a famous writer or the poet under discussion, or some poetic sentence of your own.

THE SEVEN GOLDEN RULES

1. **Read the question carefully.** This sounds obvious but I can't stress how important it is.
2. **Establish a point of view.** Do this at the beginning of your planning stage. Remember that every sentence in your essay will relate to this point of view.
3. **Structure the essay carefully.** Determine what every paragraph is going to be about before you commence writing.
4. **Begin each paragraph with a topic sentence.** Every other sentence in the paragraph will relate to this sentence.
5. **Don't paraphrase.** Don't retell the story or the action of the poem – the examiner already knows this. Just identify the two or three elements of the poem that relate to your topic.
6. **Always be quoting**
7. **Be aware of genre.** Are you being asked to write a straightforward essay or are you being asked to do something else like write a letter or give a short talk? If you are being asked to write a letter or a short talk, then the introduction and the conclusion of your essay will need to reflect this.

SAMPLE ANSWER 1

Write an essay outlining the reasons why you like or dislike the poetry of Derek Mahon.

I must say I really liked the poetry of Derek Mahon. Whereas too many poets are content simply to just go on and on about their 'feelings', Mahon engages with the world beyond himself. His poems deal with history and its victims, detailing their plight in a way that I found to be both compassionate and truly moving. I also liked the way his work focuses on individuals from history who are trapped in extreme and desperate situations, whose minds are at the 'end of their tethers'. Paradoxically, perhaps, by shifting the focus away from himself and by avoiding the discussion of his own feelings, Mahon produces work that bristles with compassion, sympathy and empathy.

One of the things I most liked about his poems was the fact that so many of them are spoken by people other than the poet himself. In 'As it Should Be', for instance, we are brought into the mind of a cold-blooded killer who 'hunted the mad bastard/ Through bog, moorland, rock, to the starlit west'. Mahon allows us, chillingly, to see this brutal and murderous act from the perpetrator's point of view and to perhaps even begin to understand how his desire to protect his children might have led him to commit this crime. All he wanted, he declared, was for the community's children to 'grow up/ To a world with method in it'. 'After the *Titanic*' also surprises us by presenting that well-known tragedy from an unfamiliar point of view. Here, we are taken into the mind of Bruce Ismay, the ship's manager who was 'humbled at the inquiry' into that tragic incident and declared to be the villain of the piece. Mahon allows us to witness first hand the suffering and humiliation this man endured as his 'costly life' went 'thundering down' to the ocean's bottom, and I felt real emotion when he beseeched us to 'Include me in your lamentations'.

Another feature of Mahon's poetry that appealed to me was its focus on individuals who are trapped in extreme situations. He specialises in describing individuals who are psychologically on the edge, whose 'minds are at the ends of their tethers'. An obvious example of this is 'Antarctica', which depicts Captain Oates 'Goading his ghost into the howling snow' as he disappears into the frozen wilderness to die. 'After the *Titanic*', meanwhile, depicts Bruce Ismay in a psychologically extreme situation as his 'poor soul/ Screams out in the starlight', tormented by the memory of the deaths for which he was at least partly responsible. Psychological suffering is also movingly depicted in 'Rathlin', which describes the anguish of Somhairle Bui trapped powerless on the 'mainland' as he listens to the screams of his tribe being slaughtered on Rathlin island. Yet the most chilling depiction of a psychological desperation is surely that

---

This is a good introduction. The essay's point of view is established in the opening sentences. The other sentences all relate to this point of view. The student presents a personal response letting us know how she was particularly moved by Mahon's work, especially by his impersonal style.

This is a fine paragraph. It opens with a clear topic sentence that the rest of the paragraph expands on. It confines its discussion to two poems, and makes clear and relevant points about each. Importantly, it doesn't fall into the trap of retelling the entire narrative of either.

This paragraph works. Once again, it opens with a definite topic sentence to which everything else relates. The student refers to four poems, which is a lot. However, she gets away with it, identifying in each a point that is relevant to her paragraph topic.

in 'Day Trip to Donegal', where the speaker dreams or hallucinates that he is 'alone far out at sea', adrift on a seething stormy ocean. I found the conclusion of this poem incredibly powerful, and I could almost see the speaker clinging to some kind of raft in the middle of an endless sea.

One of the most prominent features of Mahon's work is his over-riding concern for the victims of history. This is perhaps at its most evident in 'A Disused Shed in Co. Wexford' where the mushrooms abandoned in a shed 'deep in the grounds of a burnt-out hotel' come to represent all the people who have suffered throughout history. Mahon presents them as a symbol for the 'Lost people of Treblinka and Pompeii' – the victims of both man-made conflicts, such as the holocaust, and natural disasters, like the destruction of Pompeii by the eruption of Vesuvius in 79 BC. A similar concern for history's victims is evident in 'Rathlin', where the speaker reflects on the massacre of the people of Somhairle Bui in the sixteenth century: 'Somhairle Bui, powerless on the mainland heard the screams of the Rathlin women/ Borne to him, seconds later, upon the wind'.

Mahon also shows compassion toward the non-human world. We see this in 'Day Trip to Donegal' where the speaker pities the 'writhing glimmer of fish' as they expire on the pier in 'attitudes of agony and heartbreak'. 'A Disused Shed in Co. Wexford', meanwhile, shows real compassion for the 'thousand mushrooms' who have endured a 'half century without visitors in the dark'.

Mahon's work is so powerful because it is dedicated to speaking out on behalf of these forgotten victims who have 'come so far in darkness and in pain'. He refuses to abandon them to forgetfulness, whether they be the people of Rathlin, Pompeii and Treblinka, the hunted 'mad bastard' of 'As it Should Be' or poor old Bruce Ismay who each day is forced to 'drown again with all those dim/ Lost faces'. The triumph of his impersonal style is that it allows him to speak out on behalf of these people so movingly and with such effectiveness.

Both of these paragraphs are excellent. Once again, the student stays on topic throughout. She backs up everything with relevant quotes. There is a nice piece of linking in paragraph four. The phrase 'A similar concern for history's victims is evident in …' links her discussion of 'A Disused Shed in Co. Wexford' with her discussion of 'Rathlin'.

This is a fine conclusion. It restates the point of view established in the introduction, refers briefly to the poems mentioned in the body of the essay, and finishes with a well-executed, memorable sentence.

SAMPLE ANSWER 2

Write a letter to Thomas Kinsella telling him how you responded to some of his poems on your course. Support the points you make by detailed reference to the poems you choose to write about.

Dear Mr Kinsella,

I recently studied a number of your poems for my Leaving Cert and I just wanted to write to you and express my admiration for your work. I was especially impressed by the way your poems depicted the world of the child, perfectly capturing the innocence and vulnerability of childhood. But it was the way in which your poems set this innocence and vulnerability against the strangeness and darkness of the world that was particularly effective. In your poems, we realise how fragile the child's world is, and how very quickly in life we are exposed to experiences that are troubling and defining. I also greatly admired how you dealt with the pains and sufferings of old age, and the way in which you described interactions between the young and the old – meetings that often resulted in moments of insight and epiphany.

I found the depiction of childhood in 'Dick King' and 'Model School' very touching. The description of the young boy seeking comfort and security by leaning into Dick King's coat as they stood 'under the Fountain in James's Street' is beautiful: 'When I sheltered my nine years against your buttons/ And your own dread years were to come'. The lines wonderfully capture the fragile world of the child but also look ahead to the corresponding fragility that comes with old age. It was the extract from your work 'Settings', called 'Model School, Inchicore', however, that captured childhood most memorably. I cannot think of another poem that I have read that so perfectly renders the world of the child. The childish sense of humour ('We always tittered at each other/ when we said the adding-up table in Irish/ and came to her name') and the innocence of the child are masterfully evoked: "We are going to start/ decimals// I am going to know/ everything'.

But the innocence that your poems capture is a fragile innocence, and we always get the sense that it is only a matter of time before it will be destroyed. In 'Model School', for instance, the child who thinks sweetly of the 'fat bee ... shining amongst us' is given to darker thoughts when alone. His vulnerability is evident when he sits by himself 'in the shed' and thinks of God, who is said to be all-knowing: 'Will God judge/ our most secret thoughts and actions'. The mentioning of the 'Day of Judgement' and the way in which the poem finishes with the description of the bitter taste of ink leaves the reader with an uncomfortable feeling. 'Hen Woman' is another poem that describes a troubling moment in childhood. Just like in 'Model School', you perfectly capture the strangeness of the world as seen through the eyes of a child. Again, there are the details that

---

In this essay the student has been asked to write a letter. Note how she adheres to the conventions of the genre by beginning her essay with 'Dear Mr Kinsella' and personalising the paragraph that follows. What is most important, however, is that she does not allow the form of the letter to distract her from establishing a clear point of view and presenting a personal response.

A good paragraph. It opens with a clear topic sentence that the rest of the paragraph expands on. It confines its discussion to two poems and makes clear points about each and backs them up with relevant quotes.

The student does well in linking this paragraph with the one that came before, thereby allowing the essay to flow nicely. She makes a clear point in the topic sentence, saying that the innocence described in Kinsella's poems is fragile and inevitably destroyed. This is then backed up with reference to two poems and supported with relevant quotes.

only a child would notice: 'A beetle like a bronze leaf/ was inching across the cement,/ clasping with small tarsi/ a ball of dung bigger than its body'. But all the time there is an atmosphere of tension, an uncomfortable feeling that something odd but profoundly important is taking place: 'A mutter of thunder far off/ – time not quite stopped./ I saw the egg had moved a fraction:/ a tender blank brain/ under torsion, a clean new world'.

Encounters between the young and the old are described in a number of your poems, and often these encounters result in moments of awareness for the child. I already made reference to 'Hen Woman' and its description of a very strange encounter, but it was your poem 'Tear' that most powerfully describes the effect the old can have on the young. When I read this poem for the first time I found it almost unbearably moving. I really admire how you described unflinchingly the grandmother's suffering, and also the child's fear and repugnance at what he must encounter: 'I couldn't stir at first, nor wished to,/ for fear she might turn and tempt me'. The poem had a profound effect on me, forcing me to think of the hardships that some must endure, the 'sad dullness and tedious pain'. As I read the poem I thought back to your description of Dick King and the way in which this fondly remembered man, too, had his 'dread years', years when 'season in, season out,/ He made his wintry bed'.

What your poems revealed to me was just how important and defining some of our childhood encounters actually are. It was very touching to read of how Dick King's ghost still haunts you, how you have never been able to forget this man you knew as a child. In what I regard as one of your most beautiful lines, you suggest that when someone dies they can still inspire love in those who live: 'in your phantom vowels I read/ That death roves our memories igniting/ Love'. However, your poems also describe the unpleasant truths we must learn when we are young. In 'Tear' the child's encounter with his dying grandmother brings home to him the inevitability of sickness and death and the fact that suffering is part of life: 'the struggle/ in store for you all your life'. But it is important that we face up to these truths, acknowledge them and learn how to live.

I would just like to take this opportunity once again to thank you for the beautiful poems you have written. Much of what we had to study for the Leaving Cert I found uninspiring, but having to study your poems was both an enriching and pleasurable experience. I look forward to exploring more of your work when my exams are over.

Yours sincerely,

The student remains conscious of the fact that she is writing a letter referring to the poems as 'your poems' rather than 'his poems'. She is keeping it personal, telling the poet how the poems made her feel. Once again, she begins with a strong topic sentence, and stays on topic throughout the paragraph.

Once again, the student makes it clear how the poems made her feel. She begins the paragraph with a clear topic sentence, and fleshes this out in the sentences that follow.

The conclusion is short but it works. The student remains conscious of the fact that she is writing a letter and so tailors her lines to suit the genre. She makes some brief, personal remarks about Kinsella's work and signs off in the appropriate manner.

SAMPLE ANSWER 3

Write an essay in which you attempt to explain why the poetry of Gerard Manley Hopkins still appeals to the modern reader. Your answer should make reference to the poetry of Hopkins on your course.

In many ways, Gerard Manley Hopkins seems like a writer who has little to do with our modern world. This was a man obsessed with religion, who couldn't even see a 'dapple-dawn-drawn falcon' soaring through the morning sky without thinking about Jesus, his brave 'chevalier' who does battle against sin. Let's be honest, our age is one where religion has fallen very much by the wayside. Hopkins was a man whose greatest delight was the natural world, who could declare with a straight face that 'Nothing is so beautiful as Spring', and who delighted in watching spring lambs having 'fair their fling' over the meadows. Today, people both young and old find pleasure more in video games, television programmes and movies than we do in nature. We are more likely to be thrilled by the arrival of the latest games console or new Batman movie with Christian Bale than we are by the arrival of springtime. And yet Hopkins continues to draw readers. What brings people back to his poems again and again?

For me, there are two main reasons why Hopkins still appeals to the modern reader: the sheer beauty of his language and the unflinching manner in which he grappled with despair. As I read his work, it became clear to me that this was a poet who uncompromisingly describes 'black hours' of depression and hopelessness, emotions that are all too common in our modern world. Anyone who has ever suffered such emotions will find themselves connecting with Hopkins' 'terrible sonnets'. Modern readers no doubt also find Hopkins' work appealing because of the sheer beauty of his language. Here is a poet whose work is littered with musical phrases and with vivid imaginative descriptions. These are qualities that never go out of date.

The wonderful music of Hopkins' poetry is evident in 'The Windhover', in 'Inversnaid' and in 'Spring'. Consider the following phrase from 'The Windhover': 'rising of the rolling level underneath him steady air'. There is assonance aplenty here with the repeated 'e' and 'a' sounds, as well as alliteration with the repeated 'r' sound. Even more impressively, this majestic-sounding phrase is basically one lone adjective describing the air through which the falcon flies. A similar musical effect can be found in 'Inversnaid' where Hopkins describes a brook, or burn, flowing down a hill in the wilds of Scotland: 'This dangerous burn, horseback brown,/ His rollrock highroad roaring down'. These lines have everything: alliteration from the repeated 'r' sound, assonance from the repeated broad-vowel sounds, and even an unusual internal rhyme between 'burn' and 'brown'. In these onomatopoeic phrases, with their powerful rhythms, we can almost hear the water crashing down the highland slope. In 'Spring', meanwhile, Hopkins captures the 'descending blue' of the springtime sky, declaring 'that blue is all in a rush with richness'. Once again, assonance and alliteration combine memorably here. Who else but Hopkins could produce such rich, strange and haunting musical effects?

The second paragraph is a textbook introductory paragraph. The essay's point of view is established in this paragraph's first sentence: the modern reader likes Hopkins because of his poetic language and because of how he writes about despair. The other sentences in the paragraph all relate to this point of view. The student presents a personal response letting us know how he found Hopkins' depiction of despair compelling.

However, the student has taken a somewhat unusual approach by leading into this 'proper' introductory paragraph with a paragraph discussing Christian Bale among other things. We're told why modern readers might dislike Hopkins before the student 'comes clean' and tells us that they actually like him after all. This is a risky strategy but one that actually works in this case.

Hopkins also appeals to modern readers because of his vivid, imaginative descriptions. Who could deny the freshness and energy of the description of the falcon in 'The Windhover' with its 'wimpling wing' as it 'rebuffs the big wind' in the sky above? Equally thrilling is the depiction of the thrush in 'Spring', whose singing floats through the 'echoing timber' of the trees in the forest and is so beautiful it 'strikes like lightnings' to hear it.

As we noted, the darker side of Hopkins' work also appeals to the modern psyche. Hopkins is a writer who deals unflinchingly with depression and despair. We see this in 'Inversnaid' and in 'I Wake and Feel the Fell of Dark'. The first intrusion of despair into Hopkins' work occurs in 'Inversnaid', where he views a little whirlpool that forms in the brook as a pit of almost bottomless despair: 'Of a pool so pitch-black, fell-frowning,/ It rounds and rounds Despair to drowning.' This vision of the evil or, 'fell'-looking, pool seems to prophesise the vortex of despair into which Hopkins himself would soon be sucked. In 'I Wake and Feel the Fell of Dark' the poet feels that the 'black hours' he suffers through will never end, that the coming of light will always be delayed. He compares himself to the 'sweating selves' of the souls of the damned in hell, saying that their suffering is similar to his own, only 'worse'.

Yet perhaps the most powerful depiction of despair occurs in 'No Worst, There is None'. Hopkins uses personification to describe his mental torment, describing it as a menacing 'Fury' that pursues him. In Greek mythology, the furies were vengeful demons that relentlessly pursued their victims to the end of the earth: Fury had shrieked no ling-/ ering!' In this poem, Hopkins declares that he has been 'Pitched past pitch of grief'. His torment occupies a place on the scale of suffering that is beyond ordinary 'grief'. He is close to complete despair, and possibly even to madness. Furthermore, his mental torment keeps getting worse. Each new pain he experiences has learned from earlier pains how best to make him suffer. He describes each new 'pang', therefore, as having been 'schooled' by the pangs that went before ('forepangs'). Each new pain 'wrings' his mind in a way that is 'wilder' and more violent than the last. In a shocking conclusion, he declares that the only escape from the suffering that grips him lies in sleep or death: 'All life death does end and each day dies with sleep.'

In conclusion, then, it seems obvious to me that Hopkins' poetry will continue to be read well into the future. Readers will continue to be thrilled by his musical lines and memorable nature images. Yet modern readers will also be drawn by the darker side of his poetry. It may seem strange to suggest that people will be attracted by Hopkins' bleak portrayal of a mind on the brink of collapse. Yet we live in a world where depression, mental illness and suicide are all too common – even among the young. Hopkins' poetry provides a frank and moving depiction of these emotions that affect so many people in our modern world.

Each of the four body paragraphs in this essay are very well written. Each opens with a clear topic sentence that the rest of the paragraph expands on. Each confines its discussion to no more than three poems, and makes clear and relevant points about each. Importantly, none of these paragraphs falls into the trap of retelling the entire narrative of the poems they discuss.

It is important to note how each point is backed up with relevant quotations.

This is a fine conclusion. Its first two sentences restate the point of view established in the introduction. The remaining sentences flesh this out while referring to the poems mentioned in the body of the essay. Importantly, it doesn't go on too long, avoiding the trap of writing the whole essay all over again.

Exam Preparation

SAMPLE ANSWER 4

You have been asked to give a talk introducing your classmates to the poetry of William Wordsworth.

Fellow classmates, I would like to introduce you today to the poetry of William Wordsworth. On a personal level, I find Wordsworth's poetry very appealing because of how it depicts the natural world. At a time of great technological advancement, Wordsworth turned his attention to the 'sweet sounds and harmonies' of nature. In the 'light of setting suns,/ And the round ocean and the living air,/ And the blue sky' he found his way back to nature's beauty and mystery. Today, I would like to give you a sense of how he valued and perceived the natural world.

Wordsworth believed that spending time in nature provides us with beautiful images that we can contemplate in difficult times. In 'Tintern Abbey', the poet recalls how memories of the natural world comforted him when he found himself alone and depressed in the squalor of the city: 'oft, in lonely rooms, and 'mid the din/ Of towns and cities, I have owed to them,/ In hours of weariness, sensations sweet'. The mind, he says, is 'a mansion for all the lovely forms' of nature. When we are lonely or depressed, we can turn to these wonderful memories and feel revived. Nature fills our minds with 'quietness and beauty' and allows us to get through the 'dreary intercourse of daily life'.

Wordsworth also believed that the natural world could somehow guide and instruct us. He suggests that nature gives us a special perspective on life. To spend time in the natural world is to expose ourselves to the greater mystery and beauty of life, something that's missing from cities and factories. This enriches our minds and influences our actions in a positive way. In 'To My Sister', he declares that walking in the countryside can help our hearts to formulate certain laws: 'Some silent laws our hearts will make,/ Which they shall long obey'. In 'Tintern Abbey', he says that the natural world can have a significant impact on our conduct. The pleasure that we derive from the natural world can make us better people: 'have no slight or trivial influence/ On that best portion of a good man's life/ His little nameless, unremembered, acts/ Of kindness and of love'. Nature, he says, is 'the nurse,/ The guide, the guardian of my heart, and soul/ Of all my moral being'.

Wordsworth also suggests that there is some mysterious force or power working through nature. In a number of his poems he makes reference to a mysterious presence that he senses in the natural world. As he walks along a beach in 'It is a Beauteous Evening', he claims to hear 'the mighty Being' in the 'eternal motion' of the sea. In 'To My Sister', he speaks of 'the blessed power that rolls/ About, below, above'. In 'Tintern Abbey', he talks of feeling 'a presence' in

---

This is a very good introductory paragraph. The student is conscious that he is writing in a particular genre: the short talk. The paragraph's opening and closing sentences address his audience. He establishes a point of view early on – in fact, in the second sentence. The remainder of the paragraph fleshes out this point view. The student also 'personalises' this point of view, mentioning the impact Wordsworth's poetry had on him as an individual.

Each of these three paragraphs works very well. Each begins with a clear and definite topic sentence. The remaining sentences back up or reinforce this topic sentence. Each paragraph is clearly related to the point of view established in the introduction: 'On a personal level I find Wordsworth's poetry very appealing because of how it depicts the natural world'. The student uses quotes extensively, backing up each of his points.

nature, some strange entity that is 'interfused' with the natural world. Wordsworth does not – nor can he – say what exactly this 'power' is. It reminds us of God, but Wordsworth does not link the mysterious force he senses to any conventional Christian idea.

Wordsworth's focus on the natural world does not blind him to the plights of his fellow man. Rather than distract him from the troubles of the world, nature makes him more aware of the sadness and suffering of others. In 'Tintern Abbey', he says that as he has grown older he has become more aware of the 'still, sad music of humanity'. In 'A Slumber Did My Spirit Steal' and 'She Dwelt Among the Untrodden Ways', the poet describes the lonely death of a young woman. These short, spare poems through their simple descriptions of Lucy again reveal the sadness of life. In 'She Dwelt Among the Untrodden Ways', the poet describes how Lucy had 'lived unknown' and how 'few could know/ When Lucy ceased to be'. In 'A Slumber Did My Spirit Seal', the poet describes how death has united the young lady with the earth. She is buried in the ground and her body decays, becoming one with the earth itself: 'Rolled round in earth's diurnal course/ With rocks, and stones, and trees.' These simple poems convey the sadness and loneliness that is part of human life.

> This paragraph is considerably weaker than the others. While it does begin with a definite topic sentence, it becomes unfocused. It is not clear how the references to Lucy's body decaying and to the 'still, sad music of humanity' support or 'flesh out' the topic sentence. These references seem to have little connection to the plight of Wordsworth's fellow man. Furthermore, it is also not really clear how this topic relates to the essay's overall point of view.

I hope that in this brief talk I have given you some sense of how Wordsworth's depiction of nature is relevant to our times. The modernisation and industrialisation that Wordsworth turned away from have expanded and have corrupted the entire planet. It may seem strange to think of the natural world as some mysterious living force or to suggest that nature can somehow provide us with moral instruction. But such ideas are surely relevant to our time, an age when the earth seems like a living organism that has been fatally poisoned by human pollution. Wordsworth found meaning not in science, industry and commerce but in the natural world that surrounds us all. And that, perhaps, is his greatest lesson for the modern reader. Thank you for your time.

> This is a fine conclusion. The student remembers he is writing a short talk, and addresses his audience in the opening and closing sentences of the paragraph. He restates his point of view in the first sentence, and backs this up in the remainder of the paragraph. Importantly, he doesn't go on too long. The student manages to finish with a flourish, making a strong and urgent case for the relevance of Wordsworth's poetry.

SAMPLE ANSWER 5

'I like (or do not like) to read the poetry of Sylvia Plath.'

I really admire the poetry of Sylvia Plath because it is emotionally intense and it deals with the darker aspects of the human psyche. I also liked how the vivid and violent imagery she uses lingers in the mind long after we have read the poems. Throughout my life, I have always found poetry to be dull, boring and intellectual. The poets I read never really connected with me. However, this was definitely not the case with Sylvia Plath. This is poetry that came from the as much as from the head. Her work spoke to me immediately due to its raw and intense emotional content and its unforgettably violent imagery.

In 'Elm' and 'The Arrival of the Beebox' we see Plath expressing intense inner turmoil. 'Elm' depicts a mind at the end of its tether. The poet is tormented by the dark emotions that dwell within her psyche: 'I'm terrified by this dark thing/ That sleeps in me'. The elm tree has been 'scorched' by the 'atrocity' of 'sunsets', has been lashed by poisonous rain and blasted by 'wind of such violence'. Yet we feel that these terrible sufferings are a metaphor for the mental turmoil the poet endures. 'The Arrival of the Beebox' is another poem that deals with mental turmoil. The beebox has thrown the poet into a state of confusion and distress. She is both frightened and fascinated by this object: 'The box is locked, it is dangerous./ I have to live with it overnight/ And I can't keep away from it'. She is disgusted by the sight of the bees through the box's grill: 'Black on black, angrily clambering'. She is even more upset by the sounds that are coming from the box: 'It is noise that appals me most of all'. As in 'Elm', we feel that there is an element of metaphor to this poem. The box serves as a symbol for the darker side of the poet's psyche, for the feelings of fear and inadequacy that she keeps locked inside her and that she fears will destroy her should she set them free.

'Black Rook in Rainy Weather' and 'Poppies in July' display a desperate state of mental neutrality and numbness. In 'Black Rook in Rainy Weather', the poet expresses her 'fear/ Of total neutrality'. In one sense, this suggests her fear of writer's block, the fear that she will never again be visited by 'the angel' of inspiration, by that 'rare, random descent'. However, the mention of 'total neutrality' calls to mind the intense numbness or emptiness experienced by those suffering from depression. The grey, desolate landscape in which the poem is set serves as a metaphor for this state of 'total neutrality'. The 'desultory weather' and the 'season/ Of fatigue' calls to mind the dead inner emptiness the poet fears. In 'Poppies in July', this fear seems to have been realised. The poet is gripped by a feeling of numbness and emptiness. She longs for physical pain just so she can feel something: 'If I could bleed, or sleep! –/ If my mouth could marry a hurt like that'. She wishes the 'flames' of the poppies could burn her in order to return some sensation of feeling to her life.

This feeling of numbness surfaces again in a poem that Plath wrote about the birth of her child, called 'Morning Song'. Standing before the newborn child, the poet and her husband seem empty, devoid of the feelings we expect of parents: 'We stand round blankly as walls'. Plath's honesty here is admirable, and I really respect her for the way she writes about her feelings of inadequacy as a mother. Becoming a mother is a daunting and overwhelming experience, and Plath struggles in the role, feeling that she lacks what it takes to be an effective parent: 'I'm no more your mother/ Than the cloud that distils a mirror to reflect its own slow/ Effacement at the wind's hand'. A similar feeling of inadequacy is evident in 'Child' where the poet describes a desperate desire to fill her child's world with beauty and wonder but is unable to do so because of her struggle with depression. It is heartbreaking to read of her 'troublous/ Wringing of hands, this dark/ Ceiling without a star'.

The images of the 'Wringing of hands' and the 'dark ceiling without a star' perfectly illustrate Plath's genius for creating vivid and startling images in the minds of those who read her poems. In three short lines at the close of 'Child' she perfectly captures the horror of depression. Each of her poems is full of such memorable imagery. In 'Poppies in July', she startles us with the comparison she makes between the colour of the poppies and 'the skin of a mouth// A mouth just bloodied./ Little bloody skirts'. 'Elm' is rich with powerful and unforgettable imagery. In this poem, Plath describes the moon as being 'Diminished and flat, as after radical surgery', and speaks of branches of trees being 'a hand of wires'. Just like the bird in 'Pheasant', these images startle me still.

For me, then, Plath's poetry stands out because of its sheer emotional power. In poems like those discussed above, there is an emotional intensity like nothing else I have come across in poetry. Reading Plath's poetry, I felt she was really talking to me, that she was describing dark emotional states that I and every other human being will experience at some time. The powerful imagery, like that of the elm, the beebox and the disturbing field of poppies, will remain with me for the rest of my life.

SAMPLE ANSWER 6

'The poetry of Elizabeth Bishop appeals to modern readers for many reasons.'

Bishop's poems appeal to the modern reader because the subjects that she deals with are timeless. Her poems deal with the everyday world around us, and show how fascinating and wonderful ordinary places and objects can be if we just take the time to see them. Her poems also deal with childhood, another timeless subject, and show how it can be a troubling period, a time when we are first exposed to some of the unpleasant truths of life. And finally there is the theme of travel, something perhaps of special relevance to modern readers with the availability of cheap flights and the ease with which we can now move around the world. Bishop's poems question this constant need of ours to shift our location and explore new worlds.

Bishop's poems show how the world can be wonderfully interesting if we stop and pay attention to the details. In 'The Fish', for example, Bishop turns the rather banal experience of catching a fish into something remarkable. She firstly draws our attention to the fish's every detail, forcing us to pause and consider the strange beauty of the natural world; even that aspect of the fish that she cannot see, its insides and entrails, she imagines in intricate detail.

> I thought of the coarse white flesh
> packed in like feathers,
> the big bones and the little bones,
> the dramatic reds and blacks
> of his shiny entrails.

The eyes, too, are wonderfully described as being 'packed/ with tarnished tinfoil'. This attention to detail is also apparent in 'Filling Station'. Standing before an average, 'dirty' filling station, the poet becomes increasingly curious about the place. 'Why the extraneous plant?' she wonders. 'Why the taboret?/ Why, oh why, the doily?' Again, the poet seems to be telling us to pause and consider how strange and wonderful the world around us actually is.

Both 'The Fish' and 'Filling Station' suggest that important insights can occur when we take the time to observe the ordinary everyday world that surrounds us. In 'The Fish', for example, having inspected the fish closely and observed its every detail, the poet realises that there is something very special about the creature. The 'five big hooks' that have 'grown firmly in his mouth' from previous encounters with fishermen tell of the fish's will to survive. They are, according to the poet, the fish's 'five-haired beard of wisdom'. As such, the fish deserves to be set free. Realising this inspires the poet, gives her a great sense of 'victory', of triumph over adversity, that fills her world with a glorious 'rainbow'. A similar moment of insight occurs in 'Filling Station' when the poet realises that someone is making an effort to beautify the place. The way in which the cans of oil have been arranged is aesthetically pleasing: 'Somebody/ arranges the rows of cans/ so that they softly say:/ ESSO–SO–SO–SO// to high-strung automobiles'. Bishop considers how this has all been done for the benefit of the passing drivers, to sooth their nerves. A moment of realisation suddenly occurs: 'Somebody loves us all'.

Similar moments of awareness occur in the Bishop poems that deal with childhood, a theme relevant to every reader. What I admired about her treatment of this theme was the way in which she speaks of childhood in non-sentimental terms, and how she reveals how childhood experiences can often be troubling, traumatic and world-defining. Since every reader has undergone the painful transition from childhood to adulthood, these poems continue to hold significant appeal. 'Sestina', for example, focuses on a young child's experience of tragedy and loss, and reveals how children are extremely sensitive to the world around them without, perhaps, fully comprehending what is happening. The young child in the poem sees the drops that fall from the kettle in terms of 'small hard tears', and imagines that her grandmother's teacup is 'full of dark brown tears'. The imagination and innocence of the child are movingly evoked though her perception of the objects around her. In the child's world, 'little moons fall down like tears/ from between the pages of the almanac'. Without fully comprehending the fact of death, the little girl is all too aware of the sadness that pervades the house. 'In the Waiting Room' also focuses on the fragility of childhood innocence. Bishop's account of her own realisation as a child that she was not unique allows readers to comprehend the shock and distress that comes with such understanding.

But I felt: you are an I,
you are an Elizabeth,
you are one of them.
Why should you be one, too?

Through her focusing on one particular moment in a child's life, Bishop also reveals the complexity and commonality of our sense of identity, of who we are.

In the modern world, where so many of us are obsessed with travel, with moving from one place to another, Bishop's poems call into question the motivation behind wanting to do so. In 'Questions of Travel', she writes:

What childishness is it that while there's a breath of
    life
in our bodies, we are determined to rush
to see the sun the other way around?

As I mentioned already, poems like 'The Fish' and 'Filling Station' show us how fascinating and wonderful the everyday world can be if we only pause long enough to consider it. Considering this, we must wonder why we are so eager to travel far and wide in order to be stimulated. Bishop wonders 'Is it lack of imagination that makes us come/ to imagined places, not just stay at home'. As with many of her poems, 'Questions of Travel' does not provide any easy answers. Instead, she leaves us with many fascinating questions and, perhaps, opportunities to reassess the way we see the world.

This is the key to Bishop's appeal to the modern reader. Although her poems may have been written over fifty years ago, the questions they ask and the themes they address are still pertinent today. As I have shown above, her attentiveness to the world around her shows us how fascinating the most ordinary objects can be if we spend time with them. Her poems on childhood, with their appreciation of the complexities and difficulties of growing up, are relevant to everybody. Finally, the poetry of Elizabeth Bishop appeals to the modern reader because it asks us to slow down, to stop rushing around looking for more and more exotic experiences, and to appreciate the beauty, wonder and strangeness of the world closer to home. And this, I think, is what all great poetry does.

SAMPLE ANSWER 7

'Shakespeare's sonnets are lively reflections on Love and Time'. How true is this statement of the Shakespearean sonnets you have studied? Support your discussion by reference to or quotation from the poems.

I think that this statement is very true. These seem to be the principal themes of the sonnets, and Shakespeare returns to them again and again, each time exploring them in a lively and personal manner. I loved the way the sonnets described the pleasures and pains of being in love. Shakespeare reveals how nerve-wracking a relationship can be, but he also shows how love is ultimately the answer to life's troubles and woes. Chief among these woes is the passage of time. No other poet has so vividly described the passage of time and the horror that this can inspire. Shakespeare reflected on this again and again, trying desperately to find a way to counter time's destructive passage. Ultimately, love is pitted against time, and in the sonnets there is always a lively battle and a question hanging over which will prevail.

Shakespeare's sonnets vividly describe the emotional turmoil of being in love. In 'As an unperfect actor', the poet describes how nerve-wracking love can sometimes be. We all know how it feels to stand before someone we love and suddenly lose the ability to express ourselves coherently. Shakespeare likens the feeling to 'an unperfect actor on the stage/ Who with his fears is put beside his part'. The same sonnet also perfectly describes how love can cause us to lose the ability to function normally. The poet describes the way in which the power of his love paradoxically renders him weak and useless: 'in mine own love's strength seem to decay,/ O'ercharged with burden of mine own love's might'. All of this, of course, just leads to feelings of misery and torment, feelings that Shakespeare's sonnets record with great honesty. In 'When to the sessions', he describes how easy it is to occasionally revisit the hurt and humiliation that love has caused: 'weep afresh love's long since cancell'd woe'.

Yet in the very same sonnet, Shakespeare writes of love's ability to overcome despair. This swift and lively passage from one emotion to the next is what makes reading the sonnets so pleasurable. Just when it seems that the poet is on the verge of sinking beyond return into the pits of despair, he recovers his spirits. Thinking of the 'Fair Youth', the figure who inspired the sonnets – and, no doubt, inspired much of the poet's misery in the first place – brings an immediate end to the poet's suffering: 'But if the while I think on thee (dear friend)/ All losses are restored and sorrows end'. A similar recovery from self-loathing and doubt occurs in 'When in disgrace'. Here, again, the poet's emotional honesty is striking. He speaks of 'almost despising' himself and cursing his 'fate'. However, when he is at rock bottom he can cause his mood to lift by thinking of his beloved: 'Haply I think on thee, and then my state,/ Like a lark at break of day arising/ From sullen earth, sings hymns at heaven's gate'.

Although love causes the poet much pain and misery, it is the passage of time that truly frightens and disturbs him. Shakespeare vividly evokes the cruel passage of time in his sonnets by personifying Time. In 'When I do count the clock', he uses the classic image of the reaper to personify the power that time has to destroy all things: 'nothing 'gainst Time's scythe can make defence'. A similar image occurs in 'Let me not to the marriage of true minds' where he speaks of time's 'bending sickle's compass'. What horrifies the poet is the fact that nothing at all seems capable of surviving the passage of time. This is most vividly described in 'Since brass, nor stone' where the poet describes time's ability to destroy everything no matter how strong or vast: 'Since brass, nor stone, nor earth, nor boundless sea,/ But sad mortality o'er sways their power'.

Shakespeare's sonnets are at their most powerful when he reflects on love and time and the effect that each has on the other. In 'When I do count the clock', it is thought's of his beloved's demise that cause him greatest anguish. He is appalled at the thought that someone he loves will be destroyed by time: 'O fearful meditation! where, alack, Shall Time's best jewel from Time's chest lie hid?' A similar horror is evident in 'Let me not' where the poet speaks of 'rosy lips and cheeks' falling prey to time's destruction. But Shakespeare does not wish to give time the final say. It is love that he wishes to triumph over all. In the same sonnet, he says that 'Love is not Time's fool'. Though lovers may lose their looks and wither and die, the love they feel for each other will never alter: 'Love alters not with his brief hours and weeks,/ But bears it out even to the edge of doom'.

In conclusion, then, I would like to say that these sonnets are wonderful to read because there is such an urgent and lively energy about them. When Shakespeare writes about love and time, we really get a sense that these were themes that really mattered to him. The poet's despair and joy, his fears, doubts and longings are clearly present in his work. These are not sober and dull mediations on the passage of time and the wonder of being in love; the sonnets are alive and passionate. A battle is constantly raging between the dark forces of time and the fragile feelings of the human heart.

THE UNSEEN POEM

Hotel Room 12th Floor

by Norman MacCaig

This morning I watched from here
a helicopter skirting like a damaged insect
the Empire State Building, that
jumbo size dentist's drill, and landing
on the roof of the PanAm skyscraper.	5
But now midnight has come in
from foreign places. Its uncivilised darkness
is shot at by millions of lit windows, all
ups and acrosses.

But midnight is not	10
so easily defeated. I lie in bed, between
a radio and a television set, and hear
the wildest of warhoops continually ululating through
the glittering canyons and gulches –
police cars and ambulances racing	15
to broken bones, the harsh screaming
from frozen coldwater flats, the blood
glazed on sidewalks.

The frontier is never
somewhere else. And no stockades	20
can keep the midnight out.

SAMPLE ANSWER 1

1. **What does this poem say to you about the city? Point out the words or phrases that especially convey its message to you.**

The poem depicts the city as a rather wild and hostile place, a modern Wild West, full of danger and noise. The city's ready hostility is suggested by the metaphorical description of light coming from the many windows as bullets being wildly fired at the 'midnight' darkness: 'Its uncivilised darkness/ is shot at by a million lit windows, all/ ups and acrosses'. Though the darkness is described as 'uncivilised', the city, in turn, is hardly civilised.

The noises heard by the speaker are like those from a primitive society in the wilds of America. He tells us that he hears 'the wildest of warwhoops continually ululating through/ the glittering canyons and gulches'. We might normally associate the term 'warwhoops' with native American tribes and their 'ululating' cries, and the metaphorical description of the voids between the enormous buildings as 'glittering canyon and gulches', and the mentioning of 'The frontier' in line 19 also evoke the old American Wild West.

The city is a violent place, as primitive and dangerous as any pre-'civilised' world, and the descriptions of the 'ambulances racing/ to broken bones, the harsh screaming/ from cold-water flats, the blood/ glazed on sidewalks' all testify to this.

2. **What impresses you about this poem? Quote from or refer to the text in support of your opinion.**

What struck me initially about this poem were its many vivid images. The image of the 'blood glazed on the sidewalks' was particularly graphic, and filled me with horror as much as it impressed me. Perhaps this is because of the word 'glazed', which I associate with baking and cooking. The notion of the blood being smeared on the footpath like icing on a cake was something that really impressed me.

What I found almost equally impressive was the poet's use of metaphor and simile. The metaphor comparing the Empire State Building to a 'jumbo size dentist's drill' was both humorous and strangely accurate.

Another brilliant metaphor was the description of the city streets as 'glittering canyons and gulches' surrounded on each side by overbearing buildings. The simile comparing the helicopter to a 'damaged insect' was even more vivid. I could almost 'see' the helicopter fluttering through the sky in my mind's eye.

Another feature of this poem that impressed me was the poet's use of sound effects. We see alliteration, for instance, in 'wildest of warhoops' with its repeated 'w' sound, and in 'broken bones' with its repeated 'b' sound.

Onomatopoeia, meanwhile, features in line 13. In the word 'ululating' we can almost hear the sound made by the sirens of the police cars and ambulances as they race through the streets. These rich sound effects brilliantly convey the tapestry of noise that the poet experiences as he lies in his hotel bed, and summon up the alien, adrenaline-charged atmosphere of New York City.

Back Yard

by Carl Sandburg

Shine on, O moon of summer,
Shine to the leaves of grass, catalpa and oak,
All silver under your rain tonight.

An Italian boy is sending songs to you tonight from an accordion.
A Polish boy is out with his best girl; they marry next month;   5
    tonight they are throwing you kisses.

An old man next door is dreaming over a sheen
    that sits in a cherry tree in his back yard.

The clocks say I must go – I stay here sitting on the back porch
    drinking white thoughts you rain down.   10

    Shine on, O moon,
Shake out more and more silver changes.

SAMPLE ANSWER 2

(a) Do you like the world that the poet describes in this poem? Give reasons for your answer supporting them by reference to the text. (10)

I love the world that the poet presents in this poem. It is a magical and rather fantastical world, all coated in 'silver': 'All silver under your rain tonight'. Everything seems to have taken on a special glow or 'sheen' in the moon's light. The 'grass, catalpa and oak' and the 'cherry tree' in the neighbour's backyard are cast in a special light by the moon, beautifully transformed and altered. The poet's mood is also effected by the moon. He seems to be in a blissful state of mind, perfectly content and happy 'drinking white thoughts' that the moon inspires. Though he knows it is late, he cannot bring himself to leave this wonderful moment.

The world of the poem is also perfectly romantic. The poet thinks of others who may be appreciating the moon's special glow on this night. He imagines 'An Italian boy is sending songs to' the moon tonight 'from an accordion'. He also pictures a 'Polish boy' on a date with 'his best girl'. This couple will 'marry next month' but tonight they are out 'throwing' kisses to the moon. It seems that the world is unified on this night in its appreciation of the moon.

(b) Choose a line or two that you find particularly appealing, and explain why. (10)

I like the lines: 'The clocks say I must go – I stay here sitting on the back porch/ drinking white thoughts you rain down'. The poet sets the world of convention and propriety against the romantic world of dreams and freedom. The 'clocks' seem to represent the restricted, ordered world of responsibility whereas the poet 'sitting on the back porch' seems to have entered a place free of duty and care. The line begins with the blunt demand of the 'clocks': 'The clocks say I must go'. The terse and matter-of-fact statement is set in stark contrast against the more poetic and gentle words that follow: 'I stay here sitting on the back porch/ drinking white thoughts you rain down'. The dash in the line neatly separates the two worlds and the way that the words 'I stay' stand alongside 'I must go' makes the poet's decision all the more bold and satisfying: 'I must go – I stay'.

The poet suggests that the moon is inspiring him, feeding him 'thoughts' that are pure and joyous. It is as though the moon's rays are an intoxicating liquor that is making the poet tipsy. The image of him 'drinking white thoughts' calls to mind the term 'moonshine' that is used to describe certain illegally produced spirits. By staying out upon his back porch, the poet seems to be rebelling against what is expected of him: it is late and he should be in bed, but he does not wish to act according to convention tonight.

or

Write a personal response to the poem 'Back Yard'. (20)

This is an inspiring and romantic poem that made me feel good when I read it. The poet conjures up a magical world that is all coated in the 'silver' light of the moon: 'the leaves of grass, catalpa and oak,/ All silver under your rain tonight'. It is a world of wonder and romance peopled with lovers and dreamers. The poet mentions an Italian accordion player, a young Polish couple and an elderly neighbour, each enthralled by the moon on this summer's night. The world of the poem seems to be blissfully innocent and good, devoid of troubles.

The poem contains some lovely imagery. The poet describes the effect of the moon's soft light upon his neighbour's cherry tree: 'a sheen/ that sits in a cherry tree in his back yard'. The soft sibilant 's' and 'ch' sounds corresponds with the tranquil atmosphere of the night. I also loved the way the poet introduces images of people in other countries far away who are sharing his pleasure on this night. The 'Italian boy' and the 'Polish boy' who 'is out with his best girl' introduce a wonderful international dimension to the poem.

I especially liked the lines 'The clocks say I must go – I stay sitting on the back porch/ drinking white thoughts you rain down'. The 'clocks' seem to represent the dull and tedious world of work and responsibilty. Such a world stands in opposition to the world of romance and dream that the poet is part of on this summer's night. He knows that he ought to get to bed but he cannot resist the beauty of the moon's light and wishes to savour the moment for as long as he can. The moon's rays are like an intoxicating drink that the poet wants to keep on 'drinking'. They inspire sweet and pure thoughts ('white thoughts') that give the poet great pleasure.

I Want to Write

by Margaret Walker

I want to write
I want to write the songs of my people.
I want to hear them singing melodies in the dark.
I want to catch the last floating strains from their sob-torn

   throats.

I want to frame their dreams into words; their souls into

   notes.

I want to catch their sunshine laughter in a bowl;
fling dark hands to a darker sky
and fill them full of stars
then crush and mix such lights till they become
a mirrored pool of brilliance in the dawn.

SAMPLE ANSWER 3

1. **Write a response to the above poem, highlighting the impact it makes on you.** (20)

This poem had a powerful impact on me. It reminded me forcefully of the suffering and hardship endured by the African American community throughout the ages, bringing home the fact that the ancestors of modern African Americans were stolen from Africa and forced to endure centuries of slavery and discrimination. The poet's mention of the 'sob-torn / throats' of African Americans powerfully makes this point. We can imagine these people sobbing until their throats are sore, ravaged and exhausted. The references to darkness also suggest this history of suffering; the poet's people sing 'in the dark' and a 'darker sky' hangs over them. It's as if this darkness becomes a symbol for the suffering of her people.

This poem also impacted on me because of the skilful way the poet writes about the art of writing itself. The repetition of the phrase 'I want to write' at the beginning of the poem powerfully captures the poet's bursting, uncontainable desire to record the history of the African American community: 'I want to write the songs of my people'. Of course, the fact that the poem is entitled 'I Want to Write' also emphasises this desire.

I particularly enjoyed the fine metaphors the poet used to describe this process. She describes recording the laughter of her people as catching 'their sunshine laughter in a bowl'. The comparison of a poem to a bowl really works for me because it describes well how a poem can catch, store and preserve a people's qualities so that they will not be forgotten by future generations.

In another fine metaphor, she describes her desire to write a poem that will shine like a beacon throughout the ages. She brilliantly describes this poem she longs to create as a 'mirrored pool of brilliance in the dawn'. This poem will remember and celebrate the

African American people of which she is a part. For this reason, she imagines the 'pool of brilliance' being formed from stars African American hands have snatched from the heavens: 'fling their dark hands to a darker sky / and fill them full of stars'.

2 (a) Write down one phrase from the poem that shows how the poet feels about her people. Say why you have chosen this phrase. (10)

For me, the phrase that best sums up the poet's feelings about her people is 'their sunshine laughter'. For me, this phrase seems to work on several different levels. Firstly, it is an excellent metaphor. The comparison of laughter to sunshine is extremely clever, capturing the brightness, energy and cheerfulness we associate with the simple human act of laughing. Laughter and sunshine are, after all, linked in our imaginations.

Secondly, I liked how this phrase captures the indomitable spirit and resilience of the African American people. These people have endured incredible and unimaginable suffering since they were first enslaved in Africa all those centuries ago. Walker wonderfully and succinctly captures this grim history with her reference to the 'sob-torn / throats' of her people. Her people have cried out in suffering until their throats are sore and torn from doing so. The mention of 'sunshine laughter', therefore, wonderfully captures the spirit and resilience of the African American people. They have somehow retained their golden sense of humour in spite of all the suffering they have endured.

The phrase also introduced an element of symbolism to the poem. The brightness of this African American laughter is contrasted to the darkness that surrounds them. The sunshine of their laughter contrasts with the darkness in which they sing and the 'darker sky' that hangs over them'. It's as if their sunshine laughter represents their inner strength and resilience while the darkness represents the endless suffering that strives to wear their resistance down.

2 (b) Does this poem make you feel hopeful or not hopeful? Briefly explain why. (10)

This poem made me feel hopeful about the African American people. I would argue that it contains a great deal of optimism – optimism that the poet successfully conveys to the reader. The poem skilfully conveys the suffering endured by the African American race throughout history. It does so in a single well-chosen phrase: 'their sob-torn / throats'. Here, we can envisage the cries and lamentations of African American people throughout the centuries as they were so cruelly taken from their African homeland and forced to endure centuries of slavery and hardship in America. We powerfully imagine their 'throats' being wracked or torn with the effort of so much sobbing.

Yet despite this powerful reference to hardship, the poem retains an optimistic outlook. The African American people have not lost their pride. We sense the poet's pride in her African American heritage when she writes: 'I want to write / I want to write the songs of my people'. The African American people have not lost thei wit and brightness, their ability to laugh: 'their sunshine laughter'. The African Americans have not forgotten their traditional songs or where they came from. The poem's last image of African American hands catching stars from the night sky and forming a 'mirrored pool of brilliance' indicates that this proud people that has endured so much will have a bright and shining future.

OTHER TITLES IN THIS SERIES

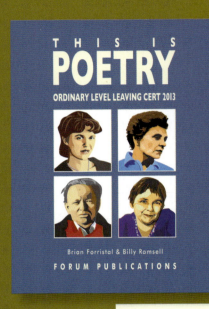
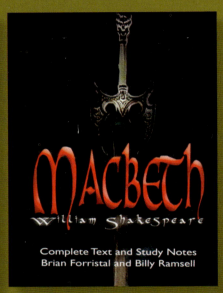
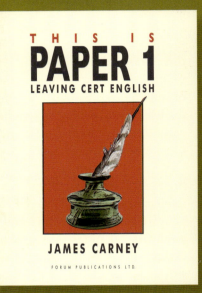
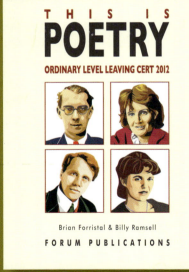
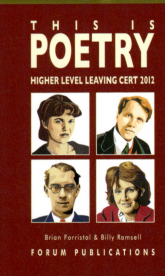

WWW.FORUM-PUBLICATIONS.COM